99 BB

18⁰⁰

New Developments in the Use of the MMPI

New Developments in the Use of the MMPI

James N. Butcher, editor

UNIVERSITY OF MINNESOTA PRESS □ MINNEAPOLIS

Published by the University of Minnesota Press,
2037 University Avenue Southeast,
Minneapolis, Minnesota 55455
Printed in the United States of America

Library of Congress Cataloging in Publication Data

Symposium on Recent Developments in the Use of the MMPI,
    14th, St. Petersburg, Fla., 1979.
    New developments in the use of the MMPI.

        "Most of the papers included in this volume are formal
articles which were invited for oral presentation at
the 14th annual Symposium on Recent Developments in
the Use of the MMPI in St. Petersburg, Florida in March
1979."
        Bibliography: p.
        Includes indexes.
        1. Minnesota multiphasic personality inventory—
Congresses. I. Butcher, James Neal, 1933–
II. Title.
BF698.8.M5S95   1979   155.2'83   79-22093
ISBN 0-8166-0894-6

The University of Minnesota is an equal-opportunity
educator and employer.

To **STARKE R. HATHAWAY**

Preface

Since its modest beginning about 40 years ago, the MMPI has gained worldwide acceptance as an effective instrument for use in making clinical decisions in diverse settings and conducting research into a variety of clinical problems. The extensive use of the MMPI is reflected in the wide range of topics included in the categorized bibliography at the end of this book.

The book focuses on several developments that have been among the most active research areas in recent years—which was determined by an extensive review of the literature from 1972 to early 1979. The authors were chosen for their special contributions to the development of the MMPI in these areas. Most of the chapters were invited for oral presentation at the 14th Annual Symposium on Recent Developments in the Use of the MMPI in St. Petersburg, Florida in March 1979 and for publication in this book.

Two of the most active research areas, addictive personality and MMPI short forms, are not included in this volume, for quite different reasons. The study of personality characteristics of alcohol and drug abusers has received a great deal of recent attention, and several excellent up-to-date reviews are available. No discussion of MMPI short forms was included because they have already received more attention in the literature than their clinical validity seems to warrant. Problems with MMPI short forms will be dealt with in Dahlstrom and Dahlstrom's *Basic Readings on the MMPI: A New Selection on Personality Measurement*, to be published later in 1979.

Since this volume owes its existence, in part, to the annual conference on Recent Developments in the Use of the MMPI, special acknowledgment goes to the Nolte Center for Continuing Education for supporting these conferences over the years. Program Director Gordon Amundson, who has been associated with the MMPI meetings since 1971, has contributed substantially to their success. In addition, he provided some much needed clerical assistance for preparing a portion of this manuscript.

I would also like to thank Dr. Susan Filskov, University of South Florida, for serving as co-coordinator of the MMPI conference in 1979, and Janet Peterson, whose rapid and accurate typing helped us meet many deadlines.

J. N. B.
August 1979

Contributors

JAMES N. BUTCHER received his Ph.D. at the University of North Carolina in 1964. In that year he accepted a position in the Department of Psychology at the University of Minnesota, where he is now director of clinical psychology training. He has been active in both clinical and industrial consultation involving the MMPI, as well as engaging in MMPI clinical research. Since 1970 he has focused his research activity on the cross-national use of the MMPI and is involved in development projects in several countries. LEE ANNA CLARK is an advanced graduate student in clinical psychology at the University of Minnesota. Before she began her graduate work in psychology, she obtained a B.A. degree in psycholinguistics and an M.A. in Asian studies at Cornell University. She taught in Japan for four years before beginning graduate work. She is specializing in clinical psychology and cross-cultural psychology. During 1979-80 she is on a Fulbright fellowship, working in Japan on a cross-cultural MMPI study.

RAYMOND D. FOWLER received his Ph.D. from Pennsylvania State University in 1957. Since 1956 he has been at the University of Alabama where he has been chairperson of the Psychology Department since 1965. He is also the director of the University of Alabama Center for Correctional Psychology and has served as a consultant to various prison systems and as an expert witness in court cases related to the rights of incarcerated people. His research interests include alcoholism, criminal behavior, and personality assessment.

MALCOLM D. GYNTHER has been professor of psychology at Auburn University in Auburn, Alabama since 1974. He received the Ph.D. degree from Duke

University in 1956. Following that, he worked as a clinical psychologist at South Carolina State Hospital and as chief psychologist at Malcolm Bliss Mental Health Center in St. Louis, Missouri. He also taught at the University of South Carolina and Washington University (St. Louis) during this period. In 1966 he was appointed professor of psychology at St. Louis University. His principal research interest is personality measurement, especially effects of demographic variables on objective personality scales, behavioral correlates of psychological test data, and psychometric variables affecting predictive validity.

STEVEN D. HOLLON is an assistant professor of psychology at the University of Minnesota. Receiving his Ph.D. from Florida State University, he served for several years as clinical coordinator at the Depression Research Unit of the University of Pennsylvania (now the Center for Cognitive Therapy). His research interests have included the development and evaluation of clinical interventions for depression and the refinement of research methodologies for use in controlled clinical trials. MONICA MANDELL is a graduate student in clinical psychology at the University of Minnesota, where she is currently assistant to the chairman of the Department of Psychology. Her major research interest is in the area of controlled treatment outcome studies.

MARY P. KOSS is an assistant professor at Kent State University. She received her Ph.D. in psychology in 1972 from the University of Minnesota. Her research interests focus on the application of the MMPI and other assessment procedures to a variety of areas including brief and crisis-oriented psychotherapy, private-practice psychotherapy, and sexual aggression and victimization.

DAVID LACHAR is director of Western Psychological Services, Los Angeles. After he received his Ph.D. from the University of Minnesota in 1970, he was a staff psychologist in the internship program at Wilford Hall USAF Medical Center, San Antonio, Texas. From 1973 to 1979 he was chief psychologist, Childrens Service, and later became director, Division of Psychology, at the Lafayette Clinic. During this time he supervised graduate research at Wayne State University. His current research interests include personality inventory construction and validation, descriptive psychopathology, prediction of treatment effects, and computer-assisted test interpretation. JAMES R. SHARP completed his internship at the Lafayette Clinic and received his Ph.D. from Wayne State University in 1979. He is presently a staff psychologist at Willard Psychiatric Center, New York. His research interests include family psychopathology, addictions, and program evaluation.

EDWIN I. MEGARGEE is professor of clinical psychology at Florida State University. He received his Ph.D. from the University of California at Berkeley in

1964 and was an assistant professor at the University of Texas before going to Florida State. Dr. Megargee's major area of research interest is personality assessment, more specifically assessment in correctional psychology. He has developed an MMPI typology for use with prisoners.

DAVID OSBORNE received his Ph.D. in clinical psychology from the University of Minnesota in 1969. Since that time, he has been a member of the Section of Psychology at the Mayo Clinic. He is currently consultant in psychology and associate professor of psychology in the Mayo Medical School. His research interests include the use of structured personality tests with medical patients, psychophysiologic disorders, and biofeedback.

PATRICIA L. OWEN is a Ph.D. candidate in clinical psychology at the University of Minnesota. She is currently working at the Hazelden Foundation in Minnesota. Her research is concerned with the interaction of personality factors and the treatment of male and female alcoholics.

Contents

New Developments in the Use of the MMPI

MMPI Item Content
Recurring Issues

Mary P. Koss

The expression "item content" refers to the semantic meanings of the words that make up a structured personality-inventory question. Item content is what a question "is about." Item content considerations form a substantial portion of the theoretical controversy that has grown up around the alternative approaches to psychological test construction. Early and recurring debates over test-construction strategy have focused on the following content issues: item responses as behavior signs versus item responses as behavior samples, the desirability of subtle versus obvious items, the utility of heterogeneous versus homogeneous item content on a scale, and stylistic versus substantive interpretations of overall test variance. These recurring item-content issues are the focus of this paper.

ITEM CONTENT AND SCALE CONSTRUCTION STRATEGY

Structured personality inventories have in the past been constructed through one of three strategies: internal, external, or intuitive. Recently, Jackson (1971) has advocated a fourth strategy that includes the successive use of the first three approaches and thus could be labeled "sequential." Each strategy of scale construction contains assumptions about the role of item content. Choosing or committing oneself to a particular strategy involves accepting the viewpoint of that approach on the following item-content issues:

3

(1) *Composition of the initial item pool.* Should the initial item pool consist mainly of items whose content is directly relevant to the trait to be measured, or is a broad item pool, reflecting the entire domain of which the trait to be measured is only a small part, preferable?

(2) *View of item responses.* Is the self-rating response viewed as a factual reflection of reality, as a truthful self-attitude, or as a new behavior in and of itself whose meaning is not related to to the item content but must be discovered empirically?

(3) *Subtle versus obvious items.* Should all the items placed on the final scales of the inventory consist of item content that is directly relevant to the trait to be measured (face valid or obvious), or are items acceptable whose psychological relevance to the trait being measured is unclear?

(4) *Homogeneous versus heterogeneous scales.* Should the scales making up the inventory consist only of items that are highly correlated and factorially pure, or are scales composed of unrelated clusters of items acceptable?

(5) *Content versus stylistic interpretations.* Are stylistic tendencies of subjects considered so major that great care must be taken to control for response sets, or are stylistic tendencies considered to be secondary to respondents' abilities to respond to item content?

Following is a review of the positions that have been taken on each of these issues in the four construction strategies.

Intuitive Strategy

The earliest psychological inventories were constructed by intuitive methods. The investigator began with an idea of what she/he wished to measure, made up test items whose item content was judged to reflect that trait, and developed a scoring key based on the response direction the investigator's personal experience or psychological knowledge indicated to be deviant. Scales were often refined further by internal consistency analysis. Intuitive methods result in scales made up of highly intercorrelated but not necessarily factorially pure items whose content has high face validity. The interpretation of a score on the scale is believed to relate directly to the item content that makes up the scale and self-rating responses are considered to reflect factual reality. The assumptions of the intuitive strategy are summarized in Table 1.

Table 1. Item Content Assumptions in Scale Construction Strategies

Approach	Item Responses	Type of Content	Scale Composition	Scale Interpretations
intuitive	samples	face valid	relatively homogeneous	item content
external	signs	face valid and subtle	heterogeneous	empirically established correlates
internal	samples	face valid and subtle	homogeneous	item content of factors
sequential	signs and samples	face valid and theoretically designed subtle items	homogeneous	item content of scales and empirical correlates

External Strategy

The assumptions about item content inherent in the external or group discrimination strategy have been clearly described by Meehl (1945) in his classic paper on the dynamics of structured personality tests. The investigator begins with a very large pool of items reflecting all facets of the general domain of which the trait to be measured is a part. Then two distinct groups are located that differ in some manner. The entire item pool is administered to the two groups and any item that is found to statistically differentiate the two groups is placed on the final scale. The scales that result from this procedure consist of subgroups of items of heterogeneous content with low overall correlations. Many items on the scale will seem related to the dimension on which the criterion groups differed, but others will seem completely unrelated. Proponents of the external strategy suggest that the presence of non-face-valid items and the use of heterogeneous scales render a test more resistant to faking by the respondent. Item responses are viewed not as behavior samples but as behavior signs (Goodenough, 1949). That is, a test response is viewed as a new behavior in and of itself and as a sign of something potentially important but not yet known. The meaning of this sign is not based on the item content but on extra-test behaviors with which the response is found to correlate. The position on item content issues embodied by the external strategy is summarized in Table 1.

Internal Strategy

The internal or factor-analytic approach involves beginning with a pool of items constructed specifically to be relevant to the traits one wishes to assess. These items are administered to as large and heterogeneous a group of people as possible. The items are then intercorrelated and factor analyzed. Items loading most highly on each factor are selected for the final scales. The resulting scales contain highly intercorrelated, factorially pure, generally highly face-valid items. The meaning of a score on a factor scale is directly related to the item-content loading on the scale. Attempts to correlate scale scores with non-test behaviors might be undertaken subsequently but only to validate interpretations based on item content. These characteristics of the internal strategy are summarized in Table 1.

Sequential Strategy

This methodology involves successive application of all the above strategies and involves the assumptions about item content that Jackson (1971) thinks are most empirically defensible at present. An intuitive approach is employed in the construction of a large initial item pool consisting of items specifically written to be relevant to the traits being assessed. Somewhat non-face-valid items are allowed only if their relevance to the trait of interest is clear to the test constructor but not to the test respondent. Next, the items are administered to a large group of individuals and factor analyzed. Then, items with the highest loadings are selected for the scales. These procedures result in items that are content relevant, mostly face-valid, highly intercorrelated, and factorially pure.

Interpretations of scores are based on the item-content loading on the scales, and item responses are viewed as behavior samples in the majority of instances. However, in the final stage of development, empirical procedures are used to validate interpretations based on item content and to establish additional behavioral correlates. The assumptions on content issues of the sequential strategy are presented in Table 1.

Following is a more detailed discussion of the controversial item-content issues and of the relevant empirical studies.

RECURRING ITEM-CONTENT ISSUES

Item Responses: Samples or Signs?

Every well-written personality-test is designed to be understood easily by the people who will be responding to it. Items must be clear so that the respondent knows which aspect of her/his behavior to evaluate and report. However, the degree to which the respondent is able to accurately interpret the test-item content in the fashion intended by the test constructor and produce a self-rating response that faithfully represents factual behavior has stirred considerable debate.

Traditional View. Woodworth (1920), who constructed the Personal Data Sheet, was credited by Meehl (1945) with formulating the "traditional view" in which item responses are viewed as descriptive of an individual's actual behavior under the circumstances described in the item content so that they can serve as a substitute for clinical interview or observation.

Meehl preferred an alternative approach to viewing test responses, which he labeled the "modern view." Meehl believed that even structured personality-test questions were somewhat projective, leading people to form a subjective interpretation of each item. For example, the word "frequently," as in "I have headaches frequently," may be interpreted quite differently by a hypochondriac than by a normal, healthy person. Under these circumstances, Meehl did not expect that test responses could possibly mirror reality as could behavior sampling. Meehl felt that item responses should be viewed as interesting bits of a person's verbal behavior. One only discovers what a particular bit "means," however, by investigating empirically the behaviors to which the particular item response is correlated.

The distinction Meehl made between the "traditional" and "modern" view of the relationship between test responses and item content has been adopted and elaborated by others. Goodenough (1949) categorized test responses as either "samples" or "signs" of behavior. Dahlstrom (1969) developed a three-level conceptualization of item responses. The prototype of what he called a "Level I" interpretation of an item response is the Woodworth Personal Data Sheet with its "straightforward acceptance of the content of the test responses as descriptive of the subject's personality (p. 3)." A "Level II" interpretation of a self-rating response involved viewing it as a truthful *self-attitude* but not as an actual fact. Dahlstrom advocated viewing test responses on "Level III," where they were seen as behavioral signs. He believed that, "Even though the subject is being asked to describe his own history or present his own self-views, the psychologist accepts these endorsements as neither reflecting factual reality nor mirroring self-attitudes but as signs of something potentially important but not yet known (1969, p. 8)."

Contemporary View. Jackson (1971) published a thorough revision of the dynamics of structured personality tests; and several other writers (Loevinger, 1957; Carson, 1969; Wiggins, 1969; and Goldberg, 1972) have expressed similar thoughts. These writers objected to aspects of the "modern view" of test responses as described by Meehl, particularly his view that personality-test items have a projective aspect that renders them unusable as a direct source of information about a respondent's factual behavior. These writers believe that in the majority of instances item responses are behavior samples. Several lines of empirical research support their position.

Empirical Research on Item Responses. The first source of relevant data is a group of studies that attempted to compare a person's item responses to other sources of factual data about that person. Landis (1936, Landis & Katz, 1934; Landis, Zubin & Katz, 1935) compared Bernreuter Personality Inventory responses to life-history data relevant to each response. Overall, 75% of the test responses were considered verified by anamnesis data, but there was an interaction between overall score level on the inventory and the agreement percentage. Agreement increased from 50% for those subjects who obtained very low scores on the whole test to 91% in the group obtaining high scores.

Koss and Butcher (1973) defined six specific crisis situations in terms of the specific behaviors manifested and complaints made by a patient in that crisis at the time of admission. Then they asked experienced psychologist-judges to identify those MMPI items that were directly relevant to the behaviors specified for each crisis group. Finally, they selected samples of newly admitted psychiatric patients who presented at the hospital with exactly the behaviors and complaints listed in the definition of one of the crisis situations, and a control group of non-crisis psychiatric patients. They found that 76% of the items judged to have content relevance to one of the crisis situations statistically differentiated each of the crisis groups from the control (p<.05). Other recent studies that compared test responses to clinical data with similar results include Campbell, Borgen, Eastes, Johannsson, and Peterson (1968), Gravitz (1968a), Morgan, Weitzel, Guyden, Robinson, and Hedlund (1972), Mlott (1973), Lachar and Alexander (1978), and Lachar and Wrobel (in press).

A second source of data stems from studies (Devries & Blau, 1972; Ewing & Thelen, 1972; Payne & Wiggins, 1972) which attempted to demonstrate that test interpretations based solely on the item content of a person's test responses were highly similar to test interpretations based on the standard statements related to scale elevations. The standard MMPI codetype interpretations were developed empirically and the correlates, descriptive adjectives, or cardinal traits found to characterize particular codetypes represent actual patient behavior. Thus, a demonstration of correspondence between the content of test responses and empirical characteristics known to be associated with the overall test score is evidence for viewing item responses as reflections of external reality.

As an example, Payne and Wiggins (1972) designed a two-phase study. First, they demonstrated that the more similar subjects were in terms of overall MMPI profile type, the more similar the subjects' content scores were. Then they compared the kind of interpretative statements that are obtained when a person's codetype is used to the type of statements suggested by the person's item content. They found a striking congruity between the interpretations based on codetype and those based on content scores for the Gilberstadt-Duker profiles 2-7-8, 7-8, and 8-6. They found definite discrepancies between the two interpretations for the type 4 profile.

Three studies that attempted to demonstrate that actual changes in behavior over time are reflected in item responses (Brozak & Erickson, 1948; Schiele & Brozek, 1948; Endicott & Endicott, 1963) are also relevant. Brozek and Erickson administered the MMPI to men before and after 6 months of experimental food deprivation. Most of the response changes that took place concerned items about anxiety, depression, lack of energy, and loss of interest, reflecting the well-known effects of restricted calorie intake. However, 20% of the response changes were on items unrelated to any observed change in the men.

The attitudes of test respondents when they take a personality test constitute an intuitive reason for viewing item responses as behavior samples. Both transcripts from the Senate hearings on personality testing (Brayfield, 1965) and data from Butcher and Tellegen's (1966) study of objectionable personality-test items indicate that test respondents are very concerned about possible improper uses of individual test items. Presumably, people express these concerns because they are convinced that their item responses reveal how they behave in certain very personal areas. Carson summarizes this point well, "Regardless of the psychologist's view of a test response, the respondent tends to view the testing situation as a opportunity for communication between himself and the testor. It is of course conceivable that many — or perhaps even most — patients in a clinical situation adopt a conscious strategy of complete honesty" (1969, p. 49).

On the other hand, a naive acceptance of the sampling view of item responses must be avoided. A reliable finding in the research on item dynamics (e.g., Landis & Katz, 1934; Koss & Butcher, 1973,

Lachar & Wrobel, in press) is that although item responses seem to function as behavior samples in the majority of instances (75%, Landis & Katz; 76%, Koss & Butcher; 75%, Lachar & Wrobel), there are still more than "isolated" examples in which self-ratings do not reflect external reality. The content of items that fail to demonstrate concurrent validity with other sources of data about a respondent does not appear upon intuitive examination to be different from the content of items that function effectively as behavior samples. No differences of length, word difficulty, item clarity, or other item characteristics have been detected. This observation indicates the necessity of subjecting items to thorough empirical validation before assuming that they operate as behavior samples.

Subtle Items: Unobtrusive Measures or Artifacts?

An "obvious" item (Weiner, 1948) is one whose psychological meaning is very clear. For example, most people could identify the item "I feel anxiety about someone or something almost all of the time" as a measure of nervousness or anxiety. A "subtle" item is one whose relevance to the scale on which it appears cannot be explained easily, even by a trained psychologist. Thus, the subtle-obvious dimension refers to the degree of relevance between item content and the psychological construct being assessed.

Tests such as the MMPI, constructed by external group-discrimination procedures from a large diverse initial item pool, usually contain a number of subtle items on each scale.

Original View. Meehl (1945) believed that subtlety was a highly positive feature of the MMPI. Subtle items in Meehl's thinking were unobtrusive measures of personality. A subject would not know what the item "was getting at" so she or he could not manipulate the direction of response in order to give one impression or another. Furthermore, Meehl suggested that the true empirical psychologist does not examine item responses or believe they reflect factual reality. Therefore, it really makes little difference what items make up a scale as long as the scale empirically differentiates two groups. Meehl has also stated that subtle items may appear to be unrelated to the scale on which they occur only because psychological theory is not yet advanced enough to explain their relevance.

The Contemporary View. Jackson (1971) argued that subtle items are statistical artifacts of the external group-discrimination procedure which would have dropped out had the original scales been subjected to cross-validation. He believes that, "ordinarily, issues, questions, or

situations directly bearing on the characteristic of interest will have
the highest probability of reflecting it" (1971, p. 232). Jackson suggested that a sample of item content relevant to a certain behavior is
the best measure of it, or, in other words, there is a positive relationship between face and empirical validity. Cronbach (1970) stated that
"separate scoring of subtle and transparent items is emphatically
needed" (p. 532) in order to perform a direct test of discriminating
power. "If the subtle keys proved to be invalid or the obvious items
carried most of the discriminating power . . . the whole criterion
keyed, empirical approach to test construction is called into question"
(Christian, Burkhart, & Gynther, 1978).

   Subtle-Obvious Classifications. There have been three attempts
to classify MMPI items along the subtle-obvious dimension. Meehl and
Hathaway (1946) classified as X items those items that are obviously
pathological and are rarely endorsed by normals, and as 0 items those
that are not especially indicative of emotional disturbance and are endorsed by normals but are even more frequently endorsed by patients.
Weiner (1948) developed subtle-obvious distinctions for scales 2, 3, 4, 6,
and 9 by intuitively dividing the items into those that indicated emotional disturbance and those that did not. Duff (1965) used 162 MMPI
items from scales 3, 4, and 8, 34 items from other clinical scales, and
30 items that appear on no clinical scale. He asked graduate students
to identify the clinical scale from which the item was drawn and the
pathological scoring direction. Items correctly identified by no more
than 10% of the judges were rated "subtle," those identified correctly
by 10-50% were rated intermediate, and those identified correctly
by more than 50% of the judges were labeled "obvious."

   Christian, Burkhart, and Gynther (in press) applied standard scal-
ing procedures to determine mean subtle-obvious ratings for all MMPI
items. College students were asked to rate the items on a scale of 1
(very subtle) to 5 (very obvious). Items were rated for subtlety twice,
once when an item was answered true and then when the item was
answered false.

   Empirical Research on Subtle Items. Burkhart, Christian, and
Gynther (1978) administered the MMPI to college students under
standard, fake-bad, and fake-good instructions. Under standard instructions, students acknowledged a small number of obvious items
and a large number of subtle items. Under fake-good instructions, the
students endorsed even fewer obvious items and slightly more subtle
items. Under fake-bad instructions, subjects endorsed many more obvious items and few subtle items. This finding is not consistent with a

view that subtle items are unobtrusive measures. Subjects were able to change their response patterns to subtle items, depending upon the impression they were trying to create.

Several investigators have examined the empirical validity of face-valid versus subtle items. McCall (1958) compared the 22 obvious and 38 subtle MMPI scale 2 items. He found that the obvious items alone could discriminate groups as well as did the entire 60-item scale. These data suggest that subtle items may even reduce the discriminating power of a scale, since here an obvious scale performed as well as a subtle and obvious scale, nearly three times as long. Duff (1965) examined the discrimination indexes for the 162 MMPI items for which he had obtained subtlety ratings. Approximately 40% of the subtle items had values over 2.00, the minimum cutoff used in the original construction of the MMPI, whereas 90% of the obvious items exceeded the cutoff. Duff's data support Jackson's (1971) contention that many subtle items are statistical artifacts that would have disappeared had the original scales been cross-validated.

Berg (1957, 1959) advanced an extreme form of blind empiricism called the "deviation hypothesis": any item content, no matter how irrelevant, can be used to construct a personality inventory. Norman (1963) accepted the challenge and used the items from the Descriptive Adjective Inventory (ADI), Occupational Preference Inventory, and Welsh Figure Preference Test to form an item pool. Several scales were empirically constructed and related to various external criteria. The only items that continued to discriminate after the first cross-validation were those ADI items that were relevant to the criteria. Goldberg and Slovic (1967) had subjects rate the face-validity of 60 verbal items related to achievement, 60 verbal items related to affiliation, and 60 irrelevant verbal items. The empirical validity of an item was determined by examining the degree to which it correlated with external criteria reflecting affiliation and achievement. They concluded that, "only scales built from items of the highest face-validity had significant cross-validity" (pp. 466-67). Duff's (1965) conclusion serves as a cogent summary of this line of research, "The results . . . raise serious questions concerning the desirability of totally disregarding the content of items selected for inventory scales. The findings imply that the discrimination of inventory scales could be markedly increased by eliminating from consideration material whose content relevance is extremely obscure" (p. 569).

It should be noted that Meehl (1972) recently re-evaluated his writings on the dynamics of structured personality tests. Although he still expresses faith in "empirical-actuarial predictive and interpretative methods" (p. 150), he suggests that the strict "criterion-statistical" view of items expressed in his 1945 paper was too strong. He now writes that the content of an item should make theoretical sense without too much ad hoc explaining. He states, "We would like the item . . . to be relatively close in the causal chain to some feature of the patient's phenomenology . . . whose 'psychological nature' is what gives the test score its interpretive name" (p. 169). However, Meehl still thinks that certain types of subtle items, namely those with stable psychometric properties, have value. He believes these items are actually content relevant, but this relationship is not explainable by present psychological theories.

Test Variance: Content or Stylistic?

Several investigators (Edwards, 1957; 1964; Jackson & Messick, 1961; Messick & Jackson, 1961) have concluded that unless one takes special precautions during test construction, personality-test items are obtained that do not result in behavior samples and do not even reflect various psychological traits, but instead reflect only a generalized orientation to test-taking (response-set) on the part of the respondent. For example, Edwards (1957, 1964) has suggested that subjects often give what they believe to be the most socially desirable answer to each question rather than responding factually. Jackson and Messick (1961; Messick & Jackson, 1961) believe that subjects tend to acquiesce to, or agree with, many items regardless of content. These authors have presented data that they believe suggest that the variance reflected by MMPI scores is not "content variance" (i.e., related to psychological traits) but reflects only "response style variance." They further suggest that the two major MMPI factor dimensions of A and R derived originally by Welsh (1956), and thought to represent the major psychological dimensions tapped by the MMPI, actually represent only the response sets of acquiescence and social desirability.

Rorer (1965) reviewed the massive literature this controversy has generated and concluded that there is no consistent support for a response-set interpretation of MMPI variance. For example, Rorer (1965) wrote reversals of all 566 MMPI items to control for the tendency to acquiesce and found no appreciable differences in test variance from standard administrations of the MMPI. Block (1965) reworked the entire MMPI to obtain scales that were balanced for mean social desirability and consisted of equal numbers of true and false keyed questions. When responses to this reworked MMPI were factor analyzed, factors very similar to the two factors of the standard MMPI were obtained. Block also determined the nontest personality characteristics of high and low scores on each of his reworked MMPI factors and found that the characteristics were highly similar to those related to the standard MMPI factors.

Thus, it appears that despite failure to balance social desirability and response alternatives in the original construction of the MMPI, respondents still reveal meaningful information about themselves. Response sets may exist, but an individual's capacity to respond to item content appears to be stronger than his or her tendency to respond stylistically.

Homogeneous vs. Heterogeneous Item Content

Scales constructed by external methods contain a much wider variety of content than do scales constructed by other procedures. For example, Harris and Lingoes (1955; 1968) found that MMPI scale 2 is composed of five separate, homogeneous content areas as are scales 3 and 4, while scale 8 is made up of six different areas of content. Wiggins (1969) has discussed several problems involved in the use of heterogeneous scales as personality-trait measures. First, the test interpretor does not know the meaning of low scores on a scale. A low score could be obtained by answering only one question from each content area or by answering many questions from one area but none from the others. Likewise, high scores are composed of a "hodgepodge of content" which "is not suggestive of any consistent personality trait or structure" (Wiggins, 1966, p. 31). With heterogeneous scales it is possible for the same configural pattern (e.g., 2-7-8 codetype) to be obtained by two subjects who endorse completely different content areas. Wiggins (1966) demonstrated hypothetically how such an outcome could occur. Payne and Wiggins (1972) demonstrated empirically that at low levels of configural complexity (i.e., high-point codes, two-point codetypes) there was wide variability in the content endorsed by individuals classified in the same category. At high levels of configural complexity, however (i.e., Marks and Seeman or Gilberstadt-Duker rules), there was marked similarity in the content endorsed by individuals in the same category. Finally, Wiggins (1969) points out that the degree of item overlap between MMPI scales is a "minor irritation" in research and interpretation.

The MMPI Item Pool: Adequate or Inadequate?

The 566 items that make up the MMPI are the result of administering an initial pool of 1000 items to various groups and choosing for the final test the items that discriminated one group from another.

The initial 1000 items were selected by Hathaway and McKinley (1940) to reflect "behaviors of significance to the psychiatrist. . . . The items were supplied from several psychiatric examination direction forms, from various textbooks of psychiatry, from certain of the directions for case taking in medicine and neurology, and from the earlier published scales of personal and social attitudes" (p. 249). The item content was clustered into the following 26 categories.

Affect, Depressive (32 items)
Social Attitudes (72 items)
Morale (33 items)
Political Attitudes, Law and Order (46 items)
Obsessive and Compulsive States (15 items)
General Neurologic (19 items)
Vasomotor, Trophic, Speech, Secretary (10 items)
Delusions, Hallucinations, Illusions, Ideas of Reference (31 items)
Phobias (29 items)
Family and Marital (26 items)
Lie Items (15 items)
Masculinity-Femininity (55 items)
General Health (9 items)
Motility and Coordination (6 items)
Gastrointestinal System (11 items)
Affect, Manic (24 items)
Occupational (18 items)
Cardiorespiratory System (5 items)
Habits (19 items)
Cranial Nerves (11 items)
Sensibility (5 items)
Educational (12 items)
Religious Attitudes (19 items)
Sadistic, Masochistic Trends (7 items)
Sexual Attitudes (16 items)
Genitourinary System (5 items)

In many content areas, such as seriously deviant psychopathology or physical symptoms, the MMPI item pool is rich. In other areas of social and psychological functioning, the item pool is seriously deficient. One cannot expect to construct valid scales from non-face-valid items (Goldberg & Slovic, 1967). Consequently, it is now generally recognized that there is a limit to the kind of scales one can construct by relying solely on the MMPI item pool. In addition, the MMPI item pool is saddled with stylistic drawbacks. For example, the vast majority of MMPI items that refer to serious psychopathology such as hallucinations, delusions, and loss of reality contact are phrased so that the deviant response is true. Scales constructed from MMPI items to measure serious psychopathology will unavoidably contain a built-in vulnerability to an acquiescent response style. Wiggins concludes, "It seems likely that the MMPI item pool which was once considered so rich and untapped, may be too limited as a source of items for building general purpose personality scales" (1966, p. 31).

EMPIRICAL EVALUATION OF TEST-CONSTRUCTION STRATEGIES

In previous sections it has been demonstrated that the positions on content issues associated with the external construction strategy are not supported by empirical data (i.e., item responses are behavior samples in the majority of instances, face-valid items are more often empirically valid than are subtle items). Perhaps one reason investigators have clung to this strategy in the face of contradictory reports is the belief that the external test-construction strategy results in more accurate prediction of external criteria than do the other strategies. Goldberg and his colleagues (Hase & Goldberg, 1967, Goldberg, 1972) have examined this issue systematically. Hase and Goldberg (1967) used the CPI items as a basic item pool, to which six different scale-construction procedures (internal, external, intuitive-theoretical, intuitive-rational, stylistic, and random) were applied. Each method was used to construct 11 scales and then 200 university women's responses to the CPI items were scored for all of the scales. Correlations between all scales and 13 criteria measures on the women were examined. The four primary strategies of test construction (internal, external, intuitive-theoretical, and intuitive-rational) were found to be equally effective and superior to stylistic or random scales. Goldberg (1972) found that external construction techniques produced a different pattern of results from the other major strategies, however. The empirical scales produced the lowest cross-validated average correlations with the two most easily predictable criteria and the highest cross-validated average correlation with the four least predictable criteria. He concluded that the externally constructed scales were "broader band-width and lower fidelity" (Cronbach & Gleser, 1965) than the other scales, although all reached an equal overall level of validity.

EXTRACTING CONTENT MEANING FROM THE MMPI

Prohibitions against viewing MMPI item responses as behavior samples and using item content to ascribe meaning to scale scores (Meehl, 1945; Dahlstrom, 1969); heterogeneous clusters of content within scales that obscure the meaning of scale scores; and the existence of subtle items that bear no content relevance to the behavior they ostensibly assess have all operated to discourage the MMPI interpretor from paying attention to the content of a subject's item responses. Nevertheless, approaches to extracting content meaning from the MMPI have emerged, and they testify to a strong desire on the part of test users to be in touch with the actual content of what respondents are communicating through their test responses. There are two major approaches to extracting content meaning from the MMPI: development of homogeneous content scales and construction of highly face-valid "critical items" designed to operate as empirically valid behavior samples (Butcher & Tellegen, 1978).

Content Subscales of Standard Clinical Scales

Harris and Lingoes Subscales. Lingoes (1960) and Harris and Lingoes (1955; 1968) have developed homogeneous content subscales for clinical scales 2, 3, 4, 6, 8, and 9. Each subscale was constructed by intuitively grouping items from a clinical scale that seemed similar in content or seemed to reflect a single attitude or trait. Labels of the subscales were developed through inspection of the item content of each subscale. Thirty-one subscales were developed, but three are not generally used in interpretation. Directions for scoring the Harris-Lingoes subscales can be found in Dahlstrom, Welsh, & Dahlstrom (1975) and Graham (1977).

The names of the Harris and Lingoes subscales are as follows:

Scale 2 (Depression)
D1 — Subjective Depression
D1 — Psychomotor Retardation
D3 — Physical Malfunctioning
D4 — Mental Dullness
D5 — Brooding

Scale 3 (Hysteria)
Hy1 — Denial of Social Anxiety
Hy2 — Need for Affection
Hy3 — Lassitude-Malaise
Hy4 — Somatic Complaints
Hy5 — Inhibition of Aggression

Scale 4 (Psychopathic Deviate)

Pd1 — Familial Discord
Pd2 — Authority Problems
Pd3 — Social Imperturbability
Pd4A — Social Alienation
Pd4B — Self-Alienation

Scale 6 (Paranoia)

Pa1 — Persecutory Ideas
Pa2 — Poignancy
Pa3 — Naivete

Scale 8 (Schizophrenia)

Sc1A — Social Alienation
Sc1B — Emotional Alienation
Sc1C — Lack of Ego Mastery, Cognitive
Sc2B — Lack of Ego Mastery, Conative
Sc2C — Lack of Ego Mastery, Defective Inhibition
Sc3 — Bizarre Sensory Experiences

Scale 9 (Hypomania)

Ma1 — Amorality
Ma2 — Psychomotor Acceleration
Ma3 — Imperturbability
Ma4 — Ego Inflation

The subscales show high intercorrelations with the parent scales (Harris & Lingoes, 1955; 1968) but this result is due in large part to the substantial item overlap between them (Graham, 1977). Internal consistency values ranged from .04 to .85 (Gocka, 1965). Approximately half the subscales have internal consistency reliabilities of less than .70, which indicates that the authors had variable success in constructing pure scales through intuitive methods. Clearly, many of the subscales need further refinement before they can be considered "homogeneous" subscales that offer interpretative advantage over the "heterogeneous" clinical scales. Validity data on the subscales — which are widely used clinically, including in several computerized interpretations — are sparse. A brief summary of sources of scoring information, and reliability and validity data on the Harris and Lingoes subscales is found in Table 2.

Masculinity-Femininity and Social Introversion Subscales. Serkownek (1975) has developed subscales for scales 5 and 0 to extend the set developed by Harris and Lingoes. However, Serkownek based his subscales on a factor analysis of these two scales (Graham, Schroe-

Table 2. Content Scale Approaches to Interpreting MMPI Content

Scale	Construction	Coverage	Norms and Scoring Directions
Harris & Lingoes sub-scales (Harris & Lingoes, 1955, 1968; Lingoes, 1960)	intuitive subgroupings of clinical scales	scales 2, 3, 4, 6, 8, 9	Dahlstrom, Welsh & Dahlstrom (1975) Graham (1977)
Si and Mf subscales (Serkownek, 1975)	factor analytic sub-groupings of scales 5, 0	scales 5, 0	Serkownek (1975) Graham (1977)
Comrey factor scales (Comrey, 1957 a-c; 1958 a-f; Comrey & Marggraff, 1958)	factor-analytic sub-groupings of clinical scales	scales F, 1, 2, 3, 4, 6, 7, 8, 9	
Wiggins content scales (Wiggins, 1969)	intuitive and internal consistency based sub-groupings of original 26 content categories (entire item pool)	13 content scales	Fowler & Coyle (1969) Wiggins (1971) Graham (1977)
Tryon, Stein & Chu cluster scales (Tryon & Bailey, 1965; Chu, 1966; Tryon, 1966; Stein, 1968)	cluster-analytic-based subgroupings of entire item pool	7 cluster scales	Stein (1968) Dahlstrom, Welsh & Dahlstrom (1975) Graham (1977)
Hunter, Overall & Butcher short-form factors (Overall, Hunter & Butcher, 1973; Hunter, Overall, & Butcher, 1974)	factor-analytic sub-groupings of first 168 and first 328 MMPI items	6 factor scales	Overall, Hunter, & Butcher (1973) Hunter, Overall & Butcher (1974)

der, & Lilly, 1971) rather than on intuitive methods. The subscales consist of the items loading higher than .30 on each factor in the factor analysis. Directions for scoring these subscales are found in Graham (1977). The subscales are labled as follows:

Scale 5 (Masculinity-Femininity)
Mf1 — Narcissism-Sensitivity
Mf2 — Stereotypic Feminine Interests
Mf3 — Denial of Stereotypic Masculine Interests
Mf4 — Heterosexual Discomfort-Passivity
Mf5 — Introspective-Critical
Mf6 — Socially Retiring

Scale 0 (Social Introversion)
Si1 — Inferiority Personal Discomfort
Si2 — Discomfort with Others
Si3 — Staid-Personal Rigidity
Si4 — Hypersensitivity
Si5 — Distrust
Si6 — Physical Somatic Concerns

No reliability and validity data are yet available on these subscales

Comrey Factor Scales. Homogeneous subgroupings of items within the clinical scales have been developed on a factor-analytic basis by Comrey (1957a, 1957b, 1957c, 1958a, 1958b, 1958c 1958d, 1958e 1958f) and Comrey and Marggraff (1958). They intercorrelated all items within an individual clinical scale and then factor-analyzed the matrix. The factors identified by this procedure are as follows:

Scale F
II — Paranoia (III)
III — Euphoria
IV — Feelings of Inferiority
V — Religious Fervor
VI — Antisocial Behavior
VII — Hostility
VIII — Religious Faith
IX — Psychopathic Personality
X — Poor Concentration
XI — Paranoia (I)
XII — Disturbed Sleep
XIII — Father Identification
XIV — Mother Identification
XV — Flight into Fantasy

Interpretive Statements	Internal Consistency Reliability	Validity
Graham (1977)	.04-.85	1. overlap with Comrey Scales: Graham (1977) 2. differentiate successful-unsuccessful therapy patients: Harris & Christiansen (1946) 3. relationship with demographic and stylistic variables: Gocka & Holloway (1963) 4. black-white differences: Panton (1959) 5. empirical, extra-test correlates: Gordon & Swart (1973), Boerger (1975), Calvin (1975)
Graham (1977)	. . .	. . .
	. . .	. . .
Wiggins (1966, 1969) Jarnecke & Chambers (1977) Lachar & Alexander (1978)	.505-.872	1. relationship to other personality inventories: Wiggins, Goldberg & Appelbaum (1971), Taylor, Ptacek, Carithers, Griffin & Coyne (1972), Derogatis, Rickels & Rock (1976) 2. empirical extra-test correlates: Payne & Wiggins (1972), Boerger (1975), Hoffman & Jackson (1976), Lachar & Alexander (1978) 3. differentiate various samples: Wiggins (1969), Kammeier, Hoffman, & Loper (1973), Mezzich, Damarin, Erickson (1974), Cohler, Weiss, & Grunebaum (1974), O'Neil, Teague, Luschene, & Davenport (1975), Jarnecke & Chambers (1977)
Graham (1977)	.85-.94	1. empirical extra-test correlates: Stein (1968) Boerger (1975)
. . .	. . .	1. factors identified similar to other studies: Barker, Fowler, & Peterson (1971), Wiggins (1969), Tryon (1966), Horn, Wanberg, & Appel (1973), Hodo & Barker (1976)

XVI — Psychotic Tendencies
XVII — Poor Physical Health
XVIII — Withdrawal
XIX — Paranoia II

Scale K

II — Cynicism
III — Euphoria
IV — Shyness
V — Hospitalization
VI — Hostility
VII — Family Dissension
XI — Feelings of Inadequacy
XIII — Worry

Scale 1

I — Poor Physical Health
II — Digestive Difficulties
III — Bad Eyesight
IV — Lung Damage
V — Poor Bowel Function
VI — Hypochondriasis
VII — Sinusitis
VIII — Hospitalization

Scale 2

I — Neuroticism
II — Cynicism
IV — Religious Fervor
V — Poor Physical Health
VI — Euphoria
VII — Repression
IX — Hostility
XI — Depression
XIV — Tearfulness

Scale 3

I — Poor Physical Health
II — Shyness
III — Cynicism
V — Headaches
IX — Neuroticism

Scale 4

I — Neuroticism

II—Paranoia
III—Psychopathic Personality
IV—Shyness
V—Delinquency
VI—Euphoria
VIII—Antisocial Behavior
XII—Family Dissension

Scale 6

I—Imaginary Persecution
II—Neuroticism
III—Cynicism
V—Antisocial Behavior
VI—Hysteria
XI—Rigidity
XIII—Actual Persecution
XV—Real Persecution

Scale 7

I—Neuroticism
II—Anxiety
III—Withdrawal
IV—Poor Concentration
V—Agitation
VI—Psychotic Tendencies
VII—Antisocial Behavior
IX—Poor Physical Health

Scale 8

I—Paranoia
II—Poor Concentration
III—Poor Physical Health
IV—Psychotic Tendencies
V—Rejection
VI—Withdrawal
VII—Father Identification
VIII—Sex Concern
IX—Repression
X—Unnamed
XI—Mother Identification
XII—Age

Scale 9

I—Shyness
II—Bitterness

III—Acceptance of Taboos
IV—Poor Reality Contact
V—Thrill Seeking
VI—Age
VII—Social Dependency
VIII—Psychopathic Personality
X—High Water Consumption
XI—Hospitalization
XII—Sex
XIII—Hypomania
XIV—Agitation
XV—Defensiveness

Graham (1977) noted the substantial item overlap between the rationally derived Harris-Lingoes subscales and the factor analytically derived Comrey scales.

The Comrey scales are not developed for clinical use. No norms exist for converting factor scores to T scores. It is likely that some of the smaller factors (several have as few as one or two items loading above .30) would have to be dropped and further refinements made to prepare the scales for clinical use. The scales have not generated any empirical research.

Content Subscales Based on Entire MMPI Item Pool

Wiggins (1969) does not believe that constructing subscales of the clinical scales is the optimal approach to content-scale development. Because of the extensive item overlap between MMPI scales, content subscales based on the clinical scales will inevitably reflect this duplication. "Such clusterings, no doubt contain meaningful dimensions of item content, but, in addition they contain variance peculiar to all dimensions along which the originally contrasted normal and psychiatric groups differed" (Wiggins, 1966, p. 3). Basing content subscales on the entire MMPI item pool avoids this problem and may reveal content dimensions obscured by the contrasted-groups methodology originally used to construct the clinical scales.

Wiggins Content Scales. The Wiggins Content Scales (Wiggins, 1966; 1969) were developed through the use of intuitive and internal-consistency procedures. Subsequently, the factorial composition of the final version of the content scales was determined through factor analysis of each content scale. Wiggins began with the 26 original content categories labeled by Hathaway and McKinley (1940). Each category was considered a scale and the items were scored in the direction of deviance (the infrequent item option chosen by the Minnesota normal population). The internal consistency reliability of each content "scale" was determined using data from 500 introductory psychology students. Using these data, Wiggins then revised the original categories by collapsing several categories, reassigning items from one scale to another, eliminating several categories, creating various new categories, and rekeying some items. These procedures resulted in 18 revised categories. Internal consistency reliabilities were determined in two new samples of college students. These data revealed that 15 current scales had promising internal consistency and a sufficient number of items on the scales; 4 scales were eliminated because they lacked these qualities. The final items to be retained on each of the 15 content scales were required to meet the following criteria: the point biserial correlation of an item with the score on that individual content scale must exceed .30, and the correlation of an item with its parent scale must exceed the correlation of the item with the 14 other content scales. These procedures resulted in the elimination of two categories with unpromising homogeneity. The final 13 content scales had internal consistency coefficients ranging from .505 to .872; 10% of the coefficients were between .50 and .59, 20% between .60 and .69, and 70% were above .70. Wiggins described his final scales as "13 mutually exclusive scales which were considered to be internally consistent, moderately independent, and representative of the major substantive clusters of the MMPI" (1966, p. 12).

MMPI booklet numbers and scoring directions can be found in Wiggins 1966; 1971); Dahlstrom, Welsh, and Dahlstorm (1975); and Graham (1977). Norms for converting raw scores to T scores are found in Graham (1977). The labels of the final 13 content scales are:

SOC—Social Maladjustment
DEP—Depression
FEM—Feminine Interests
MOR—Poor Morale
REL—Religious Fundamentalism
AUT—Authority Conflict
PSY—Psychoticism
ORG—Organic Symptoms
FAM—Family Problems
HOS—Manifest Hostility
PHO—Phobias
HY—Hypomania
HEA—Poor Health

Abbreviated versions of the content scales have been developed by Cohler, Weiss, and Grunebaum (1974). The Wiggins content scales have been subjected to a number of analyses to determine their validity. For example, the scales have been factor analyzed (Wiggins, 1966) and it was found that the five factors for men and six factors for women that account for content-scale variance were highly similar to the factors found through analysis of the entire MMPI. Reliable and meaningful nontest correlates of the content scales have been identified in a number of studies (Payne & Wiggins, 1972; Boerger, 1975; Lachar & Alexander, 1978). Sources of scoring information, reliability, and validity data are summarized in Table 2.

Tryon, Stein, and Chu Cluster Scales. The goal of factor analyzing the MMPI is to derive homogeneous factor scales that account for large proportions of the total test variance. Repeated factor analyses of the entire MMPI have demonstrated that two large factors repeesent the major dimensions of MMPI variance (Welsh, 1956; Block, 1965), but approximately five to six factors account for the largest amount of total variance (e.g., Eichman, 1962; Tryon, 1966; Wiggins, 1969; Barker, Fowler, & Peterson, 1971; Horn, Wanberg, & Appel, 1973; Overall, Hunter, & Butcher, 1973; Hunter, Overall & Butcher, 1974). Two sets of factor scales will be explored in more depth as representative examples. Dahlstrom, Welsh, and Dahlstrom (1975) review factor analytic studies of the MMPI in detail.

Tryon and his colleagues (Tryon & Bailey, 1965; Chu, 1966; Tryon, 1966; and Stein, 1968) employed cluster-analytic techniques to develop homogeneous factor scales that reflect the major MMPI dimensions. Their procedures have identifed seven homogeneous clusters of items:

   I. Social Introversion
  II. Body Symptoms
 III. Suspicion and Mistrust
  IV. Depression and Apathy
   V. Resentment and Aggression
  VI. Autism and Distruptive Thoughts
 VII. Anxiety, Worry and Fears

Sources of scoring directions, interpretative statements, reliability, and validity data are summarzied in Table 2.

Short-Form MMPI Factor Scales. Factor analytically based scales have been developed for the MMPI-168 short form (Overall, Hunter, & Butcher, 1973) and the MMPI-328 (Hunter, Overall & Butcher, 1974). Multi-stage factor analyses of both short forms resulted in six identical factors:

1. Somatization
2. Feminine Interests
3. Depression
4. Psychotic Distortion
5. Low Morale
6. Acting Out

Scoring directions and norms are contained in the original papers. The authors provide no data on extra-test correlates of the factor scales, but they do establish the comparability of their six factors to other factor analyses of the MMPI such as Horn, Wanberg, & Appel (1973); Barker, Fowler, & Peterson (1971); Wiggins (1969); and Tryon (1966). These sources are summarized in Table 2.

CRITICAL ITEM APPROACHES

An alternative way to obtain content meaning from MMPI responses is to interpret single items rather than to construct content scales. The concept of "critical item" originated in the Woodworth Personal Data Sheet which contained 10 "starred" items labeled "neurotic tendency items." The content of these items represented such severe pathology that a person responding to the item was considered neurotic regardless of the remainder of her/his responses on the inventory. Items considered to be highly indicative of disturbance have been called pathognomonic items, stop items, or critical items.

Today, a standard feature of most automated MMPI interpretation systems (RPSI, BAMMPI, Behaviordyne, and the Gilberstadt Veteran's Administration System) is a listing of the respondent's deviant responses to the "critical items." This set of 38 items was originally published by Grayson (1950). Recently, Caldwell (1969) constructed a more comprehensive list of 69 items that is less widely known. Critical-item response listings on computer printouts are often introduced by a statement indicating that deviant responses reflect serious pathology to which the clinician should be alerted. Gravitz (1968b) reported that many clinicians further utilize critical-item responses to obtain "a rapid assessment of an individual's emotional condition." Thus, critical items seem to be touted both as items capable of serving as behavior samples and as a short scale indicating the respondent's general level of psychological functioning.

Both lists of critical items were derived intuitively. The Grayson items were chosen to reflect the most serious pathology sampled by the MMPI item pool, behavior that Grayson and his co-worker considered important in their clinical setting (Veteran's Administration).

Caldwell attempted to increase the utility of the critical items by including additional content areas underrepresented in Grayson's list. Neither list was developed as a scale; thus, it was not known whether a high number of critical-item responses indicated blatant disturbance. Furthermore, individual critical items were not empirically validated to determine if responses to them relate to a respondent's actual behavior.

Characteristics of the Grayson Critical Items

Of the 38 Grayson items, 32 (85%) are scored on the F and/or Sc scale; 16 items (40%) are scored solely on F. This sizable overlap with the variance tapped by F, that is the tendency to "fake bad," raises questions about the importance of the Grayson Critical Items as an independent addition to test interpretation. The deviant direction for 35 (92%) of the Grayson items is true. Thus, they would be highly vulnerable to the person with an acquiescence response bias. The major Wiggins Content scales that are represented in the Grayson items are psychoticism (17 items), organic symptoms (4 items), and depression (4 items). There are 9 items not scored on any content scale. Only 2 Grayson items are scored on the A factor and 1 is scored on the R factor (Welsh, 1956). Yet, these are two of the major substantive dimensions of MMPI variance.

Characteristics of the Caldwell Critical Items

The 69 Caldwell items, as expected, reflect a broader range of content. Again, the major area sampled is psychoticism (21 items), but organic symptoms (9 items), family problems (7 items), depression (5 items), and poor health (4 items) are also represented. There are 14 items that do not appear on any content scale. In other respects, however, the Caldwell items show less improvement over the Grayson. There are 38 items (55%) scored on F and/or Sc, 20 items (29%) scored on F alone. Only 3 items are scored on factor A and 2 on R.

A thorough evaluation of the Grayson and the Caldwell critical items involves examining how they function as behavior samples of "critical" behavior and as a short scale of overall psychological functioning.

Empirical Data: Critical Items as Indicators of Crisis

Gravitz (1968b) and Saunders and Gravitz (1974) tabulated the frequency of deviant responses to critical items in large, normal samples. Endorsement frequencies ranged from .1% to 12.1% among males and .6% to 28.8% among females. Item-endorsement rates above 10%

in the normal population were found for five critical items. Endorsement rates this high call into question the appropriateness of these items as stop items. Furthermore, neither of these studies clarifies the meaning of a critical-item response in the normal population or improves our understanding of the operation of critical items in psychiatric populations. Newton (1968) reported T score conversions for raw numbers of critical-item responses within a small psychiatric population. No indication of how different elevations of T score related to clinical status was given.

Koss, Butcher, and Hoffmann (1976) examined the validity of both the Caldwell and the Grayson Critical Items as indicators of crisis. Samples of approximately 100 psychiatric patients who presented at admission in one of six crisis states (acute anxiety, depressed-suicidal, threatened assault, situational stress due to alcoholism, mental confusion, and persecutory ideas) were drawn and each group's MMPI item responses were compared to the responses of 300 psychiatric patients who had been admitted to the hospital under noncrisis circumstances. Item analysis revealed that 29 of the 38 (77%) Grayson items and 42 of the 69 (61%) Caldwell items differentiated some crisis group from the noncrisis controls. Conversely, 9 of the Grayson items and 32 of the Caldwell items failed to differentiate any crisis group from the controls. Although these items may be "critical" for other purposes, they are not critical for identifying types of crisis being studied. The Caldwell items were prominent among items that identified most of the crises, but the Grayson items contributed only to the identification of psychotic crises (mental confusion, persecutory ideas).

An additional analysis involved comparing the psychiatric patients as a group (crisis and noncrisis subjects combined) to a large sample of normal job applicants. The psychiatric patients responded to an average of 8 Grayson items (SD = 6.1) whereas the job applicants' mean was 2 (SD = 2). However, there was substantial overlap between the groups, owing to the extreme skew with the bulk of both samples clustering at the lower end; 43% of psychiatric patients and 94% of normals responded in the deviant direction on 5 items or fewer. The most efficient cutting score resulted in misclassification of 15% of the normals into the psychiatric group and 27% of the psychiatric patients into the normal groups. Koss et al. (1976) concluded that the critical items perform poorly when used as an index of serious malfunctioning.

Empirical Data: Critical Items as Behavior Samples

A question that is crucial to the validity of critical items is whether people reveal truthful information about themselves through their responses; and if so, do they reveal themselves on every face-valid item related to their problems or only on a subset of relevant items. To examine this issue, Koss et al. (1976) asked experienced psychologist raters to chose those MMPI items that were directly related to the six crises they studied. A majority of judges agreed that 96 items directly reflected the defining characteristics and symptoms of the crisis groups. Of these 96 face-valid items, 73 (76%) were found to be empirically valid as well. That is, these items statistically differentiated the appropriate crisis group from the controls (p<.05). There were 23 Grayson critical items that were designated by judges as relevant to the crises studied, and 16 were found to be empirically valid as well (70%). There were 41 Caldwell critical items among the relevant items, and 31 (76%) were statistically significant.

It must be noted that 7 Grayson items and 10 Caldwell items were chosen by judges as face-valid but were not found to result in empirically valid behavior samples. Recently, Lachar and Wrobel (in press) performed similar analyses employing general dimensions of problem behavior rather than crisis situations as criteria. They also found that approximately 75% of items nominated as relevant to a particular criterion were empirically valid.

The observation that many face-valid items are also empirically valid but some are not is consistent with previous studies (Goldberg & Slovic, 1967) and emphasizes the careful empirical validation that must be carried out if one chooses to employ single-item responses as behavior samples. As in previous studies, there were no *apparent* differences between those face-valid items that resulted in empirically valid behavior samples and those items that did not.

Koss et al. (1976) also found that the Grayson and Caldwell Critical Items formed only a subset of items that were rated as relevant to the crises under investigation. The critical items presently available do not necessarily represent the best subset of items that reflect behavior of potential interest to the clinician. The extremely deviant content of the critical items makes it unlikely that many deviant responses will be found among moderately disturbed or outpatient populations—two large "consumer groups" of computerized interpretation services.

Lachar-Wrobel Critical Items

Lachar and Wrobel (in press) have recently attempted to construct a new set of critical items that would cover a wider range of content, be face-valid, and result in valid behavior samples. They used a combination of intuitive and empirical procedures. First, they identified through a file search 14 problem behaviors that were most frequent in both inpatient and outpatient samples. Then 14 clinical psychologists were asked to nominate items directly related to each criterion. The proportion of psychiatric patients who met one of the criteria and who responded true to each nominated item was contrasted through chi-square analysis to the psychiatric patients not meeting the criteria who responded true to the item. Finally, the proportion of all psychiatric patients responding true to a nominated item was contrasted to the proportion of normal subjects responding true to the item. All samples employed were balanced for age, sex, race, and inpatient-outpatient status.

Of 177 items nominated by judges as relevant to one of the 14 criteria, 111 became final items. Of these items, 99 correlated at the .05 level of probability or less with the primary criterion that the item chosen to reflect; 12 items did not correlate significantly with the criterion they were chosen to reflect but did correlate with a logically related secondary criterion. The items contain prominent numbers of F (21%) and 8 (28%) scale items, and more items from other clinical scales are represented than were represented in the Grayson and Caldwell items. The deviant response category is true for 81 items (73%).

The Lachar-Wrobel Critical Items are designed to be used on computerized MMPI reports. The recommended format for presenting deviant critical-item responses to the clinician includes an introductory paragraph indicating that critical items "may suggest topics of inquiry." Then the deviant critical-item responses are presented, grouped into five intuitively derived categories.

   I. Psychological Discomfort
     A. Anxiety and Tension (11 items)
     B. Depression and Worry (16 items)
     C. Sleep Disturbance (6 items)

  II. Reality Distortion
     A. Deviant Beliefs (15 items)
     B. Deviant Thinking and Experience (11 items)

 III. Characterological Adjustment
     A. Substance Abuse (4 items)
     B. Antisocial Attitude (9 items)
     C. Family Conflict (4 items)
     D. Problematic Anger (4 items)

 IV. Sexual Concern and Deviation (8 items)

  V. Somatic Symptoms (10 Items)

Lachar and Wrobel suggest a format for presenting deviant critical-item responses to the clinician that includes the white male endorsement frequency in normal and psychiatric populations. Many of their items have rather high normal endorsement frequencies, some as high as 55%. For example, item #134 from the deviant thinking and experience category, "At times my thoughts have raced ahead faster than I could speak them," was endorsed by 55% of normal white males and 72% of psychiatric white males. In fact, 22 of the Lachar-Wrobel critical items do not reliably differentiate normals from psychiatric patients. One questions the appropriateness of such items as "stop," "pathognomic," or "critical items" in the traditional sense. It does seem very helpful to provide the clinician with the endorsement rates. Care should be taken that test users are educated in the meaning "critical item" in the Lachar-Wrobel context and that some indication is made in instances where the differences in endorsement rates for psychiatric patients and normal males are not significant.

In conclusion, Lachar and Wrobel have produced a list of critical items which at this preliminary point appear to be clinically useful, face-valid, and, for the most part, empirically valid as well. The items are too new to have stimulated empirical research. Some of the limitations of the Lachar-Wrobel items, such as preponderance of true items and high normal endorsement frequencies on some items, are the result of the inherent constraints of working within a fixed item pool. As long as one wishes to employ items from the MMPI item pool, items reflecting the most pathological behaviors will also be phrased so that true is the deviant response and items reflecting other important critical behaviors such as anxiety, depression, or suicidal thoughts will always have rather high normative base rates because of the way these items are phrased. These obstacles are unavoidable unless the researcher writes new items.

SUMMARY AND CONCLUSIONS

Considerations of item content are central to most of the major controversies of the last 25 years in psychological assessment. Early and recurring debates over test-construction strategy are an umbrella topic containing many item-content issues: item responses as behavior samples or signs, subtle versus face-valid item content, heterogeneous versus homogeneous scales, and substantive or stylistic interpretations of test variance. Most recent theoretical and empirical papers have tended to indicate that the test dynamics and content assumptions underlying the construction of the MMPI have become outmoded. Data were presented which indicated that item responses are now widely accepted as behavior samples and that homogeneous scales of relevant content are preferable clinically, if not empirically, to heterogeneous scales containing subtle items.

These developments, in conjuction with what appears to be strong motivation on the part of the clinician to be in touch with the actual verbal content of a respondent's item responses, have led to various attempts to devise strategies for extracting content meaning from MMPI data. The first approach was the construction through intuitive and/or factor-analytic procedures of homogeneous content subscales of the MMPI clinical scales (Harris and Lingoes Subscales, Scales 5 and 0 Subscales, Comrey Factor Scales). These approaches are designed to circumvent the heterogeneity of the MMPI scales, that is, to assist the clinician in determining the various subsets of content that comprise a respondent's scale score. By and large, these approaches are not fully developed or thoroughly researched. However, inclusion of content subscales on many computerized MMPI interpretation systems may indicate that clinicians desire these data. Further research on content subscales to bring them to acceptable levels of reliability and validity are urgently needed. Presently, the internal consistency reliabilities of the Harris-Lingoes subscales are too low to justify their widespread use.

A second approach to extracting content meaning from MMPI data is the construction of homogeneous content scales based on the entire MMPI item pool (Wiggins Content Scales, Tryon, Stein, & Chu Cluster Scales, and Short-Form Factor Scales). This approach avoids vast content redundancy which inevitably results when one individually factors clinical scales. The Wiggins Content Scales have been more thoroughly studied than other approaches, have acceptable evidence of reliability, growing support for validity, and wide clinical acceptance. In addition, it may be that the factor-analytic approaches, although very sound methodologically, do not offer the richness sought by the test interpretor interested in item content. In this respect, the Wiggins Content Scales are a compromise position, offering greater detail than factor scales but not the overwhelming information resulting from subgroupings based on the clinical scales.

The last major strategy for extracting content meaning from MMPI data is the critical-item approach (Grayson Critical Items, Caldwell Critical Items, Lachar-Wrobel Critical Items). Critical item approaches will always be less reliable and valid than scale approaches, owing to problems inherent in working with single-item responses. Approximately 75% of intuitively selected critical items will be found to result in valid behavior samples. Therefore, individual empirical validation of potential critical items is essential. Critical items are ineffective as indicators of overall psychological malfunctioning. Insufficient empirical validation supports the Grayson and the Caldwell Critical Items. The Lachar-Wrobel Critical Items were the result of careful intuitive and external validation procedures. However, the items suffer from several limitations that are the unavoidable result of working within the MMPI item pool.

Critical items, content scales, and content subscales for the MMPI should be viewed as essentially stopgap measures. They are techniques designed to minimize the inherent limitations of the MMPI, an outmoded but as yet unsurpassed psychopathology inventory. The expertise exists to construct a new inventory that has features such as individually empirically validated, relevant, content items and homogeneous content scales, but so far this task has proved impossible pragmatically. Until the time that such an inventory becomes available, the approaches for extracting content meaning from MMPI data reviewed in this paper can be employed to increase the clinical utility of the MMPI. However, the need for a more modern inventory is great.

REFERENCES

Barker, H. R., Fowler, R. D., & Peterson, L. P. Factor analytic structure of the short-form MMPI items. *Journal of Clinical Psychology*, 1971, 27, 228-33.

Berg, I. A. Deviant responses and deviant people: The formulation of the deviation hypothesis. *Journal of Counseling Psychology*, 1957, 4, 154-60.

Berg, I. A. The unimportance of test item content. In B. M. Bass and I. Berg (Eds.), *Objective approaches to personality assessment*. New York: Van Nostrand, 1959.

Block, J. *The challenge of response sets: Unconfounding meaning, acquiescence, and social desirability in the MMPI*. New York: Appleton-Century-Crofts, 1965.

Boerger, A. R. *The utility of some alternative approaches to MMPI scale construction*. Doctoral dissertation, Kent State University, 1975.

Brayfield, A. H. (Ed.), Special issue: Testing and public policy. *American Psychologist*, 1965, 20, 857-1002.

Brozek, J., & Erickson, N. K. Item analysis of the psychoneurotic scales of the Minnesota Multiphasic Personality Inventory in experimental semi-starvation. *Journal of Consulting Psychology*, 1948, 12, 403-11.

Burkhart, B. R., Christian, W. L., & Gynther, M. D. Item subtlety and faking on the MMPI: A paradoxical relationship. *Journal of Personality Assessment*, 1978, 42, 76-80.

Butcher, J. N., & Tellegen, A. Objections to MMPI items. *Journal of Consulting Psychology*, 1966, 30, 527-34.

Butcher, J. N., & Tellegen, A. Common methodological problems in MMPI research. *Journal of Consulting and Clinical Psychology*, 1978, 46, 620-28.

Caldwell, A. B. *MMPI critical items*. 2918 Santa Monica Boulevard, Santa Monica, California 90404. Mimeo, 1969.

Calvin, J. *A replicated study of the concurrent validity of the Harris-Lingoes subscales of the MMPI*. Doctoral dissertation, Kent State University, 1975.

Campbell, D. P., Borgen, F. H., Eastes, S. H., Johannsson, C. G., & Peterson, R. A. A set of basic interest scales for the Strong Vocational Interest Blank for men. *Journal of Applied Psychology*, 1968, 52 (6, pt. 2).

Carson, R. C. Issues in the teaching of clinical MMPI interpretation. In J. N. Butcher (Ed.), *MMPI: Research developments and clinical applications*. New York: McGraw-Hill, 1969.

Christian, W. L., Burkhart, B. R., & Gynther, M. D. Subtle-obvious ratings of MMPI items: New interest in an old concept. *Journal of Consulting and Clinical Psychology*, 1978, 46, 1178-86.

Chu, C. *Object cluster analysis of the MMPI*. Doctoral dissertation, University of California, Berkeley, 1966.

Cohler, B. J., Weiss, J. L, & Grunebaum, H. V. "Short-form" content scales for the MMPI. *Journal of Personality Assessment*, 1974, 38, 563-72.

Comrey, A. L. A factor analysis of the items on the MMPI hypochondriasis scale. *Educational and Psychological Measurement*, 1957a, 18, 568-77.

Comrey, A. L. A factor analysis of items on the MMPI depression scale. *Educational and Psychological Measurement*, 1957b, 17, 578-85.

Comrey, A. L. A factor analysis of items on the MMPI hysteria scale. *Educational and Psychological Measurement*, 1957c, 17, 586-92.

Comrey, A. L. A factor analysis of the items on the F scale of the MMPI. *Educational and Psychological Measurement*, 1958a, 18, 621-32.

Comrey, A. L. A factor analysis of the items on the K scale of the MMPI. *Educational and Psychological Measurement*, 1958b, 18, 633-39.

Comrey, A. L. A factor analysis of items on the MMPI psychopathic deviate scale. *Educational and Psychological Measurement*, 1958c, 18, 91-98.

Comrey, A. L. A factor analysis of items on the MMPI paranoia scale. *Educational and Psychological Measurement*, 1958d, 18, 99-107.

Comrey, A. L. A factor analysis of the items on the MMPI psychasthenia scale. *Educational and Psychological Measurement*, 1958e, 18, 293-300.

Comrey, A. L. A factor analysis of items on the MMPI hypomania scale. *Educational and Psychological Measurement*, 1958f, 18, 313-23.

Comrey, A. L., & Marggraff, W. A factor analysis of items on the MMPI schizophrenia scale. *Educational and Psychological Measurement*, 1958, 18, 301-11.

Cronbach, L. J. *Essentials of psychological testing*. New York: Harper and Row, 1970.

Cronbach, L. J., & Gleser, G. C. *Psychological tests and personnel decisions*. 2nd Ed. Urbana, Ill.: University of Illinois, 1965.

Dahlstrom, W. G. Recurrent issues in the development of MMPI. In J. N. Butcher (Ed.), *MMPI: Research developments and clinical applications*. New York: McGraw-Hill, 1969.

Dahlstrom, W. G., Welsh, G. S., & Dahlstrom, L. E. *An MMPI Handbook. Volume I: Clinical interpretation*. Minneapolis, University of Minnesota Press, 1972.

Dahlstrom, W. G., Welsh, G. S., & Dahlstrom, L. E. *An MMPI handbook. Volume II: Research applications*. Minneapolis: University of Minnesota Press, 1975.

Derogatis, L. R., Rickels, D., & Rock, A. F. The SCL-90 and the MMPI: A step in the validation of a new self-report scale. *British Journal of Psychiatry*, 1976, 128, 280-89.

Devries, A. G., & Blau, K. Discriminant MMPI profile versus discriminant MMPI item analysis. *International Review of Applied Psychology*, 1972, 21, 33-40.

Duff, F. L. Item subtlety in personality inventory scales. *Journal of Consulting Psychology*, 1965, 29, 565-70.

Edwards, A. L. *The social desirability variable in personality assessment and research*. New York: Dryden Press, 1957.

Edwards, A. L. Social desirability and performance on the MMPI. *Psychometrika*, 1964, 29, 295-308.

Eichman, W. J. Factored scales for the MMPI: A clinical and statistical manual. *Journal of Clinical Psychology*, 1962, 15, 363-95.

Endicott, N. A., & Endicott, J. Objective measurement of somatic preoccupation. *Journal of Nervous and Mental Disease*, 1963, 137, 427-37.

Ewing, D. R., & Thelen, M. H. Psychiatric patient self-description via self-report and the MMPI. *Journal of Clinical Psychology*, 1972, 28, 510-14.

Fowler, R. D., & Coyle, F. A. Collegiate normative data on MMPI content scales. *Journal of Clinical Psychology*, 1969, 25, 62-63.

Gocka, E. *American Lake norms for 200 MMPI scales*. Unpublished materials, 1965.

Gocka, E., & Holloway, H. *Normative and predictive data on the Harris and Lingoes subscales for a neuropsychiatric population*. Technical Report No. 7, Veteran's Administration Hospital, American Lake, Washington, 1963.

Goldberg, L. R. Parameters of personality inventory construction: A comparison of prediction strategies and tactics. *Multivariate Behavior Research Monographs*, 1972, 7, (2).

Goldberg, L. R., & Slovic, P. Importance of test item content: An analysis of a corollary of the deviation hypothesis. *Journal of Counseling*, 1967, 14, 462-72.

Goodenough, F. L. *Mental testing: Its history, principles, and applications*. New York: Rinehart, 1949.

Gordon, N. G., & Swart, E. C. A comparison of the Harris-Lingoes subscales between the original standardization population and an inpatient Veterans Administration hospital population. *Newsletter for Research in Mental Health and Behavioral Sciences*, 1973 (Nov), Vol. 15 (4), 28-31.

Graham, J. R. *The MMPI: A practical guide*. Oxford: Oxford University Press, 1977.

Graham, J. R. A review of some important MMPI special scales. In P. McReynolds (Ed.), *Advances in psychological assessment IV*. San Francisco: Jossey-Bass, 1978.

Graham, J. R., Schroeder, H. E., & Lilly, R. S. Factor analysis of items on the Social Introversion and Masculinity-femininity scales of the MMPI. *Journal of Clinical Psychology*, 1971, 27, 367-70.

Gravitz, M. A. Self-described depression scores and scores on the MMPI D scale. *Journal of Projective Techniques and Personality Assessment*, 1968a, 32, 88-91.

Gravitz, M. A. Normative findings for the frequency of MMPI critical items. *Journal of Clinical Psychology*, 1968b, 24, 220.

Grayson, H. M. *Psychological admissions testing program and manual*. Veteran's Administration Center: Neuropsychiatric Hospital, Los Angeles June, 1950.

Harris, R. E., & Christiansen, C. Prediction of response to brief psychotherapy. *Journal of Psychology*, 1946, 21, 269-84.

Harris, R., & Lingoes, J. *Subscales for the Minnesota Multiphasic Personality Inventory*. Mimeographed materials, The Langley Porter Clinic, 1955.

Harris, R., & Lingoes, J. *Subscales for the Minnesota Multiphasic Personality Inventory*. Mimeographed materials, The Langley Porter Clinic, 1968.

Hase, H. D., Goldberg, L. R. Comparative validity of different strategies of constructing personality inventory scales. *Psychological Bulletin*, 1967, 67, 231-48.

Hathaway, S. R., & McKinley, J. C. A multiphasic personality schedule (Minnesota): I. Construction of the schedule. *Journal of Psychology*, 1940, 10, 249-54.

Hodo, G. L., & Barker, R. Discriminating alcoholic and nonalcoholic patients with conventional and factored MMPI scales: A comparison. *Journal of Clinical Psychology*, 1976, 32, 495-97.

Hoffman, H., & Jackson, D. N. Substantive dimensions of psychopathology derived from MMPI content scales and Differential Personality Inventory. *Journal of Consulting and Clinical Psychology*, 1976, 44, 862.

Horn, J. L., Wanberg, K. W., & Appel, M. On the internal structure of the MMPI. *Multivariate Behavioral Research*, 1973, 8, 131-71.

Hunter, S., Overall, J. E., & Butcher, J. N. Factor structure of the MMPI in a psychiatric population. *Multivariate Behavioral Research*, 1974, 9, 283-301.

Jackson, D. N. The dynamics of structured personality tests: 1971. *Psychological Review*, 1971, 78, 239-48.

Jackson, D. N., & Messick, S. Content and style in personality assessment. *Psychological Bulletin*, 1958, 55, 243-50.

Jackson, D. N., & Messick, S. Acquiescence and desirability as response determinants on the MMPI. *Educational and Psychological Measurements*, 1961, 21, 771-90.

Jarnecke, R. W., & Chambers, E. D. MMPI content scales: Dimensional structure, construct validity, and interpretative norms in psychiatric population. *Journal of Consulting and Clinical psychology*, 1977, 45, 1126-31.

Koss, M. P., & Butcher, J. N. A comparison of psychiatric patients' self-report with other sources of clinical information. *Journal of Research in Personality*, 1973, 7, 225-36.

Koss, M. P., Butcher, J. N., & Hoffmann, N. The MMPI critical items: How well do they work? *Journal of Consulting and Clinical Psychology*, 1976, 44, 921-28.

Kammeier, M. L., Hoffman, H., & Loper, R. G. Personality characteristics of alcoholics as college freshmen and at time of treatment. *Quarterly Journal of Studies on Alcohol*, 1973, 34, 390-99.

Lachar, D., & Alexander, R. S. Veridicality of self-report: Replicated correlates of the Wiggins MMPI content scales. *Journal of Consulting and Clinical Psychology*, 1978, 46, 1349-56.

Lachar, D., & Wrobel, T. A. Validation of clinicians' hunches: Construction of a new MMPI critical item set. *Journal of Consulting and Clinical Psychology*, in press.

Landis, C. Questionnaires and the study of personality. *Journal of Nervous and Mental Disease*, 1936, 83, 125-34.

Landis, C., & Katz, S. E. The validity of certain questions which purport to measure neurotic tendencies. *Journal of Applied Psychology*, 1934, 18, 343-56.

Landis, C., Zubin, J., & Katz, S. E. Empirical evaluation of three personality adjustment inventories. *Journal of Educational Psychology*, 1935, 26, 321-30.

Lingoes, J. MMPI factors of the Harris and Weiner subscales. *Journal of Consulting Psychology*, 1960, 24, 74-83.

Loevinger, J. Objective tests as instruments of psychological theory. *Psychological Reports Monographs*, 1957, 3, 635-94.

McCall, R. J. Face validity in the D scale of the MMPI. *Journal of Clinical Psychology*, 1958, 15, 77-80.

Meehl, P. E. The dynamics of structured personality tests. *Journal of Clinical Psychology*, 1945, 1, 296-304.

Meehl, P. E. Reactions, reflections, projections. In J. N. Butcher (Ed.), *Objective personality assessment: Changing perspectives*. New York: Academic Press, 1972.

Meehl, P. E., & Hathaway, S. R. The K factor as a suppressor variable in the MMPI. *Journal of Applied Psychology*, 1946, 30, 525-64.

Messick, S., & Jackson, D. N. Acquiescence and the factorial interpretation of the MMPI. *Psychological Bulletin*, 1961, 58, 299-304.

Mezzich, J. E., Damarin, F. L., & Erickson, J. R. Comparative validity strategies and indices of differential diagnosis of depressive states from other psychiatric conditions using the MMPI. *Journal of Consulting and Clinical Psychology*, 1974, 42, 691-98.

Mlott, S. R. Degree of agreement among MMPI scores, self-ratings and staff ratings of inpatient adolescents. *Journal of Clinical Psychology*, 1973, 29, 480-81.

Morgan, D. W., Wietzel, W. D., Guyden, T. E., Robinson, J. A., & Hedlund, J. L. Comparing MMPI statements and mental status items. *American Journal of Psychiatry*, 1972, 129, 69-73.

Neill, J. A., & Jackson, D. N. An evaluation of item selection strategies in personality scale construction. *Educational and Psychological Measurements*, 1970, 30, 647-61.

Newton, J. R. Clinical normative data for MMPI special scales: Critical items, manifest anxiety, and represeeion-sensitization. *Journal of Clinical Psychology*, 1968, 24, 427-30.

Norman, W. T. Relative importance of test item content. *Journal of Consulting Psychology*, 1963, 27, 166-74.

O'Neil, H. F., Teague, M., Luschene, R. E., & Davenport, S. Personality characteristics of women's liberation activists as measured by the MMPI. *Psychological Reports*, 1975, 37, 355-61.

Overall, J. E., Hunter, S., & Butcher, J. N. Factor structure of the MMPI-168 in a psychiatric population. *Journal of Consulting and Clinical Psychology*, 1973, 41, 284-86.

Panton, J. The response of prison inmates to MMPI subscales. *Journal of Social Therapy*, 1959, 5, 233-37.

Payne, F. D., & Wiggins, J. S. MMPI profile types and the self-reports of psychiatric patients. *Journal of Abnormal Psychology*, 1972, 79, 1-8.

Rorer, L. G. The great response style myth. *Psychological Bulletin*, 1965, 63, 129-56.

Saunders, T. R., & Gravitz, M. A. Sex differences in the endorsement of MMPI critical items. *Journal of Clinical Psychology*, 1974, 30, 557-58.

Schiele, B. C., & Brozek, J. "Experimental neuroses" resulting from semi-starvation in man. *Psychosomatic Medicine*, 1948, 10, 31-50.

Serkownek, K. *Subscales for Scales 5 and 0 of the Minnesota Multiphasic Personality Inventory*. Unpublished materials, 3134 Whitehorn Road, Cleveland Heights, Ohio 44118, 1975.

Stein, K. B. The TSC scales: The outcome of a cluster analysis of the 550 MMPI items. In P. McReynolds (Ed.), *Advances in psychological assessment*. Vol. I. Palo Alto, Calif.: Science and Behavior Books, 1968.

Taylor, J. B., Ptacek, M., Carithers, M., Griffin, C., & Coyne, L. Rating scales as measures of clinical judgment. III. Judgments of the self of personality inventory scales and direct ratings. *Educational and Psychological Measurement*, 1972, 32, 543-57.

Tryon, R. C. Unrestructured cluster and factor analysis with application to the MMPI and Holzinger-Harmon problems. *Multivariate Behavioral Research*, 1966, 1, 229-44.

Tryon, R. C., & Bailey, D. (Eds.), *User's manual of the BC TRY system of cluster analysis*. Berkeley: University of California Center, 1965.

Weiner, D. N. Subtle and obvious keys for the MMPI. *Journal of Consulting Psychology*, 1948, 12, 164-70.

Welsh, G. S. Factor dimensions A and R. In G. S. Welsh and W. G. Dahlstrom (Eds.), *Basic readings on the MMPI in psychology and medicine*. Minneapolis: University of Minnesota Press, 1956, pp. 264-81.

Wiggins, J. S. Content dimensions in the MMPI. In J. N. Butcher (Ed.), *MMPI: Research developments and clinical applications*. New York: McGraw-Hill, 1969.

Wiggins, J. S. Substantive dimensions of self-report in the MMPI item pool. *Psychological Monographs*, 1966, 80 (22, Whole No. 630).

Wiggins, J. S. *Content scales: Basic data for scoring and interpretation*. Unpublished materials, 1971.

Wiggins, J. S., & Goldberg, L. R. Interrelationships among MMPI item characteristics. *Educational and Psychological Measurements*, 1965, 25, 381-97.

Wiggins, J. S., Goldberg, L. R., & Appelbaum, M. MMPI content scales: Interpretative norms and correlations with other scales. *Journal of Consulting and Clinical Psychology*, 1971, 37, 403-10.

Woodworth, R. S. *Personal Data Sheet*. Stoelting, 1920.

Aging and Personality

Malcolm D. Gynther

Aging is a ubiquitous phenomenon. Everyone has an opportunity to become an expert on this topic, either through self-examination or by observing friends and acquaintances. Such observations have been made for thousands of years. This accumulated folk wisdom has often been summarized in the form of proverbs. One famous saying is, "You can't teach an old dog new tricks," which implies that elderly people have more difficulty learning new material than younger people. We might agree with that, yet there is an equally well-known saying which claims that, "You're never too old to learn." These two proverbs obviously cancel each other. How about, "There's no fool like an old fool," a saying sometimes applied to an elderly man who is pursuing a younger woman. Before we acquiesce to that sentiment, however, perhaps we should consider the saying, "Old birds are not caught with chaff." Again, we have a case of mutually contradictory statements. Looking further for clarity, we find, "When the age is in, the wit is out," which seems a definitive statement. However, that maxim is readily countered by, "The frog is wiser than the tadpole." One could continue this exercise almost indefinitely, but it seems an unlikely means for elucidating the problem of aging.

What empirical facts about aging have been reported by contemporary students of this phenomenon? Botwinick (1970) reported that his assistant found some 2000 references related to aging in a search of the literature for the period 1963-68. The following statements represent a summary of the findings which, as he noted, were nearly all based on cross-sectional studies (i.e., comparison of a younger group of subjects with an older group). With regard to cognitive abilities, there are decrements in verbal learning, memory, intelligence, concept attainment, and creativity with advancing age. Two qualifications need to be made with regard to the intelligence-age relationship: (1) when level of education is controlled, there is less decrement associated with age, and (2) performance on verbal intelligence subtests, especially tests of stored information (e.g., the Information subtest of the Wechsler) tends to remain relatively intact, while that on psychomotor tests and tests of problem solving relatively independent of experience tend to fall with advancing adult age. As far as perception and psychophysiology are concerned, there are declines in auditory, visual, and other sense modalities with age. Also, ability to attend alertly usually decreases with advancing age. Furthermore, late life is associated with slow responding (i.e., reaction time). Observations about personality and social behavior include reports of higher frequency of depressive affect and suicide among the elderly, as well as increased cautiousness and rigidity. Also, indigent aged endorse significantly more negative statements about themselves than middle- and upper-class aged. Furthermore, survival is positively related to high social status and intelligence. Retirement constitutes stress for many people and brings about problems of adjustment. Death frequently follows admission to an institution.

Theories and hypotheses have been advanced to account for the physical, behavioral, and social phenomena just reviewed. Disengagement, which is defined as an increased tendency to dissociate oneself from people and activities, has been an important concept. As originally propounded by Cumming and Henry (1961), this tendency in aging people was considered normal or even desirable. But, according to Botwinick (1970), disengagement may be the result of rejection of older people by our youth-oriented culture. Schaie and Gribbin (1975) pointed out that disengagement theory seems inadequate to handle the behavior of successfully aging individuals. A contrasting hypothesis states that elderly people should keep busy in thought and action and that this activity will make for contentment and better adjustment. However, studies have shown that the activity-morale relationship is not as clearcut and positive as proponents of this view believe. As far as development over the life-span is concerned, three models have been proposed: decrement, stability, and decrement-with-compensation. Much of the earlier literature simply described the rise and fall of abilities, interests, and coping and adaptive mechanisms. Schaie and Gribbin (1975) argued that the implicit decrement model of aging is unduly pessimistic and not in accord with the facts. They asserted that a stability model is plausible to account for the period of adulthood and noted that many functions (e.g., crystallized mental abilities) do not show any decline over most of the life-span. Decrement-with-compensation is a position which holds that many of the difficulties of the aging person could be remedied by more favorable life-support systems (i.e., modifications of how young and middle-aged interact with their parents and grandparents).

This brief tour through the aging literature shows that the empirical facts themselves are not engraved in stone at this time. Theoretical explanations have even less consensual validation. Geropsychology, in fact, is a very lively area with much controversy about the meaning of the many findings that have been generated in the past twenty years.

What light can be cast on this complex area via studies by the Minnesota Multiphasic Personality Inventory (MMPI) and other instruments that ask subjects for self-report of their attitudes, emotions, and behaviors? Are data of this type especially relevant or should the focus be on cognitive abilities, health status, socioeconomic factors, and family support? Neugarten's (1977) comments are very pertinent. She reviewed the post-disengagement theory findings of the Chicago group and found that some elderly people sloughed off responsibilities and remained highly content with life, while others showed a drop in social interaction and a drop in life satisfaction. She reported that in one group of 70 to 79-year-olds living in the community and carrying out their usual rounds of activities, eight different patterns of aging emerged: (1) reorganizers, (2) focused, (3) disengaged, (4) holding-on, (5) constricted, (6) succorance-seeking, (7) apathetic, and (8) disorganized. These studies led to the hypothesis that personality organization or personality type is pivotal in predicting which individuals will age successfully. Health, financial status, and marital status are important; but, according to Neugarten, personality is thought to be the key element in the process of adaptation to aging.

Many MMPI studies of relationships among age, psychopathology, and personality have been carried out. One could simply report the findings in chronological order, but that would involve considerable repetition, as well as difficulties for the reader in evaluating which studies should be given the most weight from his or her particular perspective. Although other organizations of the data are certainly possible, the following breakdown by subjects studied seemed most helpful: (1) psychiatric patients, (2) medical patients, and (3) normals (from college students to elderly individuals living in the community). Within each of these major subgroups of studies, code-type or high-point scale findings, scale score presentations, and item analyses will be given separately, as available. Emphasis will be given to studies with large samples and to studies not restricted to a single diagnostic classification. After the MMPI data have been reviewed, supplementary findings from other inventories will be briefly summarized. Following that, effects of moderator variables (e.g., socio-economic status, marital status, etc.) will be considered. It should be emphasized that nearly every study employed a cross-sectional design. The few longitudinal studies located will be reviewed at the end of the following section.

MMPI STUDIES

Psychiatric Patients

One of the first large-scale studies was Aaronson's (1958) analysis of the 871 cases given in *An Atlas for the Clinical Use of the MMPI* (Hathaway & Meehl, 1951). He categorized the subjects' ages in terms of decades (i.e., 10-19, 20-29, etc.). Two percent of the total were over 60, but these were included in the 50 to 59-year-old group. He found that peaks on scales 1(*Hs*) and 2(*D*) are relatively uncommon early in life and become more common later, while the reverse is true for scales 4(*Pd*) and 8(*Sc*). These shifts were interpreted as indicating problems with impulse control for the younger patients and concerns about one's physical and mental functioning in the older group. The other study employing large numbers of subjects was Webb's (1970) analyses of two-point codes. His sample consisted of 12,174 cases, which he described as representative of outpatients of psychiatrists and psychologists nationally. Patients' ages were originally categorized as 20 and below, 21-26, 27-39, and 40 and older. But Webb found that even with his very large sample, cell frequencies were often too small for reliable analysis. Consequently, the age categories were reduced to persons below 27 and those 27 and above. Older patients obtained the following code types significantly more frequently than younger patients: 0(*Si*)-2/2-0, 1-2/2-1, 1-3(*Hy*)/3-1, 2-3/3-2, 2-7(*Pt*)/7-2, 3-4/4-3, and 3-6(*Pa*)/6-3. Younger patients obtained the following code types significantly more frequently than older patients: 4-7/7-4, 4-8/8-4, 4-9(*Ma*)/9-4, 6-8/8-6, 7-8/8-7, and

8-9/9-8. Webb interpreted his finding as supporting those reported by Aaronson. However, his subjects do not include any middle-aged, let alone elderly, people. Are troubled individuals 27 or older similar in personality to those approaching retirement?

Gynther and Shimkunas (1966) analyzed relations between MMPI scale scores and age. Data were obtained from 420 white hospitalized psychiatric patients who ranged in age from 14 to 76 (Mean = 35.7, S.D. = 13.2). The scores for scales 4, 6, 8, and 9, but not for scale 2, were significantly influenced by age. Thus, admission of rebelliousness toward authority, suspiciousness, autistic ideation, and impulsivity decrease with advancing age. However, the implication that patients admit more dysphoric behavior as they grow older (cf. Aaronson, 1958, and Webb, 1970) was not supported. Apparently scale 2 scores become more prominent as a consequence of age-linked decreases in the scores for scales 4, 6, 8, and 9.

Whitmyre and Cohen (1973) studied the MMPI scores of 373 male psychiatric patients divided into a young (less than 26), a middle-aged (30-40), and an older (50-60) group. They found that the young group of patients obtained significantly lower scores on scales 2 and 0 than the middle-aged and older groups, and significantly lower scores on scale 1 than the older group. The young subjects got significantly higher scores on scales 4 and 9 than both other groups and, in addition, got higher scores on scales 5 and 6 than the older group.

Aaronson (1960) derived an aging index (AgI) from MMPIs of 66 subjects drawn "from the files of the psychology department" (presumably hospitalized psychiatric patients when tested). The formula was $1.5 Pd + Sc + .5 Pt - Hs - D$. The scores for his group correlated $-.50$ ($p < .001$) with age. The same author (1964) published another article on the same topic. On this occasion 98 hospitalized psychiatric patients from 15 to 65 years of age participated. He found the following significant correlations with age: scale 4, $r = -.39$; scale 8, $r = -.25$; and AgI, $r = -.64$. Other studies that examined age-scale relationships with psychiatric patients have been conducted by Davis (1972), Davis, Mozdzierz, and Macchitelli (1973), Lester (1971), and Postema and Schell (1967). Studies that have examined these relationships with alcoholics or drug abusers were carried out by Hoffman and Nelson (1971), McGinnis and Ryan (1965), Weiss and Russakoff (1977), and Wilson, Mabry, and Khavari (1977). McCreary and Mensh (1977) examined relations between age and MMPI scale scores in a large group of male misdemeanor offenders referred for dispositional evaluation.

The results obtained from high-point, code-type, and scale-score analyses of younger and older psychiatric patients may be summarized as follows: rebellious, alienated, impulsive-energetic behaviors (scales 4, 8, and 9, respectively) are characteristic of youth, and hypochondriacal and depressive behaviors (scales 1 and 2, respectively) are characteristic of older samples. However, two caveats should be noted: Gynther and Shimkunas' (1966) explanation of scale 2's relative prominence in later years and the fact that few subjects over 60 were used in any of these studies.

As to item-level analyses, Devries (1966) found that endorsement patterns were strikingly affected by age. He compared 600 male psychiatric patients categorized as 0-39, 40-49, and 50+ years of age. Highly significant differences were obtained for all comparisons. However, no item data were reported in the article.

Medical Patients

One of the early MMPI studies was Guthrie's (1949) analysis of high points for over 1000 male and female medical outpatients. Although age effects were not reported, the most and least frequent high points may be of interest. The most frequent peak score for males was on scale 2 with 35.5% of the cases. Scales 1 and 3 accounted for 21.4% and 21.1%, respectively. Only 1.6% of these subjects obtained peak scores on scale 8. Scales 6 and 7 were next lowest with 2.4% and 3.6% of the total. For females, the most frequent peak score was on scale 3 with 41.3% of all cases. Scale 2 with 27.3% was the only other scale accounting for more than 10% of the cases. Scales 7 and 8 were the least frequent peaks with values of 2.0% and 2.3%, respectively.

Only three age-related MMPI studies of medical patients have been located. One study (Calden & Hokanson, 1959) included only male tuberculosis patients and hence has limited generalizability. The principal findings were rises on scale 1, 2, and 0 scores with increasing age. A second study (Colligan & Osborne, 1977) examined age changes in MMPI scale scores of 659 females and 534 males, ages 15 through 19. These data are interesting but too age-restrictive for our purposes. The other study (Swenson, Pearson, & Osborne, 1973) included 50,000 ambulatory medical patients ranging in age from younger than 20 to older than 70. This collection is undoubtedly the richest source of data available for analyzing relations between age and MMPI performance. Generalizations from these data to people-in-general are tempting, since most people do, in fact, need attention for various aches and pains on occasion. However, one might ask if traveling 25, 50, or 100 miles to the Mayo Clinic rather than going to one's own private physician makes these subjects unique in some way (e.g., socioeconomic level)? To our knowledge, no analyses have been brought forward to substantiate such a possibility, although individuals familiar with the setting seem to feel that Mayo patients are "special."

If one examines Swenson et al.'s high-point data for the younger than 20 versus the older than 70 groups, it is clear that the older subjects obtained significantly more peak scores on scales 1 and 2 and significantly fewer peak scores on scales 4, 7, 8, and 9 than the younger group. (Interactions between sex and age can also be noted, but those will be taken up in the later section on Moderator Variables). The scales that appear least affected by age of subject were 3 (*Hy*) and 6 (*Pa*). The most dramatic differences are on scales 2 and 9. Only 6% of the younger group obtained peaks on scale 2, while nearly 23% of the elderly group peaked on that scale alone. In contrast, about 21% of subjects younger than 20 peaked on scale 9, while less than 5% of the elderly peaked on that scale. These results would appear to confirm the relationships demonstrated by psychiatric patients, namely, that behaviors involving problems with health and unhappiness are the lot of the elderly, whereas strivings for independence, exuberance, impulsiveness, feeling misunderstood, and the like are characteristic of the young.

If this is the case, what is one to make of the mean scale scores for different age groupings offered in Swenson et al.? Consider the scale 2 data. It is true that those younger than 20 obtained lower scores on this scale than those 20 and older (i.e., T scores of 56 vs. 59-61, depending on age grouping). However, there are no meaningful differences between scores obtained by 20 to 29-year-olds vs. the 70+ group or any other pair of categories. For example, those in their 20's obtained an average score of slightly over 59, while those in the 70's and 80's had an average score of 60. This would hardly seem to indicate that older people are unhappier than younger people. How about scale 1? The results are very similar. The youngest group obtained lower scores than the other groups, but there were no meaningful differences between any of the other groups. Don't older people have more problems with health than younger people? Presumably the answer is yes, but they do not seem as a group to admit such problems anymore often than 20 to 30-year-olds in response to the MMPI-item stimuli.

What is the explanation for the discrepancy between peak-score and scale-score analyses? The Swenson et al. data support Gynther and Shimkunas's (1966) contention that scales 1 and 2 are more prominent in older groups not because scores on those scales have increased, but because scores on scales 4, 7, 8, and 9 have decreased. If one looks at the means for scale 9 in the Swenson data, for example, systematic decreases in scores, decade by decade, will be noted (59.29 for the < 20 group to 48.77 for the 70+ group). Correct interpretation of these findings is important. If one accepts the peak-scale results without question, the conclusion that follows is that as one grows older, one inevitably is heir to depressed moods. It is quite a different matter to state that older people are less impulsive, rebellious, and alienated than younger people, which is the conclusion that takes all the data into consideration. With the data available one can also indirectly check how well the disengagement theory applies. If we assume that scores on scale 0, which measures introversion-extraversion, are related to dissociating oneself from other people, comparison of elderly persons' scores with the mean over all ages should be enlightening. The grand mean for scale 0 is 53.15; the mean for the 70+ group is approximately 54.2. The evidence for withdrawal in these elderly medical patients is not convincing.

The most intriguing and unusual data presented in Swenson et al.'s *MMPI Source Book* are True-False endorsement rates for every item by sex and age categories. These tables probably could not have been prepared without computer assistance. As it is, the number of bits of information is truly impressive. In what appears to have been a warming-up exercise, Pearson, Swenson, and Rome (1965) published an unusual item-analytic article using a "mere" 25,000 medical patients. Figures showing % True responses by age and sex were given for 11 items. One might expect, if withdrawal in later life is typical, that % True responses to item #8, "My daily life is full of things that keep me interested," would decline with increasing age. This was not the case. Subjects 80 or older responded positively 88% of the time, whereas teen-agers agreed about 78% of the time. How about item #544, "I feel tired a good deal of the time"? Surely the older subjects would be more worn out, more tired. Again, the data do not support this common-sense view. The age period 30-49 involves the highest True response (about 56%); those 70 and older have a 46% endorsement rate. The authors assembled two scales for females and males with markedly curvilinear response patterns by age; these were labeled the "tired housewife scale" and the "worried breadwinner scale," respectively.

Which items in the *Source Book* are most affected by age? The present writer examined the % True endorsement rates given for each item by male and female medical patients. Table 1 gives the items for which the endorsement rates differed most by age for *both* males and females, and gives the keyed response for older subjects. To be included on this list, systematic increases (or decreases) in endorsement rate by decade and a percentage difference of 25 or more for extreme groups were also required. To illustrate, % True endorsement of item #9, "I am about as able to work as I ever was," by males was 75.8, 70.4, 66.7, 62.3, 53.8, 43.4, and 30.2 for subgroups identified as under 20, 20-29, 30-39, 40-49, 50-59, 60-69, and 70+, respectively. There is a 45.6% difference between the extreme groups.

Table 1. Age-Discriminating Items Extracted from *An MMPI Source Book*

9. I am about as able to work as I ever was. (F)
15. Once in a while I think of things too bad to talk about. (F)
21. At times I have very much wanted to leave home. (F)
26. I feel that it is certainly best to keep my mouth shut when I'm in trouble. (T)
30. At times I feel like swearing. (F)
39. At times I feel like smashing things. (F)
45. I do not always tell the truth. (F)
80. I sometimes tease animals. (F)
96. I have very few quarrels with members of my family. (T)
109. Some people are so bossy I feel like doing the opposite of what they request even though I know they are right. (F)
132. I like collecting flowers or growing house plants. (T)
181. When I get bored, I like to stir up some excitement. (F)
231. I like to talk about sex. (F)
232. I have been inspired to a program of life based on duty which I have since carefully followed. (T)
235. I have been quite independent and free from family rule. (T)
237. My relatives are nearly all in sympathy with me. (T)
261. If I were an artist, I would like to draw flowers. (T)
282. Once in a while I feel hate toward members of my family whom I usually love. (F)
289. I am always disgusted with the law when a criminal is freed through the argument of a smart lawyer. (T)
367. I am not afraid of fire. (F)
391. I love to go to dances. (F)
401. I have no fear of water. (F)
402. I often must sleep over a matter before I decide what to do. (T)
406. I have often met people who were supposed to be experts who were no better than I. (T)
428. I like to read newspaper editorials. (T)
432. I have strong political opinions. (T)
438. There are some people I dislike so much that I am inwardly pleased when they are catching it for something they have done. (F)
444. I do not try to correct people who express an ignorant belief. (T)
465. I have several times had a change of heart about my life work. (F)
481. I can remember "playing sick" to get out of something. (F)

Examination of these 30 items in terms of Wiggins's (1966) content categories reveals some interesting facts. First, not one of these age-related items is on Wiggins's 28-item poor health (HEA) scale. The absence of such items is quite remarkable, although one might argue that since all participants were medical patients, masking of an actual effect took place. As a second observation, one might note that the scale containing the largest number of identified items is manifest hostility (HOS). Items #39, 80, 109, 282, and 438 are members of this scale. In every case, older people endorsed the item much less frequently than younger people. Items on different scales complement the claimed decrease in hostility in older people. For example, older subjects endorsed items #96 and 237 far more frequently and item #21 far less frequently than younger subjects. These patterns imply that older people experience less turmoil and dissatisfaction at home than younger people. One might also note the responses to items #26, 132, 232, 261, 402, and 428. Wiggins (1966) classified items #132 and 261 as indicating feminine interests (FEM) and item #232 as related to psychoticism (PSY). The other items do not appear on his scales. In any case, one gets a picture of older people who are dutiful, placid, and cautious. By way of contrast, one might note the independence and/or cynicism expressed in items #235, 289, 406, and 432. This kind of analysis gives flesh to the skeletal outline provided by code-type, high-point, and scale-score analyses. These endorsements should be considered modal responses; obviously, the responses of individual subjects may differ greatly from these patterns.

Normal Subjects

No code-type or high-point analysis for normals by age was found. However, numerous sources present data relevant to T-score values. Dahlstrom, Welsh, and Dahlstrom (1972), for example, presented a T-score conversion table (pp. 384-85) based on data gathered by Swenson (1961) from normal men and women age 60 or older (median age = 71). Adjustments on scales 1 and 2 are most striking. Ordinarily, raw scores of 19 on scale 1 and 25 on scale 2 are equivalent to T scores of 70. For this age group, however, such raw scores convert to T scores of 61 and 59, respectively.

Scale-score analyses of normal samples come in two forms: comparisons of younger and older subjects, which as we have seen is the standard procedure, and studies using only elderly subjects. I will examine the findings in that order. Brozek (1955) compared 157 college males with 233 business and professional men between the ages of 45 and 55. Since his major interest was in item analysis, he reported results only for scales *L*, *F*, 1, and 0. There were no significant differences between the groups on the validity scales. Younger men obtained significantly lower scores than the older subjects on scales 1 and 0. Should one conclude that his older subjects were more introverted and concerned about health than his younger subjects? The statistical tests would be so interpreted, but it should be noted that the older subjects' mean scores on scales 1 and 0 were 49.0 and 48.1, respectively (50 is the mean of the normative group). Canter, Day, Imboden, and Cluff (1962) drew samples of males 20 to 69 years of age from a population of civilian employees in an army chemical warfare center. Analysis of variance of the MMPI scale scores for the different age groups revealed no significant differences. Furthermore, additional analyses comparing the oldest and youngest groups on all MMPI scales yielded negative results.

Thumin (1969) studied male job applicants ranging from age 19 to 56. No scale scores were reported since the investigator was primarily interested in relationships between scale scores, age, education, and intelligence. He found small but significant negative correlations between age and scores on *F*, 7, and 8 with the effects of education and intelligence partialed out. He also noted that significant relations between age and scores on scales 1, 2, 5, 9, and 0 did not occur. That is, there was no evidence of an increasing concern with bodily ailments, loss of zest or withdrawal, although, as he pointed out, his sample contained no subjects who would be described as elderly. Hardyck (1964) compared MMPI performance of 80 college women and 109 adult women between ages 30 and 55 (average = 41) at both the scale and item level. He found that the younger women obtained significantly higher scores on scales *F* and 9, and significantly lower scores on scales 1 and 3. However, neither mean profile was significantly different from the average MMPI profile (e.g., the highest mean T score was 59 for the older women on scale 3).

Slater and Scarr (1964) asked, is the personality structure of 70-year-olds the same as that of 20-year-olds? To answer this question, they gave 102 males and 109 females ranging from 47 to 88 years of age (average = 67) the MMPI, factored the resulting data, and compared their findings with those obtained from various younger male samples. They concluded that older and younger males had a common personality structure and that, within this structure, they are distinguished from each other on an impulsivity-intellectual control dimension, i.e., there is a negative relationship between age and impulsivity. Among the elderly, males and females also appeared to have a common personality structure. Osborne (1971) used Block's Ego-Resiliency (ER-0) and Ego-Control (EC-5) measures. He found a decline in ER-0 with age for males, but no age-related effect for females. EC-5 scores were not related to age for either sex.

The results for normals appear to be less clear-cut than those reported for psychiatric patients. That is, some investigators found no differences associated with age, others found differences associated with the "disinhibitory" scales (F, 8, or 9), and still others found the more typical differences associated with the "neurotic triad" (1, 2, or 3). In no case were clinically elevated scores demonstrated by the older groups, so what statistically significant differences there were may not be significant in a practical sense.

Several investigations were restricted to older populations. Swenson (1961) tested 95 nonhospitalized persons age 60 or older and found that the "median profile for this group is a neurotic one with an absence of evidence of psychotic or behavior disorder tendencies" (p. 304). Although this interpretation sounds as if he might have discovered a different pattern than did most investigators, examination of the mean scale scores in question suggests nothing novel about his findings, i.e., scale 1, 57.9, scale 2, 59.1, and scale 3, 55.9. (However, T-score conversions based on these data differ markedly from the standard conversions.) Kornetsky (1963) examined a small group of 43 males, aged 65 to 91, and concluded that elderly individuals do not deviate, except on scale 2, beyond what might be expected from an above-average IQ group of subjects. The mean score on scale 2 was 63.5. Britton and his associates published several studies using what appears to be the same sample of 80 elderly subjects (average age = 75) living at home. In the first study, Britton and Savage (1965) found that all mean T scores except for scales 4 and 0 were significantly elevated above the standardization group. The highest mean scores, 73 and 72, respectively, were on scales 1 and 3. The second study (Britton, Bergmann, Kay, & Savage, 1967) showed that age was not correlated with scores on any of the clinical scales. Of course, the age range was quite restricted, i.e., approximately 67 to 82. The third study (Britton & Savage, 1969) involved a factor analysis that yielded three major factors: general psychopathology, social withdrawal, and aggressive-asocial reaction.

Several investigators whose scale-score data we have already reviewed also examined the responses of normals to see what items might be affected by age. Brozek (1955), whose comparison involved college students versus middle-aged men, found 88 items differentiating the two groups at the .01 level or better. Obviously, we cannot deal with all these data, but we will try to convey the flavor of his findings by reporting the most discriminating items in at least some of the ten content categories that he used. Under "Health," we find that younger men endorsed item #274, "My eyesight is as good as it has been for years," and item #160, "I have never felt better in my life than I do now," far more frequently than older men. Items endorsed more frequently by the older group were #5, "I am easily awakened by noise," and #155, "I am neither gaining nor losing weight." In the "Work" category, older men endorsed "I work under a great deal of tension" (items 13 and 290) far more frequently than college males. As to "Emotional Adjustments," the following items were typically answered "True" by older men: "Criticism or scolding hurts me terribly" (#138), "I never worry about my looks" (#240), "It makes me nervous to have to wait" (#439) and "I have had periods in which I lost sleep over worry" (#442). In the same category, the college males were characterized by positive responses to: "I sometimes tease animals" (#80), "Sometimes without any reason or even when things are going wrong I feel excitedly happy, 'on top of the world'" (#248), "I have often felt that strangers were looking at me critically" (#278), and "It bothers me to have someone watch me at work even though I know I can do it well" (#416). In the "Interests" category, middle-aged men differentially endorsed "I like collecting flowers or growing house plants" (#132), "I like to read newspaper editorials" (#428), and "If I were an artist I would like to draw children" (#554); college males more often endorsed "I like to read newspaper articles on crime" (#6), "I would like to be an auto racer" (#434), and "I very much like horseback riding" (#561). Under "Norms of Conduct," young men were far more likely to endorse "If I could get into a movie without paying and be sure I was not seen I would probably do it" (#135) and "At times I have been so entertained by the cleverness of a crook that I have hoped he would get by with it" (#277); older men favored "I feel that it is certainly best to keep my mouth shut when I'm in trouble" (#26) and "I do not try to correct people who express an ignorant belief" (#444). It is difficult to summarize such myriad data, but it is clear at least for these particular samples that older men tend to be more tense, cautious, and sedentary, while younger men might be characterized as self-conscious, sensation-seeking, and against rules and regulations. If the reader will compare these data with those given in Table 1, a great deal of similarity will be found.

Hardyck (1964) contrasted the MMPI responses of college women with women who were approaching middle age (mean = 41).

Actual item endorsements will not be reported, but the gist of the findings will be summarized. The older women reported more somatic complaints, a preference for relatively sedentary pastimes, more phobias and less self-confidence, but more optimism about the future than the younger women. The younger subjects' endorsements emphasized restlessness, periods of exhilaration, excitement-seeking, assertiveness, cynicism about others' motives, yet concern about the opinions of friends and acquaintances. Hardyck compared his results with those of Brozek and concluded that, "Although the studies had very few overlapping items, the content of the items was quite similar" (p.82). The only other study we have located that compares item-level responses was conducted by Harmatz and Shader (1975) who used only scale 2 (D). Young (under 35) and old (over 65) subjects were solicited by newspaper advertisements requesting paid volunteers for psychological research. The investigators found significant differences on 25 of the 60 items. The content, however, does not support the notion that elderly people are unhappier than younger people. Those 65 and over answered "True" much more frequently than the younger group to the following items: "Everything is turning out just like the prophets of the Bible said it would" (#58), "I go to church almost every week" (#95), "I believe in the second coming of Christ" (#98), and "I believe I am no more nervous than most others" (#242). The younger subjects' "True" responses far outweighed the elderly's "True" responses to these items: "At times I feel like swearing" (#30), "At times I feel like smashing things" (#39), "I have had periods of days, weeks or months when I couldn't take care of things because I couldn't 'get going'" (#48), "At times I feel like picking a fist fight with someone" (#145), and "I like to flirt" (#208). Many of the items endorsed by the younger subjects appear to lie on the impulsivity dimension that Slater and Scarr (1964) described as the principal factor associated with age.

All the MMPI studies reviewed to this point have been cross-sectional. Very few longitudinal studies of personality have been conducted. The major MMPI study (Leon, Gillum, Gillum, & Gouze, in press) used the same subjects originally examined by Brozek in 1947. Because the original participants in this study averaged 49 years of age at that time, the survivors now range from 70 to 85 (mean age = 77). MMPI data were available for 71 men tested in 1947, 1953, 1960, and 1977. Results indicated that the largest increases over the four testing periods were on scale 2 (from 51.6 to 61.6). Significant linear increases over time were also found on scales F, K, 3, and 8. Interestingly, there were no decreases on scale 4 and 9 scores with advancing age (but what scores these men may have made on those scales while young is not known). In terms of code types, 3-5/5-3 was most prevalent in 1947, 1953, and 1960 and second most frequent in 1977. In 1977, the 2-3/3-2 code type was most prevalent. The authors interpreted these results as describing a serious, intellectual group of persons with a tendency to use denial and somatization of emotional problems. Nearly 24% of the subjects had the same two-point code type over the entire 30-year span. The greatest discrepancy in code type was found between 1953 and 1977; approximately 20% of the sample exhibited completely different code types between these two periods. Stability in scores over time on the individual scales was also examined. The findings for scale 0 were striking: a correlation of 0.74 over the 30-year period. Scores on scales 5 and 9 also were quite stable over the span of the study. The L scale was least reliable; scores on scales 1 and 8 were also relatively unstable. Although 45.5% of the sample responded positively to "I am greatly bothered by forgetting where I put things," it is noteworthy that 28% of the 71 men responded "True" to the MMPI item, "I have never felt better in my life than I do now." The authors of this study concluded that the stability of personality functioning over a 30-year period demonstrated by this group suggests that persons who manifest personality strengths in middle age generally continue to function in a positive manner in old age.

The only other longitudinal study with the MMPI has something to do with developmental psychology, but little to do with aging in the sense focused on in this review. Golden, Mandel, Glueck, and Feder (1962) reexamined 50 males who had shown a normal profile (no scale score above 55) 12 years earlier when they were 13 or 14 years of age. What we have, then, is a test-retest using teen-agers and young adults. There were slight increases on all scale scores except L and F over the 12-year period, but a panel of psychologists rated the profiles of 44 of the 50 subjects as "healthy" on retest.

Since we have already included several interpretive summaries of subsections of the MMPI research, a detailed overall summary seems unnecessary. However, a few general observations may be in order. Item data appear to yield more information about personality than scale-score or configurational data. The latter are, by the nature of the instrument, bound to psychiatric diagnostic categories. Results seem to be relatively similar for psychiatric patients, medical patients, and normals; however, more discriminating analyses may reveal unique findings associated with the separate categories. One gets the impression, at least from the cross-sectional data, that the major difference between young and older subjects lies not on an introversion-extraversion dimension, as has often been stated, but rather on an impusivity-control dimension.

FINDINGS FROM OTHER INVENTORIES

Although the major focus of this article is on age-related MMPI findings, some sampling of other sources seems desirable. As far as self-report inventories are concerned, there is little doubt that most of the research has used the MMPI. However, if one is interested in personality as opposed to psychopathology, findings with other instruments that emphasize personality variables may yield additional insights not available from MMPI research.

Schaie (1959) investigated the effects of age on a shortened version of the California Psychological Inventory's Responsibility (Re) scale. He used 500 subjects, from 20 to 70 years of age, with equal numbers of males and females at each age level. He found that mean Re scores increased up to the early 50s, after which a slight decline occurred. Analysis of variance showed that the overall between-age effect was significant at less than the .01 level. Grupp, Ramseyer, and Richardson (1968) analyzed the effects of age on CPI scales Good Impression (Gi), Self-Acceptance (Sa), Self-Control (Sc), and Socialization (So). Subjects were 246 males and 37 females with a history of drug use who were on probation or parole or incarcerated at the time of the study. Ages ranged from 19 to 51 (mean = 30.4). Sa scores were not affected by age. Scores on the other three scales typically increased as a function of age until about 40, then declined, but not to the level of the 19 to 23-year-old subgroup. Gough (1978) stated that scores on the Dominance and Well-Being scales also begin to decrease in the late 50s. All these patterns imply that personality strengths of various kinds increase from youth to middle age, then decline. No CPI data have been published on the elderly as far as the writer has been able to determine.

The 16PF Handbook (Cattell, Eber, & Tatsuoka, 1970) presents some information on age trends in primary personality factors. The authors stated that the results are based on about 7000 cases from 30 to 80 years of age. Surgency (i.e., enthusiasm, heedlessness) showed a marked and steady decline over the entire age range. There was a slight rise in superego strength (i.e., conscientiousness) as people get older. There was a rise in premsia (i.e., sensitiveness, dependency) after age 35 and in self-sentiment (control, compulsiveness) later in life. There was also a rise in radicalism (i.e., experimenting, liberalism) as a function of age. Finally, there were drops in guilt proneness (i.e., feeling insecure, worried) and in ergic tension (i.e., feeling tense, driven), especially after age 50. It is interesting to compare these findings to those adduced from the MMPI data. Although the terminology is different, there seem to be many similarities (e.g., the drop in surgency by age). Another study that employed the 16PF was directed toward the problem of age differences in the structure of personality. Costa and McCrae (1976) used data collected from the 969 male volunteers in the Veterans Administration Normative Aging Study. Three age groups were formed: 25-34 (N = 140), 35-54 (N = 711), and 55-82 (N = 118). Cluster analysis revealed three dimensions: adjustment-anxiety, introversion-extraversion, and openness to experience. The first two clusters were cross-sectionally stable, but the third cluster showed age-related differences. Young subjects showed openness to feelings, middle-aged subjects showed openness to ideas and values, and elderly subjects showed a balanced openness to both feelings and ideas. However, these intriguing findings were not replicated by longitudinal data (Costa & McCrae, 1977). More recently, Costa and McCrae (1978) found a saw-tooth effect, which peaked in the late 50s, for openness. The authors were unable to determine whether this pattern was age-related or a generational effect, but pointed out that the data are more consistent with the belief that aging involves transitional phases than with the idea that aging is a simple process of linear decline.

Findings with other inventories may be briefly noted. Garvey (1975) gave the same sample used by Costa and McCrae the Allport-Vernon-Lindzey Study of Values and found a decline in political (need for power) values and a concomitant rise in social values with increasing age. Spangler and Thomas (1962), who used the Edwards Personal Preference Schedule, found that needs for deference and affiliation increased with age, while need for heterosexuality was inversely related to age. Bendig (1960) employed the Guilford-Zimmerman Temperament Survey. He demonstrated that the scales which were involved with the social-activity factor showed decreased mean scores with age, as did general activity, ascendancy, and sociability. Increments occurred for the personal relations and restraint variables. Studies with the Eysenck Personality Inventory (Eysenck & Eysenck, 1963) have shown that both neuroticism and extraversion decline with advancing age.

Other studies might be mentioned, but those we have noted with the CPI, 16PF, and other inventories are perhaps a representative sample of non-MMPI cross-sectional investigations. The results supplement and, in many cases, complement the MMPI findings. Declines in dominance, enthusiasm, and tension, and rises in sensitiveness, social values, and restraint with age are noteworthy.

INFLUENCE OF MODERATOR VALUES

It has been difficult to summarize several of the preceding studies without reference to sex-age interactions. Numerous studies used only one sex, so comparisons were not possible. Those that used males and females often found age effects equally applicable to both sexes. However, there are cases where what happens is a function of sex as well as of age. For example, Webb (1970) presented differences in MMPI two-point code frequencies by age and sex. Many of the results are equivalent for men and women (e.g., 1-3/3-1 appears far more frequently in the older group). However, there are striking exceptions: 2-8/8-2, 5-7/7-5, and 5-8/8-5 were given much more frequently by younger males than older males, but there was no such relationship for females. Also, 0-3/3-0, 2-6/6-2, and 3-7/7-3 were given much more often by older females than younger females, but there was no age effect for men with those code types.

Table 1 reported those items in Swenson et al.'s (1973) data most age discriminating for males *and* females. However, if one uses the criteria for selecting age-related items mentioned earlier, there are 55 such items for females and 44 for males, 30 of which are shared. To give a few examples, "I never worry about my looks" (#240), "I am embarrassed by dirty stories" (#427), and "I never attend a sexy show if I can avoid it" (#548) are age-related for men, but not for women. However, "What others think of me does not bother me" (#170), "I like to flirt" (#208), and "I read in the Bible several times a week" (#490) are age-related for women, but not for men. It could also be pointed out that the 36-item "Tired housewife" scale and the 34-item "Worried breadwinner" scale (Pearson, Swenson, & Rome, 1965), have only 17 items in common.

Socioeconomic status, education, and intelligence form an interrelated set of moderator variables. As Dahlstrom, Welsh, and Dahlstrom (1975) have stated, "In general, the higher the status of the subject, the greater unwillingness to disclose any troubles and difficulties in their families, within their relationships at work, or in their emotional reactions" (p. 154). MMPI effects associated with the interaction between status and age have not been the subject of many investigations. However, Gynther and Shimkunas (1965) used data obtained from hospitalized psychiatric patients and showed that MMPI *F* scores decrease markedly as age increases for low- and high-intelligence groups, but that a relatively minor decrease in *F* scores accompanies increasing age in the average intelligence group. Thumin (1969), who used MMPIs obtained from male job applicants, found that age, education, and intelligence were all of predictive value when used in combination to predict MMPI scale scores. The three highest multiple correlations were with scales *L*, 9, and 0.

Chronic physical disability is another factor that may interact with age to influence MMPI performance. Canter et al. (1962) obtained Cornell Medical Index (CMI) Health Questionnaire data as well as MMPIs for their sample of normal male adults. They found a trend for scales 1 and 2 scores to be higher within their younger and older age groups for the highest CMI level. However, only in the case of the Morale-Loss Index did the differences reach a significant level. The authors interpreted their results as indicating that the crucial variable, regardless of age, is whether or not the individual considers himself physically ill at the time of taking the MMPI. Leon et al. (in press) asked their aged subjects to indicate whether they were presently suffering from illnesses of long duration such as arthritis, diabetes, high blood pressure, heart disease, or cancer. A "yes" response was given by nearly half the sample. Comparisons were made of MMPI scale scores of subgroups divided into those having or not having a long-standing physical illness. Significant differences between the groups were found on scales 1, 3, and 6; in each case, the mean score for the chronically ill group was significantly higher. It should be noted, however, that the "higher" scores were not particularly high (i.e., scale 1, 54.4 vs. 50.6; scale 3, 62.1 vs. 57.6; and scale 6, 54.4 vs. 50.8).

Ethnicity may also interact with age to affect MMPI scores. Fillenbaum and Pfeiffer (1976) obtained Mini-Mults from 640 individuals from 65 to 93 years of age living in a southern community. Although there are subject-by-subject discrepancies between Mini-Mult and MMPI performance, group means are relatively highly correlated. Hence, these data are included here since there are few studies that offer "a 10% random sample of noninstitutionalized persons." Among these aged community residents, blacks obtained significantly higher scores than whites on scales *F*, 4, 8, and 9. Although numerous studies have compared blacks' and whites' MMPI performance (Gynther, 1972; Gynther, 1977), none appear to have considered the interaction between age and race. It is interesting to note that the differences found by Fillenbaum and Pfeiffer (1976) are those typically noted in comparisons of much younger subjects, both institutionalized and normal.

Other moderator variables such as marital status may conceivably also interact with age to influence MMPI responding. However, the purpose of this brief review has been simply to indicate that age alone is insufficient to account for an individual's level of functioning and type of adaptation. Differences are obviously associated with being male or female. It is also clear that physical disability has effects far beyond one's ability to get around at work or play. Relatively few studies have examined the interactions between age, status, ethnicity, and MMPI performance, but those that have, suggest that differences seem to be associated with these variables. Given these kinds of influences, it appears that age differences are much more likely to emerge as significant, if the sample used is relatively homogeneous with regard to demographic variables. Furthermore, MMPI studies have yet to be done in which possible shifts in attitudes and behavior as a function of crucial life events (e.g., marriage, parenthood, job failure, widowhood) are examined. Obviously, these researches would be somewhat more difficult to put together than ones analyzing the influence of gender or educational level, but they could be done and should be done to check out these likely precipitants of personality changes. Finally, there are the stage theories as enunciated by Erikson (1950) and more recently in the best-selling popular book *Passages* (Sheehy, 1976). Is empirical validation of these theoretical statements feasible? Haan and Day (1974) in a longitudinal study examined California Q-sort performance of 136 subjects from the Oakland Growth Study (ages 12-50) and the Guidance Study (ages 12-40). The authors found that activity level, cognitive engagement, self-presentation, and socialization were essentially unchanged from adolescence to early middle age. However, there were variables that did show change. Extrapunitiveness, being bothered by demands, fantisizing, and withdrawal when frustrated decreased as a function of age. Insightfulness and evaluation of situations in motivational terms increased as the individuals grew older. Haan and Day concluded that: "Both the content of the processes of change, as well as the timing of their greatest changes, are consistent with Erikson's expectations" (p.39). Perhaps the CPI-MMPI coping and defense scales (Haan, 1965) could also be used to test hypotheses derived from these formulations.

OTHER COMPLICATIONS AND COMPLEXITIES

Nearly every study reviewed has compared younger and older subjects with a view toward casting light on the differences associated with age. Are the differences found by various investigators attributable to the effects of aging? Or do they simply reflect the different attitudes and beliefs held by people born at different times? Successive cohorts have presumably been influenced by different social events which affect their view of themselves and of the world. Consider individuals born in 1920 and 1950. If tested now, such subjects might simply be considered as middle-aged and young. But during the formative years of the older group, the Great Depression held sway, while the younger group, as teen-agers, were exposed to the vicissitudes of the war in Vietnam. Effects of such experiences might be superficial or profound, but few would deny that there are effects. As Schaie and Gribbin (1975) pointed out: "Much of our knowledge of adult development is based on the comparison of different cohorts, and consequently, for all we know, in the past we might have collected data for a psychology of generational differences rather than for a psychology of aging" (p. 65). If investigators are interested in the effects of sociocultural change, cross-sectional analyses are very appropriate. However, such procedures cannot be assumed to elucidate personality changes associated with aging.

What about longitudinal studies? These are technically far more difficult to carry out than cross-sectional studies, since, to mention two obvious points, a 30-, 40-, or 50-year span frequently extends beyond the life expectancy of the investigator and people move so frequently in our society that subjects are "lost" as the years go by. Do long-range follow-up studies such as Leon et al.'s yield an accurate picture of personality changes associated with aging? One might think so, but there are problems. For instance, if a sample is representative of a given population at the study's inception, it will become progressively less representative over time owing to the effect of sample attrition. The original group tested at the University of Minnesota consisted of 281 "physically and psychologically healthy" men. By the time Leon et al. contacted them 30 years later, only 132 were still alive. Questionnaires were completed and returned by 95 of these individuals. However, MMPIs were available at all four time periods on just 71 subjects. Schaie and Gribbin (1975) stated that: "The effects of selective dropout of subjects have been documented in a number of studies which invariably show that residual samples score higher on tests of ability and are rated more in the socially desirable direction than is true for the initial sample" (p. 68). Slater and Scarr (1964) presented data that suggested that the decrease in impulsivity among the aged is not due to aging per se, but rather to the higher mortality rate among the more impulsive individuals. Elderly people may also be considered as *survivors*, with possibly different personality traits from those characteristic of them before they reached this special status. Also, death of spouse, loss of job, and other critical incidents may complicate the picture. Longitudinal studies are valuable in tracing the relative stability or changes in individuals, but may not lead to generalizations about the aging process, owing to the reasons given.

Data collection in this area involves three factors: age of subject, time of testing, and time of birth. Cross-sectional, longitudinal, and time-lag (in which comparisons are made between samples of the same age at different points in time) methods each deal with only two of the three components. Consequently, they are likely to yield only partially correct answers and contradictory results. For a number of years, Schaie has recommended the use of designs involving the replication of cross-sectional or longitudinal procedures to tease out the variance due to chronological age from that attributable to cohort differences or non-age related environmental factors.[1] According to Schaie and Gribbin (1975), if the investigator is interested in age changes, the cross-sequential or cohort-sequential method would be required before generalization is possible. The cross-sequential method involves testing two or more cohorts at two or more common times of measurement. The cohort-sequential method requires the testing of two or more cohorts at two or more common ages. If the investigator is interested in age differences, it is necessary to employ the cross-sequential or time-sequential methods. The latter procedure involves testing two or more ages at two or more common times of measurement.

Few studies have used these designs to investigate changes in personality associated with aging. There are three notable exceptions.[2] Adolescents tested by the California Test of Personality in 1944 at the University of Southern California were contacted and retested in 1969 by Woodruff and Birren (1972). Also a group of USC students were given the same test in 1969. Finally, a group of high-school students were given the test at the same time. These three groups were referred to as the 1924, the 1948, and the 1953 cohorts, respectively. Longitudinal comparisons of the test-retest data of the 1924 cohort showed no significant differences in test scores, a result that is consistent with the stability hypothesis. Then scores achieved in 1944 by subjects in the 1924 cohort were compared with scores achieved by the 1948 and 1953 cohorts. In this case, time of testing was confounded, while age was held constant. The effect due to cohort was significant beyond the .001 level. Scores achieved in 1969 by the 1924 cohort were compared with scores of the 1948 and 1953 cohorts. In this instance, time of testing was controlled, while age varied. Here too the effect of cohort was highly significant. Members of the 1924 cohort scored higher in self and social adjustment in both comparisons than did members of the 1948 and 1953 cohort groups. The authors argued that the results reflect the "generation gap" and are a function of the different cohorts maturing in different eras with somewhat different expectations and values (e.g., the smoking commercial that states, "You've come a long way, baby"). The authors concluded that separation of the effects of age changes and cohort differences is necessary to obtain a clear picture of personality development over time.

In the second study, Schaie and Parham (1976) analyzed questionnaire data collected during 1963 and 1970 on subjects ranging in age from 21 to 84. The questionnaire contained 22 subtle and 9 obvious rigidity items as well as 44 social responsibility items. Factor-analytic procedures resulted in personality scales which estimated 13 of the factors identified by Cattell's 16PF. As the authors stated, these scales are likely to be less reliable than the 16PF scales owing to relatively few items per scale. Six attitudinal scales (e.g., humanitarian concern) were also identified. Cohort differences were found for nine of the personality factors and four of the attitude factors. Successive cohorts were found, for example, to be more outgoing, less excitable, and more coasthenic (internally restrained). Three personality factors and two attitudinal factors showed significant time trends from 1963 to 1970. There was a drop in excitability and protension (i.e., jealousy, suspiciousness), with an increase in praxernia (i.e., conventionality). These cohort differences and time-of-measurement effects were replicated in the repeated measurement part of the study. Finally, time-sequential analyses revealed stability for all variables, except excitability and humanitarian concern, both of which increased with age. Characteristic profiles for each of the eight cohorts studied were described. As the authors noted, a clear break was observed between the three oldest cohorts and the younger cohorts on protension, superego strength, and coasthenia. The latter groups obtained higher scores on these variables. A typology of 13 possible models involving biostable, acculturated, and biocultural traits was offered to account for the different developmental trends observed for the various personality factors.

The most recent study that has attempted to extricate maturational from cultural effects was conducted by Douglas and Arenberg

(1978). These investigators used Guilford-Zimmerman Temperament Survey (GZTS) data collected from participants in the Baltimore Longitudinal Study. These individuals are a highly select group of male volunteers, ages 17 to 98, who are for the most part college-educated, work in scientific, professional, or managerial positions (or did so before retirement), and are in good health. Two subsamples were formed: the first group consisted of 605 men who completed their first GZTS between 1958 and 1968; the replication group included 310 men whose GZTS was administered between 1968 and 1974. Cross-sectional analyses showed that five scales were related to age in both samples. General Activity, Ascendance, and Masculinity scores were negatively correlated with age, while Restraint and Friendliness were positively correlated with age. Longitudinal analyses of change showed declines from first to second testing on General Activity, Friendliness, Thoughtfulness, Personal Relations, and Masculinity. The magnitude of change varied linearly with age only on General Activity. Cross-sequential and time-sequential analyses were also performed. The authors attempted to attribute the results to maturation, generation (cohort), or sociocultural changes specific to the period of measurement. Within this framework, maturational change alone could account for declines on General Activity and Masculinity with increasing age. With regard to generational differences, later-born cohorts were lower in Restraint and higher in Ascendance than early-born cohorts. Time of testing differences involved Thoughtfulness and Personal Relations; both decreased during the time frame of the study. Decreases in Friendliness were attributed to an interaction between cohort and sociocultural change. Sociability, Emotional Stability, and Objectivity were not affected by maturation, generation, or time of testing.

The findings of these three studies should probably be given more weight than the many conducted without concern for or knowledge of the confounding of age changes, age differences, and sociocultural changes associated with simple cross-sectional or longitudinal designs. Do we have to discard the data so laboriously acquired over the past several decades? If we had a personality theory that took cultural and sociohistorical factors into account and actually predicted personality change as a consequence of variation in these factors, we might be able to retain the information derived from cross-sectional studies which is consistent with such predictions. In the absence of such a theory, we are probably doomed to repeat everything done previously, since there is no *a priori* way to know which data will be confirmed and which will not.

Botwinick (1970) discussed Schaie's procedural recommendations in a positive vein, but concluded that, "Unfortunately, the model is so difficult to carry out that it becomes impractical" (p. 241). This is certainly true of laboratory research on perception and memory, in which special efforts are required to collect data and recruitment for retesting years later is even more difficult. However, Botwinick's comment is less true of personality and intelligence research. In many cases, these tests are administered routinely and the resulting data are stored for years. A contemporary researcher with access to this information has a wealth of material from earlier cohorts that can now be compared with a current cohort of the same age, thus yielding easily conducted time-lag studies. Also, the investigator has the opportunity to seek out subjects tested years before and attempt retesting. If subjects are divided into various cohorts on the basis of age, sequential analyses of the test-retest data could be conducted.

If conclusions drawn about aging and personality from cross-sectional data are problematic, so are those drawn about childhood and adolescence. Cohort effects are quite possible and obviously may alter the nature of conclusions about personality development when evaluated cross-sectionally. This type of effect is clearly demonstrated in a study of adolescents by Nesselroade and Baltes (1974).

Given the considerable impact of this type of thinking on what we like to believe are the established facts of developmental psychology across the life-span, it is surprising how recently this orientation has appeared on the scene. And, to our knowledge, these replicated designs have yet to be used by MMPI researchers, despite the fact that Dahlstrom, Welsh, and Dahlstrom (1975) listed 65 references under their "Age levels" category. On the other hand, as is so often the case, we seem to be reinventing the wheel. Baltes, Reese, and Nesselroade (1977) pointed out that the importance of cohort differences for interpreting age differences was discussed in 1741 by a German demographer-minister named J. P. Süssmilch.

Although these "new" research designs seem powerful, we hope that all aging research will not be enclosed in this particular methodological straitjacket. There is a faddish aspect to methods, just as there is to theories. At one time certain approaches are in favor, at other times different approaches are. Aging is an area that superficially appears simple to investigate, but a closer look reveals numerous sources of confusion. At present we should use all data sources available, from autobiographical to genetic.

SUMMARY AND CONCLUSIONS

If the objectives of this chapter were solely to summarize and interpret the MMPI research on aging, the following data would be emphasized. Younger patients and normals obtain more peaks and higher scores on scales measuring nonconformity, rebelliousness, alienation, and energy level. Older patients and normals obtain more peaks
and higher scores on scales measuring concern with health, introversion, and to a lesser extent scales involving depression and immaturity.
Item analyses indicate that youthful subjects are sensation-seeking,
restless, anxious for the approval of others, and have problems with
impulse control. Older subjects appear to have more sedentary interests and to be more cautious and dutiful, while displaying less hostility and fewer family conflicts. The major personality dimension that
differentiates the young from the elderly may be impulsivity-intellectual control rather than the traditional introversion-extraversion.
These apparent age-related changes do not, however, appear in the
single MMPI longitudinal study that shows relative stability over a 30-
year period.

When one enlarges the scope of the task at hand and looks at
data from other sources, one finds systematic increases and decreases,
as well as rises and falls in various personality traits with age. Self-
acceptance, self-control, socialization, dominance, and well-being all
appear to increase from youth to middle age, then decline. Enthusiasm declines over the entire age range, while sensitiveness and control
increase after the mid-30s. Needs for deference and affiliation increase
with age, while needs for power and social activities decline.

All these results need to be qualified, however, owing to complex interactions with gender, health, status, ethnicity, and a host of
other as yet uninvestigated change-variables (e.g., marriage, parenthood, etc.). That is, certain values may change with age for men, but
not women. Early middle age may represent something different to
blue-collar workers than it does to white-collar workers. Certain
kinds of personalities, as yet largely unidentified, may respond favorably and successfully to retirement, while others of the same age
despair and withdraw.

Finally, if one places this review in the context of the aging literature, additional problems arise. The use of cross-sectional and longitudinal data, without replication, has been seriously questioned.
Various complex designs have been recommended to control for variation due to aging as opposed to variation due to generational (cohort) differences. Apparently, these recommendations stem from the

repeated but paradoxical observations that longitudinal studies indicate that personality is stable over time, while cross-sectional studies almost invariably demonstrate personality change.

Aging and personality have been the subject of intense scrutiny for a number of years. Much information has been generated, but it is unclear what aspects of it will hold up in more carefully designed studies. No doubt, as Robert Browning said about aging, "the best is yet to come."[3]

NOTES

1. Some writers reject the notion that sequential strategies permit the separation of age, cohort, and time-of-measurement contributions to developmental change. For a recent statement espousing this view, see Adam (1978).

2. A fourth study was brought to the writer's attention after the chapter was written. Siegler, George, and Okun (in press) gave 331 males and females Form C of the 16PF four times over an eight-year period. The subjects represented a stratified random sample of white, middle-class adults aged 45 to 70 at the first measurement in 1968-70. Significant main effects for cohort and for time were observed only for Factor B (intelligence). The oldest cohort had the lowest score and the youngest cohort had the highest score. Five traits had significant main effects for sex which tended to be in the sex-stereotyped direction and invariant over time. The authors concluded that adult personality tends to be stable in the middle years of life.

3. The writer would like to thank Anna C. Smith for her assistance in reviewing the literature. Appreciation is also expressed to Donald H. Kausler and Charles V. Lair for their helpful suggestions at different stages of manuscript preparation.

REFERENCES

Aaronson, B. S. Age and sex influence on MMPI profile peak distribution in an abnormal population. *Journal of Consulting Psychology*, 1958, 22, 203-6.

Aaronson, B. S. A dimension of personality change with aging. *Journal of Clinical Psychology*, 1960, 16, 63-65.

Aaronson, B. S. Aging, personality change, and psychiatric diagnosis. *Journal of Gerontology*, 1964, 19, 144-48.

Adam, J. Sequential strategies and the separation of age, cohort, and time-of-measurement contributions to developmental data. *Psychological Bulletin*, 1978, 85, 1309-16.

Baltes, P. B., Reese, H. W., & Nesselroade, J. R. *Life-span developmental psychology: Introduction to research methods.* Monterey, Calif.: Brooks/Cole, 1977.

Bendig, A. W. Age differences in the interscale factor structure of the Guilford-Zimmerman Temperament Survey. *Journal of Consulting Psychology*, 1960, 24, 134-38.

Botwinick, J. Geropsychology. *Annual Review of Psychology*, 1970, 21, 239-72.

Britton, P. G., Bergmann, K., Kay, D. W. K., & Savage, R. D. Mental state, cognitive functioning, physical health, and social class in the community aged. *Journal of Gerontology*, 1967, 22, 517-21.

Britton, P. G., & Savage, R. D. The MMPI and the aged—some normative data from a community sample. *British Journal of Psychiatry*, 1965, 112, 941-43.

Britton, P. G., & Savage, R. D. The factorial structure of the MMPI from an aged sample. *Journal of Genetic Psychology*, 1969, 114, 13-17.

Brozek, J. Personality changes with age: An item analysis of the MMPI. *Journal of Gerontology*, 1955, 10, 194-206.

Calden, G., & Hokanson, J. E. The influence of age on MMPI responses. *Journal of Clinical Psychology*, 1959, 15, 194-95.

Canter, A., Day, C. W., Imboden, J. B., & Cluff, L. E. The influence of age and health status on the MMPI scores of a normal population. *Journal of Clinical Psychology*, 1962, 18, 71-73.

Cattell, R. B., Eber, H. W., & Tatsuoka, M. M. *Handbook for the Sixteen Personality Factor Questionnaire*. Champaign, Ill: Institute for Personality and Ability Testing, 1970.

Colligan, R. C., & Osborne, D. MMPI profiles from adolescent medical patients. *Journal of Clinical Psychology*, 1977, 33, 186-89.

Costa, P. T., Jr. & McCrae, R. R. Age differences in personality structure: A cluster analytic approach. *Journal of Gerontology*, 1976, 31, 564-70.

Costa, P. T., Jr., & McCrae, R. R. Age differences in personality structure revisited: Studies in validity, stability, and change. *Aging and Human Development*, 1977, 8, 261-75.

Costa, P. T., Jr., & McCrae, R. R. Objective personality assessment. In M. Storandt, I. C. Siegler, & M. F. Elias (Eds.), *The clinical psychology of aging*. New York: Plenum, 1978.

Cumming, E., & Henry, W. E. *Growing old*. New York: Basic Books, 1961.

Dahlstrom, W. G., Welsh, G. S., & Dahlstrom, L. E. *An MMPI handbook*, Volume 1: *Clinical interpretation*. Minneapolis: University of Minnesota Press, 1972.

Dahlstrom, W. G., Welsh, G. S., & Dahlstrom, L. E. *An MMPI handbook*, Volume 2: *Research applications*. Minneapolis: University of Minnesota Press, 1975.

Davis, W. E. Age and the discriminative "power" of the MMPI with schizophrenic and non-schizophrenic patients. *Journal of Consulting and Clinical Psychology*, 1972, 38, 151.

Davis, W. E., Mozdzierz, G. J., & Macchitelli, F. J. Loss of discrimination "power" of the MMPI with older psychiatric patients. *Journal of Personality Assessment*, 1973, 37, 555-58.

Devries, A. G. Demographic variables and MMPI responses. *Journal of Clinical Psychology*, 1966, 22, 450-52.

Douglas, K., & Arenberg, D. Age changes, cohort differences, and cultural change on the Guilford-Zimmerman Temperament Survey. *Journal of Gerontology*, 1978, 33, 737-47.

Erikson, E. H. *Childhood and society*. New York: W. W. Norton, 1950.

Eysenck, H. J., & Eysenck, S. B. G. *Eysenck Personality Inventory*. San Diego: Educational and Industrial Testing Service, 1963.

Fillenbaum, G. G., & Pfeiffer, E. The Mini-Mult: A cautionary note. *Journal of Consulting and Clinical Psychology*, 1976, 44, 698-703.

Garvey, A. J. *Values, personality, and age*. Paper presented at the 28th Annual Meeting of the Gerontological Society, Louisville, Kentucky, October, 1975.

Golden, J. S., Mandel, N., Glueck, B. C., & Feder, Z. A summary description of fifty "normal" white males. *American Journal of Psychiatry*, 1962, 119, 48-56.

Gough, H. G. Personal communication, August 21, 1978.

Grupp, S., Ramseyer, G., & Richardson, J. The effect of age on four scales of the California Psychological Inventory. *Journal of General Psychology*, 1968, 78, 183-87.

Guthrie, G. M. *A study of the personality characteristics associated with the disorders encountered by an internist*. Unpublished doctoral dissertation, University of Minnesota, 1949.

Gynther, M. D. White norms and black MMPIs: A prescription for discrimination? *Psychological Bulletin*, 1972, 78, 386-402.

Gynther, M. D. *Ethnicity and personality: Recent findings*. Paper presented at the 12th Annual MMPI Symposium, St. Petersburg, Florida, February, 1977.

Gynther, M. D. & Shimkunas, A. M. Age, intelligence, and MMPI *F* scores. *Journal of Consulting Psychology*, 1965, 29, 383-88.

Gynther, M. D., & Shimkunas, A. M. Age and MMPI performance. *Journal of Consulting Psychology*, 1966, 30, 108-12.

Haan, N. Coping and defense mechanisms related to personality inventories. *Journal of Consulting Psychology*, 1965, 29, 373-78.

Haan, N., & Day, D. A longitudinal study of change and sameness in personality development: Adolescence to later adulthood. *International Journal of Aging and Human Development*, 1974, 5, 11-39.

Hardyck, C. D. Sex differences in personality changes with age. *Journal of Gerontology*, 1964, 19, 78-82.

Harmatz, J. S., & Shader, R. I. Psychopharmacologic investigations in healthy elderly volunteers: MMPI Depression scale. *Journal of the American Geriatrics Society*, 1975, 23, 350-54.

Hathaway, S. R., & Meehl, P. E. *An atlas for the clinical use of the MMPI*. Minneapolis: University of Minnesota Press, 1951.

Hoffman, H., and Nelson, P. C. Personality characteristics of alcoholics in relation to age and intelligence. *Psychological Reports*, 1971, 29, 143-46.

Kornetsky, C. MMPI results obtained from a population of aged men. In J. E. Birren, R. N. Butler, S. W. Greenhouse, L. Sokoloff, & M. R. Yarrow (Eds.), *Human aging: A biological and behavioral study*. Washington, D.C.: National Institute of Mental Health, 1963.

Leon, G. R., Gillum, B., Gillum, R., & Gouze, M. Personality stability and change over a 30 year period—middle age to old age. *Journal of Consulting and Clinical Psychology*, in press.

Lester, D. MMPI scores of old and young completed suicides. *Psychological Reports*, 1971, 28, 146.

McCreary, C. P., & Mensh, I. N. Personality differences associated with age in law offenders. *Journal of Gerontology*, 1977, 32, 164-67.

McGinnis, C. A., & Ryan, C. W. The influence of age on MMPI scores of chronic alcoholics. *Journal of Clinical Psychology*, 1965, 21, 271-72.

Nesselroade, J. R., and Baltes, P. B. Adolescent personality development and historical change: 1970-1972. *Monographs of the Society for Research in Child Development*, 1974, 39(1, Serial No. 154).

Neugarten, B. L. Personality and aging. In J. E. Birren & K. W. Schaie (Eds.), *Handbook of the psychology of aging*. New York: Van Nostrand Reinhold Co., 1977.

Osborne, D. Age and sex differences on MMPI factor scales E R-0 and EC-5 in a medical population. *Journal of Clinical Psychology*, 1971, 27, 245-46.

Pearson, J. S., Swenson, W. M., & Rome, H. P. Age and sex differences related to MMPI response frequency in 25,000 medical patients. *American Journal of Psychiatry*, 1965, 121, 988-95.

Postema, L. J., & Schell, R. E. Aging and psychopathology: Some MMPI evidence for seemingly greater neurotic behavior among older people. *Journal of Clinical Psychology*, 1967, 23, 140-43.

Schaie, K. W. The effect of age on a scale of social responsibility. *Journal of Social Psychology*, 1959, 50, 221-24.

Schaie, K. W., & Gribbin, K. Adult development and aging. *Annual Review of Psychology*, 1975, 26, 65-96.

Schaie, K. W., & Parham, I. A. Stability of adult personality: Fact or fable? *Journal of Personality and Social Psychology*, 1976, 34, 146-58.

Sheehy, G. *Passages*. New York: E. F. Dutton, 1976.

Siegler, I. C., George, L. K., and Okun, M. A. A cross-sequential analysis of adult personality. *Developmental Psychology*, in press.

Slater, P. E., & Scarr, H. A. Personality in old age. *Genetic Psychology Monographs*, 1964, 70, 229-69.

Spangler, D. P., & Thomas, C. W. The effects of age, sex and physical disability upon manifest needs. *Journal of Counseling Psychology*, 1962, 9, 313-19.

Swenson, W. M. Structured personality testing in the aged: An MMPI study of the gerontic population. *Journal of Clinical Psychology*, 1961, 17, 302-4.

Swenson, W. M., Pearson, J. S., & Osborne, D. *An MMPI source book: Basic item, scale, and pattern data on 50,000 medical patients*. Minneapolis: University of Minnesota Press, 1973.

Thumin, F. J. MMPI scores as related to age, education, and intelligence among male job applicants. *Journal of Applied Psychology*, 1969, 53, 404-7.

Webb, J. T. *The relation of MMPI two-point codes to age, sex and education level in a representative nationwide sample of psychiatric outpatients*. Paper presented at the Southeastern Psychological Association meetings, Louisville, Kentucky, April, 1970.

Weiss, R. W., & Russakoff, S. Relationship of MMPI scores of drug-abusers to personal variables and type of treatment program. *Journal of Psychology*, 1977, 96, 25-29.

Whitmyre, J. W., & Cohen, D. Personality characteristics of psychiatric hospitalized veterans of three age ranges. *Newsletter for Research in Mental Health and Behavioral Sciences*, 1973, 15, 12-15.

Wiggins, J. S. Substantive dimensions of self-report in the MMPI item pool. *Psychological Monographs*, 1966, 80(22, Whole No. 630).

Wilson, A., Mabry, E. A., Khavari, K. A., & Dalpes, D. Discriminant analysis of MMPI profiles for demographic classifications of male alcoholics. *Journal of Studies on Alcohol*, 1977, 38, 47-57.

Woodruff, D. S., & Birren, J. E. Age changes and cohort differences in personality. *Developmental Psychology*, 1972, 6, 252-59.

Recent Trends in Cross-Cultural MMPI Research and Application

James N. Butcher and Lee Anna Clark

The cross-cultural study of abnormal behavior has been of interest to many psychiatrists, psychologists, and anthropologists since the beginning of the twentieth century. Most of the early work in this area focused on the description of disorders within different cultures and on the study of unusual or "exotic" abnormal states. Recent years have seen a greater emphasis on comparisons of psychopathology across cultures and on improving the methodology for the cross-cultural study of abnormal behavior (Draguns, 1977).

The primary means of clinical diagnosis in cross-cultural research, the unstructured psychiatric interview, has not provided sufficiently objective and rigorous classification criteria, since the differences in diagnostic practices often make the categories not comparable. Presently, there is a great deal of emphasis on using more objective assessment procedures to obtain more comparable comparison groups. Several such approaches to classification of behavior disorders are being used, for example: psychiatric rating scales such as the Present State Examination (PSE) (Wing, 1970), the Inpatient Multidimensional Scale (IMPS) (Lorr & Klett, 1968), and the Brief Psychiatric Rating Scale (Overall & Gorham, 1962); and self-report measures like the Spielberger State-Trait Anxiety Inventory (Spielberger & Diaz-Guerrero, 1976). A number of researchers in several countries have adapted the Minnesota Multiphasic Personality Inventory (MMPI), a self-report personality questionnaire, as an aid to psychiatric diagnosis in their countries. These cross-cultural test adaptations have, for the most part, been done with the practical goals of clinical practice in mind. The MMPI has been translated into many languages, and the United States norms have been used with individuals in the target country who have sufficient reading skills. In some instances, however, it has not been translated carefully enough or studied sufficiently to warrant acceptance.

Many problems involved in the translation and adaptation of the MMPI were discussed in *A Handbook of Cross-National MMPI Research* by J. N. Butcher and Paolo Pancheri in 1976. A number of successful test adaptations were discussed and information concerning the generalizability of MMPI interpretation cross-culturally was presented. In the present chapter, we survey international MMPI research which has either been published or "come to light" since the review of Butcher and Pancheri and highlight a number of recent MMPI clinical and research applications in other countries.

RECENT DEVELOPMENTS IN CROSS-CULTURAL MMPI RESEARCH

MMPI Scales as Criteria of Psychopathology in Israel

The effect of extreme war stress on soldiers was studied by Merbaum and Hefez (1976) with a follow-up study by Merbaum (1977) using the Hebrew translation of the MMPI (Butcher & Gur, 1974). Medical and psychiatric war casualties of Israel and the United States were compared. The Israeli soldiers had been injured or suffered from disabling psychological reactions during active duty in the Yom Kippur War; the data on the United States soldiers were published by Lumry, Cederleaf, Wright, & Braatz (1972) and included veterans of the Vietnam war, not all of whom had been exposed to active combat duty.

They found that psychiatric casualties of the Yom Kippur War resembled psychiatric casualties of the Vietnam War, with prominent elevations on scales 8-2-7. The psychiatric war casualties from both countries produced MMPI profiles that differed greatly from the profiles of veterans who were physically disabled.

One year later Merbaum followed up 17 of the 24 psychological casualties of the Yom Kippur War and found no significant differences on any scale. Interview data confirmed that these men were still severely emotionally disturbed. Characteristic of the group were feelings of tenseness, physical complaints, anticipation of failure in work, lack of friendships, conflicted marriages or relationships, and guilt about their breakdown during the war. These problems often seemed to be related to the social stigma of such war-stress-induced psychological breakdown. Merbaum concluded that the profound debilitating effects of war stress are not easily overcome and require intensive therapeutic intervention, including transitional steps that take the social impact of reentry into account.

Butcher and Pancheri (1976) noted the existence of another Israeli MMPI translation (the Tel Aviv MMPI), but there were no published data on it. At present there still exists only an unpublished manuscript which was presented at the Fourth International Personality Assessment Conference in Haifa (Montag, 1977). Montag reported that the Tel Aviv version was completed in 1973 after a revision of the original 1968 translation. It was developed using several experts in both languages who made comparisons with the French and German translations. The goal in the translation was to stay as close to the original content as possible, while taking into consideration "colloquial aspects." The wording was kept simple because Hebrew is not the native language of many Israelis. Special attention was paid to Social Desirability scale values and percentage of True responses of United States samples. He reported that the content of only a few items had to be modified. The hypothesis posited in standardization research on the translation was that if the TA-MMPI functioned as the MMPI does, similar structural aspects and relationships would characterize the translation and the original. Subjects were 2,145 applicants for driver's licenses, ranging in age from 18 to 55 and in educational level from 8 to 17 years. Each was administered the MMPI and the CAQ (Clinical Analysis Questionnaire), or the EPQ (Eysenck's Personality Questionnaire), or the 16PF (16 Personality Factors).

A comparison of these normal response data with the results of the normative United States sample reveals the following:

(1) no overall difference in true responding (% T, r = .89);
(2) no overall difference in Social Desirability scale values (r = .94);
(3) high scale correlations (in the .80s and .90s) of the full instrument with various short forms;
(4) correlations between the standard scales and between these scales and the Wiggins content scales, similar to those reported with the original instrument;
(5) the same two factors (Anxiety and Repression) repeatedly reported in the United States literature; a positive loading on 0 (*Si*) and negative loadings on 9 (*Ma*) and 2 (*D*) defined a third factor (Extraversion);

(6) low positive correlations between the TA-MMPI and the CAQ; however, no comparative data exist to further elucidate these results; and

(7) expected correlations between the TA-MMPI and the EPQ and 16PF.

Montag concluded that the instrument can be considered functionally equivalent to the original MMPI. Since 1977 Montag and Raya Gur in collaboration with J. N. Butcher, who previously published work on a Hebrew version of the MMPI (Butcher & Gur, 1974), have been merging translation projects to produce one translation; they plan to publish jointly a final consolidated version of the Hebrew MMPI.

A series of studies on "desperation states" has been published by Joroff (Joroff, 1976; 1977a; 1977b). Joroff used the Hebrew MMPI to study personality factors associated with committing terrorist acts. Unfortunately, the articles were not available to us for detailed review.

Schizophrenia Research in Pakistan

Mirza (1977) continues to use his Urdu translation of the MMPI in psychopathology research in Pakistan. He found previously (see Butcher & Pancheri, 1976) that scales F and 8 (Sc) are extremely elevated (T is greater than 70) in the normal population in Pakistan, suggesting possible cultural differences in personality between Pakistani and United States normals. However, Mirza (1977) noted, "the state of knowledge is not yet sufficient to use the MMPI as an instrument of cross-cultural analysis of personality. The next best thing at this point is longitudinal study of defined groups with multiple administrations of the MMPI to discover the relationship between noticeable changes in personality and significant patterns of scores on the test." His schizophrenia research project is such a preliminary study.

At Fountain House, where the project is located, free consultation and medications (but not psychotherapy) are available to patients. The MMPI is routinely administered to new entrants and is repeated when they are considered to be free of symptoms or improved. He presented data on a sample of 40 male schizophrenics, ranging in age from 17 to 36 ($\overline{X} = 24$) with a test-retest time of 69 to 1,357 days ($\overline{X} = 604$ days or 1 year 8 months). The results showed lowered scores from first to second administration—an average difference of 4 T-score points per scale—but with practically identical profile shape. The greatest drop was in scales F, 1 (Hs), 3 (Hy), and 6 (Pa), the least in scales K and 9 (Ma).

The most notable aspects of the profiles are the high scale 3 and low scale 4 (Pd), but the normal T-score elevation for scale 3 in Pakistan is identical to that of the improved schizophrenics. He did not interpret the extremely low scale scores on scale 4. Mirza found an M-shaped distribution of scores on scale 8 (Sc) on both first and second administration, with different means for the bimodal peaks, but the same mean for the valley. He believes that this valley (T score 61-65) has a special importance for schizophrenics and corresponds to a phase of defensive "tightening up" in the face of imminent breakdown.

Mirza noted that scale 8 loses in discriminative power owing to its general elevation in the normal population, but believes that in order to preserve the usefulness of the MMPI as an instrument of cross-cultural research, it is better not to interfere with the content of the items and thus "artifically" lower the scores. For diagnostic purposes he recommends using a T-score cutoff of T = 90 on the Sc scale rather than the lower cut-off point of T = 70 used in the United States.

Group Personality Research in South Africa

Using the MMPI as "an etic research tool," Lison and Van der Spuy (1977) have attempted to support theoretical work on the personality characteristics of the three main groups in South Africa. These three groups are: the Afrikaaners, who are viewed as politically ascendant, obsessive, and authoritarian; the Coloured, who are considered to have "marginal personality," to be insecure and seeking acceptance, and the English-speaking whites, on whom no work has been done, perhaps because they are the intellectual elite (the group who does the research), although they are not politically powerful.

Lison and Van der Spuy compared three student groups (N = 263) matched for IQ, education, occupational status, but not SES, since this was believed to be a significant and important difference between the groups. They assume that "students should not be considered to be completely representative of the groups to which they belong. They in fact represent an elite who, because of their sensitive position in the society, would express personality characteristics which intensively reflect the conflicts and dynamic interplay of forces at work in South African society as experienced by their group."

On the basis of profile and content-scale differences, they develop personality descriptions they consider to be "comprehensible in relation to each group's position in the South African socio-cultural environment." Generally speaking, the scales were elevated compared with United States norms; the content scales differentiated groups better than did the standard clinical scales.

Self-Report Measures of Depression among Normal Populations of Japanese, Chinese, and Caucasian Ancestry

Marsella, Sanborn, Kameoka, Shizuru, and Brennan (1975) compared all commonly used self-report measures of depression — KAS-Hogarty Scale, Zung Depression Scale, Beck Depression Inventory, Multiple Affect Adjective Check List, and the MMPI D scale — on normal populations of different ethnic backgrounds. They investigated the question of whether some measures of depression are more effective with some groups than are other measures. Their sample consisted of 249 undergraduates of Japanese, Chinese, and Caucasian ancestry. The instruments were administered in randomized order and none of the groups' average elevations were in the clinical range for any instrument. The highest average correlation among instruments obtained was for the Caucasian females ($r = .71$); the lowest was for Chinese males ($r = .39$). For the groups as a whole, the instruments were not significantly different; the MMPI showed the lowest correlation with the other instruments ($r = .58$).

The instruments were shown to have varying degrees of generalizability and relationship to one another as a function of ethnicity and gender. In general, the measures appeared more generalizable for females than for males. Marsella et al. consider the need for systematic investigation of the influence that ethnicity and gender may exert upon the various assessment techniques. For instance, the instruments use different methods of assessing depression — symptom frequency, symptom intensity, mood adjective endorsement, or endorsement of indicator items. These may interact with ethnic response style to produce the different patterns of results obtained. Care must be taken, therefore, in generalizing from any one population to another, especially across cultures.

Personality Assessment and Test Interpretation of Mexican-Americans

There are a few studies on personality assessment of Mexican-Americans and Anglo-Americans which compare scores on standard instruments. Differences generally are attributed to individual variance rather than cultural factors. Padilla and Ruiz (1975) evaluate this assumption in the context of the limited amount of relevant empirical data available and offer recommendations for improved use of assessment techniques so that interpretation will be culturally sensitive when one is working with a Mexican-American population.

They first review several studies using the Rorschach and TAT, which will not be described here. For objective tests, they review one study using the CPI with l3 to 14-year-old Indians, Caucasians, and Mexican-Americans. The study showed differences between the Mexican-Americans and the others, but the results are questionable owing to the limited verbal facility of some subjects. Another study of social adjustment led them to question the validity of a paper-and-pencil questionnaire for Mexican-Americans. Since some Mexican-Americans are only monolingual in Spanish or partially bilingual, they note that "the translation of tests or substitution of oral instructions for written ones may seem necessary to the investigator," but that "such practices are hardly advisable in the absence of normative data on translated tests or on tests with unstandardized test procedures."

One of the major studies they review is Reilly and Knight (1970), who made 36 comparisons between 1st-year college students with Spanish surnames and those without. They found (1) Mexican-Americans had elevated L scale scores, indicating "more strict moral principles or overly conventional attitudes"; (2) non-Mexican-Americans had elevated scale 6 (Pa) scores, indicating that they were "more subjective, sensitive, concerned with self, less trusting"; (3) Mexican-American males and Anglo-American females score higher than their counterparts on scales 7 (Pa), 8 (Sc), and 0 (Si). They urge caution in interpreting these results, however, until the differences are more systematically explored.

Padilla and Ruiz concluded their review, "there is evidence that Mexican-American subjects ranging in age from 13-80 years respond differently to objective inventories than one might predict from normative data." They call for research which (1) compares test performance as a function of English and/or Spanish instructions, (2) develops norms for Mexican-American subjects, and (3) investigates the influence of examiner characteristics on test results.

In an attempt to broaden the findings of Reilly and Knight (1970), Quiroga and Besner compared the MMPI profiles of Mexican-American and Anglo-American psychiatric patients. They compared the groups using both t-tests between average scale scores and a complex ANOVA design, trying to separate out the effects of culture from those of general demographic or background variables such as "father's or husband's occupation," "religious affiliation" or IQ. Their sample (N = 200 Anglo-Americans, 400 Mexican-Americans) was chosen to include equal groups of psychotics and nonpsychotics. The reported results are not broken down by sex. They found, in support of Reilly and Knight, that the Mexican-American psychotic population, as shown by the t-test, had higher L-score evaluations than did the Anglo-Americans. The most consistent difference they found was that both Mexican-American groups scored lower on scale 0 (Si) than did the Anglo-Americans. This finding appeared in both types of analyses. Almost as robust were findings of lower scale 5 (Mf) scores in the Mexican-American nonpsychotic population and an elevated scale 4 (Pd) among Mexican-American psychotics. Finally, Mexican-American psychotics were found to have lower F scale scores by the complex ANOVA alone. Since all profiles with F greater than 80 T score were excluded, it is not surprising that differences were not more generally found on this scale. A look at the raw-score differences reported for each of the above findings, however, attenuates their strong conclusion that the influence of cultural factors "points to the need for some adjustments, development of norms or actuarial procedures for a legitimate use of the MMPI with Mexican-American patients."

	Psychotic Patients		
Scale	Mexican-Americans	Anglo-Americans	Difference
L	4.62	3.44	1.18
4 (Pd)	32.24	30.00	2.24
0 (Si)	28.87	35.94	7.00
	Non-Psychotic Patients		
5 (Mf)	28.59	32.82	4.23
0 (Si)	27.77	33.53	3.75

Adapted from Tables 2 and 3, Quiroga & Besner (undated).

Although differences are significant at the .01 level, the absolute differences are not great (except, perhaps, for scale 0 (Si) in psychotic patients) and would hardly lead to different profile interpretations, even if background were not considered. The scale 5 (Mf) scores are difficult to interpret, since they are not broken down by sex. In contrast to their conclusion, we find that the lack of significant differences is rather striking support for the high generalizability of the standard MMPI norms.

Personality Similarity of Parents and Children in Japan

Hama and Konsei (1977) examined the MMPI profiles of college students and their parents. Japanese norms were used to compute T scores, but the correlations reported were based on raw scores. Since they had too few male subjects, only the results for females were discussed. They found low but significant positive correlations between daughters and their parents, both individually and combined, on a number of scales. Only F, 5 (*Mf*), and 0 (*Si*) did not show significant correlations. Correlations ranged from .26 on scale K between mothers and daughters to .46 on scale 4 (*Pd*) between daughters and both parents combined. The significant results are reported in the accompanying tabulation.

They concluded that the results support their hypothesis of parent-child similarity, but not that of greater similarity to the same-sex parent. The significant correlations between daughters and both parents combined indicate that the parents are similar to each other. They offer several hypotheses for this finding with suggestions for further research.

Correlations between Daughters and Parents

Scale	Mother-Daughter	Father-Daughter	Parents-Daughter
L	.32**	.34**	
K	.26*		
1 (*Hs*)			.39**
2 (*D*)			.37**
3 (*Hy*)			.42**
4 (*Pd*)	.38**	.33**	.46**
7 (*Pt*)			.33**
8 (*Sc*)	.30*	.36**	
9 (*Ma*)		.31*	

Source: Hama and Konsei, 1977.
*$p < .05$
**$p < .01$

Personality Characteristics of Improved and Non-improved Heart Attack Patients in Italy

Pancheri, Bellaterra, Matteoli, Cristofari, Polizzi, and Puletti (1978) used the Italian translation of the MMPI, together with a standardized psychiatric anamnestic form and the State-Trait Anxiety Index, to compare heart-attack patients who did and did not improve after 7-10 days of hospitalization. The tests were administered three days after admission. The evaluation of improvement was a clinical judgment made on release from the hospital by the attending and head cardiologists. The average profile of the improved group (N = 25) was similar to the population norm with the exceptions of moderate elevations on scales 1 (*Hs*) and 3 (*Hy*). The non-improved group profile, on the other hand, was significantly higher on 11 of 13 scales (with T greater than or equal to 70) on scales 1 (*Hs*), 2 (*D*), and 8 (*Sc*). Together with the life-history data and higher anxiety scores, these results "give some empirical support to the hypothesis that the physiological and hemodynamic condition of the cardiac patient is in some way correlated with the patient's style of coping with stress and his history of previous life stress situation∴."

SURVEY OF RECENT USE OF THE MMPI

Several researchers and clinicians in other countries have recently undertaken MMPI translation or adaptation projects. Some of the projects will be highlighted in this section to give the reader an indication of the extent of international MMPI research and to note new projects that have been undertaken since the Butcher and Pancheri summary in 1976. An extensive project being conducted in Chile has provided a great deal of recent information on the cross-cultural use of the MMPI.

Chile

Until 1976 the MMPI was not used in Chile. In the fall of that year a group of psychologists, psychiatrists, and medical practitioners at the Student Health Service of Catholic University of Chile, with the consultation services of J. N. Butcher, launched a major translation and test adaptation project. In just two years this program produced one of the soundest MMPI translations and the most substantial data base of any translation project to date.

The MMPI research project was headed by Fernando Rissetti and included a number of other psychologists—Sergio Maltes, Carmen Gloria Hidalgo, and Marta Hermosilla—and a physician, Francisco Montiel. In addition, Patricia Hormann and Anna Marie Fleischli, linguists and translators, participated in the translation phase of the project. The success of the project owed a great deal to university officials Raul Cañas and Christian Brunner who supported the project, both financially and administratively.

The research team had several goals when the project began: (1) to develop a Spanish translation of the MMPI that could be used in Chile and other South American countries, a translation that would be both linguistically and psychologically equivalent to the English version and free of the problems in existing Spanish forms of the MMPI; (2) to develop and validate the translation so that it would be as effective a clinical instrument in South America as it is in the United States; (3) to obtain a large normal sample, similar to the target population, in order to determine whether normal subjects in Chile respond to the items as normals do in other countries, as reported in Butcher and Pancheri (1976).

The translation was carried out at the Catholic University of Chile using a committee approach to develop the initial item translation. (Initially, the Mexican translation of the MMPI [Nuñez, 1967] was tried out, but many of the translated items were problematic.) A sample of normal subjects (N = 219 males and 228 females) was administered the Chilean experimental translation of the MMPI. Item-endorsement percentages were compared with item responses of normal samples from the United States and Mexico to detect any item-response differences. Items in the Chilean MMPI for which endorsement rates differed greatly from the other normal samples were subjected to further evaluation to determine if the meaning of the item was preserved in the translation. It was found that several items were inadequately translated and required further work. Back-translation procedures were also employed to ensure that the item content and psychological meaning were maintained in the Spanish version.

The research team submitted several questionably translated items to two outside researchers (Rosa Garcia and J. N. Butcher, University of Minnesota) to determine the most adequate form of the item. At present, the inventory is being subjected to further verification—a bilingual test-retest study—before the version is finalized.

The Chilean version of the MMPI was administered to 3,088 (N = 1,557 women and N = 1,531 men) normal students at the Catholic University of Chile in spring 1978 (Rissetti et al., 1979). This is virtually the entire entering class of the university (N = 2,272) and the target population for much of the proposed MMPI work in the diagnosis and treatment planning for college students who develop psychological problems. A sample of upper-class students (N = 1,816) was also included.

Mean scores of Chilean males and females on the MMPI clinical and validity scales are given in Table 1. For comparison purposes, these scores are presented with scores of a large sample of University of Minnesota college students (Loper, Robertson, & Swanson, 1968).

A comparison of the mean MMPI scores shown in Table 1 suggests that there are few differences in the typical performance of United States and Chilean college-student populations. The small dif-

Table 1. Mean T Scores on MMPI Validity and Clinical Scales of Chilean
Normal College Students Compared with Samples of College Students
in the United States

Scale	Chilean Males (N = 1,557)	U.S. Males (N = 1,679)	Chilean Females (N = 1,531)	U.S. Females (N = 1,603)
L	54	45.9	55	46.2
F	59	53.7	55	51.8
K	54	56.0	55	56.8
Hs + .5K	52	52.0	55	49.5
D	61	52.5	57	49.2
Hy	58	56.4	56	55.1
Pd + .4K	59	59.4	56	57.0
Mfm	50	59.4		
Mff			53	47.5
Pa	56	54.7	56	55.5
Pt + 1K	59	58.1	55	55.1
Sc + 1K	61	59.1	58	56.6
Ma + 2K	61	58.3	59	56.4
Si	51	49.1	54	49.7

ference between the national groups on scale L may result from national group differences such as religion, Chilean nationals scoring higher on moral virtue. Or the difference may result from the fact that the Chilean sample was obtained from a Catholic university and the United States sample from a large state university. The analysis of item-endorsement differences may support this interpretation.

The difference between Chilean and United States normals on scale 2 (D) is consistent with studies of normals in other countries. Samples in the United States generally show lower mean elevations on the depression scale than do other national groups. This persistent finding may reflect a peculiarity in the D scale or suggest that a broader issue is involved in the measurement of depression through self-report. The latter interpretation seems to have great credibility in the study of psychopathology cross-culturally (Marsella et al., 1975).

The Chilean normal samples were scored and plotted on Mexican norms developed by Pucheu (see Butcher & Pancheri, 1976). These profiles are given in Figures 1 and 2. An inspection of the profiles reveals that the Chilean normals appear to be drawn from a population similar to the population on which Pucheu developed norms. Future work with the Chilean college-student population could well employ the T scores generated by the Mexican norms. However, a study is now under way in which special Chilean norms are being developed. We do not expect that the new norms will differ greatly from those developed in Mexico.

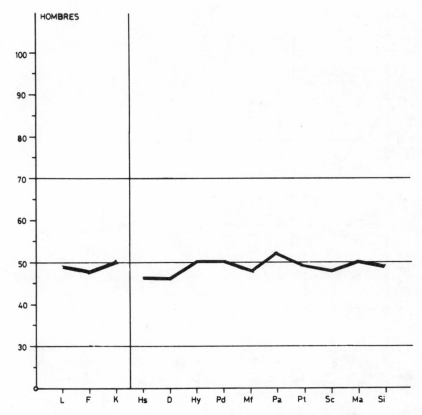

Figure 1. Group profile of Chilean normal males (N = 1,557)
plotted on Mexican norms. From Butcher & Pancheri, 1976.

The general similarity of responses to MMPI items by Chilean
and United States normals is further confirmed by item-endorsement
analysis. The percentage of True endorsements for Ss in the Chilean
sample was compared with the endorsement rates on each item reported by Loper et al. (1968), using the analysis program reported in
Butcher and Pancheri (1976). (See Table 2.)

An "extreme" item is defined as one for which there is a statistically significant difference of 25% or more in endorsement between
two national groups for males and females. In studies of "extreme"
item endorsement samples of Chilean and United States normals
and samples of Chilean and Mexican (Butcher & Pancheri, 1976)
normals, it was learned that most MMPI items are answered in the
same direction by normal subjects. Only eight items were labeled

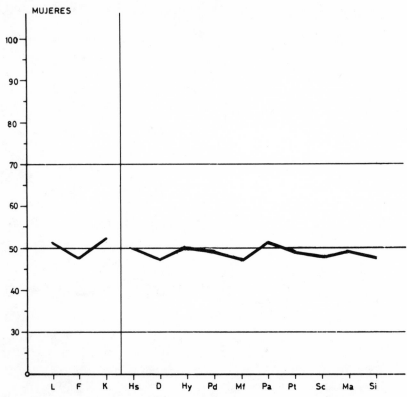

Figure 2. Mean profile of Chilean normal females (N = 1,531) plotted on Mexican norms. From Butcher & Pancheri, 1976.

Table 2. MMPI Items Answered Differently by Chilean/Mexican and Chilean/U.S. Normal Subjects (Comparisons Replicated Across Gender)

Content Category	Chilean vs. U.S. Normals	Chilean vs. Mexican Normals
Religion	249	115, 369
Morale	142, 236, 237, 264	526
Life-style	30, 112, 232, 254, 378, 406, 441, 465, 498, 529	280, 371, 455, 465
Attitudes toward law or authority	298, 376, 437, 456	376
Concerns or fears	31, 131, 179, 270, 421, 541, 560	
Miscellaneous	162, 510	

"extreme" in the Chilean/Mexican comparison, and 29 items in the Chilean/United States comparison (see Table 2). These items do not appear on a particular MMPI scale and only three scales contain more than two extreme items. They were K (3 items), 2 (D) (5 items), and 5 (Mf) (5 items). These scales have culturally sensitive items: the K scale was found to contain some items that were difficult to translate into Hebrew; the D scale has been shown to operate somewhat differently in different countries, and the Mf scale (made up of interest items) has been found sensitive to different interest patterns in other countries, e.g., Italy. The actual percentage of extreme items appearing on these scales is quite low. The fact that the majority of the MMPI items are endorsed similarly by normals in all three countries (Chile, Mexico, and the United States) is quite impressive. The

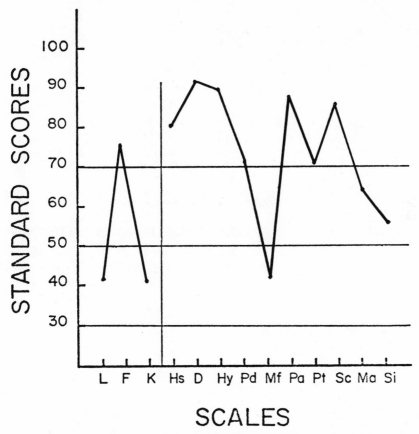

Figure 3. MMPI profile of a private-practice patient in Santiago, Chile (Case A).

content of the "extreme" items that emerged in the Chilean/U.S. and the Chilean/Mexican item comparisons is shown in Table 2. Many of the "extreme" items contain contant that would be described as differences in life-style, attitudes toward authority, and general morale.

The clinical applicability of the MMPI has been demonstrated in both private-practice and the student health service of the university. When patients' MMPIs are compared with the United States norms, their profiles match those of United States patients with similar types of problems. The young schizophrenic woman whose profile is shown in Figure 3 was seen in a private-practice setting by a psychiatrist after she experienced an acute psychotic episode. Her MMPI profile was given to an experienced clinical psychologist[1] who pro-

Besides being clearly abnormal, this profile is rather unusual in that it shows a mixture of neurotic and psychotic symptoms. On the one hand, the clinical scales indicate presence of moderate to severe depression accompanied by multiple somatic symptoms which are likely to be functional in nature.

On the other hand, the profile also shows considerable paranoid ideation, perhaps outright paranoid delusions. Reality contact is significantly impaired, and the patient probably utilizes much projection and distorts social perception. She is apt to have serious difficulties with interpersonal relationships, especially intimacy and close emotional involvement. Her communication skills are very likely quite impaired resulting in much misunderstanding. Considering the already mentioned tendency to somatize and the possibility of a psychotic condition, there may be present somatic delusions.

The combination of depression, interpersonal difficulties, and impaired reality contact would make a substantial suicide risk. It wouldn't be suprising to find suicide attempts in the patient's history. The clinical picture seems rather chronic in nature although there may be an acute element operating in addition. Judging from the unusual configuration and the presence of the acute component, it is likely that the patient's current mental status is unstable and will soon settle into a more definitive diagnostic pattern.

Impression:
1. Borderline schizophrenic with depression.
2. R/O schizoaffective disorder or paranoid schizophrenia.
3. Significant suicide potential.

Figure 4. Blind Interpretation of Case A

vided the blind interpretation given in Figure 4. The clinician was told only the patient's age, sex, and type of setting in which she was seen. He was not told that the profile was that of a Chilean patient.[2] In the translation of the case report[3] written by the psychiatrist, some of the behaviors and problems are highlighted (Figure 5).

The MMPI profile of another Chilean patient, being seen at the student health service for severe depression and inability to adjust to her present environment, is given in Figure 6 (solid line), along with the results of the MMPI she took at the first-year student orientation (dotted line) six months earlier. This profile was given to an experienced clinical psychologist[4] who provided the following blind interpretation (see Figure 7) knowing only the individual's sex, age, and type of setting in which the test was administered. The actual case description is reported in Figure 8.

History — Case A

Age: 28
Sex: Female
Reference to Psychology of General Medicine on 9/29/78.

Symptomatology
"Headache that manifests itself in the form of a triangle towards the back of the head." "I don't think this is an illness." "It is only problems . . . like everybody else. . . ." The patient indicated that when she thinks, she hears her voice perfectly inside her head, just as she would hear another person talk. "Sometimes I tell myself ridiculous things such as 'the green vase'. But this distracts me from what I really want to think. . . ." She describes this activity with a word boboso (Spanish) that could be a neologism combining the words for silly and drooling which are very similar in Spanish (bobo and baboso).

"Now I am brilliant, . . . before I wasn't." "Also in theater." "I think about my poems . . . there is a book about that." The patient says she likes mythology and interpreting the Bible. "I am full of ideas." "I have a special talent for literature, and that is my only gift." "I am not Catholic but this is a divine gift that I inherited because my father is a poet." "If I knew how to explain the reason for all things, I would be a genius . . . I would not be here."

It is difficult to ascertain precisely the beginning of her symptomatology. From some of the information provided by the patient and her moth-

Figure 5. Psychiatrist's report of a woman patient (Case A)
whose profile appears in Figure 4.

er, it seems that there has been an insidious development for the past two years.

Personal History

Normal pregnancy and delivery. No history of epileptic convulsions or high fever. No surgical interventions. Onset of menarch occurred at 12- to 13-years-old with irregular menstruation up to the present time. No history of marijuana use or alcohol abuse. She has been prone to flirting and has had multiple superficial contacts with the opposite sex since she was 14-years-old. She got married on impulse, without too much reflection. Three years ago, when she was three months pregnant, she realized that "they could not stay together" and annulled the marriage. She has not seen her ex-husband since then. She was a good student throughout primary and secondary schools, however her performance at the university has been poor. Her mother described her as having been always "somewhat strange." Lately, she has noticed that her daughter has developed a consuming interest in reading to the abandonment of other activities and obligations.

Family History

The patient is an only child who still lives with both of her parents and her two-year-old son. The only family history of psychopathology ascertained involved her maternal grandfather and uncle who were described as violent and "nervous." It appears that her family life would be good except for what is, in our opinion, the mother's excessive tolerance of her daughter's strange behavior and the fact that the mother is the one who runs the household.

Mental Exam

The patient looks old for her age. She was wearing an odd, gypsy-like outfit. However, her verbal expressions were even more bizarre than her physical appearance. She appeared agitated at times. Her speech was in the form of a monologue directed to an (audience or spectator) from whom she kept a great affective distance and indifference. Her ideas suggest megalomania (perhaps with a delirious quality). She is not only affectively removed from her situation of being mentally disturbed, but she does not recognize that she is ill. She is not really clear on why she came to the clinic.

Diagnostic Impression

Hebephrenic schizophrenia.

Treatment

Start on a phenothiazine since it has been reported that schizophrenics show fewer side effects with this drug.

Figure 5. (Continued)

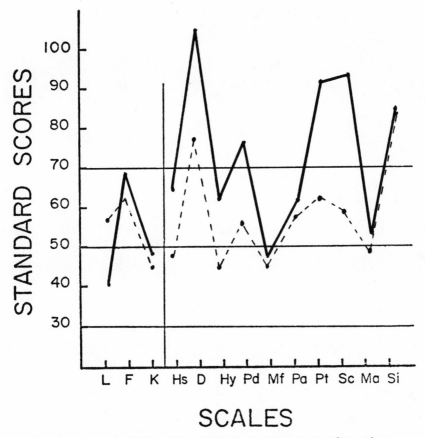

Figure 6. MMPI profile (solid line) of a female student (Case B)
at referral to the student health service. (Dotted line represents her
profile at the beginning of the school year.)

Both cases show that MMPI clinical interpretation using the original MMPI norms provides valuable diagnostic information on Chilean patients. Comparison of the average MMPI profiles of Chilean patients with those of United States normals also suggests that the MMPI is sensitive to psychological problems manifested by Chilean patients. The average patient profiles in Figures 9 and 10 show female and male patients from the student health service at the Catholic University compared with normal Chilean college students. These patient profiles resemble those of psychiatric patients in other countries (Butcher & Pancheri, 1976) and clearly differ from the normal profiles obtained from the entering class at orientation testing.

Several research projects with the MMPI are under way in Santiago. Josefina Losada Menendez and Louis Canessa Be, of the School of Education at the Catholic University in Santiago, have launched a project examining personality factors and academic attrition. Current research projects at the student health service involve increasing the information available from the MMPI by further automating the scoring. The present computer-scoring program is being expanded to score, in addition to the clinical scales, the Wiggins content scales (Wiggins, 1969) and the Koss and Butcher (1973) critical items. Efforts are being made to speed up the scoring process by using a data card MMPI form for clinic patients. Patients sort data cards, on which the items are printed. The cards can then be fed directly into the terminal, providing a more readily available input format and reduced clerical-scoring cost. The MMPI profile information can be ready for the clinician the same day.

This markedly elevated, yet technically valid, profile suggests an acute exacerbation of mixed neurotic symptoms in a chronically tense, ruminative, schizoid individual.

Symptomatically, the patient is depressed, anxious, and preoccupied with unpleasant matters pertaining to herself as a person and to her current life situation. She feels inadequate, "abnormal," and alienated from others. She is frightened by the prospect of having to deal with others, although she also desires contact and communication with at least a few selected intimates. She has, in fact, probably undergone a recent setback in her dealings with significant others, e.g., heterosexual love object, platonic friend, or family member. She characteristically overreacts to such stressful experiences, and at such times she may make overtures in the direction of suicide. She typically blames herself for her problems relating to others, thus intensifying her sense of failure, inadequacy, and differentness. Her reality testing weakens under stress, and at times her thinking becomes dereistic and highly idiosyncratic. Subtle distortions of reality, particularly in the areas of self-image, her ideas about others' views of her, and about the locus of control of her own thoughts and actions, may be detected clinically.

The patient's history may be marked by a succession of significant "losses," perhaps early loss of a parent or other significant parent-like figure, an especially close childhood friend, or, more recently, an important love object. Failure experiences in the patient's life may also be the object

Figure 7. Blind MMPI interpretation of Case B.

of much morbid rumination on her part, and she tends to think of herself as the responsible person for such losses and failures.

Diagnostically, depression seems salient at this time, though the patient's schizoid character structure suggests a significant schizophrenic diathesis. She may, in fact, be pre-schizophrenic, though there is also the possibility of a primary affective disorder of a unipolar (depressive) variety. In any case, situational stresses are very likely implicated in the current picture, and therapeutic intervention must contend with those aspects as well as with whatever endogenous components there may be. The patient must be evaluated carefully with respect to suicide risk and/or possible need for hospitalization. Chemotherapy may well be indicated, in conjunction with psychotherapy, with particular attention to alleviating the acute depression. Psychotherapy with this patient should aim at shoring up her ego defenses, improving her self image, and strengthening her abilities to cope with the stresses of everyday life as well as with the occasional occurrence of acute disappointment and/or loss. Helping her to become appropriately assertive, and to be more comfortable in her interactions with others would be additional therapeutic goals. Supportive therapy on a long-term basis is required, as she will experience continuing difficulties even after the current acute distress is ameliorated.

Figure 7. (Continued)

Case B

An 18-year-old woman first-year college student was referred to a therapist by Student Health Service and her department head after she asked to postpone her courses.

In the interview she was frightened and defensive about her academic problems. She reported that her parents strongly emphasized academic achievement. Both her parents are very strict Catholics and very traditional in their discipline. She reportedly was a good student in secondary school but was having difficulty in college. She believed that she was "no good" because she did not stand out as a student. Earlier she had hoped to study ballet but her parents discouraged it—urging her toward an academic program.

In the interview she appeared to be quite depressed. She was a frail woman who presently is neglecting her dress. Her speech was slow and hesitant. She had diffiuclty thinking and appeared confused.

She was referred to a psychotherapist for counseling for her situational problems.

Figure 8. Clinician's report on woman student patient (Case B).

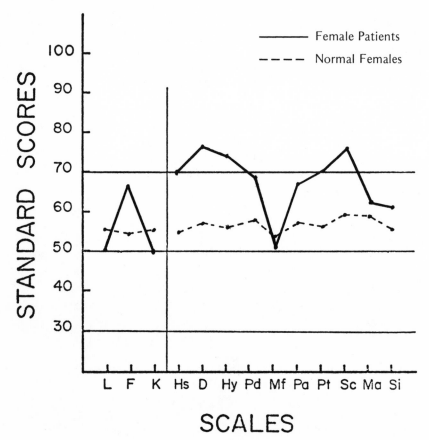

Figure 9. Average MMPI profile for female patients (N = 50)
at a student health service in Santiago compared to normal Chilean
female college students (N = 1,557)

Ultimately, the staff plans to develop decision rules that will categorize MMPI profiles for the entering class into psychopathological groups. Such information could be used to study relationships between personality factors (measured at college entrance) and the development of psychological problems during college. This system of problem identification could also be used to initiate prevention strategies—to offer psychological or educational services that would aid troubled individuals *before* they run into problems at school.

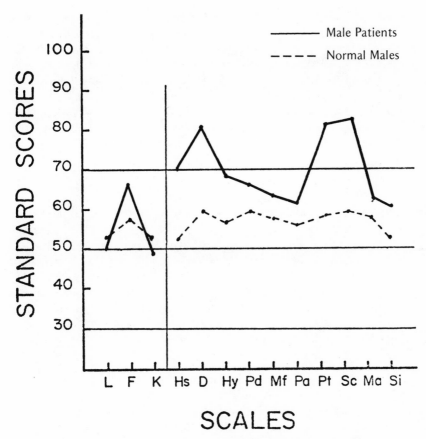

Figure 10. Average MMPI profile of male patients (N = 50)
at a college student health service in Santiago compared with
normal Chilean college males (N = 1,531)

Australia

Ian Campbell (Department of Psychology, University of Melbourne, Parkville, Victoria) recently completed a research project for his doctoral dissertaion – "The Joint Domain of the MMPI and CPI." He used the U.S. standard English version of the MMPI and examined the factor structure of the scales in Australian populations. Campbell and McGartland are also engaged in a project to define the similarities and differences in the factor structure of several MMPI short forms.

Belgium

Work on the MMPI in Belgium has broadened since the preliminary projects were described in Butcher and Pancheri (1976). De Schampheleire and Van de Mosselaer, Laboratory of Social Pathology, University of Brussels, Johannalaan 44, Brussels, Belgium, have developed new norms for the Brussels form of the MMPI based on 500 normal males and 300 normal females. They have renormed the MMPI for Belgium and have published new T scores for use with their Dutch translation. In the process of this restandardization work they rewrote the Scoremod computer program published in Butcher and Pancheri and will make it available to interested researchers.

England

In spite of the common language and shared psychological traditions, the MMPI has not been used much in England. Recently, however, Gunn, Robertson, Dell, and Way (1978) used several scales of the MMPI to evaluate men in prison. Although their choice of scales (Depression, Hypochondriasis, Manifest Anxiety, Ego Strength, and Social Introversion) does not maximally reflect the range of psychopathology in prison, they did find the MMPI useful in describing their patients. They also attempted to use the MMPI as a measure of change for their milieu treatment program.

Germany

In the past few years, the use of the MMPI in clinical practice and research has increased in Germany. Several recent projects will be highlighted here to indicate the range of work. In all cases, the translation of O. Spreen is being used.

In West Germany, Dr. Alois Angleitner (D-53 Bonn, Seehausstr. 60) is doing research on normal college-age individuals. Dr. Armin Schmidtke (Lehrstuhl Psychologie I, Universität Mannheim, Schloss, D-6800 Mannheim) has been studying clinical applications of the MMPI. An area of specific interest is suicide, described in:

Schmidtke, A. Möglichkeiten psychometrischer Verfahren bei der Abschätzung suizidalen Verhaltens Jugendlicher. *Suicidprophylaxe-Theorie und Praxis*, 1976, 3, 108-31.

Another psychologist at Mannheim, Sylvia Schalle (Lehrstuhl Psychologie I, Universität Mannheim, Schloss, D-6800 Mannheim) is using the MMPI in a correctional setting as well as with patients.

In East Germany, Dr. Claus Drunkenmölle (402 Halle/Saale, Meckelstr. 14b, German Democratic Republic/East) has been using the MMPI in marital and sexual counseling and in studies of mental and social problems in divorce. Several recent publications should be noted:

Klinische und neurosenpsychologische Untersuchungen bei funktionellen akralen. Durch-blutungsstorungen. *Psychother. Psychosom.*, 1969, 17, 343-53.

Neurosenpsychologische Untersuchungen zur essentiellen Hypertension. *Psychother. Psychosom.*, 1972, 20, 333-43.

Neurosenpsychologische Untersuchungen zum Effort-Syndrom. *Psychother. Psychosom.*, 1973, 22, 34-45.

Neurosenpsychologische Untersuchungen bei Hyperventilations-tetanie. *Zschr. arztl. Fort-bild.*, 1973, 67, 33-37.

Psychologische Untersuchungen bei Patientinnen mit Mammakarzinom (Pilotstudie). *Psychiatria clin.*, 1975, 8, 127-39.

Greece

Nikolas Manos (Department of Psychiatry, University of Thessaloniki, Thessaloniki, Greece) translated the MMPI into Greek according to the procedures suggested by Butcher and Pancheri (1976). He has completed a bilingual study of the translation and is in the process of collecting standardization data in northern Greece.

Hong Kong

The MMPI has been translated into Chinese by Fanny Miu-ching Cheung and Theodora Ting (both at the Psychology Department, Chinese University of Hong Kong) and is being used primarily for research at the moment. The "experimental" version has taken into consideration various earlier versions of the Chinese translation done independently by individual clinicians or researchers. The present version has been undergoing translation-adequacy and test-equivalence studies. The bilingual reliability studies have been difficult to conduct owing to the nonavailability of bilingual subjects with high proficiency in the English language, especially since idioms and slang are used in many items. Preliminary studies with groups of student nurses show consistency of average profiles across a number of different classrooms. As in many foreign studies, there is a general elevation of the profiles compared with United States norms, especially of scales 8 (*Sc*), 6 (*Pa*), and 2 (*D*).

Japan

The MMPI research programs in many countries are generally remarkable for their scope and coordination of efforts. There are examples, however, in which researchers have either not been in communication with each other or have for some reason chosen not to cooperate, so that numerous translations have been done and research efforts have been scattered. The most flagrant example is the MMPI work in Japan; about 15 different versions have been developed at one time or another. Since one of us (Clark) is able to read Japanese, we have been able to obtain more complete and accurate information about the state of the MMPI in Japan than was possible at the time of the publication of Butcher and Pancheri (1976). As an illustration, it is interesting to trace the development of the MMPI in Japan (Hidano, 1967).

The MMPI was first translated in 1950 by a team of workers at Japan Women's University and Keio University. Comparing a group of 570 normals with 268 psychiatric patients, they developed 10 scales: psychopathy, epilepsy, paranoid form, schizophrenia, depression, mania, psychasthenia, neurosis, hysteria, and "ismus." Later they developed a 360-item form adapted to a clinical population (N = 296). For this form they dropped some scales: mania, psychasthenia, neurosis, and hysteria and added five others: hebephrenia, catatonia, paralysis, philoponismus, and psychogenia. They then developed a research form, adding more items and including two more scales—dissimulation and ego strength—which they published in draft form.

In 1953 a team from Kyushu University translated the MMPI, changing it less than any other version has. They altered only three items, for cultural reasons: Item 70 "I used to like drop-the-handkerchief" became "I used to like 'spinning' and 'beanbags'," Item 295 "I liked 'Alice in Wonderland' by Lewis Carroll" became "I liked reading dream-like fiction stories," and Item 513 "I think Lincoln was greater than Washington" became "I like charitable politicians more than power politicians." In their basic research, they compared tuberculosis patients with healthy people. All the scales except 5 (Mf) were higher in the ill population, with scales 1 (Hs), 2(D), 3 (Hy), and 4 (Pd) significantly so. They also compared anxiety neurotics who showed elevations on scales 1 (Hs), 2 (D), 3 (Hy), and 7 (Pt).

In 1959 a team from Kanazawa University developed first a full form and then a 160-item short form. Little is known about these versions. In 1957 the 550-item "Sendai Classification Edition" was first developed by Abe and Kuroda of Tohoku University and the Sendai Juvenile Classification Office, respectively. They compared schizophrenics and anxiety neurotic patients with normals and found significant elevations on scales 1 (Hs), 4 (Pd), and 8 (Sc), as well as low scale 9 (Ma), for schizophrenics and elevations on scales 1 (Hs),

3 (Hy), and 8 (Sc) for anxiety neurotics. In 1963 the instrument was revised and published with the permission of the Psychological Corporation as the "Japan edition" (Abe, Sumita, & Kuroda, 1963). It was standardized on 560 males and 446 females over the age of 18 from a number of different regions of Japan (Abe, 1969).

In 1955 a team at Tokyo University headed by Hidano began work on still another version. They added and substituted some items, bringing the total to 576. After a number of revisions and trials on college students, normal adults, and psychiatric patients, a final version of 524 items was completed in 1962 and extensive rescaling, norming, and investigatory work was done. Clinical diagnostic groups were used as criterion groups (for example, the D-scale criterion group included endogenous depressives, periodic depressives, melancholic depressives, and cyclothymic types in the depressive state), and items distinguishing these groups from normals at the 5% level were selected. Overlap with the original MMPI scales ranged from a low of three items on scale 6 (Pa) to a high of 23 on the F scale. Test-retest reliabilities (two-week interval) of the new scales ranged from .78 (scale 0, Si) to .81 (scale 3, Hy). Cross-validation studies showed clinical populations to have generally elevated profiles with high points on the appropriate scales. From this revised version, the authors have developed the TPI (Tokyo Personality Inventory) with a similar but slightly different set of clinical scales: Dp (Depression), Hc (Hypochondriasis), Hy (Hysteria), Ob (Obsession), Pa (Paranoia), Hb (Hebephrenia), As (Anti-social), Ep (Epilepsy), Ma (Mania), and In (Introversion), as well as five validity scales: A or Nr (No response = MMPI "?"), B or Rr (Rare response = MMPI F), C or Uf (a self-criticism scale), D or Li (Lie scale = MMPI L), and E or Cr (Correction = MMPI K).

Other versions of the MMPI include translations by researchers at Osaka University, Medical Division, Gakushuin University (a shortened form), Waseda University, the National Mental Hygiene Research Institute, Maruguchi Hospital, and the Defense Department, and individual investigators Wako Okada (a short form), Haruyo Hama, Motoi Morimoto (called the NPI, Nippon Personality Inventory), and Fujio Tanaka.

No doubt one reason why so many Japanese translations of the MMPI have been done is that, as indicated by the Tokyo University rescaling project, direct translation of the instrument yields mean scores in the normal population quite elevated compared with United States norms, and each set of investigators thought they could do a better job. However, lack of communication between investigators may explain most of the new translations. Whatever the reason, the existence of many translations is not conducive to cumulative psychological research. Rescaling, altering items, etc., although admirable for use within a country, make cross-cultural studies impossible. As a result, efforts are now under way to collect all the more widely used versions, evaluate them according to the criteria to be discussed later in this chapter, determine their usage patterns in Japan, and elicit the cooperation of major developers and users in consolidating the best of each version into a single edition to be used cooperatively for research, if not for clinical purposes, throughout the country. In this way, both within-country and international research will be comparable, and research studies may build on one another, contributing to the production of a coherent picture of psychopathology around the world.

Kuwait

Three Egyptian psychologists now living in Kuwait are using an Arabic translation of the MMPI for clinical and research purposes. The psychologists are:

Attia Mahoud Hana
Professor of Counseling Psychology
Kuwait University
Kuwait, Arabia

Mostafa Ahmed Torki
Department of Psychology
Kuwait University
Kuwait, Arabia

Mohamed Emad-eddin Ismail
Department of Psychology
Kuwait University
Kuwait, Arabia

All of these researchers use the Arabic translation published by A. M. Hana, M. E. Ismail, and L. K. Melika in Egypt. Several research articles have been published, including:

Melika, L. K., Ismail, M. E., and Hana, A. M. *Personality and its measurement* (in Arabic).
Ismail, M. E. *A handbook for the use and interpretation of the MMPI* (in Arabic).
Torki, M. A. The relationship between parental care in the Kuwait family and some personality traits of university students (1974) (in Arabic).

Lithuanian SSR, USSR

Goštautas Antanas, Institute of Cardiology, Kaunas Medical Institute, translated the MMPI into Lithuanian in collaboration with Bajoras Jonas. The MMPI is being used extensively as a research instrument, as the following recent publications indicate:

Goštautas, A., Pūras, A. Evaluation of depression in paranoid schizophrenics. *Medicine, XV*. Vilnius: Scientific Works of Luthuanian Higher Schools, 1977.

Bajoras, J., & Goštautas, A. On the translation of the MMPI into Lithuanian. *Medicine, XV*. Vilnius: Scientific Works of Lithuanian Higher Schools, 1977.

Goštautas, A., Tonkonogij, J., & Vinkšna, J. An investigation of schizophrenics and neurotics by using the Lithuanian version of the MMPI. *Medicine, XIV*. Vilnius: Scientific Works of Lithuanian Higher Schools, 1973.

Goštautas, A., Daknys, R., & Grinevičius, A. A method for assessment of personality traits in patients with ischemic heart disease. *The Problems of Ischemic Heart Disease*, 1976.

Goštautas, A., Daknys, R., & Smailys, A. On the personality peculiarities with myocardiac infarction. *The psychological problems of mental hygiene, psychoprophylaxis and medical deontology (clinical psychological studies)*. Collection of scientific papers. Leningrad, 1976.

Mexico

Mexico continues to be a very active country for MMPI research. Psychologists in a number of settings have a variety of research and clinical MMPI projects under way. Mexico City and Pueblo, Mexico were sites of the 12th annual Conference on Recent Developments in the Use of the MMPI in February 1978. The conference was co-sponsored by the University of Minnesota and the University of the Americas, Miren I. de Garcia-Barcena serving as the coordinator in Mexico.

Gomez-Mont, Arias, and Acevedo (1974) correlated scores obtained from a short form (the first 366 items) with full-length scale scores for 1,021 university students. The obtained correlations were all greater than .90 (scores for K and 0 (Si) were estimated using a step-down regression analysis before correlating).

DeBarbenza, Montoya, and Borel (1978) compared differences between students in the humanities and sciences on the psychotic tetrad of the MMPI. They found no significant differences, except that in studying male students with at least one scale above $T = 60$, male science students had more elevated scores on scales 7 (Pt) and 8 (Sc) than male humanities students. "Thus, it is possible to say that students in this group are more concentrated and incommunicative; very possibly they will find difficulty in developing interpersonal relationships."

There is a diverse group of MMPI research projects currently in progress in Mexico. Research varies from improving the translation itself, to using the MMPI for selecting clinical populations, to large-scale screening for psychopathology. Some projects will be highlighted to give a picture of the work being done.

Anne Dingman (Taxqueña 1818, casa G23, Mexico 21, D.F.) studied the value of the MMPI *F* scale as a measure of invalidity in psychiatric patients' profiles. She found that psychosis was correlated with the *F* score and concluded that profiles with *F* scores of 16 should not be eliminated from interpretation.

Pablo Reyes Lopez (Rancho Nuevo No. 8, Fac. Santa Cecilia, Mexico 21, D.F.) has been using the MMPI in his work on vocational counsling. His thesis at the Universidad Nacional Autonoma de Mexico (U.N.A.M.): "El MMPI en la deteccion de psicopatologia en casos de desorientacion vocacional" (1977) serves as a basis for the work he is presently doing.

Miren I. de Garcia-Barcena (Hamburgo 250, Mexico 6, D.F.) has been using the MMPI to aid in making decisions about the placement of orphans with potential adoptive parents. She has completed a study comparing the personality characteristics associated with infertility in women.

Miguel Augel Rosado Chauvet (Presidente Carranza No. 120, Col. Coyoacan Z.P., Mexico 21, D.F.) is working on a project at the Universidad Autonoma Metropolitana Unidad Iztapalapa evaluating and counseling students.

Ofelia Rivera Jimenez (Leibnitz 83-1, Col. Anzurez, Mexico 5, D.F.) continues work on automated assessment of medical students at U.N.A.M. She is presently adapting Professor Pancheri's (University of Rome) automated interpretation system in Mexico. Recent publications include:

Pucheu, Rivera y Cols. El empleo del MMPI en un programa de prevencion de las enfermedades mentales. Undated mimeographed manuscript.

Pucheu, Rivera y Cols. The development of a method for detecting psychological maladjustment in university students. In J. N. Butcher and P. Pancheri, *A handbook of cross-national MMPI research*. Minneapolis: University of Minnesota Press, 1976.

Rivera, Ampudia y Cols. El MMPI en la deteccion precoz de las alteraciones mentales en poblaciones universitarias. *Revista de Psiquiatria*, 1976, 6, No. 2.

Rivera, Monzón y Cols. Investigacion sobre la interpretacion automatizada del MMPI para estudiantes universitarios. Reports preliminar, *Revista de Psiquiatria*, in press.

Poland

Zbigniew B. Gas of the Catholic University of Lublin has been involved in clinical and research work with the Wiskad version of the

MMPI. This translation was done by Professor Mieczyslaw Choynow-ski formerly of Poland, now living in Mexico. Further standardiza-tion and developmental work has been done by Zenomena Pluzek who published her results in *Wartość testu Wiskad-MMPI ala diagnozy różnicowej w zakresie nozologii psychiatrycznej*. Lublin: KUL, 1976.

Turkey

Nese Erol (Yucetepe mah. 6.C, Blok 28/3, I. Cadde, Anittepe/ Ankata, Turkey) and Isik Savasir (University of Hacettepe, Turkey) translated the MMPI for use in Turkey. They have been using the MMPI on a routine clinical basis at Gulhane Military Hospital since about 1972 and are presently standardizing the translation on about 1,500 normal subjects. They plan to compare these data with sam-ples available in Butcher and Pancheri (1976).

EVALUATING MMPI TRANSLATIONS

The use of any psychological test in a culture different from the one in which it was developed assumes that, or is investigating whether, the results of the test in the target culture are comparable to those obtained in the source culture—that is, whether the items and scales have the same internal structure and predict similar nontest behavior. There are numerous theoretical and methodological problems asso-ciated with the issue of psychological equivalency (Butcher & Garcia, 1978; Butcher & Pancheri, 1976; Gough, 1968; Przeworski & Teune, 1967; Sechrest, Fay, & Zaidi, 1972). The adequacy of test transla-tions is probably the most important issue in this area.

Brislin (1970) suggested a seven-step procedure for adequate translation from English to other languages, but his procedures (which involved decentering, that is, eliminating culture-specific con-tent)—as do those of Werner and Campbell (1970)—are most appli-cable when it is possible to alter both the English version and the target version. In the case of many instruments like the MMPI, which have already been standardized and researched in their origi-nal English version, the process of "decentering" is not possible.

Ultimately, questions about the cross-cultural equivalence of any psychological concept and its measurement are empirical ones. It can be argued that until a test has been translated in a rigorously literal fashion and found inadequate, there is no reason to assume that alterations other than linguistic ones need be made. If extensive revalidation were required, every major cross-cultural project would become even more difficult, involving numerous testings and retranslations. It is more expedient to bypass many of these stages and make "psychologically equivalent item substitutions" by drawing upon knowledge from other sources such as anthropological data, well-known cultural facts, and native speakers' intuitions about their language and culture. It is important to be alert to the possibility of nonequivalent constructions throughout the translation process.

For example, some items are clearly inappropriate since there are no linguistic equivalents in the target language. The MMPI item "I think Lincoln was greater than Washington" does not have the same meaning for people of any other country that it does for Americans. In such a case, what is variously known as "equivalence of inference" (Przeworski & Teune, 1967), "psychological equivalence" (Butcher & Garcia, 1978), or "experiential equivalence" (Sechrest et al., 1972) is much more important than linguistic equivalence. The translator must hypothesize what the item measures psychologically (perhaps a contrast between a war hero and a humanitarian), translate by substituting an "equivalent" concept (two people in the target culture who epitomize those qualities), and investigate how the item is answered by equivalent criterion groups in the two cultures. If the response pattern is similar, it is likely that the inference has been correctly identified and that the items have psychological equivalence.

Other items that may need "cultural translation" are those that may have linguistic "equivalents" with psychological meanings that only partly reflect the original item. For instance, if the item "My conduct is largely controlled by the customs of those about me" were translated literally, would it retain its original weight in a highly authoritarian or homogeneous culture? The translator must make the decision of whether to risk losing the import of the original item, in an effort to find a cultural difference, by translating literally, or attempt to change the item so that it is comparable in both cultures. The latter decision will lessen the probability of finding a cultural difference on the item. This translation decision exemplifies the "paradox of equivalence" (Butcher & Garcia, 1978). We believe that for the MMPI, it is better to stick fairly close to the original and allow empirical study to verify the degree of equivalence. Changing items to obtain psychological equivalence always involves the risk of mistaking the meaning of the item and distorting the data in an unknown way. This is especially true for empirically keyed inventories in which the rationale for inclusion of an item on a particular scale may not be obvious.

In light of such considerations, what are some specific criteria for evaluating translation adequacy?

(1) A basic requirement is that the translation be grammatically correct in the target language. This may seem obvious, but if the translation is done by a researcher who is not fully bilingual, it is possible for grammatical errors to slip in. We believe translation should always be performed by someone who is a native speaker of the *target* language.

(2) The translation should be accurate at the basic level of meaning. Have the translators understood the original item fully and translated it faithfully? Various techniques such as back-translation, described by Brislin (1970) and Werner and Campbell (1970), can help provide an answer to this question. Inaccuracies in meaning are quite common in MMPI translations. For example, in one Japanese translation it was discovered by back-translation that Item 241 "I dream frequently about things that are best kept to myself" had been rendered as "I often dream about things I am hiding from people." This translation would clearly change the way a person would respond to the item.

(3) The translation should read "naturally" in the target language. Butcher and Garcia (1978) and Sechrest et al. (1972) have pointed out that one of the problems of an overly literal translation is the awkward, highly stilted, or "dictionary" language. When words are chosen for their equivalence value without regard for how frequently they are used in the target culture, the result is often inaccurate or stylistically inappropriate. Phrase-level, rather than word-level, equivalence and judicious use of idiom are justified to avoid unnatural language. For example, a certain Japanese sentence literally translated into English would become "Most people make friends for the reason that friends fulfill a role," which is both grammatical and understandable; but this does not really capture the nuances of meaning of "Most people make friends because friends are likely to be useful to them," as this idea would be expressed naturally in English. The latter translation is more likely to capture the original meaning.

(4) Connotations of the words used should be the same in both cultures. Sometimes a particular word or idiom is easily translatable into another language but does not carry the same evaluative tone. It is essential for the translator to be aware of connotative as well as denotative meaning, and to choose words that are as congruent as possible on both levels. If no word of similar denotative and conno-

tative meaning exists, we have run into the problem of either experiential or conceptual inequivalence (Sechrest et al., 1972) mentioned above. For example, if the word for "shy" has a more positive connotation in Japan, Japanese respondents would find the item "I wish I were not so shy" somewhat strange. Asking them to respond to such an item would be like asking Americans to respond to the item "I wish I were not so sociable." A more serious problem is encountered when an equivalent concept simply does not exist in the target language. If the term is concrete, such as "florist," we can substitute a term which has equivalence of inference—in this case, some occupation that reflects feminine interest. If the term is abstract or subjective, such as "unpardonable," "jealousy," or "frank," the disparity is more difficult to deal with. There are also problems with the degree of specificity of words. Butcher and Garcia (1978) point out, for example, that the Spanish term "distracciones" for "hobbies" has other connotations and is, therefore, too imprecise. Since the English word is well known, it was left untranslated. In other cases, it may be necessary to give an example or two in parentheses to guide the respondents' thinking.

Many investigators have noted the difficulty that idioms cause. With idioms, as with items that need to be made relevant for the target culture, the important thing is, of course, to translate the meaning rather than the individual words. It would be helpful to translators if the authors of original instruments included in parentheses standard paraphrases of any idioms they use. Unfortunately, most inventories have been constructed without cross-cultural use in mind. There is nothing inherently wrong with using idioms either in the original or in the target version, as long as it is done carefully. The advantage of using idioms is that the translation reads naturally.

(5) Explanations of translation problems should accompany the translation, since they would help test users interpret results more adequately. Up to now, the focus has been entirely on the *product* of translation, the revised version, which is then administered to determine the degree of cross-cultural similarity and difference. However, there is much information to be gained from the *process* of translation, information that is usually lost. This could be preserved in the form of translator's notes in the test manual. Several types of information would be useful: (a) Which items were difficult to translate and why (grammatical problems, word-level or frequency differences, conceptual or experiential differences, for example)? (b) Which items were culturally modified and what was the rationale for the modification? (c) Which items were translated literally, in spite of sus-

pected cultural differences, and what were those suspected differences? (d) Which items needed grammatical (e.g., tense) modification? (e) Which items in the original contained idioms rendered into standard target language and vice versa, and what was the standard meaning in each case? (f) Which items were changed so they must be keyed oppositely? and (g) Which items translated easily but were thought to be irrelevant, uninteresting, inappropriate, or too highly (or infrequently) endorsable to be useful in the target culture?

This information could be used to predict, explain, and provide confirmatory evidence for obtained results. It would eliminate some of the suspicion that surrounds post hoc analysis. Following are a few examples of translation procedures that may provide models for future translators.

(1) MMPI item #78 "I like poetry" Japanese "Shi ga suki desu." This item was difficult to translate because there is no general word for poetry in Japanese. One must specify either Western style or traditional Japanese poetry. The former was chosen for the translation because it was thought to reflect the inference of feminine interest better than Japanese poetry which is widely enjoyed by both men and women.

(2) MMPI item #258 "I believe there is a God." Less than 10% of the American normative group responded False to this item, so it appears as an item on scale F (Infrequency). Since the Japanese generally describe themselves as nonreligious, and in any case rarely subscribe to the Western notion of "God," it was thought that this item would not function similarly in Japan. Therefore, the item was tentatively changed to "I believe I have a spirit," which it is believed will be endorsed True by most Japanese. Thus negative endorsement may be scored on the F scale.

(3) MMPI item #17 "My father was a good man." This item is translated in the present tense as well as the past tense because it is thought that many people would object to endorsing such an item if their father were still alive.

(4) MMPI item #76 "Most of the time I feel blue." A literal translation of this idiom would be ridiculous in the target language, so it is rendered as "Most of the time I feel depressed"; "depressed" is just as common in the target language as "blue" is in the original.

(5) MMPI item #188 "I can read a long while without tiring my eyes." This item is translated "My eyes get tired when I read for a long time," because it did not read smoothly in the negative. It will, therefore, be keyed oppositely.

(6) MMPI item #223 "I very much like hunting." Although hunting is not unknown in the target culture, the percentage of the population that engages in the sport is quite small. Therefore, it was assumed that the endorsement percentage of this item would be very low. However, it is associated more with men than women, and since the item is scored on scale 5 (*Mf*), it is translated literally. The translators may eventually substitute a more male-dominated sport in which more Japanese participate, if the studies of the adequacy of the translation indicate that this would be desirable.

PITFALLS OF USING LINGUISTICALLY OR PSYCHOLOGICALLY INCORRECT VERSIONS

The overriding problem of using an inadequate test is the same whether it is a poor translation or a poorly designed instrument: it does not measure what it is supposed to measure, so inferences made from results are not valid. The special problem of a poor translation is that if the original instrument has been shown to have some predictive validity, the user of the translated version expects this validity to generalize, and is likely to interpret results as though the original standardization is applicable. If such an approach were taken with a translation inadequate by the criteria outlined above, these would be the results:

(1) If the translation is ungrammatical, items will be misunderstood, subjects will lose confidence in the instrument, and a proper test-taking attitude will not be maintained, leading to increased error and random responding. Clearly, results will be contaminated and interpretation of scores questionable.

(2) If items have been inaccurately translated, both group percentages and individual endorsements will be misinterpreted. Endorsements different from the original will seem to indicate cultural differences where they may not exist. Endorsements similar to the original will be interpreted as evidence for cross-cultural similarity, again where it may not exist. These errors are more serious than the first because they cannot be detected by examining the target version alone. Although back-translation is not the only or necessarily the best method of evaluating a translation (because of problems pointed out by Gough [1968], for example), this is a case in which good back-translation might reveal errors that would otherwise go undetected. Thus, although back-translation does not ensure adequacy, it is highly useful for a check on this major type of error.

(3) Unnatural language will probably result in unnatural responding. It will necessarily force subjects to think about the items in ways
they might not, were the version closer to the way they ordinarily
use language. Most likely it will highlight the foreignness of the test,
and responders may even project their ideas of how they think for-
eigners would respond, or would want them to respond to the item.
In one sense, unnatural language changes the demand characteristics
of the item in an unpredictable way, rendering interpretation
difficult.

(4) Similar to the case of inaccurate translation, use of words with
different connotations in the two languages introduces insidious discrepancies. Unlike an unnatural translation, inspection of the target
item alone does not reveal any basis for expecting a different mode
of responding. It does not suggest any explanation for different
results in the two cultures or contain any warning that similar results
may have different meaning.

(5) If a potential test user possesses only the finished translated
instrument, he or she must make several decisions: (a) accept it as an
adequate translation and interpret results as though they correspond
to the original test; (b) suspect any results obtained of contamina-
tion in unknown directions and be conservative in the conclusions
drawn from any scores; (c) make linguistic comparisons of the two
versions before using the translation, to establish their equivalence;
or (d) treat the instrument as a new test that has no data base and
empirically investigate its correlates in the target culture. The more
common practice is to follow (a) unless the results are clearly deviant,
in which case some combination of (b) and (d) is used to explain the
obtained results. Obviously, however, neither the extreme alternatives nor the more common practice is truly satisfactory, and having
information about the process of translation, as outlined above,
would greatly facilitate decisions about the extent and validity of
generalizing interpretation.

Even with such information, and with an adequate translation,
the investigator must ultimately show that the instrument has empirical validity.

PROBLEMS OF TEST REVISION

Any time one decides to revise an existing test, a practical decision
must be made weighing the amount of effort involved against the increased benefit obtainable. For example, even though the MMPI in

its English language form has many failings (Butcher, 1972), it is so widely used and accepted in its present form, and has such an accumulated body of research and actuarial data as well as computer-based interpretation systems, that a potential reviser must be quite confident of substantially increased reliability or validity in order to justify the cost and risk of revising. With translation, however, there is rarely a substantial enough body of relevant literature to preclude revision. Nevertheless, the question of whether or not the translation is adequate must be carefully reviewed in light of the criteria outlined above, and balanced against the problems of revising. Once the decision to make changes has been made, the investigator must decide whether to revise only the inadequate items or to rewrite the whole test. As far as a translation/revision itself is concerned, the problems are not substantially different from those of the original translation process. One added difficulty is that if only some of the items are revised, care must be taken to maintain some stylistic consistency with the items that are retained in their original form. One should not be able to identify original vs. revised items when the translation is complete. The result must be an integrated test, or it will introduce stylistic response inconsistency, an unwanted source of variation.

It would be helpful in most cases if the revisor could work with the original translator of the instrument in order to understand fully the rationale of the original translation and to benefit from knowing the difficulties encountered and the considerations and compromises made. Not only would such cooperation facilitate the revision process, but it would also make acceptance of the revised version more likely. Cooperation with the original translator is especially important if he or she has obtained permission to publish the translated version from the Psychological Corporation.

GUIDELINES FOR DEVELOPING AND PUBLISHING NEW OR REVISED TRANSLATIONS

The first step to take when embarking on the translation of an instrument, once the need and scientific interest have been established, is to find out if a translation exists. As noted above in our discussion of the multiple Japanese translations, individual investigators often take this step too lightly and proceed with their translation without determining if others have already produced one. If a translation does exist, the investigator should evaluate its adequacy according to the criteria outlined above. Ideally, an appendix to the translation would exist, containing an explanation of the translating rationale and process, but this is rarely so. If the translation is deemed inaccurate, and if it is believed that incurring the cost of revision is justified, the original translator should be contacted concerning cooperation on the revision and possible copyright problems. If cooperation is obtained to revise an authorized translation of the MMPI, the Psychological Corporation (757 Third Avenue, New York, New York 10017) should be contacted about the need for revision, and be sent a report giving the reasons why the current translation is thought to be inadequate and a justification for the revision. If cooperation for a revision is not forthcoming from the original translator, and if the investigator still feels that revision is important, the Psychological Corporation should be sent cogent arguments for the value of revision. Negotiations may then be undertaken with the original translator. If these prove fruitless, the would-be translator is legally obliged to use the existing translation or produce a separate instrument of her or his own.

If, on the other hand, initial investigation confirms that the instrument has not yet been translated, the next step is to contact the Psychological Corporation for permission to undertake a translation. The investigator should state her/his qualifications for undertaking the project and outline the procedures planned for ensuring a quality translation. Native speakers of the target language should participate at every step. Ideally, the investigator will perform the task of interpreting any ambiguous items, of making decisions about the use of translation of idiom, of deciding between literal translation or "culturally equivalent" translation, and so on, making sure that the translation reflects the original in precisely the way intended. If he or she cannot fulfill this role herself or himself, he or she should entrust this most important task to someone who has the requisite bilingual capability as well as psychological sophistication. The translation itself should meet the criteria described above. The final stages of translation should include test-retest reliability studies, both monolingual (the target language alone) and bilingual (target language-source language versions). Any items that show marked differences should be checked for grammatical error, ambiguity, misinterpretation, differing connotations, and so on. The further step of developing norms will be dealt with in the next section. Once the translation is complete, every effort should be made to make it known and available to other investigators and practitioners in the field so that research efforts may be coordinated and the instrument put to practical use.

ADAPTATION AND CROSS-CULTURAL
TEST VALIDATION

The most important phase of test adaptation in a different culture or language is ensuring that the instrument measures the same constructs in the same way in the target population as it does in the culture in which the original test was developed. In most instances, when the MMPI is translated into a new language and culture, the investigator-translators are confident that the MMPI has some face validity and that the content being measured in the target population is relevant to the psychological constructs. In most cases, the original Minnesota norms are tried out with varying success with the hope of eventually developing new norms in the target population. Butcher and Garcia (1978) referred to these as *itinerant norms* and suggest that this approach might offer valuable information in the study of psychopathology cross-culturally and may aid the test adapter in re-norming the instrument in the new population. We noted in the description of the Chilean MMPI adaptation that the United States norms appeared to work quite well in the Chilean student-counseling setting and that the Chilean normals seemed to respond in a highly similar fashion to the Mexican student population. Thus it appears that in some countries, particularly Western industrialized nations, little revision of the norms may be required for routine clinical use.

However, it may be quite a different story with countries that are more "distant" from the United States in terms of language structure or culture. The work in Pakistan and Japan suggests that not only are new norms required in some instances but perhaps a different set of items may be needed to reflect the psychopathology in some countries. Two disorders that appear quite different are depression and schizophrenia. Until we have more information about self-report measures in these countries, it seems safest to operate under the assumption that the United States norms do not apply and encourage the development of local norms.

SUMMARY

The use of the MMPI for clinical and research purposes in other countries has greatly increased in recent years. Several recent publications have successfully employed the MMPI as a criterion measure for psychopathology in cross-cultural investigations.

A number of new translation projects have begun. We described, in some detail, a large project in Chile which is aimed at identifying psychopathology in a student-counseling population. We noted translation and adaptation projects in several other countries including Hong Kong, Kuwait, Greece, Turkey, and Lithuania. It is interesting to note that a great deal of the research activity involving the MMPI can be found in the Orient, Middle Eastern countries, and some Communist bloc nations. Perhaps new research studies in these countries will shed light on the differences between subjects from various countries which emerged in preliminary MMPI studies.

In general, we continue to be impressed with the robustness of the MMPI: it can be used effectively in other cultures with the same level of accuracy as it is in the United States. We expect that the use of the MMPI for objective measurement of abnormal personality will become even more widespread in the future.

NOTES

1. Dr. Zigfrids Stelmachers, Hennepin County Medical Center.

2. The different diagnoses given by the psychiatrist (hebephrenic schizophrenia) and by the clinician who made the blind MMPI interpretation (paranoid schizophrenia) raise an interesting point. The use of diagnoses in cross-cultural comparisons has been questioned by many researchers. Draguns (1977) pointed out that symptoms rather than diagnoses are the most appropriate unit for cross-cultural comparisons. In this illustration, the behavior described in the case report would more closely fit the diagnosis of paranoid schizophrenia as that term is used in the United States. The MMPI report and diagnosis *actually* fits the behavior described by the clinician but labeled paranoid schizophrenia.

3. Cases were translated from Spanish by Rosa Garcia and Alipio Sanchez.

4. Dr. Lloyd Sines, Department of Psychiatry, University of Minnesota Hospitals.

REFERENCES

Abe, M. The Japanese MMPI and its delinquency scale. *Tohoku Psychologica folia*, 1969, 28, 54-68 (Japanese).

Abe, M., Sumita, K., & Kuroda, M. *A manual of the MMPI.* Japanese standard edition. Kyoto: Sankyobo, 1963 (Japanese).

Brislin, R. W. Back-translation for cross-cultural research. *Journal of Cross-Cultural Psychology*, 1970, 1, 185-216.

Butcher, J. N., & Garcia, R. Cross-national application of psychological tests. *Personnel and Guidance*, 1978, 56, 472-75.

Butcher, J. N., & Gur, R. A Hebrew translation of the MMPI: An assessment of translation adequacy and preliminary validation. *Journal of Cross-Cultural Psychology*, 1974, 5, 220-27.

Butcher, J. N., & Pancheri, P. *A handbook of cross-national MMPI research.* Minneapolis: University of Minnesota Press, 1976.

DeBarbenza, C. M., Montoya, O. A., & Borel, M. T. The psychotic tetrad of the MMPI in a group of university students. *Revista de Psicologia General y Aplicada*, 1978, 33, 150, 79-88 (Spanish).

Draguns, J. Advances in the methodology of cross-cultural psychiatric assessment. *Transcultural Psychiatric Research Review*, 1977, 14, 125-43.

Gomez-Mont, F., Arias, R. N., & Acevedo, J. L. The MMPI 336: An abbreviated version of the Minnesota Multiphasic Personality Inventory. *Psiquiatria, Official Journal of the Mexican Psychiatric Association*, 1974, Sept.-Dec.

Gough, H. *Cross-cultural approaches to the study of delinquency*. Paper presented at the annual meeting of the American Psychological Association, San Francisco, 1968.

Gunn, J., Robertson, G., Dell, S. & Way, S. *Psychiatric aspects of imprisonment*. London: Academic Press, 1978.

Hama, H., & Konsei, A. A study on the similarity in MMPI scores between parents and children. *Doshisha Psychological Review*, 1977, 24, 21-27 (Japanese).

Hidano, T. Personality test methods—MMPI. In T. Imura (Ed.), *Clinical psychology test methods*. 2nd ed. Tokyo: Igaku Shōin, 1967.

Joroff, D. Hypotheses on terrorism and terrorists. *Journal of Psychology*, 1976, 23 (2) (French).

Joroff, D. Terror, terrorists and terrorism—the devisement of a psychology of desperation. *Journal of Psychology*, 1977, 24 (3) (French). (a)

Joroff, D. Psychological impact of terrorist activities on victims and on terrorists. *Journal of Psychology*, 1977, 24 (1) (French). (b)

Koss, M. P., & Butcher, J. N. A comparison of psychiatric patient's self-report with other sources of clinical information. *Journal of Research in Personality*, 1973, 7, 225-36.

Lison, S., & Van der Spuy, H. I. J. *Cross-national MMPI research: Group personality in South Africa*. Unpublished manuscript. University of Capetown, 1977 (Mimeograph ed).

Loper, R. G., Robertson, J. M., & Swanson, E. O. College freshman norms over a fourteen-year period. *Journal of College Student Personnel*, 1968, November, 404-7.

Lorr, M., & Klett, C. J. Major psychiatric disorders. A cross-cultural study. *Archives of General Psychiatry*, 1968, 19, 652-58.

Lumry, G. E., Cedarleaf, C. B., Wright, M. S., & Braatz, G. A. Psychiatric disabilities of the Vietnam veteran. *Minnesota Medicine*, 1972, 55, 1055-57.

Marsella, A. J. Depressive experience and disorder across cultures. A review of the literature. In H. Triandis (Ed.), *Handbook of cross-cultural psychology, Vol. 5: Culture and psychopathology*. Boston: Allyn and Bacon (in press).

Marsella, A. J., Sanborn, K. O., Kameoka, V., Shizuru, L., & Brennan, J. Cross-validation of self-report measures of depression among normal populations of Japanese, Chinese and Caucasian ancestry. *Journal of Clinical Psychology*, 1975, 31, 281-87.

Merbaum, M. Some personality characteristics of soldiers exposed to extreme war stress: A follow-up study of post-hospital adjustment. *Journal of Clinical Psychology*, 1977, 33, 558-62.

Merbaum, M., & Hefez, A. Some personality characteristics of soldiers exposed to extreme war stress. *Journal of Consulting and Clinical Psychology*, 1976, 44, 1-6.

Mirza, L. *Multiple administration of the MMPI with schizophrenics*. Unpublished manuscript. Fountain House, Pakistan, 1977.

Montag, I. *The Tel-Aviv MMPI: Some validation studies*. Paper presented at the Fourth International Personality Assessment Conference, Haifa, 1977.

Nuñez, R. *Inventario Multifasico de la Personalidad MMPI-Español, manual*. El Manual Moderno, S. A., Mexico 11, D. F., 1967.

Nuñez, R. *Aplicacion del Inventario Multifasico de la Personalidad (MMPI) a la psicopatologia*. (Application of the MMPI to psychotherapy) Mexico: El Manual Moderno, S. A., 1968.

Nuñez, R. *Aplicacion del Inventario Multifasico de la Personalidad (MMPI) a la psicopatologia* (second edition). (in press)

Overall, J. A., & Gorham, D. R. The brief psychiatric rating scale. *Psychological Reports*, 1962, 10, 799-812.

Padilla, A. M., & Ruiz, R. A. Personality assessment and test interpretation of Mexican Americans: A critique. *Journal of Personality Assessment*, 1975, 39, 103-9.

Pancheri, P., Bellaterra, M., Matteoli, S., Cristofari, M., Polizzi, C., & Puletti, M. Infarct as a stress agent: Life history and personality characteristics in improved versus not-improved patients after severe heart attack. *Journal of Human Stress*, 1978, 4, 16-42.

Przeworski, A., & Teune, N. Equivalence in cross-cultural research. *Public Opinion Quarterly*, 1967, 30, 551-68.

Quiroga, I. R., & Besner, V. F. *Cross-cultural comparison of MMPI profile differences between Anglo- and Mexican-American psychiatric patients.* Unpublished manuscript. Department of Youth and Family Development, Miami, Florida, undated.

Reilly, R. R., & Knight, G. E. MMPI scores of Mexican-American college students. *Journal of College Student Personnel*, 1970, 11, 419-22.

Rissetti, F., Butcher, J. N., Agostini, J., Elgueta, M., Gaete, S., Margulies, T., Morlans, I., & Ruiz, R. *Translation and adaptation of the MMPI in Chile: Use in a university student health service.* Paper given at the Fourteenth Annual Symposium on Recent Developments in the Use of the MMPI, St. Petersburg, 1979.

Sechrest, L., Fay, T., & Zaidi, S. Problems of translation in cross-cultural research. *Journal of Cross-Cultural Psychology*, 1972, 1, 41-56.

Spielberger, C. D., & Diaz-Guerrero, R. (Eds.) *Cross-cultural anxiety*. New York: Hemisphere, 1976.

Werner, O., & Campbell, D. T. Translating, working through interpreters, and the problems of decentering. In R. Naroll and R. Cohen (Eds.), *A handbook of cultural anthropology*. New York: American Museum of Natural History, 1970.

Wiggins, J. S. Content dimensions in the MMPI. In J. N. Butcher (Ed.), *MMPI: Research developments and clinical applications*. New York: McGraw-Hill, 1969.

Wing, J. K. A standard form of psychiatric present state examination (PSE) and a method for standardizing the classification of symptoms. In E. H. Hare and J. H. Wing (Eds.), *Psychiatric Epidemiology*. London: Oxford University Press, 1970.

POSTSCRIPT

Three additional translations came to light after this chapter was typeset: Arabic—by Dr. Adib R. Mikhail, 714 FM 1960 West, Suite 3K, Houston, Texas 77090; Greek—by Dr. Costas N. Stefanis, Professor and Head, Department of Psychiatry, Athens University Medical School; Pacificans—by Dr. Eugene Dwyer, F.M.S., 106 Holden St., North Fitzroy, Victoria 3068, Australia, who collaborates with Subhas Chandra, University of the South Pacific, Suva. They are collecting data on seminarians in Samoa, Fiji, and the Solomon Islands for both clinical and research purposes.

Jacek W. Paluchowski, 60-574 Poznan ul. Dabrowskiego 94 m. 1, Poland, has been using the MMPI in Poland. He has published a clinical manual for MMPI interpretation and has been studying actuarial interpretation of the MMPI in Poland. Shubha Thatte, Department of Psychiatry, Seth G.S. Medical College, Parel, Bombay, India, has been developing three MMPI translations for use in India: Hindi, Marathi, and Gujarati. She has collected data on over 1200 individuals and has initiated a project to refine the translations and develop normative data on these versions of the MMPI.

Ethnicity and Personality
An Update

Malcolm D. Gynther

Several years ago the writer (Gynther, 1972) reviewed all the data then available comparing MMPI performance of blacks and whites. Eighteen different articles were cited, although the actual data sources were closer to fifteen in number. Four sets of new data were also collected for the article, giving a grand total of some 20 data sources for the 33-year span from 1939 to 1972. Subjects for about half the studies were normal (often students); subjects for the other half of the studies were mental patients, prisoners, or medical patients.

The findings of the earlier article can be briefly summarized. First, there were distinctive differences between the MMPIs of blacks and whites. The amount of difference found was influenced by factors such as education and rural/urban residence; but blacks, whether young or old, male or female, normal or institutionalized, obtained higher scores than whites on scales *F*, 8, and 9 (which would typically be considered measures of nonconformity, alienation, and impulsivity respectively). Second, these differences appeared to reflect differences in values and perceptions rather than differences in adjustment. Analyses of the differentiating items were particularly revealing. Study after study showed that the principal factor distinguishing the two groups was labeled estrangement, distantiation, or mistrust of society; blacks obtained significantly higher scores on this factor. Finally, there was some evidence to suggest that prospective black employees were disadvantaged when the MMPI was used for screening and also that black psychiatric patients were less likely than white patients to be diagnosed accurately by the MMPI.

113

Recommendations for alleviating these problems were also suggested. One possibility was to develop a set of rules to modify standard interpretations when dealing with a black's MMPI. Basically, this would involve giving less weight to elevations on scales F, 8, and 9 than would ordinarily be given. Also, one could classify blacks' MMPIs into code types and then determine behavioral correlates for the types available. Most likely this would be restricted to institutionalized samples, since it is unlikely that case history or Q-sort data would be available for normals. Finally, an MMPI for blacks could be constructed. This would involve using the current set of MMPI items and the procedure originally used to develop the scales. However, the normal adults and psychiatric patients would be black. The product might resemble the current MMPI, but the scales would, presumably, contain different items and different conversions of raw to T scores.

The purpose of the present article[1] is to determine whether the MMPI findings of the past seven years confirm (or disconfirm) the previous conclusions and to see whether the recommendations have been followed and, if so, with what results. Also blacks' and whites' performance on other personality inventories and rating scales are evaluated in order to clarify questions not resolved by the MMPI data. Further, personality-inventory findings of other ethnic groups are examined to see if the findings for blacks are unique or are indistinguishable from those of American Indians, Mexican-Americans, and Asian-Americans. Finally, Sechrest's (1976) contention that race is merely a surrogate for some unknown psychological variable is examined and responded to.

COMPARISONS OF THE MMPIs
OF BLACKS AND WHITES, 1971-78

Most investigators have used deviant groups. For clinicians who are interested in black-white differences only to the extent that they affect interpretation, these studies may be helpful. However, if one is primarily interested in relationships between ethnicity and personality, the results of these investigations may be misleading. Presumably, apathy and indifference, disorganized thought processes, delusions and hallucinations will have a considerable effect on how anyone responds to a self-report inventory. Consequently, more emphasis will be placed on those few studies that used normal subjects.

MMPI Scale and Item Analyses

Normals. Fillenbaum and Pfeiffer (1976) actually used the Mini-Mult which, of course, is not the MMPI. However, the remarkable sample obtained by these investigators argues in favor of making an exception and reporting their data. Subjects consisted of nearly 1000 randomly selected community residents who ranged in age from 65 to 93. Six hundred and forty of the 997 Ss answered all 71 questions. For this subgroup, differences as a function of race were found on four scales, namely, *F*, 4, 8, and 9; in each case, the average score of blacks was higher than that of whites. Statistically significant sex-related differences were found on scales *F*, 1, 2, 3, and 7, with males obtaining higher scores than females. The authors concluded that "adjustment in scoring seems to be necessary. . . . Current sex corrections are inadequate and race-related differences are present" (p. 702).

An impressive MMPI study with normal subjects was carried out by White (1974). He compared 342 black and 288 white students from state universities in Missouri. He divided the 630 subjects into construction and validation samples, each of which contained 315 subjects (171 black, 144 white). Scores on the Social Status scale were similar for all subgroups. Significant differences by race were found in both samples for scales *F*, 4, 8, and 9. In every case, blacks' scores were higher than whites' scores. Percentage of variance accounted for ranged from 6 to 8. These findings are important because the only previous study using college students (Butcher, Ball, & Ray, 1964) found somewhat marginal differences associated with race. White (1974) also did item analyses and found 208 significantly differentiating items in the construction sample; 126 of these items were confirmed as "differentiators" in the validation sample. The magnitude of item differences is strikingly similar to Harrison and Kass's (1967) and Erdberg's (1969) results with lower-class, less educated subjects.

Another study of normals was conducted by Bull (1976) who used as subjects male and female blacks, whites, and native Americans who were attending a technical institute in a rural county of North Carolina. What is unusual or perhaps even unique about this county is that the people are almost evenly divided into these three ethnic groups. Bull predicted that blacks would have the most elevated profiles, whites would have the least elevated profiles, and Indians' profiles would fall somewhere between the blacks' and whites'.

Analysis of variance disclosed differences associated with race on scales K, 8, and 9. Follow-up statistical tests showed that black males obtained significantly higher scores than white males on scales F, 8, and 9, but whites obtained higher scores than blacks on scales K and 3. Differences were less striking among females, blacks obtaining significantly higher scores than whites only on scale 8. Indians' scale scores were more similar to whites' than to blacks' scale scores, but Bull's expectations were fulfilled only in certain cases (e.g., scale 8).

King, Carroll, and Fuller (1977) compared MMPIs of 56 black and 56 white males who were full-time employees of a large chemical company. Subjects were matched for age, education, occupation, seniority, mental-ability level, and socioeconomic level. Statistical analyses showed that blacks scored significantly higher than whites on scale 9, but whites scored higher than blacks on scale 6. Performance on several special scales was also examined. Blacks scored significantly lower than whites on the Control, Dominance, and Ego-Strength scales.

Deviant Groups. Two groups of investigators account for most of the data obtained from psychiatric patients. Davis and his colleagues (Davis, 1975; Davis, Beck, & Ryan, 1973; Davis & Jones, 1974) have found that if the two ethnic groups are divided into schizophrenic/nonschizophrenic and high-education/low-education categories, there are no significant main effects associated with race on MMPI scales. The interpretation was offered that "more advanced education appears to have either a masking or obliterating effect on culturally determined differences" and that "valid MMPIs may be obtained from Negroes . . . who have been exposed to sufficient conventional education" (Davis & Jones, 1974, p. 679).

Costello and his colleagues (Costello, 1973; Costello, Fine, & Blau, 1973; Costello, Tiffany, & Gier, 1972) account for most of the other work in this area. Their black psychiatric patients, who were carefully matched with whites on age, socioeconomic status, and duration of illness, obtained significantly higher scores than whites on scales F, 1, 5, 8, and 9; however, when stringent validity requirements were imposed on profile selection, these differences disappeared (Costello, Tiffany, & Gier, 1972). In one of their other studies (Costello, Fine, & Blau, 1973), black female psychiatric patients scored significantly higher on scales F, 4, 6, 8, and 9 than their white counterparts; black male psychiatric patients scored higher only on scale F; but there were no statistically significant differences between the scale scores of black and white prison inmates. In the third study, Costello (1973) found, as others have before him (e.g.,

Harrison & Kass, 1967), that item-level comparisons are more revealing than scale-level comparisons.

Marks, Bertelson, and May (1977) analyzed MMPIs of 232 black and 232 white psychiatric patients matched for education, marital status, employment, socioeconomic status, residence, and hospital status for differences in scale scores, items, high points, two-digit code types, number of scales with $T \geqslant 70$, and high-scale combinations. No significant main effect for race was found. Remarkably few differences at the item level, especially for adolescents, were uncovered. However, analyses of the simple effects of race showed that blacks obtained significantly higher scores than whites on scales F, 5, and 9. The authors deemphasized these results, stating that they are "difficult to interpret . . . since one scale (5, Mf) interacted with sex and another scale (Ma) interacted with age." Perhaps these findings are coincidental, but it is noteworthy that scores on scales F and 9 have more frequently yielded significant differences between blacks and whites than scores on any other scale.

Sutker, Archer, and Allain (1978) compared MMPIs of black and white drug abusers in residential treatment. Whites produced significantly higher scores than blacks on scales F, 2, 6, and 7. It was also noted that blacks used fewer drug categories and displayed lower levels of sensation-seeking than whites. Penk and Robinowitz (1974) found that black opiate groups scored lower than white opiate groups on scales F and 3, and that black opiate users scored lower than white nonopiate users (i.e., individuals using stimulants, depressants and/or hallucinogens) on scales F, 7, 8, and 0. (There were insufficient black nonopiate users to form a comparison group.) It is noteworthy that the only studies to find blacks lower than whites on scale F (out of approximately 28 references) both involve drug abusers.[2] The explanation for this anomaly appears to be that white heroin addicts are more atypical compared to their reference group than black heroin addicts, and that whites are more likely to be polydrug users than blacks. Lachar, Schoof, Keegan, and Gdowski (1978) have demonstrated that patients who use the largest variety of drugs describe themselves in the most pathological terms. Hence, the expected relationship between race and MMPI F scores is reversed because white drug abusers are, in fact, more disturbed than black drug abusers.

Reasons for Black-White MMPI Differences

Our earlier review led us to the conclusion that these scale and item differences were due to differences in values associated with the different environments that blacks and whites grow up in in the United States. Davis and Jones (1974) and Marks, Bertelson, and May (1977) focused on differences in education as the major factor underlying black-white MMPI differences. However, this explanation obviously cannot account for the striking differences White (1974) found between black and white college students. Rosenblatt and Pritchard's (1978) findings with male prisoners may be considered to complement Davis's; these investigators found that although race accounted for a significant portion of the variance, intellectual level accounted for substantially more of the variance in MMPI scores. It is interesting to note that Costello's (1973) item analysis disclosed that black prisoners and psychiatric patients reported more aspiration-reality conflict, feelings of separation and resentment, and pessimistic attitudes toward the future than their white counterparts. At a different level of analysis, Witt and Gynther (1975) showed that blacks rate predominately cynical, alienated MMPI items as "better," "more powerful," and "more active" than whites. This may be one reason why these kinds of items often differentiate blacks from whites. No doubt the differences are multi-determined. The definitive "cause and effect" study, if indeed it is possible to design one, remains in the future.

Consequences of Black-White MMPI Differences

Strauss, Gynther, and Wallhermfechtel (1974) showed that MMPI diagnosis disagrees with psychiatric diagnosis significantly more frequently for blacks than it does for whites. An implication of these findings is that, were the MMPI used to diagnose all patients, blacks would receive less adequate treatment than whites because their problems and symptoms would be less often understood. Shore (1976) has questioned Strauss et al.'s results, since his analysis, using different statistics, failed to reproduce some of the differential rates of misdiagnosis for blacks and whites. There was, unfortunately, an error in the original presentation, but the main conclusion still appears to be valid. Cowen, Watkins, and Davis (1975) also examined this issue. They found that almost half of their poorly educated black nonschizophrenics were misclassified as schizophrenics. Genthner and Graham (1976) went a step further than the other investigators. They found that although blacks appeared to be more disturbed than whites at admission (scales F, 8, and 9 were significantly more elevated) and at time of discharge (scales F and 9 were more elevated), these differences did not seem to lead to different decisions concerning discharge from the hospital nor did they appear to be related to posthospital functioning.

Two other studies have asked whether accuracy of interpretation is improved by using adolescent as compared to adult norms. Although not the major focus of either study, both compared blacks and whites in this regard. Lachar, Klinge, and Grisell (1976) found no difference in accuracy of MMPI narratives associated with race. This is encouraging since the narratives referred to are automated and are generated for cases on a commercial basis. One's positive feeling, however, has to be tempered by the fact that only 26 blacks were involved in the Lachar et al. study. Klinge and Strauss's (1976) findings may be considered as supporting those just reported. These investigators used adolescent and adult norms on profiles obtained from teen-agers to see if adult norms overestimate the degree of psychopathology in these patients. No main effects associated with race were found. Another study (Elion & Megargee, 1975) concluded that the *Pd* scale is as valid for blacks as it is for whites. However, these authors suggested that clinicians "mentally subtract" five points from the *Pd* T score of young black males to correct for racial bias. They also noted that just because *Pd* had been found to be valid for one segment of the population, the remaining clinical and validity scales should not be judged innocent by association.

New Developments for Interpretation of Blacks' MMPIs

Black-White Scales. White (1974) developed a means for adjusting blacks' MMPI profiles to reduce overinterpretation of pathology. He derived a 27-item scale (designated as *Rs*) which is composed of those statements to which blacks and whites respond most differently. A black's score on this scale provides an indication of how far he or she deviates from the modal performance of whites on the MMPI. (White factor analyzed this scale and found one factor, which he labeled 'discontent'). If the deviation is small, no adjustments to the basic scores were made. However, if a black subject obtains a T score of 60 or above (based on whites' scores on this special scale), his or her raw scores on scales *F*, 4, 8, and 9 are adjusted before K-correction and/or conversion to T score. For example, suppose an individual endorses 15 of the 27 items in the keyed direction. This raw score converts to a T score of 70. Adjustments are then applied that result in subtracting three points from the *F*-scale raw score, five points from the raw scores of scales 4 and 9, and nine points from the raw score of scale 8. With the "unwanted variance" removed, the profile can then be interpreted in the usual manner.

Costello (1977) developed a 32-item black-white scale by collating discriminating items from six prior studies. When 15 was used as a cutting score for mental-health-center clients, 81% of blacks and 87% of whites were classified correctly. Education and test score were not significantly correlated for either ethnic group. When 14 was used as a cutting score for police cadets, 51% of the blacks and 81% of the whites were classified correctly. Costello suggested that scores on this scale "might be used in an exploratory way as one quantitative estimate of functional race membership" (p. 518).

More recently, Gynther (1978) derived a 29-item scale composed of those statements answered most differently by the Minnesota norm group and a large sample of black middle-class normals (which will be described in more detail later in this chapter). Nine of these items appear on White's (1974) scale, but only four are found on the list compiled by Costello (1977). Six items are shared by White's and Costello's scales.

One might well be disturbed by the lack of agreement between the three scales. However, it should be noted that the items were derived from very different samples: White's from college students; Costello's from a mixed bag of psychiatric patients, prisoners, and normals; and Gynther's from adults averaging 35 years of age and living in the community. Also, there are more similarities than is apparent from comparison of the scales. White, for example, found 126 cross-validated discriminating items. Our analyses confirmed those results in two-thirds of the cases with only 7% reversals.

Code Type Correlates. Persons and Marks (1971) published an interesting study of the "violent 4-3 MMPI personality type." Subjects were prisoners at the Ohio State Reformatory, a maximum-security institution. The investigators found that in all comparisons with personality groups and base rates, the 4-3 Ss were significantly more violent than any other group, regardless of race. However, in addition to the MMPI Taylor's MAS, a delinquency scale, and a guilt scale were available. The key comparison disclosed that the white 4-3 Ss were significantly more anxious, showed more neurotic delinquency, and were more guilty on each of the subscales than the black 4-3 Ss. One might say that black and white 4-3s exhibited similar behavioral patterns, but closer examination revealed different personality correlates by race.

Clark and Miller (1971) attempted to validate Gilberstadt and Duker's 8-6 code type on blacks. They used 10 male VA patients whose MMPIs met the criteria for inclusion in this code type. They found 11 checklist items that significantly differentiated their black sample from the general abnormal sample of 100 Ss drawn from the Minneapolis VAH. Gilberstadt and Duker had found six such differentiating items. Only two items were on both lists. That sounds like very poor agreement, but it should be added that the separate lists did point to a similar pathological syndrome. The authors themselves seemed to have difficulty resolving these differences. At one point, they said that their results supported the conclusion that the hospitalized 8-6 code type represents a relatively homogeneous pathological entity, i.e., paranoid schizophrenia, in both black and white people. However, they then added that this pathology is superimposed on baseline behavioral characteristics that are sufficiently different to discriminate the two groups from each other and to demand the use of extreme caution in applying the white-validated criteria to a black sample for diagnostic purposes.

Gynther, Altman, and Warbin (1973a; 1973b) analyzed code-type correlates associated with $F > 25$ and 4-9/9-4 MMPI profiles for black and white psychiatric patients. The first article showed that blacks who obtain this high-ranging profile should not be expected to display the same nontest behaviors as whites who obtain this profile. In fact, blacks who generated $F > 25$ MMPI profiles were seen as no different on mental-status exams from blacks who generated $F < 26$ profiles. In the second study, which dealt with the more familiar 4-9/9-4 profiles, 15 significant discriptors were found for the original sample of white 4-9s. Thirteen significant descriptors were found for the original sample of black 4-9/9-4s. Only 3 of the 13 were in common with the 15 items found for the white patients. These differences may be more apparent than real; none of the 15 "white" items were confirmed by replication. In any case, no behavioral correlates were established for blacks' 4-9/9-4s.

Ritzema (1974) evaluated the relationships between demographic variables and behavioral correlates of MMPI two-point code types. He examined 12 reciprocal code types, e.g., 1-3/3-1, and overall found 41 correlates for his white sample and 30 correlates for his black sample. What number did the races have in common? The answer is 3. Interestingly, all 3 appeared on the 6-8/8-6 code type. He concluded that descriptors found to be applicable to one group of subjects cannot be assumed to be applicable to another group with the same profile type but differing on some major extra-test variable.

Single-Scale Correlates. Hedlund (1977) showed that MMPI *F* scores of black psychiatric patients are positively associated with scores of items assessing "disorientation," "confusion," "delusions," and other behaviors suggesting psychosis. He also found that blacks' scores on scale 2 are positively associated with "suicidal thoughts or threats," "decreased motor activity," "anxiety, tension, fearfulness," and other behaviors consistent with depression. He observed that "in other (most) instances, however, very few scale correlates of any type could be identified for the black samples" (p. 744).

Blacks' MMPI Norms. Subjects were obtained from Alabama, Michigan, and North Carolina to derive norms for blacks on the validity, clinical, and other frequently used MMPI scales (Lachar, Gynther, & Dahlstrom, in preparation). Major sources were church groups and social clubs, which were paid $5 per participant. Total sample size was 882, 321 males and 561 females. Age varied from 18 to 65, with means of 36.0 for males and 34.1 for females. Approximately 42% of the subjects had completed 12 years of schooling or less, 26% had some college, and 32% had graduated from college. Slightly over 50% of the sample were married, 30% were single, and the remainder were widowed, divorced, or separated. About 15% were unskilled, unemployed, or on welfare; 21% were semiskilled; 13% were classed as skilled manual; 18% were clerical workers, salespersons, or technicians; 8% were administrative or minor professionals; 22% were managers or lesser professionals; and 3% were executives or major professionals. Nearly 4% of the males said they had been treated for an emotional (nervous) condition, and 2.1% said they had served time in prison. The comparable figures for females were 6.2% and 0.7%. Obviously this sample is not representative of blacks in general. On the contrary, it is a substantially middle-class group which reflects a data-collection procedure that focused on socially active and community-oriented individuals.

Many analyses of code types, scale scores, and item-endorsement patterns of these data have been conducted. It would be premature to report any of the findings at this time, with two exceptions. First, it might be noted that the code types of this basically normal group, using Lachar's (1974) categories, are distributed as follows: normal, 50.8%; neurotic, 7.1%; characterological, 17.3%; psychotic, 18.8%; invalid (high *Q* or *F*), 4.2%; and other, 2.0%. Comparable figures for the Minnesota normative group are 78.3%, 10.1%, 4.4%, 4.2%, 0.2%, and 2.7%, respectively. Second, item analyses of these protocols revealed 33 items that met the 10% or less endorsement criterion used to develop the MMPI F scale (Gynther, Lachar, & Dahlstrom, 1978). White endorsement patterns agreed to a large extent with the blacks' F scale, but black endorsement patterns agreed with only one-third of the standard F-scale items. The amount of difference between responses of blacks and whites to rarely endorsed items suggested that for blacks (especially for middle-class members of this minority group), this new scale may be a more accurate measure of correlates associated with endorsement of deviant items than the standard F scale.

Summary: Research Findings and New Developments

Questions have continued to be raised about the presumed MMPI differences between blacks and whites. If one concentrates on new or older data obtained from normals, the differences and nature of the differences seem clear; however, data derived from patients is open to several interpretations. Further, some have found differences, but have then proceeded to show that the differences have no effect on diagnosis, narrative interpretation, or treatment. White's Rs scale may prove useful for removing "unwanted variance" from blacks' MMPIs. Lack of progress in the development of behavioral correlates of blacks' MMPIs is very disappointing, but the possibility of having black norms available is encouraging. Nonetheless, answers likely to be obtained via the MMPI will probably never sufficiently answer the questions that arise concerning the normal personality traits of any group. Hence, we now turn to relevant findings obtained with other instruments.

COMPARISONS OF BLACKS AND WHITES WITH OTHER INVENTORIES AND SCALES

CPI Studies. The California Psychological Inventory has been used in numerous comparisons of racial groups, but few of these studies have found their way into the published literature. A number of dissertations (e.g., Brown, 1973; Cross, 1975; Davidson, 1974; Howard, 1975) have contrasted blacks' and whites' CPI performance. Differences associated with race have been found in every case. Cross (1975) used as subjects 772 black and white freshmen and sophomores at two midwestern community colleges. He found that blacks obtained significantly lower scores than whites on Social Presence (Sp), Well-Being (Wb), Tolerance (To), Communality (Cm), Achievement via Independence (Ai), Intellectual Efficiency (Ie), and

Flexibility (*Fx*). Blacks achieved higher scores than whites on Self-Control (*Sc*) and Good Impression (*Gi*). Cross interpreted the *Sc, Gi* results as consistent with blacks' attempts to avoid negative reactions from the white majority, and, indeed, these scores would imply that blacks are more concerned about impulse management than whites. If the lower scores listed earlier are interpreted in the traditional manner, blacks would be viewed as less well-adjusted than whites, especially in terms of adaptive flexibility (*Ai, Fx, To,* and *Ie* have high loadings on this factor). However, little difference between blacks and whites in interpersonal effectiveness (except for *Sp*) would be implied by the pattern of CPI scale scores.

Cross (1975) also factor analyzed his data. He found striking differences in the factor structure of white and black males' CPI scores. The principal factor extracted for black males emphasized intrapersonal values such as impulse control, internalization of conventional values, and achievement via conformity, whereas the first factor for white males focused on interpersonal dimensions such as sociability, self-confidence, and high tolerance of stressful events. When factor structures of females' CPI results were compared, on the other hand, few differences were found. Cross (1975) interpreted these results as indicating that "the black female is more fully socialized into a stereotyped role than is the black male" (p. 67). He concluded that the differences found between black and white males are likely to work to the black male's disadvantage, especially men who are seeking opportunities in industry, colleges, and professional schools. (This study has now been published; see Cross, Barclay, & Burger, 1978.)

In a more recent study, Burger and Cross (1979) applied a Q-type factor-analytic strategy to the CPI protocols of several samples and found that black college students were classified significantly more often as constructively conventional and significantly less often as interpersonally ineffective than white college students. Approximately equal percentages of blacks and whites were classified as aggressively ascendant.

Brown's (1973) study was also carried out with college students. She found that tolerance, achievement via independence, and flexibility were the key differentiators between blacks and whites, with whites scoring higher. These results are strikingly similar to Cross's findings. She also factor analyzed her data and interpreted the results as indicating a significantly different underlying personality structure of blacks as a group. Davidson (1974) examined 12th graders in San Bernardino, California. He used the CPI, the Tennessee Self-Concept

Scale, and Rotter's I-E Scale. He found striking differences on these measures and stated that race, sex, and socioeconomic status were all significant factors. He reported, for example, that black females tend to be seen as passive, judgmental, and distrustful in social and personal outlooks. Finally, Howard (1975) also found that race was a significant discriminator for the CPI scales. She concluded that "the statistically significant general depression of scores on the CPI with regard to race introduces the question of overall social adjustment for blacks." This statement is reminiscent of Caldwell's (1954) and Ball's (1960) early MMPI articles, which reached similar conclusions on the basis of more elevated scores (but T scores less than 70) for blacks than whites.

 EPI (and ESPQ) Studies. Turning to other instruments, one finds that Jensen (1973) has analyzed the Junior Eysenck Personality Inventory scores of 2000 white, black, and Mexican-American 9 to 13-year-olds. He found that white children obtained higher Extroversion scores than blacks or Mexican-Americans over the entire age range and commented that "this is contrary to the popular stereotype of Negro children as being especially extroverted." There were no differences on Neuroticism, except in the 6th grade, where whites scored higher than the other two groups. On the Lie scale, the white children's scores were much lower than those of the black and Mexican-American children. Jensen stated that the Lie scale reflects a kind of naivete which is related to mental age, with higher mental ages achieving lower L scores and vice versa. When the Eysenck Personality Inventory was filled out by black and white adults in Detroit (Cameron, 1971), whites were found to be higher on Neuroticism, but no different from blacks on Extroversion or the Lie Scale. These results may be interpreted either as indicating lack of agreement with the Jensen study or as reflecting the personality changes that take place between childhood and adulthood. A large group which, as far as age is concerned, falls between the two just reported has also been examined via the EPI. Lowe and Hildman (1972) tested over 1600 college students in Mississippi. Black subjects obtained significantly lower Extroversion scores than whites. Furthermore, black males scored significantly lower than white males on the Neuroticism scale. The authors concluded that "race should be considered in score interpretation." Shade (1976) found that middle-class black children differed from the norms established for Cattell's Early School Personality Questionnaire, especially on measures of aloofness and shrewdness on which their scores were higher than whites. The black girls differed from the norms on twice as many of the factors as the boys did, leading the author to conclude that the "socialization of black girls . . . is substantially different from girls of other groups" (p. 273). This observation contrasts with that of Cross (1975), who noted that black and white males differed much more than black and white females.

Rating-Scale Studies. Clemente and Sauer (1976) obtained data from the National Opinion Research Center at the University of Chicago on a large-scale life satisfaction survey. Blacks scored significantly lower than whites on the four-item index used to measure this variable. It was also noted that race is a significantly more efficient predictor of life satisfaction among individuals 40 and over than for younger adults (18-39). Wen and McCoy (1976) found that black college students got significantly higher scores on the Taylor Manifest Anxiety Scale than the norms. Warheit, Holzer, and Arey (1975), in a long-range epidemiological study in the Southeastern United States, found that blacks obtained higher scores than whites on general psychopathology, phobias, anxiety symptoms, anxiety function, and depression. When controlled for socioeconomic level, however, only the difference on phobias remained. In every instance, socioeconomic status was the most powerful predictor of high scores.

Although the studies just cited appear to indicate that blacks have less life satisfaction, more anxiety, and more phobic symptoms than whites, numerous studies seem to indicate that blacks display less psychopathology than whites. For example, Lamont and Tyler (1973) found that black undergraduates reported significantly less depression than whites, Mexican-Americans, Japanese-Americans, or Chinese-Americans. Scott and Gaitz (1975), using Langer's screening scale of psychiatric symptoms with over 1400 white, black, and Mexican-American working- and lower-class adults, observed that whites reported significantly more symptoms, especially those related to anxiety, than either of the two minority groups at each age level. Whites expressed more positive and negative affect, followed by Mexican-Americans, with the least expression of either dimension by blacks. Perhaps the most interesting results were offered by Steele (1975) who evaluated the "depressive experience" in upper-class, upper-middle class, and lower-middle class gainfully employed personnel of various social service agencies. This investigator found no differences between blacks and whites on any of the depression measures, but numerous significant race by social-mobility interactions. Depression in whites was related to downward mobility, but for blacks susceptibility to depression was correlated with upward mobility. In addition, upwardly mobile blacks and downwardly mobile whites were more dependent, more externally controlled, and more self-critical, in comparison to all other groups.

Summary: Research Findings from the CPI and Other Instruments

In what ways do all these non-MMPI studies enlighten us regarding black-white MMPI differences? One point seems obvious, namely differences between blacks and whites are found on every inventory and questionnaire used. Those who would like to "explain away" racial MMPI differences as somehow due to educational, socio-economic, or subcultural factors should realize that if they should succeed in their endeavor, the MMPI would stand alone in its purity.

The second point is that the non-MMPI studies suggest that blacks-in-general differ from whites-in-general with regard to caution, defensiveness, shrewdness, and perhaps extroversion. These data also indicate that blacks are often passive, aloof, and tend to deny anxiety and depression. Yet there is evidence to indicate that some blacks are quite enthusiastic, self-confident, and emotionally stable. Is the mistrust and cynicism found for blacks via factor analysis of MMPI item differences an artifact of the many pathological statements in the MMPI, or is it really a prime characteristic of blacks?

The best evidence to date on this issue was recently reported by Jones (1978). This investigator gave 97 black and 129 white junior-college students Haan's (1965) coping and defense scales which were derived from both MMPI and CPI items. He found that 288 of the 361 items discriminated between blacks and whites, 175 at the .01 level or better. These latter items were subjected to cluster analysis resulting in ten reliable, independent clusters which accounted for 98% of the common variance. Statistical analyses of the cluster scores showed (in decreasing order of importance for racial differences) that blacks described themselves as more dominant and poised socially, more fundamentalist in their religious beliefs, more concerned with impulse management, more self-critical, psychologically tougher, more cynical and power-oriented, more conventional in moral attitudes, and more conforming than whites. Blacks also described themselves as less adventuresome and likely to take risks, and less vulnerable and tender psychologically than whites. These descriptors yield a more balanced picture of black personality than MMPI studies that have typically emphasized estrangement as the major factor distinguishing blacks from whites. Cynicism, self-criticism, and cautiousness are present, but so are dominance, poise, and toughness. More than half the items that fell into clusters in this study were from the CPI, which may account for the relatively balanced, "normal" portrait of blacks that emerged.

The third point that the CPI, EPI, and other data seem to convey is that although there probably are some basic personality differences between blacks and whites, generalizations must be tempered by numerous qualifications. Black males and females, for example, are often portrayed quite differently. Some traits seem more prevalent in children and adolescents, others are more prominent in adults. Poor and affluent blacks no doubt have different values. Brown (1973) found that black students at a predominantly white university obtained CPI scores more like their white counterparts than like other black students attending a predominantly black college. Gynther and Witt (1976) showed that black educators, especially females, feel more estranged, indulge in more impulse-ridden fantasy, are more self-conscious, and subscribe to more conservative religious beliefs than blacks with fewer educational and occupational advantages. The picture is very complex and may be changing over time. As Cronbach (1975) has said:

> A general statement can be highly accurate only if it specifies interactive effects that it takes a large amount of data to pin down. Some effects in the network will change in form, in the span of one or two generations, even before enough qualifying phrases have been added to describe the effect accurately (p. 126).

PERSONALITY STUDIES OF OTHER MINORITY GROUPS

Are the personality characteristics noted for blacks unique to blacks or simply like those one would find for any minority group in this country? To answer this question, inventory findings on three other groups will be surveyed. The first will be what has variously been called Mexican-American, Puerto Rican, or Spanish surname. The second will be American Indians, also called native Americans. The third will be Americans of Chinese, Japanese, or East Indian ancestry. To answer the question we have raised, the study should ideally include blacks, whites, and the third ethnic group. Comparisons of Mexican-Americans to whites alone, for example, would leave us in the dark concerning how similarly the minority groups responded to the inventory.

Mexican Americans. Padilla and Ruiz (1975), in a recent review, lamented the paucity of personality data on Mexican-Americans.

Covering the period from 1938 to 1974, they located only three studies that used objective inventories. Although differences were found, these writers felt that problems involving fluency in English obscured the findings. In addition to the Jensen (1973) and Scott and Gaitz (1975) articles discussed earlier, we found about 10 recent studies, seven of which were unpublished dissertations. Ewing (1971) examined relations between asocial behavior, anomie, and Jesness Inventory scores in black, white, and Mexican-American high-school boys. Values obtained by Mexican-Americans on all the measures except anomie closely resembled those found for the whites. Blacks' scores differed from those obtained by the other two ethnic groups. Jacobs (1975) studied black, white, and Chicano males selected randomly from alcoholic outpatient clinics in Los Angeles. All took the "short form MMPI." He concluded that with regard to personality characteristics, blacks differed significantly from both whites and Chicanos, who were relatively similar. McCreary and Padilla (1977) compared scale scores of white, Mexican-American, and black male offenders. Analyses of valid profiles obtained from Mexican-Americans and matched white offenders showed that the former subgroup obtained significantly higher scores on scales L and K and the Overcontrolled Hostility (OH) scale. Blacks and matched white offenders differed significantly on scales K, 3, and 9. Blacks obtained higher scores on scale 9 and lower scores on the other two scales. Weisenberg, Kreindler, Schachat, and Werboff (1975) gave white, black, and Puerto Ricans located in an outpatient dental emergency clinic the State-Trait Anxiety Inventory. Puerto Ricans had the highest trait anxiety scores, followed by blacks, then whites.

Some comparisons with fewer than three groups may also be noted. Plemons (1977) administered MMPIs to 40 bilingual Mexican-Americans and 109 Anglo-American psychiatric outpatients. There were controls for age, sex, socioeconomic status, and presenting problem. With K corrections, Mexican-Americans scored higher only on the L and K scales. Without K corrections, Mexican-Americans scored significantly lower on scales 4, 7, and 9. Fitch (1973) compared Spanish-American and Anglo-American adolescent girls on MMPI scales 1, 2, 3, and 0. He found no differences on the neurotic triad, mixed effects on scale 0, and concluded that his results did not indicate the existence of exclusive personality characteristics for statistical minority groups. Nagel (1975) evaluated the relations between anxiety and self-esteem in Spanish-surname children in grades 4 through 8. She concluded that the overall pattern of the relationships between general anxiety, test anxiety, and self-esteem is similar for

Spanish-surnamed children and the general population. Perez (1974) compared Puerto Rican college students to non-Puerto Rican college students of similar socioeconomic class on three scales of the CPI. The two groups were found to be very similar.

American Indians. Only three data sources compared Indians to non-Indians, in addition to the Bull (1976) thesis already mentioned. First, there is the work of Mason (1967, 1969, 1971), who gave the CPI to relatively small junior-high samples of American Indians, Mexican-Americans, and whites. There were marked differences between the groups: whites had the highest scale values, Mexican-American intermediate, and Indians the lowest. Then there is the Hoffman and Jackson (1973) study in which the Differential Personality Inventory was administered to Indian and non-Indian alcoholics. Indians scored higher on such scales as Cynicism, Self-Depreciation, and Ideas of Persecution. The authors recommended that separate norms be developed. Finally, Hiat (1976) gave the 16PF to 141 Pueblo children in grades 7-12. The mean scale scores, with very few exceptions, were not significantly different from those of the norm groups. Although Arthur's (1944) MMPI study of Indians took place when the basic scales were still in the process of development, very little work with objective personality inventories has followed it.

Asian-Americans. Sue and his colleagues (Sue & Kirk, 1972; Sue & Kirk, 1973; Sue & Sue, 1974) have published about half of all the articles comparing Asian-American to non-Asian-American subjects. These investigators (Sue & Kirk, 1972) compared Chinese-Americans to all other entering freshmen at the University of California by means of the Omnibus Personality Inventory. The Chinese-Americans were found to be more conforming, less extroverted, preferred concrete-tangible approaches to life, and experienced greater emotional distress than other students. When Japanese-Americans and Chinese-Americans were compared to others on the CPI (Sue & Kirk, 1973), it was noted that Chinese-Americans differed more than Japanese-Americans from scores of Caucasian college students. Sue and Sue (1974) also evaluated the MMPI scores of Asian and non-Asian students who visited a university psychiatric clinic. Asian males were significantly higher than non-Asian males on scales *L, F,* 1, 2, 4, 6, 7, 8, and 0, and Asian females were higher than non-Asian females on scales *L, F,* and 0. Conner (1974) administered the Edwards PPS to a large sample of Caucasian-Americans and Japanese-Americans. The latter group scored higher on deference, abasement, endurance, and lower on exhibition, dominance, and aggression than the Caucasians. Marsella, Sanborn, Kameoka, Shizuru, and Brennan (1975) asked students at the University of Hawaii to take five different depression measures. Overall, Chinese and Japanese females obtained the highest scores and Caucasian males the lowest scores, with the other subgroups falling in between. The only study that included blacks as well as whites in comparison with Asian-Americans is that of Lamont and Tyler (1973) which was mentioned previously. In that study, Japanese-Americans reported the most depressive symptomatology and blacks the least, with scores for Mexican-Americans, Chinese-Americans, and Caucasians falling between the extreme groups.

Summary: Research Findings on Other Minority Groups

Are the personalities of blacks distinguishable or indistinguishable from those of Mexican-Americans, American Indians, and Asian-Americans? Blacks and Mexican-Americans seem to respond differently to various personality inventories with the latter sometimes performing very similarly to white norms. Blacks may respond differently than American Indians, Japanese- and Chinese-Americans, but the evidence is too fragmentary to be certain. It is obvious that these other minority groups have been neglected even more than blacks by personality researchers.

WHAT PSYCHOLOGICAL VARIABLE IS RACE A SURROGATE FOR?

Sechrest (1976) in his chapter on Personality in a recent *Annual Review of Psychology* stated:

> Such variables as sex, race, socioeconomic status, and education are tempting additions to personality studies because they are easy to obtain, of obvious social importance, and misleadingly objective in measurement. Unfortunately, they are not *psychological* variables and they help very little in understanding most experimental outcomes; in fact, they present the danger of fostering erroneous interpretations and unjustified complacency. The problem with demographic variables in psychological studies is that they really end up being surrogate variables, but it is rarely possible to know for what real variables they are surrogates in any given case (p. 2).

Sechrest then gave examples of what he meant. Sex, he said, almost never is included as a variable because the investigator is interested in biological maleness or femaleness per se. What is of consequence are the patterns of attitudes or problems or abilities or interests that are presumed to go along with being male or female. Another example would be years of education. Sechrest stated that it cannot be of any psychological interest that someone has completed high school. Rather, completion of 12 years of school is taken as an index of social class, of intelligence, or motivation, or some other variable. What is the solution to this problem? Develop measures (or use those available) of the variables for which sex, education, and so on are surrogates. Thus, if one is interested in field-independence, then a direct measure should be included in the study.

I-E Locus of Control? Sechrest would presumably approve of using the MMPI *Mf* scale or the CPI *Fe* scale or Bem's (1974) Sex-Role Inventory as a substitute for gender. But what is race a surrogate for? Not a clue appears in Sechrest's (1976) article, though he does comment that not all blacks will have been disadvantaged. How might one go about discovering the psychological variable(s) concealed by the labels "black," "white," "Mexican-American," and so forth? One way would be to consider the major psychological variables and ask whether differences in them have been associated with race. Although there might be some disagreement, most authorities would probably list the following: anxiety, introversion-extroversion, aggression, locus of control, self-esteem, and possibly various cognitive styles. Locus of control seems the most attractive possibility for the following reasons: (1) no systematic differences between blacks, whites, or other ethnic groups have been found for anxiety, introversion-extroversion, aggression, or self-esteem; (2) differences have been demonstrated between blacks and whites on the internal-external dimension (typically, blacks obtained higher external scores, suggesting that they feel that what happens to them is not under their control); and (3) feeling helpless and at the mercy of fate or chance seems to be closely related to the estrangement, distantiation, or mistrust that item and factor analyses have shown is the principal differentiator between blacks' and whites' MMPI performance.

Different I-E Forms. If race is a surrogate for those expectancies associated with internal-external locus of control, then examination of studies of this dimension that compared racial groups should be of interest. Presumably, minority group members should get more external scores. However, it is not quite that simple. Rotter (1966) originally felt that locus of control was unidimensional and the generalization that blacks are more external than whites was established in terms of a single score. Lao (1970) later showed that there were at least two dimensions, namely personal control and ideological control. Among black college students in the deep South, for example, an "internal" belief in personal control was positively related to general competence. However, an "external" belief in social ideology, i.e., blaming the system for blacks' disadvantages in society, was related positively to creative, innovative behavior. More recently, Levenson (1974) has partitioned externality into belief in powerful others and chance. Different studies are unlikely to use exactly the same measurement procedure.

Ethnicity and I-E Scores. Examination of the abstracts from 1972 to 1976, inclusive, revealed 17 published articles or unpublished dissertations that compared whites and other ethnic groups on some version of the I-E scale. No studies compared American Indians or Chinese-Americans with Caucasians. One study (Garza & Ames, 1974) compared white and Mexican-American college students who were matched on socioeconomic background. Whites were significantly more external than the Mexican-Americans. Two studies (Bond & Tornatzky, 1973; Mahler, 1974) compared university students in Japan and the United States. In both cases, the Japanese obtained higher external scores. Where the Levenson version of the I-E scale was used, the Japanese disclosed that they felt more at the mercy of chance, but not under the control of powerful others. All but one of the other 14 studies used black and white subjects (the exception compared blacks in segregated schools with blacks in integrated schools), but several reported their data in such a way that I-E comparisons cannot be made. The box score for the remaining 10 studies (Butler, 1974; Fox, 1976; Garcia & Levenson, 1975; Jacobson, 1975; Jordan, 1973; Royer, 1976; Ryan, 1972; Segal & DuCette, 1973; Smith, 1975; Vail, 1974) is as follows: whites > blacks on E, 0, whites = blacks on E, 4, and blacks > whites on E, 6. Where no differences were found, the investigator most often used the unidimensional form of the instrument.

Summary: Race as a Surrogate for I-E Locus of Control

These results would certainly not permit one to argue that being black or white is somehow equivalent to having learned that events are contingent or noncontingent on one's behavior. That does not make sense. However, it does appear that this psychological variable is related to ethnic membership. It would be interesting to see what relationships exist between estrangement scores (Harrison & Kass, 1967), chance or powerful other externality scores (Levenson, 1974), and race-sensitive scores (White, 1974). Factor analysis of scores on these scales might reveal a personality dimension more powerfully related to race than any now known. One suggestion for those planning racial comparisons would be to partition subjects not only by the usual race, social class, and/or years of education, but also by scores on any of the race-sensitive variables just mentioned. It may well be that whites high on estrangement or externality would produce MMPI profiles more characteristic of blacks than blacks who achieve low scores on such scales. If that result were found, it would be a first step toward clarifying the psychological meaning of race.

CONCLUDING REMARKS

Recent work confirms previous observations that normal blacks present a different picture from normal whites on the MMPI. Item and factor analyses suggest that the differences are associated with different outlooks produced by different upbringing in psychologically different environments. Discontent, estrangement, and cynicism form a major portion of the "outlooks." When psychiatric patients are used as subjects, these differences tend to be obscured. Educational level, intelligence, and social status have been implicated as playing roles in black-white personality differences. There is no doubt that the differences are determined by a complex interaction of various factors. Some work suggests that the accuracy of automated narratives generated for psychiatric patients is not affected by race. Much more data are needed to confirm or reject this important relationship.

Examination of blacks' performance on other personality inventories and rating scales reveals, without exception, differences from whites' performance. The CPI results, in particular, suggest that blacks are more concerned than whites about making a good impression and impulse management at a possible cost in adaptive flexibility. Whites have also been found to be more extroverted than blacks. Blacks have admitted more phobias and anxiety, and less life satisfaction than whites; on the other hand, whites usually admit more symptoms than blacks, especially depression. Some new evidence suggests that young blacks may view themselves as more dominant and poised than their white counterparts. Attempts to see whether blacks' personalities differ from those of other minority groups in this country have not yet revealed an answer to this question. Mexican-Americans appear to differ from blacks, and Asian-Americans seem to differ from whites. More research involving at least three ethnic groups at a time is needed to clarify this issue.

We have considered Sechrest's argument that race, as well as other demographic variables, is a surrogate for some unknown psychological variable. Rotter's internal-external locus of control might serve this function. Suggestions were made to elucidate this issue.

White's device for adjusting blacks' MMPI profiles deserves an extensive trial, especially since no one is seriously trying to develop actuarial correlates for blacks' MMPI code types. Black MMPI norms, when available, should prove to be very helpful. Item endorsement tables, for example, will permit comparison of local samples, normal or deviant, with blacks-in-general rather than the less relevant Minnesota norms. In the final analysis, we are interested in having inventories that can accurately evaluate the personalities and problems of anyone whose situation legitimately calls for assessment and/or classification.

NOTES

1. An earlier version of this article titled "Personality inventory performance of various ethnic groups: Recent findings" was presented at the Twelfth Annual MMPI Symposium, St. Petersburg, Florida, on February 3, 1977.

2. Two additional studies with similar results have recently been reported (Patalano, 1978; Penk, Woodward, Robinowitz, & Hess, 1978).

REFERENCES

Arthur, G. An experience in examining an Indian twelfth-grade group with the MMPI. *Mental Hygiene*, 1944, 28, 243-50.

Ball, J. C. Comparison of MMPI profile differences among Negro-white adolescents. *Journal of Clinical Psychology*, 1960, 16, 304-7.

Bem, S. L. The measurement of psychological androgyny. *Journal of Consulting and Clinical Psychology*, 1974, 42, 155-62.

Bond, M., & Tornatzky, L. Locus of control in students from Japan and the United States: Dimensions and levels of response. *Psychologia: An International Journal of Psychology in the Orient*, 1973, 16, 209-13.

Brown, N. W. An investigation of personality characteristics of negroes attending a predominantly white university and negroes attending a black college. (Doctor's thesis, College of William and Mary, 1973). *Dissertation Abstracts International*, 1974, 34, 3980-A.

Bull, R. W. A tri-racial MMPI study. Master's thesis, University of North Carolina, 1976.

Burger, G. K., and Cross, D. T. Personality types as measured by the California Psychological Inventory. *Journal of Consulting and Clinical Psychology*, 1979, 47, 65-71.

Butcher, J. N., Ball, B., & Ray, E. Effects of socioeconomic level on MMPI differences in Negro-white college students. *Journal of Counseling Psychology*, 1964, 11, 83-87.

Butler, I. Self-concept: Race and social class in adolescent females. (Doctor's thesis, University of Washington, 1973). *Dissertation Abstracts International*, 1974, 34, 4034-B.

Caldwell, M. B. Case analysis method for the personality study of offenders. *Journal of Criminal Law, Criminology and Police Science*, 1954, 45, 291-98.

Cameron, P. Personality differences between typical urban negroes and whites. *Journal of Negro Education*, 1971, 40, 66-75.

Clark, C. G., & Miller, H. L. Validation of Gilberstadt and Duker's 8-6 profile type on a black sample. *Psychological Reports*, 1971, 29, 259-64.

Clemente, F., & Sauer, W. Racial differences in life satisfaction. *Journal of Black Studies*, 1976, 7, 3-10.

Conner, J. W. Value continuities and change in three generations of Japanese Americans. *Ethos*, 1974, 2, 232-64.

Costello, R. Item level racial differences on the MMPI. *Journal of Social Psychology*, 1973, 91, 161-62.

Costello, R. Construction and cross-validation of an MMPI black-white scale. *Journal of Personality Assessment*, 1977, 41, 514-19.

Costello, R., Fine, H., & Blau, B. Racial comparisons on the MMPI. *Journal of Clinical Psychology*, 1973, 29, 63-65.

Costello, R., Tiffany, D., & Gier, R. Methodological issues and racial (black-white) comparisons on the MMPI. *Journal of Consulting and Clinical Psychology*, 1972, 38, 161-68.

Cowen, M. A., Watkins, B. A., & Davis, W. E. Level of education, diagnosis and race-related differences in MMPI performance. *Journal of Clinical Psychology*, 1975, 31, 442-44.

Cronbach, L. J. Beyond the two disciplines of scientific psychology. *American Psychologist*, 1975, 30, 116-27.

Cross, D. T. Differential effects of ethnic membership, sex, and occupation on the California Psychological Inventory. (Doctor's thesis, St. Louis University, 1975.) *Dissertation Abstracts International*, 1976, 37, 1968-B.

Cross, D. T., Barclay, A., & Burger, G. K. Differential effects of ethnic membership, sex and occupation on the California Psychological Inventory. *Journal of Personality Assessment*, 1978, 42, 597-603.

Davidson, H. R. Personality characteristics of black high school students: An empirical and theoretical examination of interdisciplinary thought. (Doctor's thesis, California School of Professional Psychology, 1974). *Dissertation Abstracts International*, 1975, 35, 5104-B.

Davis, W. E. Race and the differential "power" of the MMPI. *Journal of Personality Assessment*, 1975, 39, 138-40.

Davis, W. E., Beck, S. J., & Ryan, T. A. Race-related and educationally-related MMPI profile differences among hospitalized schizophrenics. *Journal of Clinical Psychology*, 1973, 29 478-79.

Davis, W. E., & Jones, M. H. Negro versus Caucasian psychological test performance revisited. *Journal of Consulting and Clinical Psychology*, 1974, 42, 675-79.

Elion, V. H., & Megargee, E. I. Validity of the MMPI *Pd* scale among black males. *Journal of Consulting and Clinical Psychology*, 1975, 43, 166-72.

Erdberg, S. P. MMPI differences associated with sex, race and residence in a southern sample. (Doctor's thesis, University of Alabama, 1969). *Dissertation Abstracts International*, 1970, 30, 5236-B.

Ewing, D. B. The relations among anomie, dogmatism, and selected personal-social factors in asocial adolescent boys. *Journal of Social Issues*, 1971, 27, 159-69.

Fillenbaum, G. G., & Pfeiffer, E. The Mini-Mult: A cautionary note. *Journal of Consulting and Clinical Psychology*, 1976, 44, 698-703.

Fitch, R. S. Examination of selected MMPI profiles of four groups of Spanish-American and Anglo-American adolescent females. (Doctor's thesis, Baylor University, 1972). *Dissertation Abstracts International*, 1973, 33, 2936-A.

Fox, L. L. A comparative analysis of internal-external locus of control and sex-role concepts in black and white freshmen women. (Doctor's thesis, East Texas State University, 1975). *Dissertation Abstracts International*, 1976, 36, 5143-5144-A.

Garcia, C., & Levenson, H. Differences between blacks' and whites' expectations of control by chance and powerful others. *Psychological Reports*, 1975, 37, 563-66.

Garza, R., & Ames, R. A comparison of Anglo- and Mexican-American college students on locus of control. *Journal of Consulting and Clinical Psychology*, 1974, 42, 919.

Genthner, R. W., & Graham, J. R. Effects of short-term public psychiatric hospitalization for both black and white patients. *Journal of Consulting and Clinical Psychology*, 1976, 44, 118-24.

Gynther, M. D. White norms and black MMPIs: A prescription for discrimination? *Psychological Bulletin*, 1972, 78, 386-402.

Gynther, M. D. Item response differences and their implications. In J. R. Graham (Chair), *Minority status and MMPI scores: Empirical findings on normal blacks*. Symposium presented at the meeting of the American Psychological Association, Toronto, 1978.

Gynther, M. D., Altman, H., & Warbin, R. W. Interpretation of uninterpretable MMPI profiles. *Journal of Consulting and Clinical Psychology*, 1973, 40, 78-83. (a)

Gynther, M. D., Altman, H., & Warbin, R. W. Behavioral correlates for the MMPI 4-9, 9-4 code types: A case of the emperor's new clothes? *Journal of Consulting and Clinical Psychology*, 1973, 40, 259-63. (b)

Gynther, M. D., Lachar, D., & Dahlstrom, W. G. Are special norms for minorities needed? Development of an MMPI F scale for blacks. *Journal of Consulting and Clinical Psychology*, 1978, 46, 1403-8.

Gynther, M. D., & Witt, P. H. Windstorms and important persons: Personality characteristics of black educators. *Journal of Clinical Psychology*, 1976, 32, 613-16.

Haan, N. Coping and defense mechanisms related to personality inventories. *Journal of Consulting Psychology*, 1965, 29, 373-78.

Harrison, R. H., & Kass, E. H. Differences between negro and white pregnant women on the MMPI. *Journal of Consulting Psychology*, 1967, 31, 454-63.

Hedlund, J. L. MMPI clinical scale correlates. *Journal of Consulting and Clinical Psychology*, 1977, 45, 739-50.

Hiat, A. B. The relationship of socio-cultural variables to selected personality traits among a group of American Indians. (Doctor's thesis, University of New Mexico, 1975). *Dissertation Abstracts International*, 1976, 36, 5230-5231-B.

Hoffman, H., & Jackson, D. Comparison of measured psychopathology in Indian and non-Indian alcoholics. *Psychological Reports*, 1973, 33, 793-94.

Hokanson, J. E., & Calden, G. Negro-white differences on the MMPI. *Journal of Clinical Psychology*, 1960, 16, 32-33.

Howard, L. R. An exploratory analysis of differences in assertiveness and self-disclosure in blacks and whites. (Doctor's thesis, West Virginia University, 1975). *Dissertation Abstracts International*, 1976, 36, 5795-5796-B.

Jacobs, R. A study of drinking behavior and personality characteristics of three ethnic groups. (Doctor's thesis, California School of Professional Psychology, 1975). *Dissertation Abstracts International*, 1976, 36, 5796-B.

Jacobson, C. The saliency of personal control and racial separatism for black and white southern students. *Psychological Record*, 1975, 25, 243-53.

Jensen, A. R. Personality and scholastic achievement in three ethnic groups. *British Journal of Educational Psychology*, 1973, 43, 115-25.

Jones, E. E. Black-white personality differences: Another look. *Journal of Personality Assessment*, 1978, 42, 244-52.

Jordan, S. A comparison of black and white employees: Internal-external control expectancies (title abridged). (Doctor's thesis, Michigan State University, 1973). *Dissertation Abstracts International*, 1974, 34, 4729-B.

King, H. F., Carroll, J. L., & Fuller, G. B. Comparison of nonpsychiatric blacks and whites on the MMPI. *Journal of Clinical Psychology*, 1977, 33, 725-28.

Klinge, V., & Strauss, M. Effects of scoring norms on adolescent psychiatric patients' MMPI profiles. *Journal of Personality Assessment*, 1976, 40, 13-17.

Lachar, D. *The MMPI: Clinical assessment and automated interpretation.* Los Angeles: Western Psychological Services, 1974.

Lachar, D., Gynther, M. D., & Dahlstrom, W. G. *Minority status and test bias: A study of the relationship between ethnic membership and MMPI response and interpretation.* Book in preparation.

Lachar, D., Klinge, V., & Grisell, J. L. Relative accuracy of automated MMPI narratives generated from adult norm, and adolescent norm profiles. *Journal of Consulting and Clinical Psychology*, 1976, 44, 20-24.

Lachar, D., Schoof, K., Keegan, J., & Gdowski, C. Dimensions of polydrug use: An MMPI study. In D. Wesson, A. Carlin, K. Adams, & G. Beschner (Eds.), *Polydrug abuse: Results of a national collaborative study.* New York: Academic Press, 1978.

Lamont, J., & Tyler, C. Racial differences in rate of depression. *Journal of Clinical Psychology*, 1973, 29, 428-32.

Lao, R. C. Internal-external control and competent and innovative behavior among negro college students. *Journal of Personality and Social Psychology*, 1970, 14, 263-70.

Levenson, H. Activism and powerful others: Distinctions within the concept of internal-external control. *Journal of Personality Assessment*, 1974, 38, 377-83.

Lowe, J. D., & Hildman, L. K. EPI scores as a function of race. *British Journal of Social and Clinical Psychology*, 1972, 11, 191-92.

Mahler, I. A comparative study of locus of control. *Psychologia: An International Journal of Psychology in the Orient*, 1974, 17, 135-39.

Marks, P. A., Bertelson, A. D., & May G. D. Race and MMPI: Some new findings and considerations. Paper presented at the meeting of the American Psychological Association, San Francisco, California, August 1977.

Marsella, A. J., Sanborn, K. O., Kameoka, V., Shizuru, L., & Brennan, J. Cross-validation of self-report measures of depression among normal populations of Japanese, Chinese, and Caucasian ancestry. *Journal of Clinical Psychology*, 1975, 31, 281-87.

Mason, E. P. Comparison of personality characteristics of junior high students from American Indian, Mexican and Caucasian ethnic backgrounds. *Journal of Social Psychology*, 1967, 73, 145-55.

Mason, E. P. Cross-validation study of personality characteristics of junior high students from American Indian, Mexican and Caucasian ethnic backgrounds. *Journal of Social Psychology*, 1969, 77, 15-24.

Mason, E. P. Stability of differences in personality characteristics of junior high students from American Indian, Mexican and Anglo ethnic backgrounds. *Psychology in the Schools*, 1971, 8, 86-89.

McCreary, C., & Padilla, E. MMPI differences among black, Mexican-American, and white male offenders. *Journal of Clinical Psychology*, 1977, 33, 171-77.

Nagel, J. F. The relationship between anxiety and self-esteem among Spanish-surnamed children in grades four through eight. (Doctor's thesis, Northern Illinois University, 1975). *Dissertation Abstracts International*, 1976, 36, 6560-A.

Padilla, A. M., & Ruiz, R. A. Personality assessment and test interpretation of Mexican Americans: A critique. *Journal of Personality Assessment*, 1975, 39, 103-9.

Patalano, F. Personality dimensions of drug abusers who enter a drug-free therapeutic community. *Psychological Reports*, 1978, 42, 1063-69.

Penk, W. E., & Robinowitz, R. MMPI differences of black and white drug abusers. JSAS *Catalog of Selected Documents in Psychology*, 1974, 4, 50 (Ms. No. 630).

Penk, W. E., Woodward, W. A., Robinowitz, R., and Hess, J. L. Differences in MMPI scores of black and white compulsive heroin users. *Journal of Abnormal Psychology*, 1978, 87, 505-13.

Perez, A. A comparison of special admissions Puerto Rican students to low SES non-Puerto Rican college students on three variables: Self-concept, alienation and ethnic cohesion. (Doctor's thesis, State University of New York at Albany, 1974). *Dissertation Abstracts International*, 1975, 35, 6466-A.

Persons, R. W., & Marks P. A. The violent 4-3 MMPI personality type. *Journal of Consulting and Clinical Psychology*, 1971, 36, 189-96.

Plemons, G. A comparison of MMPI scores of Anglo- and Mexican-American psychiatric patients. *Journal of Consulting and Clinical Psychology*, 1977, 45, 149-50.

Ritzema, R. J. *The effect of demographic variables on the behavioral correlates of MMPI two point code types.* Master's thesis, Kent State University, 1974.

Rosenblatt, A. I., & Pritchard, D. A. Moderators of racial differences on the MMPI. *Journal of Consulting and Clinical Psychology*, 1978, 46, 1572-73.

Rotter, J. B. Generalized expectancies for internal versus external control of reinforcement. *Psychological Monographs*, 1966, 80, (1, Whole No. 609).

Royer, G. W. Relationship of internal, powerful others, and chance locus of control to race, socioeconomic class, sex and perceived teacher behavior. (Doctor's thesis, Ohio State University, 1975). *Dissertation Abstracts International*, 1976, 36, 7309-A.

Ryan, C. A. An examination of two internal-external locus of control dimensions and stated reinforcement preference in urban junior college students by SES and ethnic identity. (Doctor's thesis, Ohio State University, 1972). *Dissertation Abstracts International*, 1973, 34, 2316-2317-B.

Scott, J., & Gaitz, C. Ethnic and age differences in mental health measurements. *Diseases of the Nervous System*, 1975, 36, 389-93.

Sechrest, I., Personality. *Annual Review of Psychology*, 1976, 27, 1-27.

Segal, S., & DuCette, J. Locus of control and pre-marital high school pregnancy. *Psychological Reports*, 1973, 33, 887-90.

Shade, B. J. The modal personality of urban black middle-class elementary school children. *Journal of Psychology*, 1976, 92, 267-75.

Shore, R. E. A statistical note on "Differential misdiagnosis of Blacks and Whites by the MMPI." *Journal of Personality Assessment*, 1976, 40, 21-23.

Smith, G. A. Locus of control and differential reactions to interracial hostility among college students. (Doctor's thesis, Adelphi University, 1974). *Dissertation Abstracts International*, 1975, 36, 427-B.

Steele, R. E. Race, sex, and social class differences in depression among normal adults. (Doctor's thesis, Yale University, 1974). *Dissertation Abstracts International*, 1975, 36, 2485-2486-B.

Strauss, M. E., Gynther, M. D., & Wallhermfechtel, J. Differential misdiagnosis of blacks and whites by the MMPI. *Journal of Personality Assessment*, 1974, 38, 55-60.

Sue, D. W., & Kirk, B. A. Psychological characteristics of Chinese-American students. *Journal of Counseling Psychology*, 1972, 19, 471-78.

Sue, D. W., & Kirk, B. A. Differential characteristics of Japanese-American and Chinese-American college students. *Journal of Counseling Psychology*, 1973, 20, 142-48.

Sue, S., & Sue, D. MMPI comparisons between Asian-Americans and non-Asian-American students utilizing a student health psychiatric clinic. *Journal of Counseling Psychology*, 1974, 21, 423-27.

Sutker, P. B., Archer, R. P., & Allain, A. N. Drug abuse patterns, personality characteristics, and relationships with sex, race, and sensation seeking. *Journal of Consulting and Clinical Psychology*, 1978, 46, 1374-78.

Vail, I. I-E control, anxiety, frustration, and self-concept of achieving and under-achieving adolescent boys: A racial comparison. (Doctor's thesis, Fordham University, 1973). *Dissertation Abstracts International*, 1974, 34, 4062-B.

Warheit, G., Holzer, C., & Arey, S. Race and mental illness: An epidemiologic update. *Journal of Health and Social Behavior*, 1975, 16, 243-56.

Weisenberg, M., Kreindler, M., Schachat, R., & Werboff, J. Pain: Anxiety and attitudes in black, white and Puerto Rican patients. *Psychosomatic Medicine*, 1975, 37, 123-35.

Wen, S., & McCoy, R. Personal concerns and manifest anxiety in black students. *Journal of Clinical Psychology*, 1976, 32, 64-66.

White, W. G. A psychometric approach for adjusting selected MMPI scale scores obtained by blacks. (Doctor's thesis, University of Missouri, 1974). *Dissertation Abstracts International*, 1975, 35, 4669-B.

Witt, P. H., & Gynther, M. D. Another explanation for black-white MMPI differences, *Journal of Clinical Psychology*, 1975, 31, 69-70.

Use of the MMPI
with Medical Patients

David Osborne

I. EARLY USES

Very early in its history the MMPI was used to evaluate patients who had come to internists with physical complaints. Many of the early articles concerning the use of the MMPI with medical patients stated that from 30% to 70% of outpatients who sought medical attention had primarily neurotic complaints. As McKinley and Hathaway (1943) indicated, this did not mean that no concomitant organic disease was ever found; but frequently the physical complaint could not be related directly to the positive physical findings. They also pointed out that many patients with severe organic disease suffered concomitant emotional reactions that were a source of distress. Consideration of these problems was one of the factors that led to the development of the MMPI. McKinley and Hathaway initially used the MMPI with medical patients to distinguish functional from organic complaints; to identify a functional component in organic disease; and to deal with the emotional distress of patients with organic disease. These are quite similar to the purposes of those who currently use the MMPI with medical patients.

McKinley and Hathaway (1943) also addressed the reaction of medical patients to the MMPI. When the test was first used, there was some concern that the suggestion of symptoms and attitudes found in the inventory would upset patients; however, they reported very little reaction from the patients. Swenson, Rome, Pearson, and Brannick (1965) reported a similar experience. In a sample of 1,359 med-

141

ical patients who were asked to take the MMPI by an internist, 89.2% completed the test with no difficulty, 0.2% refused to cooperate, and 5.6% did not complete and return the test booklet. The remaining 5% of the patients were unable to cooperate (they were senile, acutely ill, nonreaders, etc.). It appears, therefore, that patients do accept the idea of completing a personality inventory as part of a medical evaluation. Swenson et al. (1965) used a questionnaire on the usefulness of the MMPI as part of a medical evaluation to survey 158 physicians who had used the MMPI for at least four months with all of their patients. All 14 items in the questionnaire produced a 70% to 85% endorsement of the test's utility. It appears, therefore, that the use of the MMPI as part of a medical evaluation is accepted by both patients and physicians.

Other early workers followed the lead of McKinley and Hathaway in recognizing the need to evaluate the emotional component of illness, and they presented cases in which the MMPI had been useful. In their 1943 article, McKinley and Hathaway presented four cases that illustrate the use of the MMPI. One was a 43-year-old man who had been admitted to the hospital for a probable ulcer. When the MMPI was administered, he obtained the following significant scores: *Hs* 87, *D* 83, *Hy* 78. All other scales were at normal levels. When he was interviewed further, it became apparent that neurotic factors were present. With a supportive approach and some control of the patient's diet, the symptoms of abdominal distress rapidly disappeared, and the risks of surgery were avoided. In another case, a 25-year-old woman presented with a variety of confusing neurologic symptoms. Examinations by physicians and neurologists were essentially negative. The physician's impression was that the patient's symptoms had a neurotic basis, but when she was given the MMPI, all scores were within normal limits. The highest score was on scale *Hs*, T score of 62. Eventually, the diagnosis of multiple sclerosis was made. McKinley and Hathaway used this case to make the point that when a neurotic basis for symptoms is suspected, a normal MMPI profile indicates the need for further medical evaluation. Other early papers (Houk, 1946; Kamman, 1947; Kamman & Kram, 1955) reported similar uses of the MMPI and provided further case examples of its utility in medical practice.

The first systematic study of the MMPI in medical practice was done by Guthrie (1950). Guthrie worked with an internist who used the MMPI with many of his patients. The internist took the history and recorded his impression before giving the test. Guthrie, whose sample included 365 men and 739 women, grouped the profiles according to two-point codes (the highest two clinical scales, with T scores above 54, derived from Hathaway's system). He then studied patient records in an attempt to develop a summary of the most frequently appearing physical and psychologic symptoms and the course of the disorders, and he presented summary descriptions for five code types. A validation study using 66 patients of a different internist supported Guthrie's original code-type descriptions. However, the population studied by Guthrie was not made up of all the patients seen by the internist over a given period: the internist selected cases based on his estimate of emotional difficulties. Consequently, these code-type descriptions may not hold true in a setting where all patients routinely take the MMPI.

Swenson and Pearson, at the Mayo Clinic, were faced with the need to develop a method for screening large numbers of medical patients for emotional problems. Because they thought that in previous studies of medical patients either a small number of subjects or a highly selected sample had been used, they were reluctant to generalize from these results. Therefore, they collected MMPI responses from a large number of medical patients, using automated techniques (Swenson, Pearson, & Osborne, 1973). At the time, 150,000 patients were being seen each year in the Mayo multispecialty group practice. The majority of the patients were middle-class midwesterners, and most of them came from within 400 miles of Rochester, Minnesota. During the period from 1962 to 1965, all patients seen by a group of internists at the Mayo Clinic were given the MMPI. The subjects were ambulatory outpatients, 16 years of age or older, who had sufficient reading ability in English to complete the MMPI. The physicians were conscientious in administering the MMPI to every patient who could possibly complete it, and the project continued until valid MMPI records of 50,000 medical patients had been collected.

An examination of mean scores indicated that medical patients obtained higher scores than the MMPI standardization group on a number of scales. They scored one standard deviation higher on scales *Hs*, *D*, and *Hy*. Therefore, one should not be surprised in clinical practice to find that the profile of a medical patient contains elevated scores. These should be interpreted with caution. The most common two-point code types in this population were 13 and 31. One should not conclude that these elevations were the result of emotional or physical illness. Swenson (1970) presented the mean profile of 833 males whose examination at the Mayo Clinic had revealed no symptom of any physical difficulty. Most of these patients were receiving annual physical examinations and had no medical complaints when the MMPI was administered. Even this group of patients exhibited elevations on scales *Hs* and *Hy*. It appears that when the MMPI is given as part of a medical evaluation, elevations on scales *Hs* and *Hy* can be expected and should be interpreted conservatively.

Using part of the Mayo Clinic sample, Colligan and Osborne (1977) examined the profiles of 659 female and 534 male medical patients who were less than 20 years of age. An analysis of year-by-year changes and comparison with nonmedical adolescent groups indicated that adolescent medical patients are different from other groups of adolescents in much the same way that adult medical patients are different from the adult population at large. As adolescent medical patients get older, their mean MMPI profile approaches the mean adult medical patient profile.

The Mayo sample has been used to provide medical patient norms on a variety of research scales. Swenson et al. (1973) provided raw score means and standard deviations for the 50,000 medical patients on 220 research scales. Osborne (1971) provided norms for male and female medical patients on two-factor scales developed by Block (1965) which measure ego resiliency and ego control. Schwartz (1972) reported normative information for medical patients on the repression-sensitization scale. These data have also been useful for comparing specific groups of medical patients. Osborne (1977a) compared the MMPIs of 94 pregnant women with those of female medical patients in the same age range. This type of comparison is more meaningful than comparison with the original Minnesota normals. Polley, Swenson, and Steinhilber (1970) compared rheumatoid arthritis patients with general medical patients. And the sample has been used to study emotional responses to various treatment procedures; for instance, Kutner (1978) studied the ability of the MMPI to predict recovery from surgery. These specific projects will be discussed later in this chapter.

II. PREDICTION OF FUNCTIONAL VERSUS ORGANIC DIAGNOSIS

The earliest reported use of the MMPI with medical patients was to identify neurotic illness and to assess the functional component of physical complaints. In medical settings, these are still the most common uses of the MMPI. Because large numbers of patients in a physician's practice have primarily psychologic problems or psychologic components in their physical illnesses, much research has been directed toward a simple method of identifying those psychologic problems.

Lair and Trapp (1962) investigated the utility of the MMPI in determining whether a patient's somatic symptoms were primarily organic, psychophysiologic, or functional. They studied MMPI profiles generated by patients in three groups: 20 patients with physical illnesses, 20 with psychophysiologic complaints, and 20 with neurotic problems. The groups were matched for age, education, and intelligence. The MMPI patterns were similar for all three groups. As hypothesized, the neurotic patients obtained the highest scores on the neurotic triad; the psychophysiologic patients obtained the next highest scores on these three scales; and the physically ill patients produced the lowest scores, but even their scores were significantly above normal levels. Lair and Trapp concluded that, although group differences are present on the MMPI profiles of these three groups, the large amount of overlap between the groups made predictions for an individual patient quite difficult. In evaluating the Lair and Trapp report, it would be helpful to know more about the specific diagnoses received by the patients in each group. If the study is to be relevant to the diagnostic process, patients should have complaints that might lead the diagnostician to suspect a functional basis. Chronicity of physical illness could be expected to raise the scores on the neurotic triad and increase the overlap between groups.

Gilberstadt and Jancis (1967) pursued the question of organic or functional diagnosis by using 13-31 MMPI profiles. They studied the presenting symptoms and disposition of male veterans applying for admission to a Veterans Administration hospital. Groups were formed on the basis of MMPI codes. The researchers found a high incidence of psychologic symptoms in the 13-31 group, and 7 of their 10 patients with the 13-31 code type had histories of chronic physical illness. They concluded, therefore, that it was not feasible to distinguish functional from organic complaints by using the 13-31 code type. But they did note that, as in previous studies, it was likely that profiles with higher elevations on scales 1 and 3 were obtained from patients who were being treated as psychiatric cases.

Schwartz and Krupp (1971) studied the 13-31 profile in the 50,000 MMPIs collected at the Mayo Clinic. They selected 60 male and 60 female profiles that matched slightly modified Marks and Seeman rules, and they divided the profiles into three groups on the basis of the elevation of scales *Hs* and *Hy*. The high, medium, and low groups were formed arbitrarily to place 20 males and 20 females in each group. They then abstracted the medical records for each of the patients to obtain medical diagnoses and all symptoms and complaints reported to the physician. The diagnoses were categorized into three groups: (1) organic diagnosis only, (2) functional or nonorganic diagnosis only, (3) mixed, including at least one organic and one functional diagnosis. Their purpose was to determine the relationship between the 13-31 code type and diagnosis, and, in addition, to test the statement made by Gilberstadt and Jancis (1967) that a higher elevation on scales *Hs* and *Hy* was more likely to be obtained from a patient with emotional difficulties. They concluded that the elevation of these scales was not significantly related to the likelihood of receiving a functional diagnosis. In other words, there were no significant differences between the elevation groups in the number of patients who received functional diagnoses.

In their article, Schwartz and Krupp (1971) suggested the use of moderator variables to increase the accuracy of predictions based on the 13-31 profile. Schwartz, Osborne, and Krupp (1972) followed up this suggestion by evaluating the moderating effects of age and sex on the prediction of medical diagnosis from the 13-31 MMPI profile. From 1,398 profiles at the Mayo Clinic that were classified as 13-31 by Halbower's rules, they selected a random sample of cases, stratified on the basis of age, which comprised 178 medical patients (86 males and 92 females). The patients were classified into three diagnostic categories: organic, psychologic, and mixed. The frequency of patients with the 13-31 profile in each of the three diagnostic categories was tabulated for sex and age.

It was found that age was a highly significant moderator variable within each sex. Given the presence of the 13-31 profile in males, younger men had a fairly even chance of falling into the psychologic, mixed, or organic category. Older men (beyond age 50) were highly likely to fall into the organic category. Women more than 45 years old had a fairly even chance of falling into any one of the three diagnostic categories. Younger women, on the other hand, were much more likely to fall into the psychologic category.

These results suggest that a functional or organic diagnosis cannot be predicted for either a younger male or an older female from a 13-31 profile. A younger female with this profile might best be predicted to have a psychologic diagnosis, while an older male with the profile might best be predicted to have an organic diagnosis only. The authors reported that 39% of the patients with 13-31 profiles received organic diagnoses, 34% received functional diagnoses, and 28% received mixed functional or functional-psychologic diagnoses.

These base rates point out the difficulty of interpreting the conversion V as an indicator of a functional disorder.

Calsyn, Louks, and Freeman (1976) suggested a new approach to the problem of functional versus organic diagnosis. Their experience with patients having chronic low back pain suggested that the complaints of most were neither functional nor organic exclusively. Their largest group of patients had pain with an organic basis that was clearly established but not sufficient to explain their reported degree of pain-associated behavior. The authors called this their mixed group, and they recommended that the tendency to dichotomize functional and organic pain should be deemphasized. They suggested that organic and psychologic factors in pain combine to produce the observed level of pain behavior. From a population of 62 VA patients who complained of low back pain, two groups were formed: an organic group in which the orthopedic physicians judged the organic cause to be appropriate to the reported pain level and a mixed group in which the orthopedic physicians found an organic basis for pain but thought that the organic cause did not account fully for the pain level reported. As previous studies would suggest, the mixed group had deviant responses on scales Hs, D, and Hy. They also scored higher on scale Pt. Ego strength was lower in the mixed group, and, as would be expected, the low-back-pain scale was significantly higher in the mixed group. Attempts to use the low-back-pain scale and the DOR scale to distinguish between the two groups resulted in high false-positive rates—that is, too many patients with a mixed diagnosis were placed in the organic group.

Numerous studies have been devoted to the use of the MMPI with neurologic patients. As McKinley and Hathaway pointed out in 1943, multiple sclerosis can present an extremely difficult diagnostic problem early in its course; since then, a number of attempts have been made to use the MMPI in diagnosing multiple sclerosis. Hovey (1964) reported the use of five MMPI items to identify patients with brain lesions, but several attempts to validate the Hovey index produced contradictory results (Jortner, 1965; Weingold, Dawson, & Kael, 1965, Zimmerman, 1965). Then Hovey (1967), using two additional items, attempted to distinguish cases of multiple sclerosis, cases of central-nervous-system disorders, and psychiatric cases in which central-nervous-system dysfunction had been suspected but organic problems had been ruled out. Using a cut-off score of five out of seven items answered in the scored direction, he was able to identify 64% of the multiple-sclerosis group and 28% of the central-nervous-system group. Although these figures are not high, Hovey stressed that not one member of the control group was misidentified.

Dodge and Kolstoe (1971) attempted to use the MMPI, including Hovey's index and the Pseudoneurologic Scale (Shaw & Matthews, 1965), to distinguish patients with early multiple sclerosis from patients with conversion hysteria. They were not able to do so with the clinical scales of the MMPI. Hovey's index correctly classified only 4 of the 14 early multiple-sclerosis cases and correctly identified only 8 of the 12 conversion-hysteria cases as having a nonorganic basis. The Pseudoneurologic Scale served somewhat better; it correctly identified 10 of the 14 early multiple-sclerosis patients and 11 of the 13 conversion-hysteria patients.

Schwartz and Brown (1973) did a similar study with larger groups: 70 multiple-sclerosis patients (28 men and 42 women) and 61 pseudoneurologic patients (25 men and 36 women) who had been referred for neurologic examination but had not yet been given a neurologic diagnosis. Hovey's seven items and the Pseudoneurologic Scale were used in an attempt to distinguish between the two groups. The Pseudoneurologic Scale, with the usual cut-off score of seven or greater to indicate pseudoneurologic classification, correctly identified 71% of the multiple-sclerosis patients but only 59% of the pseudoneurologic group. Duration of multiple-sclerosis symptoms was not related to errors of classification. By varying cut-off scores to isolate extreme groups on the Pseudoneurologic Scale, the authors were able to increase the percentage of accurate predictions; but this left a large group for whom no predictions were made. The seven Hovey items did not prove useful in discriminating between the two groups.

The recent development of surgical procedures to treat organic impotence has made it necessary to find effective ways of sorting organic from psychogenic factors in impotence. Beutler et al. (1975) studied 32 males—15 with psychogenic impotence and 17 with organic impotence. Nocturnal penile tumescence tests were used to determine the etiology of the impotence. Mean MMPI profiles did not distinguish the two groups; but inspection of the MMPI profiles from a subset of the patients indicated that four of six patients in the psychogenic group and only one of four patients in the organic group produced an Mf T score above 60. All six psychogenic patients and only one organic patient had any scale score above 70. Application of this index ($Mf > 60$ and any score > 70) to the remaining 22 patients in the sample resulted in correct categorization of 90% (8 of 9 psychogenic cases and 12 of 13 organic cases). This procedure, of course, needs to be validated with a larger sample.

Results of the studies reviewed here suggest that, although patients with organic diagnoses produce different mean profiles than patients with functional diagnoses, the differences cannot be relied upon to identify individual members of either group. Most of the procedures attempted have resulted in too large a number of misclassifications. Some studies suggest that age and sex, considered along with the MMPI profile, can help in the discrimination. It is also possible that particular items on the MMPI might be found that would moderate the prediction of organic versus functional diagnoses—that is, would divide the groups into those for whom accurate predictions can be made and those for whom they cannot. As suggested by Gilberstadt and Jancis (1967), this prediction might be, at least in part, a function of factors to which personality tests are not particularly sensitive.

III. RESPONSE TO TREATMENT

There have been many attempts to use the MMPI in prediction or assessment of the response to medical treatment. Beardsley and Puletti (1971) administered the MMPI and the Wechsler Adult Intelligence Scale to two groups of patients with Parkinson's disease. A group of 18 patients took these tests before and after treatment with levodopa, and a group of 12 patients (controls) took them before and after other treatments for the disease (anticholinergic drugs or thalamotomy, or both). With approximately 6 months between test administrations, the investigators found no significant group differences on the MMPI clinical scales. Clinical reports of mood and behavior disturbances associated with long-term levodopa therapy led Maskin, Riklan, and Chabot (1973) to study the differences between a group of 15 patients who had been taking levodopa for less than 18 months and a group who had been taking the drug for more than 24 months. A normal control group made up of hospital employees was also used. The groups were quite similar in sex, age, length of illness, education, dosage of levodopa, and severity of symptoms. MMPI scales D and K were compared, along with some other measures. Mean scores on scale D were significantly higher in the long-term group than in either the short-term or the control group. The investigators concluded that the initial psychologic improvement with levodopa therapy does not continue after two years of treatment and that a deterioration in mood and self-concept appeared after this length of time.

In an attempt to predict which patients might benefit from a behaviorally oriented rehabilitation program for chronic pain behavior, Maruta, Swanson, and Swenson (1978) examined differences between groups of patients who, one year after completing a pain-management program, were judged to have succeeded or failed. Success was judged by a psychologist, a psychiatrist, and a specialist in physical medicine, using three categories: attitude modification, reduction of medication, and improvement in physical function. Among 188 patients, 34 were given the highest rating by all judges and 35 were judged as complete failures by all three judges. These were the two groups studied. Statistical evaluation indicated that many nontest factors predicted success or failure. Duration of pain, work time lost, number of surgical procedures, subjective pain level, and drug dependency differentiated the two groups. MMPI T scores greater than 80 on scales *Hs* and *Hy* also helped in the prediction of failure. It is not clear from this report how much the prediction was improved by the use of the MMPI.

Several studies have used the MMPI for predicting response to surgical procedures or evaluating the psychologic effect of surgery. Ziegler, Rodgers, and Kriegsman (1966) studied the effect of vasectomy on psychologic functioning. A series of 46 men completed the MMPI after being accepted for vasectomy by private practicing urologists, and 35 of these patients completed the MMPI and follow-up questionnaires 12 to 15 months postoperatively. Even though the couples unanimously expressed satisfaction with the operation and its outcome, the MMPI suggested an increase of psychopathology and defensiveness in the men. Significant increases were found on seven of the clinical scales of the MMPI and on scale *K*.

Henrichs and Waters (1972) used the MMPI to study response to open-heart surgery. They classified preoperative MMPIs from 81 open-heart-surgery patients into groups designated as depressed, symbiotic, denying anxiety, adjusted, and significant psychologic disturbance. They reported high reliability for their classification system and stated that 97% of the total group of patients could be so classified. In comparison with previously established base rates for psychiatric complications following open-heart surgery, it was found that female patients in the adjusted category had a significantly lower probability of these complications. For male patients, predictions based on these categories yielded no significant difference from base rates.

In an attempt to predict survival of open-heart surgery, Kilpatrick et al. (1975) administered a battery of intellectual and personality tests, including the MMPI, preoperatively, to 15 patients scheduled for open-heart surgery and 72 patients for open-heart surgery with extracorporeal circulation (a higher-risk procedure). Test data, including the MMPI results, were evaluated for their ability to predict survivor or fatality status. Among both groups together, none of the MMPI validity or clinical scales, nor scales *A*, *R*, and *Es*, showed any significant difference between survivors and nonsurvivors. Examination of MMPI profiles from those patients who underwent the higher-risk procedure once again resulted in no significant differences between survivors and nonsurvivors on any of the MMPI scales.

Lair and King (1976) studied this same problem by analyzing preoperative MMPIs from 20 patients who responded successfully to open-heart surgery and 10 patients who died during or immediately after such surgery. They found no significant differences between survivors and nonsurvivors among the male patients in their sample. Among females, those who died during open-heart surgery had significantly higher elevations on scales *Hs* and *Hy* than did the survivors. All three of the women who died had an elevated conversion V profile. The authors concluded that for females, a 1-3 profile before surgery is predictive of mortality. It should be noted that there were only 3 female nonsurvivors and that 5 of the 13 female survivors also had elevations on scales *Hs* and *Hy*. Clearly, studies of personality factors in recovery from surgery must use larger groups of subjects.

Kutner (1978), in his review of studies of personality and recovery from surgery, discussed the difficulty of finding an appropriate criterion variable. The number of postsurgical days until dismissal from the hospital has been used in some studies. It appears, however, that dismissal is often an administrative rather than a medical decision. This has become increasingly true with the advent of PSRO and Utilization Review. Days until ambulation is often inappropriate, since patients are strongly encouraged to walk as soon as possible after most types of surgery. Hence there is little variation for patients having the same type of surgery. Days until temperature stabilizes is an inappropriate criterion: it is difficult to imagine the MMPI predicting postoperative infection or other conditions that would keep temperature elevated. Kutner chose the number of postoperative analgesic administrations in his study of personality factors influencing recovery from cholecystectomy. He demonstrated that, for his group of patients, there was sufficient variability to justify this criterion, although surgeons increasingly are prescribing postoperative medication on a regular schedule rather than as circumstances indicate.

Kutner (1978) employed this criterion variable in studying 243 cholecystectomy patients who had taken the MMPI shortly before surgery at the Mayo Clinic during the early 1960s. Use of the MMPI scales did not enable him to discriminate patients who received large numbers of analgesic administrations from those receiving small numbers. He found, however, that groups of individual MMPI items were able to discriminate between the two groups. A factor analysis of these items yielded the following results. The first factor appeared to be measuring sociopathic tendencies. Patients obtaining high scores on this factor requested large numbers of analgesics. He called his second factor "worry." Those who had high scores on this factor were likely also to require high levels of analgesics. The third factor, which he called "moralistic thinking," produced a high score for those patients who used few analgesic medications. Examination of these factors suggests that the conventional, moralistic, and non-worrying patients require fewer medications after surgery. These factors may measure attitudes and behavior related to use of medication rather than recovery from surgery.

Use of the MMPI to predict response to medical and surgical treatment has yielded some positive results. Although Maruta et al. (1978) found no significant differences on the MMPI between a failure and a success group in a pain-management program, they reported that extreme elevations on Hs and Hy help in predicting failure. The finding of preoperative-postoperative MMPI differences in vasectomy (Ziegler et al., 1966), the prediction of postsurgical emotional complications by using the MMPI (Henrichs & Waters, 1972), and the identification of items that predict postsurgical use of medication (Kutner, 1978) indicate some promising future directions for research and application.

IV. EMOTIONAL ASPECTS OF ILLNESS

Several investigators have used the MMPI to investigate the emotional factors involved in susceptibility to and recovery from physical illness. Bakker and Levenson (1967) evaluated 256 patients with arteriosclerotic heart disease, comparing those patients who had angina pectoris with those who did not. The MMPI was administered twice — initially during the author's initial contact with the patient and then on a six-month follow-up visit. On the initial MMPI, the group with angina had obviously higher scores on scales *Hs* and *Hy* (*p* < .05). During the next six months, angina developed in six of the patients who had not had it initially; and these six, in the second round of testing, had *Hs, Hy,* and *Hy* (obvious) scores higher than those of the patients still without angina (*p* < .05). Interpretation of these findings is complicated by the fact that the angina and non-angina groups differed significantly on a number of other variables. For example, the group with angina was more likely to have had fewer than 10 years of education, an unstable work record, and a lower-status job. These variables would be expected to influence MMPI scores.

In a 1968 study, Byrne, Steinberg, and Schwartz examined the relation between repression-sensitization and physical illness. On the basis of past findings that illness was related to stress and on indications that extreme repression involved negative physiologic consequences, they hypothesized that both sensitizers and repressors would have more frequent and more severe illnesses than persons occupying the neutral position between those groups—a curvilinear relationship. They administered the repression-sensitization scale and a health survey to two samples of undergraduates. The curvilinear hypothesis was not supported. Sensitizers had a greater frequency or severity of psychosomatic complaints and a greater total number of complaints than repressors. In a second study reported in the same article, 85 extreme scorers on the repression-sensitization scale were investigated with respect to the number of visits made to a university health center during one academic year. Among male students, sensitizers did seek medical help significantly more often than repressors, thus confirming the findings of the initial study. Among females, health-center visits were unrelated to repression-sensitization scores. These findings might suggest that repressors and sensitizers either have physiologic differences affecting susceptibility to illness or have different ways of viewing and dealing with illness. A sensitizer, for example, might be more likely to go to a clinic with a physical complaint than a repressor, who might avoid dealing with the complaint.

In another study, Schwartz, Krupp, and Byrne (1971) investigated the relationship between repression-sensitization and diagnosis in medical patients. The 366 subjects were selected at three age levels (20-29, 40-49, and 60-69) and three repression-sensitization levels (repressors, neutrals, and sensitizers), from the sample of 50,000 patients at the Mayo Clinic who took the MMPI in the project reported by Swenson et al. (1973). The repressors were found to have more purely organic diagnoses, whereas the sensitizers more often received diagnoses involving psychologic components.

In a study examining the MMPI correlates of disability in multiple sclerosis, Davis et al. (1971) found that significant disability was more frequent among patients whose *Hy* score exceeded their *Pt* score than among those whose *Hy* was lower than their *Pt*. This finding held for both vocational disability and general disability. The authors discussed several possible explanations for these results. Investigation of the *Hy-Pt* index should be extended to groups with other chronic debilitating diseases. Since this was a correlational study, it is not known whether the use of repressive defenses resulted in or was caused by greater disability.

The panic-fear scale of the MMPI, which was developed to predict scores on the panic-fear dimension of the Asthma Symptom Checklist, has been used to investigate intractability and chronicity in respiratory disease. Dirks, Jones, and Kinsman (1977a) investigated in asthmatics the relationship of the panic-fear scale to recommended dismissal drug regimens. They found that patients scoring high on the MMPI panic-fear scale were more often assigned larger and more frequent doses than those with low scores, although mean levels of pulmonary functioning did not differ between the groups. In a second study (Dirks et al., 1977b) scores on the panic-fear scale were found to have a relationship to the length of hospitalization among 65 cases of asthma and 83 cases of tuberculosis. This scale was found to be independent of pulmonary-function measurements in asthma and of bacteriologic and drug resistance in tuberculosis. The investigators concluded that the MMPI panic-fear scale is related to personality factors that influence medical intractability of chronic respiratory illness.

Several investigators have hypothesized psychogenic factors in the onset and development of cancer (Greene, 1966; Schmale & Iker, 1966). Watson and Schuld (1977) argued that much of the research used to support psychogenic theories of cancer suffers from methodologic weaknesses. They studied the MMPI responses of male psychiatric patients in a VA hospital whose diagnoses of malignant or benign neoplasms were made at least two years after taking the MMPI; and they compared them to responses of control subjects— male psychiatric patients in the same hospital with no neoplastic disease, each within five years of the age of a paired neoplastic subject. After a few subjects were dropped for the purpose of equating validity scale scores on the MMPI, there remained 17 pairs for the malignant/control comparison and 26 pairs for the benign/control comparison. There were no significant differences between mean clinical scale scores for the malignant/control comparison. Only 1 of 20 comparisons yielded a significant difference. In this case the benign neoplasm group obtained a lower mean score on scale *Hs* than did the benign controls. One significant difference out of 20 is a less-than-chance finding; therefore, the authors interpreted these results as not supporting the view that the MMPI can predict the development of neoplasms. An item analysis also failed to yield descriptions for personality characteristics that could be used to identify premorbid subjects.

A review of research involving emotional aspects of illness points to repression-sensitization as needing further investigation. The finding that medical patients who use repressive defenses tended to have purely organic diagnoses, whereas sensitizers more often received diagnoses involving psychologic components, has some similarity to the finding that panic-fear (which presumably is at the sensitizing end of the repression-sensitization scale) is related to intractability, length of hospitalization, and drug dosage in respiratory disease. Further investigation of these factors offers some promise of increasing our understanding of the emotional aspects of physical illness.

V. MMPI PROFILES OF MEDICAL PATIENT GROUPS

Most MMPI articles related to medical patients present the mean MMPI profile of patients with a given disease. These profiles are compared with those of a normal control group, a mixed medical control group, or a group of patients with a different disease. Generally, the information provided by these articles is not useful clinically, since there is usually a high degree of overlap between the control and patient groups. There is also a high degree of similarity in the MMPI profiles of patients with various diseases. Since in most of these studies the MMPI was given to patients who already had a disease, we cannot separate personality factors that might lead to development of the disease from factors that are reactions to the specific disorder or to illness in general.

West (1970) administered the MMPI to 56 patients suffering from ulcerative colitis and 122 controls who were hospitalized with a variety of psychosomatic illnesses. As would be expected, both groups of patients had elevated scores on scales *Hs, D,* and *Hy.* Group comparison, however, indicated significant differences on scales *F, Hs, D, Pd, Pt, Sc,* and *Si.* The mixed psychosomatic group received higher scores on all of these scales. West concluded that ulcerative colitis patients were significantly less disturbed psychologically than psychosomatic patients. In an attempt to identify the personality characteristics of patients with inflammatory bowel disease, McMahon et al. (1973) used clinical interviews as well as MMPI scores of 13 patients and a healthy sibling of each. The patients obtained significantly higher scores on scales *Hs* and *Hy* than did their healthy siblings.

A number of studies have focused on the MMPI profiles of patients with rheumatoid arthritis. Nalven and O'Brien (1964) presented the MMPI profiles of 35 female and 10 male outpatients with rheumatoid arthritis. They described the mean MMPI profile as "a classically neurotic pattern with major elevations on the Hypochondriasis, Depression and Hysteria scales." They believed that these elevated scores might, in part, be the result of specific symptoms of rheumatoid arthritis. In order to evaluate this assumption, they asked three experienced rheumatologists to respond to the 121 items contained in the *Hs, D,* and *Hy* scales, as if they were patients with rheumatoid arthritis but with normal psychologic adjustment. Among those items were 18 that all three rheumatologists agreed were relevant to rheumatoid arthritis; and the authors, comparing the responses to these 18 by the rheumatologists and the patients, concluded that only part of the elevation in the neurotic triad was the result of accurate reporting of somatic complaints.

An article by Polley et al. (1970) contrasted the MMPI responses of 726 patients with rheumatoid arthritis with those of the 50,000 general medical patients included in the Mayo sample and with those of 1,576 patients who were examined by a physician but had no medical complaints and no abnormal findings. The patients with rheumatoid arthritis obtained significantly higher scores on scales *Hs, D,* and *Hy* than patients in either the general medical group or the no-medical-complaint group. The authors concluded that the MMPI differences between patients with rheumatoid arthritis and other patients "are most readily explained on the basis of the symptoms and effects of a disease that is chronic, painful, and potentially disabling to various degrees."

Mean MMPI profiles for various neurologic diseases have been determined. Schwartz and Cahill (1970) presented a mean profile based on the MMPI responses of 7 males and 10 females with myasthenia gravis. Their subjects were patients who had volunteered to participate in a group counseling program, and, therefore, might not have been representative of the total population of patients with myasthenia gravis. Elevations above T score 70 were found on scales *Hs, D,* and *Hy.*

Multiple sclerosis has been a subject of considerable study with the MMPI. An early investigation (Canter, 1951) studied 33 male veterans of World War II who were in the early stages of multiple sclerosis. The mean age of the group was approximately 32, and the mean duration of symptoms four years. As is true in many studies of medical patients, highly elevated scores were found on scales *Hs, D,* and *Hy* (mean T scores 81, 79, and 75, respectively). Shontz (1955) administered the MMPI to a group of 16 patients hospitalized for multiple sclerosis and compared their mean profile to that of 16 age-matched patients hospitalized at the same institution for other chronic illnesses. Significant differences between the two groups were found on scales *Hs* and *Hy.* The profile of this multiple-sclerosis group was found to be quite similar to that obtained by Canter. Matthews, Cleeland, & Hopper (1970) compared 30 patients with multiple sclerosis to 30 individually matched patients with verified central-nervous-system impairment other than multiple sclerosis. The multiple-sclerosis group received a significantly higher T score on scales *Hs* and *Sc.* None of the other MMPI validity or clinical scales yielded a significant difference.

Boll, Heaton, and Reitan (1974) presented a number of neuro-psychologic test results and MMPI findings for patients with Huntington's chorea. They concluded that "MMPI profiles yielded strikingly consistent similarities between patients with Huntington's chorea and patients with equal ability deficit due to other types of brain damage."

The relationship between MMPI scores and menstrual irregularity was studied by Hain et al. (1970). The MMPI and a menstrual-history questionnaire were administered to 71 first-year nursing students. Extreme groups were formed of women with regular menstrual periods (21 members) and irregular menstrual periods (11 members); their MMPI scores were compared. (Premenstrual distress was significantly correlated with irregularity, and, therefore, the results obtained could be the result of either irregularity or the premenstrual symptoms.) Comparison of scores on the 3 validity and 10 clinical scales indicated significantly higher scores for the irregular group on scales *Hs, Pa, Sc,* and *Ma.* The regular group had higher scores on scale *K.*

Gruba and Rohrbaugh (1975) studied the MMPI correlates of various types of menstrual distress. Their subjects were 60 female undergraduate students who completed a menstrual questionnaire and an MMPI at the same time in the menstrual cycle. There were significant positive correlations between premenstrual symptoms and scales *Hs, Hy, Pt,* and *Sc*; but there was no significant correlation between MMPI scores and symptoms that occurred during the menstrual period.

Hooke and Marks (1962) compared MMPI characteristics of 24 women in the eighth month of their first pregnancy with those of the normative group reported by Hathaway and Briggs (1957). The mean MMPI profile of the subjects is well within normal limits; and the authors concluded that pregnancy is a time of good psychologic adjustment and emotional health, even though the pregnant women had significantly higher scores than the female norm group on five of the clinical scales (*Hy, Pd, Pa, Sc,* and *Ma*).

Osborne (1977a, 1977b, 1978) studied 94 women in the first trimester of pregnancy, comparing their mean MMPI profile with the mean profile of 1,690 female medical patients (all women between the ages of 20 and 29 years from the Mayo sample reported by Swenson et al., 1973). Osborne believed that female medical patients were a better comparison group than the female normative sample, since the pregnant women were experiencing physical symptoms and were seeing a physician regularly. On all clinical scales except *Pa* and *Si*, the female medical-patient group had significantly higher scores than the pregnant group. Scores on *Pa* and *Si* were not significantly different. The pregnant group had a lower mean T score than the medical patients on scale *F*. When the MMPI was readministered to the same 94 pregnant women in the third trimester, their scores were significantly lower than those of the medical group on scales *F, D, Mf,* factor *A*, and Tired Housewife (a scale developed at the Mayo Clinic which contains items reflecting the problems of managing households and coping with the daily problems of family life). Osborne concluded that as pregnancy continued, these women experienced less subjective distress and fewer concerns about the problems of daily life. Their interest patterns tended more in the feminine direction as the delivery date approached. When the third-trimester sample was divided into two subgroups, 52 multigravidas and 42 primigravidas, significant differences were obtained at the 5% level on only 2 of 17 MMPI scales tested. It was concluded that, insofar as the MMPI could measure, these two groups were very similar in their emotional responses to pregnancy.

Carson, Osborne, and Segura (1979) administered the MMPI to 56 women who complained of the female urethral syndrome (frequency of urination, urgency, and dysuria). These women had no other serious medical problems. Medical examinations and tests were not helpful in finding a cause for their distress. Compared with 3,474 female medical patients between the ages of 30 and 39 from the Mayo sample, the patients with the urethral syndrome had significantly higher scores on scales *F, Hs, Hy,* and *Sc.*

Swanson et al. (1976) presented MMPI profiles from 22 male and 26 female patients with chronic pain. Both male and female chronic pain patients differed significantly from general medical patients on a number of MMPI scales, the largest differences occurring on scales *Hs* and *Hy.*

The many studies of MMPI profiles in various patient groups can best be summarized in the following way. In most groups of medical patients, scales *Hs* and *Hy* are elevated. In many groups, scale *D* is also high in comparison to control groups. These scales appear to be highest among patients with chronic diseases, somewhat lower among general medical patients, and even lower—but still higher than the normative sample for the test—among persons with no physical complaints who are simply undergoing a routine medical exam.

VI. CONCLUSIONS

In their early work on the use of the MMPI with medical patients, McKinley and Hathaway (1943) hoped to distinguish functional from organic complaints. This difficult task has not been accomplished. The elevation on the neurotic triad, seen in profiles of patients with organic disease, as well as of medical patients undergoing a physical examination but having no physical complaints, precludes discrimination by use of these MMPI scales alone. Use of nontest factors improves prediction of functional versus organic diagnosis somewhat, but a large number of misclassifications still occur. Scales developed to aid in this prediction among specific patient groups—for example, the Pseudoneurologic Scale—misclassify a large number of patients unless extremely high and low cutting scores are used and no predictions are made for patients obtaining moderate scores.

McKinley and Hathaway (1943) also suggested using the MMPI to identify medical patients who have emotional difficulties. There has been much clinical use of the test for this purpose, and the MMPI seems well suited for it; but there has been little investigation of this application.

Use of the MMPI to predict response to medical and surgical treatment has yielded some promising results, but cross-validation work and studies using larger numbers of subjects are needed. Kutner's (1978) findings suggest that examination of responses to individual items might be more productive than the use of the clinical scales. A combination of test and nontest factors would have the best chance of predicting response to treatment.

The repression-sensitization and panic-fear scales offer some promise of increasing understanding of emotional and subjective aspects of physical illness. Variations in degree of disability and intractability in patients with similar disease conditions appear to be related to these personality factors.

The large number of reports that present mean profiles for specific groups of medical patients can be summarized in the following way. Scales *Hs, D,* and *Hy* were elevated in medical patient groups. They were highest in groups with chronic debilitating disease and in groups with functional complaints. General medical patients scored next highest on these scales, and then healthy people taking the MMPI in the context of a general medical examination. The latter group still scored higher on these scales than did the normative sample from which the scales were developed. There were high degrees of overlap among all of these groups.

Future investigation might best focus on a few promising areas. Studies of the use of the MMPI in screening medical patients for emotional problems are needed, since this probably is the use to which the MMPI is put most frequently in a medical setting. Investigation of repression-sensitization and panic-fear in predicting response to treatment and in evaluating emotional aspects of illness should be continued. Studies whose sole purpose is to present the mean profile of a medical patient group are unlikely to increase our understanding of either medical patients or the MMPI.

REFERENCES

Bakker, C. B., & Levenson, R. M. Determinants of angina pectoris. *Psychosomatic Medicine*, 1967, 29, 621-33.
Beardsley, J. V., & Puletti, F. Personality (MMPI) and cognitive (WAIS) changes after levodopa treatment: Occurrence in patients with Parkinson's disease. *Archives of Neurology*, 1971, 25, 145-50.

Beutler, L. E., Karacan, I., Anch, A. M., Salis, P. J., Scott, F. B., & Williams, R. L. MMPI and MIT discriminators of biogenic and psychogenic impotence. *Journal of Consulting and Clinical Psychology*, 1975, 43, 899-903.

Block, J. Cited by Osborne, D., 1971.

Boll, T. J., Heaton, R., & Reitan, R. M. Neuropsychological and emotional correlates of Huntington's chorea. *Journal of Nervous and Mental Disease,* 1974, 158, 61-69.

Byrne, D., Steinberg, M. A., & Schwartz, M. S. Relationship between repression-sensitization and physical illness. *Journal of Abnormal Psychology*, 1968, 73, 154-55.

Calsyn, D. A., Louks, J., & Freeman, C. W. The use of the MMPI with chronic low back pain patients with a mixed diagnosis. *Journal of Clinical Psychology*, 1976, 32, 532-36.

Canter, A. H. MMPI profiles in multiple sclerosis. *Journal of Consulting Psychology*, 1951, 15, 253-56.

Carson, C. C. III, Osborne, D., & Segura, J. W. Psychologic characteristics of patients with female urethral syndrome. *Journal of Clinical Psychology*, 1979, 35, 312-13.

Colligan, R. C., & Osborne, D. MMPI profiles from adolescent medical patients. *Journal of Clinical Psychology*, 1977, 33, 186-89.

Davis, L. J., Jr., Osborne, D., Siemens, P. J., & Brown, J. R. MMPI correlates with disability in multiple sclerosis. *Psychological Reports*, 1971, 28, 700-2.

Dirks, J. F., Jones, N. F., & Kinsman, R. A. Panic-fear: A personality dimension related to intractability in asthma. *Psychosomatic Medicine*, 1977, 39, 120-26. (a)

Dirks, J. F., Kinsman, R. A., Jones, N. F., Spector, S. L., Davidson, P. T., & Evans, N. W. Panic-fear: A personality dimension related to length of hospitalization in respiratory illness. *Journal of Asthma Research*, 1977, 14, 61-71. (b)

Dodge, G. R., & Kolstoe, R. H. The MMPI in differentiating early multiple sclerosis and conversion hysteria. *Psychological Reports*, 1971, 29, 155-59.

Gilberstadt, H., & Jancis, M. "Organic" *vs.* "functional" diagnoses from 1-3 MMPI profiles. *Journal of Clinical Psychology*, 1967, 23, 480-83.

Greene, W. A. The psychosocial setting of the development of leukemia and lymphoma. *Annals of the New York Academy of Sciences*, 1966, 125, 794-801.

Gruba, G. H., & Rohrbaugh, M. MMPI correlates of menstrual distress. *Psychosomatic Medicine*, 1975, 37, 265-73.

Guthrie, G. M. *A study of the personality characteristics associated with disorders encountered by an internist.* Ph.D. dissertation, University of Minnesota, 1950.

Hain, J. D., Linton, P. H., Eber, H. W., & Chapman, M. M. Menstrual irregularity, symptoms and personality. *Journal of Psychosomatic Research*, 1970, 14, 81-87.

Hathaway, S. R., & Briggs, P. F. Some normative data on new MMPI scales. *Journal of Clinical Psychology*, 1957, 13, 364-68.

Henrichs, T. F., & Waters, W. F. Psychological adjustment and response to open-heart surgery: Some methodological considerations. *British Journal of Psychiatry*, 1972, 120, 491-96.

Hooke, J. F., & Marks, P. A. MMPI characteristics of pregnancy. *Journal of Clinical Psychology*, 1962, 18, 316-17.

Houk, T. W. Use of the MMPI in diagnosis of psychoneuroses. *Northwest Medicine*, 1946, 45, 248-52.

Hovey, H. B. Brain lesions and five MMPI items. *Journal of Consulting Psychology*, 1964, 28, 78-79.

Hovey, H. B. MMPI testing for multiple sclerosis. *Psychological Reports*, 1967, 21, 599-600.

Jortner, S. A test of Hovey's MMPI scale for CNS disorder. *Journal of Clinical Psychology*, 1965, 21, 285.

Kamman, G. R. Psychosomatic diagnosis. *Journal-Lancet*, 1947, 67, 102-7.

Kamman, G. R., & Kram, C. Value of psychometric examinations in medical diagnosis and treatment. *Journal of the American Medical Association*, 1955, 158, 555-60.

Kilpatrick, D. G., Miller, W. C., Allain, A. N., Huggins, M. B., & Lee, W. H., Jr. The use of psychological test data to predict open-heart surgery outcome: A prospective study. *Psychosomatic Medicine*, 1975, 37, 62-73.

Kutner, L. A. *Psychological factors influencing pain and recovery from surgery.* Ph.D. dissertation, University of Minnesota, 1978.

Lair, C. V., & King, G. D. MMPI profile predictors for successful and expired open heart surgery patients. *Journal of Clinical Psychology*, 1976, 32, 51-54.

Lair, C. V., & Trapp, E. P. The differential diagnostic value of MMPI with somatically disturbed patients. *Journal of Clinical Psychology*, 1962, 18, 146-47.

Maruta, T., Swanson, D. W., & Swenson, W. M. *Chronic pain: Which patients may a pain-management program help?* Manuscript submitted for publication, 1978.

Maskin, M. B., Riklan, M., & Chabot, D. Emotional functions in short-term vs. long-term L-Dopa therapy in Parkinsonism. *Journal of Clinical Psychology*, 1973, 29, 493-95.

Matthews, C. G., Cleeland, C. S., & Hopper, C. L. Neuropsychological patterns in multiple sclerosis. *Diseases of the Nervous System*, 1970, 31, 161-70.

McKinley, J. C., & Hathaway, S. R. The identification and measurement of the psychoneuroses in medical practice: The Minnesota Multiphasic Personality Inventory. *Journal of the American Medical Association*, 1943, 122, 161-67.

McMahon, A. W., Schmitt, P., Patterson, J. F., & Rothman, E. Personality differences between inflammatory bowel disease patients and their healthy siblings. *Psychosomatic Medicine*, 1973, 35, 91-103.

Nalven, F. B., & O'Brien, J. F. Personality patterns of rheumatoid arthritic patients. *Arthritis and Rheumatism* 1964, 7, 18-28.

Osborne, D. Age and sex differences on MMPI factor scales ER-0 and EC-5 in a medical population. *Journal of Clinical Psychology*, 1971, 27, 245-46.

Osborne, D. Comparison of MMPI scores of pregnant women and female medical patients. *Journal of Clinical Psychology*, 1977, 33, 448-50. (a)

Osborne, D. MMPI characteristics of multigravidas and primigravidas in the third trimester of pregnancy. *Psychological Reports*, 1977, 40, 81-82. (b)

Osborne, D. MMPI changes between the first and third trimester of pregnancy. *Journal of Clinical Psychology*, 1978, 34, 92-93.

Polley, H. F., Swenson, W. M., & Steinhilber, R. M. Personality characteristics of patients with rheumatoid arthritis. *Psychosomatics*, 1970, 11, 45-49.

Schmale, A., & Iker, H. The psychological setting of uterine cervical cancer. *Annals of the New York Academy of Sciences*, 1966, 125, 807-13.

Schwartz, M. L., & Cahill, R. Personality assessment in myasthenia gravis with the MMPI. *Perceptual and Motor Skills*, 1970, 31, 766.

Schwartz, M. S. The repression sensitization scale: Normative age and sex data on 30,000 medical patients. *Journal of Clinical Psychology*, 1972, 28, 72-73.

Schwartz, M. S., & Brown, J. R. MMPI differentiation of multiple sclerosis vs. pseudoneurologic patients. *Journal of Clinical Psychology*, 1973, 29, 471-74.

Schwartz, M. S., & Krupp, N. E. The MMPI "conversion V" among 50,000 medical patients: A study of incidence, criteria, and profile elevation. *Journal of Clinical Psychology*, 1971, 27, 89-95.

Schwartz, M. S., Krupp, N. E., & Byrne, D. Repression-sensitization and medical diagnosis. *Journal of Abnormal Psychology*, 1971, 78, 286-91.

Schwartz, M. S., Osborne, D., & Krupp, N. E. Moderating effects of age and sex on the association of medical diagnoses and 1-3/3-1 MMPI profiles. *Journal of Clinical Psychology*, 1972, 28, 502-5.

Shaw, D. J., & Matthews, C. G. Differential MMPI performance of brain-damaged vs. pseudoneurologic groups. *Journal of Clinical Psychology*, 1965, 21, 405-8.

Shontz, F. C. MMPI responses of patients with multiple sclerosis. *Journal of Consulting Psychology*, 1955, 19, 74.

Swanson, D. W., Swenson, W. M., Maruta, T., & McPhee, M. C. Program for managing chronic pain. I. Program description and characteristics of patients. *Mayo Clinic Proceedings*, 1976, 51, 401-8.

Swenson, W. M. Automated personality assessment in medical practice. *Medical Clinics of North America*, 1970, 54, 835-49.

Swenson, W. M., Pearson, J. S., & Osborne, D. *An MMPI source book: Basic item, scale, and pattern data on 50,000 medical patients.* Minneapolis: University of Minnesota Press, 1973.

Swenson, W. M., Rome, H. P., Pearson, J. S., & Brannick, T. L. A totally automated psychological test: Experience in a medical center. *Journal of the American Medical Association*, 1965, 191, 925-27.

Watson, C. G., & Schuld, D. Psychosomatic factors in the etiology of neoplasms. *Journal of Consulting and Clinical Psychology*, 1977, 45, 455-61.

Weingold, H. P., Dawson, J. G., & Kael, H. C. Further examination of Hovey's "index" for identification of brain lesions: Validation study. *Psychological Reports*, 1965, 16, 1098.

West, K. L. MMPI correlates of ulcerative colitis. *Journal of Clinical Psychology*, 1970, 26, 214-19.

Ziegler, F. J., Rodgers, D. A., & Kriegsman, S. A. Effect of vasectomy on psychological functioning. *Psychosomatic Medicine*, 1966, 28, 50-63.

Zimmerman, I. L. Residual effects of brain damage and five MMPI items. *Journal of Consulting Psychology*, 1965, 29, 394.

Use of the MMPI
in Personnel Selection

James N. Butcher

The importance of personality factors in personnel-selection decisions is well established.[1] Since antiquity leaders have used judgments about personality as a basis for selecting colleagues and workers. Kings, religious groups, governments, and private businesses have
hired both leaders and followers because of personal qualities the
individuals are believed to possess. In many, if not most, instances,
the data for these important decisions were obtained from such unreliable sources as the individual's own appraisal of his/her personal
qualities or the recommendation of a friend, mentor, soothsayer, or
even court astrologer. The most likely and perhaps most useful
source of information available to prospective employers in the past
was an evaluation of the individual's reputation based on experiences
the evaluator had had with the individual in similar, previous circumstances. Only recently has it been possible to weigh objectively personality factors from outside data sources before the individual is
placed in a position of trust. Only recently have these outside personality evaluations (which may or may not have relevance and validity) of people applying for openings been accessible to prospective
employers.

PERSONALITY VARIABLES IN
PERSONNEL-SELECTION DECISIONS

Given that personality factors contribute to an individual's daily
functioning, interpersonal and job relationships, etc., which person-

165

ality variables are important in personnel-selection decisions? A great number of "general" personality theories have been set forth in an effort to account for or explain the behavior of people. The general personality theories of Freud, Jung, Adler, Erikson, Allport, Murray, Cattell, Rogers, Eysenck (to mention only a few) provide broad schemata for viewing personality. However, these theories are, for the most part, philosophical vantage points or personal world views of the individual theorist. They resemble "philosophies of life" and do not provide specific guidelines for making predictions or for developing explicit hypotheses that can withstand empirical test in trans-situational comparisons. In many instances, the principles or descriptions presented are of little value in "real-world applications" since they are often difficult to translate into explicit behavioral predictions.

Empirical research in the field of personality has specified a number of personality variables that may be useful for job-matching or job-placement decisions. Gough (1976) recently summarized a great deal of literature and noted the potential utility of a number of personality variables that are relevant for personnel-selection decisions. He described how these factors are measured and how they might be related to success on the job. These personality factors are: authoritarian values or authoritarian personality; conformity vs. independence; need-achievement; socialization and moral judgment; social maturity or social judgment; empathy; and creativity.

The use of personality information to match an individual with a particular occupation involves a number of assumptions:

(a) that certain personality or behavioral characteristics are relevant or critical for the performance of the task or position (see McCormick, 1976, for a discussion of job and task analyses);

(b) that those personality attributes are definable in an explicit enough manner to be reliable and validly measurable;

(c) that the particular tests, job samples, inferences, indexes, etc. are found to be empirically valid measures of the behavior defined in point (a) above.

Some further assumptions about the effectiveness or ethics of job matching should perhaps be made:

(d) that the selection procedures employed are economical. For example, that the test or procedure saves time, money, etc. over simply hiring anyone applying for the job and keeping those who work out. Before this assumption can be made, a great deal of information might have to be collected on cost of training, manpower availability, cost of high turnover rate, etc.;

(e) that the use of certain assessment procedures does not violate the rights or moral principles of individuals or place them in potential danger. An example of this would be determining their ability to withstand stress by requiring them to perform extraordinary or dangerous physical feats, such as ancient tests for knighthood.

Developing *inclusion* rules for matching individuals with certain personal qualities to jobs or positions that are believed to require such qualifications is a tantalizing notion. Successful person-position matching might result in such desirable outcomes as a more efficient and productive staff and more highly satisfied employees.

Job matching for specific abilities or physical characteristics may be more easily and objectively accomplished than matching for personality traits or behavioral characteristics. In their excellent recent review of personnel selection and classification systems, Dunnette and Borman (1979) examined many relevant issues, problems, and procedures concerning matching the applicant to the job. Virtually all of this review, however, deals with matching ability and interest factors; very little attention is given to matching personality characteristics. Two approaches to evaluating personality factors were discussed: (a) the old standby—the selection interview and (b) weighted application blanks and biodata information forms. Matching personality to position is often qualitatively done through job interviews, even if no attempt is made to match on the basis of objective tests. Often an employment interviewer attempts to develop an idea of the "type of personal qualities" that are demanded by a job and, using personal judgment, etc., determine whether the present applicant's judged personality attributes fit the job needs (Schmitt & Coyle, 1976). Using biodata for selection decisions is one approach to systematizing personal history (personality) data on applicants (Owens, 1976). However, there have been few attempts to develop personality measures for job-placement purposes. Attempts to measure personality characteristics related to job performance, such as those mentioned by Gough (1976), usually use instruments developed in non-industrial settings.

Dunnette (1971) discussed an approach to pre-employment job matching, multiple assessment, that proved more valid for selecting talented managers than did individual test scores alone. In his approach to assessing managerial talent, Dunnette first analyzed managerial effectiveness into its component parts, such as:

Verbal intelligence	Perception of social airs
Quantitative intelligence	Need for social approval
Divergent thinking	Interpersonal competence
Breadth of information	Forcefulness
Oral communication skills	Need achievement
Energy	Need advancement
Decisiveness	Desire to lead
Personal appearance	Need cognition
Personal impact	Inner work standards
Need security	Resistance to stress
Primacy of work	Self-esteem
Need autonomy	Tolerance of ambiguity
Behavioral stability	Attention to detail
Cognitive complexity	Organization and planning
Ability to delay gratification	Specialization orientation
Behavior flexibility	Social Awareness

Source: Dunnette, 1971

These components were determined through a review of the existing literature and a sampling of opinion from experienced managers as to what behavioral characteristics they believed were important to effective management. Next, a number of techniques were selected or developed to obtain measures on these characteristics. For example, interview, small-group problem-solving situations, paper-and-pencil tests (CPI, SVIB, EPPS, MSAT, Ghiselli Self-Description Inventory, etc.), a projective test (sentence completion), and an application blank of personal information. Dunnette concluded that the results of multiple assessment, when the assessment was done by professionals, are valid and reliable "diagnoses" of managerial talent and can be used with confidence to make recommendations about individuals.

DETECTING PSYCHOPATHOLOGY IN "NORMAL" GROUPS

The discussion thus far has centered on the use of personality measures as an aid in determining if a particular individual has a personality structure, type, or attributes that fit those believed to be important to a particular position. We now turn to a somewhat different issue regarding the suitability of personality for employment, the need to exclude some individuals from certain highly responsible or stressful occupations because of their poor mental health or adjustment problems. The believed importance of this is highlighted by the fact that a candidate for a high political office (vice presidency of the United States) was asked to resign because he had a history of manic-depressive disorder. Occupations considered so "critical" that they require higher levels of personal adjustment are positions of public trust such as police and fire personnel, airline flight crews, medical and nursing staff, clinical psychology students, ministerial candidates, etc.

Is the MMPI sensitive to psychopathology in "normal" groups? This is an important question, which requires an affirmative answer if the MMPI can justifiably be used for screening emotional disorders in a non-psychiatric context. Hedlund (1965) reviewed early applications of the MMPI in industry and concluded that the research to that point was inconclusive. Several studies she reviewed indicated that the MMPI might detect behavior problems in industry. However, it did not seem to effectively determine personality types for various occupations. Several important recent studies have demonstrated that the MMPI can be used effectively to detect psychopathology in groups of individuals not identified as patients.

Academic Environments

The MMPI does detect individuals who are likely to experience emotional maladjustment in a stressful academic environment. Lachar (1974) studied a freshman class at the United States Air Force Academy (N = 1,389) by administering the MMPI at entrance and following up dropouts after the initial period of adjustment. Lachar used the MMPI (specifically, a set of computer-based decision rules) to place cadets into four adjustment groups:

Group 1   Pathology likely (N = 30)
Group 2   Adaptation problems (N = 55)
Group 3   Deviance possible (N = 81)
Group 4   Deviance unlikely (N = 1, 223)

The mean MMPI scale scores and standard deviations for the four groups are given in Table 1.

During the period of initial adjustment 165 (11.8%) of the freshman class dropped out of the academy. Of the cadets classified by the MMPI as high risk for emotional problems (Groups 1 and 2)

Table 1. MMPI Profiles of Four Groups of Freshmen Air Force Academy Cadets Classified According to Likelihood of Emotional Maladjustment

1. Pathology likely	30	X̄	48.1	72.7	46.0	67.4	77.4	65.3	69.0	65.1	70.2	87.5	91.7	68.3	64.7	70.0	38.1
		SD	8.9	15.4	6.2	14.5	14.4	12.2	10.1	10.9	12.7	12.3	11.9	12.2	9.2	7.2	10.2
2. Adaptation problems	55	X̄	47.3	61.0	46.5	59.6	71.9	62.7	64.4	67.5	66.0	78.2	77.9	65.2	60.2	65.3	44.4
		SD	7.0	8.7	7.7	11.1	11.7	8.9	10.3	8.7	7.9	10.2	9.4	13.2	10.5	9.0	7.8
3. Deviance possible[a]	81	X̄	46.8	55.6	48.7	54.4	60.7	58.9	61.0	65.0	61.7	68.1	66.9	67.8	54.2	57.2	52.3
		SD	6.9	7.5	8.2	8.9	11.5	8.7	10.5	9.4	8.5	9.2	9.3	11.8	10.5	10.4	6.9
4. Deviance unlikely[a]	1,223	X̄	49.6	49.3	53.5	49.5	52.1	54.7	53.7	57.1	54.1	56.4	55.7	58.5	48.8	46.6	59.1
		SD	6.9	5.9	7.7	7.1	9.3	7.0	8.8	8.4	7.5	8.4	8.1	9.9	8.8	8.4	7.3

Adapted from Lachar, 1974

[a]The total sample of 1,317 low-risk controls includes 13 subjects who did not take the MMPI.

more than *twice* the number in these groups had separated from the academy than was true of the remainder of the class. Twenty-one from combined Groups 1 and 2 (N = 85) had left for emotional reasons (24.7%). Only 144 of the 1,317 low-risk controls (10.9%) had separated. Lachar concluded that elevations on scales *D, Pt, Sc,* and *A* reflected the type of psychological discomfort that made the individual susceptible to adaptation problems. Other studies that have used the MMPI to detect psychopathological tendencies or adaptation problems in student groups are cited in Butcher and Pancheri (1976); Cooke, (1967); Danet (1965); Kleinmuntz (1960 & 1963); Rissetti et al. (1979) (see Chapter 3).

The Lachar study demonstrates that a large number of individuals who develop adjustment problems drop out of the program during the initial phase of cadet training. One possible use of this information might be to develop an early intervention program in which individuals who are at high risk for psychological disorder might be given special treatment such as counseling or guidance to lessen their maladjustment. This strategy of identifying individuals at risk for psychological problems with an eye toward intervention was suggested by Pucheu's (1976) development of an MMPI screening/detection system for medical students (Butcher & Pancheri, 1976).

Job Applicants in Industry

The extent to which abnormal MMPI's are produced in an industrial setting was studied by Butcher (1977a). He analyzed MMPI profiles of 1,403 male and 323 female applicants for hourly jobs at a large industrial plant and found that both male and female employees showed a greater degree of defensiveness than was found in the original Minnesota normal sample. In fact, 8.6% of the males and 6.8% of the females produced profiles that were invalid because of high *K* scores. Thus, individuals in an employment-testing situation tend to respond to self-report questionnaires in a generally defensive and socially favorable manner.

In spite of this tendency for applicants to answer items defensively, a large number of individuals produced MMPI scales in a critical range, T ⩾ 70. In the female sample, 18% had at least one MMPI score in the pathological range; for males it was 22.2%. The distributions of single-scale and two-point codes (T = 70) of male and female job applicants are given in Tables 2 and 3. The distributions of code types of T = 60 are also given to show the frequencies of scale configural patterns at the one-standard-deviation level of elevation, since

Table 2. MMPI Code-Type Frequencies for Women Applicants (N = 323)[a]

	T = 70					T = 60			
Code	Absolute Frequency	Relative Frequency	Adjusted Frequency	Cumulative Adj. Freq.	Code	Absolute Frequency	Relative Frequency	Adjusted Frequency	Cumulative Adj. Freq.
0	4	1.2%	1.2%	1.2%	0	20	6.2%	6.2%	6.2%
1	2	.6	.6	1.9	1	1	.3	.3	6.5
2	2	.6	.6	2.5	2	2	.6	.6	7.1
4	4	1.2	1.2	3.7	3	3	.9	.9	8.0
5	8	2.5	2.5	6.2	4	25	7.7	7.7	15.8
6	1	.3	.3	6.5	5	16	5.0	5.0	20.7
7	1	.3	.3	6.8	6	5	1.5	1.5	22.3
8	2	.6	.6	7.4	8	2	.6	.6	22.9
9	11	3.4	3.4	10.8	9	22	6.8	6.8	29.7
13	2	.6	.6	11.5	10	1	.3	.3	30.0
20	2	.6	.6	12.1	12	1	.3	.3	30.3
23	1	.3	.3	12.4	13	4	1.2	1.2	31.6
26	2	.6	.6	13.0	14	1	.3	.3	31.9
27	1	.3	.3	13.3	18	1	.3	.3	32.2
38	1	.3	.3	13.6	20	12	3.7	3.7	35.9
40	1	.3	.3	13.9	23	3	.9	.9	36.8
45	1	.3	.3	14.2	24	2	.6	.6	37.5
48	3	.9	.9	15.2	25	1	.3	.3	37.8
49	2	.6	.6	15.8	26	2	.6	.6	38.4
56	1	.3	.3	16.1	27	2	.6	.6	39.0
58	1	.3	.3	16.4	29	1	.3	.3	39.3
59	1	.3	.3	16.7	34	1	.3	.3	39.6
78	1	.3	.3	17.0	35	1	.3	.3	39.9
89	3	.9	.9	18.0	36	2	.6	.6	40.6
					38	1	.3	.3	40.9

Invalid LK	22	6.8	6.8	24.8
Invalid ?	4	1.2	1.2	26.0
No high point	239	74.0	74.0	100.0
Total	323	100.0	100.0	100.0

39	1	.3	.3	41.2
40	8	2.5	2.5	43.7
45	7	2.2	2.2	45.8
46	2	.6	.6	46.4
48	3	.9	.9	47.4
49	11	3.4	3.4	50.8
50	5	1.5	1.5	52.3
56	5	1.5	1.5	53.9
58	1	.3	.3	54.2
59	9	2.8	2.8	57.0
60	5	1.5	1.5	58.5
67	1	.3	.3	58.8
68	1	.3	.3	59.1
69	3	.9	.9	60.1
70	2	.6	.6	60.7
78	4	1.2	1.2	61.9
79	2	.6	.6	62.5
80	1	.3	.3	62.8
89	5	1.5	1.5	64.4
90	2	.6	.6	65.0
Invalid LK	22	6.8	6.8	71.8
Invalid ?	4	1.2	1.2	73.1
No high point	87	26.9	26.9	100.0
Total	323	100.0	100.0	100.0

Source: Butcher, 1977.

[a]Data include Mf and Ma scale scores over $T = 70$. Since these scales are frequently above 70 for normal subjects, including them may result in an inflated estimate.

Table 3. MMPI Code-Type Frequencies for Men Applicants (N = 1,403)[a]

T = 70

Code	Absolute Frequency	Relative Frequency	Adjusted Frequency	Cumulative Adj. Freq.
0	10	.7%	.7%	.7%
1	11	.8	.8	1.5
2	12	.9	.9	2.4
3	6	.4	.4	2.8
4	23	1.6	1.6	4.4
5	20	1.4	1.4	5.8
6	3	.2	.2	6.1
7	7	.5	.5	6.6
8	7	.5	.5	7.1
9	94	6.7	6.7	13.8
12	8	.6	.6	14.3
13	8	.6	.6	14.9
14	3	.2	.2	15.1
16	2	.1	.1	15.3
18	3	.2	.2	15.5
20	1	.1	.1	15.5
23	3	.2	.2	15.8
24	7	.5	.5	16.3
25	2	.1	.1	16.4
26	3	.2	.2	16.6
27	10	.7	.7	17.3
28	3	.2	.2	17.5
29	2	.1	.1	17.7
34	2	.1	.1	17.8
45	4	.3	.3	18.1
46	2	.1	.1	18.2
47	2	.1	.1	18.4
48	12	.9	.9	19.2
49	8	.6	.6	19.8

T = 60

Code	Absolute Frequency	Relative Frequency	Adjusted Frequency	Cumulative Adj. Freq.
0	31	2.2%	2.2%	2.2%
1	1	.1	.1	2.3
2	30	2.1	2.1	4.4
3	42	3.0	3.0	7.4
4	59	4.2	4.2	11.6
5	37	2.6	2.6	14.3
6	9	.6	.6	14.9
7	9	.6	.6	15.5
8	5	.4	.4	15.9
9	145	10.3	10.3	26.2
10	1	.1	.1	26.3
12	19	1.4	1.4	27.7
13	24	1.7	1.7	29.4
14	8	.6	.6	29.9
15	2	.1	.1	30.1
16	2	.1	.1	30.2
18	5	.4	.4	30.6
19	3	.2	.2	30.8
20	29	2.1	2.1	32.9
23	16	1.1	1.1	34.0
24	34	2.4	2.4	36.4
25	12	.9	.9	37.3
26	8	.6	.6	37.8
27	21	1.5	1.5	39.3
28	8	.6	.6	39.9
29	13	.9	.9	40.8
30	1	.1	.1	40.9
34	43	3.1	3.1	44.0
35	17	1.2	1.2	45.2

57	3	.2	.2	20.0
58	1	.1	.1	20.1
59	5	.4	.4	20.5
67	1	.1	.1	20.5
68	1	.1	.1	20.6
70	2	.1	.1	20.7
78	8	.6	.6	21.3
79	1	.1	.1	21.4
89	12	.9	.9	22.2
Invalid *F*	11	.8	.8	23.0
Invalid *LK*	120	8.6	8.6	31.6
Invalid ?	17	1.2	1.2	32.8
No high point	943	67.2	67.2	100.0
Total	1,403	100.0	100.0	100.0

36	3	.2	.2	45.4
37	8	.6	.6	46.0
38	5	.4	.4	46.3
39	23	1.6	1.6	48.0
40	7	.5	.5	48.5
45	20	1.4	1.4	49.9
46	10	.7	.7	50.6
47	15	1.1	1.1	51.7
48	22	1.6	1.6	53.2
49	68	4.8	4.8	58.1
50	12	.9	.9	58.9
56	4	.3	.3	59.2
57	9	.6	.6	59.9
58	4	.3	.3	60.2
59	51	3.6	3.6	63.8
60	2	.1	.1	63.9
67	4	.3	.3	64.2
68	5	.4	.4	64.6
69	17	1.2	1.2	65.8
70	10	.7	.7	66.5
78	18	1.3	1.3	67.8
79	13	.9	.9	68.7
89	40	2.9	2.9	71.6
90	5	.4	.4	71.9
Invalid *F*	11	.8	.8	72.7
Invalid *LK*	120	8.6	8.6	81.3
Invalid ?	17	1.2	1.2	82.5
No high point	246	17.5	17.5	100.0
Total	1,403	100.0	100.0	100.0

Source: Butcher, 1977.

[a]Data include *Mf* and *Ma* scale scores over T = 70. Since these scales are frequently over 70 for normal subjects, including them may result in an inflated estimate.

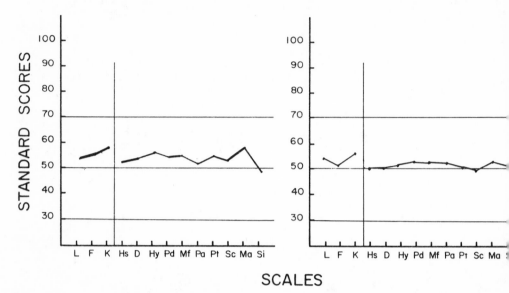

SCALES

Figure 1. Male applicants (N = 1,403)
for employment at a large industrial plant.

Figure 2. Female applicants (N = 323)
for employment at a large industrial plant.

many MMPI interpreters consider these to be interpretable scores for "normal-range" profiles, especially for defensive protocols. The group mean profiles of the male and female samples (Figures 1 and 2) present a rather normal picture. It is apparent from inspecting the code-type distributions that a moderate amount of psychopathology (as measured by the MMPI) can be found in "normal-range" populations. This point can perhaps be made more clearly by combining the pathological code types $T = 70$ into neurotic, psychotic, and character-disordered profiles (see Table 4). The rates of "psychopathology" shown by this analysis roughly approximate the more conservative estimates usually given for psychological disturbance in the community at large, 15% (President's Commission on Mental Health, 1978).

In summary, Butcher (1977) found that job applicants in an industrial-screening situation produced somewhat defensive profiles with rather low-ranging elevations. Many produced technically invalid profiles (10.8% of the men and 8.0% of the women), and no more than 18-22% of the profiles in this sample were clinically interpretable. Of the MMPIs that were interpretable, the single-point code types are distributed throughout the range of psychopathology. An earlier study by Barnabus (1948) demonstrated that many individ-

Table 4. Percentages of Employee's Profile Types
Classified as Character Disorder, Neurotic, and
Psychotic (Schizoid)

	Character Disorder	
Profile types	Male	Female
4′, 24′, 34′, 48′, 49′	3.8%	2.7%
	Neurotic	
Profile types	Male	Female
1′, 2′, 3′, 7′, 12′, 13′, 20′, 23′, 25′, 27′	4.6%	3.3%
	Psychotic (Schizoid)	
Profile types	Male	Female
8′, 16′, 18′, 26′, 28′, 58′, 67′, 68′, 78′, 79′, 89′	4.0%	3.8%

Source: Butcher, 1977.

uals identified by the MMPI as being psychopathological actually developed psychological problems that required treatment. In his study of workers in an industrial setting, all the 32 individuals requiring hospitalization had produced deviant MMPI profiles in an earlier testing.

Army Recruits

Even if it is possible to detect those individuals who are likely to encounter difficulties in a given situation, it may not be practical to act on that information. Callan (1972) pointed out that using an instrument like the MMPI for detecting pathology in army recruits was impractical. Since 80-90% of all military personnel actually perform satisfactorily, it is more profitable for the military to take all comers and use basic training to weed out the misfits. In a study to develop a practical measure of emotional disorder that could be used for screening unfit soldiers, Callan used the MMPI pool to screen 814 soliders before basic training. Following basic training, there were 712 "normal" and 102 "deviant" soldiers. The deviants were 18 discharges, 18 AWOL, who received disciplinary punishment, 22 who had to repeat basic, and 44 who had excessive sick-call attendance. He used these groups to construct a briefer inventory of potentially discriminating indexes, including an empirical scale that predicted discharges and AWOL cases. This abbreviated item set was given to 3,328 unselected trainees at the beginning of basic training. Following up the individuals who had adjustment problems, he found that the screening instrument scored 825 people as deviant; but only 96 of these were in the true deviant group which contained 236 soldiers. Thus the rate of false positives was much too high to warrant using the instrument. He found, however, that his discharge scale identified 17 of 18 individuals who separated from the army.

Police-Officer Candidates

The use of the MMPI to aid in the assessment of police-officer candidates has increased greatly in recent years. Much of the impetus for screening police candidates comes from the recognition that the potential abuse of power in that trusted position has great social implications. The traditional trust with which the public has viewed police officers has been eroded somewhat in recent years owing to bad publicity over police scandals, alleged harsh treatment of minority groups and strikers during the 1960s, etc. Many police administrators have made efforts to upgrade the quality of police personnel by initiating a more careful pre-employment psychological screening. In fact, a number of state and local political bodies have passed laws requiring that police-officer candidates be screened by psychiatric evaluation or psychological test.

Interest in excluding psychologically disturbed individuals from service on police forces has led many groups to employ objective personality tests like the MMPI. Several studies of police-officer candidates reveal that applicants for these positions typically show the "defensive" pattern on the validity scales (Sacuzzo, Higgins, & Lewandowski, 1974; McAllister, 1977) (see Figure 3). Both McAllister and Sacuzzo et al. noted further that police applicants usually had elevations on the *Pd* scale, with a 4-3-9 code type. Sacuzzo et al. also pointed out that individual applicants who were most likely to exceed "normal limits" were the character-disordered profile types (4-3-9 and 4-9).

Fenster and Locke (1973) examined sex-role orientation of policemen using the *Mf* scale of the MMPI and an interest inventory. They matched two groups of police officers (grouped according to education level) with two groups of civilians (controlling for education level). They found that patrolmen obtained higher masculinity scores than the civilian groups, indicating that sex-role identification problems are not characteristic of policemen. Earlier, Daniels and

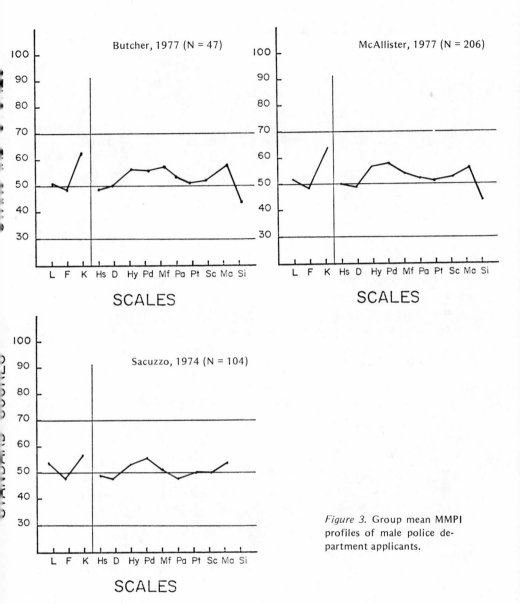

Figure 3. Group mean MMPI profiles of male police department applicants.

Hunter (1949) had shown that the *Mf* scale differentiated individuals who had high "work need of being sensitive to other people" such as social scientists, beauticians, etc., from individuals in less people-related occupations such as meat cutters and farmers.

The relationships of MMPI variables to job performance of police officers has not been clearly delineated for many reasons. For example, if the MMPI is used in the screening process, one cannot use these profiles to predict later job performance, since many officers with deviant profiles would have been eliminated from the performance study. Some studies in which pre-employment MMPIs were collected (but not used in the selection) and related to performance criteria have produced equivocal results because the job-success criteria have been weak. Several studies have reported that MMPI scores and indexes do not relate sufficiently to specific criteria to be useful in job matching (McAllister, 1977; Nowicki, 1966; Hooke & Krauss, 1971; Gottesman, 1969; and Colarelli & Siegel, 1964). However, a study by Azen, Snibbe, and Montgomery (1973), a 20-year follow-up of police officers, found that the MMPI *Ma* score successfully predicted auto accidents in which police officers were involved. This finding supports the results of a study by Parker (1953) that scale 9 (*Ma*) was inversely related to preventable accidents.

The most justifiable use of the MMPI for police selection appears to be at the initial point of recruitment in order to eliminate individuals who have obvious psychopathology. The use of the MMPI to contribute to job-matching inclusion rules or to predict complex job-performance criteria has not been established.

PREDICTING SUCCESSFUL PERFORMANCE

Personality tests like the MMPI do not predict academic success as effectively as do other measures, such as intelligence tests. Crovitz, Huse, and Lewis (1973) found that SAT scores predicted academic performance best, with the MMPI adding little to predicting the success of physician-assistants candidates. Burgess, Duffey, and Temple (1972) also found that MMPI scales added little to predicting academic success in a college nursing program. Intellectual measures such as the SCAT, WAIS, and especially GPA were the best predictors of nursing-school performance. In a study of achievement and academic variables associated with success in a psychiatric residency program, Garetz and Anderson (1973) produced interesting results. The undergraduate rank and sex of the resident best predicted success in the program. Other academic and personality variables added little to the assessment. The MMPI profiles of residents (see Figure 4) resemble those of young adults generally. However, for screening situations in which the criteria for success are influenced by personality factors, MMPI scores are often quite highly related to the criteria. That is, when the position for which the MMPI is being used to screen is one that is influenced by personality and motiva-

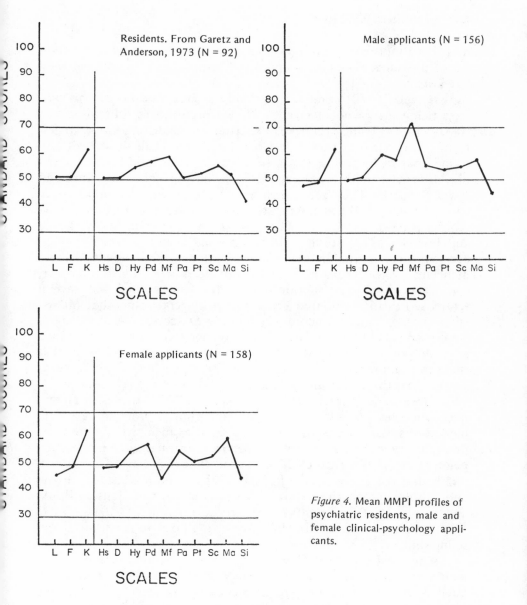

Figure 4. Mean MMPI profiles of psychiatric residents, male and female clinical-psychology applicants.

tional factors, objective personality measures like the MMPI perform well. In a well-designed study of nurses who were promoted to supervisor, Kelly (1974) found that personality factors measured by the MMPI, CPI, 16PF, and EPPS differentiated these women from those not being promoted. The results, which held up on cross-validation, indicated that promoted nurses were "independent, feminine, distant, have more capacity for status, and [are] less prone to psychological pressures. They were more self-assured and relaxed and they like nursing" (p. 41).

Harrell (1972) conducted a study of business success, his subjects being men who received a Master of Business Administration (MBA) degree. Using earnings as the criterion, he distinguished "high" from "low" success people in both large and small businesses and found that high-earning MBAs who had taken jobs in larger companies differed from low-earning MBAs by having higher *Ma* scores and lower *Si* scores. They had a high activity level and were more extroverted. These MMPI characteristics did not separate high- and low-scoring individuals in smaller companies. In a follow-up study Harrell and Harrell (1973) studied MBAs who had been promoted to managers in large nonfamily-owned corporations. They compared these men with other graduates who had not been promoted to manager, e.g., accountants, production men, etc. They found that several MMPI scores differentiated successful managers from other MBAs: High *Pd, Pa,* and *Ma* scores, and lower *Si* scores. Thus, managers were more likely to be men with a high energy level, who functioned autonomously. The elevated *Pa* score was considered to mean that these men approached their tasks more intensely. The lower *Si* scores suggest that these individuals tend to be extroverts.

Jansen and Garvey (1973) compared MMPI profiles of clergymen who were enrolled in an accredited clinical program at a state mental hospital. The clergymen were rated as high, average, and low in clinical competence by their supervisors (ratings were made independent of MMPI profile). They found that high-ranked clergymen had higher scores on an intelligence measure and less measured psychopathology than the low-rated clinical clergymen. Jansen, Bonk, and Garvey (1973) found a negative correlation of *Pa* ($-.44$), *D* ($-.40$), and *Pt* ($-.33$) with the supervisor's positive ratings of counseling skill.

The MMPI was not found to be strongly related to job performance in a study of firefighters. No MMPI scales were highly correlated with explicit job-performance criteria. However, several of the MMPI scales were related to flexibility. Thus, in positions where great flexibility is important, the MMPI scales may be effective predictors (Arvey, Mussio, & Payne, 1972).

Although it is not clear from their article which MMPI scales or indexes were used, Solway, Hays, and Zieben (1976) reported that probation officers appeared rigidly conventional, controlling, and hyper-responsible, while unwittingly idealizing behavior (in their counselees) that is oppositional and unconventional. Evans (1976) found that by using linear discriminant function, the MMPI could significantly discriminate conscientious hotline paraprofessionals from non-conscientious workers.

Stone, Bassett, Brosseau, Demers, and Stiening (1972) found that the MMPI (scales *Mf* and *Es*) were successful in predicting success in a MEDEX (medical assistant) training program using a multiple regression technique. The predictors held in a cross-validation study (Stone & Brosseau, 1973).

Muha and May (1973) attempted to discriminate groups of men and women who were "fit" for employment in a government agency from those who, by interview, were deemed unfit. Using multiple regression, they determined a formula that predicted the criterion of fitness well. In comparisons of unfit and fit women there were more significant MMPI differences than in comparisons of fit-unfit men.

Efforts to match the personality of applicants with a desired "employee type" have not been very productive. Butcher (1977) developed a subset of items that significantly differentiated "good employees" through the use of item analysis. This analysis was performed by determining which items differentiated (and held up on cross-validation across sex) employees for a large industrial plant from the Minnesota normative sample. Since the original Minnesota sample responded to only 504 items (without *Si* and *Mf*), the analysis could not be performed on the full 566 items of the MMPI. In general, it should be noted that the item-endorsement percentages for the industrial job applicants and the Minnesota normals were quite close. The 23-item scale is given in Table 5.

The item content suggests the following: that "good" employees deny personal problems, they claim feelings of well-being and self-confidence, they assert their ability to get along with others, and claim to have a great deal of social tolerance. It may be that the items on this scale have some utility for measuring social adaptiveness or denial of social problems in an employment-screening context. Further, efforts to validate the MMPI in selection settings might find this subset of items useful in measuring applicant attitudes.

It is apparent from this review of studies using the MMPI in personnel selection that several factors limit the effectiveness of this use of the test:

(1) Applicants for positions tend to be quite defensive on the MMPI, about 10-12% of all candidates producing invalid protocols.

(2) About 85% of the profiles submitted for evaluation would not be clinically interpretable (unless one makes evaluative statements on scores in the 60-70 range).

(3) There are no clearcut guidelines or inclusion procedures for matching profile type with occupation. At best, some general criteria might be employed that designate an individual as adjusted, flexible, non-pathological, or extroverted.

THE PROBLEM OF "DEFENSIVE" PROFILES

The persistent finding is that many applicants for employment or entrance to an academic program produce technically invalid MMPI profiles. The pattern of invalidity usually involves some elevation on the L scale (e.g., T = 55-60) and marked elevation on the K scale (T = 68-75) and indicates the individual's attempt to present a highly favorable picture of his or her adjustment. This response pattern resembles the results of studies in which normals have taken the MMPI with instructions to make the most favorable impression they can. The typical clinical pattern involves *no* elevation or submerged scores on F, 1 (*Hs*), 2 (*D*), 4 (*Pd*), 6 (*Pa*), 7 (*Pt*), and 8 (*Sc*), with moderate elevation on scales 3 (*Hy*) and 9 (*Ma*) at T = 55-65, and with scale 0 (*Si*) being quite low (T = 40-45). The individual is communicating a lack of psychological problems, a high energy level, high self-confidence, and an outgoing personality.

The usual practice, since this is a modal pattern for employment situations, is to accept this pattern as "normal" unless either the L or K scale reaches an elevation of T = 70 or greater. For technically invalid cases, the recommendation is to avoid interpreting the profile and evaluate the candidate through other means, e.g., interview. There are clear limitations to the use of self-report measures for employment screening. In many respects, it is surprising that as many as 15% of the profiles in this setting actually provide useful diagnostic information. The value of the MMPI in a screening situation occurs when pathological profiles *are* actually obtained. When the MMPI profile is valid and shows abnormal behavior—for example, an airline pilot applicant who produces at 4-6 profile or a police applicant with

Table 5. Cross-Sex Validated Items That Significantly Discriminate between
Industrial Job Applicants (N = 1,403 males and 323 females) and the
Minnesota Normative Group

Item No.
26(F) I feel that it is certainly best to keep my mouth shut when I'm in trouble.
136(F) Criticism or scolding hurts me terribly.
127(T) I know who is responsible for most of my troubles.
237(F) My relatives are nearly all in sympathy with me.
383(F) People often disappoint me.
389(F) My plans have frequently seemed so full of difficulties that I have had to give them up.
400(T) If given the chance I could do some things that would be of great benefit to the world.
411(F) It makes me feel like a failure when I hear of the success of someone I know well.
148(F) It makes me impatient to have people ask my advice or otherwise interrupt me when I am working on something important.
234(F) I get mad easily and then get over it soon.
89(F) It takes a lot of argument to convince most people of the truth.
265(F) It is safer to trust nobody.
46(T) My judgment is better than it ever was.
73(T) I am an important person.
240(F) I never worry about my looks.
418(F) At times I think I am no good at all.
270(F) When I leave home I do not worry about whether the door is locked and windows closed.
378(F) I do not like to see women smoke.
430(T) I am attracted by members of the opposite sex.
470(F) Sexual things disgust me.
427(F) I am embarrassed by dirty stories.
69(F) I am very strongly attracted by members of my own sex.
558(F) A large number of people are guilty of bad sexual conduct.

Source: Butcher, 1977.

a *Pd* spike at T = 80—the test results should be believed. The use of the MMPI as an exclusion criterion for critical or sensitive occupations when high-scale elevations are obtained is quite appropriate. The problem with self-report instruments is that individuals with pathological tendencies, if they choose to be "defensive," may prevent the assessment officer from discovering his or her secrets. At least, they may thwart the assessment somewhat by being guarded—requiring that the test results be thrown out. Thus, one limitation of the MMPI in selection is the inability to distinguish *some*, unknown, numbers of pathological cases.

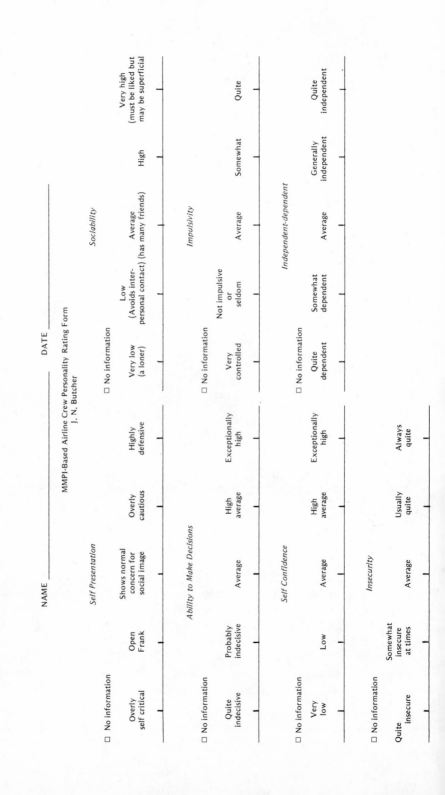

Potential Problem of Addiction

☐ No information

Very unlikely	Low indication	Average	Above average	Moderate	High	Extreme

Checklist of Potential Problems

___ control of anger   ___ legal difficulties
___ aloof   ___ manipulative
___ autocratic   ___ marital problems
___ aggressive   ___ suspicious of others
___ acting out   ___ superficial relations
___ disorganized   ___ moody
___ financial problems   ___ resentful

Areas that Require Further Inquiry in Interview

___ absenteeism   ___ insubordination
___ accident proneness   ___ somatic problems
___ irresponsibility   ___ extreme defensiveness

Stability

☐ No information

Quite unstable	Somewhat unstable	Average	Usually quite	Always quite

Flexibility

☐ No information

Rigid thinking	Somewhat rigid	Average	Usually quite flexible	Always quite flexible

Tolerance for Stress

☐ No information

Very low	Somewhat low	Average	High	Quite high

Energy Level

☐ No information

Very low	Low	Average	High	Very high

Figure 5. MMPI-based rating form for airline crews. From Butcher, 1977.

MMPI CLINICAL INTERPRETATION IN
PERSONNEL SELECTION

Rather than use the MMPI as a psychometric predictor for employment, some individuals use it qualitatively or descriptively to provide
hypotheses about the applicant to be tested in interview or background check. The MMPI consultant provides a written psychological
report about the individual's self-presentation, personality traits, possible problem areas, coping strengths, etc., based on a clinical interpretation of the profile. In some instances, the MMPI is interpreted
by electronic computer, which provides a clinical report based on
clinical norms.

Another way of summarizing MMPI-based inferences and describing the applicant's personality attributes is through the use of
checklists (see Figures 5 and 6). These checklists summarize MMPI-
based inferences in a concise manner and provide ratings on several
relevant personality dimensions.

It should be noted that the use of these checklists is based on
clinical guesswork as opposed to actuarially based empirical findings.
No empirical studies have been published on the relevance and validity of the checklists.

ISSUES IN THE USE OF PERSONALITY TESTS IN
PERSONNEL SELECTION

Invasion of Privacy

Is it appropriate for a prospective employer to administer psychological tests or other measures that involve asking personal questions that the applicant might rather not answer? Are business or
government institutions justified in evaluating an individual's personal
life through lie detection tests (GSR), credit checks, security investigations, in-depth stress interviews, etc.? Is the individual's right to
privacy (as guaranteed by the Constitution of the United States)
being violated by such individual personal-history or personality
evaluations.

There is very little question that many of these procedures pry
into the private lives of job applicants, and it is also quite likely that
many of these procedures: (a) seek information that is irrelevant for
the screening decision, e.g., some personal questions on the MMPI are
not actually used in any of the routinely used scores or indexes, and

NAME OR CODE_____ REFERRED BY_____ DATE_____

ABBREVIATIONS FOR RATINGS:

M/O = MILD/OCCASIONAL
BOR = BORDERLINE
EXC = EXCESSIVE

1. VALIDITY AND ACCEPTABILITY OF MMPI PROFILE

M/O   BOR   EXC
☐   ☐   ☐   denied common, trivial moral faults
☐   ☐   ☐   excessively minimizing of psychological problems
☐   ☐   ☐   serious psychological problems may have been covered over

Acceptable   1 2 3 4 5 6 7 8 9 10   Not Acceptable

2. SERIOUS PSYCHOLOGICAL-EMOTIONAL PROBLEMS

M/O   BOR   EXC
☐   ☐   ☐   overconcern about own health, potential medical absence and disability problems
☐   ☐   ☐   prone to pain and other body complaints without sufficient physical basis, overreactive to injuries
☐   ☐   ☐   depressed, low morale would interfere with functioning
☐   ☐   ☐   slowed down pace, may not keep up
☐   ☐   ☐   lacks emotional stability and self-regulation
☐   ☐   ☐   could misinterpret the motives of others and act on wrong beliefs
☐   ☐   ☐   insecure, fearful, lacks mature identity
☐   ☐   ☐   unable to handle hostility from others, may disorganize under intense hostility
☐   ☐   ☐   overexcitable and easily distracted
☐   ☐   ☐   unrealistic optimism, apt to get "carried-away"
☐   ☐   ☐   starter but non-finisher
☐   ☐   ☐   deficits of practical coping

Not indicated   1 2 3 4 5 6 7 8 9 10   Serious Disorder

3. STABILITY AND JUDGMENT

M/O   BOR   EXC
☐   ☐   ☐   deficits of conscience and integrity
☐   ☐   ☐   potential for over-reactions and loss of judgment under stress
☐   ☐   ☐   potential antagonism to normal discipline
☐   ☐   ☐   impulsive, failures to anticipate consequences
☐   ☐   ☐   accident prone
☐   ☐   ☐   serious longterm risk of alcoholism and/or drug abuse

Good   1 2 3 4 5 6 7 8 9 10   Unacceptable

4. SELF-CONTROL AND ANGER CONTROL

M/O   BOR   EXC
☐   ☐   ☐   undercontrolled aggression under stress
☐   ☐   ☐   could be dangerous to others
☐   ☐   ☐   irritable, hasty reactions
☐   ☐   ☐   "chip-on-the-shoulder" attitude
☐   ☐   ☐   could be self-righteous and punitive
☐   ☐   ☐   rigid and brittle controls; potentially explosive

Favorable   1 2 3 4 5 6 7 8 9 10   Poor risk

5. WORK FACTORS

M/O   BOR   EXC
☐   ☐   ☐   risk of undue "time off sick"
☐   ☐   ☐   moodiness, could drag others down
☐   ☐   ☐   inhibited, lacks needed assertiveness
☐   ☐   ☐   problems in handling criticism
☐   ☐   ☐   lacks flexibility, rule-bound
☐   ☐   ☐   potentially irritating or disturbing of staff morale
☐   ☐   ☐   lacks longterm persistence, vocational stability
☐   ☐   ☐   lacks warmth, sensitivity
☐   ☐   ☐   distant and slow to trust others
☐   ☐   ☐   rationalizer
☐   ☐   ☐   manipulative of others
☐   ☐   ☐   lacks realistic self-appraisal
☐   ☐   ☐   overly ambitious, unrealistic
☐   ☐   ☐   likely to seek responsibilities beyond training and experience
☐   ☐   ☐   low overall effectiveness

Favorable   1 2 3 4 5 6 7 8 9 10   Bad risk

OVERALL ACCEPTABILITY

☐   ACCEPTABLE
☐   PROBABLY ACCEPT
☐   BORDERLINE, LEAN TOWARD ACCEPT
☐   BORDERLINE, LEAN TOWARD NOT ACCEPT
☐   PROBABLY NOT ACCEPT
☐   NOT ACCEPT

Figure 6. MMPI-based rating form for police personnel.
From Caldwell, 1978.

(b) use some data for which there is no valid basis to expect that they will assist employers in making the intended decision.

When used in a personnel-selection situation, the MMPI has been considered an invasion of privacy (Brayfield, 1965). Many of the MMPI items were found objectionable by subjects in a personnel-selection situation that were not considered inappropriate in a clinical context (Butcher & Tellegen, 1966). The MMPI items that subjects considered inappropriate for an employment-selection situation are shown in Table 6. These items fall into four broad content domains: religion, sex, bladder and bowel functioning, and family relationships. They are items that people feel are not relevant to the general question of their suitability for employment and should not be asked by employers.

But, even if the use of these procedures can be justified, could invasion of privacy be shown to be warranted under some circumstances?

A recent court decision, McKenna vs. Fargo (*Federal Supplement 1355* [1978]), concerning the use of the MMPI for selecting firemen, speaks to the legal side of the issue. Several firefighters sued the personnel manager and the city of Jersey City, N.J. for infringing their rights under the 1st and 14th amendments:

(a) Several MMPI items with religious content violated their right to freedom of religious belief.

(b) Administering the MMPI in this setting constituted an invasion of privacy.

The opinion read by Judge Coolahan was against the plaintiffs. It read:

> Rarely does a case involve conflicting interests as important and difficult to reconcile as those in this litigation. The psychological testing which Jersey City uses to screen applicants for its fire department has been challenged by plaintiffs as an invasion of the applicants' constitutional rights. In plaintiffs' view, conditioning employment on psychological testing of questionable validity puts the applicants to a prohibited choice of sacrificing constitutional freedoms to secure prized employment or of looking for work elsewhere. Defendants contend that the condition is a reasonable and necessary one because the task of fighting fires is no ordinary job in difficulty or importance and because its success depends critically on the psychological capabilities of firemen.
>
> There is good reason to scrutinize a government requirement which

Table 6. Content Classification of MMPI Items
(Listed by Booklet No.) with Objection Rates of .20 or More

Category	General Condition	Selection Condition
Sex	20, 133, 297	20, 37, 69, 101, 133, 179, 199, 208, 231, 239, 297, 300, 302, 320, 324, 427, 441, 470, 485, 514, 519, 548, 558, 566
Religion and religious beliefs	58, 483	27, 50, 53, 58, 95, 98, 115, 206, 249, 258, 369, 373, 387, 413, 420, 464, 476, 483, 488, 490, 491
Family relationships	237	65, 216, 220, 224, 237, 325, 421, 478, 562
Bladder and bowel function	14, 63, 512	14, 18, 63, 462, 474, 486, 542
Other	61, 287, 513	15, 61, 311, 19, 70, 73, 127, 184, 232, 244, 287, 303, 358, 511, 513, 533

Source: Butcher & Tellegen, 1966.

joins the words psychology and testing. Psychology is not yet the science that medicine is and tests are too frequently used like talismanic formulas. The Court has, therefore, carefully reviewed the extensive evidence generated by a long trial and has not arrived lightly at the conclusion that the defendants' psychological testing is constitutional.

Meehl (1969) stated this position:

Now let me play the other role for a moment. Consider the use of the MMPI for selecting Northwest Orient Airlines electrical inspectors. The psychopathic component on the MMPI is largely validated in a psychiatric context. For the moment, pretend that no studies of behaviors like accident-proneness or goofing off in school had ever been done. Under these circumstances, I would say there is an ethical problem in industry—when you extrapolate the behavior domain into a new context. Whether it is illicit to use the instrument under these circumstances is dependent upon the sensitivity of the job. If the job is one which affects whether airplanes crash, then I would say, "Look, if you are an industrial psychologist using the MMPI in the airline industry, you ought to try to validate it. But, even before you validate the instrument, if a high degree of judgment and responsibility is required in the position for which you're screening and if your selection ratio is running reasonably small, then you should give a Mult. If it's a matter of selecting a shoe salesman, eliminating the 49's isn't that important. But, when I fly, I would feel more comfortable knowing that some screening of the crew, even with imperfect tests, has been done— I would prefer not having 49's at the helm."

Can the MMPI be made less objectionable? Butcher and Tellegen (1966), in their study of objectionable item content, suggested that the incidence of objections to the item content could be reduced without drastically altering the validity of the scales. They examined the scale membership of the objectionable items and found that some scales—particularly *F*, *Pd*, and *Sc*—contained a high percentage of the items. Altering the scales by deleting controversial items would reduce the effectiveness of several important scales (particularly *Pd* and *Sc*) without making the scales much less objectionable (see Table 7).

The overall objectionableness of the MMPI might be reduced somewhat by improving administration procedures—for example, by requiring that candidates answer only the first 399 items of Form R

Table 7. Objection Statistics of Selected Scales

Scale	General Condition Mean Item Objection Rate	Selection Condition Mean Item Objection Rate	Selection Condition Percentage of OI's[a]	Mean Item Objection Rate with OI's Eliminated
L	04	12	06	11
F	05	14	19	11
K	03	09	00	09
Hs	04	11	06	08
D	04	11	12	08
Hy	03	08	03	07
Pd	06	13	22	10
Mf	05	13	18	09
Pa	05	13	08	12
Pt	04	09	06	08
Sc	05	13	17	11
Ma	05	11	09	10
Si	04	09	06	08
A	04	08	02	08
R	03	11	02	11
So-r	04	10	05	09

Source: Butcher & Tellegen, 1966.

[a]OI's: objectionable items, a group of 76 items with objection rates −.20.

(since the validity and clinical scales can be scored from this reduced item set) and by providing an appropriate explanation to applicants of why the questions need to be asked and how the results are going to be used.

Potential Misuses of Psychological Tests

The use of psychological tests to assess individual personality is generally based on the assumption that the results of the tests or procedures will in some way benefit the individual taking the test. That is, the testee is the client in most applications of psychological tests. However, in personnel screening the client becomes the organization conducting the assessment and the individual benefits only indirectly from submitting to testing. Ethical guidelines for psychologists ensure that this relationship is not unethical. The individuals, who are the objects of evaluation, are willing participants and are treated with appropriate consideration. Using psychological tests in personnel decisions may, in fact, be the most beneficial procedure available, since they may allow for the "eventual actualization of processes leading to an optimal utilization of human resources for the total economy" (Dunnette & Borman, 1979, p. 514).

The ethical use of psychological assessment procedures assumes that tests are being administered, scored, interpreted, and, in general, controlled in a professionally responsible manner. The guidelines for psychological tests, like the MMPI, are more strict than are those recommended for interests tests, values tests, job-related achievement tests, etc. (American Psychological Association, 1974), since the level of training and professional background required for their use are high and the potential for misuse is great. Sound professional application of a personality instrument requires extensive training in abnormal psychology, psychometric theory, and clinical psychological practice.

In large corporations or institutions, procedures are developed by qualified professionals. But sometimes the tests are administered or managed by less well-trained personnel. The relatively objective administrative format of the MMPI makes it well suited for large-scale use since clerks can be trained to score the test in a few minutes. Because the MMPI can often be interpreted by reference to the published MMPI codebooks, this step in the analysis of test performance becomes a temptation for unqualified individuals. The author is aware of several instances in which important decisions about an applicant's life were made by clerks who had neither the expertise nor the acquired professional "responsibility" for such decisions. The following unfortunate situation will illustrate this problem.

Applicants seeking admission to the graduate program in clinical psychology at the University of Minnesota are asked to take the MMPI. Most individuals take it at a university counseling bureau or at a similar agency, which sends the score profile to our admissions committee. The MMPI profile given in Figure 7, with the accompanying interpretation, was sent by an industrial psychology firm (which incidentally charged the woman a high fee for the disservice).

The psychological interpretation represents an unethical use of the psychological test for a number of reasons: (1) The test interpretation was *incorrect*. Actually, the candidate's normal-limits profile fits quite closely the modal female applicant to graduate psychology programs (see Figure 4; (2) Thus it is the *base rate* profile; (3) It was analyzed by a *secretary* who simply scored the answer sheet and looked up the "personality" descriptions in a reference book. No psychologist examined the profile for accuracy or verified the relevance and appropriateness of the interpretations; (4) The interpretation is *sexist*, including incorrect and harmful anti-female speculations about the person being described in the report. The unethical practice reported here is perhaps an extreme example. However, other examples could be given in which psychologists who are untrained in the interpretation of the MMPI and unaware of its limitations employ the instrument in questionable ways.

Fairness to Minority Applicants

There has been a great deal of concern in recent years about fairness in hiring practices of businesses and government agencies. Equal-employment opportunity has been a central issue for employment officers as well as for the individual minority group member or female who applies for employment. One focus of attention has been the use of psychological tests that allegedly favor one group over another. Although much of the debate has raged over the use of intellectual or ability measures, other types of tests have not escaped criticism. For example, the MMPI has been considered to have "racially sensitive" items (Harrison & Kass, 1967; Gynther, Chapter 4 this volume). Minority group members are believed to answer items in certain MMPI content domains differently from the way in which white subjects answer. Blacks and poor people in general have been shown to have more highly elevated profiles on the MMPI simply because of their minority group membership and not because they are psychologically disturbed. Thus, the elimination of blacks from a

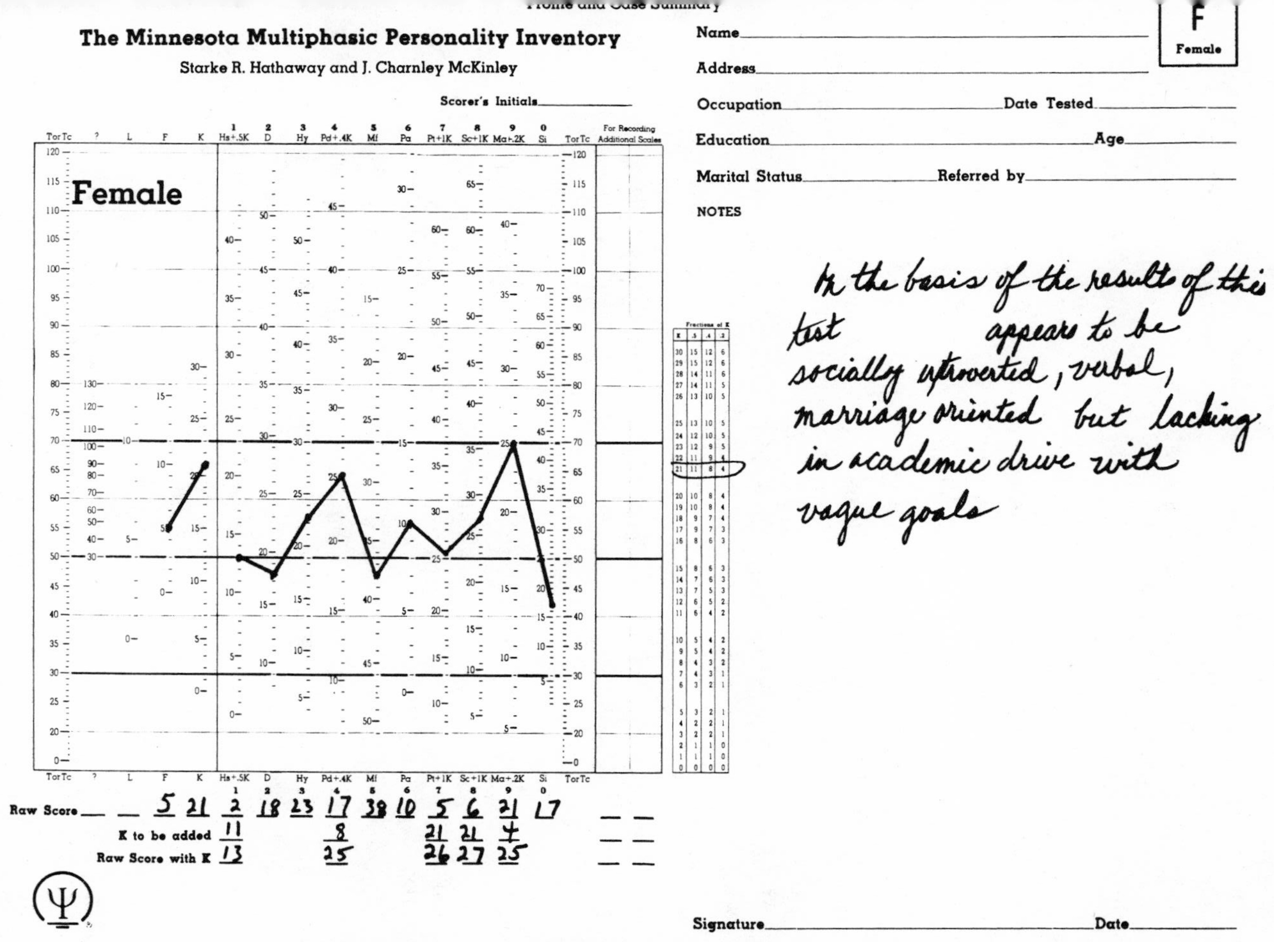

The Minnesota Multiphasic Personality Inventory

Starke R. Hathaway and J. Charnley McKinley

Female

Scorer's Initials

Name
Address
Occupation   Date Tested
Education   Age
Marital Status   Referred by
NOTES

On the basis of the results of this test appears to be socially extroverted, verbal, marriage oriented but lacking in academic drive with vague goals

Raw Score ___ L 5 F 21 K ___ Hs+.5K 2 D 18 Hy 23 Pd+.4K 17 Mf 38 Pa 10 Pt+1K 5 Sc+1K 6 Ma+.2K 21 Si 17
K to be added ___   11   21   24
Raw Score with K ___   13   38 25   26 27

Signature _____ Date _____

Figure 7. Inappropriate MMPI profile and report submitted on a normal, female, graduate-school applicant.

job on the basis of an MMPI elevation may be considered an unfair application. Gynther (1972) expressed concern about this problem and suggested that there have been instances in which the MMPI has been unfairly used. These conclusions are not unanimously accepted, however. Dahlstrom (1978) pointed out that analyses have not identified consistent differences associated with ethnicity alone and that the differences reported in various studies could be attributed to socio-economic factors.

An important study that bears on the use of the MMPI in a personnel-selection situation was published by King, Carroll, and Fuller (1977). They examined MMPI profiles of black and white full-time employees of a large industrial company. They found that the mean profiles were within normal limits and produced no clinically significant scale differences. Scores on three scales were significant, with blacks slightly higher on *Ma* and whites slightly higher on *Pa* and *Es*.

Can the MMPI be used to select job applicants and comply with government equal-opportunity recommendations? Yes, if the indexes have been shown to be related to performance on the job and if they do not punish minority applicants. The most recent Guidelines provided by the Equal Employment Opportunity Commission (*Federal Registry*, December, 1977) for psychological tests in selection do not argue against the use of psychological tests for personnel screening but do offer stringent suggestions about their use.

Dunnette and Borman (1979) pointed out that:

> Provision 703 of title VII of the 1964 CRA assured employers that Congress did not intend that employers be required to give preferential treatment to individuals just because they belonged to protected classes no matter what imbalances their current work force might show. By implication, legal proof of unfair discrimination would require a showing of intent to discriminate against particular individuals. But, enforcement of the equal employment opportunity goals of title VII could not, in practice, rely exclusively on such a difficult burden of proof; thus, it is that additional regulations and correct interpretations have been promulgated such that the abstraction *equal opportunity* might be defined according to results achieved (statistical *parity*) by an employer's personnel practices (p. 502).

Computerized Personality Assessment: Potentials and Problems

The development of computer-based objective psychological test interpretation has revolutionized clinical assessment in the past

15 years. A movement that began with Meehl's (1954) demonstration that actuarial rules result in more sound predictions than interpretations generated by the clinician has culminated in a large number of commerically available diagnostic MMPI programs. Subscribers to a particular automated MMPI system can send protocols to the service and receive, usually by return mail, a full clinical diagnostic report. Many of these clinical reports provide, in addition to scoring and drawing the profile, a descriptive narrative report that reviews the individual's symptoms, traits, and conflicts, and frequently provides a prognostic statement and treatment recommendations.

Most of these programs were developed with clinical or psychiatric patients as the target population and were constructed with data generated from patient groups. A few programs were written with non-psychiatric populations in mind, e.g., Mayo program (medical) and Fowler's Psychological Assessment Service (corrections). However, they employ clinically based constructs and correlates. (For reviews of computer systems, see Butcher (1978) and Adair (1978) in the *Eighth Mental Measurements Yearbook*).

Attempts to use these computer-assessment systems in the "normal-range" employment-selection population have resulted in questionable practices. Some instances in which pathological personality descriptions have been routinely applied to normal-range profiles in employment screening have been noted (Butcher, 1978). Mass personality assessments can be done with computerized programs, thus presenting a temptation for managers to employ psychological screening on a grand scale—for purposes and with populations not suitable for MMPI assessment. Any computer application, industrial or otherwise, should be justified on the basis of relevancy of the test interpretation for the employment task and the actual validity of the prediction or reports. It falls upon the consumer of the computer-based interpretation and the management of the MMPI service (see APA guidelines for automated personality assessment, Fowler, 1969) to ensure that the psychological application is appropriate and valid.

SUMMARY

The importance of personality factors in personnel selection decision-making was discussed. Although personality theories, per se, do not provide practical guidelines to aid in the selection process, several personality areas believed important to applicant selection were mentioned—authoritarian value structure, conformity, need achievement, socialization, social judgment, empathy, and creativity.

The use of personality tests to aid in making personnel decisions was examined. The most tenable conclusion at this time is that no personality scales have been developed that have relevant indexes and valid predictors for personality/job matching decisions. The MMPI has been studied as a candidate for this use, but psychometric limitations inherent in the test, and limited data, prohibit it. It has not been shown that the MMPI can be used effectively to select certain personality types for specific occupations. Two uses of the MMPI in personnel selection have proved valuable:

(a) Providing empirical descriptions of the types of personalities who apply for given positions. However, the MMPI item content focuses on strange behavior and personality problems, most of which are irrelevant to most job applicants. Thus, the utility of the MMPI in this type of study is somewhat limited.

(b) Detecting psychopathology in the pool of applicants for employment. In this way, the MMPI operates as an exclusion criterion. Studies have shown that when the MMPI is used in populations of normal job applicants, a large percentage of cases (8-10%) produce invalid MMPI's and most individuals (about 85%) produce profiles in the normal range. Thus, the MMPI may aid in detecting aberrant personality patterns in a small percentage of the population.

The cost of testing needs to be weighed against the potential gain from using an instrument like the MMPI. Personnel-selection decisions for most occupations may not require the kind of information the MMPI provides. However, with critical occupations in which great responsibility, personality stability, honesty, etc., are highly desired characteristics (airline crew, police, etc.), the benefits of close personality evaluations may offset the costs involved. The MMPI appears to offer useful information about potential personality problems that could interfere with performance in some occupations.

Several issues that bear upon the use of personality tests in personnel selection were discussed. These include invasion of privacy, fairness to minority applicants, and the use of clinically based computerized narrative reports. Although these issues are quite complicated and the problems as yet not fully resolved, I tried to define the issues and present some recent information to help clarify them. The use of personality assessment in personnel selection remains a controversial area: the procedures require much greater empirical verification and important questions require answers.

NOTE

1. I appreciate the helpful comments Marvin Dunnette made on an earlier version of this paper.

REFERENCES

Adair, F. L. Reviews of MMPI automated systems. In Buros, O. K. (Ed.), *Eighth Mental Measurements Yearbook.* Vol. I. New Jersey: Gryphon Press, 1978, 940-42.

American Psychological Association. Standards for educational and psychological tests. Washington, D.C.: *American Psychological Association*, 1974.

Arvey, R. D., Mussio, S. J., & Payne, G. Relationships between MMPI scores and job performance measures of fire fighters. *Psychological Reports*, 1972, 31, 199-202.

Azen, S. P., Snibbe, H. M., & Montgomery, H. R. A longitudinal predictive study of success and performance of law enforcement officers. *Journal of Applied Psychology*, 1973, 57, 190-92.

Barnabus, B. Validity of personality and interest tests in selection and placement situations. *Trans. Kan. Acad. Sci.*, 1948, 51, 335-39.

Brayfield, A. H. (Ed.). Testing and public policy. *American Psychologist*, 1965, 20, 857-1005.

Burgess, M. M., Duffey, M., & Temple, F. G. Two studies of prediction success in a collegiate program of nursing. *Nursing Research*, 1972, 21, 357-66.

Butcher, J. N. *Use of the MMPI for industrial medical screening.* Unpublished manuscript, 1977. (a)

Butcher, J. N. MMPI based rating form for selection of airline crews. Unpublished manuscript, 1977. (b)

Butcher, J. N. Reviews of MMPI automated systems. In Buros, O. K. (Ed.), *Eighth Mental Measurements Yearbook.* Vol. I. New Jersey: Gryphon Press, 1978, 942-45.

Butcher, J. N., & Pancheri, P. *Handbook of cross-national MMPI research.* Minneapolis: University of Minnesota Press, 1976.

Butcher, J. N., & Tellegen, A. Objections to MMPI items. *Journal of Consulting Psychology*, 1966, 30, 527-34.

Caldwell, A. *Caldwell Report: Police Rating Form.* Unpublished manuscript, 1978.

Callan, J. P. An attempt to use the MMPI as a predictor of failure in military training. *British Journal of Psychiatry*, 1972, 121, 553-57.

Colarelli, N. J., & Siegel, S. M. A method of police personnel selection. *The Journal of Criminal Law, Criminology and Police Science*, 1964, 55, 287-89.

Cooke, J. K. MMPI in actuarial diagnosis of psychological disturbance among college males. *Journal of Counseling Psychology*, 1967, 4, 474-77.

Crovitz, E., Huse, M. N., & Lewis, D. E. Selection of physician's assistants. *Journal of Medical Education*, 1973, 48, 551-55.

Dahlstrom, W. G. *Minority status and MMPI scores: MMPI score patterns and background characteristics.* Paper given at the American Psychological Association Convention, Toronto, 1978.

Danet, B. N. Prediction of mental illness in college students on the basis of "nonpsychiatric" MMPI profiles. *Journal of Consulting Psychology*, 1965, 29, 577-80.

Daniels, E. E., & Hunter, W. A. MMPI personality patterns for various occupations. *Journal of Applied Psychology*, 1949, 33, 559-65.

Dunnette, M. D. The assessment of managerial talent. In P. McReynolds (Ed.), *Advances in psychological assessment.* Vol. II. Palo Alto, California: Science and Behavior Books, 1971.

Dunnette, M. D., & Borman, W. C. Personnel selection and classification systems. *Annual Review of Psychology*, 1979, 30, 477-525.

Equal Economic Opportunity Commission Uniform Guidelines on Employee Selection Procedures. *Federal Registry*, 1977, 42, 65512-52.

Evans, D. R. The use of the MMPI to predict conscientious hotline workers. *Journal of Clinical Psychology*, 1976, 32, 684-86.

Fenster, C. A., & Locke, B. Patterns of masculinity-femininity among college and non-college-oriented police officers: An empirical approach. *Journal of Clinical Psychology*, 1973, 29, 27-28.

Fowler, R. D. Automated interpretation of personality test data. In J. N. Butcher (Ed.), *MMPI: Research developments and clinical applications*. New York: McGraw-Hill, 1969.

Garetz, F. K., & Anderson, R. W. Patterns of professional activities of psychiatrists: A follow-up of 100 psychiatric residents. *American Journal of Psychiatry*, 1973, 130, 981-84.

Gottesman, J. *Personality patterns of urban police applicants as measured by the MMPI*. Hoboken, N. J. Laboratory of Psychological Studies, Steven Institute of Technology, 1969.

Gough, H. Personality and personality assessment. In M. D. Dunnette (Ed.), *Handbook of industrial and organizational psychology*. Chicago: Rand-McNally, 1976.

Gynther, M. D. White norms and black MMPI's: A prescription for discrimination? *Psychological Bulletin*, 1972, 78, 386-402.

Harrell, T. W. High earning MBA's. *Personnel Psychology*, 1972, 25, 523-30.

Harrell, T. W., & Harrell, M. S. The personality of MBA's who reach general management early. *Personnel Psychology* 1973, 26, 127-34.

Harrison, R. H., & Kass, E. H. Differences between negro and white pregnant women on the MMPI. *Journal of Consulting psychology*, 1967, 31, 454-63.

Hedlund, D. E. A review of the MMPI in industry. *Psychological Reports*, 1965, 17, 875-89.

Hooke, J. F., & Krauss. H. H. Personality characteristics of highly rated policemen. *Personnel Psychology*, 1971, 24, 679-86.

Jansen, D. G., Bonk, E. C., & Garvey, F. J. MMPI characteristics of clergymen in counseling training and their relationship to supervisor's and peers' ratings of counseling effectiveness. *Psychological Reports*, 1973, 33, 695-98.

Jansen, D. G., & Garvey, F. J. High-, average-, and low-rated clergymen in a state hospital clinical program. *Journal of Clinical Psychology*, 1973, 29, 89-92.

Kelly, W. L. Psychological prediction of leadership in nursing. *Nursing Research*, 1974, 23, 38-42.

King, H. F., Carroll, J. L., & Fuller, G. B. Comparison of nonpsychiatric blacks and whites on the MMPI. *Journal of Clinical Psychology*, 1977, 33, 725-28.

Kleinmuntz, B. Identification of maladjusted college students. *Journal of Counseling Psychology*, 1960, 7, 209-11.

Kleinmuntz, B. MMPI decision rules for the identification of college maladjustment: A digital computer approach. *Psychological Monographs*, 1963, 77(14, Whole No. 577).

Lachar, D. Prediction of early U.S. Air Force freshmen cadet adaptation with the MMPI. *Journal of Counseling Psychology*, 1974, 21, 401-8.

Marks, P. A. *Some methodological problems in intra-cultural research*. Paper given at the 13th Annual MMPI Symposium. Mexico City, 1978.

McAllister, L. *The MMPI as a selection instrument for law enforcement officers in Dakota County, 1969-77*. Oral presentation at Police Officer Training Board Seminar, Willmar, Minnesota, October 12, 1977.

McCormick, E. J. Job and task analysis. In M. D. Dunnette (Ed.), *Handbook of industrial and organizational psychology*. Chicago: Rand-McNally, 1976.

McKenna, V. Fargo. *451 F. Supplement*, 1355, 1978.

Meehl, P. E. *Clinical versus statistical prediction*. Minneapolis: University of Minnesota Press, 1954.

Meehl, P. E. Comments on the invasion of privacy. In J. N. Butcher (Ed.), *MMPI: Research developments and clinical applications*. New York: McGraw-Hill, 1969.

Muha, T. M., & May, J. R. An employment index for identifying unfit job applicants. *Journal of Community Psychology*, 1973, 1, 362-65.

Nowicki, S. A study of the personality characteristics of successful policemen. *Police*, 1966, 10, 39-41.

Owens, W. A. Background data. In M. D. Dunnette (Ed.), *Handbook of industrial and organizational psychology*. Chicago: Rand-McNally, 1976.

Parker, J. W. Psychological and personal history data related to accident records of commercial truck drivers. *Journal of Applied Psychology*, 1953, 37, 317-20.

Pucheu, C., & Riviera, O. Use of the MMPI in Mexico. Quoted in J. N. Butcher & P. Pancheri, *Handbook of cross-national MMPI research*. Minneapolis: University of Minnesota Press, 1976.

President's Commission on Mental Health. *Report to the President 1978*. U.S. Government Printing Office, October, 1978.

Rissetti, F:, Butcher, J. N., et al. *Translation and adaptation of the MMPI in Chile*. Paper given at the 14th Annual MMPI Symposium, St. Petersburg, 1979.

Sacuzzo, D. P., Higgins, G., & Lewandowski, D. Program for psychological assessment of law enforcement officers: Initial evaluation. *Psychological Reports*, 1974, 35, 651-54.

Schmitt, N. Social and situational determinants of interview decisions. Implications for the employment interview. *Personnel Psychology*, 1976, 29, 79-101.

Schmitt, N., & Coyle, B. W. Applicant decisions in the employment interview. *Journal of Applied Psychology*, 1976, 61, 184-92.

Solway, K. S., Hays, J. R., & Zieben, M. Personality characteristics of juvenile probation officers. *Journal of Community Psychology*, 1976, 4, 152-56.

Stone, L. A., Bassett, G. R., Brosseau, J. D., Demers, J., & Stiening, J. A. Psychological test scores for a group of MEDEX trainees. *Psychological Reports*, 1972, 31, 827-31.

Stone, L. A., & Brosseau, J. D., Cross-validation of a system for predicting training success of MEDEX trainees. *Psychological Reports*, 1973, 33, 917-18.

Use of Parents' MMPIs in the Research and Evaluation of Children

A Review of the Literature and Some New Data

David Lachar and James R. Sharp

Hafner, Butcher, Hall, and Quast (1969) noted that MMPI profiles from parents may "reflect, more or less adequately, a map of the child's psychological environment insofar as it is determined by parental personalities" (p. 187). This measurement of parents' personalities has potential theoretical and pragmatic value. Some investigators have studied the influence of parental characteristics on the subsequent behavior of children, and have measured the effects that the atypical behavior of children has upon parents. Their hope has been to shed additional light on the etiology of childhood disorders. By contrast, clinicians in child-guidance settings administer the MMPI to parents to meet more immediate needs. The MMPI profile provides information that will help the clinician understand the presenting complaints and design an effective treatment plan. The MMPI is an important source of information about the parents, who are often not willing to focus on their own behavior when their presence at a clinic is motivated by their child's problem behavior. Clinicians evaluate the profiles of parents to accurately assess the child's current problems, identify possibly deviant parent-child interactions, structure their contact with parents to establish a "therapeutic relationship," and determine the degree to which parents can become effectively involved in their child's treatment.

Because reported findings were inconsistent and because there was only a limited amount of information available to be derived from studies with methodological deficiencies, Hafner et al. (1969)

limited their conclusion to the general one that the parents of be-haviorally disturbed children appear to be more disturbed than parents in general, but not as disturbed as adult psychiatric patients.

In this chapter, we will present studies that evaluate MMPI pro-files of parents, discuss methodological issues, and explore some of the more promising approaches used with a sample of MMPI proto-cols of parents seen by the staff of the Division of Child and Ado-lescent Psychiatry at Lafayette Clinic, an urban psychiatric training and research facility. We hope to provide more specific conclusions about the role of parental psychopathology in childhood disorder than it was possible for Hafner et al. to provide.

THE LAFAYETTE CLINIC SAMPLE

Subjects

The sample included 190 children and adolescents and their mothers, fathers, or guardians who accompanied them to the Lafay-ette Clinic for psychiatric evaluation during the years 1976 and 1977. Evaluation had been arranged by the recommendation of par-ents (29%), mental health agencies (27%), school personnel (25%), private psychiatrists (12%), courts (4%), or family physicians (3%). These disturbed children ranged in age from 4 to 17 years and in-cluded 117 males and 73 females, 129 of whom were white, 61 black. The parents were composed of 184 mothers and 73 fathers; 48% of the parents were married, 28% divorced, 11% separated, 8% single, and 5% widowed. Some additional data were available to ex-pand the number of mothers in one analysis to 218 (maternal MMPI X Personality Inventory for Children scores (Wirt, Lachar, Klinedinst, & Seat, 1977). The distribution of the traditionally established components of socioeconomic status for these 190 families is given in Table 1.

Distribution of primary GAP diagnoses (Group for the Ad-vancement of Psychiatry, 1966) for this sample may be estimated from a concurrent study of a sample of 431 evaluations of children and adolescents at Lafayette Clinic (Lachar & Gdowski, 1979b). In that study, GAP diagnoses reflected a variety of presenting problems for children and adolescents, respectively: healthy responses, 8.5% and 8.2%; reactive disorders, 12.5% and 24.2; developmental devia-tions, 35.5% and 14.3%; psychoneurotic disorders, 18.5% and 22.1%; personality disorders, 10.5% and 17.3%; psychotic disorders, 1.0% and 6.5%; psychophysiologic disorders, .5% and 1.3%; and brain syndromes and mental retardation, 11.0% and 3.0%.

Table 1. Education and Occupation of the Household's
Highest Income-Earner

Educational Attainment	N	%
Graduate or professional training	5	2.6
College graduate	10	5.3
Partial college training	31	16.3
High-school graduate	72	37.9
Partial high school	36	18.9
Junior high school (grades 7-9)	18	9.5
Less than 7 years of school	2	1.1
Missing data	16	8.4
Total	190	100.0

Current Occupation	N	%
Executive or major professional	4	2.1
Manager or lesser professional	10	5.3
Administrative personnel or semi-professional	11	5.8
Clerical, salesworker, or technician	24	12.6
Skilled manual worker	23	12.1
Semi-skilled worker, machine operator	33	17.4
Unskilled worker or unemployed	72	37.9
Missing data	13	6.8
Total	190	100.0

MMPI Data

MMPIs of the parents were obtained at various points in the diagnostic process. For approximately half the cases, the MMPI was administered within the first few weeks of hospitalization of the child or adolescent; the remaining MMPIs were administered during one of the early outpatient visits. MMPI responses were obtained through the sorting of Inventory items printed on computer cards, and the 13 profile, *ES* (Barron, 1953), *A, R* (Welsh, 1965) scales, profile code category, and code type were generated by an automated scoring and interpretation program (Lachar, 1974a, b; Lachar, Klinge, & Grisell, 1976).

Criteria

Information on the child's behavior, family interaction, and parental characteristics was available as part of the systematic validation of a new objective multidimensional child-behavior instrument, the Personality Inventory for Children (PIC) (Wirt, et al., 1977). Data on physical, intellectual, and social development and current behavior problems were systematically gathered in the form of an application for diagnostic services This form was usually completed by the child's parents several weeks before their initial clinic appointment.

A second data form was completed by a psychiatric resident following an interview with the parent(s) of the child, review of material provided by the child's school, and consultation with a supervising psychiatrist. This form included checklist items concerning the child's self-concept, affect, cognitive functioning, interpersonal relations, physical development and health, parent-child relationships, and parent characteristics.

A third source of information on the status of the child and family was the PIC profile scale scores. These 16 scales reflect informant response style, general adjustment, intellectual status, and academic achievement, as well as a broad range of behavioral and personality trait dimensions. In each case, this 600-item inventory was completed by the child's mother, usually on the day of her first diagnostic interview.

RELATIVE PSYCHOPATHOLOGY OF PARENTS OF DEVIANT CHILDREN

Parents of Children with Limited or Specific Disabilities

The earliest published research evaluated the parents of stuttering children. Comparing parents of 100 stuttering children with normal controls matched on age and sex of the child and socioeconomic status of the parents yielded limited results (Goodstein & Dahlstrom, 1956). In two of the three significant mean scale differences, the parents of stuttering children obtained *lower* scale scores than did parents of normal children. In addition, children whose stuttering symptoms were more severe tended to have parents with more normal profiles. A follow-up study using children with stuttering problems of longer duration reported a similar lack of mean scale score differences (Goodstein, 1956). In addition, no relationship was found between scale scores and severity of stuttering.

Parents of children with cleft palates obtained lower mean scale scores than the control group in three of the five significant differences; none of the differences were of great magnitude (Goodstein, 1960a, 1960b). Although parental adjustment, judged on the basis of the MMPI profile, was not related to the adjustment of the child, parental adjustment was significantly related to the age of the physically deformed child. This finding supported the notion that the effect upon the parent of having a physically handicapped child may be cumulative.

Parents of very young retarded children obtained significantly greater mean scale scores in comparison to the norm samples for all clinical scales except *Hs* and *Ma* for mothers, and *Hs*, *Pa*, and *Sc* for fathers (Erickson, 1969). High-point codes were tabulated for these parents, and scales *Hy* and *Pd* classified over 40% of the profiles. In a second study conducted in a pediatric clinic, no mean scale score differences were found between parents of older retarded children and children of average intelligence, nor was the age of the child related to scale elevation (Routh, 1970). Further analysis indicated that parental education related to several scales for both mothers and fathers. A recent study found that mothers of retarded children obtained lower mean *K* and higher mean *Ma* scores than mothers of normal children, while no differences were found between mothers of retarded and emotionally disturbed children (Miller & Keirn, 1978). A lack of comparability in these three studies makes it difficult to draw any conclusions. Comparison groups varied from the MMPI standardization sample, parents of nonretarded children seen at a pediatric clinic, to parents of normal children recruited from the same geographic area as study parents. In addition, the behaviors and child-rearing needs subsumed by the term "retardation" may have differed across studies. It is likely that children labeled retarded at a young age display more deviant behavior and make more demands on parents than children labeled retarded at an older age. It is also likely that retarded children seen at a pediatric clinic manifest less behavioral disturbance than retarded children seen at a psychiatric clinic. The lack of differences between parents of retarded and emotioanlly disturbed children may very well reflect the fact that the former were seen for "a variety of adaptive, behavioral, and emotional problems . . . but the primary reason for referral to the clinic was the child's developmental disability" (Miller & Keirn, 1978, p. 687).

Comparison of the mean profiles of parents of asthmatic children with parents of children with diverse physical ailments resulted in significant differences for only 2 of 28 comparisons (Fitzelle, 1959). The mothers of enuretic children differed on only one scale, *Pa*, from a group of volunteers (Stehbens, 1970). Pinneau and Hopper (1958) examined the relation between maternal scale scores and incidence of gastrointestinal disturbance in their infants. The surprising results suggested an inverse relation between admission of pathology and rates of burping and regurgitation in the infants.

Parents of Children with Emotional Disorders

Analysis of Mean Scale Score Data. Seven studies were published between 1959 and 1966 that compared the mean profiles of parents of children seen in guidance clinics with normal controls (Adrian, Vacchiano, & Gilbart, 1966; Goodstein & Rowley, 1961; L'Abate, 1960; Lauterbach, London, & Bryan, 1961; Liverant, 1959; Marks, 1961; Wolking, Quast, & Lawton, 1966). In all but one study, children were excluded who were mentally deficient or organically impaired. Four of the studies used the Goodstein and Dahlstrom (1956) sample of normal parents for their control group, two used the MMPI norm sample, and Adrian et al. (1966) recruited parents of normal children from PTA organizations. Unlike the results of the studies with parents of children with limited or specific disabilities, the results of these studies are very consistent, in that the mean MMPI profiles of parents of children seen at child guidance agencies are elevated in comparison to control samples. Tabulation of the frequency of obtained significant differences across the seven cited studies revealed that mothers of behaviorally disturbed children were uniformly found to have higher mean scores on scales *D* and *Hy*; five to six studies documented higher mean scores on scales *Hs*, *Pd*, and *Pa*; and four studies found higher mean scores for scales *Pt* and *Sc*. Tabulation of the results of these analyses of MMPI scales for fathers revealed that in five to six studies the fathers of behaviorally disturbed children were found to have higher mean scores on scales *Hs*, *D*, *Pd*, and *Sc*, and four studies found higher mean scores on *Hy*. It is important to note that the magnitude of the scale differences obtained was not large; the modal difference was only four T-score units. In no case did the difference exceed the standard deviation of the scale.

Three studies compared mean parent profiles to those of adult psychiatric patients. Lauterbach et al. (1961) found that parents of children seen in guidance clinics obtained significantly lower MMPI scores in 17 of 24 comparisons when contrasted with neurotic VA inpatients. McAdoo and Connolly (1975) and McAdoo and DeMeyer (1978) used adult psychiatric outpatients who were also parents as a control group, and found that parents who were patients themselves obtained higher scores on all scales measuring symptomatology, and were less defensive, as measured by *K*.

Analysis of Configural Data. A number of studies have reported the frequency of primed parent profiles (⩾1 clinical scale ⩾70T), or the proportion of mothers and fathers generating profiles generally considered to suggest significant disability. Mothers seen in child-guidance clinics obtained more primed profiles than did mothers in control samples: 46 vs. 18% (Liverant, 1959); 52 vs. 24% (Goodstein & Rowley, 1961); and 50 vs. 14% (Marks, 1961). Studies without controls have reported similar frequencies: 27% (Lauterbach et al., 1961), and 40% (Wolking et al., 1966). Fathers seen in child guidance clinics obtained more primed profiles than did fathers in control samples: 53 vs. 31% (Liverant, 1959); 46 vs. 26% (Goodstein & Rowley, 1961); and 44 vs. 15% (Marks, 1961). The fathers described by Lauterbach et al. (1961) and Wolking et al. (1966) obtained 28% and 36% of primed profiles, respectively. McAdoo and DeMeyer (1978) found that the percentages of child-guidance parent profiles similar to those obtained by psychiatric outpatients (McAdoo, 1976) was 21% for mothers and 18% for fathers.

Tabulation of profile *high-point* (highest scale >54T) by Marks (1961) revealed that child-guidance mothers had a significantly greater proportion of *Hy* and *Pd* high points than controls, and that combined these two scales classified nearly 50% of clinic mothers. Wolking et al. (1966) found significant differences not only for *Hy* and *Pd*, but also for *D* and *Pa*. Clinic fathers have been found to have greater proportions of high points on scales *D* and *Hy* (Marks, 1961; Wolking et al., 1966) and *Pd* (Wolking et al., 1966). Wolking et al. (1966) also found a significantly smaller proportion of *Ma* high points for clinic mothers and fathers. In contrast, Lauterbach et al. (1961) found no significant differences in high-point frequencies between clinic parents and controls.

Reciprocal two-point code types are frequently the basis for profile classification in MMPI interpretive systems (Lachar, 1974b). Both Marks (1961) and Wolking et al. (1966) found that the 3-4/4-3 code was among the most common of profile types for both clinic mothers and fathers. Other frequent code types reported included 1-3/3-1, 0-2/2-0, and 2-4/4-2 for clinic mothers, and 0-2/2-0, 1-3/3-1, 5-9/9-5, and 3-5/5-3 for clinic fathers.

Methodological Considerations

The amount of information conveyed by the preceding studies has been limited by the methodology used in the studies. Basically, the classification of parents and their MMPI results have been global and diffuse. In studies of the etiology of the behavior problems of children, it is usually assumed that the degree of parental influence varies as a function of the disorder of the child. By placing all behaviorally disturbed children in one sample, one may entirely mask the potential differences between disorders with possibly greater genetic influence, and, therefore, fewer environmental components (such as hyperactivity and psychosis) and disorders with possibly greater relationship to the environment (such as reactive depressions and antisocial behavior).

In none of these studies were separate analyses completed by either sex or age of the child being evaluated. Social learning theory would suggest that the same-sex parent might have a greater influence on the behavior of the child (Bandura & Walters, 1963). The effects of parental behavior on older children might be either attenuated owing to increased peer influence or stronger owing to more years of parent-child interaction. Jacob (1975), when comparing the literature on family interaction in normal and disturbed families, noted the potential importance of family size, social class, religion, and ethnicity; age and sex of parent; and sex, age, and birth order of child. Since a high proportion of father-absent families are seen in guidance clinics, it may be that the mother's influence on her children varies as a function of the presence of her husband in the home.

In many studies, the effect of demographic variables was neither controlled nor evaluated. Because studies have mainly used samples of lower-middle-class white families, it is uncertain to what extent these results can be generalized to other populations. A tentative answer to this question is provided by Verinis (1976), who compared the MMPI profiles of mothers of clinic and control children in an urban ghetto. The absence of significant differences (a majority of profiles in both samples were clinically elevated) suggests that great caution should be exercised in generalizing results to different populations. Research by Shectman (1970, 1971) suggests some important factors that may influence the relation of the MMPIs of parents and the problem behavior of children across ethnic groups. In contrast to findings with white children, the mean number of checklist symptoms did not differ between clinic and nonclinic black children, and a smaller proportion of referrals were initiated by black compared to white parents. In addition, there is evidence that the scale scores of the MMPI may need to be adjusted for minority groups (Gynther, 1972; Gynther, Lachar, & Dahlstrom, 1978).

The analysis of mean profile data has proven problematic here as well as in other areas of MMPI research. In averaging profiles, the frequency of meaningful profile characteristics and the relationships among MMPI scales may be obscured. It is impossible to determine the frequency of primed profiles from an average group profile that is within normal limits (T < 70). Even the code of an elevated mean profile may not suggest that this code type predominates, or is even frequent (cf. Hodo & Fowler, 1976). Such "configural masking" will occur as a result of the averaging procedure if there is simply a large proportion of unique profiles in a given sample, or if two or more distinct configural patterns predominate.

An additional issue is raised by the comparison of method of data collection, which is concurrent for parent protocols and child classification, and the method of interpretation, which often assumes a causational frame of reference. Traditionally, clinicians and research- ers have labeled indications of parental psychopathology as causative factors in the development of a child's behavioral disorder. More re- cent literature has stressed the interaction of the effects of parent on child and child on parent. In the MMPI literature on parents, Erick- son (1968, 1969) has been the major proponent of the interpretation that "at least some of the profile elevation may be due to the parents' reaction to the stress of having a deviant child" (1968, p. 704).

A general evaluative strategy of the "stress reaction" hypothesis has been to evaluate the parents of deviant children for whom parent pathology is unlikely to be causative (e.g., retardation), and to com- pare them to parents of deviant children for whom parent pathology is hypothesized to be causative. Erickson (1968) found similar pro- files from parents of retarded children who were emotionally dis- turbed and parents of retarded children having organic involvement but displaying no signs of emotional disturbance. Miller and Keirn (1978) found no differences between the profiles of parents of re- tarded and emotionally disturbed children, who were evaluated at an outpatient psychiatric clinic, although a greater number of significant differences were found between mothers of normal and emotionally disturbed children than between mothers of mentally retarded and normal children. Alley, Snider, Forsyth, and Opitz (1974) after co- varying child age and family socioeconomic status found no differ- ences between the fathers of children with "minimal cerebral dys- function" and fathers of children with behavior disorders, but the two groups of mothers did differ on four of the MMPI scales. Dee and Dee (1972) reported only minimal differences among the MMPIs of parents of motor dysfunctional, emotionally disturbed, and boys referred for evaluation but later classified as normal.

Erickson's (1969) findings that the parents of retarded children have elevated MMPIs in comparison to a normative sample was also interpreted as supporting the stress-reaction hypothesis. In this study, many of the same scales that have often differentiated parents of emotionally disturbed children from control samples were found to be elevated in the profiles of parents of retarded children. In contrast, Wolking et al. (1966) reported that parents of retarded children had a lower mean MMPI profile than their sample of clinic parents.

Although Erickson (1969) stated that the stress-reaction hypothesis would predict greater parental abnormality with increased behavioral deviancy in the child, MMPI scale elevations of parents have not been found to be positively related to the severity of the problems of stuttering children (Goodstein, 1956; Goodstein & Dahlstrom, 1956), children with cleft palates (Goodstein, 1960b), and asthmatic children (Fitzelle, 1959). McAdoo and DeMeyer (1978) compared the parents of autistic and non-autistic, non-psychotic guidance clinic children. Parents were matched on marital status, race, relationship to child, age, education, number of children in the family, social class, and sex of the child. Although the stress-reaction hypothesis would predict greater deviancy in the parents of the more disturbed autistic children, this was not found.

Ideally, longitudinal studies could determine if parental MMPI profile elevations develop as a reaction to the child's deviance or if such elevations predate the existence of the child's problems. In the absence of such research, investigators need to obtain measures of the subjective stress caused by the child's problems. Johnson and Lobitz (1974), for example, found significant positive relationships for fathers and their sons between the amount of disruptive behavior and the elevation of scales *F*, *Hy*, *Pd*, and *Sc*. Recent research (e.g., Smith, Johnson & Sarason, 1978) suggests that subjective measures of stress may be more pertinent, as perceived stress is probably a function of the interaction between life events and personality factors.

Essentially, the analysis of MMPI data as related to the stress-reaction hypothesis may be restated in terms of whether the MMPI profile elevations of clinic parents reflect either state or trait variables. As Spielberger (1966) notes, measures of personality constructs such as anxiety may fluctuate with changing environmental stresses, thus reflecting the current "state" of the individual, or they may represent predispositions for the individual to act in similar ways across a variety of situations (i.e., they may act as "trait" measures). Research that has experimentally examined the relation between MMPI scale elevations and various forms of stress suggests that (1) there is an interaction between the effects of stress and the personality of the subject (e.g., Roessler, Alexander, & Greenfield, 1963), and (2) MMPI profile changes resulting from stress appear to vary with the particular form of the stressor. Research that examines the finer grain of the relation of parental personality to the behavior of children, and documents both positive and negative relationships, may begin to tease apart the effects of, and on, parent personality.

The Lafayette Clinic Sample

The code-type classification of the MMPI profiles of 184 mothers and 73 fathers appears in Tables 2 and 3. Consistent with previous studies, from 36% to 56% of the profiles in this study are in the clinical range by the criterion of having one or more clinical scales T ≥ 70. Examination of the frequency of code types indicated that half of the clinical-range profiles for fathers and mothers included only one scale T ≥ 70 (spikes), while the other half of these profiles had two or more scales so elevated. Chi-square analysis revealed no significant differences in frequency of clinical-range profiles of mothers and fathers by sex of child. Examination of individual profile code types revealed that the *Pd* spike (9.8%), *Hy* spike (4.9%), and 1-3/3-1 (3.8%) were among the most frequent for mothers. For fathers the *Pd* spike was also the most frequent (5.5%). A comparison of mean profile scale scores suggests a high degree of similarity with previous studies (e.g., Hanvik & Byrum, 1959; Marks, 1961; Wolking et al., 1966). Mothers obtained the highest mean elevation on scales *D*, *Hy*, *Pd*, and *Pa*, with the lowest for scale *Mf*. Fathers obtained the highest mean elevation of scales *Hy*, *Pd*, and *Mf*, a result consistent with past research. All highest elevations have means T > 60, one standard deviation above the original normative group means.

Table 2. Maternal MMPI Code Type Category by Child Age and Sex (N = 184)

	Male				Female					
	Child (N = 73)		Adolescent (N = 40)		Child (N = 36)		Adolescent (N = 35)		Total (N = 184)	
Profile Type	N	%	N	%	N	%	N	%	N	%
Normal limits	38	52.0	18	45.0	16	44.5	17	48.6	89	48.4
Neurotic	11	15.1	7	17.5	7	19.5	6	17.1	31	16.8
Characterological	14	19.2	8	20.0	7	19.5	10	28.6	39	21.2
Psychotic	8	11.0	5	12.5	5	13.7	1	2.8	19	10.3
Other	2	2.7	2	5.0	1	2.8	1	2.8	6	3.3

Note: Normal limits = *Hs-Pd*, *Pa-Si* all < 70T;
    Neurotic = 1 Spike, 2 Spike, 3 Spike, 7 Spike, 1-2/2-1, 1-3/3-1, 2-3/3-2, 2-7/7-2, 2-0/0-2;
    Characterological = 4 Spike, 9 Spike, 2-4/4-2, 3-4/4-3, 4-6/6-4, 4-7/7-4, 4-8/8-4;
    Psychotic = 6 Spike, 8 Spike, 2-8/8-2, 6-8/8-6, 7-8/8-7, 8-9/9-8;
    Other = 0 Spike, 1-9/9-1

Table 3. Paternal MMPI Code Type Category by Child Age and Sex

Profile Type	Male Child (N = 29) N	Male Child (N = 29) %	Male Adolescent (N = 23) N	Male Adolescent (N = 23) %	Female Child (N = 11) N	Female Child (N = 11) %	Female Adolescent (N = 10) N	Female Adolescent (N = 10) %	Total (N = 73) N	Total (N = 73) %
Normal limits	15	51.7	12	52.2	7	63.6	6	60.0	40	54.8
Neurotic	2	6.9	6	26.1	1	9.1	3	30.0	12	16.4
Characterological	11	37.9	3	13.0	2	18.2	1	10.0	17	23.3
Psychotic	1	3.5	2	8.7	0	0.0	0	0.0	3	4.1
Other	0	0.0	0	0.0	1	9.1	0	0.0	1	1.4

Note: Normal limits = *Hs-Pd*, *Pa-Si* all < 70T;
  Neurotic = 1 Spike, 2 Spike, 3 Spike, 1-2/2-1, 1-3/3-1, 2-3/3-2;
  Characterological = 4 Spike, 9 Spike, 1-4/4-1, 2-4/4-2, 3-4/4-3, 4-7/7-4,
    4-8/8-4, 4-9/9-4;
  Psychotic = 8 Spike, 6-8/8-6;
  Other = 0 Spike

COMPARISONS AMONG GROUPS OF DEVIANT CHILDREN AND THE RELATION OF THE PERSONALITY DIMENSIONS OF CHILDREN AND PARENTS

Children Classified by Standard Diagnostic Procedures

Several investigators first attempted to reduce the heterogeneity of children's behavior by placing children in subgroups on the basis of the classifications of some diagnostic system and subsequently evaluated the relation between scale elevations on the MMPIs of parents, and the variation in the behavior of children that is assumed by different diagnostic classifications. Liverant (1959) and Goodstein and Rowley (1961) divided clinic children into four diagnostic subgroups based on predominant symptoms. Three of these subgroups (schizophrenic, acting-out, neurotic) appreared in both studies, and Liverant included a physical-complaint group and Goodstein and Rowley included a "personality trait" group composed of children diagnosed adjustment reaction or enuretic. Liverant (1959) found more differences between the fathers of these groups of children than between the mothers, but Goodstein and Rowley (1961) obtained significant differences only on maternal MMPIs for groups of children selected by predominant symptoms.

Hanvik and Byrum (1959) found no relation between the MMPIs of fathers of 12 groups of children formed on the basis of "primary problems." In contrast, mothers with *Hy* high-point profiles and *Mf* as a low point tended to have children with the primary problem of "rebelliousness at home or school." Wolking et al. (1966) also found that the *Hy* high point in maternal profiles was associated with diagnosis of the child as primary behavior disorder. A combination of *Hy* and *Pd* high points in paternal profiles was also related to this diagnosis. Wolking et al. (1966) also found that the mean MMPI codes of clinic fathers obtained greater variability across eight diagnostic groups than did the maternal codes. In fact, scales *Hy* and *Pd* were the highest maternal mean scale elevations in 7 of 8 diagnostic groups. The parents of children with organic brain syndromes obtained the highest mean profiles, and the parents of retarded children had the lowest.

Wolking, Dunteman, and Bailey (1967) tested for differences in mean profiles across five groups of parents divided on the basis of their children's psychiatric diagnosis. Four separate multivariate analyses controlled for the sex of the parent and sex of the child. Significant differences were obtained only for mothers of male children, although attempts to predict the male child's diagnostic classification from the discriminant scores of the mother's profiles suggested that the magnitude of these differences was not of pragmatic value.

Wolff and Morris (1971) compared the mean profiles of parents of seven autistic children with the clinic parent profiles of Wolking et al. (1966). Only one significant difference was obtained in each comparison: these seven mothers obtained lower *Mf* scores, and the fathers of autistic children obtained lower *L* scores. McAdoo and De-Meyer (1978), using Goldfarb's (1961) criteria for organicity, compared the parents of 24 organic autistic children with the parents of 15 nonorganic autistic children. Although Goldfarb (1961) had observed a greater incidence of psychopathology in the parents of nonorganic schizophrenic children, this conclusion was not supported by the MMPI scale analysis.

Bradley, Wakefield, Yom, Doughtie, Cox, and Kraft (1974) evaluated by canonical analysis the relationship of six pathological behaviors of children to parental MMPI scale scores. For mothers, "pica" and "excessive breath-holding" were associated with scales *Sc* and *Pa*, and "holding self rigid" was associated with scales *D* and *F*. For fathers only, pica was found to clearly relate to MMPI scale elevation (*Sc* and *F*).

Children Classified by Empirical Clustering Techniques

Three studies have classified children into "internalizing" and "externalizing" categories based upon factor ratings obtained from behavior and symptom checklist data. These two categories reflect symptom ratings associated with withdrawn neurotic behaviors, and delinquent acting-out behaviors, respectively (Achenbach, 1966). Butcher (1966) noted that the mothers of internalizing adolescent sons more frequently had primed elevations on scales *Hs, D, Hy, Pa,* and *Si,* but only the mean *Pa* score was significantly higher than that of mothers of externalizers. Fathers of adolescent externalizing sons obtained significantly higher scores on scales *F* and *Pd* than fathers of internalizers. In addition, 37% of the fathers of these externalizing adolescents had a *Pd* scale score ⩾70 T, but this was true for none of the fathers of internalizers.

Anderson (1969) found that parents of externalizing pre-adolescent boys had significantly higher scores on scales *Hs, Pd, Pt, Sc,* and *Ma,* and parents of internalizers obtained significantly higher scores on scale *K.* Configural analyses were completed separately for mothers and fathers. Fathers of externalizers had significantly more profiles with *Pd* ⩾ 70 T than did fathers of internalizers, while the reverse was true for scale *K.* Fathers of externalizers were higher on *Pd* than on *Hy,* and fathers of internalizers were higher on *Hy.* This latter finding may be important in view of the frequent elevation of scales *Hy* and *Pd* for clinic parents. The two groups of clinic mothers did not differ on these configural comparisons, although mothers of externalizing children did have significantly more profiles with *Mf* as the low point.

The scores of mothers of internalizing preschool children in Friedman's (1974) study were significantly higher than the scores of control mothers on scales *D, Pd, Sc,* and *Ma.* The scores of mothers of externalizing preschool children were higher than controls only on *Ma.* In direct comparisons of the two groups, mothers of internalizers obtained more elevated *Pt* scores.

Comparison of Adolescent and Parental MMPIs

Similarities among personality dimensions of parents and their children can be measured by independent administration of the MMPI to both. Sopchak (1958) found a greater number of significant correlations between the scale scores of mothers and their college-age daughters, and between fathers and their college-age sons, than between parents and opposite-sex children. Lauterbach, Vogel, and Hart (1962) reported correlations lower than Sopchak's within the families of male adolescents referred for psychiatric evaluation, as did Mlott (1972) for a sample of families of male and female adolescent psychiatric inpatients. Lauterbach et al. (1962) also found that the correlation between the profiles of husbands and wives were also lower than those reported by Sopchak (1958).

Archer, Sutker, White, and Orvin (1978) evaluated the relation of parental MMPI and adolescent psychiatric inpatient profiles classified as normal, conduct disorder, psychotic, and invalid. The greatest dissimilarity was found between the MMPIs of children who were placed in the invalid and psychotic classifications and the MMPI profiles of their parents. Butcher and Messick (1966) reported the greatest similarity between the profiles of parents and eighth-grade boys occurred when the boys were rated medium in manifest aggression, as opposed to low or high manifest agression.

Methodological Considerations

In addition to highlighting the methodological issues previously discussed, new concerns are raised by these studies. When children are categorized into discrete groups, researchers assume that this process will increase within-group similarity and facilitate the identification of parent-child relationships. Researchers, however, have seldom provided a detailed description of the diagnostic procedures, and have not presented data regarding the reliability of the diagnostic system. In a review of the research on diagnostic systems, Zubin (1967) concluded that the reliability of diagnoses is quite low, particularly in regard to the classification of children. Other researchers have classified children on the basis of behavioral problems or specific symptoms. However, matching subjects on such limited information may, as noted by Meehl (1971), systematically "unmatch" them on other variables. In order to avoid these problems, some investigators have employed variations in empirically based behavioral dimensions (Achenbach, 1966) to dichotomize samples of children. Although this approach has produced substantial results, it may be argued that the use of only two classifications does not do justice to the variety of childhood disorders. In addition, it may be argued that the division of children into discrete groups may mask potential linear relationships between dimensions of parental and children's behavior.

The correlation of the MMPIs of parents and children allows the evaluation of dimensions across a variety of combinations of children's behavior, but limits these studies to adolescent offspring. It is also likely that other MMPI indexes, such as the Wiggins content scales (Wiggins, 1969; Lachar & Alexander, 1978), may provide estimates of more homogeneous personality dimensions, or behavior patterns. Future research will also need to adjust adolescent protocols for adolescent norms (Marks, Seeman, & Haller, 1974; Lachar et al., 1976).

The Lafayette Clinic Sample

Data were available for the exploratory study of the relation between parental MMPI scales and children's behavior in two ways. The dimensions of children's behavior were represented by the 16 scales of the PIC profile. These scales have established reliability and favorable psychometric characteristics (Wirt et al., 1977) as well as stable correlates and empirically determined interpretive guidelines (Lachar, Butkus, & Hryhorczuk, 1978; Lachar & Gdowski, 1979a, 1979b). The 16 scales include three measures of informant response style: Lie (L), F, and Defensiveness (DEF); one general screening scale: Adjustment (ADJ); three measures of cognitive ability: Achievement (ACH), Intellectual Screening (IS), and Development (DVL); two measures of behavioral and emotional control: Delinquency (DLQ) and Hyperactivity (HPR); as well as 7 other scales that measure internalizing and other clinically relevant dimensions: Somatic Concern (SOM), Depression (D), Family Relations (FAM), Withdrawal (WDL), Anxiety (ANX), Psychosis (PSY), and Social Skills (SSK).

Also, checklist items selected from the clinic application and clinician rating forms were submitted to factor analysis to identify dimensions of children's behavior. Items were selected from each form in a manner consistent with Comrey's (1978) recommendations. The number of items selected from each checklist was limited by the size of the sample. Infrequently endorsed items were excluded, and items were selected to represent the variety of content present in each form. Forty-two clinic application and 50 clinician rating items were separately evaluated, using the principal components method with iteration and varimax rotation. Factors were extracted with eigenvalues greater than one, and a factor score was calculated for each child to represent each factor. The factor scores thus reflected each child's relative standing for each behavior dimension for the total sample.

PIC Profile Scales. Tables 4 and 5 present the significant correlations between the MMPI scales of mothers and fathers and the PIC profile scales for sons and daughters. Comparison of obtained results suggests a stronger relation between parental MMPI scores and the behavior of daughters than of sons. This result is all the more significant in view of the fact that fewer daughters were available for this analysis. Maternal MMPI scales were significantly ($p < .05$) related to

PIC scores 41 times for sons and 86 times for daughters. Paternal MMPI scales were significantly ($p < .10$) related to PIC scores 23 times for sons and 42 times for daughters.

Inspection of table columns suggests which dimensions of children's behavior are related to, and which independent of, parental personality. The multiple correlations between MMPI scales and *FAM* support the notion that individual parental deviance contributes to problematic family relationships. Maternal deviance appears to be related to those behaviors associated with child somatization, depression, anxiety, and delinquency, but little or no evidence supported a relationship between maternal pathology and children's cognitive ability, activity level, social skills, and withdrawal, represented by scales *ACH, IS, DVL, WDL, HPR,* and *SSK*. Inspection of the rows of the table suggests that behavior problems of children are inversely related to maternal scales *K* and *ES* and positively related to scales *Hs, D, Pt,* and *A*, as well as *Hy* and *Si*, although the latter two relations are limited to daughters.

Although the relationship between the MMPIs of fathers and the problem behavior of children appears attenuated, and the results obtained are based on one-third of the parent-child pairs available in evaluating maternal MMPIs, several observations are possible. In this sample, elevation of fathers' scales *L* and *K* was negatively related to problems of academic achievement, somatization, and hyperactivity for their daughters. Elevation of scale *Hs* appears to be negatively related to behavior problems for daughters, and *Si* appears to be positively related. Fathers who obtained higher *Mf* scores are more likely to have sons with internalizing symptomatology (*SOM, D, WDL, ANX, PSY*), and are less likely to have daughters with externalizing behaviors (*ADJ, DLQ*). In contrast to maternal MMPIs, the paternal Ego Strength scale elevation was not related to reduced psychopathology of the children, and was, in fact, positively related to children's acting-out and family conflict for sons.

Problem Behavior Factor Scores. Seven factors were extracted in the factor analysis of the 42 parental application items accounting for 78.6% of the total variance. Eight factors were extracted in the factor analysis of the 50 clinician rating items, accounting for 81% of the total variance. Factors, item composition, and relative variance represented are given in Table 6. These 15 problem-behavior factors were correlated with the 13 MMPI profile scales separately for mothers and fathers for groups selected by child's sex and age (child = 4-12 years; adolescents = 13-17 years). Because group size ranged from 73 to 10, all correlations significant at $p < .10$ were retained as

Table 4. Correlations between Maternal MMPI Scales and PIC Scale Descriptions of Problem Behavior Children as a Function of Sex of Child

MMPI Scale	Sex[a]	PIC SCALES															
		L	F	DEF	ADJ	ACH	IS	DVL	SOM	D	FAM	DLQ	WDL	ANX	PSY	HPR	SSK
L	m	.26	.20				.22	.24			-.31					.27	
	f		.23								-.27						
F	m		.29						.21		.45			.28	.25		
	f								.38	.23							
K	m	.22								-.22	-.29						
	f									-.35	-.22			-.39	-.27		
Hs	m				.27	.26			.22		.24	.26					
	f		.47						.52			.29					
D	m									.23	.39			.20	.30		
	f		.38		.30				.43	.33	.39	.22		.36	.33		
Hy	m		.38		.33				.43	.24	.27			.22			
	f	-.23									.29						
Pd	m	-.24	.38						.35		.32	.21					
	f		.25								.54	.25					
Mf	m	.21								-.21							-.20
	f				-.26												
Pa	m			-.20					.23		.32						
	f		.22						.34	.29	.40			.33			
Pt	m		.35		.22				.24	.20	.27			.21			
	f								.47	.26	.40			.34	.32		
Sc	m		.32						.29		.24						
	f								.43		.41						
Ma	m	-.26															
	f								.21		.29						
Si	m		.29		.24					.31	.21			.40	.33		.25
	f								.34	.27	.29			.32			
A	m			-.22	.25					.27	.37						
	f		.33						.36	.42	.37			.53	.38		.22
R	m			.21													
	f																
ES	m	.24			-.29				-.23	-.24	-.31			-.39			
	f	-.46			-.27			-.22	-.44	-.35	-.28				-.46		-.22

[a] males: N = 131, females: N = 87. All correlates $p < .05$

Table 5. Correlations between Paternal MMPI Scales and PIC Scale Descriptions of Problem Behavior Children as a Function of Sex of Child

MMPI Scale	Sex[a]	PIC SCALES														
		L	F	DEF	ADJ	ACH	IS	DVL	SOM	D	FAM	DLQ	WDL	ANX	PSY	HPR	SSK
L	m																
	f	.59				-.38			-.39				.38			-.41	
F	m																
	f																
K	m																
	f										.40						
Hs	m																
	f					-.44			-.49	-.55						-.43	
D	m																
	f				-.38	-.40	-.40				.40			-.50	-.42		-.55
Hy	m								.27								
	f										.62						
Pd	m											-.25					
	f						-.43				.66	.41				-.30	
Mf	m		.34						.25								
	f		-.44		-.51					.35			.32	.39	.33		
Pa	m		.45		-.38				.24						.26	-.24	
	f											-.44	.45			-.42	
Pt	m										-.29					-.27	
	f						.24										
Sc	m						.26										
	f						-.40								.32	-.28	
Ma	m																
	f													-.40			
Si	m								.27								
	f																
A	m		.49		.45	.59	.50	.43									
	f															.42	.42
R	m					.28		.38	.41								
	f			-.38			.38					.40					
ES	m	.54								-.45							
	f										.31	.25					

[a]males: N = 50, females, N = 20. All correlations $p < .10$.

Table 6. Composition of Problem Behavior Factors

Factor and % Variance	Ratings and Factor Loadings (≥ .30)	
I. Preappointment information		
1. Hostility-dyscontrol	Can't be trusted	.75
30.1%	Lies	.70
	Steals	.69
	Disobeys parents	.63
	Talks back to grown-ups	.56
	Won't obey school rules	.45
	Fights with other children	.45
	Acts without thinking	.43
	Runs away from home	.39
	Sets fires	.32
	Hangs around with a "bad crowd"	.31
2. Dysphoria	Is sad or unhappy most of the time	.68
14.6%	Doesn't trust other people	.57
	Mood changes quickly	.36
	Tired most of the time	.30
3. Slow development	Slow to speak first sentences	.93
10.2%	Slow to speak first words	.67
	Slow to sit up	.42
4. Socialized delinquency	Often skips school	.65
7.3%	Uses drugs	.54
	Has threatened or attempted suicide	.51
	Runs away from home	.44
	Hangs around with a "bad crowd"	.43
	Is afraid to go to school	.37
5. Deviant behavior	Daydreams a lot	.75
6.5%	Is often confused and in a daze	.67
	Says or does strange or peculiar things	.32
6. Social withdrawal	Plays alone most of the time	.88
5.3%	Has few or no friends	.69
	Hangs around with a "bad crowd"	−.30
7. Distractibility	Doesn't finish things (short attention span)	.72
4.5%	Has problems learning in school	.57
	Acts without thinking	.40
	Acts younger than real age	.38
	Won't obey school rules	.36
	Can't sit still	.32
II. Clinician ratings		
1. Socialized delinquency	Stealing	.87
25.9%	Truancy	.87
	Blames others for his/her problems	.86
	Involved with police	.86
	Displays irresponsible behavior	.86
	Teases peers	.86
	Lying	.81
	Poor judgment/needs much supervision	.35
	Expresses a dislike for school	.31

Table 6. (Continued)

Factor and % Variance	Ratings and Factor Loadings ($\geq$ .30)	
2. Poor reality testing 14.7%	Delusions of persecution/paranoia	.84
	Poor recent or remote memory	.68
	Impulsive behavior	.68
	Disorganized (bizarre) behavior	.62
	Frequently unresponsive to surroundings	.54
	Achievement in school at least one year below chronological age-grade placement	.31
3. Poor motor skills 10.9%	Fine motor ataxia	.73
	Speech disturbance	.70
	Gross motor ataxia	.55
	Displays expressive aphasic symptoms	−.50
4. Hostility-overactivity 8.8%	Verbally hostile or argumentative	.53
	Often a poor sport or poor loser	.50
	Easily upset or irritable	.49
	Overactive or irritable	.47
	Disobedience to teachers or breaks school rules	.45
	Temper tantrums	.40
	Rapid mood shifts (sad or angry one day, happy the next	.37
5. Withdrawal 7.0%	Decreased verbal communication/seldom talks	.59
	Excessive daydreaming	.55
	Isolative (usually plays alone, stays in room, etc.)	.48
	Excessive shyness	.47
6. Substance abuse 5.5%	History of problematic alcohol abuse	.76
	History of problematic substance (drug) abuse	.56
	Running away from home	.35
7. Depression-anxiety 4.3%	Expresses feelings of sadness or unhappiness	.64
	Frequent crying	.51
	Worries a great deal	.45
	Listless and continually tired	.37
	Sleep disturbance: has nightmares/bad dreams	.32
	Expresses feelings of anxiety, tension, nervousness, or restlessness	.32
8. Somatization 4.0%	Somatic response to stress (e.g., stomachaches)	.74
	Headaches	.58

suggestive of parent-child relationships. These correlations are presented in Table 7.

Inspection of the eight columns of Table 7 reveals those problem-behavior dimensions that manifest some relation to parental MMPI scale scores. It becomes readily apparent that: (1) these relationships vary considerably by sex of parent, as well as age and sex of child; (2) the results obtained are not dependent on group size, since in many cases, smaller groups obtained more significant correlations than larger groups; and (3) parental deviance may, in some cases, be *negatively* related to childhood psychopathology. When MMPI scale elevation is positively related to the problem behavior of children, the relation can be interpreted as representing the effect of children's behavior on parental stability, as well as the effect of disturbed parents on the personality development of children. When this relationship is a negative one, the "stress-reaction hypothesis" is not tenable, because it would be illogical to postulate that the abnormal behavior of children promotes good parental adjustment, or that limited disturbance of children promotes parental pathology. The parsimonious explanation is that parental pathology inhibits certain kinds of problem behavior in children. Inspection of table rows identifies those dimensions of children's behavior that are more likely to be relatively independent of parental psychopathology.

Behavior dimensions of slow development, distractibility, and withdrawal were positively correlated for male children to maternal profile elevation, and paternal pathology was positively related to somatization and negatively related to social withdrawal in this group. Maternal pathology appeared to clearly relate to behaviors reflective of depression and anxiety in their female children. Paternal scale elevation appeared to be negatively related to the presence of hostility-dyscontrol, social withdrawal, and distractibility in their female children, and demonstrated some positive relation to the dimensions of socialized delinquency, substance abuse, and somatization.

Limited relationships were noted between the MMPI scales of parents and the rated behavior of their adolescent sons. Maternal profile elevation was found to be positively related to son's behavior reflecting hostility-dyscontrol, and negatively related to withdrawal. Paternal pathology appears to be negatively related to behavior of adolescent sons characterized by hostility-dyscontrol and socialized delinquency. Although the samples of parents of adolescent daughters were quite small, the relationships obtained were substantial. The elevation of maternal profile scales was positively related to children's behavior characterized by socialized delinquency, deviant be-

Table 7. Correlations between Parent MMPI Scales and Child Problem Behavior Factor Scores ($p < .10$)

Preappointment Information

Problem Behavior Factor Scores	Male Children		Female Children		Male Adolescents		Female Adolescents	
	Mother (N = 73)	Father (N = 29)	Mother (N = 36)	Father (N = 11)	Mother (N = 40)	Father (N = 23)	Mother (N = 35)	Father (N = 10)
1. Hostility dyscontrol			Pd (.34)	K (−.60) Hs (−.63) Hy (−.66) Pa (−.50) Sc (−.60)	Hs (.28) Hy (.28) Mf (.29)	F (−.37) D (−.35)		Si (.67)
2. Dysphoria		K (−.35) Ma (.32)	Pd (−.27)	L (.54) Hy (−.48)	Mf (−.30) Pa (.28) Ma (−.31)		Pa (.37)	
3. Slow development	F (.33) Hs (.29) Hy (.25) Pd (.34) Pa (.27) Pt (.24) Sc (.29)	K (.45) Ma (−.45)		Pa (−.52) Sc (−.62)		Hs (.40)		K (−.56)
4. Socialized delinquency	Pd (.30)	L (.36) Si (.37)	Mf (.32)			Pd (−.35) Ma (−.50)	Hs (.35) Hy (.42) Sc (.33)	Si (.72)
5. Deviant behavior	Hy (.26) Si (−.23)		D (.37) Si (.48)	K (.53) Mf (−.60)	F (.35) K (−.26)		F (.29) Hs (.43) D (.38) Hy (.35) Pa (.42) **Pt** (.44) Sc (.51)	Mf (.70)

Table 7. (Continued)

Problem Behavior Factor Scores	Male Children		Female Children		Male Adolescents		Female Adolescents	
	Mother (N = 73)	Father (N = 29)	Mother (N = 36)	Father (N = 11)	Mother (N = 40)	Father (N = 23)	Mother (N = 35)	Father (N = 10)
6. Social withdrawal	D (.25) Mf (−.30)	F (−.33) Pa (−.30) Sc (−.36)	K (.30) Ma (−.29)	L (−.53) Hs (−.61) D (−.57) Mf (−.67)		Ma (−.37)		
7. Distractibility	L (.26) Hs (.28) Hy (.19)		Sc (−.29)	Pa (−.70) Sc (−.74) Ma (−.53)	L (−.28) Pa (.26)		L (−.47) F (.29) Hs (.31) Hy (.35) Pd (.37) Mf (−.40) Pa (.30) Pt (.31) Sc (.34) Si (.34)	

Clinicians Ratings

Problem Behavior Factor Scores	Male Children		Female Children		Male Adolescents		Female Adolescents	
	Mother (N = 73)	Father (N = 29)	Mother (N = 36)	Father (N = 11)	Mother (N = 40)	Father (N = 23)	Mother (N = 35)	Father (N = 10)
1. Socialized delinquency			L (.27) Hs (.31)	L (−.54) F (.49) K (−.58) Si (.49)				F (−.56) Pd (−.52) Mf (−.60) Pa (−.63) Pt (−.50)
2. Poor reality testing	K (.21)	L (−.32) D (−.35)						K (−.61) Pd (−.58) Mf (−.50) Pa (−.69) Pt (−.51)

3. Poor motor skills	Hy (.19), Ma (.26)	Si (−.30)		Si (−.56)		Hy (−.52), Pt (−.42)	L (.32), Pt (−.34)	F (.68), Pa (.78), Pt (.59), Sc (.70), Si (.66)
4. Hostility-overactivity	Hs (.19), D (.41), Hy (.24), Pt (.22), Si (.20)	Mf (.34)	Mf (.34), Pt (.29)	K (−.49), Hy (−.66)	K (−.26)			Pd (.68), Ma (.76)
5. Withdrawal		Si (.37)	D (.29), Ma (−.43)		D (−.31), Hy (−.27), Mf (.34)		L (.29), Pa (−.32)	F (.72), Sc (.53)
6. Substance abuse	Sc (−.19), Ma (.24)	Pd (−.42), Mf (−.32), Si (.38)		Pa (.77), Sc (.50), Ma (.48)	Mf (−.30), Si (−.38)	L (−.35), Pa (−.35)	Mf (−.31), Pa (.31)	L (−.56), Hs (−.50)
7. Depression-anxiety	L (−.20), Ma (.28)	Pa (.30), Si (−.31)	F (.44), D (.45), Pd (.41), Pa (.28), Pt (.46), Sc (.41), Si (.37)	L (.50)	L (−.28)			
8. Somatization		F (.58), K (−.33), Pa (.57), Sc (.55), Ma (.36), Si (.38)	Pd (−.30)	Pa (.58), Sc (.48)	K (−.33)	Ma (.49)	K (−.34)	D (.61), Si (.56)

havior, and distractibility. Paternal scale elevations were found to clearly relate to the presence of behavior reflecting poor motor skills and hostility-overactivity in their adolescent daughters as well as to the absence of behavior reflecting socialized delinquency and poor reality testing.

CLINICAL INTERPRETATION OF PARENTS' MMPIs

Although it is clear that there are stable, significant relationships between parents' MMPI scales or configurations and children's behavior dimensions or types, parents' MMPIs may be able to predict a number of parental behaviors that would have direct relevance on the design and selection of intervention techniques. These behaviors might include the degree of cooperation displayed in complying with treatment requirements, the consistency manifest in carrying out recommendations, as well as severe, disabling psychopathology and interactional patterns that would necessitate evaluation of the need to remove the child from the home to reach treatment objectives. Most investigators have not collected or reported data pertaining to the nontest behavior of parents, and much of the information that has been reported has either not been analyzed in a systematic fashion, or has relied on extrapolations from the behavioral and descriptive correlates of the MMPI profiles of psychiatric patients.

Parents' MMPIs and Marital Adjustment

Hanvik and Byrum (1959) noted the frequent elevation of the index *Pd* minus *Ma* in the profiles of clinic parents. This often occurred with "situationally maladjusted individuals reacting adversely and with intense hostility to a portion of the social environment, i.e., persons with severe marriage problems" (p. 429). Johnson and Lobitz (1974) administered the Locke-Wallace Marital Adjustment Test (Locke & Wallace, 1959) as well as the MMPI to clinic parents of externalizing boys. The *Pd* minus *Ma* index was found to be negatively related to marital adjustment for both mothers and fathers, as were several profile scales including *Pd*. The *Pd* scale has also been associated with incidence of marital discord in two other studies that contrasted the MMPI profiles of married mothers seen in clinics with separated or divorced mothers seen in clinics (Dunteman & Wolking, 1967; Loeb & Price, 1966). In both studies the *Pd* scale was significantly more elevated in the profiles of separated or divorced mothers. In addition, Loeb and Price (1966) noted that children of separated or divorced mothers had problems that were more likely to involve aggression and acting-out.

Johnson and Lobitz (1974) also reported that incidence of marital discord in parents seen at clinics was negatively related to *Mf* elevation for mothers and positively related to *Mf* elevation for fathers. That is, the more each parent responded to items in the "feminine" direction, the greater the likelihood of problems in the marital relationship. Hanvik and Byrum (1959) commented on the tendency for clinic fathers to have elevated *Mf* scores, and mothers, relatively low scores on this scale. Just as Rutter (1971) has reported that marital discord has been found to be related to the antisocial behavior of children, so the findings of Hanvik and Byrum (1959) and Anderson (1969) that low *Mf* elevations in maternal profiles were associated with externalizing symptoms in their children may also support the notion that *Mf* relates to marital adjustment.

Prognostic Implications of Parents' MMPIs

Marks (1961) related therapists' ratings of treatment effectiveness with parents' MMPI configurations. Case improvement was associated with maternal MMPI profiles classified with *Ma* as the high point, or classified as 1-3/3-1; the 2-0/0-2 maternal code type was associated with partial improvement following treatment. An unfavorable prognosis was associated with code types 2-4/4-2 and 3-4/4-3. Marks also noted that mothers who obtained 3-4/4-3 profiles typically cancelled many interviews and rarely remained in treatment for more than three months. Marks also noted that the *Pd* minus *Ma* index was negatively related to degree of therapeutic improvement. Hanvik and Byrum (1959) reported that mothers with low *Mf* elevations were very difficult to influence therapeutically. Marks (1961) found that case improvement was associated with paternal profiles with a *Pd* high point or a 9-5/5-9 code type, although fathers with the former profiles rarely participated in the treatment process. Lack of improvement was noted in children whose father's profiles were coded 2-0/0-2 or 1-3/3-1.

In contrast to these findings, McAdoo and Roeske (1973) were unable to demonstrate MMPI differences between the parents in families who, following a diagnostic evaluation, either continued in treatment or declined treatment at a child-guidance clinic. These results are not directly comparable to Marks (1961) who limited his efforts to the study of families in treatment.

Parents' MMPIs and Parenting Attitudes

Zuckerman and Oltean (1959) correlated MMPI scale scores of mothers who were hospitatalized psychiatric patients with their factor scores on the Parental Attitude Research Inventory (PARI) (Schaefer & Bell, 1958). The "Authoritarian-Control" factor was positively related to elevations on *Mf*, and six scales (*F, Hs, Pa, Pt, Sc,* and *Ma*) were significantly related to "Hostility-Rejection" factor scores. The PARI scales composing the Hostility-Rejection factor include Irritability with Children, Rejection of the Homemaking Role, and Marital Conflict, suggesting that "a woman who is high on this factor would be expected to have needs for achievement outside of the home, lack of motivation to care for and devote herself to others, and show aggressiveness in interpersonal relations" (p. 29).

Methodological Considerations

It is a rather surprising finding that so few studies have compared the relationship of parents' MMPI scales to parents' behavior. It must be assumed that clinicians generally apply the established clinical lore and actuarial information on scale elevation and profile configuration obtained from adult psychiatric patients to the profiles of parents seen in child-guidance settings—certainly a questionable procedure considering the differences between these two populations.

The Lafayette Clinic Sample

The clinician rating form and PIC Family Relations (*FAM*) and individual inventory items provide an opportunity to study the relation of parents' MMPI scores to their behavior.

Parents' Psychopathology. Table 8 presents the significant point biserial correlations between MMPI profile scales, scales *A, R,* and Ego Strength (*ES*), and clinicians' ratings of parents' status and behavior. The relation of scale elevation to parents' adjustment is most successfully captured by independent clinicians' ratings of presence of a degree of parental emotional disturbance that would justify the need for individual treatment. Correlation analysis, mean profiles presented in Figure 1, and code-type classification clearly document that scale elevation is associated with judged psychopathology, although the relationship is clearer for mothers than for fathers. Need for individual treatment was significantly related to 12 maternal and 7 paternal scales; mothers rated as emotionally disturbed (N = 70) obtained significantly higher scores on *F, Hs, D, Hy, Pd, Pa, Pt, Sc,*

Ma, and *Si* than mothers not rated as emotionally disturbed (N = 68); while fathers rated as emotionally disturbed (N = 11) obtained significantly higher scores on *F*, *Pd*, and *Sc*, and lower scores on *K* compared to fathers not so rated (N = 25). Analysis of frequency of rated emotional disturbance by code-type classification was significant for mothers ($X^2(4) = 32.22$, p $<$ .0001), but not for fathers. Although no differences were obtained between frequencies of the code-type categories of neurotic, psychotic, characterological, and indeterminate, 75% of mothers with primed profiles were rated as emotionally disturbed, but only 26% of mothers with profiles within normal limits were so rated. For fathers, frequency of this rating was 38% for primed profiles and 20% for profiles within normal limits. Scale elevation was related to clinician's rating of alcoholism/substance abuse for fathers tested during their daughter's evaluation. This relation was also supported by the significant point-biserial correlations between PIC item #317: "The child's father drinks too much." (T), and scales *F*, *D*, *Pd*, *Mf*, *Pt*, and *Sc*. Scale elevation was also related to family history of mental illness for the mothers tested during their sons' evaluation. PIC items #240, 286, and 468 for all mothers; item #484 for mothers and sons; and item #430 for fathers of daughters were significantly related to 5-10 MMPI scales. These findings associate elevated profiles with maternal crying spells, admission of mental illness, and dislike of the traditional homemaker role, as well as paternal dissatisfaction with current job.

Parent Interactional Family Climate. Clinicians' ratings of marital discord appeared to have some relationship to MMPI elevations of the parents of daughters, as did documentation of their daughters' birth out of wedlock. Maternal MMPI scale elevation was significantly related to PIC items #89, 290, 466, 535, 559, 583, suggesting such profile elevation may be associated with swearing, quarreling, financial concerns, and lack of communication between parents. Maternal profile elevation also related to family isolation (#29) and admission by the child that he was ashamed of his family (#345) for sons seen in evaluation, while paternal profile elevation was related to these items only for daughters.

Parenting Behaviors and Attitudes. Ratings of "Inconsistent in setting limits" and "Overly permissive, difficulty in setting limits" were significantly related to maternal scale elevation, suggesting maternal deviance is associated in child-guidance populations to inefficient parenting behavior. By contrast, a substantial relationship between paternal profile and ratings of parenting behavior was not found. Maternal MMPI scale elevation was found to relate to admis-

Table 8. MMPI Correlates of Parents of Behaviorally Disturbed Children by Sex of Parent and Child

Correlate	Sex of Child	n	BR[a]	Mothers' MMPI Scales ($p < .05$)	n	BR[a]	Fathers' MMPI Scales ($p < .05$)
I. Psychopathology							
Emotionally disturbed (in need of individual treatment)	m	83	48	$F(.42)$, $Hs(.40)$, $D(.39)$, $Hy(.43)$, $Pd(.50)$, $Mf(-.28)$, $Pa(.49)$, $Pt(.45)$, $Sc(.50)$, $Ma(.24)$, $A(.31)$, $ES(-.44)$	26	35	$F(.45)$, $K(-.41)$, $Pa(.40)$, $Pt(.40)$, $Sc(.47)$, $Si(.43)$, $A(.52)$
	f	55	56	$L(-.28)$, $F(.32)$, $Hs(.37)$, $D(.41)$, $Hy(.40)$, $Pd(.44)$, $Pa(.33)$, $Pt(.39)$, $Sc(.35)$, $Si(.33)$, $A(.42)$, $ES(-.34)$	10	20	none
Alcoholic or other substance abuser	m	94	12	$Ma(.38)$, $R(-.26)$, $ES(-.24)$	26	26	$L(-.49)$, $Pa(.44)$
	f	55	13	none	16	25	$Hs(.49)$, $D(.57)$, $Pd(.53)$, $Pt(.51)$, $Si(.53)$, $A(.51)$
Family history of mental illness or epilepsy	m	89	24	$F(.28)$, $Hs(.23)$, $Hy(.27)$, $Mf(-.22)$, $Sc(.23)$, $Ma(.28)$	27	41	$ES(-.50)$
	f	57	26	none	13	8	none
II. Interview Behavior							
Defensive (about self) in interview	m	102	44	none	32	59	none
	f	65	35	none	16	56	$F(.56)$, $K(-.67)$, $A(.53)$
Minimizes child's problems	m	101	26	none	32	22	$Pa(.40)$, $ES(-.39)$
	f	66	17	$Hs(.28)$, $Hy(.27)$	16	13	none
III. Parental Interaction							
History of marital discord	m	102	75	$Ma(.22)$	46	70	$Hs(-.29)$, $Pt(-.39)$, $Sc(-.32)$,

	f	65	74	Hs(.27), Pd(.29), Sc(.25), Si(.29), A(.29), ES(-.29)	19	68	F(.51), K(-.52), A(.66)

Descriptor							
Child was born out of wedlock	m	112	19	Mf(.19)	51	17	none
	f	68	22	F(.47), K(-.29), Hs(.34), D(.29), Pd(.30), Pa(.31), Pt(.33), Sc(.39), Ma(.24), Si(.30), A(.41), ES(-.31)	18	6	F(.55), D(.47), Pd(.56), Sc(.56)
IV. Parenting Behavior							
Overly concerned or overly protective	m	97	40	none	31	13	Hs(.44), ES(-.44)
	f	64	28	D(-.29), Pd(-.24), Si(-.34), ES(.24)	15	27	Pt(-.61), Ma(.56)
Strict disciplinarian	m	97	15	none	29	38	none
	f	60	12	L(-.26), R(-.26)	15	20	D(-.55), Si(-.51), R(-.62)
Uses excessive physical punishment	m	90	11	none	26	19	none
	f	60	12	K(-.26), A(.26), ES(-.35)	15	0	none
Inconsistent in setting limits	m	83	69	F(.26), Hs(.23), D(.28), Hy(.23), Pd(.23), Pa(.25), Sc(.25), ES(-.25)	30	60	none
	f	57	51	F(.38), D(.37), Pd(.37), Pt(.43), Sc(.33), Si(.36), A(.43)	14	50	F(.65), D(-.74), Hy(-.52), A(.71)
Overly permissive, difficulty in setting limits	m	89	51	F(.27), Hs(.25), D(.22), Hy(.32), Pd(.30), Mf(-.25), Pa(.31), Pt(.25)	30	37	none
	f	58	45	F(.29), D(.37), Pd(.30), Pt(.33), Sc(.27)	14	29	F(.61), Si(.58)

[a]BR = base rate, i.e., frequency of descriptor in parent subgroup studied.

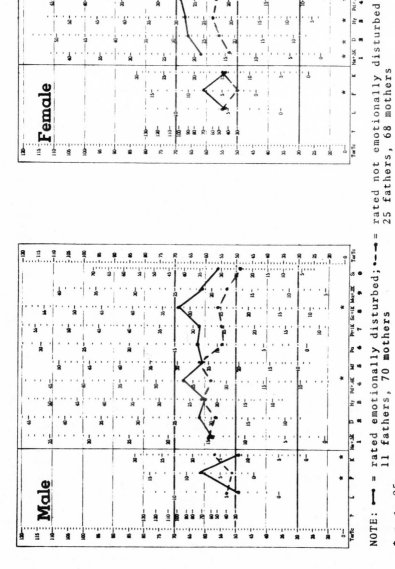

NOTE: ——— = rated emotionally disturbed; - - - = rated not emotionally disturbed
11 fathers, 70 mothers   25 fathers, 68 mothers

* p < .05

Figure 1. Mean Profiles of Mothers and Fathers Rated for Presence of
Emotional Disturbance (Need for Individual Treatment)

sion on the PIC of misunderstanding (#528), "blowing up" at (#268), and babying (#166) the child evaluated. Maternal profile elevation also related to her admission of excessive use of punishment (#s 327, 565) and control over her child's allowance (#183). Paternal MMPI scales were significantly related to wives' descriptions of their husbands as jealous of (#68), and excessively strict in dealing with (#497), the daughter evaluated. These results suggest that the lack of significant paternal MMPI correlates reflecting parent-child interaction may reflect relatively less accuracy in the clinicians' ratings of the fathers, rather than the lack of association between profile elevation and deviant parenting behavior.

Inspection of the pattern of all significant MMPI scales to PIC item correlations suggested that elevations on scales *F, D, Pd, Mf, Pa, Pt,* and *Sc* most frequently related to various manifestations of paternal deviance. Maternal scales *F, D, Pa, Pt, Sc,* and *A* frequently related to the presence of various manifestations of maternal deviance. Elevation of *Es,* and to a lesser extent *L* and *K,* were found to be related to a reduced frequency of deviant maternal marital and familial behavior and attitudes.

CONCLUSIONS AND RECOMMENDATIONS FOR FUTURE RESEARCH

The Relation of Parents' Psychopathology to the Problem Behavior of Children

Studies of parental influence, or of the stress-reaction hypothesis, that have taken the form of comparison of mean profiles of parents of clinic children with mean control profiles, or between mean profiles of clinic subgroups, have yielded few consistent results. A further limitation of this study paradigm lies in the subsequent attribution of specific meaning to the group differences obtained. That is, the data generated in this manner do not identify the sources of these differences. In contrast, the potential value of analyzing parents' MMPI scores against ratings of children's behavior has been documented in Tables 4, 5, and 7 of the current study, as well as in the work of Butcher (1966), Anderson (1969), and Friedman (1974). It is clear that future studies that employ samples of convenience globally characterized or selected by readily available information, such as traditional diagnoses, are unlikely to yield new information, and that prospective data collection that includes ratings or other measures of children's behavior will prove to be the most productive.

When the study design includes multiple measures of children's behavior, researchers may find that the application of multivariate statistical techniques, such as factor analysis and cluster analysis, will be necessary to form homogeneous groups of children that reflect these multiple measures. In the study of parent-child relationships, however, the comparison of parent personality differences between homogeneous groups of disturbed children may not be the optimal approach to the measurement of these relationships. This chapter clearly documents the importance of children's age and sex, as well as sex of parent in identifying these relationships. Future research must take into account these variables, as well as other demographic characteristics.

The exploratory analysis of the Lafayette Clinic sample tentatively identified three conclusions that deserve further evaluation: (1) the relation between parental psychopathology and children's problem behavior may be stronger for daughters than sons, perhaps reflecting a greater physiological or genetic component to the problem behavior of male children; (2) mother-child interactions may have a greater influence on childrens' behavior than do father-child interactions; and (3) the relations between parental personality and children's behavior may be negative as well as positive. Such relationships identify situations where parental psychopathology may be associated with a reduced probability of certain problem behaviors.

Researchers need to consider the appropriateness of the thirteen traditional profile scales in these studies. Rather than employing preexisting parental estimates of personality, more homogeneous MMPI-derived measures such as the Wiggins Content Scales (Wiggins, 1969) may provide useful information. The finding that at least half of parental profiles are within normal limits may suggest that the MMPI is not the instrument of choice to measure parental personality, since the MMPI is less likely to be sensitive to "normal-range" personality attributes than other measures, such as the California Personality Inventory or the Personality Research Form (Butcher & Tellegen, 1978). If the intent of the research is to estimate the relative influence of parental behavior on children's behavior and vice versa, the identification of inverse relationships between parental and childrens' psychopathology, as well as the collection of separate trait and state measures of known validity, may prove helpful.

The Clinical Interpretation of Parents' MMPIs

It can be stated with some certainty that a substantial proportion (27-55%) of the MMPI profiles obtained from parents of behaviorally disturbed children include scale elevations in the clinical range (T > 69), and that 20-25% of parents' profiles are similar to those obtained from psychiatric patients. This also means, however, that the majority of profiles obtained will be within normal limits, and not readily suggestive of clinical hypotheses. The analysis of the Lafayette Clinic sample suggests that deviant profiles reflect significant parental psychological disability as well as pathological parent-child interaction. These initial results suggest that efforts to construct actuarial guides for interpreting the MMPIs of parents will be productive and that such projects should include descriptors that reflect parental adjustment, parental interaction, and parent-child relationships. These data also suggest that stable and pragmatic correlates will be found for scales such as Ego Strength (Barron, 1953) and factor A (Welsh, 1965).

REFERENCES

Achenbach, T. M. The classification of children's psychiatric symptoms: A factor-analytic study. *Psychological Monographs*, 1966, 80 (7, Whole No. 615).

Adrian, R. J., Vacchiano, R. B., & Gilbart, T. E. Linear disciminant function classification of accepted and rejected adoptive applicants. *Journal of Clinical Psychology*, 1966, 22, 251-54.

Alley, G. R., Snider, B., Forsyth, R. A., & Opitz, E. Comparative parental MMPI protocols of children evaluated at a child development clinic. *Psychological Reports*, 1974, 35, 1147-54.

Anderson, L. M. Personality characteristics of parents of neurotic, aggressive and normal preadolescent boys. *Journal of Consulting and Clinical Psychology*, 1969, 33, 575-81.

Archer, R. P., Sutker, P. B., White, J. L., & Orvin, G. H. Personality relationships among parents and adolescent offspring in inpatient treatment. *Psychological Reports*, 1978, 42, 207-14.

Bandura, A., & Walters, R. H. *Social learning and personality development.* New York: Holt, Rinehart & Winston, 1963.

Barron, F. An ego-strength scale which predicts response to psychotherapy. *Journal of Consulting Psychology*, 1953, 17, 327-33.

Bradley, P. E., Wakefield, J. A., Yom, B. L., Doughtie, E. B., Cox, J. A., & Kraft, I. A. Parental MMPIs and certain pathological behaviors in children. *Journal of Clinical Psychology*, 1974, 30, 379-82.

Butcher, J. N. *MMPI characteristics of externalizing and internalizing boys and their parents.* Paper presented at the First Conference on Recent Developments in the Use of the MMPI, Minneapolis, March, 1966.

Butcher, J. N., & Messick, D. M. Parent-child profile similarity and aggression: A preliminary study. *Psychological Reports*, 1966, 18, 440-42.

Butcher, J. N., & Tellegen, A. Common methodological problems in MMPI research. *Journal of Consulting and Clinical Psychology*, 1978, 46, 620-28.

Comrey, A. L. Common methodological problems in factor analytic studies. *Journal of Consulting and Clinical Psychology*, 1978, 46, 648-59.

Dee, C., & Dee, H. L. MMPIs of parents of emotionally disturbed, motor dysfunctional, and normal children. *Journal of Consulting and Clinical Psychology*, 1972, 38, 464.

Dunteman, G. H., & Wolking, W. D. Relationship between marital status and the personality of mothers of disturbed children. *Journal of Consulting Psychology*, 1967, 31, 220.

Erickson, M. T. MMPI comparisons between parents of young emotionally disturbed and organically retarded children. *Journal of Consulting and Clinical Psychology*, 1968, 32, 701-6.

Erickson, M. T. MMPI profiles of parents of young retarded children. *American Journal of Mental Deficiency*, 1969, 73, 728-32.

Fitzelle, G. T. Personality factors and certain attitudes toward child rearing among parents of asthmatic children. *Psychosomatic Medicine*, 1959, 21, 208-17.

Friedman, R. J. MMPI characteristics of mothers of preschool children who are emotionally disturbed or have behavior problems. *Psychological Reports*, 1974, 34, 1159-62.

Goldfarb, W. *Childhood schizophrenia*. Cambridge, Mass.: Harvard University Press, 1961.

Goodstein, L. D. MMPI profiles of stutterers' parents: A follow-up study. *Journal of Speech and Hearing Disorders*, 1956, 21, 430-35.

Goodstein, L. D. MMPI differences between parents of children with cleft palates and parents of physically normal children. *Journal of Speech and Hearing Research*, 1960, 3, 31-38. (a)

Goodstein, L. D. Personality test differences in parents of children with cleft palates. *Journal of Speech and Hearing Research*, 1960, 3, 39-43. (b)

Goodstein, L. D., & Dahlstrom, W. G. MMPI differences between the parents of stuttering and nonstuttering children. *Journal of Consulting Psychology*, 1956, 20, 365-70.

Goodstein, L. D., & Rowley, V. N. A further study of MMPI differences between parents of disturbed and nondisturbed children. *Journal of Consulting Psychology*, 1961, 25, 460.

Group for the Advancement of Psychiatry. *Psychopathological disorders in childhood: Theoretical considerations and a proposed classification*. New York: The Authors, 1966.

Gynther, M. D. White norms and black MMPIs: A prescription for discrimination? *Psychological Bulletin*, 1972, 78, 386-402.

Gynther, M. D., Lachar, D., & Dahlstrom, W. G. Are special norms for minorities needed?: Development of an MMPI F scale for blacks. *Journal of Consulting and Clinical Psychology*, 1978, 46, 1403-8.

Hafner, A. J., Butcher, J. N., Hall, M. D., & Quast, W. Parent personality and childhood disorders: A review of MMPI findings. In J. N. Butcher (Ed.), *MMPI: Research developments and clinical applications*. New York: McGraw-Hill, 1969.

Hanvik, L. J., & Byrum, M. MMPI profiles of parents of child psychiatric patients. *Journal of Clinical Psychology*, 1959, 15, 427-31.

Hodo, G., & Fowler, R. Frequency of MMPI two-point codes in a large alcoholic sample. *Journal of Clinical Psychology*, 1976, 32, 487-89.

Jacob, R. Family interaction in disturbed and normal families: A methodological and substantive review. *Psychological Bulletin*, 1975, 82, 33-65.

Johnson, S. M., & Lobitz, G. K. The personal and marital adjustment of parents as related to observed child deviance and parenting behaviors. *Journal of Abnormal Child Psychology*, 1974, 2, 193-207.

L'Abate, L. The effect of paternal failure to participate during the referral of child psychiatric patients. *Journal of Clinical Psychology*, 1960, 16, 407-8.

Lachar, D. Accuracy and generalizability of an automated MMPI interpretation system. *Journal of Consulting and Clinical Psychology*, 1974, 42, 267-73. (a)

Lachar, D. *The MMPI: Clinical assessment and automated interpretation*. Los Angeles: Western Psychological Services, 1974. (b)

Lachar, D., & Alexander, R. S. Veridicality of self-report: Replicated correlates of the Wiggins MMPI content scales. *Journal of Consulting and Clinical Psychology*, 1978, 46, 1349-56.

Lachar, D., Butkus, M., & Hryhorczuk, L. Objective personality assessment of children: An exploratory study of the Personality Inventory for Children (PIC) in a child psychiatric setting. *Journal of Personality Assessment*, 1978, 42, 529-37.

Lachar, D., & Gdowski, C. L. *Actuarial assessment of child and adolescent personality: An interpretive guide for the Personality Inventory for Children profile*, Los Angeles: Western Psychological Services, 1979. (a)

Lachar, D., & Gdowski, C. L. Problem behavior factor correlates of Personality Inventory for Children profile scales. *Journal of Consulting and Clinical Psychology*, 1979, 47, 39-48. (b)

Lachar, D., Klinge, V., & Grisell, J. L. Relative accuracy of automated MMPI narratives generated from adult norm and adolescent norm profiles. *Journal of Consulting and Clinical Psychology*, 1976, 44, 20-24.

Lauterbach, C. G., London, P., & Bryan, J. MMPIs of parents of child guidance cases. *Journal of Clinical Psychology*, 1961, 17, 151-54.

Lauterbach, C. G., Vogel, W., & Hart, J. Comparison of the MMPIs of male problem adolescents and their parents. *Journal of Clinical Psychology*, 1962, 18, 485-87.

Liverant, S. MMPI differences between parents of disturbed and nondisturbed children. *Journal of Consulting Psychology*, 1959, 23, 256-60.

Locke, H. J., & Wallace, K. M. Short marital and adjustment tests: Their reliability and validity. *Marriage and Family Living*, 1959, 21, 251-55.

Loeb, J., & Price, J. Mother and child personality characteristics related to parental marital status in child guidance cases. *Journal of Consulting Psychology*, 1966, 30, 112-17.

Marks, P. A. An assessment of the diagnostic process in a child guidance setting. *Psychology Monographs*, 1961, 75 (3, Whole No. 507).

Marks, P. A., Seeman, W., & Haller, D. *The actuarial use of the MMPI with adolescents and adults.* Baltimore: Williams & Wilkins, 1974.

McAdoo, W. G. *Measures of parental psychopathology and their correlates.* Unpublished manuscript, 1976.

McAdoo, W. G., & Connolly, F. J. MMPIs of parents in dysfunctional families. *Journal of Consulting and Clinical Psychology*, 1975, 43, 270.

McAdoo, W. G., & DeMeyer, M. K. Personality characteristics of parents. In M. Rutter & E. Schopler (Eds.), *Autism: A reappraisal of concepts and treatment.* New York: Plenum, 1978.

McAdoo, W. G., & Roeske, N. A. A comparison of defectors and continuers in a child guidance clinic. *Journal of Consulting and Clinical Psychology*, 1973, 40, 328-34.

Meehl, P. E. High school yearbooks: A reply to Schwarz. *Journal of Abnormal Psychology*, 1971, 77, 143-48.

Miller, W. H., & Keirn, W. C. Personality measurement in parents of retarded and emotionally disturbed children: A replication. *Journal of Clinical Psychology*, 1978, 34, 686-90.

Mlott, S. R. Some significant relationships between adolescents and their parents as revealed by the Minnesota Multiphasic Personality Inventory. *Adolescence*, 1972, 7, 169-82.

Pinneau, S. R., & Hopper, H. E. The relationship between incidence of specific gastro-intestinal reactions in the infant and psychological characteristics of the mother. *Journal of Genetic Psychology*, 1958, 93, 3-13.

Roessler, R., Alexander, A. A., & Greenfield, N. S. Ego strength and physiological responsivity: I, the relationship of the Barron Es Scale to skin resistance, finger blood volume, heart rate, and muscle potential responses to sound. *Archives of General Psychiatry*, 1963, 8, 142-54.

Routh, D. K. MMPI responses of mothers and fathers as a function of mental retardation of the child. *American Journal of Mental Deficiency*, 1970, 75, 376-77.

Rutter, M. Parent-child separation: Psychological effects on the child. *Journal of Child Psychology and Psychiatry*, 1971, 12, 233-60.

Schaefer, E. S., & Bell, R. Q. Development of a parental attitude research instrument. *Child Development*, 1958, 29, 339-61.

Shectman, A. Psychiatric symptoms in normal and disturbed children. *Journal of Clinical Psychology*, 1970, 26, 38-41.

Shectman, A. Psychiatric symptoms observed in normal and disturbed black children. *Journal of Clinical Psychology*, 1971, 27, 445-47.

Smith, R. E., Johnson, J. H., & Sarason, I. G. Life change, the sensation of seeking motive, and psychological distress. *Journal of Consulting and Clinical Psychology*, 1978, 46, 348-49.

Sopchak, A. L. Spearman correlations between MMPI scores of college students and their parents. *Journal of Consulting Psychology*, 1958, 22, 207-9.

Spielberger, C. D. Theory and research on anxiety. in C. D. Spielberger (Ed.), *Anxiety and behavior*. New York: Academic Press, 1966.

Stehbens, J. A. Comparison of MMPI scores of mothers of enuretic and control children. *Journal of Clinical Psychology*, 1970, 26, 496.

Verinis, J. S. Maternal and child pathology in an urban ghetto. *Journal of Clinical Psychology*, 1976, 32, 13-15.

Welsh, G. S. MMPI profiles and factor scales A and R. *Journal of Clinical Psychology*, 1965, 21, 43-47.

Wiggins, J. Content dimensions in the MMPI. In J. N. Butcher (Ed.), *MMPI: Research developments and clinical applications*. New York: McGraw-Hill, 1969.

Wirt, R. D., Lachar, D., Klinedinst, J. K., & Seat, P. D. *Multidimensional description of child personality. A manual for the Personality Inventory for Children*. Los Angeles: Western Psychological Services, 1977.

Wolff, W. M., & Morris, L. A. Intellectual and personality characteristics of parents of autistic children. *Journal of Abnormal Psychology*, 1971, 77, 155-61.

Wolking, W. D., Dunteman, G. H., & Bailey, J. P. Multivariate analysis of parents' MMPIs based on the psychiatric diagnosis of their children. *Journal of Consulting Psychology*, 1967, 31, 521-24.

Wolking, W. D., Quast, W., & Lawton, J. J. MMPI profiles of the parents of behaviorally disturbed children and parents from the general population. *Journal of Clinical Psychology*, 1966, 22, 39-48.

Zubin, J. Classification of behavior disorders. In P. R. Farnsworth, D. McNewmar, & Q. McNemar (Eds.), *Annual Review of Psychology*, Palo Alto, California: Annual Reviews, Inc., 1967.

Zuckerman, M., & Oltean, M. Some relationships between maternal attitude factors and authoritarianism, personality needs, psychopathology, and self-acceptance. *Child Development*, 1959, 30, 27-36.

Use of the MMPI
in the Evaluation
of Treatment Effects

Steven Hollon and Monica Mandell

INTRODUCTION

What properties must a measure possess to be useful as a measure of therapeutic change? Not only must such a measure meet all of the traditional requirements for reliability and validity, it must also be sensitive to real fluctuations, "true" change, in the phenomenon of interest. The measure must change when the phenomenon of interest changes and remain relatively constant when the phenomenon of interest is stable.

In this chapter, we shall evaluate the relative adequacy of the MMPI as a measure of change following therapeutic interventions. Our question will be a comparative one: How adequate is the MMPI relative to other existing indexes of change? By adequate, we mean both sensitivity in the detection of fluctuations and the ease with which those observed fluctuations lend themselves to interpretation.

We shall focus our attention on syndrome depression. Efforts to apply an intensive analysis of any broad-spectrum instrument such as the MMPI would be beyond the scope of any single chapter. We shall make some general comments about the utility of the MMPI in several types of patient samples, including mixed outpatients, schizophrenics, alcoholics, drug addictions, and sociopathy, but shall focus our attention on syndrome depression as a model for intensive comparative reviews in other areas.

HISTORICAL BACKGROUND

Since its introduction in the 1940s, the MMPI has been associated with literally thousands of published studies. Most of the investigations have explored questions of differential diagnosis and/or differential prediction of subsequent psychopathology. Table 1 presents a classification of MMPI uses organized along two major dimensions. The first dimension of interest involves concern with the status of the individual at (or retrospective to) the time of assessment vs. interest in the status of the individual at some future date (detection vs. prediction). The second dimension involves concern with the delineation of some state of the individual vs. some change in the state of the individual (concurrent vs. future status). Our primary interest in this chapter will lie with the upper right-hand cell, the detection of changes that at the time of the final assessment have already occurred following intervention with individuals who initially showed some type of psychopathology.

Schofield (1950; 1953) has argued that any measure which provides a sensitive measure of a phenomenon at one point in time can reasonably be expected to provide a sensitive assessment of change in that phenomenon. It is not enough, however, that a measure reliably sorts individuals into known diagnostic groups (the predominant methodology used for initial item selection and scale construction). It is necessary that the measure be sensitive to real fluctuations in the phenomena measured. The logic of our analyses will be similar to that used in reviews of therapeutic efficacy: (1) Can the MMPI be said to detect changes over time detected by other measures? (2) Can the MMPI be said to evidence changes between differentially treated groups? and (3) Can the changes detected above, if any, be related meaningfully to current clinical knowledge. The first two issues involve questions of the detection of internally valid changes (Campbell & Stanley, 1963), issues best addressed by comparing the relative sensitivities of two or more measures *in the same study*. The third question involves the issue of construct validity; given that we can

Table 1. Classification of Uses of the MMPI

Purpose	Phenomenon	Change in Phenomenon
Detection	Establishment of differential diagnosis	Detection of change in phenomenon (outcome)
Prediction	Identification of high-risk cases	Prediction of change in phenomenon (prognosis)

reliably detect a phenomenon, can we accurately interpret that phenomenon? With a multidimensional tool like the MMPI, change may be easier to detect than to understand (Lewinsohn, 1965; Lewinsohn & Nichols, 1964; 1967). In all instances, the crucial determination will be whether the MMPI outperforms other available measures of the same phenomenon.

AN INDEX OF INSTRUMENT SENSITIVITY

In a recent paper, Smith and Glass (1977) conducted what they termed a meta-analysis of the effects of various therapeutic interventions. In brief, the authors calculated the magnitude of change associated with various treatments, using the formula:

$$\text{Effect Strength (ES)} = \frac{\overline{X} \text{ treatment} - \overline{X} \text{ control}}{\sigma \text{ control}}$$

The authors then averaged the calculated effect strengths across instances of similar interventions, calculating an average effect strength for "behavior therapy," a separate effect strength for "psychodynamic therapy," etc. The averaged effect strengths for the respective treatments were then compared in an effort to draw conclusions regarding the efficacy of the respective treatments.

Smith and Glass's reasoning appears flawed in several respects; populations vary across studies and treatment types, poorly designed studies are uncritically combined wtih well-designed studies, and "powerful" control groups are uncritically equated with less "powerful" control groups. In effect, their statistics confound treatment efficacy with population variance, design adequacy, and control-condition efficacy.

Nonetheless, the concept of meta-analysis may have considerable merit if put to a different use. Specifically, a meta-analysis of the effect sizes associated with different measures of the same phenomena might well yield an interpretable index of sensitivity to change associated with those different measures. A meta-analysis within given studies avoids several of the problems inherent in Smith and Glass's exploration of treatment effects. By restricting analysis to studies utilizing multiple measures, any given pair of *measures of effect sizes* will be based on identical samples exposed to identical procedures. The analysis becomes, essentially, a matter of analyzing indexes of *sensitivity* unconfounded by design, control, or population variance.

All studies chosen for such an analysis must meet the following requirements: (a) subjects randomly assigned to conditions; (b) two or more conditions compared; and (c) two or more measures of the same hypothetical variable utilized, with at least one based on the MMPI. Studies to be reviewed will be grouped in the following general domains: anxiety, depression, schizophrenia, psychopathy, alcoholism, drug abuse, and miscellaneous phenomena of interest. These domains roughly parallel the major nosological categories of the new *Diagnostic and Statistics Manual* (DSM-III) of the American Psychiatric Association (Task Force of the American Psychiatric Association, Note 1). The following discussion is not intended to be exhaustive; rather, it concerns representative research on the MMPI. In recent review, Butcher and Owen (1978) noted that most recent research involving the MMPI focused on either alcoholism and drug abuse or depression.

Throughout the remainder of this section, the following conventions will be utilized. Effect sizes for within-group comparisons over time will be calculated as follows according to Smith and Glass's formula, previously discussed. Once effect sizes are calculated for any given pair of measures, they can be converted to *sensitivity indexes* (SI's) by simply dividing the calculated effect size for one instrument by the effect size of another for any given comparison:

$$\frac{SI}{\text{Sensitivity Index}} = \frac{ES_{\text{Scale 1}}}{ES_{\text{Scale 2}}}$$

The closer the index to unity (1.0), the greater the comparability between the scales.

Our initial desire had been to calculate sensitivity indexes for the various MMPI scales *vis-à-vis* alternative instruments used in the controlled-outcome literature. Unfortunately, the tendency for investigators to report data only in the form of summary statistics forestalled such an effort. In most instances, scales can be compared only by means of dichotomous "significant/non-significant" criteria. Nonetheless, the concept of sensitivity indexes appears to provide a useful technique for future comparisons between competing outcome measures.

WHAT MEASURES TO UTILIZE?

The potential user of the MMPI as an index of change is confronted by an embarrassment of riches. In addition to the 10 basic clinical scales and three basic validity scales, the inventory can be used to provide profile clusters, sets of critical items, and a seemingly endless supply of subsidiary scales. The dilemma lies in specifying what index is relevant to the research question being asked. Typically, the existing published reports include one or more of the original clinical scales. Less often, subscales or derivative scales have been utilized, such as the Manifest Depression scale (Overall, Hollister, Pokorny, Casey, & Katz, 1962), the D-30 (Dempsey, 1964), both shortened forms of the longer 60-item depression scale. The Taylor Manifest Anxiety Scale (Taylor, 1953) is an example of a subscale that pulls items from several of the original clinical scales. Not infrequently, investigators have utilized a global pathology index, e.g., averaging across T scores for the clinical scales (e.g., Donnelly, Murphy, & Goodwin, 1976). Sines and Silver (1963) have developed a pathology index based on weighted combinations of several selected clinical indexes. Using such empirically derived combinations would appear to be superior to unvalidated global indexes, although we know of no studies directly comparing the respective validities and interpretabilities of the two types of combinatorial indexes.

Selection from among these various indexes depends largely on the question being asked and the purposes to which it is to be put. One very common practice, administering the full battery pre- and post-treatment and analyzing for changes across all clinical scales, while practical, can foster conceptually inadequate research. As a general rule of thumb, it would seem useful to have some initial hypotheses of what types of change would be interpretable if detected, if for no other reason than to ensure that the expensive venture of hypothesis testing is not entered into in a haphazard fashion. Further, reliance on multivariate analyses, or other adjustments for consideration of error rates when making multiple comparisons, would seem essential in such instances, although, in practice, is rarely done.

Content scales (Wiggins, 1966; Goldberg, 1974) may prove more satisfactory than existing indexes. Derived from multivariate analyses, the content scales presumably represent factorially pure indexes of basic dimensions of psychopathology. Although various reviewers have called for an increased reliance on such indexes (e.g., Butcher & Tellegen, 1978), we are unaware of any studies that have used such measures to assess change.

PSYCHOMETRIC PROPERTIES

Schofield (1966) and Dahlstrom, Welsh, and Dahlstrom (1975, Chapter 7) have reviewed in depth the substantive issues surrounding the psychometric properties of the MMPI as an index of change. Dahlstrom et al. (1975) argue that care must be exercised in applying criteria like internal consistency or test-retest notions of reliability to a measure like the MMPI. Briefly, with respect to internal consistency, the authors argue that many of the phenomena studied, e.g., depression, anxiety, etc., are conceptualized at the syndrome level and may well represent multifactorial processes. With regard to notions of test-retest reliability, the authors point out that the only reasonable process for assessing the reliability of a change measure lies in assessing the concordance of two or more change measures over time. If one simply calculates test-retest correlations on a single instrument, one risks attributing reliable sensitivity in detecting a "true" change to unreliability of the instrument.

Several studies have evaluated the stability of various MMPI indexes over time in the absence of strong reasons to expect change (cf. Fiske, 1957; Goldberg & Jones, 1969; Holzberg & Alessi, 1949; Lichtenstein & Bryan, 1966; Mauger, 1972; Mills, 1954; Newmark, 1971; Pauker, 1965; Pepper, 1964; Rosen, 1953; Stone, 1965; Ullman & Wiggins, 1962). In general, the findings suggest fairly strong test-retest correlations, both in normal and in clinical samples, at least over brief periods. Fiske (1957), in a reanalysis of earlier data involving from 9 to 18 retestings on a normative population, found greater stability for more extreme scores—a remarkable finding since one must assume there were offsetting factors decreasing reliability at the extremes related to sample regression artifacts. Such data appear to indicate the operation of different means for different individuals which became detectable with repeated testing. In short, such findings point to consistency within individuals across time in the same testing situation, with, perhaps, a suggestion that the more extreme scores fluctuate in a stable fashion around more elevated baselines than do less extreme scores.

For the purposes of change assessment, item instability may be less a problem than item stability. Schofield (1953) has demonstrated that only a small portion of specific items ($\simeq 14\%$) are likely to change over time for individuals. Stable items tended to represent a greater proportion of some scales than others (e.g., scales F and Sc showed the greatest stability), to be obvious rather than subtle, to involve no estimate of the frequency of specific behaviors, and to be stated in past rather than present tenses. Fully 86% of all specific items proved stable over time. Such stability, of course, may cause special problems when the MMPI is used as a measure of change. Just as a high-water mark may register valid flood-water peaks yet fail to reflect subsequent recessions in water levels, so a measure dominated by historical or characterological items may reliably classify along previous trait dimensions without being sensitive enough to state fluctuations or even more permanent changes in trait variables. The overall length of the inventory appears to compensate for such potential deficiencies; 14% of a 550-item measure still leaves a working pool of over 70 items for change purposes. What does seem to be affected, however, are the relative magnitudes of the sensitivity indexes calculated for the MMPI and alternative measures used to detect within-group and between-group changes. Table 2 presents sensitivity indexes calculated for three instruments, the MMPI *D* scale, the Beck Depression Inventory (BDI), and the Hamilton Rating Scale of Depression (HRS-D), based on a recent controlled comparison of drugs (imipramine hydrochloride) and a psychosocial intervention (cognitive therapy) in the treatment of outpatient depressives (Rush, Beck, Kovacs, & Hollon, 1977). Pre- and post-treatment means and standard deviations are first converted to relative effect sizes using the formula presented in Table 2. Separate effect sizes are calculated for within-group (pre-post)

Table 2. Analysis of Change Measures

Group	Measure	Pre-treatment	Post-treatment
Drug (N = 17)	MMPI-D	95.18 (11.56)	83.56 (14.57)
	BDI	32.00 (5.86)	14.82 (12.88)
	HRS-D	22.71 (4.25)	10.24 (6.84)
Cognitive therapy (N = 18)	MMPI-D	88.65 (18.10)	71.00 (14.64)
	BDI	30.28 (6.82)	5.94 (5.33)
	HRS-D	21.20 (3.34)	5.80 (3.67)

Effect Sizes

	Within Groups		Between Groups
Scale	Drug	C/B	Drug vs. C/B (Post)
MMPI-D	.89	1.08	.86
BDI	1.83	4.01	.98
HRS-D	2.25	4.39	.84

Sensitivity Ratios

	Within Groups		Between Groups
Comparison	Drug	C/B	Drug vs. C/B (Post)
MMPI-D vs. BDI	.49	.27	.88
MMPI-D vs. HRS-D	.39	.25	1.02
BDI vs. HRS-D	.81	.91	1.17

Source: Rush, Beck, Kovacs, and Hollon, 1977.

Key: MMPI-D: Depression Scale (scale 2)
BDI: Beck Depression Inventory
HRS-D: Hamilton Rating Scale for Depression

changes for each measure in each treatment cell (drug vs. cognitive therapy) and for between-group differences at post-treatment (drug vs. cognitive therapy). These effect sizes are directly analogous to the ratio of mean group differences to group variability used by Cohen (1969) in calculating power ratios for a given study. Since sample sizes are held constant across measures, these effect sizes for the different measures can themselves be cast as ratios of sensitivity. The closer to unity the ratio, the greater the comparability between the two pairs of measures.

As can be seen, between-group effect sizes are relatively comparable across all three measures, while the MMPI *D* scale appears to be far less sensitive than either the BDI or HRS-D to within-group changes from pre- to post-treatment. How are we to account for such differences? Our preferred explanation involves the ratio of potentially change-detecting, or "working," scale items to stable items. The larger item pool of the MMPI *D* scale appears less sensitive to changes over time, since a greater proportion of items are unlikely to change. For between-group comparisons, where the absolute number of "working" items is roughly equivalent to the shorter BDI (21 items) or HRS-D (only the first 14 items scored), and stable items in the two samples cancel each other out, the MMPI *D* scale approaches unity, or comparable sensitivity. It remains to be seen whether such an explanation retains viability in similar studies, but it does point toward an interesting non-concordance between within- and between-group means for measures mixed with respect to item stability/instability over time.

In the sections to follow, we shall evaluate the relative sensitivity of the MMPI *vis-à-vis* alternative measures. Our desire to conduct a series of sensitivity analyses across studies has been blocked by the frequent absence of reported means and standard deviations in the published literature. Investigators frequently report only summary statistics, e.g., ANOVA's or t-tests, rather than those descriptive statistics required for such a fine-grained analysis. We opted for a dichotomous categorization, significant/nonsignificant, in our comparisons of measures. Although less satisfying, such a procedure at least approximates the more elaborate calculation of sensitivity ratios. Such ratios, however, appear to have much to recommend them, and we would encourage subsequent investigators to provide both such indexes and the requisite descriptive statistics for their calculation as an aid to researchers in the field. With these considerations in mind, we turn now to a review of the MMPI as an index of change in syndrome depression.

DEPRESSION

Recent reviews have not been favorable with regard to the utility of the MMPI as a measure of change in syndrome depression. After comparing the relative sensitivities of various self-report indexes across 72 controlled, double-blind pharmacological trials published in 1955-72, McNair (1974) found the MMPI D scale detected significant placebo-drug or drug-drug differences in only 11 of 63 relevant comparisons, or 17% of the time. The Manifest Depression scale (Overall, Hollister, Pokorny, Casey, & Katz, 1962), an abbreviated version of the D scale, was even less impressive, detecting differences in only 2 of 13 comparisons (15%). Meanwhile, global ratings made by patients proved sensitive to treatment effects in 11 of 31 relevant comparisons (35% detection), clearly outperforming the MMPI, as did three other scales, the Beck Depression Inventory (BDI) (Beck, Ward, Mendelsohn, Mock, & Erbaugh, 1961), with a 29% detection ratio, the Zung Self-Rating Depression Scale (SDS) (Zung, 1965), at 26% and the Clyde Mood Scale (Clyde, 1963), at 25% detection. McNair concluded that although the MMPI D scale "has been used in more trials than any other measure . . . it is difficult to regard its performance as more than disappointing" (p. 290).

McNair's conclusions were flawed in two respects. First, he simply tallied incorrectly. Although he lists 63 comparisons involving the MMPI D scale, 27 involving placebo-drug comparisons and 36 involving drug-drug comparisons, after several readings of the 24 relevant publications cited by McNair, we can locate only 40 total comparisons. Our tallies are in close accord with his for drug-placebo comparisons, where we locate 24 comparisons, but wildly divergent with respect to the drug-drug comparisons, of which we can locate only 13. Although a small margin of disagreement is not unreasonable (it is, for example, not clear whether McNair regarded the occasional cross-over designs as two discrete comparisons or only one), a discrepancy of 23 comparisons (36 vs. 13) clearly requires explanation. We suspect that some error in the author's clerical tabulations is responsible. Whatever the nature of the error, its effects are obvious. Recalculating the sensitivity of the MMPI D scale based on our count, we find the detection of significant differences in 3 of 13 drug-drug comparisons, 23% of the relevant instances. Combined with the 8 of 27 significant placebo-drug comparisons observed (30% detection), the overall sensitivity ratio for the MMPI D scale becomes 27.5%, moving it from a poor fifth to a strong third on the list.

The second flaw in McNair's review was more subtle and largely because of this subtlety, more problematic. Specifically, McNair's procedure for determining the sensitivity of an index—dividing the total number of observed significant findings across studies by the total number of observed comparisons across studies—confounds the sensitivity of the measure with the power of the trials in which it is utilized. The error in logic is similar to that of Smith and Glass (1977) detailed earlier in our discussion of their attempt to conduct a meta-analysis of the average effects of various approaches to psychosocial interventions. The viability of comparisons based on indexes generated by pooling results across different sets of discrete studies depends upon the validity of the assumption that all other factors contributing to outcome (e.g., sample size, sample characteristics, treatment type, trial length, procedural rigor, statistical competence, etc.) are randomly distributed with respect to the measures to be compared. The tenuousness of such an assumption is evident. There are a variety of ways to design a study that evidences no differences between comparisons besides selecting a "poor" measure of change.

The converse is, of course, also true. In McNair's review, patient self-ratings of syndrome depression proved to be the most sensitive index of change, producing a 35% detection rate based on significant differences in 11 of 31 comparisons. However, 7 of the 12 published reports from which those 31 comparisons were drawn involved studies done by a single research group on analogue populations of community volunteers solicited, in part, by newspaper advertisements (Rickels, Gordon, Weise, Bazilian, Feldman, & Wilson, 1970; Rickels, Hutchinson, Weise, Csanalosi, Chung, & Case, 1972; Rickels, Laquer, Rial, Rosenfeld, Schneider, & Wagner, 1971; Rickels, Perloff, Stepansky, Dion, Case, & Sapra, 1969; Rickels, Ward, & Schut, 1965; Rickels, Ward, & Snow, 1963; Snow & Rickels, 1964), while an eighth (Brick, Doub, & Perdue, 1962) involved a volunteer sample drawn from prison inmates. Although we are not questioning the internal validity of those designs, nor the potential generalizability of findings in such populations to more strictly defined clinical samples (an issue too often resolved on the basis of polemics rather than empirical research), we would question the wisdom of conducting any direct comparisons (e.g., between scales or between treatments) when such comparisons so clearly confound the phenomena of interest with systematic differences in samples. Although 8 of 12 published trials (67%) utilizing global self-report indexes of depression were based on analogue populations, only 4 of 24 published trials (25%) utilizing the MMPI *D* scale were similarly based. Does the distinction between subclinical and clinical populations make a difference? Perhaps. Of the 11 significant differences detected in the 37 MMPI *D* scale comparisons, 4 came from comparisons involving such subclinical populations. In fact, 4 of 7 such comparisons were significant, indicating a clearly greater tendency for significant differences to have been detected in analogue, as opposed to clinical samples (x^2, = 4.10, p < .05).

Rather than basing comparisons between measures on averaged outcomes across different sets of studies, more satisfying comparisons can be obtained if attention is restricted to comparisons between measures within specific studies. Table 3 lists the studies surveyed by McNair, providing information on other depression measures utilized in addition to the MMPI D scale. As can be seen, despite the relatively small number of studies comparing any specific pair of measures, concordance between measures is relatively high. Only 5 of the 37 comparisons involve any discordance between measures (Hollister, Overall, Johnson, Katz, Kimbell, & Honigfeld, 1963; Overall, Hollister, Shelton, Johnson, & Kimbell, 1966; Roulet, Alvarez, Duffy, Lenkoski, & Bidder, 1962; Wittenborn, Plante, Burgess, & Livermore, 1961; and Wittenborn, Plante, Burgess, & Maurer, 1962). The results? In those five instances, the D scale was outperformed once by the Wittenborn Psychiatric Rating Scale (Wittenborn, et al., 1961) and once by the MMPI Manifest Depression Scale; the D scale outperformed the Clyde Mood Scale, a clinician rating, and the Inpatient Multidimensional Psychiatric Rating Scale (IMPS) once each.

Making specific pair-wise comparisons with self-report measures is difficult owing to the limited number of relevant studies. Nonetheless, it is evident that the MMPI D scale fared well in most comparisons. The sole exception is provided by the MMPI Manifest Depression Scale, which is concordant with the MMPI D scale on one significant outcome and four "no differences," while detecting a difference not detected by the D scale in one other instance. The D scale is totally concordant with patient global ratings, both measures evidencing three significant outcomes and one nonsignificant outcome. Similar concordance is demonstrated in single pair-wise comparisons with the BDI, SDS, and Johnson Temperament Scale (Depression) (JTD); all are nonsignificant. The D scale appears to outperform the Clyde Mood Scale, detecting one significant difference not detected by the Clyde, while being concordant on a second, nonsignificant finding. The Global ratings, BDI, Zung SDS, and Clyde scales were the four scales initially listed by McNair as more sensitive than the MMPI D scale; yet, in no instance where pair-wise comparisons appeared within any single study did any of those scales detect a difference not detected by the MMPI D scale.

What of D-scale comparisons with physician-rated scales? Again, examination of specific pair-wise comparisons indicates at least relative comparability for the D scale. Most frequent are D-IMPS comparisons, with the two scales concordant on 13 nonsignificant outcomes. The only disconcordant outcome favors the MMPI. In one other instance, the D scale detects a difference not detected by a clinician rating scale. The only instance in which the D scale does not detect a difference detected by a clinician-rated measure involves the Wittenborn rating scale.

Comparable results are evident for the MMPI Manifest Depression Scale. Table 4 lists the pair-wise comparisons involving the Manifest Depression Scale in studies cited by McNair. As can be clearly seen, the only disconcordance occurring in any of the 13 total comparisons actually favors the MMPI Manifest Depression Scale, and that at the expense of the MMPI D scale (Hollister et al., 1963).

Clearly, indexes of instrument sensitivity that confound instrument variance with any of the myriad of alternate sources of variance risk misconstruing the sensitivity of the instruments involved. A far more satisfying approach involves either straightforward pair-wise concordance comparisons between measures used in the same study or the even more sophisticated meta-analyses of measured affect sizes within studies.

Several additional studies, not reviewed by McNair, exist that also involve the concomitant use of the MMPI and alternative measures of syndrome depression. In general, these studies, listed in Table 5, appear to confirm the impression from the pharmacological literature that the MMPI D scale provides a valid measure of change in syndrome depression, one comparably sensitive to alternative measures.

Taylor and Marshall (1977) compared a cognitive-behavioral therapy, strictly behavioral therapy, and waiting-list control in the treatment of syndrome depression. All subjects were undergraduate college students volunteering for an analogue therapy experience and scoring above a set psychometric criterion for minimum level of depression. All subjects were assessed on the MMPI-D(30), a shortened (30-item) version of the 60-item MMPI D scale (Dempsey, 1964), the Beck Depression Inventory (BDI) (Beck et al., 1961), and. the Visual Analogue Scale (VAS) (Aiken, 1969). All three measures were taken at pre-treatment, post-treatment (six weeks), and post-treatment follow-up (one month) points. All groups except the waiting-list control showed significant decreases in level of syndrome depression from pre- to post-treatment on all three depression measures. Similarly, all three treatment groups showed significantly greater reductions in syndrome depression than did patients in the waiting-list control,

Table 3. Comparative Studies Listed in McNair, 1975, as Using the MMPI D Scale

Study	Type	Placebo-Drug			Drug-Drug		
		No.	Self-Report Measure	Clinician-Rated Measure	No.	Self-Report Measure	Clinician-Rated Measure
Brick, Doub, & Perdue, 1962	Mixed	2	D ++ Global Rating ++		1	D + Global Rating +	
Brick, Doub, & Perdue, 1964[a]					2	D == JTD ==	
Brick, Doub, & Perdue, 1966	PI-Rx	1	D +	Clinical Rating +			
Burke & Templar, 1968	Rx-Rx				1	D = SDS =	Clinical Rating = (Wechsler)
DiMascio, Meyer, & Stifler, 1968[b]	PI-Rx	2	D + =				
Fryer & Timberlake, 1963[a]	PI-Rx	2	D ==				
Gallant, Bishop, Scrignar, Hornsby, Moore & Inturrisi, 1966	PI-Rx	1	D =	HRS-D = Global Rating =			
Hollister & Overall, 1965[c]	Rx-Rx				1	MD =	IMPS = BPRS =
Hollister, Overall, Johnson, Katz, Kimbell, & Honigfeld, 1963	PI-Rx	1	D == MD +	IMPS =			
Hollister, Overall, Johnson, Pennington, Katz & Shelton, 1964	Mixed	2	D == MD ==	IMPS ==	1	D = MD =	IMPS =
Hollister, Overall, Johnson, Shelton, Kimbell & Brunse, 1966	Rx-Rx				1	D = MD =	IMPS = BPRS =

Table 3, cont.

Study	Type	Placebo-Drug			Drug-Drug		
		No.	Self-Report Measure	Clinician-Rated Measure	No.	Self-Report Measure	Clinician-Rated Measure
Malitz & Kanzler, 1971	PI-Rx	1	D +	BPRS + Clinician Rating +			
Mandell, Markham, Tallman, Mandell, 1962	PI-Rx	1	D +				
Nussbaum, Wittig, Hanlon & Kurland, 1963	PI-Dr	1	D =	Global Clinician Rating =			
Overall, Hollister, Pokorny, Casey, & Katz, 1962c	Mixed	3	MD = = =	IMPS = = = PRP = = =	3	MD = = =	IMPS = = = PRP = = =
Overall, Hollister, Shelton, Johnson, & Kimbell, 1966	Rx-Rx	1	D		1	D + MD +	IMPS =
Robin & Wiseberg, 1958	PI-Rx	1	D = Global Rating =	Global Rating =			
Roulet, Alvarez, Duffey, Lenkoski, & Bidder, 1962	PI-Rx	1	D +	Clinician Rating =			
Sandifer, Wilson, & Gambill, 1965	Rx-Rx				1	D =	HRS-D =
Schenker, Marjerrison, Schlachet, Freedman, Hankoff, & Engelhardt, 1961	PI-Rx	1	D =	Clinician Rating =			
Shaffer, Freinek, McCusker, & DeFelice, 1964	Rx-Rx				1	D +	IMPS = BPRS = Global Clinician Rating =
Wilson, Vernon, Guin, & Sandifer,	PI-Rx	1	D =	HRS-D =			

Study	Comparison	n	Measures	Sig		
Wittenborn, Plante, Burgess, & Livermore, 1961e	Pl-Rx	1	D Clyde	= =	Wittenborn	+
Wittenborn, Plante, Burgess, & Maurer, 1962	Pl-Rx	1	D Clyde	+ =	Wittenborn	+

Totals (all studies)	24	D (8/24) MD (1/3) Global (2/3) BDI (0/1)	Clinical Rating (2/7) HRS-D (0/3) IMPS (0/5) BPRS (1/1) Wittenborn (2/2)	13

D (2/13) MD (1/3) Global Rating (1/1) SDS (0/1) JTD (0/2)	Clinician Rating (0/2) BPRS (0/3) IMPS (0/8) PRP (0/3) HRS-D (0/1)

aSecond comparison based on cross-over design, all patients entering second comparison had just completed first comparison under different treatment conditions. Many patients had already showed marked symptom reductions.

bSecond comparison based on "normal" subjects low on syndrome-depression measures.

cReported in McNair (1974) as involving the MMPI D Scale, when the actual scale reported in the source article was the MMPI Manifest Depression Scale.

dTwo separate trials (study 1 and study 2) reported in the published report.

eFactorial design included ECT vs. no ECT. It is not clear from McNair's report whether combined cells (e.g., drug plus ECT or placebo plus ECT) were included or excluded from the count. In this review, ECT in combination is considered to "not exist," hence placebo plus ECT is considered equivalent to placebo alone.

Key:
Pl-Rx: Placebo vs. Drug
Rx-Rx: Drug vs. Drug
Mixed: Both Placebo-Drug and Drug-Drug comparisons included.

BG: Between Groups
WG: Within Groups

+ : significant differences between treatment groups
= : no significant differences between treatment groups
− : significant differences between drug vs. placebo, favoring placebo

Multiple signs are used when multiple comparisons were made.

BPRS: Brief Psychiatric Rating Scale
Clyde: Clyde Mood Scale (MMPI)
D: Depression Scale (MMPI)
HRS-D Hamilton Rating Scale for Depression
IMPS: Inpatient Multidimensional Psychiatric Rating Scale
JTD: Johnson Temperament Scale (Depression)
MD: Manifest Depression Scale (MMPI)
PRP: Psychotic Reaction Profile
SDS: Zung Self-Rating Depression Scale

Table 4. Studies Listed in McNair (1975) as Using the MMPI Manifest Depression Scale

Study	Type	Placebo vs. Drug			Drug vs. Drug		
		No.	Self-Report Measure	Clinician-Rated Measure	No.	Self-Report Measure	Clinician-Rated Measure
Hollister, Overall, Johnson, Katz, Kimbell, & Honigfeld, 1963	Pl-Rx	1	MD + D =	IMPS =			
Hollister, Overall, Johnson, Pennington, Katz, & Shelton, 1964	Mixed	2	MD = = D = =	IMPS = =	1	MD = D =	IMPS =
Hollister, Overall, Johnson, Shelton, Kimbell, & Brunse, 1966	Rx-Rx				1	MD = D =	IMPS = BPRS =
Overall, Hollister, Meyer, Kimbell, & Shelton, 1964	Rx-Rx				1	MD =	BPRS =
Overall, Hollister, Pokorny, Casey, & Katz, 1962	Mixed	3	MD = = =	IMPS = = =	3	MD = =	IMPS = =
Overall, Hollister, Shelton, Johnson, & Kimbell, 1966	Rx-Rx				1	MD + D +	IMPS =
Totals (all studies)		6	MD (1/6) D (0/3)	IMPS (0/6) PRP (0/3)	7	MD (1/7) D (1/3)	IMPS (1/6) PRP (0/3) BPRS (0/2)

Study	Population	Comparison	Measure	Outcome	
Cole, Patterson, Craig, Thomas, Ristine, Stahly, & Pasamanick, 1959	Depressed Inpatients	Drug (Iproniazid) vs. Psychotherapy (traditional) vs. Pill-Placebo	MMPI-D -Pt Lorr MSRRP	NS NS NS	(0) (0) (0)
Fuchs & Rehm, 1977	Depressed Volunteers (Adult)	Psychotherapy (self-control) vs. Psychotherapy (nondirective) vs. Waiting List	MMPI-D BDI	SC < ND < WL SC < ND < WL	(+) (+)
McClure, Low, & Gent, 1973	Depressed Inpatients	Drug (Clomipramine) vs. Drug (Imipramine)	MMPI-Welsh Anx IPAT BDI (Clinician-rated) HRS-D	NS NS NS NS	(0) (0) (0) (0)
McDonald, Perkins, & Marjerrison, 1966	Depressed Inpatients	ECT vs. Drug (Amitriptyline) vs. Pill-Placebo	MMPI Depression Rating Scale Ward Observation Index	ECT = Dr < PI NS ECT = Dr < PI	(+) (0) (+)
Mormont, 1974	Depressed Inpatients	Drug (Noveril) vs. Drug (Noveril—time released)	MMPI-D Breulet Depression Scale HRS-D	Dr < Dr-TR Dr < Dr-TR Dr < Dr-TR	(+) (+) (+)
Olson, 1962	Depressed Inpatients	Drug (Nialamide—300 mg) vs. Drug (Nialamide—100 mg) vs. Drug (nonantidepressant)	MMPI-D Nurses' Ratings of Behavior	$Dr_{300} < Dr_{100} =$ N-AD $Dr_{300} < Dr_{100} =$ N-AD	(+) (+)
Rush, Beck, Kovacs, & Hollon, 1977	Depressed Outpatients	Drug (Imipramine) vs. Psychotherapy (cognitive-behavioral)	MMPI-D BDI HRS-D (Raskin)[a]	C/B < Dr C/B < Dr C/B < Dr NS	(+) (+) (+) (0)
Spreche, 1963	Depressed Inpatients	ECT vs. Drug CT (Indoklon)	MMPI Clinical Observation	NS NS	(0) (0)
Taylor & Marshall, 1977	Depressed Volunteers (College Students)	Psychotherapy (cognitive-behavioral) vs. Psychotherapy (cognitive) vs. Psychotherapy (behavioral) vs. Waiting List	MMPI-D (3) BPI VAS MAACL	C/B < C = B > WL C/B << C = B > WL NS NS	(+) (+) (0) (0)

Table 5, cont.

Study	Population	Comparison	Measure	Outcome	
		Depression in Related Populations			
Equi & Jabara, 1976	Depression in Alcoholic sample	Inpatient Treatment Program	MMPI-D Zung SDS	Not reported (?) Not reported (?)	
Lauer, 1976	Depression in Passive-dependent out-patients and inpatients	Drug (imipramine) vs. Drug (nortriptyline) vs. No Drug	MMPI-D Edwards PPS	NS NS (except Endurance subscale) (?)	(0) (0)
Marsh & Markham, 1973	Depression in Parkinsonism patients	Drug (levadopa – 3 months) vs. Drug (levadopa – 15 months)	MMPI-D	No changes (?)	(0)
Maskin, Riklan, & Chabot, 1973	Depression in Parkinsonism patients	Drug (levadopa) vs. Control	MMPI-D MAACL	Dr > control Dr > control	(+) (+)
Overall, Brown, Williams, & Neill, 1973	Depression in Alcoholic sample	Drug vs. Pill-Placebo	MMPI-D -Pt	Dr < Pl Dr < Pl	(+) (+)
Shaw, Donley, Morgan, & Robinson, 1975	Depression in Alcoholic sample	Inpatient Treatment Program	MMPI-D SDS	Reported as correlations between measures (?)	

aBased on reduced sample size owing to missing data points.

Key: BDI: Beck Depression Inventory
HRS-D: Hamilton Rating Scale for Depression
IPAT: Institute for Personality and Ability Testing: Anxiety Scale
VAS: Visual Analogue Scale

NS: Nonsignificant
Dr: Drug
Pl: Placebo

while patients in combined cognitive-behavior therapy showed greater reductions than that shown by patients treated in either the strictly cognitive or the strictly behavioral cells. As in the within-group comparisons, the same patterns of results were evident for all three depression measures. Sensitivity ratios on the within-group comparisons for the MMPI-*D* (30) were comparable to those shown by the BDI or the VAS in relevant comparisons in this study. Similarly, between-group differences were equally well detected by the MMPI-*D* (30). Calculation of the sensitivity ratios for all possible comparisons between the three measures utilized suggest a slight advantage for the BDI (average SI ratio = – 1.93, with a range from – 1.6 to – 2.5). As in the earlier drug comparisons reviewed by McNair, the MMPI-*D* (30) appeared to provide a reasonably sensitive index of change in syndrome depression (as measured). Further, the comparisons between the MMPI-*D* (30) and the BDI and VAS, both widely used self-report indexes of depression, indicated that the former scale compared quite favorably with the latter two scales.

Fuchs and Rehm (1977) randomly assigned adult female community volunteers to six weeks of self-control therapy (SC), a nonspecific treatment control (NSp), or a waiting-list control (WL). All subjects were assessed pre- and post-treatment on the MMPI-*D* and the BDI. Subjects in the two treatment cells were also assessed on both measures at a one-month post-treatment follow-up. The data indicated significant within-group decreases in depression symtomatology from pre- to post-treatment for both the SC and the NSp treatment groups on both the MMPI-*D* and the BDI. Similarly, both measures evidenced comparable results, no change, for the WL group over the same interval. Differences between the groups favoring SC over NSp and NSp over WL were significant on both measures. Nonsignificant treatment-group differences at one-month follow-up were found in both self-report syndrome depression measures. Although the absence of reported standard deviations precluded the calculation of sensitivity and/or power ratios, comparisons of the magnitudes of the respective ANOVA's indicated a relative comparability of the MMPI-*D* and BDI as indexes of differential change between groups. As in the two earlier studies (Rush et al., 1977; Taylor & Marshall, 1977), within-group changes initially do not appear as striking for the MMPI-*D* as for the BDI, but power-ratio estimations suggest that either measure would detect changes in samples as small as eight per cell. Overall, these three studies suggest that, in subclinical populations, the MMPI-*D* (or D(30)) appears to be a sensitive self-report-based index of either within- or between-group differences in measured syndrome depression, comparing favorably to the BDI or VAS. A pattern of near comparable between-group ratios and somewhat less power on within-group ratios appears to emerge.

What of clinical populations and other than self-report measures? Our predominant interest in this discussion has been to assess the comparative utility of the MMPI for assessing change in clinical populations, with that assessed change reflecting real changes in clinical phenomena of interest. Although evidence on the adequacy of the instrument with subclinical populations is suggestive, more direct evidence in an actual clinical sample would be required before clinical utility could be assessed. Similarly, all of the comparative measures discussed in these three studies were essentially self-report measures; changes detected across such similar measures may well have reflected only factors associated with test-taking rather than real change in syndrome depression or other related phenomena of clinical interest.

Rush, Beck, Kovacs, and Hollon (1977) reported a comparison between cognitive (behavior) therapy (C/B) versus imipramine hydrochloride plus brief supportive psychotherapy in a sample of non-bipolar, non-psychotic, primary depressed outpatients (see also Hollon, Beck, Kovacs, & Rush, 1977) for a more complete description of scores on the MMPI). All patients were either self- or physician referrals for psychiatric treatment, hence representative of an outpatient clinical population. Diagnoses were made in accordance with the Feighner research diagnostic criteria (Feighner, Robins, Guze, Woodruff, Winokur, & Munoz, 1972). All patients were assessed at pre- and post-treatment (12 weeks) with the MMPI and BDI (as self-report measures), and with two clinician-rated measures, the Hamilton Rating Scale for Depression (HRS-D) (Hamilton, 1960) and the Raskin Depression Scale (Raskin, Schulterbrandt, Reatig, & Rice, 1967).

Within-group scores on the MMPI D scale and the other three syndrome depression measures listed above all reflected significant decreases in depression scores for both groups from pre- to post-treatment. As shown earlier in Table 2, sensitivity ratios on the within-group comparisons tend to favor the other measures somewhat, although power calculations indicate that within-group changes of a magnitude demonstrated would have been detected with sample sizes of eight and six, respectively, for the C/B and drug-treated cells.

Examination of the between-group sensitivity-index ratios of the various measures indicated that only the clinician-rated Raskin did not indicate greater change for the C/B group than the drug-treated group. Examination of the power ratios suggests that this was the result of the combination of missing data points and lower measured differential change for that instrument. Comparisons between the MMPI-*D*, BDI, and the clinician-rated HRS-D scale indicate a relative comparability between those three measures. All three measures indicated significantly greater change in the C/B than in the drug-treated cells, and all sensitivity-index ratios were within one standard unit of one another. These findings are consistent with those noted for the three analogue studies reported above; the MMPI-*D* appears to fare well when compared to alternative syndrome depression measures in detecting between-group changes. Although sensitivity-index ratios are somewhat less favorable to the MMPI-*D* when based on within-group analyses, the greater power of such analyses typically overrides this concern. In essence, any comparative study with a design powerful enough to generate meaningful between-group changes should also prove significantly powerful to allow detection of clinically meaningful changes on any of the major syndrome-depression measures, including the MMPI-*D*. Because comparable changes were found on at least one clinician-rated measure, the HRS-D, the differences detected cannot be attributed solely to nonrelevant changes in measurement-method factors.

Several additional points regarding the use of the MMPI in such populations and studies are relevant. First, unlike the two analogue studies reported above, the Rush et al. comparison involved the administration of the full MMPI. Significant within-group decreases were obtained for the C/B cell on subscales *F, Hs, D, Hy, Pt, Sc,* and *Si,* while within-group increases emerged on scales *K* and *ES.* For the drug-treatment group, within-group decreases emerged on subscales *F, D, Pt, Sc,* and *Si,* while increases were apparent on *K* only. Between-group differences in post-treatment scores favored the C/B group not only on *D,* but also on *F, Pt, Sc, and Si.* This pattern of within- and between-group changes is quite similar to that shown in similar studies involving mixed outpatient populations, even if not specifically on the basis of primary depressive symptomatology.

Second, the composite four-point code type for both cells was a 2-4-7-8 (*D-Pd-Pt-Sc*) profile. This composite profile is quite similar to that found by Andreasen (1976), Donnelly and Murphy (1973), and Donnelly, Murphy, and Goodwin (1976) for samples of inpatient non-bipolar, nonpsychotic primary depressives also selected in accordance with the Feighner criteria. Although these mean group profiles obscure considerable heterogeneity in individual profile types, the model four-point code in the Rush et al. samples was that same 2-4-7-8 profile, and over 50% of the sample showed various combinations of those four scales as their four highest peaks. It appears likely that the use of operationally defined criteria in selecting samples of non-bipolar nonpsychotic primary depression, e.g., the Feighner criteria or the highly similar research Diagnostic Criteria (Spitzer, Endicott, & Robins, 1978) and DSM-III criteria (Task Force on Nomenclature and Statistics of the American Psychiatric Association, 1977), will generate similar composite 2-4-7-8 profiles.

Third, earlier literature, e.g., Rosen (1958), suggests that such a profile is most often associated with patients designated as neurotic, or at least nonpsychotic, depressives. Psychotic depressives were more likely to show composite scale elevations on scale 2, with all remaining scales below a T score of 70. Individual profiles did not necessarily show peaks only on scale 2, but elevations on other scales were not common enough to be reflected in the average group profile. It is not clear exactly how the distinction between nonpsychotic and psychotic depressions was drawn in such earlier studies, but in the later, Feighner-based diagnoses, discrete indications of delusions, hallucinations, or stuporous conditions were typically required for such a designation. By scoring the Rush et al. sample on the Goldberg rules for distinguishing nonpsychotic from psychotic profiles (Goldberg, 1965), 21 patients were classified as "psychotic" and 21 were classified as "nonpsychotic." This despite the absence of any patients classified as "psychotic" under newer diagnostic systems. Given the greater differential responsivity of "psychotic" patients to somatic interventions such as electroconvulsive therapy (ECT) (Dana, 1957; Feldman, 1952), attention to such classificatory discrepancies may be warranted.

Several additional pharmacological comparisons (McClure, Low, & Gent, 1973; Mormont, 1974) provide additional data regarding the utility of the MMPI in clinical trials. In the McClure et al. study, inpatient depressions were treated with either imipramine or clomipramine HCL over a 44-day period. Pre-treatment and periodic re-evaluation assessments were made with the BDI, HRS-D, and Institute for Personality and Ability Testing, anxiety scale questionnaire (IPAT) (Scheier & Cartell, 1960). Unfortunately for the purposes of this survey, the only subscale from the MMPI administered was the Welsh anxiety index (A) (Welsh, 1952). Data on all measures indicated progressive, but deaccelerating, symptomatic improvement over the course of treatment. The two medication cells did not differ on any of the two measures.

Mormont (1974) compared ordinary Noveril versus time-released Noveril in a sample of depressed inpatients. Pre- and two post-treatment evaluations (three and six months) were made using the HRS-D (rated by both the treating and an independent clinical observer), the Breulet Depression measure (Bobon, Bourdouxle, Breulet, Mormont, & Parent, 1972) (also rated by treating clinician and an independent clinical observer), and the MMPI. Although the absence of cell means and standard deviations precludes calculating sensitivity indexes, the author does report significant cell differences on all clinician-rated measures, except three-month therapist-rated HRS-D's and three-month observer-rated Breulet's. Three month MMPI-*D*'s show comparable symptomatic decreases. The absence of cell means precludes full analysis of the data, but, on the whole, the MMPI-*D* appears to compare favorably with the clinician-rated measures.

Cole, Patterson, Craig, Thomas, Ristine, Stahly, and Pasamanick (1959) provided an early comparison of iproniazid, psychotherapy, and inert pill-placebo in a group of inpatient depressives. Treatment lasted over six weeks, with outcome assessed on the MMPI *D* and *Pt* scales and on the Lorr Multidimensional Scale for Rating Psychiatric Patients (MSRPP) (Lorr, 1953). No differences were found between the groups on any of the measures, with massive dropout rates (44%) vitiating treatment comparisons. Olson (1962) compared drug (Nialamide) at low (100 mg.) vs. high (300 mg.) daily dosage levels, with a third cell consisting of physician's choice of medication excluding anti-depressants. Measures included the MMPI-*D* and a nurses' behavior rating. High dosages of Nialamide proved superior to either of the other conditions on both measures.

Two studies evaluated convulsive therapies in depressed samples. McDonald, Perkins, and Marjerrison (1966) found that either electroconvulsive therapy or amitriptyline was superior to a pill-placebo on both the MMPI *D* scale and a Ward Observation Index in a sample of depressed inpatients. No differences were detected on a clinician's Depression Rating Scale designed specifically for the trial. Spreche (1963) compared ECT with drug-induced convulsions (hexafluorodiemyl ether) in a sample of depressed patients. Both groups improved significantly over time, but no between-group differences were apparent on either the MMPI *D* scale or on structured clinical observations.

Three additional populations are of interest by virtue of their frequency of associated depressive psychopathology. Lauer (1976) studied clinically identified "passive-dependent" patients drawn from both inpatient and outpatient settings. Patients were treated with either imipramine or nortriptyline, while a separate control group was kept drug-free. Pre-treatment assessments were made on the MMPI and the Edwards Personality Preference Schedule (EPPS) (Edwards, 1954). Significant between-group differences were found only on the Hypochondriasis (*Hs*) and Paranoia (*Pa*) subscales of the MMPI, and the Endurance subscale of the EPPS. The absence of other relevant depression measures, the absence of reported within-group changes, and the absence of mean scores make analysis of these results problematic.

Equi and Jabara (1976), Overall, Brown, Williams and Neill (1973), and Shaw, Donley, Morgan, and Robinson (1975) investigated levels of depressive symptomatology in alcoholic samples. Although none of the three studies reports data in formats suitable for Sensitivity Index analysis, all three suggest comparability between the MMPI *D* scale and various other depression measures. Equi and Jabara (1976) report a pre-treatment correlation between the MMPI *D* scale and the Zung SDS of r = .71. At post-treatment, the two measures correlated at r = .84. Overall et al. reported significant decreases in both MMPI *D*-scale and MMPI *Pt*-scale levels following pharmacological treatment. Shaw et al. reported comparable sensitivity for the MMPI and the Zung SDS in between-group changes in withdrawal symptoms in alcoholics.

Two studies (Marsh & Markham, 1973; Maskin, Riklan, & Chabot, 1973) investigated affective symptomatology associated with Parkinsonism. Marsh and Markham found no changes following either three or 15 months of treatment with levadopa on syndrome depression, as measured by the MMPI *D* scale. There was some indication of increases in subtle measures of thinking disorder (as measured by *Pa* and *Sc*) with prolonged levadopa treatment. Maskin et al. (1975) found comparable between-group differences and comparable absences of within-group changes over time on the MMPI *D* scale and the MAACL. Again, the MMPI *D* scale compared favorably with yet another self-report index of depression.

Overall, these studies appear to provide relatively consistent support for the utility of the MMPI as an index of change in syndrome depression and as an index of more generalized change in identified depression. Based on sensitivity index analyses, the MMPI *D* scale appears to compare favorably with the BDI (Fuchs & Rehm, 1977; Rush et al., 1977; Shaw & Hollon, 1978; Taylor & Marshall, 1977), the VAS (Taylor & Marshall, 1977), and the MAACL (Maskin et al., 1975), all self-report measures. Similarly, sensitivity index analyses suggest a relative comparability for the MMPI *D* scale with the HRS-D (Rush et al., 1977). It appears that any of several measures, including the MMPI, may provide relatively useful, sensitive indexes of levels and changes in levels of syndrome depression.

One caveat is in order. Donnelly et al. (1976) reported data suggesting that the MMPI may be relatively insensitive to both absolute levels and changes in absolute levels of syndrome depression for bipolar depression when in the depressed phase. Although recently hospitalized non-bipolar depressives showed the composite 2-4-7-8 profile typical of that diagnostic group changing to a less symptomatic profile at discharge, recently hospitalized depressed bipolar patients evidenced a relatively flat profile at both admission and discharge. Observer ratings on the Bunney-Hamburg Ward Behavior Rating Scale (Bunney & Hamburg, 1963) indicated that both non-bipolar and bipolar samples were comparably symptomatic at admission and comparably less symptomatic at discharge. It is not clear whether this phenomenon involving the relative insensitivity of the MMPI D scale to levels of depression in bipolar depressions, if a replicable finding, is specific to the MMPI or a general attribute of self-report measures in this depressive subtype. The authors favor the latter interpretation. It should be noted that these findings have yet to be replicated. Lumry (1978) reported archival data based on previous administrations of the MMPI which were at variance with the Donnelly et al. findings. Bipolar patient profiles evidenced clear-cut elevations on scale 2 (as well as elevations on Pt and Sc), with comparable reductions during symptom-free intervals. Clearly, insensitivity of the MMPI to depression levels of bipolar depressives would be quite important clinically. However, at this time, these findings must be viewed with considerable caution.

On the whole, then, the MMPI appears to compare quite favorably with other available measures of syndrome depression as a potential measure of change. These favorable comparisons seem to hold whether considering other self-report or clinician-rated measures. Instances of disconcordance within the same study are rare and, when they do occur, are as likely to favor the MMPI D scale as not. Only the Wittenborn Psychiatric Rating Scale appeared to outperform the MMPI D scale, and then only in one of two comparisons. The apparent sensitivity of the MMPI D scale to changes in syndrome depression, combined with the full instrument's utility as a multiphasic descriptive and predictive tool, has led to a recommended inclusion of the MMPI, along with the Beck Depression Inventory and at least one clinician-rated measure, in trials comparing treatment efficacy in syndrome depression (Coordinating Committee for Comparative Trials in Depression, 1976).

Overall, the approach of restricting comparisons across measures to those studies using multiple measures appears more rigorous than simple "box score" approaches. In this instance, such a procedure produced markedly different conclusions than did McNair's early "box score" review. Although more precise calculations of measured effect sizes and sensitivity ratios could be extracted from only a few reports, such indexes may prove to be a useful heuristic in the future, and adequate reporting of descriptive statistics, or, minimally, deposition of such information in central archives (see Bryant & Wortman, 1978) would appear desirable.

ADDITIONAL TYPES OF PSYCHOPATHOLOGY

The following sections briefly review studies speaking to the utility of the MMPI in detecting changes in phenomena other than depression. These reviews are neither intensive nor exhaustive; rather, they have been designed to be illustrative of current usage and knowledge.

Mixed Outpatient Populations

Traditionally, mixed outpatient populations have provided some of the earliest trials of the utility of the MMPI as a measure of change. In this population, symptomatology is frequently phenomenological rather than strictly behavioral. Patients meeting these criteria are rarely, if ever, incapable of meaningful self-report, as is sometimes true of psychotic individuals.

Rashkis and Shaskin (1946) provided one of the earliest clinical trials utilizing the MMPI in an outcome measure. Twenty-two mixed outpatients were treated with dynamically oriented group psychotherapy over a six-week period. Significant decreases in average elevation were noted on scales *Hs, D, Hy,* and *Pt,* scales typically elevated in "neurotic" profiles. The absence of alternate treatment cells makes it impossible to attribute the observed change to intervention, while the absence of alternative measures precluded the interruption of observed changes.

Schofield (1950, 1953) evaluated changes over time on the MMPI associated with four groups; nonpsychiatric college students, college students in individual treatment at a university counseling center, hospitalized psychoneurotics, and hospitalized psychotics treated with electroconvulsive therapy. As in the Rashkis and Shaskin study cited above, the absence of untreated (or treated) matched control groups at each level of psychopathology and the absence of other measures and/or ratings preclude meaningful interpretation of the data. Schofield observed that different subscales did show different proportions of relatively stable scores; scales *F* and *Sc* showed the least change from pre- to post-testing, while scale *Pt* the greatest variability over time.

While interesting, it is not clear exactly how much can be made of such findings. Item stability is likely to prove to be a complex function varying, at least, across types of psychiatric diagnosis, types of interventions, and length of interval between test and retest. Clearly related is the issue of initial elevation; the more items answered in a "deviant" direction at the initial test, the greater the likelihood that items will be answered in a "non-deviant" direction. This is not simply an artifact based on statistical regression; rather, this phenomenon is largely based on the notion that it is difficult to correct a problem that does not exist. Although stability figures for MMPI items are frequently cited (e.g., Butcher & Tellegen, 1978), it would be inappropriate to assume that such figures necessarily restrain the capacity of specific subscales to reflect real change in populations accurately elevated on those subscales.

Further, it may also be inappropriate to conclude that other measures are better suited to measurement of the change process. Mosak (1950), for example, compared global clinical ratings, a sign approach based on the Rorschach, and the MMPI in the evaluation of changes in a mixed outpatient group treated with individual client-centered therapy over a 28-day period. The author noted significant decreases in scales *Hs, D, Hy, Pa,* and *Sc* in the sample as a whole. The MMPI scales and global clinician ratings correlated well, while Rorschach signs were essentially unrelated to either of the other clinical measures.

Kaufmann (1950) similarly followed the course of college students treated in a university counseling center. Studying only those students rated "improved" following treatment (the vast majority of the sample), the author noted significant decreases in subscales *F, Hs, D, Pa, Pt,* and *Sc,* with a significant increase in *K*. Gallagher (1953) noted somewhat similar changes in outpatient college students treated with client-centered therapy at a university counseling center. The author observed significant decreases in scales *F, Hs, D, Pt,* and *Si,* with a significant increase on scale *K*. Further, the author constructed a *Maladjustment Index*, composed of the sums of the raw item scores from scales *Hs, D, Hy, Pd, Pa, Pt,* and *Sc*. This index correlated moderately well with other client ratings; a global improvement rating, $r = .58$ ($p < .05$), and the client's rated ratio of positive vs. negative feelings, $r = .44$ ($p < .05$), and poorly with the therapists' rating of improvement, $r = .15$ (n.s.). Discrepancies between global improvement ratings made by clients or therapists, and independent ratings made by client, therapist, and independent clinician are hardly unusual (Garfield, 1978; Strupp & Hadley, 1977). The relatively adequate correlations between the MMPI and alternative self-report measures do appear to buttress claims for the utility of the MMPI.

Barron and Leary (1955) provided one of the earliest controlled comparative trials utilizing the MMPI as an outcome measure. One hundred and fifty psychoneurotic outpatients were treated with either analytically oriented group psychotherapy or individual psychotherapy, or they were assigned to a waiting-list control. The authors reported no apparent differences between the three cells at post-test. The absence of ratings on any other indexes makes it difficult to determine whether apparent nondifferences were attributable to the MMPI's lack of sensitivity as a measurement instrument or to the lack of power of the types of therapy utilized. Analysis of these data by Cartwright (1956) suggested a third alternative. Noting that variances were significantly greater for those patients treated with individual therapy than for those in the waiting-list control on scales F, Hs, D, Pt, Sc, and Es, Cartwright interpreted the combination of the lack of mean differences with the increased variance as an indication of treatment-induced improvement plus treatment-induced deterioration; some treated patients get better than an untreated control while other treated patients get worse. Deterioration effects have been discussed in detail elsewhere (Bergin, 1971). For purposes of this survey, it is evident that the MMPI must be adequately reflecting real *changes* in symptomatology for such phenomena to be detected.

Although mean scale scores did not differ across treatment cells, there were differences in the patterns of within-cell, pre-post treatment changes shown by the different interventions. For individual-therapy patients, scores on scales L, Hs, D, and Hy decreased significantly and scales K and Es increased significantly following treatment. Patients treated in group psychotherapy decreased significantly on L, Hs, D, Hy, Pa, and Pt scale scores, but increased significantly on scale Es scores. Patients assigned to the waiting-list control decreased significantly on scales L and Pd, and increased significantly on scale Es. It is interesting that the pattern of within-group changes appeared to be more comparable between the two psychotherapy cells than between either psychotherapy cell and the waiting-list control group.

Mogar and Savage (1964) reported an investigation of the utility of LSD-assisted supportive psychotherapy in a mixed sample of psychoneurotics and character-disordered personalities. Significant decreases in F, D, Pt, Sc, and Si were noted, along with significant increases on *K, Ma,* and *Es.* Unfortunately, the absence of control groups or alternate-treatment measures precluded the adequate evaluation of either the internal or construct validity of the measured changes.

Slawson (1965) utilized the MMPI to evaluate the contribution of psychodrama as an adjunct to general ward milieu in the treatment of mixed inpatients. Testing on selected subscales of the MMPI (*D, Pd, Pt,* and *Si*) failed to indicate any between-group differences between psychodrama plus general ward milieu and general ward milieu alone. Again, the absence of alternate means of assessment makes it unclear whether the absence of group differences is best attributed to the insensitivity of the instrument or the importance of the treatment.

With the exception of the Mosak (1950) and Gallagher (1953) studies, most studies reviewed so far have failed to utilize measures other than the MMPI. Controlled studies including multiple measures are listed in Table 6. Brill, Koegler, Epstein, and Forgy (1964) reported a major comparative study involving multiple assessment measures and multiple interventions in the treatment of a heterogenous outpatient sample. Adult psychiatric outpatients were assigned to one of six treatment cells; prochlorperazine, meprobamate, phenobarbital, waiting list control, an analytically oriented psychotherapy, and pill-placebo. All patients were assessed pre- and post-treatment (treatment lasting up to 12 months) on ratings made by the patient, the therapist, and some close relative, as well as on the MMPI. Between-group differences emerged only on scale *Pt,* with the waiting-list cell having higher mean scores. In general, these findings are consistent with the findings on the other measures, where rated anxiety reflected the greatest treatment-related variation.

Endicott and Endicott (1964) utilized both the MMPI and therapists' ratings of improvement in a comparison between treated (analytically oriented psychotherapy) and untreated mixed outpatients. The authors reported within-group changes for the treated patients on subscales *Hs, D, Hy, Pd, Pa, Pt,* and *Sc.* The authors divided patients into those rated improved vs. those rated unimproved by their therapists, and reported a near identical outcome of findings. The "improved" patients showed significant improvment on all clinical scales (*Hs, D, Hy, Pd, Pa, Pt,* and *Sc*) except *Mf* and *Ma.* These findings, consistent as they were with clinical ratings, suggest that the MMPI is sufficiently sensitive to treatment-related change.

Brick, Doub, and Perdue (1966) utilized the MMPI and clinician and/or nurses' ratings to evaluate response to an experimental medication (tybamate) in a double-blind, placebo-controlled trial involving

Table 6. Studies with Mixed Outpatient Samples

Study	Population	Comparison	Measure	Outcome
Boudewyns & Wilson, 1972	Mixed Inpatients	Implosion vs. Sys. D. vs. Control	MMPI Mooney Prob. Checklist Clinician Progress Ratings	Changes on several scales consistent with Mooney and clinician ratings (+)
Brick, Doub, & Perdue, 1966	Mixed Outpatients (analogue)	Drug (Tybamate) vs. Placebo	MMPI Nurses Ratings	
Brill, Koegler, Epstein, & Forgy, 1964	Mixed Outpatients	Drug (prochloperazine), vs. Drug (meprobamate) vs. Drug (phenobarbital) vs. Psychotherapy vs. Placebo vs. Waiting List	MMPI Ratings: therapist, patient significant other	Rated anxiety differed across measures (+)
Endicott & Endicott, 1964	Mixed Outpatients	Psychotherapy (analytic) vs. No Psychotherapy	MMPI Ratings: therapist	Changes on several scales consistent with therapist ratings (+)
Endicott & Endicott, 1963	Mixed Outpatients		MMPI TAT Rorschach	
Horowitz, 1970	Mixed Outpatients	Relaxation + Imaginal vs. Arousal + Imaginal vs. Posthypnotic vs. No Threat	MMPI (MAS) Fear Checklist Behavioral Approach Measure	MAS failed to detect changes shown by other measures (−)
Kelly, Walter, Mitchell-Heggs, & Sargent, 1972	Mixed Outpatients	Psychosurgery	MAS	
Sherman, 1972	Mixed Outpatients	Exposure vs. Nonexposure by Desensitization vs. No Desensitization	MMPI Willoughby IPAT TMAS	Comparable changes on all measures (+)

Study	Population	Treatment	Measures	Results
Simon & Gilberstadt, 1954	Mixed Neurotics	Carbon Dioxide Inhalation		Greater changes in patients rated "better" clinically (+)
Solyom, Heseltine, McClure, Ledwidge, & Kenny, 1971	Mixed Outpatients	Aversion Relief vs. Desensitization	MMPI IPAT Wolpe-Lange FSS Self-Ratings Psychiatric Ratings	Changes on psychiatric ratings, but not on self or psychometric ratings (−)
Stoudenmire, 1972	Mixed Outpatients	Muscle Relaxation vs. No Muscle Relaxation	TMAS STAI-St STAI-Tr MAACL	Group differences on STAI-St and MAACL, but not STAI-Tr or TMAS (−)
Vernallis, Shipper, Butler, & Tomlinson, 1970	Mixed Outpatients	Saturation Group vs. No-Treatment Control	MMPI ISB Clinician ratings (non-blind)	MMPI and clinician ratings significant, not ISB (+)

an analogue prison population. Pre- to post-treatment changes (over a 60-day interval) indicated significant decreases in the drug-treated cell on scales *Hs, D,* and *Pt,* while the placebo-treated cell decreased significantly only on scale *Ma.* Since tybamate was proposed as an anti-anxiety, anti-depressant medication, these changes were interpreted as reflecting the treatment efficacy of the medication. Unfortunately, no between-group analyses were presented to support these claims.

The authors did compare improvement percentages calculated from the MMPI with percentages generated from clinical ratings. The two sets of ratings compared quite favorably; 87% of the "patients" were considered improved in the drug cell on the basis of the MMPI, with 82% in that same cell rated improved by the clinicians. In the placebo-treated cell, 50% of the patients were considered improved on the basis of the MMPI, vs. 38% by clinicians' ratings. In general, it appears that the MMPI compared favorably to the more extensive clinicians' ratings in this study.

Levis and Carera (1967) used the MMPI as the sole outcome measure in a comparison of implosive and traditional psychotherapies, with a waiting-list control cell. Patients were mixed outpatients of unknown diagnosis. The authors reported significant between-group differences favoring the implosive treatment cell on scales *Mf* and *Sc,* as well as a total elevation measure composed of the sum of T scores across all the clinical scales. Inadequate descriptions of the populations sampled and the assignment procedures used, as well as the failure to report within-group changes and the absence of alternative measures, make the evaluation of the adequacy of the MMPI on the basis of this study quite problematic.

Finally, McCall (1974) evaluated pre- to post-therapy changes for obese women in terms of both pounds lost and MMPI changes. The authors reported that within-group reductions on scales *Hs, D, Hy, Pd, Sc, A, Ca,* and *Dy,* and increases on *Es,* were associated with weight loss in a TOPS (Take Off Pounds Sensibly) weight-control program. It is, of course, difficult to specify the nature of correlated data, but it would seem unlikely that a nonprofessional self-help approach to weight control would directly ameliorate clinical levels of psychiatric symptomatology. Rather, it seems more reasonable to speculate that reductions in general distress were attributable to loss of weight. It is unclear how the MMPI could facilitate the direct assessment of such specific goals as weight loss, other than as a prediction measure, ensuring function that either facilitates or retards weight gain.

Although it has been many years since the MMPI was first used as a tool to evaluate treatment response in mixed outpatient populations, relatively few adequately controlled studies utilizing alternate means of assessment have been conducted. This makes it difficult to adequately evaluate the clinical utility of the MMPI in these populations. In part, these deficiencies reflect a failure on the part of investigators to select and describe homogeneous patient samples, to clearly conceptualize what is meant by change and provide adequate assessment perspectives to distinguish real from artificial change, and to attend to issues of control for the sake of subsequent comparison. In sum, the fact that it is impossible to make clear generalizations reflects an uninformed and/or inadequate approach to research design.

On the whole, such data as do exist appear to be mildly supportive of the MMPI as a valid measure of change in these populations. The Taylor Manifest Anxiety Scale seemed to fare poorly as an outcome measure. Interpreting internally valid changes, however, is quite a different matter from detecting them. Although most of the observed changes occurred on scales that might be expected to change with decreases in "neurotic" symptomatology (e.g., decreases in the neurotic triad, *Hs*, *D*, and *Hy*, and less often *Pt*; and increases on *K* and *Es*), it is not clear how closely such changes correspond to behavioral and/or other observable phenomena of interest. The trends in the outcome therapy literature over the last 25 years have clearly emphasized increased homogeneity and reliance on operationalized criteria for sample selection and increasingly careful application of multiple assessment procedures (cf. Hollon & Beck, 1978: Luborsky, Singer, & Luborsky, 1975). Although the rate of outcome research has not declined, the percentage of studies reported utilizing the MMPI as clearly dropped over the years. Later, we shall describe the kinds of studies that, we would argue, would be required before the MMPI could be utilized as a meaningful measure of change in these populations.

Schizophrenia

Remarkably few studies have utilized the MMPI to evaluate treatment-related changes in schizophrenia. Most of these studies have been associated with early biochemical or somatic interventions. Doubtless, this paucity of evidence is related to the notion that schizophrenic patients lack the ability to understand, conceptualize, and interpret material required by self-report measures such as the MMPI (May, 1968; Sehdev & Olson, 1974). For a variety of reasons, it appears that these concerns may be unfounded for all but the most severely disturbed psychotic individuals. Presumably invalid profiles, those with highly elevated F scales, may accurately reflect the conceptual disorganization of such patients.

Similarly, evidence indicating poor concordance of self-report with clincian-rated scales has been interpreted as reflecting the inability of severely disturbed patients to give a valid self-report (Prusoff, Klerman, & Paykel, 1972). Such evidence based on low correlations between pairs of measures, is more accurately attributed to joint range restrictions on all pairs of measures, rather than the lack of validity for any single scale (Hollon, Rush, Beck & Kovacs, 1979).

A study of Sehdev and Olson (1974) (see also Table 7) illustrates the effects of rationally derived biases. In this study, the authors examined the efficacy of nicotinic acid in the treatment of diagnosed schizophrenics. Pre-post outcome measures included the MMPI, an Interpersonal Checklist (ICL), and a nurse's Behavior Rating Scale (BRS). No evidence of treatment-related change was noted on any of the measures. Pre- and post-treatment scores were presented for the MMPI and ICL only. The conclusions drawn? That "the MMPI employed alone . . . as an indicator of clinical improvement in schizophrenic patients, would not seem adequate." The ICL? "It could also be concluded that the absence of change observed on the test accurately reflected absence of significant change in the clinical condition of the subjects." The BRS? "The BRS, on the other hand, provided a simple valuable tool in recording observable clinical changes in the patients." The data? None were presented based on the BRS.

What empirical evidence exists regarding the utility of the MMPI as a measure of change in schizophrenia? Martin, Moore, Sterne, and McNairy (1977) utilized the MMPI and the Brief Psychiatric Rating Scale (BPRS) (Overall & Gorham, 1962) to evaluate hypotheses relating therapist expectations to outcome. All patients were diagnosed schizophrenic, most of them psychotic at the time of admission. MMPI scales and the clinician-rated BPRS were not provided. Clinicians' ratings of prognosis were significantly, and equivalently, related for both indexes of psychopathology. It is not clear how a self-report measure of psychopathology could correlate with clinician-rated indexes if that former measure either (1) could not be obtained for uncooperative, severely disturbed patients, or (2) reflected only random, unreliable, or invalid information.

Several studies have utilized the MMPI as one of a battery of measures to investigate potential changes associated with various non-somatic interventions. Sines, Silver, and Lucero (1961) assigned one

Table 7. Studies with Schizophrenic Samples

Study	Population	Comparison	Measure	Outcome
Kraus, 1959	Schizophrenics	Psychotherapy (group) vs. No Treatment	MMPI Ratings: clinician, ward behavior	MMPI detected changes not detected on other measures (+)
Mendelsohn, Penman, & Schiele, 1959	Schizophrenics (chronic)	Drug (chlorpromazine) vs. Placebo	MMPI Wittenborn Manifest Behav. Scale	MMPI did not detect changes shown by other measures (−)
Michaux, Chelet, Foster, & Pruim, 1972	Mixed inpatients (predominantly schizophrenic)	Drug vs. Full Hospitalization	MMPI IMPS	Only the K scale evidenced change, several on IMPS (−)
Murillo & Exner, 1973	Schizophrenics (nonrandom assignment)	Regressive Electroshock Therapy (REST) vs. No Treatment	MMPI IMPS KAS-R SFSC	Significant differences on all measures, including MMPI (Hs, Hy, Pa, and Ma) (+)
Rittenhouse, 1970	Mixed inpatients (predominantly schizophrenic)	Family Therapy vs. Inpatient Therapeutic Community	MMPI MACC Self-Rating Readmission Family Pathology Community Functioning	Differences in readmission rates between groups, few differences on various scales (−)
Roback, 1972	Schizophrenic Inpatients (20 of 24)	Insight & Interaction vs. Insight vs. Interaction vs. Control (graduate student therapists)	MMPI Symptom CL Adj. CL Hosp. Adj. Scale Wittenborn Days Out of Hospital	No differences on any measure (0)
Sehdev & Olson, 1974	Chronic Schizophrenics	Nicotinic Acid vs. No Pill	MMPI ICL Below Rating Scale	Some changes on MMPI, none on ICL, no data reported on BRS (+)
Simon, Wirt, Wirt, Holloran, Hinckley, Lund, & Hopkins, 1958	Schizophrenics	Clinician's Treatment of Choice vs. Chlorpromazine, vs. Nercipine, vs. Milieu only	MMPI Clinician Interview Ward Behavior	All measures showed 1 > 2 > 3 = 4 (+)

group of chronic schizophrenic inpatients to paraprofessional helpers, while a second group of patients had no such contact. Assessment on the MMPI, L-M Behavior Rating Scale, and a Q-sort failed to reveal any differences between the two groups. Kraus (1959), however, found the MMPI to be the only instrument to indicate improvement for good-prognosis schizophrenics treated in group psychotherapy vs. an untreated control group. Measures that indicated no differences included therapist ratings, behavior ratings, and a projective ink-blot technique. Although the ward behavior ratings did not differ significantly between the groups, differences on these measures were consistent with those on the MMPI, suggesting that both measures were detecting similar changes, but that the MMPI did so more powerfully. Johnston and McNeal (1965) took pre- and post-treatment MMPI's from a generalized group of inpatient schizophrenics. The patients showed significant pre-post treatment decreases on scales F, Pd, Pa, and Sc, exactly those scales on which schizophrenic psychopathology would be reflected. Although the three studies provide insufficient evidence on which to base any firm conclusions, there appears to be no instance in which any other measures "outperformed" the MMPI in this population. Changes, when detected, were consistent with those that might be expected in this population. Finally, generalized change in these populations did not reflect the Hs, D, Hy, Pt cluster that appears to be very labile in mixed outpatient populations.

Earlier studies investigating response to insulin-coma shock therapy provide additional data supportive of these general conclusions. Pacella, Piotrowski, and Lewis (1947) contrasted schizophrenics, psychotic depressives, and psychoneurotics before, immediately after (one week), and following (four to eight weeks) insulin-coma therapy. The psychotic depressives (characterized by elevations on scale 2) showed the greatest change at the one week reassessment. The psychoneurotics (characterized by multiple elevations on scales Hs, D, Hy, and Pt) showed little change. The absence of other measures precluded evaluating the sensitivity of the MMPI.

Hales and Simon (1948) studied 20 inpatient schizophrenics treated with insulin-shock therapy. Although the group as a whole showed no overall change, clinically rated improved patients decreased on F, Pa, Pt, and Sc, and clinically rated unimproved patients actually increased on those same scales. Carp (1950) observed changes on a similar set of scales, F, Pd, Pa, Pt, and Sc, for schizophrenics also treated with insulin-coma therpay.

In general, these data suggest that the MMPI is reasonably sensitive to treatment-related changes in schizophrenic individuals, a sensitivity to change different from that shown with depressed or mixed outpatients. In general, scales *F*, *Pa*, and *Sc* change most reliably, scales *Pd* and *Pt* appearing to be involved less frequently. In no study did any other measure prove more sensitive to treatment changes than the MMPI.

Alcoholism

As noted by Butcher and Owen (1978), there has been a proliferation of articles using the MMPI in investigations of alcoholism. However, most of these studies have employed the MMPI exclusively as a tool for detection and differential diagnosis. Few studies have reported both pre- and post-treatment MMPI scores in conjunction with alternate measures, and fewer still have done so in connection with two or more intervention modalities. Finally, most of the relevant studies have been conducted with male populations, further hampering efforts to evaluate the relative adequacy of the MMPI as an assessment of change in alcoholic populations.

Only five studies appear to conform to our criteria for inclusion in the sensitivity index analysis (see Table 8). In the first of these studies Ends and Page (1959) examined the MMPI scores of two groups of 28 male hospitalized alcoholics. Both groups participated in the hospital's alcoholism rehabilitation program, which emphasized education and AA participation. In addition to the rehabilitation program, the experimental group received 30 sessions of Rogerian group therapy. The experimental group showed significant decreases on *F*, *D*, *Pa*, and *Pt*, and increases on *Es* and *K*. Only *Pa* showed a significantly greater decrease for the experimental group as compared to the control group. A Q-sort technique was also employed to measure treatment effects. Both the Rogerian therapy group and the control group moved in the favorable direction on a number of the Q-sort indexes. Statistically significant differences in movement between the two groups were obtained on five of the eight indexes, favoring the therapy group. Although this apparently greater sensitivity of the Q-sort in registering between-group differences might well be a function of this instrument being specifically geared toward evaluation of Rogerian therapy, the apparent lesser sensitivity of the MMPI is best considered an unfavorable finding for the MMPI.

Shaffer, Yeganeh, Foxwell, and Kurland (1968) utilized the MMPI as part of a larger battery including the Clyde Mood Scale, the

Table 8. Studies with Alcoholic Samples

Study	Population	Comparison	Measure	Outcome
Denson & Sydiaha, 1970	Alcoholics	LSD vs. No LSD	MMPI EPI IPAT Lorr (0) MPS	No significant BG differences on any measure (0)
Ends & Page, 1959	Alcoholics	Rogerian Group Therapy vs. No Treatment in Inpatient Education and AA Program	MMPI Q-Sort	BG differences more apparent on Q-sort (5 of 8 indexes) than on MMPI (only scale Pa discriminated treated from non-treated) (−)
Shaffer, Yeganeh, Foxwell, & Kurland, 1968	Alcoholics	Drug (1 = prazepam, 2 = chlordiazepoxide) vs. Placebo	MMPI Clyde Mood Scale Psychiatric Eval. Profile	NS (−) $p < .05$ $p < .05$
Smith, Johnson, & Burdick, 1971	Alcoholics	Drug (NAD) vs. Placebo	MMPI SDS DACL MAS	all NS (0)
Soskin, 1970	Alcoholics	LSD vs. Human Relations Training	MMPI 16-PF PHN Elmore Anomie Scale (EAS)	BG: on 16-PF (2 of 16 changed), on MMPI Si and F favored LSD; no differences on PHN or EAS WG: on 16-PF (5 of 16 TH), n MMPI (Es and K increased; D and Pt decreased) PHN and EAS (0 → +)

Psychiatric Evaluation Profile (based on clinician ratings), and ward-behavior ratings to evaluate the efficacy of various medications in reducing *withdrawal symptoms* in hospitalized alcoholics. Medication conditions involved prozepam vs. chlordiazepoxide vs. pill placebo in a double-blind trial. The authors observed significant between-group differences on both the psychiatric and ward-behavior ratings, but not on the MMPI scales or the Clyde Mood scale. Failure to detect changes registered by both sets of ratings suggests a lesser sensitivity for the MMPI on the phenomena studied. It should be noted, however that these phenomena involved withdrawal-related symptomatology which may have been more specifically related to items rated than to more general indexes of psychopathology.

Smith, Johnson, and Burdick (1971) similarly investigated the amelioration of withdrawal symptoms via medication (MAD) vs. pill-placebo in a double-blind design. In addition to the MMPI, the assessment battery included the Zung SDS, the Lubin Depression Objectives Checklist (DACL) (Lubin, 1967), and the Taylor MAS. No differences were evident between the groups on any of the measures. Given the absence of differences (all self-report psychometric indexes), it is unclear whether no measure was sensitive to change or no differential change was associated with treatment. In this study, as opposed to the Shaffer et al. design, it can be said that the MMPI fared no worse (or no better) than any of the other measures utilized.

Two studies (Denson & Sydiaha, 1970; Soskin, 1970) utilized the MMPI as part of larger batteries to evaluate the efficacy of LSD-medicated abreaction in the treatment of alcoholics. Denson and Sydiaha found no differences between LSD abreaction and no such abreaction on any MMPI indexes, or on the Eysenck Personality Inventory (EPI) (Eysenck & Eysenck, 1968), IPAT, or Lorr IMPS (adjusted for use with outpatients). As in the Smith et al. design, the absence of any treatment effects across all measures was considered by the authors to indicate a lack of any clinical effect associated with the specific treatment. The same conclusion can be drawn regarding the MMPI as in the Smith et al. design; although it is not certain that the MMPI is "as good as" other measures utilized, it is evident that none of the other measures were demonstrably more sensitive to between-group differences.

Finally, Soskin (1970) utilized the MMPI, Cattell's 16-PF (Cattell & Eber, 1957), Philosophies of Human Nature Scale (PHN) (Wrightsman, 1964), and Elmore Anomie Scale (EAS) (Elmore, 1952) to compare LSD-mediated abreaction with human-relations training. Within- and between-group changes on both the MMPI and IPAT favored the LSD-treated group (e.g., the LSD-treated group had significantly lower scores on scales *F* and *Si*; within-group reductions were significant on *D* and *Pt*, and within-group increases were significant on *Es* and *K* for the LSD group, but not for the alternative-treatment groups). No between-group differences were evident on either the PHN or EAS. These findings suggest comparable sensitivity of the MMPI and IPAT, the PHN and EAS being less sensitive to changes.

Overall, these data do not appear to provide overwhelmingly compelling indications of clinical utility for the MMPI as an index of treatment-related change in alcoholic populations. One study indicated greater sensitivity for an alternate measure (Ends & Page, 1959), albeit one perhaps more closely tied to the theoretical rationale underlying treatment than in processes clearly related to alcoholism. In two pharmacological studies investigating the amelioration of withdrawal symptoms, specific clinical ratings proved more sensitive than psychometric indexes in one study (Shaffer et al., 1968), but in the second study there were no differences on any measure, a "weak" tie score. A similarly "weak" tie score resulted from one of two investigations of LSD-assisted abreaction, the second of these two designs providing some evidence of scale sensitivity. In none of these studies were measures of drinking behavior provided. In general, each design can be viewed as focusing more on corollary symptomatology (e.g., withdrawal symptoms, anxiety, etc.) than on drinking per se. There appears to be little evidence documenting the utility of the MMPI as an index of treatment-related changes in this population.

Examining the pattern of MMPI scale changes in studies not meeting sensitivity-index criteria yields some interesting findings. One of the earlier studies exploring the use of the MMPI as a tool for evaluating the effects of an alcoholism treatment program was conducted by Rohan, Tatro, and Rotman (1969). The MMPI was administered to 58 hospitalized veterans at admission to and discharge from the Alcoholic Rehabilitation Program (ARP). The ARP is described as a mixed-treatment approach including group discussions, objective information, AA meetings, and some drug therapy. Patients who used alcohol while in treatment were discharged. The investigators found significant pre- and post-treatment score differences on a number of scales. Scores on scales *Hs, D, Hy, Pd, Pt,* and *Si* decreased significantly. According to the authors this reduction in symptomatology as indicated by the MMPI was consistent with a clinical impression of reduced depression and somatic preoccupation and increased impulse control and social skills. No other outcome measure was reported. A second investigation of 40 veterans participating in the same Alcoholic Rehabilitation Program (Rohan, 1972) yielded somewhat different results. Significant decreases occurred on *F, D, Hy, Mf, Pa, Pt,* and *Si,* whereas *K* increased. Again no other measure of treatment effects was included. Rohan(1972) concluded that substantial agreement existed between the two studies in regard to MMPI profile changes.

Wilkinson, Prado, Williams, and Schnadt (1971) studied score changes for 85 males who completed 90 days at the Alcoholic Rehabilitation Unit. The unit utilized a multidisciplinary treatment approach including group therapy and vocational counseling. Significant differences computed for MMPI raw scores were found on *F, Hs, D, Hy, Pd, Pa, Pt, Sc,* and *Ma,* all of which decreased, and *Es,* which increased. Pre- and post-treatment measures were also obtained on the Allport-Vernon Scale of Values and the Worchel Self-Activity Inventory. No significant differences were found on either of these two instruments. A very similar pattern of change in MMPI scores has been reported by Huber and Danahy (1975). Their population consisted of 67 hospitalized veterans, who participated for 90 days in an educational rehabilitation program utilizing individual and group therapy. Significant decreases in *K*-corrected T scores occurred on *F, Hs, D, Hy, Pd, Pa, Pt, Sc,* and *Si.* Apart from the MacAndrew Alcoholism Scale and the Unitary Alcoholism Factor Scale, both of which are MMPI-derived and will be discussed later, no other measures of relative treatment success were reported.

Kraft and Wijesinghe (1970) utilized systematic desensitization in the treatment of alcoholics, finding significant pre-post reductions on scales *D, Pa, Pt, Sc, Ma,* and *Si.* These changes were paralleled on the Taylor MAS and Eysenck EPI neuroticism scale. Kurland, Unger, Shaffer, and Savage (1967) utilized only the MMPI to evaluate LSD-assisted depth psychotherapy in 69 male alcoholics. Significant pre-post-treatment reductions were evident on all clinical scales except scale *Ma.*

The effects of another multiple-approach program consisting of group psychotherapy, encounter exercises, and transactional analysis were investigated by Bean and Karasievich (1975). The authors followed 80 male alcoholics through three stages of treatment administering tests approximately 5, 30, and 60 days after admission. The assessment battery consisted of the Wechsler Memory Scale, the Bender-Gestalt Test, the Draw-A-Person Test, and the MMPI. Significant changes in the direction of improvement were obtained between stage I and III for the Wechsler Memory Scale and the Bender-

Gestalt. The Draw-A-Person Test indicated reduced regression, but no significant overall change was found between the first and the last stages of treatment. The MMPI registered significant decreases on *F*, *Hs*, *D*, *Hy*, *Pd*, *Pt*, and *Sc* between stages I and III. The authors point out that an orderly relationship existed between reduction in symptomatology on the MMPI and time spent in the program.

An examination of the pattern of MMPI scale changes reveals a consistent decrease on scales *D* and *Pt* across all studies. This phenomenon has also been reported by Rohan (1972), who theorized that the length and type of treatment would differentially affect other scale changes. Following this hypothesis for a moment, it is interesting to note that the two studies (Huber & Danahy, 1975; Wilkinson et al., 1971) which reported significant changes on the largest number of scales evaluated the effect after 90 days in mixed rehabilitation programs. However, the consistent decrease on *D* and *Pt* across studies is not surprising as a result of hospitalization alone. As indicated by Kaufmann (1950) the *D* and *Pt* scales are the two clinical MMPI scales most sensitive to change. However, the question remains whether the reduction in psychological discomfort and dysphoria as reflected in the two scales also reflects a decrease in alcohol abuse. Are the measures detecting generalized treatment effects or treatment effects pertaining to alcoholic rehabilitation? To answer such a question standardized and generally accepted outcome criteria for successful treatment of alcoholism must first be established.

Another recurring pattern is that the score on the MacAndrew scale (MAC) does *not* change significantly as a result of treatment. This observation has also been discussed previously in the literature. Butcher and Owen (1978) stress that the MacAndrew Scale not only measures the current pattern of addiction but also registers a past history of alcohol abuse and indicates the potential for future dependency problems. Chang, Caldwell, and Moss (1973) report that chronic alcoholics who have not been drinking for an extended period of time still score above the 24-item cutoff on the MacAndrew Scale. The authors interpret this to mean that the scale measures a characterological trait of addictiveness rather than the effects of current drinking. Huber and Danahy (1975) suggest that the MacAndrew Scale might prove to be a useful measure of treatment success if administered concurrently with treatment. However, given the scale's ability to register present as well as past and future alcohol addiction its utility as an outcome measure needs to be explored further. Huber and Danahy also compared the MacAndrew Scale with the Unitary Alcoholism Factor Scale, which showed a significant decrease from pre- to post-treatment scores. However, the authors concluded that the information provided by the scale as an outcome measure is redundant with the MMPI since the Unitary Factor Scale decreases parallel the MMPI decreases.

Clear interpretation of alcoholism outcome studies using the MMPI is confounded by the heterogeneity of a number of variables. First, the alcoholic population is not homogeneous. The psychological literature is filled with attempts to identify and classify subcategories and clusters of alcoholics (Bean et al., 1975; Goldstein & Linden, 1969; Jellinek, 1952; Rohan, 1972; Rohan et al., 1969). Some of these attempts will be discussed below. Second, the treatment programs are in most instances mixed and multidisciplinary. Research on specific treatment methods is rather uncommon, one exception being Soskin's (1970) comparison of two different treatment programs. Often a particular intervention technique is simply added to the general rehabilitation program (Ends et al., 1959; Greer & Callis, 1975). Few if any studies incorporate a no-treatment control group in the research design. Finally, the MMPI scales, the majority being empirically derived, are not content homogeneous (Graham, 1977).

Some attempts have been made to remedy these methodological difficulties. In both studies on the Alcoholic Rehabilitation Program (Rohan, 1972; Rohan et al., 1969) a specific analysis was made of the subjects' scores on scale *Pd* both before and after treatment. The investigators identified three different groups. The first group had T scores below 70 on scale *Pd* both before and after treatment. The second group maintained an above 70 score at both pre- and post-testing, whereas the third group scored above 70 at admission with a subsequent drop below 70 after treatment. Rohan (1972) suggests that there is some resemblance between these three groups and three of the four types reported by Goldstein and Linden (1969). Bean and Karasievich (1975) also identified four different clusters. Again there is a certain amount of agreement between their four clusters and Goldstein and Linden's four types. In studies where both pre- and post-testing were performed, the subgroups were found to respond differentially to treatment. Thus a more fruitful approach to pre- and post-score analysis of the effects of treatment could be done by first dividing the alcoholic sample into more homogeneous subgroups.

A detailed discussion of the heterogeneity of most alcoholism treatment programs is beyond the scope of this section. Bowman and Jellinek (1941) wrote: "One could infer that if the indiscriminate application of psychotherapeutic methods results in 25 percent success, variation of treatment based on selective principles would bring a considerably better result" (p. 169). Goldstein and Linden hypothesized that their four different types of alcoholics may benefit from differential treatment programs. The same notion has been put forth by other investigators (Bean et al., 1975; Rohan, 1972). Thus it appears that initial classification of an alcoholic patient sample into homogeneous subtypes could lead to the identification and selection of more specific and appropriate treatment modalities for that particular subgroup. The MMPI appears to be a suitable instrument for such pre-screening. Butcher and Tellegen (1978) suggest that content-homogeneous MMPI scales are potentially more useful as indicators of change that has occurred than the more heterogeneous standard MMPI scales. A more meaningful interpretation of particular scale changes can thus be performed relating the respective increase, decrease, or lack of change to a particular problem area. Examples of existing content-homogeneous scales are the Wiggins content scales (Wiggins, 1966). However, as discussed above, it is still not known if changes in pre- and post-treatment MMPI scores measure the effect of treatment of alcoholism. Changes in MMPI scores following participation in alcoholism rehabilitation programs need to be cross-validated against independent outcome measures. The present lack of any such standardized criteria detrimentally affects our ability to reach any meaningful conclusions regarding the relative merits of the MMPI as a tool for evaluating the therapeutic success of alcoholism treatment programs. As stated by Lowe and Thomas (1976) "the evaluation of various treatment programs for alcoholics has been hampered by the lack of well-defined criteria of what constitutes recovery or successful treatment. If we are to evaluate the effectiveness of our various treatment programs according to commonly accepted goals and expected outcomes, it will be necessary to standardize our evaluative measures and procedures" (p. 888). Completion of an alcoholism rehabilitation program in and of itself does not constitute a valid indication of treatment success. Thus lower MMPI scores between admission and discharge do not necessarily indicate a corresponding recovery from alcohol addiction.

Drug Abuse

As is true of the MMPI literature on alcoholism, most of the MMPI studies conducted with drug abusers pertain to the establishment of differential diagnosis rather than the evaluation of treatment effects. Another similarity between the two areas is that neither alcoholics nor drug abusers are homogeneous groups. This within-group heterogeneity is even more apparent among drug abusers, who are often further classified according to type of substance abused.

Graf, Baer, and Comstock (1977) divided their sample of 42 non-narcotic male and female drug users into four primary drug-of-abuse groups. They were grouped according to the subjects' drug preference: stimulant (N = 9), barbiturate (N = 9), sedative (N = 9), and multidrug (N = 15) users. The MMPI was administered before and after two weeks of hospitalization and group therapy. The stimulant group showed significant pre- and post-treatment decreases on *Hs, Hy,* and *Pd.* The sedative group decreased their scores on *D, Hy, Pa, Pt,* and *Sc.* The barbiturate group on *F, Hs, D, Hy, Pa, Pt, Sc,* and *Si,* whereas *L* and *K* increased. The multidrug group produced decreases on *F, Hs, D, Hy, Pd, Pa, Pt, Sc,* and *Si.* The entire sample showed significant decreases on *F, Hs, D, Hy, Pd, Pa, Pt, Sc,* and *Si,* whereas *L* and *K* increased. Thus fairly different patterns of change emerged for the different subgroups. The only scale that decreased consistently for *all* four groups was *Hy,* whereas *Ma* remained unchanged for all four groups. In addition to the MMPI the patients were evaluated on the Brief Psychiatric Rating Scale (BPRS). According to the authors the change in the MMPI profile for the entire sample was paralleled by an improvement on the BPRS. On both instruments the majority of the patients, regardless of the primary drug abused, appeared "psychotic" at admission with a subsequent reduction in psychopathology. However, at discharge the stimulant group showed a "psychotic" slope, whereas the sedative, barbiturate, and, to some extent, the mixed-drug group appeared to be primarily psychopathic.

Sutker, Allain, and Cohen (1974) compared long-term and short-term hospitalization of heroin addicts. Their sample consisted of 58 male subjects from two different treatment facilities. The patients were institutionalized for either six weeks (N = 28) or six months (N = 30). Significant decreases on MMPI scores after short-term hospitalization were obtained on *F, Hs, D, Hy, Pa, Pt, Sc,* and *Si,* whereas *L* and *Es* increased. After long-term confinement there were significant decreases on *Hs* and *Hy,* whereas *L, K,* and *Es* increased. The authors suggest that this difference in outcome between the two treatment conditions might be due to early sweeping changes which then tended to level off. Presumably, the difference in intensity and frequency of treatment between the two facilities might also account for some of the discrepancy. Only *Hs* and *Hy* decreased in both settings, with *Ma* remaining unchanged.

In the only study meeting the criteria for inclusion in sensitivity index calculations, Ross, McReynolds, and Berzins (1974) (see Table 9) compared the effects of one 17-hour marathon group psychotherapy session with daily psychotherapy sessions over a period of two weeks in one of the few controlled studies using multiple measures. The subjects were 12 female narcotic addicts who were equally divided between the two treatment conditions. The assessment battery consisted of 20 scales from the Lexington Personality Inventory including the eight clinical MMPI scales and Rotter's Internal-External Locus of Control Scale (Rotter, 1966). Both groups showed significant reductions on *Hs, D,* and *Hy* as well as on the Rotter's Locus of Control Scale. A between-group analysis of variance yielded lower *Hs* and *Ma* scores and higher *Es* scores for the marathon group as compared to the daily-sessions group. It is interesting to note that again *Ma* remained unchanged, whereas *Hs* and *Hy* decreased for both groups.

Zuckerman, Sola, Masterson, and Angelone (1975) studied 145 male and female drug abusers. The subjects were members of three different therapeutic communities: a hard-drug center and a soft-drug center for males and mixed-hard or soft-drug center for females. All three programs consisted of two phases. The first phase included confrontive group interactions and problem-oriented counseling. During the second or reentry phase the participants worked outside the center but returned at night and continued to take part in group sessions and counseling. The MMPI was administered at entry and reentry for all subjects. The male soft-drug users showed decreases on *F, Hs, D, Pd, Pa, Pt, Sc,* and *Si,* whereas *K* and *Ma* increased. The male hard-drug users decreased their scores on *F, Hs, D, Hy, Pd, Pt, Sc,* and *Si,* and increased their scores on *K.* The female users decreased between entry and three months of treatment on *F, Hs, D, Hy, Pd, Pa, Pt, Sc,* and *Si,* and increased on *K.* There were additional changes between three months and reentry on *F, Pa, Pt, Sc,* and *Si,* all of which decreased, whereas *K* increased. The authors interpreted the reduction of depressive and neurotic patterns to suggest that these problems are more reactive to than causal of drug abuse.

Thus it appears from the studies reviewed that a reduction in *Hs* and *Hy* is a common effect of drug-abuse rehabilitation programs. Similarly, there is a fairly consistent resistance to change in the *Ma.* However, as discussed previously in the alcoholism section, owing to limitations in the study designs it is still not clear how these results should be interpreted. Other appropriate outcome measures are needed to verify that changes occurring in the MMPI are an indication of change in the subject and not a function of the tool itself. Furthermore, the change should not be attributed to treatment until an adequate control group is included to rule out the effects of mere passage of time and spontaneous remission.

Psychopathy

Few if any studies exist utilizing the MMPI to investigate treatment-related changes in measured psychopathy. Only two studies (Persons, 1966; Sowles & Gill, 1970) that conformed to our criteria for inclusion could be located (see Table 10). Both studies involved institutionalized adolescents rather than more rigorously defined "psychopaths." For neither study did data presentation permit the calculation of sensitivity ratios.

Persons (1966) assigned 82 institutionalized adolescents to either individual psychotherapy or a no-treatment control. Measures administered included the MMPI, Taylor MAS, and Delinquency Scale (Peterson, Quay, & Cameron, 1959). Behavioral changes were assessed by monitoring institutional adjustment, interpersonal skills, and scholastic performance. Results across all measures favored the treated group, with specific between-group differences on all 10 MMPI clinical scales except scale 5. Comparable between-group differences were evident on the Taylor MAS and on the Delinquency Scale. Parallel findings were obtained for the behavioral and community-adjustment measures. It thus appears that a generalized reduction in psychopathology, paralleled by specific changes in behavior, was detected by the MMPI. It is, of course, not clear whether such reported improvements on both the psychometric and the behavioral measures constitute a "recovery" from delinquency or an adjustment to institutionalization.

Sowles and Gill (1970) assigned institutionalized adolescents to either individual or group psychotherapy, or to a no-treatment control. Psychometric measures included the Taylor MAS, California F Scale (Adorno, Frenkel-Brunswik, Levinson, & Sanford, 1950), Ethnocentrism Scale, Eysenck Intolerance for Ambiguity Scale (IAS) (Eysenck, 1954), and the California Test of Personality (Glaser, 1949). Behavioral changes were assessed by monitoring adjustment in the institution (number of fights, running away incidents) and adjustment after discharge. In general, most psychometric indexes showed small but significant changes favoring the treated groups, changes not paralleled by the behavior-adjustment measures. Although the psychometric indexes appeared to show relatively concordant change,

Table 9. Studies Utilizing the MMPI to Evaluate Changes in Drug Addiction Samples

Study	Population	Comparison	Measure	Outcome
Ross, McReynolds, & Berzins, 1974	Narcotic Addicts	Marathon Group vs. Daily Group Therapy	MMPI IE	Several MMPI clinical scales (Hs, D, Hy) and ISB appear comparably sensitive to WG change. MMPI scales Hs, Ma, and Es detected BG change; ISB did not (+)

Table 10. Studies Utilizing the MMPI to Evaluate Changes in Psychopathic Samples

Study	Population	Comparison	Measure	Outcome
Persons, 1966	Psychopaths (adolescents)	Psychotherapy vs. No Treatment	MMPI TMAS Delinquency scale (DS)	BG differences on all MMPI clinical scales except 5, TMAS, and DS. (0)
Sowles & Gill, 1970	Psychopaths (adolescents)	Individual Counseling vs. Group Counseling vs. No Treatment	TMAS California F Scale Ethnocentrism Scale IAS CTP Behavior in Institution Behavioral Adjustment after Release	Doesn't clearly report outcome on TMAS, but generally found some reductions on paper-and-pencil measures, little or no correspondence with behavioral measures (−)

the lack of concordance with behavioral measures appears to minimize the clinical relevance of the findings. For the purpose of this review, it is unfortunate that the full MMPI was not utilized, since several of the clinical scales, e.g., scale *Pd*, have been of greater interest than the Taylor MAS in this specific population.

From this cursory look at MMPI research pertaining to the rehabilitation of institutionalized populations, it appears that treatment may be associated with specific decreases on MMPI scales. Concordance with changes in behavioral indexes of adjustment is unclear, although some support can be drawn from Persons's study. In this regard, it is important to discriminate concordance between different measures of change from the difficulties encountered in producing change. There may well be instances when lack of change in a measure, e.g., *Pd*, accurately mirrors an absence of change on other measures or underlying processes.

The issue of change following incarceration needs to be distinguished from change associated with treatment programs. Bauer and Clark (1976) have suggested that length of imprisonment is positively correlated with increased psychopathology as measured by the MMPI. Similar findings indicating a general increase in scale elevation after incarceration have been reported by Dahlstrom et al. (1975). However, Warman and Hannum (1965) found no significant changes between immediate post-incarceration administration and six-month post-readministrations in a sample of 50 female prisoners, and Torterella (1973) found significant decreases in indexes of psychopathology during long-term incarceration, specifically on clinical scales *Hs, D, Hy, Pa, Pt, Sc,* and *Si*. It is of interest that no decrease in scale *Pd*, perhaps the most specific index for this population, was evident. It is unclear what factors influence changes related to incarceration, although it is quite possible that relatively temporary factors (e.g., the initial stress of incarceration) may produce somewhat unstable changes on more state-sensitive indexes. At this time, it is clear only that additional controlled longitudinal research is needed to explicate the relationship between changes on the MMPI and changes related to incarceration.

Homosexuality

At least two existing studies utilize the MMPI to evaluate the efficacy of shock-avoidance conditioning paradigms in the reversal of homosexual preference. Results from these two studies are inconclusive regarding the utility of the MMPI, particularly scale *MF*.

Birk, Huddleston, Miller, and Cohler (1971) contrasted shock-mediated avoidance conditioning with a bogus "associative" conditioning control for two groups of homosexual males (N = 8). Outcome measures included the MMPI, reported indexes of sexual behavior, clinician ratings, and self-ratings of feelings and sexual interests. As shown in Table 11 reported behavior clearly discriminated the avoidance from the associative control patients. Both self and clinician ratings favored the avoidance-conditioning group, but neither set of measures as significant. No significant differences emerged on the MMPI, although scales F and Sc showed a trend (p < .10) in favor of the avoidance-treated patients. Scale Mf showed no difference between the groups, despite the reported corollary between-group behavioral changes, nor was there any evidence of significant within-group decreases in scale Mf for either treated or control patients. Given the apparent changes in self-reported sexual behavior, the failure of the MMPI (or self-report and/or clinician ratings) to indicate differential treatment effects may be telling. It would appear that existing MMPI subscales, or at least the Mf scale, may be relatively insensitive to potential changes in homosexual behavior.

A second study (Tanner, 1973; 1974) utilized a battery consisting of the MMPI Mf scale, reported sexual behavior, verbal ratings of arousal to heterosexual and homosexual erotic stimuli, and measured penile circumference to those same erotic stimuli to investigate changes following eight weeks of shock-mediated aversive conditioning vs. a waiting-list, no-treatment control. With eight male homosexual volunteers in each condition, significant between-group differences were found on each of the sets of measures listed above, including scale Mf of the MMPI.

These two studies appear to give somewhat contradictory conclusions about the utility of MMPI scale Mf for detecting changes in sexual orientation. Unfortunately, neither study presented data in a format permitting the calculation of sensitivity indexes. One potentially important distinction between the two designs may account for the disparity; the Birk et al. design involved a comparison of active treatment and a presumably inert control procedure, but the Tanner study compared active treatment with a waiting-list control. It is probable that the control procedure would have been associated with greater nonspecific change than the waiting-list control, reducing the magnitude of treatment-control differences to be detected in the Birk et al. study.

It appears that no firm conclusions can be drawn regarding the differential sensitivity of the MMPI to treatment-related changes in

Table 11. Studies Utilizing the MMPI to Evaluate Changes in Homosexual Samples

Study	Population	Comparison	Measure	Outcome
Birk, Huddleston, Miller, & Cohler, 1971	Male homosexuals (N = 8)	Shock-avoidance conditioning vs. associational conditioning (non-specific control)	MMPI Sexual behaviors (self-report) Clinician ratings Self-ratings	Group differences on reported behaviors, not MMPI scales, self, or clinician ratings—no WG changes on MMPI scale 5 (−)
Tanner, 1974	Male homosexuals (N = 8)	Shock avoidance conditioning vs. waiting list (no-treatment control)	MMPI (scale 5 only) Sexual behaviors (self-report) Verbal ratings of arousal to erotic stimuli Autonomic index of arousal to erotic stimuli	Both WG and BG changes on all measures, including MMPI scale 5 (0)

Note: Of course, where sample sizes are equivalent, such statistics as ANOVA's or t-tests can be directly compared to provide a rough, relative index.

homosexual orientation and/or behavior. Given that other, more direct measures of such phenomena are available (e.g., penile circumference, behavioral reports, self-ratings, etc.), it does not seem likely that the MMPI will receive much attention as a primary outcome measure in this area. The available data, however, are mixed, suggesting that additional attention to the potential merits of scale *Mf* as an outcome measure in this area may be warranted. We are unaware of any controlled studies utilizing the MMPI to evaluate therapeutic outcomes in attempts to alter other types of sexual preferences.

CONCLUSIONS

Overall, the sensitivity of the MMPI to changes in clinically relevant phenomena appears to be quite varied. Much of this variance seems to be attributable to the types of phenomena being studied. Thus, the *D* scale appears to fare well *vis-à-vis* other measures of change in syndrome depression. Although individual scales or combinations of scales appear to perform adequately in mixed outpatient samples, efforts toward ensuring greater homogeneity in problem definition may make the scales obsolete. The MMPI seems sensitive to change in schizophrenic samples, but problems remain in using the instrument with those more severely disturbed patients who often comprise a large portion of this population. Use of the MMPI with alcoholic and addictive populations probably will continue to focus on prediction, sample designation, and change in general psychological discomfort, rather than on changes in core addictive processes. The MMPI does not seem to detect changes in psychopathy or sexual orientation, but it is not clear that detectable changes in these phenomena actually occur. Overall, the utility of the MMPI in detecting changes in *some* phenomena, combined with its utility for sample designation, sample description, and prediction seem to suggest that it is advisable to use the MMPI as an adjunctive measure in outcome studies, rather than as the sole measure.

Three recommendations can be made, based on this review. First, it is unclear why content measures have not received greater attention in the MMPI treatment-outcome literature. Although there is no guarantee that such measures will prove more sensitive than existing scales, such a possibility would seem to merit empirical exploration.

Second, it is particularly discouraging that so few studies have been explicitly designed to explore the validity of the MMPI as an index of change. Such studies would minimally involve concurrent pre- and post-treatment assessment on theoretically relevant MMPI and alternative measures. The most striking aspect of the preceding review was the real paucity of such studies in the extensive MMPI literature.

Finally, sensitivity index analyses appear to have much to recommend them. Such analyses are clearly superior to traditional "box-score" methods, the latter confounding sample, design, and efficacy of the control-group sources of variance with indexes of instrument sensitivity. Whether pursued as dichotomous "significant/ nonsignificant" outcome counts across studies using similar measures, or as the more precise calculation of sensitivity indexes, these analyses may well facilitate a more intelligent selection of outcome measures than has been possible previously.

REFERENCES

Abuzzahab, F. S., & Kulkarni, A. S. A pilot investigation of clinical effects of PM-33, a new anti-anxiety agent. *Current Therapeutic Research*, 1974, 16, 1181-86.

Adorno, T. W., Frenkel-Brunswik, E., Levinson, D. J., & Sanford, R. N. *The authoritarian personality*. New York: Harper & Row, 1950.

Aiken, R. C. B. Measurement of feeling using visual analogue scales. *Proceedings of the Royal Society of Medicine*, 1969, 62, 989-93.

Andreasen, N. C. Do depressed patients show thought disorder? *Journal of Nervous and Mental Disease*, 1976, 163, 186-92.

Barron, F., & Leary, T. F. Changes in psychoneurotic patients with and without psychotherapy. *Journal of Consulting Psychology*, 1955, 19, 239-45.

Bauer, G. E., & Clark, J. A. Personality deviancy and prison incarceration. *Journal of Clinical Psychology*, 1976, 32, 279-83.

Bean, K. L., & Karasievich, G. D. Psychological test results at three stages of inpatient alcoholism treatment. *Journal of Studies on Alcohol*, 1975, 36, 838-52.

Beck, A. T., Ward, C. H., Mendelsohn, M., Mock, J. E., & Erbaugh, J. K. An inventory for measuring depression. *Archives of General Psychology*, 1961, 4, 561-71.

Bergin, A. E., The evaluation of therapeutic outcomes. In A. E. Bergin and S. L. Garfield (Eds.), *Handbook of Psychotherapy and Behavior Change*. New York: Wiley, 1971.

Birk, L., Huddleston, W., Miller, E., & Cohler, B. Avoidance conditioning for homosexuality. *Archives of General Psychiatry*, 1971, 25, 314-23.

Boudewyns, P. A., & Wilson, A. E. Implosive therapy and desensitization therapy using free association in the treatment of inpatients. *Journal of Abnormal Psychology*, 1972, 79, 259-68.

Bowman, K. M., & Jellinek, E. M. Alcohol addiction and its treatment. *Quarterly Journal of Studies on Alcohol*, 1941, 2, 98-176.

Brick, H., Doub, W. H., & Perdue, W. C. Effects of amitriptyline on depressive and anxiety states in penitentiary inmates. *Diseases of the Nervous System*, 1962, 23, 572-78.

Brick, H., Doub, W. H., & Perdue, W. C. A comparison of the effects of amitriptyline and protriptyline on anxiety and depressive states in female prisoners. *International Journal of Neuropsychiatry*, 1964, 1, 325-36.

Brick, H., Doub, W. H., & Perdue, W. C. Effects of tybamate on depressive and anxiety states in penitentiary inmates: A preliminary report. *International Journal of Neuropsychiatry*, 1966, 2, 637-44.

Brill, N. Q., Koegler, R. R., Epstein, L. J., & Forgy, E. W. Controlled study of psychiatric outpatient treatment. *Archives of General Psychiatry*, 1964, 10, 581-95.

Bryant, F. B., & Wortman, P. M. Secondary analysis: The case for data archives. *American Psychologist*, 1978, 33, 381-87.

Bunney, W. E., Jr., & Hamburg, D. A. Methods for reliable longitudinal observation of behavior. *Archives of General Psychiatry*, 1963, 9, 280-94.

Burke, T. F., & Templar, D. I. Comparison of Abbott A-10749 with imipramine. *Current Therapeutic Research*, 1968, 10, 335-41.

Butcher, J. N., & Owen, P. L. Objective personality inventories: Recent research and some contemporary issues. In B. B. Wolman (Ed.), *Clinical diagnosis of mental disorders: A handbook*. New York: Plenum, 1978.

Butcher, J. N., & Tellegen, A. Common methodological problems in MMPI research. *Journal of Consulting and Clinical Psychology*, 1978, 46, 620-28.

Campbell, D. T., & Stanley, J. C. *Experimental and quasiexperimental designs for research*. Chicago: Rand McNally, 1963.

Carp, A. L. MMPI performance and insulin shock therapy. *Journal of Abnormal and Social Psychology*, 1950, 45, 721-26.

Cartwright, D. S. Notes on "changes in psychoneurotic patients with and without psychotherapy." *Journal of Consulting Psychology*, 1956, 20, 403-4.

Cattell, R. B., & Eber, H. W. *Handbook for the Sixteen Personality Factor Questionnaire*. Champaign, Illinois: Institute for Personality and Ability Testing, 1957. (With 1964 supplement).

Chang, A. F., Caldwell, A. B., & Moss, T. Stability of personality traits in alcoholics during and after treatment as measured by the MMPI: A one-year followup study. *Proceedings of the 81st Annual Convention of the American Psychological Association*, 1973, 8, 387-88. (Summary).

Clyde, D. J. *Manual for the Clyde Mood Scale*. Biometric Laboratory, University of Miami, Coral Gables, Florida, 1963.

Cohen, J. *Statistical power analysis for the behavioral sciences*. New York: Academic Press, 1969.

Cole, C. E., Patterson, E. M., Craig, J. B., Thomas, W. E., Ristine, L. P., Stahly, M., & Pasamanick, B. A. A controlled study of efficacy of iproniazid in treatment of depression. *Archives of General Psychiatry*, 1959, 1, 513-18.

Coordinating Committee for Comparative Trials in Depression, Washington, D. C.: September, 1976.

Dahlstrom, W. G., Welsh, G. S., & Dahlstrom, L. E. *An MMPI handbook. Volume II: Research applications*. Minneapolis: University of Minnesota Press, 1975.

Dana, R. H. MMPI performance and electroshock treatment. *Journal of Clinical Psychology*, 1957, 350-55.

Dempsey, P. A unidimensional depression scale for the MMPI. *Journal of Consulting Psychology*, 1964, 28, 364-70.

Denson, R., & Sydiaha, D. A controlled study of LSD treatment in alcoholism and neurosis. *British Journal of Psychiatry*, 1970, 116, 443-45.

DiMascio, A., Meyer, R. E., & Stifler, L. Effects of imipramine on individuals varying in level of depression. *American Journal of Psychiatry*, 1968, 8, 55-58.

Donnelly, E. F., & Murphy, D. L. Primary affective disorder: MMPI differences between unipolar and bipolar depressed subjects. *Journal of Clinical Psychology*, 1973, 29, 303-6.

Donnelly, E. F., Murphy, D. L., & Goodwin, F. K. Cross-sectional and longitudinal comparisons of bipolar and unipolar depressed groups on the MMPI. *Journal of Consulting and Clinical Psychology*, 1976, 44, 233-38.

Edwards, A. L. *Manual for the Edwards Personal Preference Schedule*. New York: Psychological Corporation, 1954.

Elmore, T. M. *The development of a scale to measure psychological anomie*. Unpublished Doctoral Dissertation, Ohio State University, 1962.

Endicott, N. A., & Endicott, J. Objective measures of somatic preoccupation. *Journal of Nervous and Mental Disease*, 1963, 137, 427-37.

Endicott, N. A., & Endicott, J. Prediction of improvement in treated and untreated patients using the Rorschach prognostic rating scale. *Journal of Consulting Psychology*, 1964, 28, 342-48.

Ends, E. J., & Page, C. W. Group psychotherapy and concomitant psychological change. *Psychological Monographs*, 1959, 73, (Whole No. 480).

Equi, P. J., & Jabara, R. F. Validation of the self-rating depression scale in an alcoholic population. *Journal of Clinical Psychology*, 1976, 32, 504-7.

Eysenck, H. J. *The psychology of politics*. New York: Prager, 1954.

Eysenck, H. J., & Eysenck, S. *Manual for the Eysenck Personality Inventory*. San Diego: Educational and Industrial Testing Service, 1968.

Feighner, J. P., Robins, E., Guze, S. B., Woodruff, R. A., Winokur, G., & Munoz, R. Diagnostic criteria for use in psychiatric research. *Archives of General Psychiatry*, 1972, 26, 57-63.

Feldman, M. J. The use of the MMPI profile for prognosis and evaluation of shock therapy. *Journal of Consulting Psychology*, 1952, 16, 376-82.

Fiske, D. W. The constraints on intraindividual variability in test responses. *Educational and Psychological Measurement*, 1957, 17, 317-37.

Fryer, D. G., & Timberlake, W. H. A trial of imipramine (tofpranil) in depressed patients with chronic physical disease. *Journal of Chronic Disease*, 1963, 16, 173-78.

Fuchs, C. Z., & Rehm, L. P. A self-control behavior therapy program for depression. *Journal of Consulting and Clinical Psychology*, 1977, 45, 206-15.

Gallagher, J. J. MMPI changes concomitant with client-centered therapy. *Journal of Consulting Psychology*, 1953, 17, 334-38.

Gallant, D. M., Bishop, M. P., Scrignar, C. B., Hornsby, L., Moore, B., & Inturrisi, B. B. A double-blind study of thozalinone (Cl 39, 808) in depressed outpatients. *Current Therapeutic Research*, 1966, 8, 621-22.

Garfield, S. Research problems in clinical diagnosis. *Journal of Consulting and Clinical Psychology*, 1978, 46, 596-607.

Glaser, R. A methodological analysis of the inconsistency of response to test items. *Educational and Psychological Measurement*, 1949, 14, 727-39.

Goldberg, L. R. Diagnosticians vs. diagnostic signs: The diagnosis of psychosis vs. neurosis from the MMPI. *Psychological Monographs*, 1965, 79 (9, Whole No. 602).

Goldberg, L. R. Objective diagnostic tests and measures. *Annual Review of Psychology*, 1974, 25, 343-66.

Goldberg, L. R., & Jones, R. R. The reliability of reliability: The generality and correlates of intra-individual consistency in responses to structured personality inventories. *Oregon Research Institute Monograph*, 1969, 9, No. 2.

Goldstein, S. G., & Linden, J. D. Multivariate classification of alcoholics by means of the MMPI. *Journal of Abnormal Psychology*, 1969, 74, 661-69.

Graf, X., Baer, P. E., & Comstock, B. S. MMPI changes in briefly hospitalized non-narcotic drug users. *Journal of Nervous and Mental Disease*, 1977, 165, 126-33.

Graham, J. R. *The MMPI: A practical guide.* New York: Oxford University Press, 1977.

Greer, R. M., & Callis, R. The use of videotape models in an alcohol rehabilitation program. *Rehabilitation Counseling Bulletin*, 1975, 18, 154-59.

Hales, W. M., & Simon, W. MMPI patterns before and after insulin shock therapy. *American Journal of Psychiatry*, 1948, 105, 254-58.

Hamilton, M. A rating scale for depression. *Journal of Neurology, Neurosurgery, and Psychiatry*, 1960, 23, 56-62.

Hollister, L. E., & Overall, J. E. Reflections on the specificity of action of anti-depressants. *Psychosomatics*, 1965, 6, 361-65.

Hollister, L. E., Overall, J. E., Johnson, M., Katz, G., Kimbell, I., & Honigfeld, G. Evaluation of desipramine in depressive states. *Journal of New Drugs*, 1963, 3, 161-66.

Hollister, L. E., Overall, J. E., Johnson, M., Pennington, Y., Katz, G., & Shelton, J. Controlled comparison of amitriptyline, imipramine, and placebo in hospitalized depressed patients. *Journal of Nervous and Mental Disease*, 1964, 139, 370-75.

Hollister, L. E., Overall, J. E., Johnson, M. H., Shelton, J., Kimbell, I., & Brunse, A. Amitryptiline alone and combined with perphenazine in newly admitted depressed patients. *Journal of Nervous and Mental Disease*, 1966, 142, 460-69.

Hollon, S. D., & Beck, A. T. Psychotherapy and drug therapy: Comparisons and combinations. In S. L. Garfield and A. E. Bergin (Eds.), *The handbook of psychotherapy and behavior change* (2nd ed.). New York: Wiley, 1978.

Hollon, S. D., Beck, A. T., Kovacs, M., & Rush, A. J. *Cognitive therapy versus pharmacotherapy of depression: Outcome and follow-up.* Paper presented at the annual meeting of the American Psychological Association, San Francisco, August, 1977.

Hollon, S. D., Rush, A. J., Beck, A. T., & Kovacs, M. *Poor concordance between different methods of assessing psychopathology: Fact or artifact?* Unpublished manuscript, University of Minnesota, Minneapolis, Minnesota, 1979.

Holzberg, J. D., & Alessi, S. Reliability of the shortened MMPI. *Journal of Consulting Psychology*, 1949, 13, 288-92.

Horowitz, S. L. Strategies within hypnosis for reducing phobia behavior. *Journal of Abnormal Psychology*, 1970, 75, 104-12.

Huber, N. A., & Danahy, S. Use of the MMPI in predicting completion and evaluating changes in a long-term alcoholism treatment program. *Journal of Studies on Alcohol*, 1975, 36, 1230-37.

Jellinek, E. M. The phases of alcohol addiction. *Quarterly Journal of Studies on Alcohol*, 1952, 13, 673-84.

Johnston, R., & McNeal, B. F. Residual psychopathology in released psychiatric patients and its relation to readmission. *Journal of Abnormal Psychology*, 1965, 70, 337-42.

Kaufmann, P. Changes in the Minnesota Multiphasic Personality Inventory as a function of psychiatric therapy. *Journal of Consulting Psychology*, 1950, 14, 458-64.

Kelly, D. H., Walter, C. J., Mitchell-Heggs, N., & Sargent, W. Modified leucotomy assessed clinically, physiologically and psychologically at six weeks and eighteen months. *British Journal of Psychiatry*, 1972, 120, 19-29.

Kraft, T., & Wijesinghe, B. Systematic desensitization of social anxiety in the treatment of alcoholism: A psychometric evaluation of change. *British Journal of Psychiatry*, 1970, 117, 443-44.

Kraus, A. R. Experimental study of the effect of group psychotherapy with chronic psychotic patients. *International Journal of Group Psychotherapy*, 1959, 9, 293-302.

Kurland, A. A., Unger, S., Shaffer, J. W., & Savage, C. Psychedelic therapy utilizing LSD in the treatment of the alcoholic patient: A preliminary report. *American Journal of Psychiatry*, 1967, 123, 1202-9.

Kurtz, R. R., & Grummon, D. L. Different approaches to the measurement of therapist empathy and their relationship to therapy outcome. *Journal of Consulting and Clinical Psychology*, 1972, 39, 106-15.

Lauer, J. W. The effect of tricyclic antidepressant compounds on patients with passive-dependent personality traits. *Current Therapeutic Research*, 1976, 19, 495-505.

Levis, D. J., & Carrera, R. Effects of ten hours of implosive therapy in the treatment of outpatients. *Journal of Abnormal Psychology*, 1967, 72, 504-8.

Lewinsohn, P. M. Dimensions of MMPI change. *Journal of Clinical Psychology*, 1965, 21, 37-43.

Lewinsohn, P. M., & Nichols, R. C. The evaluation of changes in psychiatric patients during and after hospitalization. *Journal of Clinical Psychology*, 1964, 20, 272-79.

Lewinsohn, P. M., & Nichols, R. C. Dimensions of change in mental hospital patients. *Journal of Clinical Psychology*, 1967, 23, 498-503.

Lichtenstein, E., & Bryan, J. H. Short-term stability of MMPI profiles. *Journal of Consulting Psychology*, 1966, 30, 172-74.

Lorr, M. *Multidimensional scale for rating psychiatric patients: Hospital form*. Veterans Administration Technical Bulletin, 1953, TB 10-507 6, 1-44.

Lowe, W. C., & Thomas, S. D. Assessing alcoholism treatment effectiveness: A comparison of three evaluative measures. *Journal of Studies on Alcohol*, 1976, 37, 883-89.

Lubin, B. *Manual for the Depression Adjective Check Lists*. San Diego: Education and Industrial Testing Service, 1967.

Luborsky, L., Singer, B., & Luborsky, L. Comparative studies of psychotherapies: Is it true that everyone has won and all must have prizes? *Archives of General Psychiatry*, 1975, 32, 995-1008.

Lumry, A. E. *Bipolar affective disorder: A clinical-genetic study*. Unpublished doctoral dissertation, University of Minnesota, Minneapolis, Minnesota, 1978.

Malitz, S., & Kanzler, M. Are antidepressants better than placebo? *American Journal of Psychiatry*, 1971, 127, 1605-11.

Mandell, A. J., Markham, C. H., Tallman, F. F., & Mandell, M. P. Motivation and ability to move. *American Journal of Psychiatry*, 1962, 119, 544-49.

Marsh, G. G., & Markham, C. H. Does levodopa alter depression and psychopathology in Parkinsonism patients? *Journal of Neurology, Neurosurgery, and Psychiatry*, 1973, 36, 925-35.

Martin, P. J., Moore, J. E., Sterne, A. L., & McNairy, R. M. Therapists prophesy. *Journal of Clinical Psychology*, 1977, 33, 502-10.

Maskin, M. B., Riklan, M., & Chabot, D. Emotional functions in short-term vs. long-term L-DOPA therapy in Parkinsonism. *Journal of Clinical Psychology*, 1973, 29, 493-95.

Mauger, P. A. *The test-retest reliability of persons: An empirical investigation utilizing the Minnesota Multiphasic Personality Inventory and the Personality Research Form*. Unpublished doctoral dissertation, University of Minnesota, 1972.

May, P. R. A. *Treatment of schizophrenia*. New York: Science House, 1968.

McCall, R. J. Group therapy with obese women of varying MMPI profiles. *Journal of Clinical Psychology*, 1974, 30, 467-70.

McClure, D. J., Low, G. L., & Gent, M. Clomipramine HCL—a double-blind study of a new antidepressant drug. *Canadian Psychiatric Association Journal*, 1973, 18, 403-8.

McDonald, I. M., Perkins, M., & Marjerrison, G. A controlled comparison of amitriptyline and electroconvulsive therapy in the treatment of depression. *American Journal of Psychiatry*, 1966, 122, 1427-31.

McNair, D. M. Self evaluations of antidepressants. *Psychopharmacologia*, 1974, 37, 281-302.

Meltzoff, J., & Kornreich, M. *Research in psychotherapy*. New York: Atherton, 1970.

Mendelsohn, R. M. Penman, A. S. & Schiele, B. C. Massive chlorpromazine therapy: The nature of behavioral changes. *Psychiatric Quarterly*, 1959, 33, 55-76.

Michaux, M. H., Chelet, M. R., Foster, S. A., & Pruim, R. J. Day and full-time psychiatric treatment: A controlled comparison. *Current Therapeutic Research*, 1972, 14, 279-92.

Mills, W. W. MMPI profile pattern and scale stability throughout four years of college attendance. Doctoral dissertation, University of Minnesota, 1954 (*Dissertation Abstracts*, 1954, 14, 1259).

Mogar, R. E., & Savage, C. Personality change associated with psychiatric (LSD) therapy: A preliminary report. *Psychotherapy, Theory, Research, and Practice*, 1964, 1, 154-62.

Mormont, C. Evaluation des effets psychologiques du Noveril simple et du Noveril TR. *Psychopharmacologia*, 1974, 37, 365-70.

Mosak, H. *Evaluation of psychotherapy: A study of some current measures.* Unpublished doctoral dissertation: University of Chicago, 1950. (Cited in Meltzoff & Kornreich, 1971)

Murillo, L. G., & Exner, J. E. The effect of regressive ECT with process schizophrenia. *American Journal of Psychiatry*, 1973, 130, 269-73.

Newmark, C. S. MMPI comparison of the oral form presented by a live examiner and the booklet form. *Psychological Reports*, 1971, 29, 797-98.

Nussbaum, K., Wittig, B. A., Hanlon, T. E., & Kurland, A. A. Intravenous nialamide in the treatment of depressed female patients. *Comprehensive Psychiatry*, 1963, 4, 105-16.

Olson, G. W. Application of an objective method for measuring the action of antidepressant medications. *American Journal of Psychiatry*, 1962, 118, 1044-45.

Overall, J. E., Brown, D., Williams, J. D., & Neill, L. T. Drug treatment of anxiety and depression in detoxified alcoholic patients. *Archives of General Psychiatry*, 1973, 29, 218-21.

Overall, J. E., & Gorham, D. R. The brief psychiatric rating scale. *Psychological Reports*, 1962, 10, 799-812.

Overall, J. E., Hollister, L. E., Meyer, F., Kimbell, I., & Shelton, J. Imipramine and thioridazine in depressed and schizophrenic patients. Are there specific antidepressant drugs? *Journal of the American Medical Association*, 1964, 189, 605-8.

Overall, J. E., Hollister, L. E., Pokorny, A. D., Casey, J. F., & Katz, G. Drug therapy in depression. Controlled evaluation of imipramine, isocarboxazide, dextroamphetamine-amobarbitol, and placebo. *Clinical Pharmacology and Therapeutics*, 1962, 3, 16-22.

Overall, J. E., Hollister, L. E., Shelton, J., Johnson, M., & Kimbell, I. Tranylcypromine compared with dextroamphetamine in hospitalized depressed patients. *Diseases of the Nervous System*, 1966, 27, 653-59.

Pacella, B. L., Piotrowski, Z. A., & Lewis, N. D. The effects of convulsive therapy on certain personality traits in psychiatric patients. *American Journal of Psychiatry*, 1947, 104, 83-91.

Paulker, J. D. MMPI profile stability in a psychiatric inpatient population. *Journal of Clinical Psychology*, 1965, 21, 281-82.

Pepper, L. J. *The MMPI: Initial test predictors of retest changes.* Unpublished doctoral dissertation, University of North Carolina, 1964.

Persons, R. W. Psychological and behavioral change in delinquents following psychotherapy. *Journal of Clinical Psychology*, 1966, 22, 337-40.

Peterson, D. R., Quay, N. C., & Cameron, G. R. Personality and background factors in juvenile delinquency as inferred from questionnaire responses. *Journal of Consulting Psychology*, 1959, 23, 395-99.

Prusoff, B. A., Klerman, G. L., & Paykel, E. S. Concordance between clinical assessments and patients' self report in depression. *Archives of General Psychiatry*, 1972, 26, 546-52.

Rashkis, H. A., & Shaskin, D. A. The effects of group therapy on personality scores. *American Journal of Orthopsychiatry*, 1946, 16, 343-49.

Raskin,, A., Schulterbrandt, J., Reatig, N., & Rice C. E. Factors of psychotherapy in interview, ward behavior, and self-report ratings of hospitalized depressives. *Journal of Consulting Psychology*, 1967, 31, 270-78.

Rickels, K., Gordon, P. E., Weise, C. C., Bazilian, S. E., Feldman, H. S., & Wilson, D. A. Amitriptyline and trimipramine in neurotic depressed outpatients: A collaborative study. *American Journal of Psychiatry*, 1970, 127, 208-18.

Rickels, K., Hutchinson, J. C., Weise, C. C., Csanalosi, I., Chung, H. R., & Case, W. G. Doxapin and amitriptyline-perphenazine in mixed anxious-depressed neurotic outpatients: A collaborative controlled study. *Psychopharmacologia*, 1972, 23, 305-18.

Rickels, K., Laquer, K. G., Rial, W. Y., Rosenfeld, H., Schneider, B., & Wagner, I. G. The combination of protriptyline and oxazepam in depressed neurotic general practice patients. *Psychosomatics*, 1971, 12, 341-48.

Rickels, K., Perloff, M., Stepansky, W., Dion, H. S., Case, W. G., & Sapra, R. K. Doxepin and diazepam in general practice and hospital clinic neurotic patients: A collaborative controlled study. *Psychopharamacologia*, 1969, 15, 265-79.

Rickels, K., Ward, C. H., & Schut, L. Different populations, different drug responses. A comparative study of two anti-depressants, each used in two different patient groups. *American Journal of Medical Science*, 1965, 247, 548-50.

Rickels, K., Ward, C. H., & Snow, L. Nialamide and placebo in depressed psychiatric clinic patients (a controlled double-blind study). *Diseases of the Nervous System*, 1963, 24, 548-50.

Rittenhouse, J. D. Endurance of effect: Family unit treatment compared to identified patient treatment. *Proceedings of the 78th Annual Convention of the American Psychological Association*, 1970, 5, 535-36. (Summary)

Roback, H. B. Experimental comparison of outcomes in insight- and non-insight-oriented therapy groups. *Journal of Consulting and Clinical Psychology*, 1972, 38, 411-17.

Robin, A. A., & Wiseberg, S. A controlled trial of methylphenidate (ritalin) in the treatment of depressive states. *Journal of Neurology, Neurosurgery, and Psychiatry*, 1958, 21, 55-57.

Rohan, W. P. MMPI changes in hospitalized alcoholics. *Quarterly Journal of Studies on Alcohol*, 1972, 33, 65-76.

Rohan, W. P., Tatro, R. L. & Rotman, S. R. MMPI changes in alcoholics during hospitalization. *Quarterly Journal of Studies on Alcohol*, 1969, 30, 389-400.

Rosen, A. Test-retest stability of MMPI scales for a psychiatric population. *Journal of Consulting Psychology*, 1953, 17, 217-21.

Rosen, A. Differentiation of diagnostic groups by individual MMPI scales. *Journal of Consulting Psychology*, 1958, 22, 453-57.

Ross, W. F., McReynolds, W. T., & Berzins, J. I. Effectiveness of marathon group psychotherapy with hospitalized female narcotics addicts. *Psychological Reports*, 1974, 34, 611-16.

Rotter, J. B. Generalized expectancies for internal versus external control of reinforcement. *Psychological Monographs*, 1966, 80, 1-28.

Roulet, N., Alvarez, R. R., Duffy, J. P., Lenkoski, L. D., & Bidder, T. G. Imipramine in depression: A controlled study. *American Journal of Psychiatry*, 1962, 119, 427-31.

Rush, A. J., Beck, A. T., Kovacs, M., & Hollon, S. D. Comparative efficacy of cognitive therapy and pharmacotherapy in the treatment of depressed outpatients. *Cognitive Therapy and Research*, 1977, 1, 17-38.

Sandifer, M. G., Wilson, I. C., & Gambill, J. M. The influence of care selection and dosage in an antidepressant drug trial. *British Journal of Psychiatry*, 1965, 111, 142-48.

Scheier, I. H., & Cattell, R. B. *The Forty-item Anxiety Scale.* Institute for Personality and Ability Testing, 1602 Coronado Drive, Champaign, Illinois, 1960.

Schenker, V. J., Marjerrison, G., Schlachet, P., Freedman, N., Hankoff, L. D., & Engelhardt, D. M. Monoamine oxidase inhibition and antidepressive correlates. *Third World Congress of Psychiatry, Proceedings* (Vol. 1), Montreal, 1961.

Schofield, W. Changes in responses to the Minnesota Multiphasic Inventory following certain therapies. *Psychological Monographs*, 1950, 64 (No. 5, Whole No. 311).

Schofield, W. A further study of the effects of therapies on MMPI responses. *Journal of Abnormal and Social Psychology*, 1953, 48, 67-77.

Schofield, W. The structured personality inventory in measurement of effects of psychotherapy. In L. A. Gottschalk & A. H. Auerbach (Eds.), *Methods of research in psychotherapy.* New York: Appleton-Century-Crofts, 1966.

Sehdev, H. S., & Olson, J. L. Nicotinic acid therapy in chronic schizophrenia. *Comprehensive Psychiatry*, 1974, 15, 511-17.

Shaffer, J. W., Freinek, W. R., McCusker, J. K., & DeFelice, E. A. A comparison of modaline sulfate (W 3207 B) and imipramine in the treatment of depression. *Journal of New Drugs*, 1964, 4, 288-94.

Shaffer, J. W., Yeganeh, M. L., Foxwell, N. H., & Kurland, A. A. A comparison of the effects of prazipam, chlordiazepoxide, and placebo in the short-term treatment of convalescing alcoholics. *The Journal of Clinical Pharmacology and the Journal of New Drugs*, 1968, 8, 392-99.

Shaw, B. F., & Hollon, S. D. *Cognitive therapy in a group format with depressed outpatients.* Unpublished manuscript, University of Western Ontario, 1978.

Shaw, J. A., Donley, P., Morgan, D. W., & Robinson, J. A. Treatment of depression in alcoholics. *American Journal of Psychiatry*, 1975, 132, 641-44.

Sherman, A. R. Real-life exposure as a primary therapeutic factor in the desensitization treatment of fear. *Journal of Abnormal Psychology*, 1972, 79, 19-28.

Simon, W., & Gilberstadt, H. MMPI patterns before and after carbon dioxide inhalation therapy. *Journal of Nervous and Mental Disease*, 1954, 119, 523-29.

Simon, W., Wirt, R. D., Wirt, A. L., Holloran, A. V., Hinckley, R. G., Lund, J. B., & Hopkins, G. W. A controlled study of the short-term differential treatment of schizophrenia. *American Journal of Psychiatry*, 1958, 114, 1077-85.

Sines, L. K., & Silver, R. J. An index of psychopathology (Ip) derived from clinicians' judgements of MMPI profiles. *Journal of Clinical Psychology*, 1963, 19, 324-26.

Sines, L. K., Silver, R. J., & Lucerno, R. J. The effect of therapeutic intervention by untrained "therapists." *Journal of Clinical Psychology*, 1961, 17, 394-96.

Slawson, P. F. Psychodrama as a treatment for hospitalized patients: A controlled study. *American Journal of Psychiatry*, 1965, 122, 530-33.

Smith, J. W., Johnson, L. C., & Burdick, J. A. Sleep, psychological and clinical changes during alcohol withdrawal in NAD-treated alcoholics. *Quarterly Journal of Studies in Alcoholism*, 1971, 32, 982-84.

Smith, M.L., & Glass, G. V. Meta-analysis of psychotherapy outcome studies. *American Psychologist*, 1977, 32, 752-60.

Snow, L. H., & Rickels, K. The controlled evaluation of imipramine and amitriptyline in hospitalized depressed psychiatric patients. A contribution to the methodology of drug evaluation. *Psychopharmacologia*, 1964, 5, 409-16.

Solyom, L., Heseltine, G. R., McClure, D. J., Ledwidge, B., & Kenny, F. A comparative study of aversion relief and systematic desensitization in the treatment of phobias. *British Journal of Psychiatry*, 1971, 119, 299-303.

Soskin, R. A. Personality and attitude change after two alcoholism treatment programs: Comparative contributions of lysergide and human relations training. *Quarterly Journal of Studies on Alcohol*, 1970, 31, 920-31.

Sowles, R. C., & Gill, J. H. Institutional and community adjustment of delinquents following counseling. *Journal of Consulting and Clinical Psychology*, 1970, 34, 398-402.

Spitzer, R. L., Endicott, J., & Robins, E. *Research diagnostic criteria.* New York: New York State Department of Mental Hygiene, New York State Psychiatric Institute, Biometrics Research, 1978.

Spreche, D. A quantitative comparison of ECT with hexafluorodiethyl ether. *Journal of Neuropsychiatry*, 1963, 5, 132-37.

Stone, L. A. Test-retest stability of the MMPI scales. *Psychological Reports*, 1965, 16, 619-20.

Stoudenmire, J. Effects of muscle relaxation training on state and trait anxiety in introverts and extroverts. *Journal of Personality and Social Psychology*, 1972, 24, 273-75.

Strupp, H. H., & Hadley, S. W. A tripartite model of mental health and therapeutic outcomes. *American Psychologist*, 1977, 32, 187-96.

Sutker, P. B., Allain, A. N., & Cohen, G. N. MMPI indices of personality change following short- and long-term hospitalization of heroin addicts. *Psychological Reports*, 1934, 34, 495-500.

Tanner, B. A. The modification of male homosexual behavior by avoidance learning. Doctoral dissertation, University of North Carolina, 1972 (*Dissertation Abstracts International*, 1973, 33, 3923B).

Tanner, B. A. A comparison of automated aversive conditions and a waiting list control in the modification of homosexual behavior in males. *Behavior Therapy*, 1974, 5, 29-32.

Task Force on Nomenclature and Statistics of the American Psychiatric Association. *Diagnostic and statistical manual of metnal disorders – III draft*, Washington, D.C.: American Psychiatric Association, 1978.

Taylor, F. G., & Marshall, W. L. Experimental analysis of a cognitive-behavioral therapy for depression. *Cognitive Therapy and Research*, 1977, 1, 59-72.

Taylor, J. A. A personality scale of manifest anxiety. *Journal of Abnormal and Social Psychology*, 1953, 48, 285-90.

Tortorella, W. M. Personality and intellectual changes in delinquent girls following long-term institutional placement. *Journal of Community Psychology*, 1973, 1, 288-91.

Ullman, L. P., & Wiggins, J. S. Endorsement frequency and the number of differentiating MMPI items to be expected by chance. *Newsletter of Research in Psychology*, 1962, 4, 29-35.

Vernallis, F. F., Shipper, J. C., Butler, D. C., & Tomlinson, T. M. Saturation group psychotherapy in a weekend clinic: An outcome study. *Psychotherapy: Theory, Research and Practice*, 1970, 7, 144-52.

Warman, R. E., & Hannum, T. E. MMPI pattern changes in female prisoners. *Journal of Research in Crime and Delinquency*, 1965, 2, 72-76.

Welsh, G. S. An anxiety index and an internalization ratio for the MMPI. *Journal of Consulting Psychology*, 1952, 16, 65-72.

Wiggins, J. S. Substantive dimensions of self-report in the MMPI item pool. *Psychological Monographs*, 1966, 80 (22, Whole No. 630).

Wilkinson, A. E., Prado, W. M., Williams, W. O., & Schnadt, F. W. Psychological test characteristics and length of stay in alcoholism treatment. *Quarterly Journal of Studies on Alcohol*, 1971, 32, 60-65.

Wilson, I. C., Vernon, J. T., Guin, T., & Sandifer, M. G. A controlled study of treatments of depression. *Journal of Neuropsychiatry*, 1963, 4, 331-37.

Wittenborn, J. R., Plante, M., Burgess, F., & Livermore, N. The efficacy of electroconvulsive therapy, iproniazid and placebo in the treatment of young depressed women. *Journal of Nervous and Mental Disease*, 1961, 133, 316-32.

Wittenborn, J. R., Plante, M., Burgess, F., & Maurer, H. A comparison of imipramine, electroconvulsive therapy and placebo in the treatment of depressions. *Journal of Nervous and Mental Disease*, 1962, 135, 131-37.

Wrightsman, L. S. Measurement of philosophies of human nature. *Psychological Reports*, 1964, 14, 743-51.

Zuckerman, M., Sola, S., Masterson, J., & Angelone, J. V. MMPI patterns in drug abusers before and after treatment in therapeutic communities. *Journal of Consulting and Clinical Psychology*, 1975, 43, 286-96.

Zung, W. W. A self-rating depression scale. *Archives of General Psychiatry*, 1965, 12, 63-70.

Development and Validation of an MMPI-Based System for Classifying Criminal Offenders

Edwin I. Megargee

In its 1973 *Report on Corrections*, the National Advisory Commission on Criminal Justice Standards and Goals called for the immediate implementation of comprehensive classification programs at all levels of the criminal justice system, noting: "classification can make handling large numbers of offenders more efficient through a grouping process based on needs and problems. From an administrative standpoint, classification systems can provide for more orderly processing and handling of individuals. From a financial standpoint, classification schemes can enable administrators to make more efficient use of limited resources and to avoid providing resources for offenders who do not require them" (1973, p. 201).

In 1975, ten million adults were arrested in the United States; for each a decision had to be made regarding whether they should be diverted from the criminal justice system or prosecuted, detained in jail, or released. One million were tried and convicted; for each a decision on the most appropriate sentence, ranging from probation to the death penalty, had to be made. For the 190,000 who entered prison, decisions had to be made regarding the custody level required and the optimum facility for placement, ranging from open community-based placements to maximum-security penitentiaries. In addition,

Note: Preparation of this paper was supported by Grant No. MH29911 (Center for Studies of Crime and Delinquency: NIMH). The research reported in this chapter was supported by Grant No. 18468 (Center for Studies of Crime and Delinquency, NIMH), by Subcontract No. 75-AS-33-E401 from the Florida Bureau of Criminal Justice Planning and Assistance (LEAA), and by contracts from the Federal Bureau of Prisons (J100c-Z3,631).

rehabilitation programs had to be designed. For the quarter million individuals in prison, parole decisions had to be made and community plans formulated for the 165,000 who were released (Gottfredson, Hindelang, & Parisi, 1978). The National Advisory Commission's recommendations made it clear that classification should play a central role in making such decisions.

How should these offenders be classified? Dozens of typologies of criminal offenders have been proposed over the last century by behavioral scientists from a number of disciplines. Virtually every measurable aspect of humankind—physique, personality structure, socioeconomic class, criminal behavior patterns, and many more—have been used as the basis for these taxonomic systems, but few can be used in applied criminal justice settings. The writer recently proposed a minimum set of standards for judging the usefulness of a typology of juvenile or adult offenders in correctional decision-making:

> First, (a good classification system) should be sufficiently *complete* so that most of the offenders or clients in the agency or setting can be classified. Equally important is the need for *clear operational definitions* of the various types so that each person can be classified with a minimum of ambiguity. Third, the system must be *reliable* so that two different raters will arrive at the same classification of a given individual. Fourth, it must be *valid*; it must be demonstrated that the individuals falling within a given classification actually have the attributes they are hypothesized to possess. Fifth, it should be *dynamic*, so that changes in an individual, such as improvement as a result of correctional treatment, will be reflected by a change in his or her classification. Sixth, each classification should carry with it *implications for treatment*. Finally, it should be *economical* so that large numbers of offenders can be classified with minimal expense and personnel (1977, p. 108; italics in original).

A recent survey of a broad array of typologies of criminal offenders showed that the vast majority had been deductively derived from sociological or psychological theories or were based on informal observations of select groups of offenders (Megargee, Bohn, Meyer, & Sink, 1979). Virtually none had been tested for validity; except for anecdotal data, there was rarely any empirical evidence that the proposed types actually existed. Indeed, it would have been difficult even to attempt to validate most typologies because the descriptions of the proposed groups were far too vague to be used as operational definitions.

The few systems that had been validated and implemented in correctional settings had other drawbacks. They typically relied on information that took a significant amount of time and expertise to gather, such as structured clinical interviews by specially trained individuals, extensive life-history data, or detailed behavioral observations. Such systems would be difficult to implement in settings that require rapid classification or that lack adequate funds or suitably trained personnel.

To meet the need for a reliable, valid, economical typology for classifying criminal offenders, the present investigator and his colleagues have spent the last nine years deriving and testing a taxonomy of offenders based on the MMPI. It was thought that an MMPI-based classification system would have a number of significant advantages. First, those systems that, like the MMPI, focus on personality variables had proved to be the most useful in correctional decision-making. Second, the MMPI would provide a uniform data base, so classification procedures would not vary from one jurisdiction to the next as a function of the records available (as in life-history systems) or plea-bargaining (as in offense-based systems). Third, the ease and economy of MMPI administration would make it possible to obtain the requisite data easily and efficiently; indeed, since the MMPI was already routinely administered in all federal and many state correctional systems, offenders in such settings could be classified with no additional effort or expense. Fourth, the MMPI would provide quantitative data that would be especially amenable to statistical analysis and that could form the basis for clear, precise operational definitions, and perhaps even economical, computer-based classification. Fifth, since changes in the MMPI profile reflect significant changes in personality functioning or attitudes, an MMPI-based system would probably be dynamic, reflecting changes in clients that are associated with correctional treatment in a way not possible in systems based on life history, offense patterns, demographic characteristics, or physique. Sixth, whereas some of the best existing classification systems had been created for use with juveniles, the MMPI was designed for adults, who make up the bulk of the offender population. Seventh, cross-cultural and cross-national research with the MMPI (Butcher & Pancheri, 1976) suggested that an MMPI-based system, if it could be derived, might be broadly generalizable. Thus, it seemed that an MMPI-based typology, if one could be constructed, could well meet the requirements of a useful classification system and also have a high degree of cost-effectiveness.

The fact that several MMPI-based systems for the classification and diagnosis of adolescent and adult psychiatric patients and normals had been constructed was a further indication that an MMPI-based system for classifying criminal offenders might be viable (Gilberstadt & Duker, 1965; Marks, Seeman, & Haller, 1974). It was also encouraging that a number of studies, including the writer's own research on overcontrolled and undercontrolled assaultive offenders, had indicated that the MMPI was useful in differentiating among groups of criminal offenders (Dahlstrom, Welsh, & Dahlstrom, 1972; Hathaway & Monachesi, 1953; Wirt & Briggs, 1959; Megargee, 1966, 1973; Megargee, Cook, & Mendelsohn, 1967).

At the same time, it was recognized the relatively narrow, quickly obtained, data base that would make an MMPI-based system inexpensive and efficient could also prove to be a fatal weakness if the MMPI item pool proved to be an inadequate basis for a typology of criminal offenders. A particular concern was that the MMPI's emphasis on psychopathology might make it inappropriate for the broad range of psychologically "normal" offenders.

These were, of course, empirical questions that could be resolved only through research. Although the initial notion of an MMPI-based taxonomy had occurred to the present investigator in the mid-1960s, it was not until 1970 that an opportunity to derive and validate such a typology arose. Under the auspices of a grant from the Center for Studies of Crime and Delinquency (NIMH) and with the cooperation, support, and assistance of the Federal Bureau of Prisons, a research laboratory was established at the Federal Correctional Institution at Tallahassee, Florida, (FCI), a medium-security prison then housing approximately 500 to 600 youthful male felons ages 18 to 27, most of whom were drawn from the southeastern United States; 65% of the inmates were white, 34% were black, and the remaining 1% were primarily American Indians.

As part of the routine admissions program at the FCI, the MMPI had been administered to every incoming inmate since 1967 with the resulting data retained for research purposes. From 1970 to 1974, a greatly expanded program of research was undertaken. For every inmate who entered from November 3, 1970 through November 2, 1972, 1,345 men in all, a broad array of social, psychological, physiological, attitudinal, behavioral, and historical data were collected by means of psychological tests, structured interviews, an autonomic screening procedure, and a detailed study of case records. Each man was followed throughout the course of his incarceration, and systematic data were obtained on his adjustment to the institution, including records of disciplinary infractions, periodic ratings by correctional personnel and work supervisors, grades in various academic and vocational courses, and records of sick-call attendance. Before leaving the institution, additional tests and interviews were administered, and several years later, follow-up data on the subsequent criminal careers of the men were obtained from the National Crime Information Center (NCIC) under the auspices of a grant obtained from the Florida Bureau of Criminal Justice Planning and Assistance (LEAA).

RATIONALE OF THE STUDIES

Most of the typologies of juvenile and adult criminals to be found in the literature have been heuristic; the types have been established by fiat based on theoretical deductions, informal observations, or, possibly, divine revelation. Such matters as operational definitions, reliability, and validity have been left to future investigators, if any, to establish.

The present investigator and his colleagues chose to reverse this method and proceed inductively rather than deductively, determining empirically the existence of clusters of MMPI profiles that could form the basis for a typology, testing the reliability of such groups, formulating clear operational definitions, and later determining the characteristics of any such types. The task of integrating the typology with existing theory, or formulating new theoretical explanations, was left to last, on the grounds that a typology that did not meet these preliminary empirical tests would not be worth integrating with criminological or sociological theory.[1]

As noted above, the present investigator had serious reservations about whether the MMPI could constitute a sufficiently broad data base for a comprehensive classification system for criminal offenders. For this reason, the research program was formulated as a series of steps in which progressively more difficult questions would be posed. A negative answer at any point in the sequence would indicate that further research efforts should be abandoned. These questions were:

(1) Do the MMPI profiles of youthful offenders in a federal correctional institution fall into distinct groups or clusters?

(2) Are such groups reliable? That is, does one obtain the same basic groupings in different samples?

(3) Is it possible for a clinician to sort individual MMPI profiles into such groups reliably?

(4) Is it possible to define such groups operationally so that other clinicians, or even a computer, can sort individual MMPI profiles validly?

(5) Assuming that an MMPI-based system can be derived and reliable classification is possible, do such groups differ significantly on non-MMPI variables, e.g., in their life-styles, social history, behavior, dynamics, adjustment to prison, and possibly even recidivism?

(6) If the groups do differ in their behavior, are there clear implications for treatment?

(7) Is such treatment effective? Does each group respond better to the prescribed treatment than to other treatment modes?

(8) Can a system derived on data collected on incarcerated youthful offenders in a federal institution be generalized to offenders in other settings who differ in age, sex, and offense patterns (Megargee, 1977, p. 111)?

DERIVATION OF THE TYPES

The first questions to be answered were whether there were naturally occurring clusters of offenders' MMPI profiles and whether such groups were reliable. These questions were answered in a Master's thesis by James Meyer, Jr. Meyer drew three random samples of 100 profiles each from the MMPIs Megargee had collected at the FCI in 1968 and 1969. Although these protocols, like all our MMPIs, were scored on over 100 scales and indexes, we limited our attention to the 10 standard clinical scales that would be routinely scored in most settings.

Each of these samples was subjected to Veldman's (1967) "hierarchical profile analysis," a multivariate statistical procedure that considers all the salient aspects of an MMPI profile, including elevation, phasicality, and slope, and groups those profiles that are most similar to one another. In the course of this analysis, the error term associated with combining individual profiles into groups increases abruptly if fundamentally dissimilar profiles are being combined. Such an abrupt increase indicates the number of naturally occurring clusters, if any, within the sample. Such an increase was found in each of the three samples at about the same point, indicating that there were about the same number of natural clusters in each sample (Meyer & Megargee, 1972; 1977).

Groups with fewer than five profiles were discarded; Meyer and Megargee clinically inspected the rest and matched them across samples. The first group in the first sample was arbitrarily named Group "A" or "Able." The profiles in this group were plotted, a mean profile was computed, and the Welsh codes were carefully examined. Then Sample Two was surveyed until a group was located that matched the essential characteristics of Group Able. It, too, was studied, and then the profiles in Sample Three were inspected until a group with the same basic characteristics was identified. In similar fashion, the remaining eight groups in Sample I were given arbitrary alphabetical names (Baker, Charlie, Delta, Easy, Foxtrot, George, How, and Item) and were matched with groups in the other two samples. In the process, rules for the identification of each type were written. This answered affirmatively the first two questions, showing that a typological system based on the MMPI could be derived and that the groups established were consistent across samples.

The next question was whether psychologists could sort individual MMPI profiles into such groups reliably. Individual profiles often deviate markedly from average or mean profiles; if psychologists could not classify individual profiles reliably, the system would obviously be worthless. Meyer drew a new sample of 85 profiles, and he and Megargee independently sorted them into groups. They agreed on the classification of 86% of the profiles and could easily resolve their differences on the others. It was concluded that, for these two investigators at least, the system was reliable (Meyer & Megargee, 1972; 1977).

REVISING AND PROGRAMMING
THE CLASSIFICATORY RULES

The next question was whether the operational definitions of the groups, as embodied in the original Meyer-Megargee (1972) rules, were sufficiently precise so that other clinicians, or even a computer, could validly classify individual profiles. When Martin Bohn, Jr. arrived and assumed the role of chief psychologist at the FCI in 1973, he undertook to learn the classificatory system. At the same time, Megargee began to work with Brent Dorhout, a computer programmer, on devising a program that could take over much of the tedious task of profile classification, a project that gained much impetus from the fact that there were over 1,200 research subjects who had taken the MMPI whose profiles were waiting to be classified.

It soon became apparent that considerable refinement and expansion of the initial Meyer-Megargee (1972) rules was necessary. Although the initial set of rules had enabled Meyer and Megargee to sort profiles reliably, they had apparently served as short-hand re-minders of a more comprehensive gestalt of implicit characteristics and conventions. Those who had not participated in the derivation of the groups or studied the profiles of the types as intensively could not apply the rules satisfactorily without a great deal of further coaching and training—an expensive, time-consuming process that the system had been intended to eliminate.

In the months that followed, Megargee would classify a random-ly selected set of MMPI profiles of FCI inmates using the original Meyer and Megargee rules plus his clinical judgment and knowledge of the system. As he classified these profiles, he would "think out loud" about the reasons why a given profile would fit into one type and not another. Dorhout listened, took notes, and then attempted to translate Megargee's comments into rules for a computerized clas-sification program. With this program, a different set of profiles was classified, and Megargee then indicated which profiles the program had classified correctly and which incorrectly, explaining the reasons for his judgment while Dorhout took more notes for a revised pro-gram. Bohn, too, contributed suggestions for new rules based on his experiences in learning the system. Through this tedious trial-and-error process, the rules became more sophisticated and were refined until finally we arrived at our present rules and a computer program embodying them.

Although space does not permit listing the rules for classifying all the groups, their nature and application can be illustrated by re-ferring to the rules for one of the types, Group Charlie. The mean profile for Group Charlie is presented in Figure 1. The rules are as follows:

Set I (1) Top scale $\geq 80\%$ and $\leq 110T$
     (2) Scale $8 \geq 80T$
     (3) Scale $6 \geq 65T$
     (4) Scale 4 or Scale $6 > 70T$

		Points
Set II (1)	Scale $2 > 50T$	(+1)
(2)	Scale $6 > 70T$	(+1)
(3)	Scale 6 one of the top two scales	(+1)
(4)	Scale 8 one of the top two scales	(+1)
(5)	Profile slopes up to the right	(+1)

It can be seen that the rules are divided into two sets. After a profile has been screened for validity, the clinician or the computer program scans the Set I rules for each group sequentially. If a profile fails to meet any of the basic Set I rules, it cannot be classified into the group in question. If the profile does meet the basic rules, the accessory, Set II, rules are examined to determine goodness of fit. For every rule that is met, one or two points are awarded.

Next, the "Point Chart" associated with each group is consulted. For Group Charlie, a profile that earns five points fits the group at the "High" level, one that earns three or four points fits at the "Medium" level, one that earns only one or two points fits at the "Low" level, and one that meets only the Set I rules and none of the accessory rules fits the group at the "Minimum" level.

Some profiles meet the basic (Set I) rules for two or more different groups; in such instances, the profile is classified into the group in which it meets the accessory rules at the highest level. A profile meeting the rules for Group Charlie at the "High" level and

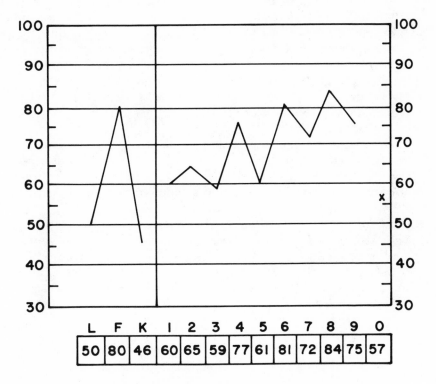

L	F	K	1	2	3	4	5	6	7	8	9	0
50	80	46	60	65	59	77	61	81	72	84	75	57

Figure 1. Mean MMPI Profile for Group Charlie.
Reprinted from *Classifying Criminal Offenders: A New System Based on the MMPI*, by E. I. Megargee, M. J. Bohn, J. Meyer, and F. Sink c. 1979 by permission of the Publishers, Sage Publications, Inc. Beverly Hills.

the rules for Group How at the "Medium" level would be assigned to Charlie.

These rules, as embodied in the computer program, are designed to classify only the clear-cut cases. More difficult decisions are reserved for a clinician familiar with the system and reasonably sophisticated in the use of the MMPI, who can go beyond the rules and consult published guidelines, tables of ranges, and the mean profiles of each group (Megargee & Dorhout, 1977; Megargee et al., 1979).

Mechanical application of the rules results in the classification of about two-thirds of the profiles of criminal offenders. The remaining one-third are about equally divided between profiles that meet the rules for two groups at the same level (ties) and those that fail to meet the basic Set I rules for any group. With the published guidelines and additional data, it is a simple matter to resolve the ties. Many profiles that fail to meet the exact requirements of the Set I rules in every detail nevertheless match the essential configuration of a group and can be classified into it without doing violence to the system. In applied settings in which each inmate must, perforce, be assigned to *some* group, it is more likely that such exceptions will be made and individuals will be classified into the group they most nearly approximate even if the rules are not all met. However, researchers will no doubt prefer to use only clearly classifiable profiles in their studies.

The number of profiles classifiable under the system is, of course, partly determined by the methods used in administering the MMPI and the care that was taken to minimize invalid or random responding. At the FCI, using oral administration for poor readers and with the computer program classifying the easy profiles and the clinician the more difficult ones, it has been found over the years that 90-95% of the profiles can be classified. Investigators who have applied the system in other settings and to other populations have reported that 85-89% of their profiles can be classified (Cassady, 1978; Edinger, 1979; Miller, 1978; Nichols, 1978). (See Table 1.) These data have laid to rest our fears that an MMPI-based system might not be extensive enough to be useful in criminal justice settings. The fact that the largest single group (Item) was the one with an essentially normal MMPI profile also relieved our concern that an MMPI-based system might overemphasize psychopathology.

CHARACTERISTICS OF THE GROUPS

At this stage, all of the first four questions had been answered af-

Table 1. Distribution of Offenders over Types in Three Samples

Groups		Men			Women	
		Federal (Megargee)	State (Nichols)	County (Cassady)	Federal (Sink)	State (Sink)
Able	N	204	54	27	34	50
	%	(16.8)	(14.4)	(16.2)	(17.5)	(14.0)
Baker	N	51	10	9	1	6
	%	(4.2)	(2.7)	(5.4)	(0.5)	(1.7)
Charlie	N	103	30	11	16	44
	%	(8.5)	(8.0)	(6.6)	(8.3)	(12.3)
Delta	N	120	47	20	18	38
	%	(9.9)	(12.5)	(12.0)	(9.3)	(10.6)
Easy	N	84	26	14	6	12
	%	(6.9)	(6.9)	(8.4)	(3.1)	(3.4)
Foxtrot	N	100	25	8	17	14
	%	(8.2)	(6.7)	(4.8)	(8.8)	(3.9)
George	N	85	35	10	15	17
	%	(7.0)	(9.3)	(6.0)	(7.7)	(4.8)
How	N	155	30	13	15	40
	%	(12.8)	(8.0)	(7.8)	(7.7)	(11.2)
Item	N	225	69	29	47	82
	%	(18.5)	(18.4)	(17.4)	(24.2)	(22.9)
Jupiter	N	37	4	8	2	5
	%	(3.0)	(1.1)	(4.8)	(1.0)	(1.4)
Unclassified	N	50	45	10	23	49
	%	(4.1)	(12.0)	(6.0)	(11.8)	(13.7)
Total		1,214	375	167	194	357

Source: Reprinted from *Classifying Criminal Offenders: A New System Based on the MMPI*, by E. I. Megargee, M. J. Bohn, J. Meyer, and F. Sink, c. 1979 by permission of the Publishers, Sage Publications, Inc. Beverly Hills.

firmatively. The value of the system, however, would rest heavily on the answer to Question Five, "Assuming an MMPI-based system can be derived and reliable classification is possible, do such groups differ significantly on non-MMPI variables?" If this question was not answered affirmatively, the five years of work that had gone into establishing the existence and reliability of the groups and formulating the operational definitions would prove to be nothing more than a sterile academic exercise.

An indication that such differences would be obtained had been provided by James Meyer in his dissertation research. Comparing 20 subjects from five of the groups on 20 social and demographic variables, Meyer had found significant differences on 16 of the 20 measures (Meyer, 1974).

To answer this question definitively, Megargee and Bohn (1977) used the data collected as part of the extensive longitudinal project and compared all ten groups. Of the 1,345 men who entered the FCI during the two-year intake period, 1,214 had taken the MMPI; 204 (16.8%) were classified into Group Able, 51 (4.2%) in Baker, 103 (8.5%) in Charlie, 120 (9.9%) in Delta, 84 (6.9%) in Easy, 100 (8.2%) in Foxtrot, 85 (7.0%) in George, 155 (12.8%) in How, 225 (18.5%) in Item, and 37 (3.0%) in Jupiter, a new group identified in the course of classifying the cohort. Fifty profiles (4.1%) were not classifiable into any group.

Background information included demographic data such as race, marital status, and offense categories, and academic and intellectual data including the Beta, the GATB, the Stanford Achievement Test, and reports of grade level. The presentence investigation report and a specially structured hour-long intake interview provided a great deal of developmental, familial, and social data. A number of quantitative scales based on these instruments were constructed, assessing such areas as family cohesiveness and child-rearing practices, social deviance of the various members of the nuclear family, and the socioeconomic status of the parents as well as the individual offender. Other scales focused on educational, vocational, and military achievement and activities as well as overall achievement motivation. Yet another set of scales focused on interpersonal relations, including problems of getting along with peers, race relations, and authority conflicts. Maladjustment and deviance was another focal point, and scales were constructed to assess these patterns in childhood, adolescence, and adulthood, and to measure marital instability, social marginality, and physical health. Naturally, the criminal career was of considerable interest and the prior criminal records as a juvenile and adult were scaled, as were propensities to violence, drug usage, and adjustment in previous incarcerations. Analyses of variance followed by Duncan Multiple Range Tests were used to compare the groups on all these measures.

In addition to the presentence investigation and the structured intake interview, we had available standardized psychological reports in the form of Q-sorts conducted by the psychologists who had administered the intake interview. We also had a variety of other personality tests and attitude scales including the California Psychological Inventory, Itkin's scales assessing attitudes toward mother and father, Spielberger et al.'s trait and state anxiety scales, Quay and Peterson's scales for neurotic, subcultural, and psychopathic delinquency, and Ballard et al.'s scale of interpersonal maturity level.

From the beginning of the study until July 1974, information was systematically collected on the institutional adjustment and achievement of every member of the research cohort. These data included such measures as disciplinary infractions, time spent in the cell house, assaultive behavior, reports to sick call, and monthly grades in all academic and vocational courses. In addition, every dormitory officer filled out scales assessing each subject's interpersonal adjustment and behavior patterns at 90-day intervals. These ratings assessed such areas as response to supervision, authority conflicts, interpersonal relations, maturity, self-control, aggressiveness, and dependability. Work crew supervisors filled out similar ratings in such areas as ability to learn, willingness to work with others, dependability, response to and need for supervision, quantity and quality of work, and overall job performance. The teachers of the academic and vocational courses supplied monthly assessments of goal motivation, response to supervision, emotional stability, and overall achievement.

At the time of classification and throughout the period of incarceration, no staff members were aware of any offender's MMPI type. (In fact, because of the time required to revise the classificatory rules and develop the computer program, none of the inmates' MMPIs were even typed until a year after all the ratings had been collected.)

In July 1976, a comprehensive study of recidivism was undertaken. The computerized F.B.I. fingerprint arrest records maintained by the National Crime Information Center were used to determine the post-release criminal activity of each offender. A total of 1,011 subjects satisfied the basic criteria of having been released to the community at least 18 months before the cut-off date and having sufficient data in the NCIC records to permit a determination of recidivism (Megargee, 1978). For each inmate, the number of subsequent arrests, convictions, and incarcerations was determined, as well as an overall rating of recidivism, which considered the amount of time before a subsequent offense and the seriousness of new infractions. The total number of lines of NCIC printout constituted a fifth measure of recidivism.

A detailed description of the results of this study is, obviously, far beyond the scope of this chapter. Suffice to say that the 10 groups were compared on 116 different variables, ranging from disciplinary practices and adjustment in early childhood to eventual recidivism several years after the MMPI was administered. Of the 116 statistical comparisons performed, 97 were statistically significant, and most of the probability values were extremely low. Moreover, the data were internally consistent; information from all the different data sources—case histories, interviews, psychologists' evaluations, psychological tests, institutional adjustment measures, correctional and educational staff ratings, and even eventual recidivism—converged providing a consistent picture of each of the 10 groups. (For a complete report see Megargee et al., 1979.)

IMPLICATIONS FOR TREATMENT

The study outlined above provided an unequivocal, affirmative answer to Question Five. The 10 groups defined solely on the basis of their MMPI profile characteristics clearly differed not only in their test-taking behavior but in many other aspects of their behavior and functioning as well. These findings led directly to Question Six, "If the groups do differ in their behavior, are there clear implications for treatment?"

To answer this question, Megargee and Bohn independently studied the patterns of significant differences for each of the 10 individual groups and then collaborated in characterizing each group's typical patterns of behavior and functioning. Again, these detailed descriptions are beyond the scope of this chapter and may be found elsewhere (Megargee & Bohn, 1977; Megargee et al., 1979).

Although detailed descriptions of the 10 groups based on empirical data are now available, we have decided not to substitute descriptive names for the alphabetic designations originally assigned each group. In the beginning, we resisted labels such as "psychopathic" or "subcultural" because there were insufficient data to support such designations. This decision proved wise, later research showing that some of the suggested labels were inaccurate.

Our present decision to retain the neutral alphabetic designations instead of using more convenient short-hand labels stems in large measure from the experience of the developers and early users of the MMPI who learned the pitfalls associated with scale names such as "schizophrenia" and "psychasthenia." Over the years, it proved wiser to refer to MMPI scales by number and allow the MMPI user to learn through experience and the literature exactly what constructs each scale assessed.

By retaining the admittedly frustrating phonetic names of our criminal types, we hope that users of the system will, perforce, have to study the empirical data, free of expectations or bias, and learn for themselves the unique constellation of characteristics associated with each group. Moreover, as additional data accumulate, it will be easier for our clinical understanding of groups Able, Baker, Charlie, and the rest to grow and develop than it would be had labels such as "neurotic" or "professional criminal," with all their surplus meaning, been affixed.

Once the unique characteristics of each group had been delineated, Bohn took the lead and worked with Megargee using these data to formulate recommendations for management and treatment, focusing on such issues as the most appropriate setting (institutional or community), the optimal change agent, and the treatment program most likely to be effective with individuals from each group. These recommendations were based not only on the statistical comparisons of the 10 types, but also on Bohn's continuing clinical interactions with offenders of each type at the FCI, Tallahassee, where the inmates are now classified into MMPI types as a matter of course. These recommendations can be found in the complete report of the research to date (Megargee et al., 1979).

EFFECTIVENESS OF MANAGEMENT AND
TREATMENT RECOMMENDATIONS

The seventh question asked whether the recommendations regarding management and treatment were effective. Many years of research using experimental procedures and randomly selected groups of offenders will be required to answer this question definitively. Indeed, given the constraints on experimentation and treatment in correctional settings, it is questionable when it will be possible to resolve this issue rigorously.

Bohn (1978; 1979) recently evaluated the application of the system to the management of criminal offenders. In an effort to reduce violence at the FCI, Tallahassee, by separating those inmates most likely to prey upon their fellows from those inmates most likely to be exploited, Bohn (1978) classified the population into three broad groups, those most likely to be predatory, those most likely to be preyed upon, and average inmates who were at neither extreme. Each of the two extreme groups comprised about 15% of the inmate population, and the middle group made up the remaining 70%.

Three open dormitories were used in the experiment. All the possibly predatory inmates were assigned to one dormitory and all those deemed most likely to be victimized to another. The average inmates filled out the remaining spaces in these two dorms and filled up a third.

The classification of the initial population was based primarily on the Quay Correctional Adjustment Check List (CACL) and secondarily on the MMPI types. Bohn found that the CACL was of limited usefulness in assigning newly arrived inmates because the officers who were to make the behavioral ratings had insufficient time to make the necessary observations. Hence, after the initial classification, the MMPI-based typology became the primary classification instrument.

Bohn (1978) compared the number of incident reports and the rate of institutional violence during the first three quarters (nine months) under the new system with the same period for the preceding year when random assignments had been made. Since no other important changes had been made in the FCI's program or personnel during that period, it seemed reasonable to attribute any differences to the classification program

The primary goal of the classification and reassignment had been to reduce violence and to isolate the more troublesome inmates, so that they would not interfere with the progress of the general population. Bohn reported that the overall number of assaults decreased from 22 to 13, a 46% reduction, reversing a trend toward increasing violence before the change. Most interesting, all of the assaults took place in the two dormitories housing the two extreme groups, 69% in the group housing those thought most likely to be aggressors, and 31% in the unit housing those thought most likely to be victims. The difference in the distribution of the assaults among the three dormitories before and after the transition was highly significant ($\chi^2 = 10.96$, df = 2, $p < .001$). Commenting on these results, Bohn (1978, p. 33) concluded, "It seems evident that the absolute level of violence within the institution was lessened after the introduction of the classification system and assignments to living units. As expressed by one administrator, a serious assault has become a rare event rather than an expected occurrence in the institution."

Bohn went on to observe, "the remarkable decrease in assaults noted in the non-extreme unit was actually accomplished with a lessened amount of staff coverage. This reduction in need for staff coverage in the unit composed of middle group inmates permitted extra coverage in the other units housing the inmates predicted to need more support and security" (1978, p. 35).

More recently, Bohn (1979) examined the incidence of violence and other forms of maladaptive behavior for the second year after

the classification system had been introduced, by which time virtually all the inmates in the institution had been assigned to dormitories primarily on the basis of their MMPI type. He found that the
gains made in the first year had been maintained; in fact one quarter
had passed without a single assault taking place in the entire institution, an event unprecedented in the history of the FCI.

Fowler (1979) has reported on the use of the MMPI-based
typology in conjunction with computerized MMPI interpretations in
providing data for correctional decision-making in Mississippi. (See
Chapter 10.) Although the initial reports on its usefulness are promising, and, in conjunction with Bohn's studies, suggest that the
system can provide useful information in applied correctional settings, much more research on its usefulness and validity in guiding
differential management and treatment decisions needs to be done.
Well-controlled, rigorous studies of inmate adjustment and change as
a function of the interaction of MMPI type, program, setting, and
change agent need to be carried out. Nevertheless, the data thus far
indicate that the system does have the potential to make a positive
contribution to decisions regarding differential management and
treatment.

GENERALIZABILITY OF THE TYPOLOGY

Most of the research thus far described took place in a single setting, the Federal Correctional Institution at Tallahassee, Florida. The
eighth question posed at the beginning of our research was whether a
classification system based on youthful male offenders in a federal
institution could be successfully generalized to other populations in
other settings.

County jails are reserved for misdemeanants, and state prisons
contain a much larger proportion of felons convicted of crimes
against persons such as assault, homicide, and rape, whereas the FCI
was composed almost wholly of property offenders. State and local
institutions also house a much greater age range than the 18- to 27-
year-old FCI population. The applicability of the typology in these
settings had to be determined, as did its usefulness among female
offenders of all ages in all settings.

Two studies have been completed thus far (Edinger, 1979;
Miller, 1978) and preliminary data have been provided from two
others that are currently in progress (Cassady, 1978; Nichols, 1978).
Edinger applied the system to 2,063 male inmates at the Federal
Correctional Institution at Petersburgh, Virginia, and to 1,455 Ala-

bama State offenders, including 1,291 men and 164 women whose MMPIs had been obtained by Raymond Fowler in conjunction with Fowler's ongoing classification projects in Alabama and Mississippi. Miller (now Sink) reported on the applicability of the typology to 194 women confined at the Federal Correctional Institution at Alderson, West Virginia, and 357 women confined at the Florida Correctional Institution at Lowell, Florida.

Preliminary results of ongoing investigations have also been generously supplied by two other researchers. Wyatt Nichols, an associate of Fowler's, has applied the system to 375 male Mississippi State Offenders and John Cassady has employed it in the classification of 167 male inmates sentenced to terms of confinement at the Orange County (Florida) jail.

None of these investigations employed the Megargee-Dorhout computer program, which only recently became available in sufficiently general form to be usable on other computers. Fowler and Edinger wrote their own programs, Fowler corresponding extensively with Megargee and Edinger working independently. Edinger relied exclusively on his program, Nichols used Fowler's program followed by clinical inspection, and Cassady and Miller classified their protocols clinically.

Despite the diverse settings—including local, state, and federal institutions—the changes in racial composition—ranging from 33% to 81% whites—the wide span of ages represented—ranging from 15 to 85 years—as well as the different ways of applying the classificatory rules, the results of these studies have been remarkably similar. As shown in Table 1, in every sample studied thus far, 85 to 89% of the profiles have been classifiable. Moreover, in every study all 10 types were represented. From these data, it appears very likely that the MMPI-based typological system may prove to be applicable to most incarcerated offenders in American penal institutions, although much more extensive research is obviously needed to adequately establish the system's generalizability. With the publication of extended guidelines (Megargee et al., 1979) and the availability of the Megargee-Dorhout computer program for use on other computers, such research will be easier to perform and to interpret in the future.

DIRECTIONS FOR FURTHER RESEARCH

All the questions posed at the beginning of our research program in 1970 have now been answered affirmatively in some degree. It appears that an MMPI-based classification system of criminal offenders is viable and that it has the potential to supply correctional administrators with information that should be useful in correctional decision-making.

So far, the system meets all the criteria for a useful classification system outlined at the beginning of this chapter. The studies showing that over 85% of the offenders in a wide range of settings can be classified indicate that the typology is sufficiently complete so that most clients can be assigned to a type. The system has clear operational definitions and Sink's studies have shown high inter-rater reliability. Empirical studies have established the validity of the system, and the fact that MMPI profiles are known to change as a function of changes in individuals suggests that it should be dynamic, although this aspect of the typology remains to be investigated. The different types have clear implications for differential management and treatment. And, finally, because it is based on the MMPI and uses computer technology, the typology permits large numbers of offenders to be rapidly classified with minimal expense and personnel.[2]

Much remains to be done. Studies of the characteristics of the 10 types need to be undertaken in other settings and populations. Preliminary results have been promising. Independent investigations in other populations have found the types to differ with respect to age (Edinger, 1979), educational level (Cassady, 1978; Nichols, 1978; Sink, 1978), offense patterns (Edinger, 1979; Nichols, 1978), criminal history (Sink, 1978), and institutional adjustment (Edinger, 1979; Edinger & Auerbach, in press; Fowler, 1979). Sink (1979) recently reported that the demographic characteristics of women in the various types approximated the characteristics of the men studied by Megargee and Bohn (1977). Although more research is required, Sink's (1979) investigation indicated the classification system can be extended to women. More systematic and extensive research is needed to determine whether the characteristics of offenders in other settings classified into the various groups are the same as those found for the members of that group studied at the Tallahassee FCI. Is a 50-year-old "Charlie" in a state institution the same as a 20-year-old one in a federal facility? Do the same management and treatment implications apply? These questions must be answered if the system is to be generalized or applied to other settings and groups.

The effectiveness of the treatment and management implications must be tested empirically. Although the applications of the system thus far have been encouraging (Bohn, 1978, 1979; Fowler, 1979), much more extensive and rigorous research needs to be performed in this area.

Changes in individuals' typological designations over time have yet to be examined. Preliminary comparisons of the intake and exit MMPIs in the FCI research cohort indicate that changes do take place, but no studies have yet investigated the nature or extent of these changes or whether they are associated with observable changes in behavior or attitudes.

Most of the studies outlined above continue the applied research tradition that has characterized this program from the outset. The time has come to begin theoretical studies. The first step is cross-classification research, attempting to determine the correspondence of our MMPI-based types with other typologies of criminal offenders. Bohn is currently planning a study of the relationship of the MMPI types and the adult types delineated by Quay; Joyce Carbonell is undertaking a similar investigation of the typology's convergence with Warren's Interpersonal Maturity Level system.

Several of the types of criminal offenders derived in the present research program resemble MMPI code types found in the literature on psychiatric patients and normals (Gilberstadt & Duker, 1965; Marks et al., 1974). There are some noteworthy differences in the behavioral descriptions and case histories, however. Some interesting etiological inferences could well be derived from the systematic comparison of individuals with similar MMPI profile configurations who are found in psychiatric as opposed to criminal justice settings.

In addition to cross-classification research, laboratory studies of the differences and similarities among the types need to be undertaken. It is hoped that the data collected as part of the autonomic screening conducted by Jack Hokanson as part of the FCI research project might prove enlightening. Other laboratory studies should test the differences among the types with respect to impulsivity, ability to delay gratification, need for sensory stimulation, cognitive and perceptual styles, and other variables that have been found to have etiological significance in criminal justice settings. Such research is needed if we are to progress beyond the questions of *how* the types differ, and begin to answer the more important issue of *why* they differ from one another and from the general population. With answers to the questions "Why?," we should be able to formulate treatment plans more rationally, and eventually even undertake research aimed at primary prevention.

NOTES

1. The conceptual chasm between this inductive empirical approach and the more common deductive, heuristic technique was illustrated at a meeting of a national criminological society at which Megargee presented a preliminary report of this research. One member of the audience, seeking some epithet that would adequately express his outrage, finally denounced the enterprise as "pure empiricism." So naive was the investigator that he felt complimented rather than insulted.

2. Moorhead (1979) recently investigated whether a short form of the MMPI, the MMPI-168, would provide the same typological designations as the standard long form. She found agreement in less than half of the cases, despite the use of locally derived conversion equations. Moreover, the disagreements were often ones that were rated as being clinically "serious," i.e., resulting in substantially different treatment and management prescriptions. She concluded that MMPI short forms should not be used as a basis for classification in the Megargee system.

REFERENCES

Bohn, M. J., Jr. , *Classification of offenders in an institution for young adults.* Paper presented at the 19th International Congress of Applied Psychology, Munich, Germany, July 31, 1978.

Bohn, M. J., Jr. *New data on the application of the MMPI-based classification system in a correctional institution.* Paper presented at the 3rd annual meeting of the International Differential Treatment Association, Rennselaerville, N.Y., April, 1979.

Butcher, J. N., & Pancheri, P. *A handbook of cross-national MMPI research.* Minneapolis: University of Minnesota Press, 1976.

Cassady, J. Personal communication, May, 1978.

Dahlstrom, W., Welsh, G., & Dahlstrom, L. *An MMPI handbook.* Vol. I. Minneapolis: University of Minnesota Press, 1972.

Edinger, J. D. Cross-validation of the Megargee et al. MMPI typology for prisoners. *Journal of Consulting and Clinical Psychology*, 1979, 47, 234-42.

Edinger, J. D., & Auerbach, S. M. Development and validation of a multidimensional-multivariate model for accounting for infractionary behavior in a correctional setting. *Journal of Personality and Social Psychology*, in press.

Fowler, R. *Use of a computerized MMPI for correctional decisions.* Paper presented at the MMPI Symposium, Tampa, Fla., April, 1979.

Gilberstadt, H., & Duker, J. *A handbook for clinical and actuarial MMPI interpretation.* Philadelphia: W. B. Saunders, 1965.

Gottfredson, M. R., Hindelang, M. J., & Parisi, N. *Sourcebook of criminal justice statistics – 1977.* Washington, D. C.: U. S. Department of Justice, 1978.

Hathaway, S. R., & Monachesi, E. D. *Analyzing and predicting juvenile delinquency with the MMPI.* Minneapolis: University of Minnesota Press, 1953.

Marks, P. A., Seeman, W., & Haller D. *The actuarial use of the MMPI with adolescents and adults.* Baltimore: Williams and Wilkins, 1974.

Megargee, E. I. Undercontrolled and overcontrolled personality types in extreme antisocial aggression. *Psychological Monographs*, 1966, 80 (3, Whole No. 611).

Megargee, E. I. Recent research on overcontrolled personality patterns among violent offenders. *Sociological Symposium*, 1973, No. 9, 37-50.

Megargee, E. I. A new classification system for criminal offenders, I: The need for a new classification system. *Criminal Justice and Behavior*, 1977, 4, 107-14.

Megargee, E. I. *A comprehensive investigation of recidivism*. Final report on subcontract 75-A5-33-E401 submitted to the Florida Bureau of Criminal Justice Planning and Assistance (LEAA). Tallahassee, Fla., April, 1978.

Megargee, E. I., & Bohn, M. J., Jr. A new classification system for criminal offenders, IV: Empirically determined characteristics of the ten types. *Criminal Justice and Behavior*, 1977, 4, 149-210.

Megargee, E. I., & Bohn, M. J., Jr. with Meyer, J. E. Jr. & Sink F. *Classifying criminal offenders: A new system based on the MMPI*. Beverly Hills, Calif.: Sage Publishing, 1979.

Megargee, E. I., Cook, P. E., & Mendelsohn, G. A. Development and validation of an MMPI scale of assaultiveness in overcontrolled individuals. *Journal of Abnormal Psychology*, 1967, 72, 519-58.

Megargee, E. I., & Dorhout, B. A new classification system for criminal offenders, III: Revision and refinement of the classificatory rules. *Criminal Justice and Behavior*, 1977, 4, 125-48.

Meyer, J., Jr. Empirical correlates of five Meyer-Megargee types of youthful offenders. *FCI Research Reports*, 1974, 6(1), 1-43. Federal Correctional Institution, Tallahassee, Fla., 32303.

Meyer, J., Jr., & Megargee, E. I. Development of an MMPI-based typology of youthful offenders. *FCI Research Reports*, 1972, 4(2), 1-21. Federal Correctional Institution, Tallahassee, Fla., 32303.

Meyer, J., Jr., & Megargee, E. I. A new classification system for criminal offenders, II: Initial development of the system. *Criminal Justice and Behavior*, 1977, 4, 115-24.

Miller, F. S. *The applicability of the Megargee MMPI-based offender typology to female offenders*. Unpublished Master's thesis, Florida State University, 1978.

Moorhead, K. *Application of the MMPI-168 to the Megargee typology system*. Paper presented at the 3rd annual meeting of the International Differential Treatment Association, Rennselaerville, N. Y., April, 1979.

National Advisory Commission on Criminal Justice Standards and Goals. *Report on corrections*. Washington, D. C.: Law Enforcement Assistance Administration, U. S. Department of Justice, 1973.

Nichols, W. Personal communication, 1978.

Sink, F. *New developments in the classification of female offenders*. Paper presented at the 3rd annual meeting of the International Differential Treatment Association, Rennselaerville, N. Y., April, 1979.

Veldman, D. J. *Fortran programming for the behavioral sciences*. New York: Holt, Rinehart & Winston, 1967.

Wirt, R. D., & Briggs, P. F. Personality and environmental factors in the development of delinquency. *Psychological Monographs*, 1959, 73 (Whole No. 485).

Use of the Computerized MMPI in Correctional Decisions

Raymond D. Fowler

The use of the MMPI in correctional settings has been reviewed extensively by Dahlstrom and Welsh (1960) Dahlstrom, Welsh, and Dahlstrom (1975), and Haven (1970). Haven noted that the MMPI has been used extensively in prisons for diagnosis, program planning, and research purposes. Dahlstrom, Welsh, and Dahlstrom (1975) include 389 references to the MMPI in criminal-justice settings, none of which refers to the computerized MMPI. The material that follows deals exclusively with the use of the computerized MMPI with law offenders.

The early 1960s saw the development of several systems for computerized MMPI interpretation. The system developed by Fowler was designed to assess mental-health patients and to provide a report similar in content and style to those written by experienced clinicians (Fowler, 1969). In 1966, the Roche Psychiatric Service Institute (RPSI) was established by Roche Laboratories to make reports based on the Fowler system nationally available. RPSI has subsequently processed well over a million reports from a variety of mental-health facilities. The interpretation system has been translated into several languages and used in a number of countries outside the United States (Fowler, 1971).

Several studies demonstrated the validity of reports generated by the Fowler system. In these studies psychiatrists and psychologists rated the reports on patients from a variety of clinical settings. In one study (Webb, Miller, & Fowler, 1969), 697 psychiatrists rated one report each on a 16-item, 5-point rating scale. The results indicated that the reports gave valid overall descriptions of the patient (87%), accurately represented the patient's interpersonal relations (78%), and correctly predicted the patient's response to treatment (75%). In comparing the computerized reports with most non-computerized reports they had seen, the judges rated 38% of the reports equal, 27% better, and 13% much better. Judges agreed with the reports 70%-85% of the time, a remarkable contrast with Tallent's (1963) finding that mental-health workers were often quite critical of traditional psychological reports, and that the reports often were not highly regarded by the users for whom they were prepared. The results of several other studies with different rater groups were substantially equivalent (Webb, Miller, & Fowler, 1970; Webb, 1970).

The Fowler MMPI interpretation system is currently being used by the Roche Psychiatric Service Institute in the United States and by the Hans Hüber Psychodiagnostic Service in Europe to provide services to health and mental-health facilities. The Psychological Assessment Services (PAS) was organized in 1971 to provide reports based on the Fowler system for facilities that were not primarily health-related. The original system has been modified for use with a number of populations, including industrial employees, college students (Fowler, 1968), and law offenders (Fowler, 1972).

The law-offender version of the system was developed for use in jails, juvenile facilities, probation and parole departments, and as a part of presentence investigations. Development of the system was prompted by a study (Fowler, 1972) in which RPSI reports on prisoners in a midwestern state prison were rated for accuracy by the psychology staff. The results of the rating-scale study compared favorably with previous studies with psychiatric/mental-health populations, but suggested that some modifications of the statements were necessary. The statement library was rewritten, in collaboration with experienced correctional psychologists, with particular emphasis on management and treatment issues. A follow-up rating-scale study resulted in markedly higher ratings.

The psychological Assessment Service (PAS) computer print-out (Figures 1-5) consists of several sections.

(a) *The Narrative Report* (Figure 1)

The narrative report, one to two pages long, is a compilation of the paragraphs selected by the computer on the basis of the decision rules. It contains statements about the validity of the test, predicted behavior of the subject, and descriptions of current behavior, symptoms, and psychological functioning.

NUMBER: 77813   AGENCY: 1000
AGE: 31   MALE   SEPTEMBER 29, 1977

THE TEST RESULTS OF THIS PERSON APPEAR TO BE VALID. HE SEEMS TO
HAVE MADE AN EFFORT TO ANSWER THE ITEMS TRUTHFULLY AND TO FOLLOW THE
INSTRUCTIONS ACCURATELY. TO SOME EXTENT, THIS MAY BE REGARDED AS A
FAVORABLE PROGNOSTIC SIGN SINCE IT INDICATES THAT HE IS CAPABLE OF
FOLLOWING INSTRUCTIONS AND ABLE TO RESPOND RELEVANTLY AND TRUTHFULLY TO
PERSONAL INQUIRY.

THIS PERSON TENDS TO BE ACTIVE AND IMPULSIVE. HE SEEKS EXCITEMENT
AND AROUSAL AND IS CHARACTERIZED BY HIGH ENERGY LEVEL. HE MAY EXPEND
GREAT EFFORT TO ACCOMPLISH HIS OWN DESIRES, BUT HE FINDS IT DIFFICULT TO
STICK TO DUTIES IMPOSED BY OTHERS. HE MAY BE SOCIABLE AND OUTGOING, BUT
HIS POOR JUDGMENT AND LACK OF CONSIDERATION TEND TO ALIENATE OTHERS.
POOR WORK ADJUSTMENT AND EXCESSIVE DRINKING ARE LIKELY. AMONG
ADOLESCENTS AND VARIOUS LOW SOCIOECONOMIC GROUPS, THIS PATTERN OCCURS
FAIRLY FREQUENTLY AND MAY HAVE LESS SERIOUS IMPLICATIONS. HOWEVER, SOME
IMPULSIVENESS MAY BE ANTICIPATED. THIS IS A PATTERN WHICH OCCURS QUITE
FREQUENTLY AMONG PEOPLE WHOSE IMPULSIVENESS AND LACK OF INTERNALIZED
RESTRAINTS CAUSE THEM TO COME INTO CONFLICT WITH THE LAW. CONTROLS WHICH
ARE FIRM AND WELL DEFINED, ESPECIALLY WHEN ACCOMPANIED BY IMMEDIATE
RECOGNITION AND REWARD OF APPROPRIATE BEHAVIOR, CAN BE HIGHLY EFFECTIVE
IN BUILDING THE ABILITY TO ASSUME RESPONSIBILITY AND TO TOLERATE DELAY OF
GRATIFICATION. HE NEEDS HELP IN DEVELOPING SOCIAL AND VOCATIONAL
COMPETENCY.

HE UTILIZES REPRESSION AND DENIAL IN RESPONSE TO EMOTIONAL PROBLEMS.
HE MAY RESPOND TO SUGGESTION AND REASSURANCE, BUT HE PROBABLY WILL RESIST
A PSYCHOLOGICAL EXPLANATION OF HIS DIFFICULTIES. IN PERIODS OF PROLONGED
EMOTIONAL STRESS SUCH AS LEGAL PROCEEDINGS OR INITIAL INCARCERATION, HE
MAY DEVELOP ANXIETY ATTACKS AND FUNCTIONAL COMPLAINTS.

THERE ARE SOME UNUSUAL QUALITIES IN THIS PERSON'S THINKING WHICH MAY
REPRESENT AN ORIGINAL OR INVENTIVE ORIENTATION OR PERHAPS SOME SCHIZOID
TENDENCIES. FURTHER INFORMATION WOULD BE REQUIRED TO MAKE THIS
DETERMINATION.

NOTE: THE MMPI CAN BE USED AS AN OBJECTIVE AID IN PLANNING
REHABILITATION AND CUSTODY PROGRAMS. HOWEVER, IT SHOULD NOT BE USED AS
THE SOLE BASIS FOR DECISIONS, AND RECOMMENDATIONS BASED ON THE TEST
INFORMATION SHOULD BE SUPPORTED BY OTHER INDICES. THIS REPORT SHOULD BE
REGARDED AS CONFIDENTIAL, AND ONLY PERSONS WITH APPROPRIATE
PROFESSIONAL QUALIFICATIONS SHOULD HAVE ACCESS TO IT.

Figure 1. Narrative report.

(b) *The Critical Item List* (Figure 2)
The critical item list is a subset of 55 MMPI items that sometimes suggest special problems that should be directly investigated by the clinician. Only those items answered in the deviant direction are printed. The items are grouped into content

SCALE SCORES FOR MMPI

NUMBER: 77813   AGENCY: 1000
AGE: 31   MALE   SEPTEMBER 29, 1977

SCALE	?	L	F	K	HS	D	HY	PD	MF	PA	PT	SC	MA	SI
RAW	0	2	7	17	13	21	27	33	32	12	27	30	28	31
K-C					13			33			27	30	28	
T-C	OK	44	60	59	54	60	69	83	73	62	58	65	78	56

SCALE	A	R	ES	LB	CA	DY	DO	RE	PR	ST	CN	AT	SO-R	MT
RAW	11	23	46	12	10	21	19	16	15	25	31	18	29	11
T-C	49	65	53	61	51	52	62	40	56	67	65	57	36	58

SCALE	SOC	DEP	FEM	MOR	REL	AUT	PSY	ORG	FAM	HOS	PHO	HYP	HEA
RAW	10	7	14	5	4	15	16	5	5	6	8	17	5
T-C	53	50	64	44	42	64	64	49	56	43	56	62	50

WELSH CODE: *4 95´3862-701/:=

CRITICAL ITEMS (EXTENDED LIST)

THESE MMPI TEST ITEMS, WHICH WERE ANSWERED IN THE DIRECTION INDICATED,
MAY REQUIRE FURTHER INVESTIGATION BY THE CLINICIAN. THE CLINICIAN IS
CAUTIONED, HOWEVER, AGAINST OVERINTERPRETATION OF ISOLATED RESPONSES.

347   I HAVE NO ENEMIES WHO REALLY WISH TO HARM ME. (FALSE)

33   I HAVE HAD VERY PECULIAR AND STRANGE EXPERIENCES. (TRUE)

302   I HAVE NEVER BEEN IN TROUBLE BECAUSE OF MY SEX BEHAVIOR. (FALSE)
133   I HAVE NEVER INDULGED IN ANY UNUSUAL SEX PRACTICES. (FALSE)

156   I HAVE HAD PERIODS IN WHICH I CARRIED ON ACTIVITIES WITHOUT KNOWING
      LATER WHAT I HAD BEEN DOING. (TRUE)
215   I HAVE USED ALCOHOL EXCESSIVELY. (TRUE)

152   MOST NIGHTS I GO TO SLEEP WITHOUT THOUGHTS OR IDEAS BOTHERING ME.
      (FALSE)

Figure 2. Critical item list.

categories: suspicion and ideas of reference; unusual thoughts
and ideas; depression, guilt, and self-destructive feelings; health
and bodily concerns; sexual concerns and problems; alcohol
and drug use.

(c) *The Content Scale Statements* (Figure 3)
The content scales (Wiggins, 1969) are made up of items that
are clearly and obviously related to the characteristic being
measured. The content-scale statements are brief paragraphs
based on the subject's content-scale scores. These statements

CONTENT SCALES

THE FOLLOWING STATEMENTS ARE BASED UPON AN ANALYSIS OF THE CONTENT
OF THE SUBJECT'S RESPONSES TO THE MMPI ITEMS. THE CONTENT SCALES
MAY BE REGARDED AS A MEASURE OF HOW THE SUBJECT VIEWS HIMSELF OR
WISHES TO PRESENT HIMSELF IN THESE AREAS, AND THUS MAY DIFFER FROM THE
DESCRIPTIONS FOUND IN THE NARRATIVE REPORT OP FROM THE CLINICAL
IMPRESSION.

ABOVE EACH STATEMENT IS AN INDICATION OF WHETHER THE SUBJECT'S
PROFESSED TENDENCY TOWARD THE CHARACTERISTICS DESCRIBED IS HIGH,
(T SCORE 70 OR HIGHER), MODERATE, (60-69), OR LOW (40 OR LOWER).
SCALE SCORES BETWEEN 40 AND 60 ARE NOTED AS AVERAGE.

1. DEPRESSION (DEP)   AVERAGE   T=   50

2. POOR MORALE (MOR)   AVERAGE   T=   44

3. PSYCHOTICISM (PSY)   MODERATE   T=   64

HE ADMITS TO SOME SYMPTOMS WHICH ARE CHARACTERISTIC OF PSYCHOTIC
THINKING. HE MAY HAVE FEELINGS OF UNREALITY, DELUSIONARY THOUGHT, AND
STRANGE AND PUZZLING EXPERIENCES SUCH AS SEEING AND HEARING THINGS
THAT OTHERS DO NOT.

4. PHOBIAS (PHO)   AVERAGE   T=   56

5. ORGANIC SYMPTOMS (ORG)   AVERAGE   T=   49

6. AUTHORITY CONFLICT (AUT)   MODERATE   T=   64

HE IS CYNICAL AND DISTRUSTFUL OF PEOPLE IN AUTHORITY. HE SEES
OTHER PEOPLE AS HYPOCRITICAL AND MOTIVATED PRIMARILY BY PERSONAL GAIN,
EVEN IF UNFAIRLY OBTAINED. HE EXPECTS OTHERS TO TRY TO GET THE BEST
OF HIM AND FEELS JUSTIFIED IN TRYING TO PROTECT HIMSELF BY WHATEVER
MEANS ARE AVAILABLE.

7. MANIFEST HOSTILITY (HOS)   AVERAGE   T=   43

8. FAMILY PROBLEMS (FAM)   AVERAGE   T=   56

9. HYPOMANIA (HYP)   MODERATE   T=   62

HE IS AN ENERGETIC ENTHUSIASTIC PERSON WITH BROAD INTERESTS AND A
TENDENCY TO BECOME INVOLVED IN A VARIETY OF ACTIVITIES. HE IS
RESTLESS, ENJOYS CHANGE, AND HAS LITTLE TOLERANCE FOR MONOTONY. HE
MAKES UP HIS MIND FAST, CHANGES IT FREQUENTLY, GENERALLY MAINTAINS A
HIGH LEVEL OF ACTIVITY, SOMETIMES TO THE POINT OF EXHAUSTION.

10. SOCIAL MALADJUSTMENT (SOC)   AVERAGE   T=   53

Figure 3. Content scale statements.

are often more closely related to the patient's self-perceptions
than are the statements in the narrative report.

(d) *The Profile* (Figure 4)
The MMPI scale scores are presented in graphic form, permitting visual inspection of the scale patterns.

(e) *The Technical Section* (Figure 5)
A final page is printed to facilitate the use of the data for re-

```
NUMBER:    77813              MMPI  PROFILE              AGENCY:      1000
AGE: 31    MALE                                          SEPTEMBER 29, 1977
```

```
120:?    L    F    K      HS   D    HY   PD   MF   PA   PT   SC   MA   SI:120
 :                    :    1    2    3    4    5    6    7    8    9    0 :
 :                    :                                                  :
 :                    :                                                  :
110:-   -    -    -   :    -    -    -    -    -    -    -    -    -    - :110
 :                    :                                                  :
 :                    :                                                  :
 :                    :                                                  :
100:-   -    -    -   :    -    -    -    -    -    -    -    -    -    - :100
 :                    :                                                  :
 :                    :                                                  :
 :                    :                                                  :
 90:-   -    -    -   :    -    -    -    -    -    -    -    -    -    - : 90
 :                    :                                                  :
 :                    :                                                  :
 :                    :                   X                              :
 80:-   -    -    -   :    -    -    -    -    -    -    -    -    -    - : 80
 :                    :                                            X     :
 :                    :                                                  :
 70:-----------------:--------------------X-----------------------------: 70
 :                    :              X                                   :
 :                    :                                                  :
 :                    :                             X                    :
 60:-   -    X    -   :    -    X    -    -    -    X -    -    -    - : 60
 :             X      :                                  X              :
 :                    :    X                                       X  :
 50:-----------------:---------------------------------------------: 50
 :        X           :                                                  :
 40:-   -    -    -   :    -    -    -    -    -    -    -    -    -    - : 40
 :                    :                                                  :
 30:-----------------:---------------------------------------------: 30
 :                    :                                                  :
 20:.................:..............................................: 20
R      0    2    7   17    13   21   27   33   32   12   27   30   28   31
K-C                       13             33             27   30   28
T-C  OK  44   60   59     54   60   69   83   73   62   58   65   78   56
```

Figure 4. Profile.

search. This page includes scores on 14 special scales, a numerical code to classify the profile, the score on the MacAndrews Scale (alcoholism or addiction proneness), along with a statement interpreting the scale and a matrix of true-false responses by which the subject's answer to any item can be determined.

MMPI SUMMARY DATA

NUMBER: 77813   AGENCY: 1000
AGE: 31   MALE   SEPTEMBER 29, 1977

SCALE	?	L	F	K	HS	D	HY	PD	MF	PA	PT	SC	MA	SI
RAW	0	2	7	17	13	21	27	33	32	12	27	30	28	31
K-C					13			33			27	30	28	
T-C	OK	44	60	59	54	60	69	83	73	62	58	65	78	56

SCALE	A	R	ES	LB	CA	DY	DO	RE	PR	ST	CN	AT	SO-R	MT
RAW	11	23	46	12	10	21	19	16	15	25	31	18	29	11
T-C	49	65	53	61	51	52	62	40	56	67	65	57	36	58

SCALE	SOC	DEP	FEM	MOR	REL	AUT	PSY	ORG	FAM	HOS	PHO	HYP	HEA
RAW	10	7	14	5	4	15	16	5	5	6	8	17	5
T-C	53	50	64	44	42	64	64	49	56	43	56	62	50

SCALE	AP	HC	HX	PV	EC	I	II	III	IV	V	VI	VII	VIII	IX
RAW	16	38	13	11	18	9	9	21	8	12	2	3	9	2
T-C	72	70	65	61	67	47	52	66	77	0	40	50	59	54

SCALE	O-H	ED	AM
RAW	20	8	25
T-C	74	65	65

INDICES: AI =   56   IR = .748   FT = 1.248   GI =   44   MFI =   27

WELSH CODE: *4 95´3862-701/:=

ANSWERS		10		20		30		40		50
1	FTTFF	FFTTF	FFTFF	FTTTT	FFFFF	TFFFT	FFTFF	TTTFT	FFFFT	TFFFF
51	TFFTT	FTFTT	TFTFT	FFTFT	TFTFT	FFTFF	FFTTF	FFTTT	FFTFF	TFFFF
101	FTTFT	FTFFF	FTTFF	TTTFT	FTFTF	TTFFT	FFFTT	FFFFT	FFTFF	FFFFT
151	FFTTF	TTFFF	FFTTT	FTFTF	TFTFT	FTTFF	TFFFF	FTTFT	TTTFT	TFFTF
201	FFFTF	FTFFF	FFFFT	FTFFT	TFFTT	FFTTF	FTTFF	FTTTF	FFTTF	FFFFT
251	FTTFF	FTTFF	FFFTF	FFTTF	FTFTF	TTTFT	FFFFT	FTTFT	FFFFF	TFFTF
301	FFTTT	FFFTT	TTFFF	TTTFF	TTTFF	FFTFT	FFFFF	FFTFT	FFFFF	FFTFF
351	FTTFF	FFFFF	FTFFF	FTFFF	TTTFF	FTFTT	TFTTF	TFFTT	FFFTF	FFFFT
401	TFTTT	FFTTT	FFFFT	FFTFT	FFTFF	TFFTT	FTTFF	TTTFT	TTTFT	FFFFF
451	FFFTF	TFFFT	FFFTT	FFFFF	FFTTF	FTFTF	FTFFF	TFTTF	FFFFT	TTTTT
501	FTFTF	FFTFF	TFFFT	FFFFT	TTTTT	FFFFF	FFTTF	FFFTT	FFFFF	TFFFF
551	FFFTF	TFFFF	FFTFF	F						

CODE: 147 200 204 491 504 512 521 524 528 530 533 547 550 552
      556 561 564 568 573 576 580 585 588 634 637 640 642 645 649
      653 699

Figure 5. Technical section.

The PAS law-offender interpretation system has been introduced in a number of criminal-justice programs in the United States
and Canada, including state and federal prisons, probation and parole
departments, and youthful-offender facilities. Its use in two unique
system-wide applications will be described.

THE ALABAMA PRISON SYSTEM

In 1974 the PAS system was adopted by the Alabama prison system as part of the admissions procedure at the Diagnostic and Reception Center. The testing program, the first ever initiated in the Alabama system, was interrupted in the summer of 1975 when dangerous levels of overcrowding in all state prisons precluded further testing except on an occasional basis. In 1976 the entire state-prison system came under federal court orders that required major reforms. The court, noting that the classification system was nonfunctional, ordered the state to develop, in cooperation with the University of Alabama Psychology Department, a plan for the reclassification of all inmates. When the state failed to develop an adequate plan, the court authorized an alternative plan calling for the reclassification to proceed under the direction of the author. The Prison Classification Project was directed by the author and staffed by over 50 psychology department faculty members, graduate students, recent graduates, and temporary employees from a variety of disciplines. Interviews, tests, and thorough file reviews were conducted for every inmate, and inmates were present in staff conferences in which decisions were made concerning educational, vocational, health, and security needs. All inmates with adequate reading ability were given the MMPI, and the PAS computerized reports contributed to decisions made about custody levels and the need for mental-health care or referral. From July to November 1976, over 4,000 inmates were classified. Over one-third of the incarcerated prisoners were found to be suitable for community placement, and were transferred to appropriate facilities. The large data base that resulted is still being analyzed in a variety of ongoing studies, some of which are described in another section of this chapter.

THE MISSISSIPPI DEPARTMENT OF CORRECTIONS

The Mississippi Department of Corrections introduced the PAS MMPI service in 1974 as a part of the admissions and classification procedure in the state penitentiary. In July 1977, the department, with funding from the Law Enforcement Assistance Administration, introduced a unique state-wide program of psychological testing as a part of presentence investigation and evaluation for convicted felons. The system was designed to provide district judges with information to assist them in making sentencing decisions. The primary objective of the program was to increase the use of community alternatives to imprisonment by more accurately assessing the risk a convicted person might present, and to identify special needs an offender might have in order to facilitate his/her eventual reintegration into society.

A state-wide network was organized to provide service to all of the state's judicial districts, with referrals made at the option of the presiding judge. Three MA level psychologists were employed to serve the northern, central, and southern areas of the state, and a fourth served as state-wide coordinator. The author served as general consultant to the project.

Before initiating the service, in-service training was provided by the author to the area coordinators and by the coordinators and the author to the presentence investigators in each of the state's judicial districts. Presentence investigators were taught to administer the MMPI, the Wide Range Achievement Test (WRAT), and the Slosson Intelligence Test (SIT) under standard conditions. The Wide Range Achievement Test provides an estimate of the school grade level (year and month) in the areas of reading (word recognition and pronunciation), written spelling, and arithmetic computation. The Slosson Intelligence Test is a short screening test that provides a gross measure of intellectual functioning. Individuals with unusually low SIT scores ordinarily do not take the MMPI and may be referred to the area coordinator for individual testing.

Procedures

The procedures established called first for a decision on the part of the judge about whether or not a convicted offender would be tested. Some judges request testing for all offenders, some for selected cases, and some use the service rarely or not at all. After referral by the judge, the presentence investigator administers the tests as part of the presentence evaluation and investigation. Completed MMPI answer sheets are forwarded to the author for computer processing, and the computerized reports are sent to the area coordinator. The area coordinator, after integrating the personal history, crime record, and psychological test results, visits the referring judge and presents a verbal summary and recommendation. The degree to which recommendations are accepted depends upon the personal style of the judge and his confidence in the testing program and the coordinator. It has been observed that the judges place increasing confidence in the reports and recommendations as they have more contact with the testing program and the coordinators. The coordinators report that some judges who had previously sentenced virtually all offenders to the state penitentiary have begun to make use of probation and community placements. New leadership in the department of corrections has promoted the development of numerous community alternatives that did not exist previously, and the testing program has helped select appropriate candidates for the new facilities. The new policies of the department of corrections have resulted in a sharply decreased prison population.

Megargee Classification System

The constructive use of the MMPI reports in both the presentence program and the state penitentiary encouraged the introduction, as part of the PAS computerized report, of the classification system developed by E. I. Megargee (1975, 1977). The Megargee rules were programmed and the classifications verified by a comparison with the classifications of Megargee's computer program.

Two kinds of output were designed. First, the descriptive information for each of the types was rewritten into a two- to three-page prototype description called the *extended report*. Second, the primary features of each type were summarized in a set of descriptive phases, called the *offender profile and recommendations*. Both the extended report and the brief report were divided into two sections, *psychological description* and *treatment and management considerations*. The brief report, never more than one page, included, for convenience, a summary of the results of the Slosson Intelligence Test and the Wide Range Achievement Test.

The total output provided to the area coordinator includes:

(1) The PAS print-out containing narrative report, critical items, profile, content scales, and summary data.

(2) The offender profile and recommendations, containing a psychological description, treatment and management considerations based on the Megargee typology, and a summary of intelligence, reading, and arithmetic level.

Figures 6 and 7 are a sample offender profile and extended report. To reduce computer time and postage costs, the extended reports are not routinely printed out. Instead each area coordinator is provided with a booklet containing an extended report for each of the types.

Since the initiation of the Megargee classification report in the presentence procedure, similar reports have been provided to the prison classification team. Because there is full cooperation between the two assessment groups, the test reports of offenders sentenced to the state penitentiary are immediately forwarded to the prison classification team to facilitate rapid classification. Offenders not tested

PSYCHOLOGICAL ASSESSMENT SERVICE

OFFENDER PROFILE AND RECOMMENDATIONS

NUMBER   77813   AGENCY   1000
AGE 31   MALE   SEPTEMBER 29, 1977

TYPE IV (GROUP ABLE)

THIS INDIVIDUAL IS CLASSIFIED AS TYPE IV ON THE BASIS OF HIS MMPI. THE
FOLLOWING REPORT DESCRIBES BEHAVIOR AND EXPERIENCES WHICH ARE TYPICAL OF
TYPE IV INMATES. IT SHOULD BE KEPT IN MIND THAT THIS IS A GENERAL
PICTURE AND NOT ALL TYPE IV CHARACTERISTICS WILL APPLY TO EVERY GROUP
MEMBER.

SUMMARY

PSYCHOLOGICAL DESCRIPTION

.... CLEVER, OPPORTUNISTIC, DARING, AND SELF-ASSURED.

.... HIGH IN SOCIABILITY AND DOMINANCE.

.... OUTGOING, FORCEFUL, BUT NOT EXCESSIVELY AGGRESSIVE.

.... LACK THE PATIENCE TO ACHIEVE CONSTRUCTIVE GOALS OR TO RESIST
      IMPULSES.

.... WILL NOT SEEK FIGHTS BUT WILL RETALIATE AGGRESSIVELY IF ATTACKED.

TREATMENT AND MANAGEMENT CONSIDERATIONS

.... HIGH IN SELF-ACCEPTANCE; LITTLE DESIRE TO CHANGE.

.... MAY HAVE NEGATIVE EFFECT ON EASILY INFLUENCED INMATES.

.... DIFFICULT TO WORK WITH IN A COMMUNITY SETTING OR LOOSELY STRUCTURED
      SITUATION.

.... NEED DEFINITE STRUCTURE AND GUIDELINES.

.... MAY PROFIT FROM A DIRECT, CONFRONTIVE TREATMENT APPROACH.

.... CHANGES MADE IN TREATMENT ARE LIKELY TO BE SUPERFICIAL AND
      SHORT-LIVED AFTER RELEASE.

INTELLIGENCE AND ACHIEVEMENT

.... INTELLIGENCE

.... READING LEVEL IS EQUIVALENT TO 10TH   GRADE 4TH   MONTH.

.... SPELLING LEVEL IS EQUIVALENT TO 9TH   GRADE 6TH   MONTH.

.... ARITHMETIC LEVEL IS EQUIVALENT TO 11TH   GRADE 4TH   MONTH.

SCALE SCORES FOR MMPI

NUMBER   77813   AGENCY   1000
AGE 31   MALE   SEPTEMBER 29, 1977

SCALE		L	F	K	HS	D	HY	PD	MF	PA	PT	SC	MA	SI
RAW	0	2	7	17	4	21	27	26	32	12	10	13	25	31
K-C					13			33			27	30	28	
T-C	0K	44	60	59	54	60	69	83	73	62	58	65	78	56

WELSH CODE   *4 95'3862-701/ =

GROUP(S) CLASSIFICATION
        POINTS LEVEL

ABLE   2   MEDIUM

PROGRAM REV.(11-14-77)

Figure 6. Offender profile.

PSYCHOLOGICAL ASSESSMENT SERVICE

OFFENDER PROFILE AND RECOMMENDATIONS

EXTENDED REPORT

Type IV (Group Able)

Inmates in this group tend to be clever, opportunistic, daring, and amoral people who risk taking illegal shortcuts to gratify their wants as soon as possible. They are significantly higher than other prison groups in sociability and social presence. They tend to be charming, popular, and manipulative. They have the ability to form good interpersonal relations with few conflicts, and are consistently evaluated as being one of the better adjusted groups in prison. They are active, forceful, and self-assured with a strong drive for dominance, coupled with imagination and smooth, persuasive verbal skills. Unfortunately, they lack the patience and achievement motivation necessary to achieve their goals through conventional means, as well as the social values and internal constraints that might inhibit their impulsive pleasure seeking. They give the impression of being a happy-go-lucky group, and, indeed, they seem to have less anxiety than any other prison groups. Over all, they are average in their history of violence and in their use of drugs. They are relatively high in the use of marijuana, but below average in the use of LSD. Although below average in their adjustment to prior incarcerations, they are quite optimistic about their ability to adjust to the present incarceration. They are one of the more outgoing, dominant groups. They are not excessively aggressive, but they do little to avoid hostile interactions. Their aggressive encounters seem to be primarily of a reactive type. They will not seek out fights, but they retaliate aggressively to attacks by others. They have generally good relations with authorities and are seen as friendly and adaptable.

Unfortunately, the men in this group are high in self-acceptance. They are charming, popular, and manipulative. Having little desire to change, they probably feel that the best way to cope with prison is to manipulate the staff and the parole board. They may appear contrite, but there are no signs of sincere remorse or guilt, and any changes they make are apt to be superficial and short-lived once they are released. Given their social skills, the men in this group probably are frequently successful in their attempts to subvert the system and will be reluctant to abandon this habit.

Treatment and Management

Members of this group, being sociable, manipulative, and persuasive, will be difficult to work with without some external control over their coming and going. They would probably be difficult to treat in a community or loosely structured situation. It could be that incarceration for relatively short periods would get their attention and induce them to at least consider alternative ways of gratifying their needs. Being interpersonally dominant and ascendant, these men influence other inmates within an institution. This relative strength could be used in a positive direction in considering the needs of the more disturbed groups. In dealing with relatively well adjusted but easily influenced groups, it could be that members of this group would have a negative influence.

Men in this group would not respond positively or be helped by warm, supportive, insight-oriented approach. They are not particularly interested in insight, and they tend to manipulate relationships for their own purposes. They may profit more from a direct confrontive approach which challenges them. They are not reluctant to get involved in stressful interpersonal interactions, and dealing in those terms would enable them to use some of the skills they have already mastered. Clear cut and definite structure and guidelines to any program would be required to place some boundaries on the extent of this group's manipulation. Staff members assigned to work with these individuals should be self-assured and comfortable in their own roles and personalities, with a good sense of humor, so that they do not over-react to situations in which manipulation is successful.

The men in this group can relate well in group settings, and it would not be surprising to see the men in this group emerge as leaders and pace-setters of a group. An approach with its own language, procedure, and stages, such as transactional analysis, would seem particularly appealing as an approach for this group.

The goal for this group is to get the men to live within values that they have been taught but which they have thus far elected to ignore or go around. If the men in this group could channel their interpersonal energy and talent into constructive legitimate activities, there is good indication that they could be leaders.

Figure 7. Extended report.

before imprisonment are tested as part of the admissions procedure, and some prisoners are retested when decisions are to be made such as parole, transfer to community programs, and referral to mental-health care.

Within the institution, the MMPI reports and the offender profile are used as part of the classification procedure. The test information is used, along with behavioral observations and history, to determine custody level and assignment to work, education, and rehabilitation programs.

CURRENT RESEARCH

Several studies using the PAS MMPI system have been recently completed or are currently under way. In an unpublished exploratory study, Howell and Geiselman (1978) examined the PAS reports on 40 inmates housed in one of the Mississippi community restitution centers. The subjects ranged in age from 17 to 33. Thirty-three of the subjects were white, six were black, and one was an American Indian. The purpose of the study was to identify test characteristics associated with behavior and outcome in the community facility. The group was divided into three management categories according to observed behavior: No Problems (fewer than 2 rule infractions), Occasional Problems (3 to 8 infractions), Frequent Problems (more than 8 infractions or one major violation). The Frequent Problem group was the youngest, lowest in I.Q., and had the poorest WRAT performance. The more deviant Megargee types predominated. The No Problem group was the oldest, was approximately equal to the Occasional Problem group in I.Q. and WRAT scores, but had a predominance of the least deviant Megargee types. The Occasional Problem group fell midway between the other two groups in the deviancy of Megargee types and partially overlapped both. There was no overlap between the first and third groups: all the subjects in the first group (No Problem) fell in types 1-4, and all the subjects in the third group (Frequent Problems) fell in types 5-10. Similarly, no subjects in types 7-10 successfully completed the program, and no subjects in types 1-5 were involuntarily terminated from the program.

The authors concluded that the Megargee/MMPI classification seemed to be the best single criterion for predicting outcome in a community-restitution program. In terms of correctional decision-making, these pilot results, if confirmed, suggest that individuals in types 6-10 should not be placed in the relatively open community centers, since their pattern of rule infractions, escape, and early termination poses risks for the program and the community, and may subject the offender to added penalties as a result of his/her inability to maintain adequate behavioral controls.

Osterhoff (1973), in a study designed to identify positive and negative personality change in prisoners, examined initial and retest MMPIs in the same prison population used to develop the PAS law-offender interpretation system. He found little difference between the initial and retest mean profile for the total sample, and, using Ward's hierarchical grouping technique (1961), he identified four discrete subgroups, one of which had strongly positive changes, one no changes, and two slight positive changes.

Using the Megargee system to classify the mean profiles for the four subgroups in Osterhoff's study, Nichols (1979) found that the "no change group" stayed in the same Megargee type (Type IV) as did one of the moderate change groups (Type V). The other moderate change group, initially seen as having made positive changes on the basis of reduced profile elevation, actually moved, on the basis of configuration, to a more deviant Megargee type (I to IV). The group with greatest change moved an extremely deviant type (X) to the more moderate IV. In terms of Megargee types, it would appear that prisoners may change for the better, for the worse, or remain the same, depending upon prior personality characteristics.

Jones (1977) studied four groups of prisoners from the Alabama prison study who differed in how well they had adjusted in prison. The groups were classified according to their behavior while in prison. The extremely violent group had committed murder or several extremely assaultive acts in prison. The moderately violent group had committed one or two extremely assaultive acts, but not murder. The disciplinary group had committed nonviolent rule infractions and the nondisciplinary group had no record of rule violations. In a multivariate analysis of the data, Jones found significant differences among the MMPI profiles of the three groups. The extremely violent group showed marked elevations on scales 6, 7, and 8 as well as the elevations on scales 4 and 9 found in most prison groups. The mean profile of the most violent group was classified into Type IX, an aggressive, psychologically disturbed type. The moderately violent group was classified Type VIII, a violent, dominant type. The nonviolent group with disciplinary infractions, surprisingly, fell into Type VIII, although the mean profile was obviously less elevated than the moderately violent group. The nondisciplinary group fell into the least pathological Type I.

Nichols (1979) in a pilot study classified 293 inmates from the Alabama sample into Megargee types. He found that the distribution of types differed significantly from the distribution in Megargee and Dorhout's original sample (1976). The major difference was in the larger number of unclassifiable profiles, indicating that the Megargee system was not completely applicable to a state-prison population and suggesting the possible existence of types not identified by the Megargee group.

Nichols is currently analyzing the profiles of a much larger sample of Alabama and Mississippi inmates. His preliminary findings suggest that the Megargee system accounts for most of the types found within a state-prison population, although some groups not found in Megargee's restricted sample (youthful, federal offenders) emerge in this much more heterogeneous sample. Identification and description of these "missing elements" might well result in a modified system with even more power for decision-making in correctional settings.

REFERENCES

Dahlstrom, W. G., & Welsh, G. S. *An MMPI handbook: a guide to use in clinical practice and research*. Minneapolis: University of Minnesota Press, 1960.

Dahlstrom, W. G., Welsh, G. S., & Dahlstrom, L. E. *An MMPI handbook, Volume II: Research applications*. Minneapolis: University of Minnesota Press, 1975.

Fowler, R. D. MMPI computer interpretation for college counseling. *The Journal of Psychology*, 1968, 69, 201-207.

Fowler, R. D. Automated interpretation of personality test data. In J. N. Butcher (Ed.), *MMPI: Research developments and clinical applications*. New York: McGraw-Hill, 1969.

Fowler, R. D. The interpretation of personality tests by computer: The Minnesota Multiphasic Personality Inventory. In L. Goodstein & R. Lanyon (Eds.), *Readings in personality assessment*. New York: Wiley, 1971.

Fowler, R. D. *The use of computer-produced MMPI reports with a prison population*. Unpublished paper, 1972.

Haven, H. The MMPI with incarcerated adult and delinquent offenders. *FCI Technical and Treatment Notes*, 1970, 1, 1-46.

Hodo, G. *Clinical validation of the factored MMPI*. Unpublished dissertation, University of Alabama, 1973.

Howell, G., & Geiselman, J. *A psychodiagnostic study of restitution inmates*. Unpublished paper, 1978.

Jones, M. T. *Classification of violent and nonviolent prison inmates using selected MMPI scales*. Unpublished dissertation, University of Alabama, 1977.

Megargee, E. I. An MMPI-based classification system for young adult male offenders. *Proceedings of the 104th Annual Congress of Correction*. College Park, Md.: American Correctional Association, 1975, 382-92.

Megargee, E. I. A new classification system for criminal offenders, I: The need for a new classification system. *Criminal Justice and Behavior*, 1977, 4, 107-14.

Megargee, E. I., & Dorhout, B. Revisions and refinement of an MMPI-based typology of youthful offenders. *FCI Technical and Treatment Notes*, 1976, 6(1).

Nichols, W. *Application of the Megargee classification system to state inmates*. Unpublished paper, 1979.

Osterhoff, W. *MMPI changes in youthful offenders during incarceration*. Unpublished dissertation, University of Alabama, 1973.

Tallent, N. *Clinical psychological consultation: A rationale and guide to team practice*. Englewood Cliffs, N.J.: Prentice-Hall, 1963.

Ward, J. *A hierarchical grouping procedure applied to a problem of grouping profiles*. Lackland Air Force Base, Texas: Personnel Laboratory, Wright Air Development Division, A.S.D. Technical Note, October, 1961.

Webb, J. T. *Validity and utility of computer produced MMPI reports with V.A. psychiatric populations*. Paper presented to the American Psychological Association, Miami, 1970.

Webb, J. T., Miller, M. L., & Fowler, R. D. Validation of a computerized MMPI interpretation system. *Proceedings of the 77th Annual Convention of the APA*, 1969, 4, 523-24.

Webb, J. T., Miller, M. L., & Fowler, R. D. Extending professional time: a computerized MMPI interpretation service. *Journal of Clinical Psychology*, 1970, 26, 210-14. (Also in *Ontario Psychologist*, 1969, 1, 256-71).

Wiggins, J. S. Content dimensions in the MMPI. In J. N. Butcher (Ed.), *MMPI: Research developments and clinical applications*. New York: McGraw-Hill, 1969.

Bibliography of MMPI Research

Patricia L. Owen

The purpose of this bibliography is to provide a comprehensive reference source for researchers and clinicians who use the MMPI. An attempt was made to gather all articles using or discussing the MMPI since 1972. The references were obtained through two computerized searches (PSYCHOLOGICAL ABSTRACTS and ERIC) and through manual searches of the individual journals.

Each reference has been placed in what appeared to be the most relevant category, although many articles could easily fit into several. Users should be aware that some references are categorized by the content of the title, rather than by the more subtle content of the articles. And, although an attempt was made to be thorough, some articles may have been omitted inadvertently.

Bibliography

GENERAL GUIDES AND MANUALS

Butcher, J. N. (Ed.). *Objective personality assessment: Changing perspectives.* New York: Academic Press, 1972.

Butcher, J. N., & Owen, P. L. Objective personality inventories: Recent research and some contemporary issues. *Clinical diagnosis of mental disorders: A handbook.* New York: Plenum, 1978.

Butcher, J. N., & Pancheri, P. *Handbook of cross-national MMPI research.* Minneapolis: University of Minnesota Press, 1976.

Butcher, J. N., & Tellegen, A. Common methodological problems in MMPI research. *Journal of Consulting and Clinical Psychology,* 1978, *46,* 620-628.

Dahlstrom, W. G., Welsh, G. S., & Dahlstrom, L. E. *An MMPI handbook, Volume I: Clinical interpretation.* Minneapolis: University of Minnesota Press, 1972.

Dahlstrom, W. G., Welsh, G. S., & Dahlstrom, L. E. *An MMPI handbook, Volume II: Research applications.* Minneapolis: University of Minnesota Press, 1975.

Duckworth, J., & Duckworth, E. *MMPI interpretation manual for counselors and clinicians.* Muncie, Ind.: Accelerated Development, 1975.

Faschingbauer, T. R., & Newmark, C. S. *Short forms of the MMPI.* Lexington, Mass: D. C. Heath & Co., 1977.

Good, P. K.-E., & Branter, J. P. *A practical guide to the MMPI.* Minneapolis: University of Minnesota Press, 1974.

Graham, J. R. *The MMPI: A practical guide.* New York: Oxford University Press, 1977.

Graham, J. R. The Minnesota Multiphasic Personality Inventory (MMPI). In B. B. Wolman (Ed.), *Clinical diagnosis of mental disorders: A handbook.* New York: Plenum, 1978.

Lachar, D. *The MMPI: Clinical assessment and automated interpretation.* Los Angeles: Western Psychological Services, 1974.

Marks, P. A., Seeman, W., & Haller, D. L. *The actuarial use of the MMPI with adolescents and adults.* Baltimore: Williams & Wilkins, 1974.

Swenson, W. M., Pearson, J. S., & Osborne, D. *An MMPI source book: Basic items scale, and pattern data on 50,000 medical patients.* Minneapolis: University of Minnesota Press, 1973.

PSYCHOMETRIC CHARACTERISTICS
Alternate Forms

Bassos, C., Seeman, W., & Schumsky, D. Context effect in the MMPI. *Journal of Clinical Psychology,* 1977, *33,* 178-180.

Clavelle, P. R., & Butcher, J. N. An adaptive typological approach to psychiatric screening. *Journal of Consulting and Clinical Psychology,* 1977, *45,* 851-859.

Cochran, M. L. Abbreviated MMPI booklet forms: The 300- & 366-item scales with K-correction. *Journal of Clinical Psychology,* 1975, *31,* 298-300.

Henning, J. J., Levy, R. H., & Aderman, M. Reliability of MMPI tape recorded and booklet administrations. *Journal of Clinical Psychology,* 1972, *28,* 372-373.

Milligan, W. L. Computer controlled oral test administration: A method and example. *Educational and Psychological Measurement,* 1978, *38,* 823-828.

Taylor, J. F., & Graham, J. R. A simplified MMPI form with reduced reading difficulty level. *Journal of Clinical Psychology,* 1974, *30,* 182-185.

Internal Consistency

Barker, B. M., & Barker, H. R. Norms for MMPI factor scales. *Journal of Clinical Psychology,* 1978, *34,* 429-430.

DeWolfe, A. S., & Davis, W. E. Pattern analysis and deviation scores in clinical research: Mean scatter revisited. *Journal of Personality Assessment,* 1972, *36,* 307-313.

Gold, E. M., & Hoffman, P. J. Flange detection cluster analysis. *Multivariate Behavioral Research,* 1976, *11,* 217-235.

Gravitz, M. A., & Gerton, M. I. An empirical study of internal consistency in the MMPI. *Journal of Clinical Psychology,* 1976, *32,* 567-568.

Horn, J. L., Wanberg, K. W., & Appel, M. On the internal structure of the MMPI. *Multivariate Behavioral Research,* 1973, *8,* 131-171.

Hunter, S., Overall, J. E., & Butcher, J. N. Factor structure of the MMPI in a psychiatric population. *Multivariate Behavioral Research,* 1974, *9,* 283-302.

Kolton, M. S., & Dwarshuis, L. A clinical factor analytic method for inferring construct meaning. *Educational and Psychological Measurement,* 1973, *33,* 653-661.

Stewart, R. A. C. Factor analysis and rotation of the 566 MMPI items. *Social Behavior and Personality,* 1974, *2,* 147-154.

Items

Characteristics of

Jackson, D. N., & Messick, S. Judged frequency of endorsement and frequency of occurrence scale values and dispersions for MMPI items. *Psychological Reports,* 1973, *33,* 183-191.

Koss, M. P., Butcher, J. N., & Hoffmann, N. G. The MMPI critical items: How well do they work? *Journal of Consulting and Clinical Psychology,* 1976, *44,* 921-928.

Lachar, D., & Wrobel, T. A. Validating clinicians' hunches: Construction of a new MMPI critical item set. *Journal of Consulting and Clinical Psychology,* 1979, *47,* 277-284.

Saunders, T. R., Jr., & Gravitz, M. A. Sex differences in the endorsement of MMPI critical items. *Journal of Clinical Psychology,* 1974, *30,* 557-558.

Smith, R. C. Item ambiguity in the 16 PF and MMPI: An assessment and comparison. *Journal of Consulting and Clinical Psychology,* 1972, *38,* 460.

Vesprani, G. J., & Seeman, W. MMPI X and zero items in a psychiatric outpatient group. *Journal of Personality Assessment,* 1974, *38,* 61-64.

Objections to

Barna, J. D. Invasion of privacy as a function of test set and anonymity. *Perceptual and Motor skills,* 1974, *38,* 1028-1030.

Fink , A. M. & Butcher, J. N. Reducing objections to personality inventories with special instructions. *Educational and Psychological Measurement,* 1972, *32,* 631-639.

Gynther, M. D. MMPI items for invasion of privacy studies. *Journal of Clinical Psychology,* 1972, *28,* 76-77.

Gynther, M. D., & Ullom, J. Objections to MMPI items as a function of interpersonal trust, race and sex. *Journal of Consulting and Clinical Psychology,* 1976, *44,* 1020.

MMPI in Relationship to Other Instruments

Abbott, R. D. Improving the validity of affective self-report measures through constructing personality scales unconfounded with social desirability: A study of the Personality Research Form. *Educational and Psychological Measurement,* 1975, *35,* 371-377.

Apfeldorf, M., Smith, W. J., Peixotto, H. E., & Hunley, P. J. Is the representation of the objective body-image in figure drawings related to the personality characteristics of the drawer? *Psychological Reports,* 1974, *34,* 1015-1020.

Bartlett, F. E., & Cooke, P. E. A correlational study of the Community Adaptation Schedule and the MMPI. *Community Mental Health Journal,* 1972, *8,* 189-195.

Bush, M. Relationship between color-word test interference and MMPI indices of psychoticism and defense rigidity in normal males and females. *Journal of Consulting and Clinical Psychology,* 1975, *43,* 926.

Coché, E., & Taylor, S. Correlations between the Offer Self-image Personality Inventory in a psychiatric hospital population. *Journal of Youth and Adolescence,* 1974, *3,* 145-152.

D'Agostino, C. A. Performance of psychopathic and non-psychopathic delinquent girls on the Kahn Test of Symbol Arrangement. *Perceptual and Motor Skills,* 1976, *43,* 1020-1022.

Derogatis, L. R., Rickets, K., & Rock, A. F. The SCL-90 and the MMPI: A step in the validation of a new self-report scale. *British Journal of Psychiatry,* 1976, *128,* 280-289.

Dudley, H. K., Ellis, M. C., Mason, M., & Hirsch, S. M. Drawings of the opposite sex: Continued use of the Draw-A-Person test and young state hospital patients. *Journal of Youth and Adolescence,* 1976, *5,* 201-219.

Gendreau, P., Gibson, M., Surridge, C. T., & Hug, J. J. The application of self-esteem measures in corrections: A further report on the SEI. *Journal of Community Psychology,* 1973, *1,* 423-425.

Helmes, E., Reed, P. L., & Jackson, D. N. Desirability and frequency scale values and endorsement proportions for items of Personality Research Form E. *Psychological Reports,* 1977, *41,* 435-444.

Higdon, J. F., & Brodsky, S. L. Validating Hand Test acting out ratios for overt and experimentally induced aggression. *Journal of Personality Assessment,* 1973, *37,* 363-368.

Hoffmann, H., & Jackson, D. N. Substantive dimensions of psychopathology derived from MMPI content scales and the Differential Personality Inventory. *Journal of Consulting and Clinical Psychology,* 1976, *44,* 862.

Johnson, D. T., Workman, S. N., Neville, C. W., Jr., & Beutler, L. E. MMPI and 16PF correlates of the A-B Therapy Scale in psychiatric inpatients. *Psychotherapy: Theory Research and Practice,* 1973, *10,* 270-272.

McCraw, R. K., & White, R. B., Jr. Social introversion - extraversion and Rorschach human responses in adult psychiatric patients. *Psychological Reports,* 1974, *35,* 932-934.

Nichols, M. P., Gordon, T. P., & Levine, M. D. Development and validation of the Life Style Questionnaire. *Journal of Social Psychology,* 1972, *86,* 121-125.

Oldroyd, R. J. A principle components analysis of the BPI and MMPI. *Criminal Justice and Behavior,* 1975, *2,* 85-90.

Rhodes, R. J., & Rice, A. S. MMPI correlates of the Popoff Index of Depression. *Psychological Reports,* 1977, *40,* 35-41.

Rice, L. N. & Gaylin, N. L. Personality processes reflected in client vocal style and Rorschach performance. *Journal of Consulting and Clinical Psychology,* 1973, *40,* 133-138.

Scott, D. P., & Severance, L. J. Relationship between the CPI, MMPI, and locus of control in a nonacademic environment. *Journal of Personality Assessment,* 1975, *39,* 141-145.

Spaulding, W. The relationship of some information-processing factors to severely disturbed behavior. *Journal of Nervous and Mental Disease,* 1978, *166,* 417-427.

Trott, D. M., & Morf, M. E. A multimethod factor analysis of the Differential Personality Inventory, Personality Research Form, and MMPI. *Journal of Counseling Psychology,* 1972, *19,* 94-103.

Turner, R. G., Willerman, L., & Horn, J. M. A test of some predictions from the Personality Assessment System. *Journal of Clinical Psychology,* 1976, *32,* 631-643.

Von Hilsheimer, G., Levy, A., Tucker, J. T., & Moore, L. S. HOO-MMPI: A Comparison. *Journal of Orthomolecular Psychiatry,* 1977, *6,* 8-17.

Wakefield, J. A., Jr., Yom, B. L., Bradley, P. E., Doughtie, E. B., Cox, J. A., & Kraft, I. A. Eysenck's personality dimensions: A model for the MMPI. *British Journal of Social and Clinical Psychology,* 1974, *13,* 413-420.

Whitaker, L. C. Validity and usefulness in four WIST studies recently reported in the Journal. *Journal of Clinical Psychology,* 1978, *34,* 588-594.

Wildman, R. W., & Wildman, R. W., II. An investigation into the comparative validity of several diagnostic tests and test batteries. *Journal of Clinical Psychology,* 1975, *31,* 455-458.

Williams, J. D., Dudley, H. K., Jr., & Overall, J. E. Validity of the 16PF and the MMPI in a mental hospital setting. *Journal of Abnormal Psychology,* 1972, *80,* 261-270.

Wilson, J. P. & Aronoff, J. A sentence completion test assessing safety and esteem motives. *Journal of Personality Assessment,* 1973, *37,* 351-354.

Yarnell, T. Validation of the Seeking of Noetic Goals Test with schizophrenic and normal Ss. *Psychological Reports,* 1972, *30,* 79-82.

MMPI in Relation to Other Patient Information

Clum, G. A. Relations between biographical data and patient symptomatology. *Journal of Abnormal Psychology,* 1975, *84,* 80-83.

Ewing, D. R., & Thelen, M. H. Psychiatric patient self-description via self-report and the MMPI. *Journal of Clinical Psychology,* 1972, *28,* 510-514.

Griffiths, R. D. The accuracy and correlates of psychiatric patients' self-assessment of their work behavior. *British Journal of Social and Clinical Psychology,* 1975, *14,* 181-189.

Koss, M. P., & Butcher, J. N. A comparison of psychiatric patients' self-report with other sources of clinical information. *Journal of Research in Personality,* 1973, *7,* 225-236.

Payne, F. D., & Wiggins, J. S. MMPI profile types and the self-report of psychiatric patients. *Journal of Abnormal Psychology,* 1972, *79,* 1-8.

Sappington, A. A., & Michaux, M. H. Prognostic patterns in self-report, relative report, and professional evaluation measures for hospitalized and day-care patients. *Journal of Consulting and Clinical Psychology,* 1975, *43,* 904-910.

Zimmerman, R. L., Vestre, N. D., & Hunter, S. H. Validity of family informants' ratings of psychiatric patients: General validity. *Psychological Reports,* 1975, *37,* 619-630.

Zimmerman, R. L., Vestre, N. D., & Hunter, S. H. Validity of family informants' ratings of psychiatric patients: Differential validity. *Psychological Reports,* 1976, *38,* 555-564.

Profiles and Code Types

Altman, H., Warbin, R. W., Sletten, I. W., & Gynther, M. D. Replicated empirical correlates of the MMPI 8-9/9-8 code type. *Journal of Personality Assessment,* 1973, *37,* 369-371.

Dworkin, R. H., & Widom, C. S. Undergraduate MMPI profiles and the longitudinal prediction of adult social outcome. *Journal of Consulting and Clinical Psychology,* 1977, *45,* 620-624.

Goldberg, L. R. Man versus mean: The exploitation of group profiles for the construction of diagnostic classification systems. *Journal of Abnormal Psychology,* 1972, *79,* 121-131.

Golden, C. J., & Golden, E. E. Resistance to cognitive interference as a function of MMPI profile. *Journal of Consulting and Clinical Psychology,* 1975, *43,* 749.

Gynther, M. D., Altman, H., & Sletten, I. W. Development of an empirical interpretive system for the MMPI: Some after-the-fact observations. *Journal of Clinical Psychology,* 1973, *29,* 232-234.

Gynther, M. D., Altman, H., & Sletten, I. W. Replicated correlates of MMPI two-point code types: The Missouri actuarial system. *Journal of Clinical Psychology,* 1973, *29,* 263-289.

Gynther, M. D., Altman, H., & Warbin, R. W. Behavioral correlates for the MMPI 4-9/9-4 code types: A case of the emperor's new clothes? *Journal of Consulting and Clinical Psychology,* 1973, *40,* 259-263.

Gynther, M. D., Altman, H., & Warbin, R. W., & Sletten, I. W. A new actuarial system for MMPI interpretation: Rationale and methodology. *Journal of Clinical Psychology,* 1972, *28,* 173-179.

Kelley, C. K., & King, G. D. Behavioral correlates for within-normal-limit MMPI profiles with and without elevated K in students at a university mental health center. *Journal of Clinical Psychology,* 1978, *34,* 695-699.

King, G. D., & Kelley, C. K. Behavioral correlates for spike-4, spike-9, and 4-9/9-4 MMPI profiles in students at a university mental health center. *Journal of Clinical Psychology,* 1977, *33,* 718-724.

Kunce, J. T., & Anderson, W. P. Normalizing the MMPI. *Journal of Clinical Psychology,* 1976, *32,* 776-780.

Lewandowski, D., & Graham, J. R. Empirical correlates of frequently occurring two-point MMPI code types: A replicated study. *Journal of Consulting and Clinical Psychology,* 1972, *39,* 467-472.

Newmark, C. S., & Finkelstein, M. Maximizing classification rates of Marks and Seeman code types. *Journal of Clinical Psychology,* 1973, *29,* 61-62.

Newmark, C. S., Konanc, J., Aponte, C., & Gard, B. Changes in psychiatric admission MMPI profiles over a period of 15 to 20 years. *Journal of Clinical Psychology,* 1977, *33,* 741-743.

Newmark, C. S., & Sines, L. K. Characteristics of hospitalized patients who produce "floating" MMPI profiles. *Journal of Clinical Psychology,* 1972, *28,* 74-76.

Overall, J. E. Comparison of error rates associated with alternative MMPI profile classification schemes. *Educational and Psychological Measurement,* 1973, *33,* 255-266.

Overall, J. E., & Higgins, C. W. An application of actuarial methods in psychiatric diagnosis. *Journal of Clinical Psychology,* 1977, *33,* 973-980.

Reilley, R. R., & Little, D. K. Hierarchial grouping of MMPI group profiles. *Psychological Reports*, 1977, *41*, 1323-1330.

Rice, J. A. The psychodiagnostic profile. *Journal of Special Education*, 1974, *8*, 193-203.

Schneider, L. J., & Cherry, P. MMPI patterns of college males from 1969 to 1973. *Journal of College Student Personnel*, 1976, *17*, 417-419.

Skinner, H. A. Differentiating the contribution of elevation, scatter and shape in profile similarity. *Educational and Psychological Measurement*, 1978, *38*, 297-308.

Subotnik, L. "Spontaneous remission" of deviant MMPI profiles among college students. *Journal of Consulting and Clinical Psychology*, 1972, *38*, 191-201.

Watson, C. G., & Klett, W. G. A validation of the psychotic inpatient profile. *Journal of Clinical Psychology*, 1972, *28*, 102-109.

Woodward, C. A., & Armentrout, J. A. MMPI profile characteristics of psychiatric patients in an urban Canadian setting. *Canadian Journal of Behavioral Science*, 1974, *6*, 192-198.

Young, R. C. Profile generalizability in the use of the MMPI with psychiatric inpatients. *Journal of Clinical Psychology*, 1974, *30*, 552-557.

Repression Sensitization

Abbott, R. D., Fry, R. M., & Abbott, S. K. The R scale of the MMPI as a measure of acquiescence: Replication for non-pathological content trait adjectives. *Psychological Reports*, 1972, *31*, 806.

Abbott, R. D., Fry, R. M., & Kiem-Abbott, S. Tests of an alternative explanation of data supporting the R scale of the MMPI as a measure of acquiescence. *Psychological Reports*, 1973, *32*, 1243-1246.

Bergquist, W. H., & Klemm, H. D. Acquisition of verbal concepts as a function of explicit and implicit experimental demands and repression-sensitization. *Journal of General Psychology*, 1973, *89*, 67-80.

Carlson, R. W. Dimensionality of the Repression Sensitization Scale. *Journal of Clinical Psychology*, 1979, *35*, 78-84.

Merbaum, M. Simulation of normal MMPI profiles by repressors and sensitizers. *Journal of Consulting and Clinical Psychology*, 1972, *39*, 171.

Millimet, C. R., & Cohen, H. J. A test of the homogeneous versus heterogeneous categorization of the repression-sensitization dimension. *Educational and Psychological Measurement*, 1973, *33*, 773-785.

Shavit, H., & Shouval, R. Repression-sensitization and processing of favorable and adverse information. *Journal of Clinical Psychology*, 1977, *33*, 1041-1044.

Starbird, D. H., & Biller, H. B. An exploratory study of the interaction of cognitive complexity, dogmatism, and repression-sensitization among college students. *Journal of Genetic Psychology*, 1976, *128*, 227-232.

Response Consistency

Coché, E., & Steer, R. A. The MMPI response consistencies of normal, neurotic, and psychotic women. *Journal of Clinical Psychology*, 1974, *30*, 194-195.

Jones, F. W., Neuringer, C., & Patterson, T. W. An evaluation of an MMPI response consistency measure. *Journal of Personality Assessment*, 1976, *40*, 419-421.

Schubert, D. S. P. Increase of personality consistency by prior response. *Journal of Clinical Psychology*, 1975, *31*, 651-658.

Schubert, D. S. P., & Fiske, D. W. Increase of item response consistency by prior item response. *Educational and Psychological Measurement*, 1973, *33*, 113-121.

Response Styles

Anthony, N. Malingering as role-taking. *Journal of Clinical Psychology,* 1976, *32,* 32-41.

Burkhart, B. R., Christian, W. L., & Gynther, M. D. Item subtlety and faking on the MMPI: A paradoxical relationship. *Journal of Personality Assessment,* 1978, *42,* 76-80.

Burkhart, B. R., Gynther, M. D., & Christian, W. L. Psychological mindedness, intelligence, and item subtlety endorsement patterns on the MMPI. *Journal of Clinical Psychology,* 1978, *34,* 76-79.

Calhoun, L. G., & Selby, J. W. Help-seeking attitudes and severity of psychological distress. *Journal of Clinical Psychology,* 1974, *30,* 247-248.

Christian, W. L., Burkhart, B. R., & Gynther, M. D. Subtle-obvious ratings of MMPI items: New interest in an old concept. *Journal of Consulting and Clinical Psychology,* 1978, *46,* 1178-1186.

Cohen, J., & Lefkowitz, J. Development of a biographical inventory blank to predict faking on personality tests. *Journal of Applied Psychology,* 1974, *59,* 404-405.

Davis, D. A., & Widseth, J. C. Prediction of help-seeking with the MMPI: The problem of base rates. *Journal of Clinical Psychology,* 1977, *33,* 995-1000.

Davis, D. A., & Widseth, J. C. A MMPI indicator of psychological distress in male students. *Journal of Counseling Psychology,* 1978, *25,* 469-472.

Groesch, S. J., & Davis, W. E. Psychiatric patients' religion and MMPI responses. *Journal of Clinical Psychology,* 1977, *33,* 168-171.

Harvey, M. A., & Sipprelle, C. N. Demand characteristics effects on the subtle and obvious subscales of the MMPI. *Journal of Personality Assessment,* 1976, *40,* 539-544.

Hunt, H. The differentiation of malingering, dissimulation, and pathology. In M. Hammer, K. Salzinger, S. Sutton, (Eds.), *Psychopathology: Contributions from the social, behavioral, and biological sciences.* New York: John Wiley and Sons, 1973.

Jones, R. R., & Rorer, L. G. Response biases and trait descriptive adjectives. *Multivariate Behavioral Research,* 1973, *8,* 313-330.

Kroger, R. O. Faking in interest measurement: A social-psychological perspective. *Measurement and Evaluation Guide,* 1974, *7,* 130-134.

Match, J., & Wiggins, N. Individual viewpoints of social desirability related to faking good and desirability estimation. *Educational and Psychological Measurement,* 1974, *34,* 591-606.

Morf, M. E., & Jackson, D. N. An analysis of two response styles: True responding and item endorsement. *Educational and Psychological Measurement,* 1972, *32,* 329-353.

Petroni, F. A. Correlates of the psychiatric sick role. *Journal of Health and Social Behavior,* 1972, *13,* 47-54.

Rios-Garcia, L. R., & Cook, P. E. Self-derogation and defense style in college students. *Journal of Personality Assessment,* 1975, *39,* 273-281.

Sacks, J. M., & Kirtley, D. D. Some personality characteristics related to response to subtle and obvious items on the MMPI. *Journal of Consulting and Clinical Psychology,* 1972, *38,* 66-69.

Schwartz, S., & Giacoman, S. Convergent and discriminant validity of three measures of adjustment and three measures of social desirability. *Journal of Consulting and Clinical Psychology,* 1972, *39,* 239-242.

Taylor, J. B., Carithers, M., & Coyne, L. MMPI performance, response set, and the "self-concept hypothesis." *Journal of Consulting and Clinical Psychology,* 1976, *44,* 351-362.

Wales, B., & Seeman, W. Instructional sets and MMPI items. *Journal of Personality Assessment,* 1972, *36,* 282-286.

Wilcox, P., & Dawson, J. G. Role-played and hypnotically induced simulation of psychopathology on the MMPI. *Journal of Clinical Psychology,* 1977, *33,* 743-745.

Scale Development

Boerger, A. R., Graham, J. R., & Lilly, R. S. Behavioral correlates of single-scale MMPI code types. *Journal of Consulting and Clinical Psychology,* 1974, *42,* 398-402.

Brown, P. M. The congruence between moral judgment and selected scales of the MMPI. *Journal of Clinical Psychology,* 1976, *32,* 627-630.

Burish, T. G., & Houston, B. K. Construct validity of the Lie scale as a measure of defensiveness. *Journal of Clinical Psychology,* 1976, *32,* 310-314.

Clayton, M. R., & Graham, J. R. Predictive validity of Barron's *Es* scale: The role of symptom acknowledgment. *Journal of Consulting and Clinical Psychology,* 1979, *47,* 424-425.

Clopton, J. R. MMPI scale development methodology. *Journal of Personality Assessment,* 1978, *42,* 148-151.

Clopton, J. R., & Neuringer, C. MMPI Cannot Say scores: Normative data and de-ized MMPI scales. *Journal of Consulting and Clinical Psychology,* 1978, *46,* 1436-1438.

Clopton, J. R., & Neuringer C. MMPI Cannot Say scores: Normative data and degree of profile distortion. *Journal of Personality Assessment,* 1977, *41,* 511-513.

Finch, A. J., Jr., Griffin, J. L., Jr., & Edwards, G. L. Abbreviated Mf and Si scales: Efficacy with parents of emotionally disturbed children. *Journal of Clinical Psychology,* 1974, *30,* 80.

Graham, J. R. A review of some important MMPI special scales. In P. McReynolds (Ed.), *Advances in psychological assessment IV.* San Francisco: Jossey-Bass, 1978.

Graham, J. R., & Schroeder, H. E. Abbreviated Mf and Si scales for the MMPI. *Journal of Personality Assessment,* 1972, *36,* 436-439.

Greene, R. L. An empirically derived MMPI Carelessness Scale. *Journal of Clinical Psychology,* 1978, *34,* 407-410.

Gynther, M. D., Burkhart, B. R., & Hovanitz, C. Do face-valid items have more predictive validity than subtle items? The case of the MMPI *Pd* scale. *Journal of Consulting and Clinical Psychology,* 1979, *47,* 295-300.

Hedlund, J. L. MMPI clinical scale correlates. *Journal of Consulting and Clinical Psychology,* 1977, *45,* 739-750.

Jarnecke, R. W., & Chambers, E. D. MMPI content scales: Dimensional structure, construct validity, and interpretive norms in a psychiatric population. *Journal of Consulting and Clinical Psychology,* 1977, *45,* 1126-1131.

King, G. D., & Kelley, C. K. MMPI behavioral correlates of spike-5 and two-point code types with scale 5 as one elevation. *Journal of Clinical Psychology,* 1977, *33,* 180-185.

Klingler, D. E., Johnson, J. H., Giannetti, R. A., & Williams, T. A. Comparisons of the clinical utility of the MMPI basic scales and specific MMPI state-trait scales: A test of Dahlstrom's hypothesis. *Journal of Clinical and Consulting Psychology,* 1977, *45,* 1086-1092.

Kroger, R. O., & Turnbull, W. Invalidity of validity scales: The case of the MMPI. *Journal of Consulting and Clinical Psychology,* 1975, *43,* 48-55.

Lachar, D., & Alexander, R. S. Veridicality of self-report: Replicated correlates of the Wiggins MMPI content scales. *Journal of Consulting and Clinical Psychology,* 1978, *46,* 1349-1356.

Levitt, E. E. A note on "MMPI scale development methodology." *Journal of Personality Assessment,* 1978, *42,* 503-504.

Listiak, R. L., Stone, L. A., & Coles, G. J. Clinicians' multidimensional perceptions of MMPI scales. *Journal of Clinical Psychology,* 1973, *29,* 29-32.

Martin, J. D., Blair, G. E., Grah, C. R., & Shoaff, J. E. Correlation of the scores on Barron's Ego Strength Scale with the scores of the Bender-Gestalt Test. *Educational and Psychological Measurement,* 1979, *39,* 187-191.

Stephens, F. G., & Valentine, M. MMPI and clinical scales compared. *British Journal of Psychiatry,* 1974, *125,* 42-43.

Templer, D. I., & Lester, D. An MMPI scale for assessing death anxiety. *Psychological Reports,* 1974, *34,* 238.

Vestre, N. D., & Watson, C. G. Behavioral correlates of the MMPI paranoia scale. *Psychological Reports,* 1972, *31,* 851-854.

Wakefield, J. A., Bradley, P. E., Doughtie, E. B., & Kraft, I. A. Influence of overlapping and non-overlapping items on the theoretical interrelationships of MMPI scales. *Journal of Consulting and Clinical Psychology,* 1975, *43,* 851-857.

Zuckerman, M., Bone, R. N., Neary, R., Mangelsdorff, D., & Brustman, B. What is the sensation seeker? Personality trait and experience correlates of the sensation-seeking scales. *Journal of Consulting and Clinical Psychology,* 1972, *39,* 308-321.

Short Forms

Bassett, J. E., Schellman, G. C., Gayton, W. F., & Tavormina, J. Efficacy of the Mini-Mult validity scales with prisoners. *Journal of Clinical Psychology,* 1977, *33,* 729-731.

Bolton, B. Homogeneous subscales for the Mini-Mult. *Journal of Consulting and Clinical Psychology,* 1976, *44,* 684-685.

Caslyn, D. A., Spengler, D. M., & Freeman, C. W. Application of the somatization factor of the MMPI-168 with low back pain patients. *Journal of Clinical Psychology,* 1977, *33,* 1017-1020.

Dean, E. F. A lengthened Mini: The Midi-Mult. *Journal of Clinical Psychology,* 1972, *28,* 68-71.

Elsie, R. D., & McLachlan, J. F. Reliability of the Maxi-Mult and scale equivalence with the MMPI. *Journal of Clinical Psychology,* 1976, *32,* 67-70.

Erickson, R. C., & Freeman, C. Using the MMPI-168 with medical inpatients. *Journal of Clinical Psychology,* 1976, *32,* 803-806.

Erickson, R. C., & O'Leary, M. Using the MMPI-168 with alcoholics. *Journal of Clinical Psychology,* 1977, *33,* 133-135.

Faschingbauer, T. R. A 166-item short form of the group MMPI: The FAM. *Journal of Consulting and Clinical Psychology,* 1974, *42,* 645-655.

Faschingbauer, T. R. Some clinical considerations in selecting a short form of the MMPI. *Professional Psychology,* 1976, *7,* 167-176.

Faschingbauer, T. R. Substitution and regression models, base rates, and the clinical validity of the Mini-Mult. *Journal of Clinical Psychology,* 1976, *32,* 70-74.

Faschingbauer, T. R., Johnson, D. T., & Newmark, C. S. The interpretative validity of the FAM: Long-term psychotherapists' ratings of psychiatric inpatients. *Journal of Personality Assessment,* 1978, *42,* 74-75.

Fillenbaum, G. G., & Pfeiffer, E. The Mini-Mult: A cautionary note. *Journal of Consulting and Clinical Psychology,* 1976, *44,* 698-703.

Finch, A. J., Jr., Edwards, G. L., & Griffin, J. L., Jr. Utility of the Mini-Mult with parents of emotionally disturbed children. *Journal of Personality Assessment,* 1975, *39,* 146-150.

Finch, A. J., Jr., Kendall, P. C., Nelson, W. M., & Newmark, C. S. Application of Fauschingbauer's abbreviated MMPI to parents of emotionally disturbed children. *Psychological Reports,* 1975, *37,* 571-574.

Freeman, C., Caslyn, D., & O'Leary, M. Application of Faschingbauer's abbreviated MMPI with medical patients. *Journal of Consulting and Clinical Psychology,* *45,* 706-707.

Freeman, C. W., O'Leary, M. R., & Caslyn D. Application of the Faschingbauer Abbreviated MMPI with alcoholic patients. *Journal of Clinical Psychology,* 1977, *33,* 303-306.

Gaines, L. S., Abrams, M. H., Toel, P., & Miller, L. M. Comparison of the MMPI and the Mini-Mult with alcoholics. *Journal of Consulting and Clinical Psychology,* 1974, *42,* 619.

Gayton, W. F., Bishop, J. S., Citrin, M. M., & Bassett, J. S. An investigation of the Mini-Mult validity scales. *Journal of Personality Assessment,* 1975, *39,* 511-513.

Gayton, W. F., Fogg, M. E., Tavorimina, J., Bishop, J. S., Citrin, M. M., & Bassett, J. F. Comparison of the MMPI and Mini-Mult with women who request abortion. *Journal of Clinical Psychology,* 1976, *32,* 648-650.

Gayton, W. F., Ozman, K. L., & Wilson, W. T. Investigation of a written form of the Mini-Mult. *Psychological Reports,* 1972, *30,* 275-278.

Gilroy, F. D., & Steinbacher, R. Extension of the Mini-Mult to a college population. *Journal of Personality Assessment,* 1973, *37,* 263-266.

Griffin, J. L., Finch, A. J., Edwards, G. L., & Kendall, P. C. MMPI-Midi-Mult correspondence with parents of emotionally disturbed children. *Journal of Clinical Psychology,* 1976, *32,* 54-56.

Harford, T., Lubetkin, B., & Alpert, G. Comparison of the standard MMPI and the Mini-Mult in a psychiatric outpatient clinic. *Journal of Consulting and Clinical Psychology,* 1972, *39,* 243-245.

Hedberg, A. G., Campbell, L. M., Weeks, S. R., & Powell J. A. The use of the MMPI (Mini-Mult) to predict alcoholics' response to a behavioral treatment program. *Journal of Clinical Psychology,* 1975, *31,* 271-274.

Hedlund, J. L., Cho, D. W., & Wood, J. B. Comparative validity of MMPI-168 factors and clinical scales. *Multivariate Behavioral Research,* 1977, *12,* 327-329.

Hedlund, J. L., Cho, D. W., & Wood, J. B. MMPI-168 factor structure: A replication with public health mental patients. *Journal of Consulting and Clinical Psychology,* 1977, *45,* 711-712.

Hedlund, J. L., Cho, D. W., & Powell, B. J. Use of MMPI short forms with psychiatr: patients. *Journal of Consulting and Clinical Psychology,* 1975, *43,* 924.

Hobbs, T. R. Scale equivalence and profile similarity of the Mini-Mult and MMPI in an outpatient clinic. *Journal of Clinical Psychology,* 1974, *30,* 349-350.

Hobbs, T. R., & Fowler, R. D. Reliability and scale equivalence of the Mini-Mult and MMPI. *Journal of Consulting and Clinical Psychology,* 1974, *42,* 89-92.

Hoffmann, N. G., & Butcher, J. N. Clinical limitations of three MMPI short forms. *Journal of Consulting and Clinical Psyghology,* 1975, *43,* 32-39.

Huisman, R. E. Correspondence between Mini-Mult and standard MMPI scale scores in patients with neurological disease. *Journal of Consulting and Clinical Psychology,* 1974, *42,* 149.

Jabara, R. F., & Curran, S. F. Comparison of the MMPI and Mini-Mult with drug users. *Journal of Consulting and Clinical Psychology,* 1974, *42,* 739-740.

McLachlan, J. F. C. Test-retest stability of long and short MMPI scales over two years. *Journal of Clinical Psychology,* 1974, *30,* 189-191.

Mlott, S. R. The Mini-Mult and its use with adolescents. *Journal of Clinical Psychology,* 1973, *29,* 376-377.

Mlott, S. R., & Mason, R. L. The practicability of using an abbreviated form of the MMPI with chronic renal dialysis patients. *Journal of Clinical Psychology,* 1975, *31,* 65-68.

Newmark, C. S., Boas, B., & Messervy, T. An abbreviated MMPI for use with college students. *Psychological Reports,* 1974, *34,* 631-634.

Newmark, C. S., Conger, A. J., & Faschingbauer, T. R. The interpretive validity and effective test length functioning of an abbreviated MMPI relative to the standard MMPI. *Journal of Clinical Psychology,* 1976, *32,* 27-32.

Newmark, C. S., Cook, L., Clarke, M., & Faschingbauer, T. R. Application of Faschingbauer's abbreviated MMPI to psychiatric inpatients. *Journal of Consulting and Clinical Psychology,* 1973, *41,* 416-421.

Newmark, C. S., Cook. L., & Greer, W. Application of the Midi-Mult to psychiatric inpatients. *Journal of Clinical Psychology,* 1973, *29,* 481-484.

Newmark, C. S., Falk, R., & Finch, A. J. Interpretive accuracy of abbreviated MMPIs. *Journal of Personality Assessment,* 1976, *40,* 10-12.

Newmark, C. S., & Faschingbauer, T. R. Bibliography of short forms of the
    MMPI. *Journal of Personality Assessment,* 1978, *42,* 496-502.
Newmark, C. S., & Finch, A. J. Comparing the diagnostic validity of an ab-
    breviated and standard MMPI. *Journal of Personality Assessment,* 1976, *40,*
    10-12.
Newmark, C. S., Galen, R., & Gold, K. Efficacy of an abbreviated MMPI as a
    function of type of administration. *Journal of Clinical Psychology,* 1975,
    31, 639-642.
Newmark, C. S., & Glenn, L. Sensitivity of the Faschingbauer Abbreviated MMPI
    to hospitalized adolescents. *Journal of Abnormal Child Psychology,* 1974,
    2, 299-306.
Newmark, C. S., Newmark, L., & Cook, L. The MMPI-168 with psychiatric patients.
    Journal of Clinical Psychology, 1975, *31,* 61-64.
Newmark, C. S., Newmark, L., & Faschingbauer, T. R. Utility of three abbrevia-
    ted MMPIs with psychiatric outpatients. *Journal of Nervous and Mental
    Disease,* 1974, *159,* 438-443.
Newmark, C. S., Owen, M., Newmark, L., & Faschingbauer, T. R. Comparison of
    three abbreviated MMPIs for psychiatric patients and normals. *Journal of
    Personality Assessment,* 1975, *39,* 261-270.
Newmark, C. S., & Raft, D. Using an abbreviated MMPI as a screening device for
    medical patients. *Psychosomatics,* 1976, *17,* 45-48.
Ogilvie, L. P., Kotin, J., & Stanley, D. H. Comparison of the MMPI and the
    Mini-Mult in a psychiatric outpatient clinic. *Journal of Consulting and
    Clinical Psychology,* 1976, *44,* 497-498.
Overall, J. E., Butcher, J. N., & Hunter, S. Validity of the MMPI-168 for
    psychiatric screening. *Educational and Psychological Measurement,* 1975,
    35, 393-400.
Overall, J. E., & Gomez-Mont, F. The MMPI-168 for psychiatric screening. *Ed-
    ucational and Psychological Measurement,* 1974, *34,* 315-319.
Overall, J. E., Higgins, W., & De Schweinitz, A. Comparison of differential
    diagnostic discrimination for abbreviated and standard MMPI. *Journal of
    Clinical Psychology,* 1976, *32,* 237-245.
Overall, J. E., Hunter, S., & Butcher, J. N. Factor structure of the MMPI-168
    in a psychiatric population. *Journal of Consulting and Clinical Psychology,*
    1973, *41,* 284-286.
Palmer, A. B. A comparison of the MMPI and Mini-Mult in a sample of state men-
    tal hospital patients. *Journal of Clinical Psychology,* 1973, *29,* 484-485.
Pantano, L. T., & Schwartz, M. L. Differentiation of neurologic and pseudo-
    neurologic patients with combined MMPI Mini-Mult and Pseudo-Neurologic
    Scale. *Journal of Clinical Psychology,* 1978, *34,* 56-60.
Percell, L. P., & Delk, J. L. Relative usefulness of three forms of the Mini-
    Mult with college students. *Journal of Consulting and Clinical Psychology,*
    1973, *40,* 487.
Platt, J. J., & Scura, W. C. Validity of the Mini-Mult with male reformatory
    inmates. *Journal of Clinical Psychology,* 1972, *28,* 528-529.
Poythress, N. G., Jr. Selecting a short form of the MMPI: Addendum to
    Faschingbauer. *Journal of Consulting and Clinical Psychology,* 1978, *46,*
    331-334.
Poythress, N. G., & Blaney, P. H. The validity of MMPI interpretations based
    on the Mini-Mult and the FAM. *Journal of Personality Assessment,* 1978, *42,*
    143-147.
Rusk, R., Hyerstay, B. J., Calsyn, D. A., & Freeman, C. W. Comparison of the
    utility of two abbreviated forms of the MMPI for psychiatric screening of
    the elderly. *Journal of Clinical Psychology,* 1979, *35,* 104-107.
Rybott, G. A., & Lambert, J. A. Correspondence of the MMPI and Mini-Mult with
    psychiatric inpatients. *Journal of Clinical Psychology,* 1975, *31,* 279-281.
Scott, N. A., Mount, M. K., & Kosters, S. A. Correspondence of the MMPI and
    the Mini-Mult among female reformatory inmates. *Journal of Clinical Psy-
    chology,* 1976, *32,* 792-794.

Simono, R. B. Comparison of the standard MMPI and the Mini-Mult in a university counseling center. *Educational and Psychological Measurement,* 1975, *35,* 401-404.

Streiner, D. L., Goodman, J. T., & McLean, A. Correspondence between the MMPI and the Midi-Mult. *Psychological Reports,* 1977, *40,* 551-554.

Streiner, D. L., Woodward, C. A., Goodman, J. T., & McLean, A. Comparison of the MMPI and Mini-Mult. *Canadian Journal of Behavioral Science,* 1973, *5,* 76-82.

Taulbee, E. S. Mini-Mult vs. MMPI. *Journal of Personality Assessment,* 1974, *38,* 479.

Taulbee, E. S., & Samelson, J. Mini-Mult vs. MMPI. *Journal of Personality Assessment,* 1972, *36,* 590.

Thornton, L. S., Finch, A. J., & Griffin, J. L. The Mini-Mult with criminal psychiatric patients. *Journal of Personality Assessment,* 1975, *39,* 394-396.

Trybus, R. J., & Hewitt, C. W. The Mini-Mult in a non-psychiatric population. *Journal of Clinical Psychology,* 1972, *28,* 371.

Tsushima, W. T. Relationship between the Mini-Mult and the MMPI with medical patients. *Journal of Clinical Psychology,* 1975, *31,* 673-675.

Turner, J., & McCreary C. Short forms of the MMPI with back pain patients. *Journal of Consulting and Clinical Psychology,* 1978, *46,* 354-355.

Vincent, K. R. Validity of the MMPI-168 on private clinic subpopulations. *Journal of Clinical Psychology,* 1978, *34,* 61-62.

Walls, R., McGlynn, F. D., & Tingstrom, D. H. An evaluation of three short forms extracted from the group form MMPI responses of incarcerated offenders. *Journal of Clinical Psychology,* 1977, *33,* 431-435.

RESEARCH AREAS

Academic Achievement

Banreti-Fuchs, K. M., & Meadows, W. M. Interest, mental health, and attitudinal correlates of academic achievement among university students. *British Journal of Educational Psychology,* 1976, *46,* 212-219.

Banreti-Fuchs, K. M. Attitudinal, situational and mental health correlates of academic achievement at the undergraduate university level. *British Journal of Educational Psychology,* 1975, *45,* 227-231.

Clopton, J. R., & Neuringer, C. An MMPI scale to measure scholastic personality in women. *Perceptual and Motor Skills,* 1973, *37,* 963-966.

Faunce, P. S., & Loper, R. G. Personality characteristics of high ability college women and college women-in-general. *Journal of College Student Personnel,* 1972, *13,* 499-504.

Felton, G. S. Use of the MMPI Underachievement Scale as an aid in counseling academic low achievers in college. *Psychological Reports,* 1973, *32,* 151-157.

Levine, R. V., Megargee, E. I. Prediction of academic success with the MMPI and Beta Intelligence Test in a correctional institution. *Catalog of Selected Documents in Psychology,* 1975, *5,* 343.

Maudal, G. R., Butcher, J. N., & Mauger, P. A. A multivariate study of personality and academic factors in college attrition. *Journal of Counseling Psychology,* 1974, *21,* 560-567.

Newton, M., & Krauss, H. H. The health-engenderingness of resident assistants as related to student achievement and adjustment. *Journal of College Student Personnel,* 1973, *14,* 321-325.

Adolescents and College Students

Chase, T. V., Chaffin, S., Morrison, S. D. False positive adolescent MMPI profiles. *Adolescence,* 1975, *40,* 507-519.

Eddy, G. L., & Sinnett, E. R. Behavior setting utilization by emotionally disturbed college students. *Journal of Consulting and Clinical Psychology*, 1973, *40*, 210-216.

Feinberg, L. Faculty-student interaction: How students differ. *Journal of College Student Personnel*, 1972, *13*, 24-27.

Jones, F. H. A 4-year follow-up of vulnerable adolescents: The prediction of outcome in early adulthood from measures of social competence, coping style, and overall level of psychopathology. *Journal of Nervous and Mental Disease*, 1974, *159*, 20-39.

Klinge, V., & Strauss, M. Effects of scoring norms on adolescent psychiatric patients' MMPI profiles. *Journal of Personality Assessment*, 1976, *40*, 13-17.

Mlott, S. R. Degree of agreement among MMPI scores, self-ratings, and staff ratings of inpatient adolescents. *Journal of Clinical Psychology*, 1973, *29*, 480-481.

Oshman, H., & Manosevitz, M. The impact of the identity crisis on the adjustment of late adolescent males. *Journal of Youth and Adolescence*, 1974, *3*, 207-216.

Rychlak, J. F. Time orientation in the positive and negative free phantasies of mildly abnormal versus normal high school males. *Journal of Consulting and Clinical Psychology*, 1973, *41*, 175-180.

Schubert, D. S. P. Increase of apparent adjustment in adolescence by further ego identity formation and age. *College Student Journal*, 1973, *7*, 3-5.

Schubert, D. S. P., & Wagner, M. E. A subcultural change of MMPI norms in the 1960s due to adolescent role confusion and glamorization of alienation. *Journal of Abnormal Psychology*, 1975, *84*, 406-411.

Spellacy, F. Neuropsychological differences between violent and nonviolent adolescents. *Journal of Clinical Psychology*, 1977, *33*, 966-969.

Aging

Alpaugh, P. K., & Birren, J. E. Are there sex differences in creativity across the adult life span? *Human Development*, 1975, *18*, 461-465.

Davis, W. E., Mozdzierz, G. J., & Macchitelli, F. J. Loss of discriminative "power" of the MMPI with older psychiatric patients. *Journal of Personality Assessment*, 1973, *37*, 555-558.

Edwards, A. E., & Husted, J. R. Penile sensitivity, age, and sexual behavior. *Journal of Clinical Psychology*, 1976, *32*, 697-700.

Fracchia, J., Sheppard, C., & Merlis, S. Treatment patterns in psychiatry: Clinical and personality features of elderly hospitalized patients during milieu, single-drug and multiple-drug programs. *Journal of American Geriatrics Society*, 1974, *22*, 212-216.

Harmatz, J. S., & Shader, R. I. Psychopharmacologic investigations in healthy elder volunteers: MMPI depression scale. *Journal of the American Geriatrics Society*, 1975, *23*, 350-354.

Lewinson, P. M., & MacPhillamy, D. J. The relationship between age and engagement in pleasant activities. *Journal of Gerontology*, 1974, *29*, 290-294.

Cross-Cultural and Subcultural

Baughman, E. E., & Dahlstrom, W. G. Racial differences on the MMPI. In S. S. Guterman (Ed.), *Black psyche: The modal personality patterns of black Americans*. Berkeley, Calif.: Glendessary Press, 1972.

Butcher, J. N., & Gur, R. Hebrew translation of the MMPI: An assessment of translation adequacy and preliminary validation. *Journal of Cross-Cultural Psychology*, 1974, *5*, 220-227.

Costello, R. M. Item level racial differences on the MMPI. *Journal of Social Psychology*, 1973, *91*, 161-162.

Costello, R. M. Construction and cross-validation of an MMPI Black-White scale. *Journal of Personality Assessment*, 1977, *41*, 514-519.

Costello, R. M., Fine, H. J., & Blau, B. I. Racial comparisons on the MMPI. *Journal of Clinical Psychology,* 1973, *29,* 63-65.

Costello, R. M., Tiffany, D. W., & Gier, R. H. Methodological issues and racial (black-white) comparisons on the MMPI. *Journal of Consulting and Clinical Psychology,* 1972, *38,* 161-168.

Cowan, M. A., Watkins, B. A., & Davis, W. E. Level of education, diagnosis and race-related differences in MMPI performance. *Journal of Clinical Psychology,* 1975, *31,* 442-444.

Davis, W. E. Race and differential "power" of the MMPI. *Journal of Personality Assessment,* 1975, *39,* 138-140.

Davis, W. E., Beck, S. J., & Ryan T. A. Race-related and educationally-related MMPI profile differences among hospitalized schizophrenics. *Journal of Clinical Psychology,* 1973, *29,* 478-479.

Davis, W. E., & Jones, M. H. Negro versus Caucasian test performance revisited. *Journal of Consulting and Clinical Psychology,* 1974, *42,* 675-679.

Elion, V. H. The validity of the MMPI as a discriminator of social deviance among black males. FCI Research Reports, Vol. 6, No. 3. Tallahassee, Fla.: Federal Correctional Institution, 1974.

Elion, V. H., & Megargee, E. I. Validity of the MMPI Pd scale among black males. *Journal of Consulting and Clinical Psychology,* 1975, *43,* 166-172.

Gendreau, P. Psychological test usage in corrections in English-speaking Canada: 1972-1973. *Canadian Journal of Criminology and Corrections,* 1975, *17,* 215-220.

Genther, R. W., & Graham, J. R. Effects of short-term public psychiatric hospitalization for both black and white patients. *Journal of Consulting and Clinical Psychology,* 1976, *44,* 118-124.

Ghei, S. N. A cross-cultural comparison of the social desirability variable. *Journal of Cross-Cultural Psychology,* 1973, *4,* 493-500.

Gynther, M. D. White norms and black MMPIs: A prescription for discrimination? *Psychological Bulletin,* 1972, *78,* 386-402.

Gynther, M. D., Altman, H., & Warbin, R. Interpretation of uninterpretable MMPI profiles. *Journal of Consulting and Clinical Psychology,* 1973, *40,* 78-83.

Gynther, M. D., Lachar, D., & Dahlstrom, W. D. Are special norms for minorities needed? Development of an MMPI F scale for blacks. *Journal of Consulting and Clinical Psychology,* 1978, *46,* 1403-1408.

Gynther, M. D., & Witt, P. H. Windstorms and important persons: Personality characteristics of black educators. *Journal of Clinical Psychology,* 1976, *32,* 613-616.

Jones, E. E. Black-White personality differences: Another look. *Journal of Personality Assessment,* 1978, *42,* 244-252.

King, H. F., Carroll, J. L., & Fuller, G. B. Comparison of nonpsychiatric Blacks and Whites on the MMPI. *Journal of Clinical Psychology,* 1977, *33,* 725-728.

Lamont, J., & Tyler, C. Racial differences in rate of depression. *Journal of Clinical Psychology,* 1973, *29,* 428-432.

Marsella, A. J., Sanborn, K. O., Kameoka, V., Shizuru, L., & Brennan, J. Cross validation of depression among normal populations of Japanese, Chinese, and Caucasian ancestry. *Journal of Clinical Psychology,* 1975, *31,* 281-287.

McCreary, C., & Padilla, E. MMPI differences among Black, Mexican-American, and White male offenders. *Journal of Clinical Psychology,* 1977, *33,* 171-177.

Murray, L., Heritage, J., & Holmes, W. Black-White comparisons of the MMPI Mini-Mult. *Southern Journal of Educational Research,* 1976, *10,* 105-114.

Pandey, R. E. Personality characteristics of successful, dropout, and probationary black and white university students. *Journal of Counseling Psychology,* 1972, *19,* 382-386.

Patil, V., & Manerikar, V. The personality profile of Indian executives using the MMPI. *Indian Journal of Applied Psychology,* 1976, *13,* 16-20.

Plemons, G. A comparison of MMPI scores of Anglo- and Mexican American psychiatric patients. *Journal of Consulting and Clinical Psychology*, 1977, *45*,
149-150.

Powell, L., & Johnson, E. H. The black MMPI profile: Interpretive problems.
Journal of Negro Education, 1976, *45*, 27-36.

Rosenblatt, A. I., & Pritchard, D. A. Moderators of racial differences on the
MMPI. *Journal of Consulting and Clinical Psychology*, 1978, *46*, 1572-1573.

Sappington, A., & Grizzard, R. Self-discrimination responses in black school
children. *Journal of Personality and Social Psychology*, 1975, *31*, 224-231.

Scott, J., & Gaitz, C. Ethnic and age differences in mental health measurement.
Diseases of the Nervous System, 1975, *36*, 389-393.

Shore, R. E. A statistical note on "differential misdiagnosis of blacks and
whites by the MMPI." *Journal of Personality Assessment*, 1976, *40*, 21-23.

Strauss, M. E., Gynther, M. D., & Wallhermfechtel, J. Differential misdiagnosis of blacks and whites by the MMPI. *Journal of Personality Assessment*,
1974, *38*, 55-60.

Sue, S., & Sue, D. W. MMPI comparisons between Asian-American and non-Asian
students utilizing a student health psychiatric clinic. *Journal of Counseling Psychology*, 1974, *21*, 423-427.

Thomas, J. E. A cross validation study of the Hy scale of the MMPI in India.
Psychological Studies, 1973, *18*, 50-52.

Witt, P. H., & Gynther, M. D. Another explanation for black-white MMPI differences. *Journal of Clinical Psychology*, 1975, *31*, 69-70.

Families--Parents, Children, and Couples

Alley, G. R., Snider, B., Forsyth, R. A., & Opitz, E. Comparative parental
MMPI protocols of children evaluated at a child development clinic.
Psychological Reports, 1974, *35*, 1147-1154.

Armentrout, J. A. Repression-sensitization and MMPI correlates of retrospective reports of parental child-rearing behaviors. *Journal of Clinical
Psychology*, 1975, *31*, 444-448.

Bradley, P. E., Wakefield, J. A., Jr., Yom, B. L., Doughtie, E. B., Cox,
J. A., & Kraft, I. A. Parental MMPIs and certain pathological behaviors in
children. *Journal of Clinical Psychology*, 1974, *30*, 379-382.

Briggs, P. F., Rouzer, D. L., Hamberg, R. L., & Holman, T. R. Seven scales for
the Minnesota-Briggs History Record with reference group data. *Journal of
Clinical Psychology*, 1972, *28*, 431-448.

Burger, G. K., Armentrout, J. A., & Rapfogel, R. G. Recalled parental behavior
and objective personality measures: A canonical analysis. *Journal of
Personality Assessment*, 1975, *39*, 514-522.

Byong-Hee, L. Y., Bradley, P. E., Wakefield, J. A., Jr., Kraft, I. A.,
Doughtie, E. B., & Cox, J. A. A common factor in the MMPI scales of married
couples. *Journal of Personality Assessment*, 1975, *39*, 64-69.

Catlin, N., Croake, J. W., & Keller, J. F. MMPI profiles of cohabiting college
students. *Psychological Reports*, 1976, *38*, 407-410.

Cohler, B. J., Grunebaum, H. U., Weiss, J. L., Robbins, D. M., Shader, R. I.,
Gallant, D., & Hartman, C. R. Social role performance and psychopathology
among recently hospitalized and nonhospitalized mothers: 2, correlates with
life stress and life-reported psychopathology. *Journal of Nervous and Mental Disease*, 1974, *159*, 81-90.

Dee, C., & Dee, H. L. MMPIs of parents of emotionally disturbed, motor dysfunctional, and normal children. *Journal of Consulting and Clinical Psychology*, 1972, *38*, 464.

Friedman, R. J. MMPI characteristics of mothers of pre-school children who are
emotionally disturbed or have behavior problems. *Psychological Reports*,
1974, *34*, 1159-1162.

Gartner, D., & Goldstein, H. S. Some characteristics of mothers of severely disturbed children in a therapeutic nursery. *Psychological Reports,* 1972, *30,* 901-902.

Heilbrun, A. B., Jr., & Norbert, N. Style of adaptation to aversive maternal control and paranoid behavior. *Journal of Genetic Psychology,* 1972, *120,* 145-153.

Horn, J. H., & Turner, R. G. MMPI profiles among subgroups of unwed mothers. *Journal of Consulting and Clinical Psychology,* 1976, *44,* 25-33.

McAdoo, W. G. The application of Goldberg's classification rules to parents in a child guidance clinic and in an adult psychiatric clinic. *Journal of Community Psychology,* 1974, *2,* 174-175.

McAdoo, W. G., & Connolly, F. J. MMPIs of parents in dysfunctional families. *Journal of Consulting and Clinical Psychology,* 1975, *43,* 270.

McAdoo, W. G., & Roeske, N. A. A comparison of defectors and continuers in a child guidance clinic. *Journal of Consulting and Clinical Psychology,* 1973, *40,* 328-334.

McKay, M. J., & Richardson, H. Personality differences between one-time and recidivist unwed mothers. *Journal of Genetic Psychology,* 1973, *122,* 207-210.

Meikle, S., & Gerritse, R. A comparison of husband-wife responses to pregnancy. *Journal of Psychology,* 1973, *83,* 17-23.

Miller, W. H., & Gottlieb, F. Predicting behavioral treatment outcome in disturbed children: A preliminary report on the Responsivity Index of Parents (RIP) *Behavior Therapy,* 1974, *5,* 210-214.

Miller, W. H., & Keirn, W. C. Personality measurement in parents of retarded emotionally disturbed children: A replication. *Journal of Clinical Psychology,* 1978, *34,* 686-690.

Mlott, S. R. Some significant relationships between adolescents and their parents as revealed by the MMPI. *Adolescence,* 1972, *7,* 169-182.

Newmark, C. S., & Toomey, T. The MF scale as an index of disturbed marital interaction: A replication. *Psychological Reports,* 1972, *31,* 590.

Paulson, M. J., Afifi, A., Chaleff, A., Thomason, M., & Lui, V. An MMPI scale for identifying at risk abusive parents. *Journal of Clinical Child Psychology,* 1975, *4,* 22-24.

Paulson, M. J., Afifi, A. A., Thomason, M. L., & Chaleff, A. The MMPI: A descriptive measure of psychopathology in abusive parents. *Journal of Clinical Psychology,* 1974, *30,* 387-390.

Paulson, M. J., Schwemer, G. T., & Bendel, R. B. Clinical application of the Pd, Ma and (OH) experimental MMPI scales to further understanding of abusive parents. *Journal of Clinical Psychology,* 1976, *32,* 558-564.

Rodgers, D. A., & Ziegler, F. J. Social role theory, the marital relationship, and the use of ovulation suppressors. *Journal of Marriage and Family,* 1968, *30,* 584-591.

Verinis, J. S. Maternal and child pathology in an urban ghetto. *Journal of Clinical Psychology,* 1976, *32,* 13-15.

Wright, L. The sick but slick syndrome as a personality component of parents of battered children. *Journal of Clinical Psychology,* 1976, *32,* 41-45.

Field Dependency

Fine, B. J. Field-dependent introvert and neuroticism: Eysenck and Witkin united. *Psychological Reports,* 1972, *31,* 939-959.

Morris, L. A., & Shapiro, A. K. MMPI scores for field-dependent and field-independent psychiatric outpatients. *Journal of Consulting and Clinical Psychology,* 1974, *42,* 364-369.

Stansell, V., Beutler, L. E., Neville, C. W., & Johnson, D. T. MMPI correlates of extreme field independence and field dependence in a psychiatric population. *Perceptual and Motor Skills,* 1975, *40,* 539-544.

Genetics

Goldsmith, H. H., & Gottesman, I. I. An extension of construct validity for personality scales using twin-based criteria. *Journal of Research in Personality*, 1977, *11*, 381-397.

Gottesman, I. I., & Shields, J. *Schizophrenia and genetics: A twin study vantage point*. New York: Academic Press, 1972.

Haier, R. J., Rosenthal, D., & Wender, P. H. MMPI assessment of psychopathology in the adopted-away offspring of schizophrenics. *Archives of General Psychiatry*, 1978, *35*, 171-175.

Hill, M. S. Heredity influence on the normal personality using the MMPI: 2, prospective assortative mating. *Behavior Genetics*, 1973, *3*, 225-232.

Hill, M. S., & Hill, R. N. Heredity influence on the normal personality using the MMPI: 1, age-corrected parent-offspring resemblances. *Behavior Genetics*, 1973, *3*, 133-144.

Horn, J. M., Green, M., Carney, R., & Erickson, M. T. Bias against genetic hypotheses in adoption studies. *Archives of General Psychiatry*, 1975, *32*, 1365-1367.

Wender, P. H., Rosenthal, D., Rainer, J. D., Greenhill, L., & Sarlin, B. Schizophrenics' adopting parents. *Archives of General Psychiatry*, 1977, *34*, 777-784.

Homosexuality

Adelman, M. R. A comparison of professionally employed lesbians and heterosexual women on the MMPI. *Archives of Sexual Behavior*, 1977, *6*, 193-201.

Birk, L., Huddleston, W., Miller, E., & Cohler, B. Avoidance conditioning for homosexuality. *Archives of General Psychiatry*, 1971, *25*, 314-323.

Horstman, W. R. MMPI responses of homosexual and heterosexual male college students. *Homosexual Counseling Journal*, 1975, *2*, 68-76.

Lopiccolo, J., & Blatt, S. J. Cognitive style and sexual identity. *Journal of Clinical Psychology*, 1972, *28*, 148-151.

Pierce, D. M. Test and nontest correlates of active and situational homosexuality. *Psychology*, 1973, *10*, 23-26.

Rosen, A. C. Brief report of MMPI characteristics of sexual deviation. *Psychological Reports*, 1974, *35*, 73-74.

Ross, M. W. Relationship between sex role and sex orientation in homosexual men. *New Zealand Psychologist*, 1975, *4*, 25-29.

Tanner, B. A. A comparison of automated aversive conditioning and a waiting list control in the modification of homosexual behavior in males. *Behavior Therapy*, 1974, *5*, 29-32.

Tanner, B. A. Avoidance training with and without booster sessions to modify homosexual behavior in males. *Behavior Therapy*, 1975, *6*, 649-653.

Locus of Control

Gray-Little, B. Attitudes toward conflict with authority as a function of sex, I-E, and dogmatism. *Psychological Reports*, 1974, *34*, 375-381.

Lottman, T. J., Davis, W. E., & Gustafson, R. C. MMPI correlates with locus of control in a psychiatric population. *Journal of Personality Assessment*, 1973, *37*, 78-82.

Powell, A., & Gable, P. Adult locus of control and self-righteous attitudes. *Psychological Reports*, 1973, *32*, 302.

Masculinity-Femininity

Constaninople, A. Masculinity-femininity: An exception to a famous dictum? *Psychological Bulletin*, 1973, *80*, 389-407.

Fenster, C. A., & Locke, B. Patterns of masculinity-femininity among college- and noncollege-oriented police officers: An empirical approach. *Journal of Clinical Psychology,* 1973, *29,* 27-28.

Lunneborg, P. W. Dimensionality of MF. *Journal of Clinical Psychology,* 1972, *28,* 313-317.

Russell, M. A., & Sines, J. O. Further evidence that M-F is bipolar and multi- dimensional. *Journal of Clinical Psychology,* 1978, *34,* 643-649.

Sines, J. O. M-F: Bipolar and probably multidimensional. *Journal of Clinical Psychology,* 1977, *33,* 1038-1041.

Sines, J. O., & Russell, M. A. The BSRI M, F, and androgeny scales are bipolar. *Journal of Clinical Psychology,* 1978, *34,* 53-56.

Suter, B., & Domino, G. Masculinity-femininity in creative college women. *Journal of Personality Assessment,* 1975, *39,* 414-420.

Wakefield, J. A., Sasek, J., Friedman, A. F., & Bowden, J. D. Androgeny and other measures of masculinity-femininity. *Journal of Consulting and Clinical Psychology,* 1976, *44,* 766-770.

Sleep

Cartwright, R. D. Sleep fantasy in normal and schizophrenic persons. *Journal of Abnormal Psychology,* 1972, *80,* 275-279.

Cartwright, R. D., & Ratzel, R. W. Effects of dream loss on waking behaviors. *Archives of General Psychiatry,* 1972, *27,* 277-280.

Coursey, R. D., Buchsbaum, M., & Frankel, B. L. Personality measures and evoked responses in chronic insomniacs. *Journal of Abnormal Psychology,* 1975, *84,* 239-249.

Hartmann, E., Baekeland, F., & Zwilling, G. R. Psychological differences be- tween long and short sleepers. *Archives of General Psychiatry,* 1972, *26,* 463-468.

Kales, A., Caldwell, A. B., Preston, T. A., Healey, S., & Kales, J. D. Person- ality patterns in insomnia: Theoretical implications. *Archives of General Psychiatry,* 1976, *33,* 1128-1134.

McDonald, D. G., Shallenberger, H. D., Koresko, R. L., & Kinzy, B. G. Studies of spontaneous electrodermal responses in sleep. *Psychophysiology,* 1976, *13,* 128-134.

Monroe, L. J., & Marks, P. A. MMPI differences between adolescent poor and good sleepers. *Journal of Consulting and Clinical Psychology,* 1977, *45,* 151-152.

Roth, T., Kramer, M., & Lutz, T. The nature of insomnia: A descriptive summary of a sleep clinic population. *Comprehensive Psychiatry,* 1976, *17,* 217-220.

Wagner, M. K., & Mooney, D. K. Personality characteristics of long and short sleepers. *Journal of Clinical Psychology,* 1975, *31,* 434-436.

Webb, W. B., Bonnet, M. H., & White, R. M. State and trait correlates of sleep stages. *Psychological Reports,* 1976, *38,* 1181-1182.

Weiss, M. F. The treatment of insomnia through the use of electrosleep: An EEG study. *Journal of Nervous and Mental Disease,* 1973, *157,* 108-120.

Woerner, M. G., & Klein, D. F. 14 and 6 per second positive spiking. *Journal of Nervous and Mental Disease,* 1974, *159,* 356-361.

DIAGNOSIS OF PSYCHOPATHOLOGY

Automated Interpretation

Adams, K. M., & Shore, D. L. The accuracy of an automated MMPI interpretation system in a psychiatric setting. *Journal of Clinical Psychology,* 1976, *32,* 80-82.

Altman, H., Gynther, M. D., Warbin, R. W., & Sletten, I. W. A new empirical automated MMPI interpretive program: The 6-8/8-6 code type. *Journal of Clinical Psychology,* 1972, *28,* 495-498.

Bringmann, W. G., Balance, W. D. G., & Giesbrecht, C. A. The computer vs. the technologist: Comparison of psychological reports on normal and elevated MMPI profiles. *Psychological Reports,* 1972, *31,* 211-217.

Clopton, J. R. A computer program for MMPI scale development with contrasted groups. *Educational and Psychological Measurement,* 1974, *34,* 161-163.

Clopton, J. R., & Neuringer, C. FORTRAN computer programs for the development Gilberstadt's code book. *Journal of Clinical Psychology,* 1975, *31,* 648-651.

Clopton, J. R., & Neuringer, C. FOTRAN computer programs for the development of new MMPI scales. *Educational and Psychological Measurement,* 1977, *37,* 783-786.

Colligan, R. C. Atypical response sets and the automated MMPI. *Journal of Clinical Psychology,* 1976, *32,* 76-78.

Dunn, T. G., Lushene, R. E., & O'Neil, H. F., Jr. Complete automation of the MMPI and a study of its response latencies. *Journal of Consulting and Clinical Psychology,* 1972, *39,* 381-387.

Fowler, R. D. Automated psychological test interpretation: The status in 1972. *Psychiatric Annual,* 1972, *2,* 10-17.

Goldstein, A. M., & Reznikoff, M. MMPI performance in chronic medical illness: The use of computer-derived interpretations. *British Journal of Psychiatry,* 1972, *120,* 157-158.

Grayson, H. M., & Backer, T. E. Scoring accuracy of four automated MMPI interpretation report agencies. *Journal of Clinical Psychology,* 1972, *28,* 366-370.

Gynther, M. D., Altman, H., & Warbin, R. W. A new empirical automated MMPI interpretive program: The 2-4/4-2 code type. *Journal of Clinical Psychology,* 1972, *28,* 498-501.

Gynther, M. D., Altman, H., Warbin, R. W., & Sletten, I. W. A new empirical automated MMPI interpretive program: The 1-2/2-1 code type. *Journal of Clinical Psychology,* 1973, *29,* 54-57.

Gynther, M. D., Altman, H., & Warbin, R. W. A new empirical automated MMPI interpretive program: The 2-7/7-2 code type. *Journal of Clinical Psychology,* 1973, *29,* 58-59.

Gynther, M. D., Altman, H., & Warbin, R. W. A new empirical automated MMPI interpretive program: The 6-9/9-6 code type. *Journal of Clinical Psychology,* 1973, *29,* 60-61.

Gynther, M. D., Altman, H., & Warbin, R. W. A new actuarial-empirical automated MMPI interpretive program: The 4-3/3-4 code type. *Journal of Clinical Psychology,* 1973, *29,* 229-231.

Hedlund, J. L., Morgan, D. W., & Master, F. D. The Mayo Clinic automated MMPI program: Cross-validation with psychiatric patients in an Army hospital. *Journal of Clinical Psychology,* 1972, *28,* 505-510.

Kleinmuntz, B. The computer as clinician. *American Psychologist,* 1975, *30,* 379-387.

Lachar, D. Accuracy and generalizability of an automated MMPI interpretation system. *Journal of Consulting and Clinical Psychology,* 1974, *42,* 267-273.

Lachar, D., Klinge, V., & Grisell, J. L. Relative accuracy of automated MMPI narratives generated from adult norm and adolescent norm profiles. *Journal of Consulting and Clinical Psychology,* 1976, *44,* 20-24.

Lushene, R. E., O'Neil, H. F., Jr., & Dunn, T. Equivalent validity of a completely computerized MMPI. *Journal of Personality Assessment,* 1974, *38,* 353-361.

Miller, D. A., Johnson, J. H., Klingler, D. E., Williams, T. A., & Giannetti, R. A. Design for an on-line computerized system for MMPI interpretation. *Behavior Research Methods and Instrumentation,* 1977, *9,* 117-122.

Warbin, R. W., Altman, H., Gynther, M. D., & Sletten, I. W. A new empirical automated MMPI interpretive program: 2-8 and 8-2 code types. *Journal of Personality Assessment,* 1972, *36,* 581-584.

Clinical Judgment

Block, J. An illusory interpretation of the first factor of the MMPI: A reply to Shweder. *Journal of Consulting and Clinical Psychology,* 1977, *45,* 930-935.

Conger, A. J., & Jackson, D. N. Supressor variables, prediction, and the interpretation of psychological relationships. *Educational and Psychological Measurement,* 1972, *32,* 579-599.

Davis, D. A. On being detectably sane in insane places: Base rates and psychodiagnosis. *Journal of Abnormal Psychology,* 1976, *85,* 416-422.

Dowling, J. F., & Graham, J. R. Illusory correlation and the MMPI. *Journal of Personality Assessment,* 1976, *40,* 531-538.

Edwards, A. L. Comments on Shweder's "Illusory correlation and the MMPI controversy." *Journal of Consulting and Clinical Psychology,* 1977, *45,* 925-929.

Fitzgibbons, D. J., & Hokanson, D. T. The diagnostic decision-making process: Factors influencing diagnosis and changes in diagnosis. *American Journal of Psychiatry,* 1973, *130,* 972-975.

Fowler, R. D., & Hodo, G. L. A comparison of classification rates of the original and revised Marks and Seeman rules. *Journal of Clinical Psychology,* 1975, *31,* 665-667.

Giannetti, R. A., Johnson, J. H., Klingler, D. E., & Williams, T. A. Comparison of linear and configural MMPI diagnostic methods with an uncontaminated criterion. *Journal of Consulting and Clinical Psychology,* 1978, *5,* 1046-1052.

Goodson, J. H., & King, G. D. A clinical and actuarial study on the validity of the Goldberg Index for the MMPI. *Journal of Clinical Psychology,* 1976, *32,* 328-335.

Holland, T. R., & Watson, C. G. Utilization of the Goldberg MMPI profile classification rules for the assessment of psychopathology in different clinical populations. *Journal of Clinical Psychology,* 1978, *34,* 893-901.

Johnson, J. H., Williams, T. A., & Klingler, D. E. An exploratory study of the interaction between personality and psychopathology. *Journal of Clinical Psychology,* 1978, *34,* 371-379.

Lichtenstein, S. Conditional non-independence of data in a practical Bayesian decision task. *Organizational Behavior and Human Performance,* 1972, *8,* 21-25.

Loro, B., & Woodward, J. A. The dependence of psychiatric diagnosis on psychological assessment. *Journal of Clinical Psychology,* 1975, *31,* 635-639.

Lorr, M., & Gilberstadt, H. A comparison of two typologies for psychotics. *Journal of Nervous and Mental Disease,* 1972, *155,* 144-148.

Messick, S., & Jackson, D. N. Judgmental dimensions of psychopathology. *Journal of Consulting and Clinical Psychology,* 1972, *38,* 418-427.

Moxley, A. W. Clinical judgment: The effects of statistical information. *Journal of Personality Assessment,* 1973, *37,* 86-91.

Neziroglu, F. The relationships among the Hoffer-Osmond Diagnostic Test, the MMPI, and independent clinical diagnoses. *Journal of Clinical Psychology,* 1975, *31,* 430-433.

Nichols, D. S. The Goldberg Rules in the detection of MMPI codebook modal diagnoses. *Journal of Clinical Psychology,* 1974, *30,* 186-188.

Ritter, D. R. Concurrence of psychiatric diagnosis and psychological diagnosis on the MMPI. *Journal of Personality Assessment,* 1974, *38,* 52-54.

Schinka, J. A., & Sines, J. O. Correlates of accuracy in personality assessment. *Journal of Clinical Psychology,* 1974, *30,* 374-377.

Shweder, R. A. Illusory correlation and the MMPI controversy. *Journal of Consulting and Clinical Psychology,* 1977, *45,* 917-924.

Shweder, R. A. Illusory correlation and the MMPI controversy: Reply to some of the allusions and elusions in Block's and Edwards' commentaries. *Journal of Consulting and Clinical Psychology,* 1977, *45,* 936-940.

Skinner, H. A., & Jackson, D. N. A model of psychopathology based on an integration of MMPI actuarial systems. *Journal of Consulting and Clinical Psychology,* 1978, *46,* 231-238.

Stenson, H., Kleinmuntz, B., & Scott, B. Personality assessment as a signal detection task. *Journal of Consulting and Clinical Psychology,* 1975, *43,* 794-799.

Taylor, J. B., Ptacek, M., Carithers, M., Griffin, C., & Coyne, L. Rating scales as measures of clinical judgment III: Judgments of the self on personality inventory scales and direct ratings. *Educational and Psychological Measurement,* 1972, *32,* 543-557.

Turner, R. G., & Horn, J. M. Effects of employing Goldberg's Ambdex statistic in the development of personality scales. *Psychological Reports,* 1976, *39,* 527-530.

Young, R. C. Clinical judgment as a means of improving actuarial prediction from the MMPI. *Journal of Consulting and Clinical Psychology,* 1972, *38,* 457-459.

Zeldow, P. B. Clinical judgment: A search for sex difference. *Psychological Reports,* 1975, *37,* 1135-1142.

TREATMENT OUTCOME

Patient, Therapist, and Treatment Variables

Abramowitz, C. V., Abramowitz, S. I., Roback, H. B., & Jackson, C. Differential effectiveness of directive and nondirective group therapies as a function of client internal-external control. *Journal of Consulting and Clinical Psychology,* 1974, *42,* 849-853.

Berzins, J. I., Bednar, R. L., & Severy L. J. The problems of intersource consensus in measuring therapeutic outcomes: New data and multivariate perspectives. *Journal of Abnormal Psychology,* 1975, *84,* 10-19.

Bierenbaum, H., Nichols, M. P., & Schwartz, A. J. Effects of varying session length and frequency in brief emotive psychotherapy. *Journal of Consulting and Clinical Psychology,* 1976, *44,* 790-798.

Bolton, B. A factor analysis of personal adjustment and vocational measures of client change. *Rehabilitation Counselor Bulletin,* 1974, *18,* 99-104.

Brown, J. B., & Dunbar, P. W. MMPI differences between fee-paying and non-fee-paying psychotherapy clients. *Journal of Clinical Psychology,* 1978, *34,* 953-954.

Coché, E., & Flick, A. Problem-solving training groups for hospitalized psychiatric patients. *Journal of Psychology,* 1975, *91,* 19-29.

Coie, J. D., Costanzo, P. R., & Cox, G. Behavioral determinants of mental illness concerns: A comparison of gatekeeper professions. *Journal of Consulting and Clinical Psychology,* 1975, *43,* 626-636.

Cooper, E. B., Eggertson, S. A., & Galbraith, S. A. Clinician personality factors and effectiveness: A three-study report. *Journal of Communication Disorders,* 1972, *5,* 270-274.

Crowder, J. E. Relationship between therapist and client interpersonal behaviors and psychotherapy outcome. *Journal of Counseling Psychology,* 1972, *19,* 68-75.

Davis, H. M. Psychometric prediction of institutional adjustment: A validation study. *British Journal of Social and Clinical Psychology,* 1974, *13,* 269-276.

Dekker, D. J., & Webb, J. T. Relationships of the Social Readjustment Rating scale to psychiatric patient status, anxiety, and social desirability. *Journal of Psychosomatic Research,* 1974, *18,* 125-130.

Dietzel, C. S., & Abeles, N. Client-therapist complementarity and therapeutic outcome. *Journal of Counseling Psychology,* 1975, *22,* 264-272.

Doherty, E. G. Labeling effects in psychiatric hospitalization: A study of diverging patterns of inpatient self-labeling processes. *Archives of General Psychiatry,* 1975, *32,* 562-568.

Dreger, R. M., & Johnson, W. E., Jr., Characteristics of volunteers, nonvolunteers, and no shows in a clinical follow-up. *Journal of Consulting and Clinical Psychology,* 1974, *42,* 746-747.

Evans, R. G., & Dinning, W. D. Future outlook and psychopathology among psychiatric patients. *Psychological Reports*, 1977, *41*, 1309-1310.

Garfield, S. L., Prager, R. A., & Bergin, A. E. Some further comments on evaluation of outcome in psychotherapy. *Journal of Counseling and Clinical Psychology*, 1974, *42*, 296-297.

Ginsburg, A. B., & Goldstein, S. G. Age bias in referral for psychological consultation. *Journal of Gerontology*, 1974, *29*, 410-415.

Gomes-Schwartz, B. Effective ingredients in psychotherapy: Prediction of outcome from process variables. *Journal of Consulting and Clinical Psychology*, 1978, *5*, 1023-1035.

Graham, J. R., Friedman, I., Paolino, A. F., & Lilly, R. S. An appraisal of the therapeutic value of the mental hospital milieu. *Journal of Community Psychology*, 1974, *2*, 153-160.

Graham, J. R., Lilly, R. S., Konick, D. S., Paolino, A. F., & Friedman, I. MMPI changes associated with short-term psychiatric hospitalization. *Journal of Clinical Psychology*, 1973, *29*, 69-73.

Jansen, D. G., & Johnson, L. E. Patients who schedule meetings with a state hospital review board. *Psychological Reports*, 1975, *36*, 283-286.

Jansen, D. G., & Nickles, L. A. Variables that differentiate between single- and multiple-admission psychiatric patients at a state hospital over a 5-year period. *Journal of Clinical Psychology*, 1973, *29*, 83-85.

Jansen, D. S. Personality characteristics of state hospital patients' rights office visitors. *Journal of Clinical Psychology*, 1974, *30*, 347-349.

Jeske, J. O. Identification and therapeutic effectiveness in group therapy. *Journal of Counseling Psychology*, 1973, *20*, 528-530.

Joanning, H. Behavioral rehearsal in group treatment of socially nonassertive individuals. *Journal of College Student Personnel*, 1976, *17*, 313-318.

Klingler, D. E., Johnson, J. E., & Williams, T. A. A retest of MMPI prediction of admission to a psychiatric hospital. *Journal of Clinical Psychology*, 1977, *33*, 1029-1031.

Kurtz, R. R., & Grummon, D. L. Different approaches to the measurement of therapist empathy and their relationship to therapy outcomes. *Journal of Consulting and Clinical Psychology*, 1972, *39*, 106-115.

Leve, R. M. A comment on Garfield, Prager, and Bergin's evaluation of outcome in psychotherapy. *Journal of Consulting and Clinical Psychology*, 1974, *42*, 293-295.

Lindsey, C. J., Martin, P. J., & Sterne, A. L. Patient characteristics and expectancy measures as factors that influence the expectancy-improvement relationship. *Journal of Clinical Psychology*, 1977, *33*, 1125-1127.

Longabaugh, R., & Eldred, S. H. Pre-morbid adjustments, schizoid personality and onset of illness as predictors of post-hospitalization functioning. *Journal of Psychiatric Research*, 1973, *10*, 19-29.

Martin, P. J., & Sterne, A. L. Prognostic expectations and treatment outcomes. *Journal of Consulting and Clinical Psychology*, 1975, *43*, 572-576.

Martin, P. J., & Sterne, A. L. Subjective objectivity: Therapists' affection and psychotherapy. *Psychological Reports*, 1976, *38*, 1163-1169.

Martin, P. J., Sterne, A. L., Moore, J. E., & Friedmeyer, M. H. Patient's and therapists' expectancies and treatment outcome: An elusive relationship reexamined. *Research Communications in Psychology, Psychiatry and Behavior*, 1976, *1*, 301-314.

Melnick, B. Patient-therapist identification in relation to both patient and therapist variables and therapy outcome. *Journal of Consulting and Clinical Psychology*, 1972, *38*, 97-104.

Mintz, J., Luborsky, L., & Christoph, P. Measuring the outcomes of psychotherapy: Findings of the Penn Psychotherapy Project. *Journal of Consulting and Clinical Psychology*, 1979, *47*, 319-334.

Nichols, M. P. Outcome of brief cathartic psychotherapy. *Journal of Consulting and Clinical Psychotherapy*, 1974, *42*, 403-410.

Prager, R. A., & Garfield, S. L. Client initial disturbance and outcome in psychotherapy. *Journal of Consulting and Clinical Psychology*, 1972, *38*, 112-117.

Roback, H. B., & Strassberg, D. S. Relationship between perceived therapist-offered conditions and therapeutic movement in group psychotherapy. *Small Group Behavior*, 1975, *6*, 345-352.

Roback, H. B., Webb, W. W., & Strassberg, D. Personality differences between fee-paying and non-fee-paying patients seen for psychological testing. *Journal of Consulting and Clinical Psychology*, 1974, *42*, 734.

Rosen, A. C., & Golden, J. S. The encounter-sensitivity training group as an adjunct to medical education. *International Review of Applied Psychology*, 1975, *24*, 61-70.

Schonfield, J., & Donner, L. The effect of serving as a psychologist on students with different specialty preferences. *Journal of Medical Education*, 1972, *47*, 203-209.

Schubert, D. S., & Wagner, M. E. "A" therapists as creative and personally involved with other people. *Journal of Consulting and Clinical Psychology*, 1975, *43*, 266.

Shapiro, A. K., Struening, E., Shapiro, E., & Barten, H. Prognostic correlates of psychotherapy in psychiatric outpatients. *American Journal of Psychiatry*, 1976, *133*, 802-808.

Shows, W. D., Gentry, W. D., & Wyrick, L. C. Social constriction in psychiatric patients: A normative study. *American Journal of Psychiatry*, 1974, *131*, 1287-1288.

Sloan, R. B., Staples, F. R., Cristol, A. H., Yorkston, N. J., & Whipple, K. Patient characteristics and outcome in psychotherapy and behavior therapy. *Journal of Consulting and Clinical Psychology*, 1976, *44*, 330-339.

Strupp, H. H., & Bloxom, A. L. An approach to defining a patient population in psychotherapy research. *Journal of Counseling Psychology*, 1975, *22*, 231-237.

Treppa, J. A., & Fricke, L. Effects of a marathon group experience. *Journal of Counseling Psychology*, 1972, *19*, 466-467.

Truax, C. B., Altmann, H., & Wittmer, J. Self-disclosure as a function of personal adjustment and the facilitative conditions offered by the target person. *Journal of Community Psychology*, 1973, *1*, 319-322.

Tuma, A. H., May, P. R. A., Yale, C., & Forsythe, A. B. Therapist experience, general clinical ability, and treatment outcome in schizophrenia. *Journal of Consulting and Clinical Psychology*, 1978, *5*, 1120-1126.

Pharmacological Studies

Biro, M. Evaluation by means of the MMPI of residual syndromes in antidepressive drug therapy. *Revija Za Psihologiju*, 1975, *5*, 3-14.

Capone, T., Brahen, L. S., & Wiechert, V. Personality factors and drug effects in a controlled study of cyclazocine. *Journal of Clinical Psychology*, 1976, *32*, 489-495.

Haier, R. L., Buchsbaum, M. S., & Murphy, D. L. Screening young adults for psychiatric vulnerability: A preliminary comparison of biological and clinical measures. *Psychopharmacology Bulletin*, 1979, *15*, 7-9.

Henry, B. W., Overall, J. E., & Woodward, J. A. Actuarial justification for choice of drug treatment for psychiatric patients. *Diseases of the Nervous System*, 1976, *37*, 555-557.

Klapper, J. A., & McColloch, M. A. Personality and reactivity to stimulants and depressants. *Journal of Nervous and Mental Disease*, 1972, *154*, 439-444.

Klapper, J. A., McColloch, M. A., & Merkey, R. P. The relationship of personality to tolerance of an irritant compound. *Journal of Personality and Social Psychology*, 1973, *26*, 110-112.

Klapper, J. A., McColloch, M. A., & Sidell, F. R. The effect on personality of reactivity to 1,2-dimethyl-heptyl-tetrahydrocannabinol. *Archives of General Psychiatry*, 1972, *26*, 483-485.

Lauer, J. W. The effect of tricyclic antidepressant compounds on patients with passive-dependent personality traits. *Current Therapeutic Research,* 1976, *19,* 495-505.

Murphy, D. L., Belmaker, R., Buchsbaum, M. S. Biogenic amine-related enzymes and personality variations in normals. *Psychological Medicine,* 1977, *7,* 149-157.

Schooler, C., Zahn, T. P., Murphy, D. G., & Buchsbaum, M. S. Psychological correlates of monoamine oxidase activity in normals. *Journal of Nervous and Mental Disease,* 1978, *166,* 177-186.

Shader, R. I., Harmatz, J. S., Kochansky, G. E., & Cole, J. O. Psychopharmacologic investigations in healthy elderly volunteers: Effects of pipradol-vitamin (Alertonic) elixir and placebo in relation to research design. *Journal of the American Geriatrics Society,* 1975, *23,* 277-279.

Soskin, R. A. The use of LSD in time-limited psychotherapy. *Journal of Nervous and Mental Disease,* 1973, *157,* 410-419.

Wittenborn, J. R., & Kiremitci, N. A comparison of antidepressant medications in neurotic and psychotic patients. *Archives of General Psychiatry,* 1975, *32,* 1172-1176.

Wittenborn, J. R., Kiremitci, N., & Weber, E. S. P. The choice of alternative antidepressants. *Journal of Nervous and Mental Disease,* 1973, *156,* 97-108.

DISORDERS

Addiction

Code Types

Apfeldorf, M. Contrasting assumptions and direction in MMPI research on alcoholism. *Quarterly Journal of Studies on Alcoholism,* 1974, *35,* 1375-1379.

Apfeldorf, M., & Hunley, P. J. Exclusion of subjects with F scores at or above 16 in MMPI research on alcoholism. *Journal of Clinical Psychology,* 1976, *32,* 498-500.

Black, F. W., & Heald, A. MMPI characteristics of alcohol- and illicit drug-abusers enrolled in a rehabilitative program. *Journal of Clinical Psychology,* 1975, *31,* 572-575.

Clopton, J. R. Alcoholism and the MMPI: A review. *Journal of Studies on Alcohol,* 1978, *39,* 1540-1558.

Collins, H. A., Burger, G. K., & Taylor, G. A. Personality patterns of drug abusers as shown by MMPI profiles. *Journal of Clinical Psychology,* 1977, *33,* 897-900.

Crowley, T. J., Chesluk, D., Dilts, S., & Hart, R. Drug and alcohol abuse among psychiatric admissions: A multidrug clinical-toxicologic study. *Archives of General Psychiatry,* 1974, *30,* 13-20.

Davis, W. E., Pursell, S. A., & Burnham, R. A. Alcoholism, sex-role orientation and psychological distress. *Journal of Clinical Psychology,* 1979, *35,* 209-212.

Donovan, D. M., Chaney, E. F., & O'Leary, M. R. Alcoholic MMPI subtypes: Relationship to drinking styles, benefits, and consequences. *Journal of Nervous and Mental Disease,* 1978, *166,* 553-561.

English, G. E., & Tori, C. A. Psychological characteristics of drug abuse clients seen in a community mental health center. *Journal of Community Psychology,* 1973, *1,* 403-407.

Equi, P. J., & Jabara, R. F. Validation of the self-rating depression scale in an alcoholic population. *Journal of Clinical Psychology,* 1976, *32,* 504-507.

Eshbaugh, D. M., Tosi, D. J., & Hoyt, C. Some personality patterns and dimensions of male alcoholics: A multivariate description. *Journal of Personality Assessment,* 1978, *42,* 409-417.

Fitzgibbons, D. J., Berry, D. F., & Shearn, C. R. MMPI and diagnosis among hospitalized drug abusers. *Journal of Community Psychology,* 1973, *1,* 79-81.

Freed, E. X. Alcohol and mood: An updated review. *International Journal of the Addictions,* 1978, *13,* 173-200.

Graf, K., Baer, P. E., & Comstock, B. S. MMPI changes in briefly hospitalized non-narcotic drug users. *Journal of Nervous and Mental Disorders,* 1977, *165,* 126-133.

Hodo, G. L., & Fowler, R. D. Frequency of MMPI two-point codes in a large alcoholic sample. *Journal of Clinical Psychology,* 1976, *32,* 487-489.

Hoffmann, H. MMPI changes for a male alcoholic state hospital population-- 1959-1971. *Psychological Reports,* 1973, *33,* 139-142.

Hoffmann, H., & Borynge, E. R. Personalities of female alcoholics who become counselors. *Psychological Reports,* 1977, *41,* 37-38.

Hoffmann, H., Jackson, D. N., & Skinner, H. A. Dimensions of psychopathology among alcoholic patients. *Journal of Studies on Alcohol,* 1975, *36,* 825-837.

Hoffmann, H., & Jansen, D. G. Relationships among discharge variables and MMPI scale scores of hospitalized alcoholics. *Journal of Clinical Psychology,* 1973, *29,* 475-477.

Hoffmann, H., Jansen, D. G., & Wefring, L. R. Relationships between admission variables and MMPI scale scores of hospitalized alcoholics. *Psychological Reports,* 1972, *31,* 659-662.

Hoffmann, H., & Miner, B. B. Personality of alcoholics who become counselors. *Psychological Reports,* 1973, *33,* 878.

Jansen, D. G. Use of the psychological screening inventory with hospitalized alcoholics. *Journal of Consulting and Clinical Psychology,* 1972, *39,* 170.

Jansen, D. G., & Hoffmann, H. Demographic and MMPI characteristics of male and female state hospital alcoholic patients. *Psychological Reports,* 1973, *33,* 561-562.

Jansen, D. G., & Hoffmann, H. MMPI scores of counselors on alcoholism prior to and after training. *Journal of Consulting and Clinical Psychology,* 1975, *43,* 271.

Jarvis, L. G., Simnegar, R. R., & Traweek, A. R. An MMPI comparison of U.S.A.F. groups identified as drug users. *Psychological Reports,* 1975, *37,* 1339-1345.

Kammeier, M. L., Hoffmann, H., & Loper, R. G. Personality characteristics of alcoholics as college freshmen and at time of treatment. *Quarterly Journal of Studies on Alcohol,* 1973, *34,* 390-399.

Kline, J. A., Rozynko, V. V., Flint, G., & Roberts, A. C. Personality characteristics of male native American alcoholic patients. *International Journal of the Addictions,* 1973, *8,* 729-732.

Knox, W. J. Objective psychological measurement and alcoholism; review of the literature, 1971-1972. *Psychological Reports,* 1976, *38,* 1023-1050.

Kristianson, P. Classification of the MMPI profiles of two alcoholic groups. *Acta Psychiatrica Scandinavica,* 1976, *54,* 359-380.

Lachar, D., Gdowski, C. L., & Keegan, J. F. MMPI profiles of men alcoholics, drug addicts and psychiatric patients. *Journal of Studies on Alcohol,* 1979, *40,* 45-56.

Loper, R. G., Kammeier, M. L., & Hoffmann, H. MMPI characteristics of college freshman males who later become alcoholics. *Journal of Abnormal Psychology,* 1973, *82,* 159-162.

MacAndrew, C. Women alcoholics' responses to scale 4 of the MMPI. *Journal of Studies on Alcohol,* 1978, *39,* 1841-1855.

McAree, C. P., Steffenhagen, R. A., & Zheutlin, L. S. Personality factors and patterns of drug usage in college students. *American Journal of Psychiatry,* 1972, *128,* 890-893.

McLachlan, J. F. Classification of alcoholics by an MMPI actuarial system. *Journal of Clinical Psychology,* 1975, *31,* 145-147.

Mozdzierz, G. J., Macchitelli, F. J., & Lottman, T. J. Personality correlates of coffee consumption in an alcoholic population. *Psychological Reports,* 1973, *32,* 550.

Mozdzierz, G. J., Macchitelli, F. J., Planek, T. W., & Lottman, T. J. Personality and temperament differences between alcoholics with high and low records of traffic accidents and violations. *Journal of Studies on Alcohol,* 1975, *36,* 395-399.

O'Leary, M. R., Chaney, E. F., Brown, L. S., & Schuckit, M. A. The use of the Goldberg indices with alcoholics: A cautionary note. *Journal of Clinical Psychology,* 1978, *34,* 988-990.

O'Leary, M. R., Donovan, D. M., & Hauge W. H. Relationships between locus of control and MMPI scales among alcoholics: A replication and extension. *Journal of Clinical Psychology,* 1974, *30,* 312-314.

Overall, J. E. MMPI personality patterns of alcoholics and narcotic addicts. *Quarterly Journal of Studies on Alcohol,* 1973, *34,* 104-111.

Overall, J. E., Brown, D., Williams, J. D., & Neill, L. T. Drug treatment of anxiety and depression in detoxified alcoholic patients. *Archives of General Psychiatry,* 1973, *29,* 218-221.

Overall, J. E., & Patrick, J. H. Unitary alcoholism factor and its personality correlates. *Journal of Abnormal Psychology,* 1972, *79,* 303-309.

Penk, W. E., Robinowitz, R., & Fudge, J. W. Differences in interpersonal orientation of heroin, amphetamine, and barbiturate users. *British Journal of Addiction,* 1978, *73,* 82-88.

Ross, S. M. Fear, reinforcing activities and degree of alcoholism: A correlational analysis. *Quarterly Journal of Studies on Alcohol,* 1973, *34,* 823-828.

Schoolar, J. C., White, E. H., & Cohen, C. P. Drug abusers and their clinic-patient counterparts: A comparison of personality dimensions. *Journal of Consulting and Clinical Psychology,* 1972, *39,* 9-14.

Skinner, H. A., Jackson, D. N., & Hoffmann, H. Alcoholic personality types: Identification and correlates. *Journal of Abnormal Psychology,* 1974, *83,* 658-666.

Skinner, T. J., & Charalampous, K. D. Interpretive procedures entailed in using the Michigan Alcoholism Screening Test. *British Journal of Addiction,* 1978, *73,* 117-123.

Smith, R. B., Burgess, A. D., Guinee, V. J., & Reifsnider, L. C. A curvilinear relationship between alcoholic withdrawal tremor and personality. *Journal of Clinical Psychology,* 1979, *35,* 199-203.

Steffenhagen, R. A., McCann, H. G., & McAree, C. P. Personality and drug use: A study of the usefulness of the Mf scale of the MMPI in measuring creativity and drug use. *Journal of Alcohol and Drug Education,* 1976, *21,* 8-16.

Sutker, P. B., Archer, R. B., & Allain, A. N. Drug abuse patterns, personality characteristics, and relationships with sex, race, and sensation seeking. *Journal of Consulting and Clinical Psychology,* 1978, *46,* 1374-1378.

Tarter, R. E. Personality of wives of alcoholics. *Journal of Clinical Psychology,* 1976, *32,* 741-743.

Tarter, R. E., McBride, H., Buonpane, N., & Schneider, D. U. Differentiation of alcoholics: Childhood history of minimal brain dysfunction, family history, and drinking pattern. *Archives of General Psychiatry,* 1977, *34,* 761-768.

Templer, D. I., Ruff, C. F., Barthlow, V. L., Halcomb, P. H., & Ayers, J. L. Psychometric assessment of alcoholism in convicted felons. *Journal of Studies on Alcohol,* 1978, *39,* 1948-1951.

Weiss, R. W., & Russakoff, S. The sex role identity of male drug abusers. *Journal of Clinical Psychology,* 1978, *34,* 1010-1013.

Wilson, A. S., Mabry, E. A., & Khavari, K. A. Use of MMPI profiles for occupational classification of alcoholics. *Journal of Studies on Alcohol,* 1977, *38,* 471-476.

Wilson, A. S., Mabry, E. A., Khavari, K. A., & Dalpes, D. Discriminant analysis of MMPI profiles for demographic classifications of male alcoholics. *Journal of Studies on Alcohol,* 1977, *38,* 47-57.

Narcotic

Berzins, J. I., Ross, W. F., English, G. E., & Haley, J. V. Subgroups among opiate addicts: A typological investigation. *Journal of Abnormal Psychology,* 1974, *83,* 65-73.

Black, F. W. Personality characteristics of Viet Nam veterans identified as heroin abusers. *American Journal of Psychiatry,* 1975, *132,* 748-749.

Collins, H. A., Burger, G. K., & Taylor, G. A. An empirical typology of heroin abusers. *Journal of Clinical Psychology,* 1976, *32,* 473-476.

DeLeon, G., Skodol, A., & Rosenthal, M. S. Phoenix House: Changes in psychopathological signs of resident drug addicts. *Archives of General Psychiatry,* 1973, *28,* 131-135.

Fracchia, J., Sheppard, C., & Merlis, S. Some comments about the personality comparison of incarcerated and street heroin addicts. *Psychological Reports,* 1973, *33,* 413-414.

Gendreau, P., & Gendreau, L. P. A theoretical note on personality characteristics of heroin addicts. *Journal of Abnormal Psychology,* 1973, *82,* 139-140.

Hampton, P. T., & Vogel, D. B. Personality characteristics of servicemen returned from Viet Nam identified as heroin abusers. *American Journal of Psychiatry,* 1973, *130,* 1031-1032.

Kojak, G., Jr., & Canby, J. P. Personality and behavior patterns of heroin-dependent American servicemen in Thailand. *American Journal of Psychiatry,* 1975, *132,* 246-250.

Mott, J. The psychological bases of drug dependence: The intellectual and personality characteristics of opiate users. *British Journal of Addiction,* 1972, *67,* 89-100.

Penk, W. E., & Robinowitz, R. Personality differences of volunteer and non-volunteer heroin and nonheroin drug users. *Journal of Abnormal Psychology,* 1976, *85,* 91-100.

Ross, W. F., & Berzins, J. I. Personality characteristics of female narcotic addicts on the MMPI. *Psychological Reports,* 1974, *35,* 779-784.

Sheppard, C., Ricca, E., Fracchia, J., & Merlis, S. Personality characteristics of urban and suburban heroin abusers: More data and another reply to Sutker and Allain. *Psychological Reports,* 1973, *33,* 999-1008.

Sutker, P. B. Personality characteristics of heroin addicts: A response to Gendreau and Gendreau. *Journal of Abnormal Psychology,* 1974, *83,* 463-464.

Sutker, P. B., & Allain, A. N. Incarcerated and street heroin addicts: A personality comparison. *Psychological Reports,* 1973, *32,* 243-246.

Other Drug Abuse

Brodsky, L., & Zuniga, J. Nitrous oxide: A psychotogenic agent. *Comprehensive Psychiatry,* 1975, *16,* 185-188.

Burke, E. L., & Eichberg, R. H. Personality characteristics of adolescent users of dangerous drugs as indicated by the MMPI. *Journal of Nervous and Mental Disease,* 1972, *154,* 291-298.

Carlin, A. S., Detzer, E., & Stauss, F. F. Psychopathology and nonmedical drug use: A comparison of patient and nonpatient drug users. *International Journal of the Addictions,* 1978, *13,* 337-348.

Harmatz, J. S., Shader, R. I., & Salzman, C. Marihuana users and nonusers: Personality test differences. *Archives of General Psychiatry,* 1972, *26,* 108-112.

Heaton, R. K., & Victor, R. G. Personality characteristics associated with psychedelic flashbacks in natural and experimental settings. *Journal of Abnormal Psychology,* 1976, *85,* 83-90.

Holland, T. R. Dimensions, patterns, and personality correlates of drug abuse in an offender population. *Journal of Consulting and Clinical Psychology,* 1978, *46,* 577-578.

Keller, J., & Redfering, D. L. Comparison between the personalities of LSD users and nonusers as measured by the MMPI. *Journal of Nervous and Mental Disease*, 1973, *156*, 271-277.

Kochansky, G. E., Hemenway, T. S., Salzman, C., & Shader, R. I. Methaqualone abusers: A preliminary survey of college students. *Diseases of the Nervous System*, 1975, *36*, 348-351.

Matefy, R. E., & Krall, R. G. An initial investigation of the psychedelic drug flashback phenomena. *Journal of Consulting and Clinical Psychology*, 1974, *42*, 854-860.

Matefy, R. E., & Krall, R. Psychedelic drug flashbacks: Psychotic manifestation or imaginative role playing? *Journal of Consulting and Clinical Psychology*, 1975, *43*, 434.

McCabe, O. L., Savage, C., Karland, A., & Unger, S. Psychedelic (LSD) therapy of neurotic disorders: Short term effects. *Journal of Psychedelic Drugs*, 1972, *5*, 19-28.

McGlothlin, W., Cohen, S., & McGlothlin, M. S. Long lasting effects of LSD on normals. *Archives of General Psychiatry*, 1976, *17*, 521-532.

McGuire, J. S., & Megargee, E. I. Personality correlates of marijuana use among youthful offenders. *Journal of Consulting and Clinical Psychology*, 1974, *42*, 124-133.

Naditch, M. P. Ego functioning and acute adverse reactions to psychoactive drugs. *Journal of Personality*, 1975, *43*, 305-320.

Panton, J. H., & Behre, C. Characteristics associated with drug addiction within a state prison population. *Journal of Community Psychology*, 1973, *1*, 411-416.

Phillips. B. J., Phillips, I. F., & Davidson, E. E. Juvenile delinquent drug abuse in females: A clinical study. *Australian and New Zealand Journal of Psychiatry*, 1975, *9*, 281-286.

Salzman, C., Lieff, J., Kochansky, G. E., & Shader, R. I. The psychology of hallucinogenic drug discontinuers. *American Journal of Psychiatry*, 1972, *129*, 755-761.

Scott, N. A., Mount, M. K., & Kosters, S. A. Correspondence of the MMPI and Mini-Mult among female reformatory inmates. *Journal of Clinical Psychology*, 1976, *32*, 792-794.

Silver, A. M. Some personality characteristics of groups of young drug misusers and delinquents. *British Journal of Addiction*, 1977, *72*, 143-150.

Stein, K. B., & Rozynko, V. Psychological and social variables and personality patterns of drug abusers. *International Journal of the Addictions*, 1974, *9*, 431-446.

Trevithick, L., & Hosch, H. M. MMPI correlates of drug addiction based on drug of choice. *Journal of Consulting and Clinical Psychology*, 1978, *46*, 180.

Winstead, D. K., Anderson, A., Eilers, M. K., Blackwell, B., & Zaremba, A. L. Diazepam on demand: Drug-seeking behavior in psychiatric inpatients. *Archives of General Psychiatry*, 1974, *30*, 349-351.

Winstead, D. K., Lawson, T., Abbott, D. Diazepam use in military sick call. *Military Medicine*, 1976, *141*, 180-181.

Special Scales

Apfeldorf, M. Alcoholism scales of the MMPI: Contributions and future directions. *International Journal of the Addictions*, 1978, *13*, 17-55.

Apfeldorf, M., & Hunley, P. J. Application of MMPI alcoholism scales to older alcoholics and problem drinkers. *Journal of Studies on Alcohol*, 1975, *36*, 645-653.

Burke, H. R., & Marcus, R. MacAndrew MMPI Alcoholism Scale: Alcoholism and drug addictiveness. *The Journal of Psychology*, 1977, *96*, 141-148.

DeGroot, W. G., & Adamson, J. D. Responses of psychiatric inpatients to the MacAndrew Alcoholism Scale. *Quarterly Journal of Studies on Alcohol*, 1973, *34*, 1133-1139.

Friedrich, W. N., & Loftsgard, S. O. Comparison of two alcoholism scales with alcoholics and their wives. *Journal of Clinical Psychology,* 1978, *34,* 784-786.

Friedrich, W. N., & Loftsgard, S. O. A comparison of the MacAndrew Alcoholism Scale and the Michigan Alcohol Screening Test in a sample of problem drinkers. *Journal of Studies on Alcohol,* 1978, *39,* 1940-1944.

Hodo, G. L., & Barker, H. R. Discriminating alcoholic and nonalcoholic patients with conventional and factored MMPI scales: A comparison. *Journal of Clinical Psychology,* 1976, *32,* 495-497.

Hoffmann, H., Loper, R. G., & Kammeier, M. L. Identifying future alcoholics with MMPI alcoholism scales. *Quarterly Journal of Studies on Alcohol,* 1974, *35,* 490-498.

Kranitz, L. Alcoholics, heroin addicts and nonaddicts: Comparisons on the MacAndrew Alcoholism Scale of the MMPI. *Quarterly Journal of Studies on Alcohol,* 1972, *33,* 807-809.

Kwant, F., Rice, J. A., & Hays, J. R. Use of Heroin Addiction Scale to differentiate addicts from rehabilitation clients. *Psychological Reports,* 1976, *38,* 547-553.

Lachar, D., Berman, W., Grisell, J. L., & Schoof, K. The MacAndrew alcoholism scale as a general measure of substance abuse. *Journal of Studies on Alcohol,* 1976, *37,* 1609-1615.

MacAndrew, C. MAC Scale scores of three samples of men under conditions of conventional versus independent scale administration. *Journal of Studies on Alcohol,* 1979, *40,* 138-141.

McLachlan, J. F. An MMPI discriminant function to distinguish alcoholics from narcotic addicts: Effects of age, sex, and psychopathology. *Journal of Clinical Psychology,* 1975, *31,* 163-165.

Miller, W. R. Alcoholism scales and objective assessment methods: A review. *Psychological Bulletin,* 1976, *83,* 649-674.

Rhodes, R. J., & Chang, A. F. A further look at the Institutionalized Chronic Alcoholic Scale. *Journal of Clinical Psychology,* 1978, *34,* 779-780.

Rosenberg, N. MMPI alcoholism scales. *Journal of Clinical Psychology,* 1972, *28,* 515-522.

Ruff, C. F., Ayers, J., & Templer, D. I. Alcoholics' and criminals' similarity of scores on the MacAndrew alcoholism scale. *Psychological Reports,* 1975, *36,* 921-922.

Sheppard, C., Ricca, E., Fracchia, J., Rosenberg, N., & Merlis, S. Cross-validation of a heroin addiction scale from the MMPI. *Journal of Psychology,* 1972, *81,* 263-281.

Treatment

Bean, K. L., & Karasievich, G. O. Psychological test results at three stages of inpatient alcoholism treatment. *Journal of Studies on Alcohol,* 1975, *36,* 838-852.

Berzins, J.I., & Ross, W. F. Experimental assessment of the responsiveness of addict patients to the "influence" of professionals versus other addicts. *Journal of Abnormal Psychology,* 1972, *80,* 141-148.

Bess, B., Janus, S., & Rifkin, A. Factors in successful narcotics renunciation. *American Journal of Psychiatry,* 1972, *128,* 861-865.

Cummings, R. E. A three-year study of V.A. inpatient alcoholic treatment using demographic and psychological data. *Rehabilitation Literature,* 1977, *38,* 153-156.

DeCourcy, P., & Duerfeldt, P. H. The impact of number and type of models on claimed success rate and mood of adult alcoholics. *Journal of Genetic Psychology,* 1973, *122,* 63-79.

Frankel, A., & Murphy, J. Physical fitness and personality in alcoholism: Canonical analysis of measures before and after treatment. *Quarterly Journal of Studies on Alcohol,* 1974, *35,* 1272-1278.

Gellens, H. K., Gottheil, E., & Alterman, A. I. Drinking outcome of specific alcoholic subgroups. *Journal of Studies on Alcohol*, 1976, *37*, 986-989.

Greer, R. M., & Callis, R. The use of videotape models in an alcohol rehabilitation program. *Rehabilitation Counseling Bulletin*, 1975, *18*, 154-159.

Hoffmann, H., & Wehler, R. Pre- and post-training MMPI scores of women alcoholism counselors. *Journal of Studies on Alcohol*, 1978, *39*, 1952-1955.

Huber, W. A., & Danahy, S. Use of the MMPI in predicting completion and evaluating changes in a long-term alcoholism treatment program. *Journal of Studies on Alcohol*, 1975, *36*, 1230-1237.

Kamback, M. C., Bosma, W. G. A., & D'Lugoff, B. C. Family surrogates? The drug culture or the methadone maintenance program. *British Journal of Addiction*, 1977, *72*, 171-176.

Kaplan, R., Blume, S., Rosenberg, S., Pitrelli, J., & Turner, W. J. Phenytoin, Metronidazole and multivitamins in the treatment of alcoholism. *Quarterly Journal of Studies on Alcohol*, 1972, *33*, 97-104.

Krasnoff, A. Differences between alcoholics who complete or withdraw from treatment. *Journal of Studies on Alcohol*, 1976, *37*, 1666-1671.

Krasnoff, A. Failure of MMPI scales to predict treatment completion. *Journal of Studies on Alcohol*, 1977, *38*, 1440-1442.

Lin, T. Use of demographic variables, WRAT, and MMPI scores to predict addicts' types of discharge from a community-like hospital setting. *Journal of Clinical Psychology*, 1975, *31*, 148-151.

Lowe, W. C., & Thomas, S. D. Assessing alcoholism treatment effectiveness: A comparison of three evaluation measures. *Journal of Studies on Alcohol*, 1976, *37*, 883-889.

Martin, W. R., Jasinski, D. R., Haertzen, C. A., Kay, D. C., Jones, B. E., Mansky, P. A., & Carpenter, R. W. Methadone - a re-evaluation. *Archives of General Psychiatry*, 1973, *28*, 286-295.

Mozdzierz, G. J., Macchitelli, F. J., Conway, J. A., & Krauss, H. H. Personality characteristic differences between alcoholics who leave treatment against medical advice and those who don't. *Journal of Clinical Psychology*, 1973, *29*, 78-82.

Ottomanelli, G. A. MMPI and Pyp prediction compared to base rate prediction of six-month behavioral outcome for methadone patients. *British Journal of Addiction*, 1977, *72*, 177-186.

Ottomanelli, G. A. Patient improvement, measured by the MMPI and Pyp, related to paraprofessional and professional counselor assignment. *International Journal of the Addictions*, 1978, *13*, 503-507.

Ottomanelli, G., Wilson, P., & Whyte, R. MMPI evaluation of 5-year methadone treatment status. *Journal of Consulting and Clinical Psychology*, 1978, *46*, 579-581.

Paredes, A., Gregory, D., & Jones, B.M. Induced drinking and social adjustment in alcoholics: Development of a therapeutic model. *Quarterly Journal of Studies on Alcohol*, 1974, *35*, 1279-1293.

Price, R. H., & Curlee-Salisbury, J. Patient-treatment interaction among alcoholics. *Journal of Studies on Alcohol*, 1975, *36*, 659-669.

Pugliese, A. C. A study of methadone maintenance patients with the MMPI. *British Journal of Addiction*, 1975, *70*, 198-204.

Rae, J. B. The influence of the wives on the treatment outcome of alcoholics: A follow-up study at two years. *British Journal of Psychiatry*, 1972, *120*, 601-613.

Resnick, R., Orlin, L., Geyer, G., Schuyten-Resnick, E., Kestenbaum, R. S., & Freedman, A. M. L-alpha-acetylmethadol (LAAM): Prognostic considerations. *American Journal of Psychiatry*, 1976, *133*, 814-819.

Rohan, W. P. MMPI changes in hospitalized alcoholics: A second study. *Quarterly Journal of Studies on Alcohol*, 1972, *33*, 65-76.

Ross, S. M. Fear, reinforcing activities and degree of alcoholism: A correlational analysis. *Quarterly Journal of Studies on Alcohol*, 1973, *34*, 823-828.

Ross, W. F., McReynolds, W. T., & Berzins, J. I. Effectiveness of marathon group psychotherapy with hospitalized female narcotic addicts. *Psychological Reports,* 1974, *34,* 611-616.

Shaw, J. A., Donley, P., Morgan, D. W., & Robinson, J. A. Treatment of depression in alcoholics. *American Journal of Psychiatry,* 1975, *132,* 641-644.

Sheppard, C., Fracchia, J., Ricca, E., & Merlis, S. Indications of psychopathology in male narcotic abusers, their effects and relation to treatment effectiveness. *Journal of Psychology,* 1972, *81,* 351-360.

Sheppard, C., Ricca, E., Fracchia, J., & Merlis, S. Indications of psychopathology in applicants to a county methadone maintenance program. *Psychological Reports,* 1973, *33,* 535-540.

Sutker, P. B., Allain, A. N., & Cohen, G. H. MMPI indices of personality change following short- and long-term hospitalization of heroin addicts. *Psychological Reports,* 1974, *34,* 495-500.

Weiss, R. W., & Russakoff, S. Relationships of MMPI scores of drug-abusers to personal variables and type of treatment program. *Journal of Psychology,* 1977, *96,* 25-29.

Ziegler, R., Kohutek, K., & Owen, P. A multimodal treatment approach for incarcerated alcoholics. *Journal of Clinical Psychology,* 1978, *34,* 1005-1008.

Zuckerman, M., Sola, S., Masterson, J., & Angelone, J. V. MMPI patterns in drug abuse before and after treatment in therapeutic communities. *Journal of Consulting and Clinical Psychology,* 1975, *43,* 286-296.

Affective Disorders and Related Studies

Anxiety and Fear

Adams, J., Rothstein, W., & McCarter, R. E. A canonical-correlation analysis of 16 fear factors and the MMPI. *Journal of Personality Assessment,* 1973, *37,* 156-164.

Boudewyns, P. A., & Levis, D. J. Autonomic reactivity of high and low ego-strength subjects to repeated anxiety eliciting scenes. *Journal of Abnormal Psychology,* 1975, *84,* 682-692.

Boudewyns, P. A., & Wilson, A. E. Implosive therapy and desensitization therapy using free association in the treatment of inpatients. *Journal of Abnormal Psychology,* 1972, *79,* 259-268.

Justice, B., McBee, G., & Allen, R. Social dysfunction and anxiety. *Journal of Psychology,* 1977, *97,* 37-42.

Levitt, E. A. Procedural issues in the systematic desensitization of air-travel phobia. *New Zealand Psychologist,* 1975, *4,* 2-9.

Newmark, C. S., Faschingbauer, T. R., Finch, A. J., & Kendall, P. C. Factor analysis of the MMPI-STAI. *Journal of Clinical Psychology,* 1975, *31,* 449-452.

Newmark, C. S., Hetzel, W., & Frerking, R. A. The effects of personality tests on state and trait anxiety. *Journal of Personality Assessment,* 1974, *38,* 17-20.

Newmark, C. S., Ray, J., Lyman, R. A. F., & Paine, R. D. Test-induced anxiety as a function of psychopathology. *Journal of Clinical Psychology,* 1974, *30,* 261-264.

Patton, G. W. R., & Kotrick, C. A. Visual exploratory behavior as a function of manifest anxiety. *Journal of Psychology,* 1972, *82,* 349-353.

Rappaport, E. The relation between trait anxiety and the Harris MMPI Pd sub-scales among psychiatric inpatients. *Journal of Clinical Psychology,* 1978, *34,* 388-390.

Sherman, A. R. Real life exposure as a primary therapeutic factor in the desensitization treatment of fear. *Journal of Abnormal Psychology,* 1972, *79,* 19-28.

Tudor, T. G., & Holmes, D. S. Differential recall of successes and failures: Its relationship to defensiveness, achievement motivation, and anxiety. *Journal of Research in Personality,* 1973, *7,* 208-234.

Wennerholm, M. A., & Zarle, T. H. Internal-external control, defensiveness, and anxiety in hypertensive patients. *Journal of Clinical Psychology,* 1976, *32,* 644-648.

Depression

Birtchnell, J. The personality characteristics of early-bereaved psychiatric patients. *Social Psychiatry,* 1975, *10,* 97-103.

Burns, B. H., & Nichols, M. A. Factors related to the localization of symptoms to the chest in depression. *British Journal of Psychiatry,* 1972, *121,* 405-409.

Cerbus, G., & Dallara, R. F., Jr. Seasonal differences of depression in mental hospital admissions as measured by the MMPI. *Psychological Reports,* 1975, *36,* 737-738.

Donnelly, E. F., & Murphy, D. L. Primary affective disorder: Delineation of a unipolar depressive subtype. *Psychological Reports,* 1973, *32,* 744-746.

Donnelly, E. F., & Murphy, D. L. Primary affective disorder: MMPI differences between unipolar and bipolar depressed subjects. *Journal of Clinical Psychology,* 1973, *29,* 303-306.

Donnelly, E. F., & Murphy, D. L. Primary affective disorder: Bender-Gestalt sequence of placement as an indicator of impulse control. *Perceptual and Motor Skills,* 1974, *38,* 1079-1082.

Donnelly, E. F., Murphy, D. L., & Goodwin, F. K. Cross-sectional and longitudinal comparisons of bipolar and unipolar depressed groups on the MMPI. *Journal of Consulting and Clinical Psychology,* 1976, *44,* 233-237.

Donnelly, E. F., Murphy, D. L., & Scott, W. H. Perception and cognition in patients with bipolar and unipolar depressive disorders: A study in Rorschach responding. *Archives of General Psychiatry,* 1975, *32,* 1128-1131.

Donnelly, E. F., Murphy, D. L., Waldman, I. N., & Reynolds, T. D. MMPI difference between unipolar and bipolar depressed subjects: A replication. *Journal of Clinical Psychology,* 1976, *32,* 610-612.

Donovan, D. M., & O'Leary, M. R. Relationship between distortions in self-perception of depression and psychopathology. *Journal of Clinical Psychology,* 1976, *32,* 16-19.

Gurney, C., Roth, M., Garside, R. F., Kerr, T. A., & Schapira, K. Studies in the classification of affective disorders: The relationship between anxiety states and depressive illnesses - II. *British Journal of Psychiatry,* 1972, *121,* 162-166.

House, K. M., & Martin, R. L. MMPI delineation of a subgroup of depressed patients refractory to lithium carbonate therapy. *American Journal of Psychiatry,* 1975, *132,* 644-646.

Johnson, J. H. Bender-Gestalt constriction as an indicator of depression in psychiatric patients. *Journal of Personality Assessment,* 1973, *37,* 53-55.

Lewinson, P. M., & Graf, M. Pleasant activities and depression. *Journal of Consulting and Clinical Psychology,* 1973, *41,* 261-268.

Lewinson, P. M., Lobitz, W. C., & Wilson, S. "Sensitivity" of depressed individuals to aversive stimuli. *Journal of Abnormal Psychology,* 1973, *81,* 259-263.

Mendels, J., Weinstein, N., & Cochrane, C. The relationship between depression and anxiety. *Archives of General Psychiatry,* 1972, *27,* 649-653.

Mezzich, J. E., Damarin, F. L., & Erickson, J. R. Comparative validity of strategies and indices for differential diagnosis of depressive states from other psychiatric conditions using the MMPI. *Journal of Consulting and Clinical Psychology,* 1974, *42,* 691-698.

Pardue, L. H. Familial unipolar depressive illness: A pedigree study. *American Journal of Psychiatry,* 1975, *132,* 970-972.

Persky, H. Tetrahydrocortisol/tetrahydrocortisone ratio (H-sub-4F/H-sub-4E) as an indicator of depressive feelings. *Psychosomatic Medicine,* 1976, *38,* 13-18.

Roth, M. Gurney, C., Garside, R. F., & Kerr, T. A. Studies in the classification of affective disorders: The relationship between anxiety states and depressive illnesses-I. *British Journal of Psychiatry*, 1972, *121,* 147-161.

Schless, A. P., Mendels, J., Kipperman, A., & Cochrane, C. Depression and hostility. *Journal of Nervous and Mental Disease*, 1974, *159,* 91-100.

Shipley, C. R., & Fazio, A. F. Pilot study of a treatment for psychological depression. *Journal of Abnormal Psychology*, 1973, *82,* 372-376.

Steinmeyer, E. M. An experimental evaluation of self-descriptions of depressive symptoms by psychopathological groups. *Zeitschrift Fur Experimentelle und Angewandte Psychologie*, 1975, *22,* 290-315.

Tharp, R. G., Watson, D., & Kaya, J. Self-modification of depression. *Journal of Consulting and Clinical Psychology*, 1974, *42,* 624.

Waxer, P. Nonverbal cues for depth of depression: Set versus no set. *Journal of Consulting and Clinical Psychology*, 1976, *44,* 493.

Wener, A. E., & Rehm, L. P. Depressive affect: A test of behavioral hypothesis. *Journal of Abnormal Psychology*, 1975, *84,* 221-227.

White, R. B. Variations of Bender-Gestalt constriction and depression in adult psychiatric patients. *Perceptual and Motor Skills*, 1976, *42,* 221-222.

White, R. B., & McCraw, R. K. Note on the relationship between downward slant of Bender figures 1 and 2 and depression in adult psychiatric patients. *Perceptual and Motor Skills*, 1975, *40,* 152.

Wollert, R. W., & Buchwald, A. M. Subclinical depression and performance expectations, evaluations of performance and actual performance. *Journal of Nervous and Mental Disease*, 1979, *167,* 237-242.

Stress

Butcher, J. N., & Ryan, M. Personality stability and adjustment to an extreme environment. *Journal of Applied Psychology*, 1974, *59,* 107-109.

Ford, C. V., & Spaulding, R. C. The Pueblo incident: A comparison of factors related to coping with extreme stress. *Archives of General Psychiatry*, 1973, *29,* 340-343.

Hendrie, H. C., Lachar, D., & Lennox, K. Personality trait and symptom correlates of life change in a psychiatric population. *Journal of Psychosomatic Research*, 1975, *19,* 203-208.

Klonoff, H., Clark, C., Horgan, J., Kramer, P., & McDougall, G. The MMPI profile of prisoners of war. *Journal of Clinical Psychology*, 1976, *32,* 623-627.

Merbaum, M., & Hefez, A. Some personality characteristics of soldiers exposed to extreme war stress. *Journal of Consulting and Clinical Psychology*, 1976, *44,* 1-6.

Suicide

Clopton, J. R. Suicidal risk assessment via the MMPI. In C. Neuringer (Ed.), *Psychological assessment of suicide risk*. Springfield, Ill.: Charles C Thomas Publishers, 1974.

Clopton, J. R. A note on the MMPI as a suicide predictor. *Journal of Consulting and Clinical Psychology*, 1978, *46,* 335-336.

Clopton, J. R., & Jones, W. C. Use of the MMPI in the prediction of suicide. *Journal of Clinical Psychology*, 1975, *31,* 52-54.

Clopton, J. R., Pallis, D. J., & Birtchnell, J. MMPI profile patterns of suicide attempters. *Journal of Consulting and Clinical Psychology*, 1979, *47,* 135-139.

Hoey, H. P. Lethality of suicidal behavior and the MMPI. *Psychological Reports*, 1974, *35,* 942.

Kissinger, J. R. Women who threaten suicide: Evidence for an identifiable personality type. *Omega*, 1973, *4,* 73-84.

Leonard, C. V. Self-ratings of alienation in suicidal patients. *Journal of Clinical Psychology*, 1973, *29,* 423-428.

Leonard, C. V. The MMPI as a suicide predictor. *Journal of Consulting and Clinical Psychology*, 1977, *45,* 367-377.

Leonard, C. V. Response to "A note on the MMPI as a suicide predictor."
    Journal of Consulting and Clinical Psychology, 1978, *46,* 337-338.
Marks, P. A., & Haller, D. L. Now I lay me down for keeps: A study of adole-
    scent suicide attempts. *Journal of Clinical Psychology,* 1977, *33,* 390-400.
Pallis, D. J., & Birtchnell, J. Personality and suicidal history in psychia-
    tric patients. *Journal of Clinical Psychology,* 1976, *32,* 246-253.
Poeldinger, W. J., Gehring, A., & Blaser, P. Suicide risk and MMPI scores,
    especially as related to anxiety and depression. *Life-Threatening Behavior,*
    1973, *3,* 147-153.
Tarter, R. E., Templer, D. I., & Perley, R. L. Social role orientation and
    pathological factors in suicide attempts of varying lethality. *Journal of
    Community Psychology,* 1975, *3,* 295-299.

Physical and Medical Disorders

General Considerations

Colligan, R. C., & Osborne, D. MMPI profiles of adolescent medical patients.
    Journal of Clinical Psychology, 1977, *33,* 186-189.
Fracchia, J., Sheppard, C., Ricca, E., & Merlis, S. MMPI performance in
    chronic medical illness: The use of computer-derived interpretations.
    British Journal of Psychiatry, 1973, *122,* 242-243.
Harper, D. C. Personality characteristics of physically impaired adolescents.
    Journal of Clinical Psychology, 1978, *34,* 97-103.
Harper, D. C., & Richman, L. C. Personality profiles of physically impaired
    adolescents. *Journal of Clinical Psychology,* 1978, *34,* 636-642.
Newmark, C. S., & Raft, D. Using an abbreviated MMPI as a screening device for
    medical patients. *Psychosomatics,* 1976, *17,* 45-48.
Osborne, D., & Swenson, W. M. Muscle tension and personality. *Journal of
    Clinical Psychology,* 1978, *34,* 391-392.
Page, R. D., & Schaub, L. H. EMG biofeedback applicability for differing per-
    sonality types. *Journal of Clinical Psychology,* 1978, *34,* 1014-1020.
Pattison, E. M., Lapins, N. A., & Doerr, H. A. Faith healing: A study of per-
    sonality and function. *Journal of Nervous and Mental Disease,* 1973, *157,*
    397-409.
Schwartz, M. S. The Repression-Sensitization Scale: Normative, age, and sex
    data on 30,000 medical patients. *Journal of Clinical Psychology,* 1972, *28,*
    72-73.
Schwartz, M. S., Osborne, D., & Krupp, N. E. Moderating effects of age and sex
    on the association of medical diagnoses and 1-3/3-1 MMPI profiles. *Journal
    of Clinical Psychology,* 1972, *28,* 502-505.
Shaffer, J. W., Nussbaum, K., & Little, J. M. MMPI profiles of disability in-
    surance claimants. *American Journal of Psychiatry,* 1972, *129,* 403-407.
Sharp, M. W., & Reilley, R. R. The relationship of aerobic physical fitness
    to selected personality traits. *Journal of Clinical Psychology,* 1975, *31,*
    428-430.
Shershow, J. C., King, A., & Robinson, S. Carbon dioxide sensitivity and per-
    sonality. *Psychosomatic Medicine,* 1973, *35,* 155-160.
Spielberger, C. D., Auerbach, S. M., Wadsworth, A. P., Dunn, T. M., &
    Taulbee, E. S. Emotional reactions to surgery. *Journal of Consulting and
    Clinical Psychology,* 1973, *40,* 33-38.
Stewart, D. J., Powers, J., & Gouaux, C. The Wechsler in personality assess-
    ment: Object Assembly subtest as predictive of bodily concerns. *Journal of
    Consulting and Clinical Psychology,* 1973, *40,* 488.
Verberne, T. J. P. MMPI performance in chronic medical illness. *British Jour-
    nal of Psychiatry,* 1972, *121,* 235.

Cancer

Achterberg, J., & Lawlis, G. F. Psychological factors and blood chemistries as disease outcome predictors for cancer patients. *Multivariate Experimental Clinical Research*, 1977, *3*, 107-122.

Drunkenmolle, C. Psychological investigations of patients with breast carcinoma: A pilot study. *Psychiatria Clinica*, 1975, *8*, 127-139.

Kellerman, J. A note on psychosomatic factors in the etiology of neoplasms. *Journal of Consulting and Clinical Psychology*, 1978, *46*, 1522-1523.

Schonfield, J. Psychological and life-experience differences between Israeli women with benign and cancerous breast lesions. *Journal of Psychosomatic Research*, 1975, *19*, 229-234.

Schonfield, J. Psychological factors related to delayed return to an earlier life-style in successfully treated cancer patients. *Journal of Psychosomatic Research*, 1976, *20*, 41-46.

Watson, C. G., & Schuld, D. Psychosomatic factors in the etiology of neoplasms. *Journal of Consulting and Clinical Psychology*, 1977, *45*, 455-461.

Watson, C. G., & Schuld, D. Psychosomatic etiological factors in neoplasms: A response to Kellerman. *Journal of Consulting and Clinical Psychology*, 1978, *46*, 1524-1525.

Weisman, A. D., & Worden, J. W. The existential plight in cancer: Significance of the first 100 days. *International Journal of Psychiatry in Medicine*, 1976-77, *7*, 1-15.

Cardiac

Henrichs, T. F., & Waters, W. F. Psychological adjustment and response to open-heart surgery: Some methodological considerations. *British Journal of Psychiatry*, 1972, *120*, 491-496.

Jenkins, C. D., Zyzanski, S. J., Ryan, T. J., Flessas, A., & Tannenbaum, S. I. Social insecurity and coronary-prone Type A responses as identifiers of severe atherosclerosis. *Journal of Consulting and Clinical Psychology*, 1977, *45*, 1060-1067.

Kilpatrick, D. G., Miller, W. C., Allain, N., Huggins, M. B., & Lee, W. H., Jr. The use of psychological test data to predict open-heart surgery outcome: A prospective study. *Psychosomatic Medicine*, 1975, *37*, 62-73.

Lair, C. V., & King, G. D. MMPI profile predictors for successful and expired open-heart surgery patients. *Journal of Clinical Psychology*, 1976, *32*, 51-54.

Lebovits, B., Licher, E., & Moses, V. K. Personality correlates of coronary heart disease: A re-examination of the MMPI. *Social Science and Medicine*, 1975, *9*, 207-219.

Shealy, A. E., & Walker, D. R. MMPI prediction of intellectual changes following cardiac surgery. *Journal of Nervous and Mental Disease*, 1978, *166*, 263-267.

Stephans, J. H., Harris, A. H., Brady, J. V., & Shaffer, J. W. Psychological and physiological variables associated with large magnitude voluntary heart rate changes. *Psychophysiology*, 1975, *12*, 381-387.

Eating

Abram, H. S., Meixel, S. A., Webb, W. W., & Scott, H. W. Psychological adaptation to jejunoileal bypass for morbid obesity. *Journal of Nervous and Mental Disease*, 1976, *162*, 151-157.

Held, M. L., & Snow, D. L. MMPI, internal-external control, and Problem Checklist scores of obese adolescent females. *Journal of Clinical Psychology*, 1972, *28*, 523-525.

McCall, R. J. MMPI factors that differentiate remediably from irremediably obese women. *Journal of Community Psychology*, 1973, *1*, 34-36.

McCall, R. J. Group therapy with obese women of varying MMPI profiles. *Journal of Clinical Psychology*, 1974, *30*, 466-470.

Pierloot, R. A., Wellens, W., & Houben, M. E. Elements of resistance to a combined medical and psychotherapeutic program in anorexia nervosa: An over-
view. *Psychotherapy and Psychosomatics*, 1975, *26*, 101-117.
Pomerantz, A. S., Greenberg, I., & Blackburn, G. L. MMPI profiles of obese men
and women. *Psychological Reports*, 1977, *41*, 731-734.
Snow, D. L., & Held, M. L. Relation between locus of control and the MMPI with
obese female adolescents. *Journal of Clinical Psychology*, 1973, *29*, 24-25.

Epilepsy

Kristianson, P. A comparison between the personality changes in certain forms
of psychomotor and grand mal epilepsy. *British Journal of Psychiatry*, 1974,
125, 34-35.
Lachar, D., Lewis, R., & Kupke, T. MMPI in differentiation of temporal lobe
and nontemporal lobe epilepsy: Investigation of three levels of test
performance. *Journal of Consulting and Clinical Psychology*, 1979, *47*,
186-188.
Matthews, C. G., Dikmen, S., & Harley, J. P. Age of onset and psychometric
correlates of MMPI profiles in major motor epilepsy. *Diseases of the Nervous System*, 1977, *38*, 173-176.
Rennick, P. M. Psychosocial evaluation of individuals with epilepsy. In G. N.
Wright (Ed.), *Epilepsy rehabilitation*. Boston, Mass.: Little, Brown, 1975.
Rodin, E. A., Rim, C. S., Kitano, H., Lewis, R., & Rennick, P. M. A comparison
of the effectiveness of primadone versus carbamazepine in epileptic outpatient. *Journal of Nervous and Mental Disease*, 1976, *163*, 41-46.
Stevens, J. R., Milstein, V., & Goldstein, S. Psychometric test performance
in relation to the psychopathology of epilepsy. *Archives of General Psychiatry*, 1972, *26*, 532-538.

Hemodialysis

Malmquist, A., Kopfstein, J. H., Frank, E. T., Picklesimer, K., Clements, G.,
Ginn, E., & Cromwell, R. L. Factors in psychiatric prediction of patients
beginning hemodialysis: A follow-up of 13 patients. *Journal of Psychosomatic Research*, 1972, *16*, 19.
Pierce, D. M., Freeman, R., Lawton, R., & Fearing, M. Psychological correlates
of chronic hemodialysis estimated by MMPI scores. *Psychology*, 1973, *10*,
53-57.
Pierce, D. M., Freeman, R., Lawton, R., & Fearing, M. Longitudinal stability
of psychological status of hemodialysis patients. *Psychology*, 1973, *10*,
66-69.

Pain

Caslyn, D. A. Louks, J., & Freeman, C. W. The use of the MMPI with chronic low
back pain patients with a mixed diagnosis. *Journal of Clinical Psychology*,
1976, *32*, 532-536.
Freeman, C., Caslyn, D., & Louks, J. The use of the MMPI with low back pain
patients. *Journal of Clinical Psychology*, 1976, *32*, 294-298.
Gentry, W. D., Shows, W. D., & Thomas, M. Chronic low back pain: A psychological profile. *Psychosomatics*, 1974, *15*, 174-177.
Louks, J. L., Freeman, C. W., & Caslyn, D. A. Personality organization as an
aspect of back pain in a medical setting. *Journal of Personality Assessment*,
1978, *42*, 152-158.
Maruta, T., Swanson, D. W., & Swenson, W. M. Low back pain patients in a psy-
chiatric population. *Mayo Clinic Proceedings*, 1976, *51*, 57-61.
Rhodes, R. J. Failure to validate an MMPI headache scale. *Journal of Clinical
Psychology*, 1973, *29*, 237-238.
Shipman, W. G., Greene, C. S., & Laskin, D. M. Correlation of placebo re-
sponses and personality characteristics in myofascial pain-dysfunction
(MPD) patients. *Journal of Psychosomatic Research*, 1974, *18*, 475-483.

Swanson, D. W., Swenson, E. M., Maruta, T., & McPhee, M. C. Program for managing chronic pain. I. *Mayo Clinic Proceedings,* 1976, *51,* 401-408.

Thomas, M. R., & Lyttle, D. Development of a diagnostic checklist for low back pain patients. *Journal of Clinical Psychology,* 1976, *32,* 125-129.

Timmermans, G., Sternbach, R. A. Factors of human chronic pain: An analysis of personality and pain reaction variables. *Science,* 1974, *184,* 806-808.

Towne, W. S., & Tsushima, W. T. The use of the Low Back and the Dorsal scales in the identification of functional low back pain patients. *Journal of Clinical Psychology,* 1978, *34,* 88-91.

Whilfling, F. J., Klonoff, H., & Kokan, P. Psychological, demographic, and orthopedic factors associated with prediction of outcome of spinal fusion. *Clinical Orthopedics,* 1973, *90,* 153-160.

Wiltse, L. L., & Rocchio, P. D. Preoperative psychological tests as predictors of success of chemonucleolysis in the treatment of low back syndrome. *Journal of Bone and Joint Surgery,* 1975, *57,* 478-483.

Zaretsky, H. H., Lee, M. H., & Rubin, M. Psychological factors and clinical observations in acupuncture analgesia and pain abatement. *Journal of Psychology,* 1976, *93,* 113-120.

Ziesat, H. A., Jr., & Gentry, W. D. The Pain Apperception Test: An investigation of concurrent validity. *Journal of Clinical Psychology,* 1978, *34,* 786-789.

Sexual Dysfunction, Pregnancy, Menstruation

Beutler, L. E., Karacan, I., Anch, A. M., Salis, P. J., Scott, F. B., & Williams, R. L. MMPI and MIT discriminators of biogenic and psychogenic impotence. *Journal of Consulting and Clinical Psychology,* 1975, *43,* 899-903.

Bloom, L. J., Shelton, J. L., & Michaels, A. C. Dysmenorrhea and personality. *Journal of Personality Assessment,* 1978, *42,* 272-276.

Brown, R. S., Haddox, V., Posada, A., & Rubio, A. Social and psychological adjustment following pelvic exenteration. *American Journal of Obstetrics and Gynecology,* 1972, *114,* 162-171.

Ford, C. V., Castelnuovo-Tedesco, P., & Long, K. D. Women who seek therapeutic abortion: A comparison with women who complete their pregnancies. *American Journal of Psychiatry,* 1972, *129,* 546-552.

Gruba, G. H., & Rohrbaugh, M. MMPI correlates of menstrual distress. *Psychosomatic Medicine,* 1975, *37,* 265-273.

Kane, F. J., Jr., Moan, C. A., & Bolling, B. Motivation factors in pregnant adolescents. *Diseases of the Nervous System,* 1974, *35,* 131-134.

Kutner, S. J., & Brown, W. L. Types of oral contraceptives, depression, and premenstrual symptoms. *Journal of Nervous and Mental Disease,* 1972, *155,* 153-162.

Kutner, S. J., & Brown, W. L. History of depression as a risk factor for depression with oral contraceptives and discontinuance. *Journal of Nervous and Mental Disease,* 1972, *155,* 163-169.

Munjack, D. J., & Staples, F. R. Psychological characteristics of women with sexual inhibition (frigidity) in sex clinics. *Journal of Nervous and Mental Disease,* 1976, *163,* 117-123.

Osborne, D. Comparison of MMPI scores of pregnant women and female medical patients. *Journal of Clinical Psychology,* 1977, *33,* 448-450.

Osborne, D. MMPI characteristics of multigravidas and primigravidas in the third trimester of pregnancy. *Psychological Reports,* 1977, *40,* 81-82.

Osborne, D. MMPI changes between the first and third trimester of pregnancy. *Journal of Clinical Psychology,* 1978, *34,* 92-93.

Perez-Reyes, M. G., & Falk, R. Follow-up after therapeutic abortion in early adolescence. *Archives of General Psychiatry,* 1973, *28,* 120-126.

Shader, R. I., & Harmatz, J. S. Molindone: A pilot evaluation during the premenstruum. *Current Therapeutic Research,* 1975, *17,* 403-406.

Yamamoto, K. J., & Kinney, D. K. Pregnant women's ratings of different factors influencing psychological stress during pregnancy. *Psychological Reports*, 1976, *39*, 203-214.

Other Disorders

Crary, W. G., & Wexler, M. Meniere's Disease: A psychosomatic disorder. *Psychological Reports*, 1977, *41*, 603-645.

Dirks, J. F., Jones, N. F., & Kinsman, R. A. Panic-fear. A personality dimension related to intractability in asthma. *Psychosomatic Medicine*, 1977, *39*, 120-126.

Ford, C. V., Bray, G. A., & Swerdloff, R. S. A psychiatric study of patients referred with a diagnosis of hypoglycemia. *American Journal of Psychiatry*, 1976, *133*, 290-294.

Hoffman, A. L. Psychological factors associated with rheumatoid arthritis: Review of the literature. *Nursing Research*, 1974, *23*, 218-234.

Jones, N. F., Kinsman, R. A., Schum, R., & Resnikoff, P. Personality profiles in asthma. *Journal of Clinical Psychology*, 1976, *32*, 285-291.

Jordon, J. M., & Whitleer, R. A. Atopic dermatitis anxiety and conditioned scratch responses. *Journal of Psychosomatic Research*, 1974, *18*, 297-299.

Jurko, M. F., Andy, O. J., & Giurintano, L. P. Changes in the MMPI as a function of thalamotomy. *Journal of Clinical Psychology*, 1974, *30*, 569-570.

Kendall, P. C., Edinger, J., & Eberly, C. Taylor's MMPI correction factor for spinal cord injury: Empirical endorsement. *Journal of Consulting and Clinical Psychology*, 1978, *46*, 370-371.

Kuha, S., Moilanen, P., & Kampman, R. The effects of social class on psychiatric psychological evaluations in patients with pulmonary tuberculosis. *Acta Psychiatrica Scandinavica*, 1975, *51*, 249-256.

McMahon, A. W., Schmitt, P., Patterson, J. F., & Rothman, E. Personality differences between inflammatory bowel disease patients and their healthy siblings. *Psychosomatic Medicine*, 1973, *35*, 91-103.

Mlott, S. R., Lira, F. T., & Miller, W. C. Psychological assessment of the burn patient. *Journal of Clinical Psychology*, 1977, *33*, 425-430.

Schmidt, R. T. Personality and fainting. *Journal of Psychosomatic Research*, 1975, *19*, 21-25.

Organicity and Intellectual Functioning

Ayers, J., Templer, D. I., & Ruff, C. F. The MMPI in the differential diagnosis of organicity vs. schizophrenia: Empirical findings and a somewhat different perspective. *Journal of Clinical Pscyhology*, 1975, *31*, 685-686.

Black, F. W. Use of the MMPI with patients with recent war-related head injuries. *Journal of Clinical Psychology*, 1974, *30*, 571-573.

Black, F. W. Unilateral brain lesions and MMPI performance: A preliminary study. *Perceptual and Motor Skills*, 1975, *40*, 87-93.

Bloom, R. B., & Entin, A. D. Intellectual functioning and psychopathology: A canonical analysis of WAIS and MMPI relationships. *Journal of Clinical Psychology*, 1975, *31*, 697-698.

Boll, T. J., Heaton, R., & Reitan, R. M. Neuro-physiological and emotional correlates of Huntington's Chorea. *Journal of Nervous and Mental Disease*, 1974, *158*, 61-69.

Chaney, E. F., Erickson, R. C., & O'Leary, M. R. Brain damage and five MMPI items with alcoholic patients. *Journal of Clinical Psychology*, 1977, *33*, 307-308.

Crumpton, E., & Mutalipassi, L. R. The veteran NP patient: Past and present. *Journal of Clinical Psychology*, 1972, *28*, 94-101.

Dikman, S., & Reitan, R. M. MMPI correlates of dysphasic language disturbances. *Journal of Abnormal Psychology*, 1974, *83*, 675-679.

Dikman, S., & Reitan, R. M. MMPI correlates of localized cerebral lesions. *Perceptual and Motor Skills*, 1974, *39*, 831-840.

Dikman, S., & Reitan, R. M. MMPI correlates of adaptive ability deficits in patients with brain lesions. *Journal of Nervous and Mental Disease,* 1977, *165,* 247-254.

Fruhauf, K. Psychometric determination of behavioral maturity in the brain-damaged. *Zeitschrift Fur Psychologie,* 1975, *183,* 279-293.

Gocka, E. F. MMPI item responses for male neuropsychiatric patients. *Catalog of Selected Documents in Psychology,* 1976, *6,* 12.

Halperin, K. M., Neuringer, C., Davies, P. S., & Goldstein, G. Validation of the schizophrenia-organicity scale with brain-damaged and non-brain-damaged schizophrenics. *Journal of Consulting and Clinical Psychology,* 1977, *45,* 949-950.

Heaton, R. K., Smith, H. H., Jr., Lehman, R. A. W., & Vogt, A. T. Prospects for faking believable deficits on neuropsychological testing. *Journal of Consulting and Clinical Psychology,* 1978, *46,* 892-900.

Holland, T. R., Lowenfeld, J., & Wadsworth, H. M. MMPI indices in the discrimination of brain-damaged and schizophrenic groups. *Journal of Consulting and Clinical Psychology,* 1975, *43,* 426.

Judd, L. L., & Grant, I. Brain dysfunction in chronic sedative users. *Journal of Psychedelic Drugs,* 1975, *7,* 143-149.

Louks, J., Caslyn, D., & Lindsay, F. Personality dysfunction and lateralized deficits in cerebral functions as measured by the MMPI and Reitan-Halstead Battery. *Perceptual and Motor Skills,* 1976, *43,* 655-659.

Lyle, O. E., & Gottesman, I. I. Premorbid psychometric indicators of the gene for Huntington's disease. *Journal of Consulting and Clinical Psychology,* 1977, *45,* 1011-1022.

Malec, J. Neuropsychological assessment of schizophrenia versus brain damage: A review. *Journal of Nervous and Mental Disease,* 1978, *166,* 507-516.

Marsh, G. G. Parkinsonian patients' scores on Hovey's MMPI scale for CNS disorder. *Journal of Clinical Psychology,* 1972, *28,* 529-530.

Maskin, M. B., Riklan, M., & Chabot, D. A preliminary study of selected emotional changes in Parkinsonians on L-Dopa therapy. *Journal of Clinical Psychology,* 1972, *28,* 604-605.

Maskin, M. B., Riklan, M., & Chabot, D. Emotional functions in short-term vs. long-term L-Dopa therapy in Parkinsonism. *Journal of Clinical Psychology,* 1973, *29,* 493-495.

Morgan, D. W., Weitzel, W. D., Guyden, T. E., Robinson, J. A., & Hedlund, J. L. Comparing MMPI statements and mental status items. *American Journal of Psychiatry,* 1972, *129,* 693-697.

Neuringer, C., Dombrowski, P. S., & Goldstein, G. Cross-validation of an MMPI scale of differential diagnosis of brain damage from schizophrenia. *Journal of Clinical Psychology,* 1975, *31,* 268-271.

Norton, J. C. Patterns of neuropsychological test performance in Huntington's disease. *Journal of Nervous and Mental Disease,* 1975, *161,* 276-279.

Norton, J. C., & Romano, P. O. Validation of the Watson-Thomas rules for MMPI diagnosis. *Diseases of the Nervous System,* 1977, *38,* 773-775.

Perkins, C. W. Some correlates of Category Test scores for nonorganic psychiatric patients. *Journal of Clinical Psychology,* 1974, *30,* 176-178.

Reitan, R. M. MMPI studies in brain damage. *Annual Review of Psychology,* 1976, *27,* 204-208.

Rice, R. G., & Narus, L. R., Jr. The WAIS vocabulary subscale as a reading test. *Newsletter of Research in Mental Health and Behavioral Science,* 1975, *17,* 12-13.

Riklan, M., Halgin, R., Maskin, M., & Weissman, D. Psychological studies of longer range L-Dopa therapy in Parkinsonism. *Journal of Nervous and Mental Disease,* 1973, *157,* 452-464.

Ruff, C. F., Ayers, J. L., & Templer, D. I. The Watson and the Hovey MMPI scales: Do they measure organicity or functional psychopathology? *Journal of Clinical Psychology,* 1977, *33,* 732-734.

Russell, E. W. Validation of a brain damage vs. schizophrenia MMPI key. *Journal of Clinical Psychology,* 1975, *31,* 659-661.

Russell, E. W. MMPI profiles of brain-damaged and schizophrenic subjects. *Journal of Clinical Psychology,* 1977, *33,* 190-193.

Ryan, J. J., & Souheaver, G. T. Further evidence that concerns the validity of an MMPI key for separation of brain-damaged and schizophrenic patients. *Journal of Clinical Psychology,* 1977, *33,* 753-754.

Sand, P. L. Performance of medical patient groups with and without brain damage on the Hovey (0) and Watson, (Sc-0) MMPI scales. *Journal of Clinical Psychology,* 1973, *29,* 235-237.

Schwartz, M. S. Separate versus full MMPI method: Reliability of the pseudoneurologic scale. *Journal of Clinical Psychology,* 1974, *30,* 79.

Schwartz, M. S., & Brown, J. R. MMPI differentiation of multiple sclerosis vs. pseudoneurologic patients. *Journal of Clinical Psychology,* 1973, *29,* 471-474.

Shapiro, A. K., Shapiro, E., Wayne, H., & Clarkin, J. The psychopathology of Gilles de la Tourette's Syndrome. *American Journal of Psychiatry,* 1972, *129,* 427-434.

Siskind, G. Hovey's 5-item MMPI scale and psychiatric patients. *Journal of Clinical Psychology,* 1976, *32,* 50.

Storms, L. H. Relationships among patients' emotional problems, neurologists' judgments, and psychological tests of brain dysfunction. *Journal of Clinical Psychology,* 1972, *38,* 54-60.

Templer, D. I., & Connolly, W. Affective vs. thinking disturbance related to left- vs. right-sided brain functioning. *Psychological Reports,* 1976, *38,* 141-142.

Turner, R. G., & Horn, J. M. MMPI correlates of WAIS subtest performance. *Journal of Clinical Psychology,* 1976, *32,* 583-594.

Watson, C. G. A simple bivariate screening technique to separate NP hospital organics from other psychiatric groups. *Journal of Clinical Psychology,* 1973, *29,* 448-450.

Watson, C. G., Davis, W. E., & Gasser, B. The separation of organics from depressives with ability- and personality-based tests. *Journal of Clinical Psychology,* 1978, *34,* 393-397.

Watson, C. G., Davis, W. E., & McDermott, M. T. MMPI-WAIS relationships in organic and schizophrenic patients. *Journal of Clinical Psychology,* 1976, *32,* 539-540.

Watson, C. G., & Plemel, D. An MMPI scale to separate brain-damaged from functional psychiatric patients in neuropsychiatric settings. *Journal of Consulting and Clinical Psychology,* 1978, *44,* 1127-1132.

Watson, C. G., Plemel, D., & Jacobs, L. An MMPI sign to separate organic from functional psychiatric patients. *Journal of Clinical Psychology,* 1978, *34,* 399-401.

Wiens, A. N., & Matarazzo, J. D. WAIS and MMPI correlates of the Halstead-Reitan Neuropsychology Battery in normal male subjects. *Journal of Nervous and Mental Disease,* 1977, *164,* 112-121.

Personality Disorders

Brandsma, J. M., & Ludwig, A. M. A case of multiple personality: Diagnosis and therapy. *International Journal of Clinical and Experimental Hypnosis,* 1974, *22,* 216-233.

Button, J. H., & Reivich, R. S. Obsessions of infanticide: A review of 42 cases. *Archives of General Psychiatry,* 1972, *27,* 235-240.

Kristianson, P. The personality in psychomotor epilepsy compared with the explosive and aggressive personality. *British Journal of Psychiatry,* 1974, *125,* 221-229.

Liskow, B. I., Clayton, P., Woodruff, R., Guze, S., & Cloninger, R. Briquet's syndrome, hysterical personality and the MMPI. *American Journal of Psychiatry,* 1977, *134,* 1137-1139.

Ludwig, A. M., Brandsma, J. M., Wilbur, C. B., Bendfeldt, F., & Jameson, D. N.

The objective study of a multiple personality: Or, are four heads better than one? *Archives of General Psychiatry,* 1972, *26,* 298-310.

Rogers, R., & Wright, E. W. Behavioral rigidity and its relationship to authoritarianism and obsessive-compulsiveness. *Perceptual and Motor Skills,* 1975, *40,* 802.

Slavney, P. R., & McHugh, P. R. The hysterical personality: An attempt at validation with the MMPI. *Archives of General Psychiatry,* 1975, *32,* 186-190.

Warner, R. The diagnosis of anti-social and hysterical personality disorders: An example of sex bias. *Journal of Nervous and Mental Disease,* 1978, *166,* 839-845.

Watson, C. G., & Buranen, C. The frequency and identification of false positive conversion reactions. *Journal of Nervous and Mental Disease,* 1979, *167,* 243-247.

Psychopathy, Criminals, and Aggression

Adams, T. C. Some MMPI differences between first and multiple admissions with a state prison population. *Journal of Clinical Psychology,* 1976, *32,* 555-558.

Adams, T. C., & West, J. E. Another look at the use of the MMPI as an index to "escapism." *Journal of Clinical Psychology,* 1976, *32,* 580-582.

Bauer, G. E., & Clark, J. A. Personality deviancy and prison incarceration. *Journal of Clinical Psychology,* 1976, *32,* 279-283.

Beck, E. A., & McIntyre, S. C. MMPI patterns of shoplifters within a college population. *Psychological Reports,* 1977, *41,* 1035-1040.

Blackburn, R. Dimensions of hostility and aggression in abnormal offenders. *Journal of Consulting and Clinical Psychology,* 1972, *38,* 20-26.

Blackburn, R. An empirical classification of psychopathic personality. *British Journal of Psychiatry,* 1975, *127,* 456-460.

Christensen, L., & Le Unes, A. Discriminating criminal types and recidivism by means of the MMPI. *Journal of Clinical Psychology,* 1974, *30,* 192-193.

Climent, C. E., Rollins, A., Ervin, F. R., & Plutchik, R. Epidemiological studies of women prisoners: 1, Medical and psychiatric variables related to violent behavior. *American Journal of Psychiatry,* 1973, *130,* 985-990.

Cubitt, G. H., & Gendreau, P. Assessing the diagnostic utility of MMPI and 16 PF indexes of homosexuality in a prison sample. *Journal of Consulting and Clinical Psychology,* 1972, *39,* 342.

Deiker, T. E. A cross-validation of MMPI scales of aggression on male criminal criterion groups. *Journal of Consulting and Clinical Psychology,* 1974, *42,* 196-202.

Edinger, J. D. Cross-validation of the Megargee MMPI typology for prisoners. *Journal of Consulting and Clinical Psychology,* 1979, *47,* 234-242.

Emmons, T. D., & Webb, W. W. Subjective correlates of emotional responsivity and stimulation seeking in psychopaths, normals, and acting-out neurotics. *Journal of Consulting and Clinical Psychology,* 1974, *42,* 620.

Eron, L. D., Huesmann, L. R., Lefkowitz, M. M., & Wolder, L. O. Does television violence cause aggression? *American Psychologist,* 1972, *27,* 253-263.

Flanagan, J. J., & Lewis, G. R. First prison admissions with juvenile histories and absolute first offenders: Frequencies and MMPI profiles. *Journal of Clinical Psychology,* 1974, *30,* 358-360.

Gallemore, J. L., Jr., & Panton, J. H. Inmate responses to lengthy death row confinement. *American Journal of Psychiatry,* 1972, *129,* 167-172.

Gendreau, P., Irvine, M., & Knight, S. Evaluating response set styles on the MMPI with prisoners: Faking good adjustment and maladjustment. *Canadian Journal of Behavioral Science,* 1973, *5,* 183-194.

Godfrey, E. A., & Schulman, R. E. Age and a group test battery as predictors of type of crime. *Journal of Clinical Psychology,* 1972, *28,* 339-342.

Hawk, S., & Peterson, R. A. Do MMPI psychopathic deviancy scores reflect psychopathic deviancy or just deviance? *Journal of Personality Assessment*, 1974, *38*, 362-368.

Hindelang, M. J. The relationship of self-reported delinquency to scales of the CPI and MMPI. *Journal of Criminal Law, Criminology, and Police Science*, 1972, *63*, 75-81.

Hindelang, M. J. Variations in personality attributes of social and solitary self-reported delinquents. *Journal of Consulting and Clinical Psychology*, 1973, *40*, 452-454.

Holland, T. R., & Holt, N. Prisoner intellectual and personality correlates of offense severity and recidivism probability. *Journal of Clinical Psychology*, 1975, *31*, 667-672.

Holland, T. R., & Holt, N. Personality patterns among short-term prisoners undergoing presentence evaluations. *Psychological Reports*, 1975, *37*, 827-836.

Huesmann, L. R., Lefkowitz, M. M., & Eron, L. D. Sum of MMPI Scales F, 4, and 9 as a measure of aggression. *Journal of Consulting and Clinical Psychology*, 1978, *5*, 1071-1078.

Joesting, J., Jones, N., & Joesting, R. Male and female prison inmates' differences on MMPI scales and revised beta IQ. *Psychological Reports*, 1975, *37*, 471-474.

Johnson, J. H. A cross validation of seventeen experimental MMPI scales related to antisocial behavior. *Journal of Clinical Psychology*, 1974, *30*, 564-565.

Knott, P. D., Lasater, L., & Shuman, R. Aggression-guilt and conditionability for aggressiveness. *Journal of Personality*, 1974, *42*, 332-344.

Lester, D., Perdue, W. C., & Brookhart, D. Murder and the control of aggression. *Psychological Reports*, 1974, *34*, 706.

Leunes, A., & Christensen, L. A comparison of forgers with other criminals. *Journal of Community Psychology*, 1975, *3*, 285-288.

Leventhal, G. Female criminality: Is "Women's Lib" to blame? *Psychological Reports*, 1977, *41*, 1179-1182.

Lothstein, L. M., & Jones. P. Discriminating violent individuals by means of various psychological tests. *Journal of Personality Assessment*, 1978, *42*, 237-243.

McCreary, C. P. Trait and type differences among male and female assaultive and nonassaultive offenders. *Journal of Personality Assessment*, 1976, *40*, 617-621.

McCreary, C. P., & Mensh, I. N. Personality differences associated with age in law offenders. *Journal of Gerontology*, 1977, *32*, 164-167.

McCreary, C., & Padilla, E. MMPI differences among black, Mexican-American, and white male offenders. *Journal of Clinical Psychology*, 1977, *38*, 171-177.

Panton, J. H. Personality characteristics of management problem prison inmates. *Journal of Community Psychology*, 1973, *1*, 185-191.

Panton, J. H. Personality differences between male and female prison inmates measured by the MMPI. *Criminal Justice and Behavior*, 1974, *1*, 332-339.

Panton, J. H. Personality characteristics of death-row prison inmates. *Journal of Clinical Psychology*, 1976, *32*, 306-309.

Panton, J. H. Significant increase in MMPI Mf scores within a state prison population. *Journal of Clinical Psychology*, 1976, *32*, 604-606.

Panton, J. H. Longitudinal post-validation of the MMPI Escape (EC) and Prison Adjustment (AP) scales. *Journal of Clinical Psychology*, 1979, *35*, 101-103.

Penner, L. A., Summers, L. S., Brookmire, D. A., & Dertke, M. S. The lost dollar: Situational and personality determinants of a pro- and antisocial behavior. *Journal of Personality*, 1976, *44*, 274-293.

Spellacy, F. Neuropsychological discrimination between violent and nonviolent men. *Journal of Clinical Psychology*, 1978, *34*, 49-52.

Sutker, P. B., Allain, A. N., & Geyer, S. Female criminal violence and differential MMPI characteristics. *Journal of Consulting and Clinical Psychology*, 1978, *5*, 1141-1143.

Sutker, P. B., & Moan, C. E. A psychosocial description of penitentiary inmates. *Archives of General Psychiatry*, 1973, *29*, 663-667.

Sutker, P. B., & Moan, C. E. Prediction of socially maladaptive behavior within a state prison system. *Journal of Community Psychology*, 1973, *1*, 74-78.

Sutker, P. B., Moan, C. E., & Swanson, W. C. Porteus Maze Test qualitative performance in pure sociopaths, prison normals, and antisocial psychotics. *Journal of Clinical Psychology*, 1972, *28*, 349-353.

Syndulko, K., Parker, D. A., Jens, R., Maltzman, I., & Ziskind, E. Psychophysiology of sociopathy: Electrocortical measures. *Biological Psychology*, 1975, *3*, 185-200.

Tamayo, A., & Raymond, F. Self-concept of psychopaths. *Journal of Psychology*, 1977, *97*, 71-77.

Verberne, T. J. P. Blackburn's typology of abnormal homicides: Additional data and a critique. *British Journal of Criminology*, 1972, *12*, 88-89.

Weiss, J. M. A. The natural history of antisocial attitudes: What happens to psychopaths? *Journal of Geriatric Psychiatry*, 1973, *6*, 236-242.

Wilkins, J. L., Scharff, W. H., & Schlottmann, R. S. Personality type, reports of violence, and aggressive behavior. *Journal of Personality and Social Psychology*, 1974, *30*, 243-247.

Hostility Control

Johnston, N., & Cooke, G. Relationship of MMPI alcoholism, prison escape, hostility control, and recidivism scales to clinical judgments. *Journal of Clinical Psychology*, 1973, *29*, 32-34.

Mallory, C. H., & Walker, C. E. MMPI O-H Scale responses of assaultive and nonassaultive prisoners and associated life history variables. *Educational and Psychological Measurement*, 1972, *32*, 1125-1128.

McLachlan, J. F. C. A hostility scale for Form R of the MMPI. *Journal of Clinical Psychology*, 1974, *30*, 369-371.

Megargee, E. I. Recent research on overcontrolled and undercontrolled personality patterns among violent offenders. *Sociological Symposium*, 1973, *No. 9*, 37-50.

Megargee, E. I., & Cook, P. E. Negative response bias and the MMPI over controlled-hostility scale: A response to Deiker. *Journal of Consulting and Clinical Psychology*, 1975, *43*, 725-729.

Vanderbeck, D. J. A construct validity study of the O-H (Overcontrolled-Hostility) scale of the MMPI, using a social learning approach to the catharsis effect. *FCI Research Reports*, 1973, *5*, 1-18. Federal Correctional Institution, Tallahassee, Florida, 32304.

VanDeventer, J., & Webb, J. T. Manifest hostility as modified by the K and SO-R scales of the MMPI. *Journal of Psychology*, 1974, *87*, 209-211.

White W. C., Jr. Validity of the overcontrolled-hostility (O-H) scale: A brief report. *Journal of Personality Assessment*, 1975, *39*, 587-590.

White W. C., Jr., McAdoo, W. G., & Megargee, E. I. Personality factors associated with over- and undercontrolled offenders. *Journal of Personality Assessment*, 1973, *37*, 473-478.

Juvenile Delinquents

Devore, J. E., & Fryrear, J. L. Analysis of juvenile delinquents' hole drawing responses on the tree figure of the House-Tree-Person technique. *Journal of Clinical Psychology*, 1976, *32*, 731-736.

Montague, D. J., & Prytula, R. E. Human figure drawing characteristics related to juvenile delinquents. *Perceptual and Motor Skills*, 1975, *40*, 623-630.

Rawlings, M. L. Self-control and interpersonal violence: A study of Scottish adolescent male severe offenders. *Criminology*, 1973, *11*, 23-48.

Tortorella, W. M. Personality and intellectual changes in delinquent girls following long-term institutional placement. *Journal of Community Psychology*, 1973, *1*, 288-291.

Wenk, E. A., & Emrich, R. B. Assaultive youth: An exploratory study of the assaultive experience and assaultive potential of California Youth Authority wards. *Journal of Research on Crime and Delinquency*, 1972, *9*, 171-196.

Sex Offenders

Armentrout, J. A., & Hauer, A. L. MMPIs of rapists of adults, rapists of children, and non-rapist sex offenders. *Journal of Clinical Psychology*, 1978, *34*, 330-332.

Karacan, I., Williams, R. L., Guerrero, M. W., Salis, P. J., Thornby, J. I., & Hursch, C. J. Nocturnal penile tumescence and sleep of convicted rapists and other prisoners. *Archives of Sexual Behavior*, 1974, *3*, 19-26.

McCreary, C. P. Personality differences among child molesters. *Journal of Personality Assessment*, 1975, *39*, 591-593.

McCreary, C. P. Personality profiles of persons convicted of indecent exposure. *Journal of Clinical Psychology*, 1975, *31*, 260-262.

Rader, C. M. MMPI profile types of exposers, rapists, and assaulters in a court services population. *Journal of Consulting and Clinical Psychology*, 1977, *45*, 61-69.

Silver, S. N. Outpatient treatment for sexual offenders. *Social Work*, 1976, *21*, 134-140.

Smukler, A. J., & Schiebel, D. Personality characteristics of exhibitionists. *Diseases of the Nervous System*, 1975, *36*, 600-603.

Schizophrenia and Paranoia

Cash, T. F., & Stack, J. J. Locus of control among schizophrenics and other hospitalized psychiatric patients. *Genetic Psychology Monographs*, 1973, *87*, 105-122.

Davis, W. E. Age and the discriminative "power" of the MMPI with schizophrenic and nonschizophrenic patients. *Journal of Consulting and Clinical Psychology*, 1972, *38*, 151.

Fine, H. K. Studying schizophrenia outside the psychiatric setting. *Journal of Youth and Adolescence*, 1973, *2*, 291-301.

Fishkin, S. M., Lovallo, W. R., & Pishkin, V. Relationship between schizophrenic thinking and MMPI for process and reactive patients. *Journal of Clinical Psychology*, 1977, *33*, 116-119.

Koh, S. D., & Peterson, R. A. Perceptual memory for numerousness in "nonpsychotic schizophrenics." *Journal of Abnormal Psychology*, 1974, *83*, 215-226.

Newmark, C. S., Gentry, L., Simpson, M., & Jones, T. MMPI criteria for diagnosing schizophrenia. *Journal of Personality Assessment*, 1978, *42*, 366-373.

Newmark, C. S., Raft, D., Toomey, T., Hunter, W., & Mazzaglia, J. Diagnosis of schizophrenia: Pathognomic signs or symptom clusters. *Comprehensive Psychiatry*, 1975, *16*, 155-163.

Routh, D. K., & Keller, W. Instructions, word association, and the hospitalized psychiatric patient. *Psychological Reports*, 1973, *32*, 579-585.

Ryan, D. V., & Neale, J. M. Test-taking sets and the performance of schizophrenics on laboratory tests. *Journal of Abnormal Psychology*, 1973, *82*, 207-211.

Sappington, J. Psychometric correlates of defensive style in process and reactive schizophrenics. *Journal of Consulting and Clinical Psychology*, 1975, *43*, 154-156.

Scagnelli, J. The significance of dependency in the paranoid syndrome. *Journal of Clinical Psychology*, 1975, *31*, 29-34.

Storms, L. H., & Acosta, F. X. Effects of dynamometer tension on stimulus generalization in schizophrenic and nonschizophrenic patients. *Journal of Abnormal Psychology,* 1974, *83,* 204-207.

Tarter, R. E., & Perley, R. N. Clinical and perceptual characteristics of paranoids and paranoid schizophrenics. *Journal of Clinical Psychology,* 1975, *31,* 42-44.

Templer, D. I., Ruff, C. F., & Armstrong, G. Cognitive functioning and degree of psychosis in schizophrenics given many electroconvulsive treatments. *British Journal of Psychiatry,* 1973, *123,* 441-443.

Watson, C. G. Psychopathological correlates of anthropometric types in male schizophrenics. *Journal of Clinical Psychology,* 1972, *28,* 474-478.

Watson, C. G. Roles of impression management in the interview, self-report, and cognitive behavior of schizophrenics. *Journal of Consulting and Clinical Psychology,* 1972, *38,* 452-456.

OCCUPATIONAL GROUPS

Arvey, R. D., Mussio, S. J., & Payne, G. Relationships between MMPI scores and job performance measures of fire fighters. *Psychological Reports,* 1972, *31,* 199-202.

Azen, S. P., Snibbe, H. M., & Montgomery, H. R. A longitudinal predictive study of success and performance of law enforcement officers. *Journal of Applied Psychology,* 1973, *57,* 190-192.

Best, C. L., & Kilpatrick, D. G. Psychological profiles of rape crisis counselors. *Psychological Reports,* 1978, *40,* 1127-1134.

Bloom, W. Relevant MMPI norms for young adult Air Force trainees. *Journal of Personality Assessment,* 1977, *41,* 505-510.

Bonynge, E. R., & Hoffmann, H. Personality measurements in selection of applicants for an alcohol counselor training program. *Psychological Reports,* 1977, *41,* 493-494.

Burgess, M. M., Duffey, M., & Temple, F. G. Two studies of prediction of success in a collegiate program of nursing. *Nursing Research,* 1972, *21,* 357-366.

Callan, J. P. An attempt to use the MMPI as a predictor of failure in military training. *British Journal of Psychiatry,* 1972, *121,* 553-557.

Campbell, H. G., Clarkson, Q. D., & Sinsabaugh, L. L. MMPI identification of nonrehabilitants among disabled veterans. *Journal of Personality Assessment,* 1977, *41,* 266-269.

Crovitz, E., Huse, M. N., & Lewis, D. E. Selection of physician's assistants. *Journal of Medical Education,* 1973, *48,* 551-555.

Delk, J. L. Some personality characteristics of skydivers. *Life-Threatening Behavior,* 1973, *3,* 51-57.

Evans, D. R. The use of the MMPI to predict conscientious hotline workers. *Journal of Clinical Psychology,* 1976, *32,* 684-686.

Evans, D. R. Use of the MMPI to predict effective hotline workers. *Journal of Clinical Psychology,* 1977, *33,* 1113-1114.

Garetz, F. K., & Anderson, R. W. Patterns of professional activities of psychiatrists: A follow-up of 100 psychiatric residents. *American Journal of Psychiatry,* 1973, *130,* 981-984.

Garrard, J., & Weber, R. G. Comparison of three- and four-year medical school graduates. *Journal of Medical Education,* 1974, *49,* 547-553.

Harrell, T. W. High earning MBA's. *Personnel Psychology,* 1972, *25,* 523-530.

Harrell, T. W., & Harrell, M. S. The personality of MBA's who reach general management early. *Personnel Psychology,* 1973, *26,* 127-134.

Heath, D. H. Adolescent and adult predictors of vocational adaptation. *Journal of Vocational Behavior,* 1976, *9,* 1-19.

Heaton, R. K., Chelune, G. J., & Lehman, R. A. Using neuropsychological and personality tests to assess the likelihood of patient employment. *Journal of Nervous and Mental Disease,* 1978, *166,* 408-416.

Heikkinen, C. A., & Wegner, K. W. MMPI studies of counselors: A review. *Journal of Counseling Psychology,* 1973, *20,* 275-279.

Jansen, D. G., Bonk, E. C., & Garvey, F. J. MMPI characteristics of clergymen in counseling training and their relationship to supervisor's and peers' ratings of counseling effectiveness. *Psychological Reports,* 1973, *33,* 695-698.

Jansen, D. G., & Garvey, F. J. High-, average-, and low-rated clergymen in a state hospital clinical program. *Journal of Clinical Psychology,* 1973, *29,* 89-92.

Jansen, D. G., & Hoffmann, H. MMPI scores of counselors on alcoholism prior to and after training. *Journal of Consulting and Clinical Psychology,* 1975, *43,* 271.

Kelly, W. L. Psychological prediction of leadership in nursing. *Nursing Research,* 1974, *23,* 38-42.

Lachar, D. Prediction of early U. S. Air Force freshman cadet adaptation with the MMPI. *Journal of Counseling Psychology,* 1974, *21,* 404-408.

Lester, D., & Narkunski, A. An exploratory study of correlates of success in a vocational training program for ex-addicts. *Psychological Reports,* 1975, *37,* 1212-1214.

Machota, P., Ott, J. E., Moore, V., Dungy, C., & Fine, L. Predictors of clinical performance of child health associates. *Journal of Allied Health,* 1975, *4,* 25-31.

Muha, T. M., & May, J. R. An employment index for identifying unfit job applicants. *Journal of Community Psychology,* 1973, *1,* 362-365.

Oldroyd, R. J., Pappas, J. P., & Hart, D. A comparison of three personality inventories as screening instruments to select effective teachers. *Journal of Student Personnel Association and Teaching Education,* 1973, *12,* 45-53.

Richards, J. M., Jr., Calkins, E. V., McCanse, A., & Burgess, M. M. Predicting performance in a combined undergraduate and medical education program. *Educational and Psychological Measurement,* 1974, *34,* 923-931.

Saccuzzo, D. P., Higgins, G., & Lewandowski, D. Program for psychological assessment of law enforcement officers: Initial evaluation. *Psychological Reports,* 1974, *35,* 651-654.

Saunders, B. T., & Fenton, T. MMPI profiles of child care applicants at a children's residential treatment center. *Devereux Forum,* 1975, *10,* 16-19.

Schaffer, K. F. Evaluating job satisfaction and success for emotionally maladjusted men. *Journal of Vocational Behavior,* 1976, *9,* 329-335.

Schoenfield, L. S., Preston, J., & Adams, R. L. Selection of volunteers for telephone crisis intervention centers. *Psychological Reports,* 1976, *39,* 725-726.

Simono, R. B. Careers in the clergy: The myth of femininity. *Educational and Psychological Measurement,* 1978, *38,* 507-511.

Solway, K. S., Hays, J. R., & Zieben, M. Personality characteristics of juvenile probation officers. *Journal of Community Psychology,* 1976, *4,* 152-156.

Stone, L. A., Bassett, G. R., Brosseau, J. D., DeMers, J., & Stiening, J. A. Psychological test scores for a group of MEDEX trainees. *Psychological Reports,* 1972, *31,* 827-831.

Stone, L. A., Bassett, G. R., Brosseau, J. D., DeMers, J., & Stiening, J. A. Psychological test characteristics associated with training-success in a MEDEX (physician's extension) training program. *Psychological Reports,* 1972, *32,* 231-234.

Stone, L. A., & Brosseau, J. D. Cross-validation of a system for predicting training success of MEDEX trainees. *Psychological Reports,* 1973, *33,* 917-918.

MISCELLANEOUS STUDIES

Adams, H. B., Cooper, G. D., & Carrera, R. N. Individual differences in behavioral reactions of psychiatric patients to brief partial sensory deprivation. *Perceptual and Motor Skills,* 1972, *34,* 199-217.

Cerbus, G., & Travis, R. J. Seasonal variation of personality of college students as measured by the MMPI. *Psychological Reports,* 1973, *33,* 665-666.

Collins, J. F., Newman, P. A., & Hutson, S. P. Personality correlates of visual perceptual responses. *Perceptual and Motor Skills,* 1974, *38,* 1183-1187.

Davis, H. What does the P scale measure? *British Journal of Psychiatry,* 1974, *125,* 161-167.

Erickson, R. C., Post, R. D., & Paige, A. B. Hope as a psychiatric variable. *Journal of Clinical Psychology,* 1975, *31,* 324-330.

Finney, J. C. Therapist and patient after hours. *American Journal of Psychotherapy,* 1975, *29,* 593-602.

Finney, J. C., Brandsma, J. M., Tondow, M., & LeMaistre, G. A study of transsexuals seeking gender reassignment. *American Journal of Psychiatry,* 1975, *132,* 962-964.

Finney, J. C., Skeeters, D. E., Auvenshine, C. D., & Smith, D. F. Phases of psychopathology after assassination. *American Journal of Psychiatry,* 1973, *130,* 1379-1380.

Fisher, S., & Greenberg, R. P. Selective effects upon women of exciting and calm music. *Perceptual and Motor Skills,* 1972, *34,* 987-990.

French, A. P., Russell, T. L., & Tupin, J. P. Subjective changes with the Sentic Cycles of Clynes: A preliminary psychometric study. *Diseases of the Nervous System,* 1972, *33,* 598-602.

Fromme, D. K., & Schmidt, C. K. Affective role enactment and expressive behavior. *Journal of Personality and Social Psychology,* 1972, *24,* 413-419.

Golden, C. J., & Golden, E. E. A note on self-reported behavioral correlates of resistance to interference. *Journal of Genetic Psychology,* 1976, *128,* 299-300.

Hartlage, L. C., & Tollison, C. D. MMPI correlates of looking left or right during mental tasks. *Journal of Clinical Psychology,* 1979, *35,* 92-94.

Herzberg, F., Mathapo, J., Wiener, Y., & Wieson, L. E. Motivation-hygiene correlates of mental health: An examination of motivational inversion in a clinical population. *Journal of Consulting and Clinical Psychology,* 1974, *42,* 411-419.

Hood, R. W. The construction and preliminary validation of a measure of reported mystical experience. *Journal for the Scientific Study of Religion,* 1975, *14,* 29-41.

Husted, J. R., & Edwards, A. E. Personality correlates of male sexual arousal and behavior. *Archives of Sexual Behavior,* 1976, *5,* 149-156.

Johnson, D. W., & Norem-Hebeisen, A. Attitudes toward interdependence among persons and psychological health. *Psychological Reports,* 1977, *40,* 843-850.

McLachlan, J. F. C. Revised scale for estimating ability to judge complex behavior. *Perceptual and Motor Skills,* 1972, *35,* 250.

Markel, N. N., Phillis, J. A., Vargas, R., & Howard, K. Personality traits associated with voice types. *Journal of Psycholinguistic Research,* 1972, *1,* 249-255.

Mendelsohn, G. A., & Lindholm, E. P. Individual differences and the role of attention in the use of cues in verbal problem solving. *Journal of Personality,* 1972, *40,* 226-241.

O'Neil, H. F., Teague, M., Lushene, R. E., & Davenport, S. Personality characteristics of women's liberation activists as measured by the MMPI. *Psychological Reports,* 1975, *37,* 355-361.

Powell, L., Cameron, H. K., Asbury, C. A., & Johnson, E. H. Some characteristics of a special urban educational program. *Journal of Negro Education,* 1975, *44,* 361-367.

Rapfogel, R. G., & Armentrout, J. A. Inner- versus other-directedness and hypomanic tendencies in a nonpsychiatric population. *Journal of Clinical Psychology,* 1972, *28,* 526-527.

Reynolds, W. M., & Sundberg, N. D. Recent research trends in testing. *Journal of Personality Assessment,* 1976, *40,* 228-233.

Roll, S., & Hertel, P. Arrow-dot measures of impulse, ego, and superego functions in noncheaters, cheaters, and super cheaters. *Perceptual and Motor Skills,* 1974, *39,* 1035-1038.

Rosenbluh, E. S., Owens, G. B., & Pohler, M. J. Art preference and personality. *British Journal of Psychology,* 1972, *63,* 441-443.

Shweder, R. A. How relevant is an individual difference theory of personality? *Journal of Personality,* 1975, *43,* 455-484.

Spaulding, W. The relationships of some information-processing factors to severely disturbed behavior. *Journal of Nervous and Mental Disease,* 1978, *166,* 417-428.

Stricker, L. J., Jacobs, P. I., & Kogan, N. Trait interrelations in implicit personality theories and questionnaire data. *Journal of Personality and Social Psychology,* 1974, *30,* 198-207.

Tancredi, F. N., & Wagner, M. E. Women volunteers for dormitory coeducational living. *College Student Journal,* 1975, *9,* 19-22.

Wagner, M. E., & Schubert, D. S. Increasing volunteer representativeness by recruiting for credit or pay. *Journal of General Psychology,* 1976, *94,* 85-91.

Wessman, A. E. Personality and the subjective experience of time. *Journal of Personality Assessment,* 1973, *37,* 103-114.

Indexes

Name Index

Subject Index